The Sources of Husserl's 'Ideas I'

The Sources of Husserl's 'Ideas I'

Edited by
Andrea Staiti and Evan Clarke

DE GRUYTER

ISBN 978-3-11-052782-7
e-ISBN (PDF) 978-3-11-055159-4
Set-ISBN 978-3-11-055160-0

Library of Congress Control Number: 2018940939

Bibliographic information published by the Deutsche Nationalbibliothek
The Deutsche Nationalbibliothek lists this publication in the Deutsche Nationalbibliografie;
detailed bibliographic data are available on the Internet at http://dnb.dnb.de.

© 2019 Walter de Gruyter GmbH, Berlin/Boston
This volume is text- and page-identical with the hardback published in 2018.
Cover image: Edmund Husserl, manuscript F III 1-3a,
© Husserl Archive Leuven
Printing and binding: CPI books GmbH, Leck

www.degruyter.com

Table of Contents

Andrea Staiti and Evan Clarke
Introduction —— 1

Part I Background (1905–1913)

Rodney Parker
Theodor Elsenhans —— 13

Translated by Erin Stackle
Theodor Elsenhans. Selections from *Textbook of Psychology* —— 17

Will Britt
Henry Jackson Watt —— 35

Translated by Will Britt
Henry J. Watt. Literature Review: Second General Review On New Research in the Psychology of Memory and Association from the Year 1905 —— 39

R. Brian Tracz
Carl Stumpf —— 79

Translated by R. Brian Tracz
Carl Stumpf. Appearances and Psychic Functions —— 81

Adam Knowles
Jonas Cohn —— 115

Translated by Adam Knowles
Jonas Cohn. The Fundamental Questions of Psychology —— 117

Rodney Parker
Theodor Ziehen —— 151

Translated by Erin Stackle
Theodor Ziehen. Selections from *Epistemology on the Basis of Psychophysiological and Physical Grounds* —— 153

Andrea Staiti
August Messer —— 213

Translated by Andrea Staiti
August Messer. Husserl's Phenomenology in Its Relation to Psychology —— 215

Part II Responses (1913–1918)

Rodney Parker
Heinrich Maier —— 229

Translated by Rodney Parker
Heinrich Maier. Psychology and Philosophy —— 231

Translated by Andrea Staiti
August Messer. Husserl's Phenomenology in its Relation to Psychology (Second Essay) —— 239

Translated by Evan Clarke
Edmund Husserl. Draft of a Letter to August Messer (1914) —— 255

Translated by Andrea Staiti
Edmund Husserl. Remark on Messer and Cohn (February/March 1913: First Draft) —— 261

Andrea Staiti
Heinrich Gustav Steinmann —— 267

Translated by Andrea Staiti
Heinrich Gustav Steinmann. On the Systematic Position of Phenomenology —— 269

Michaela Sobrak-Seaton
Edith Stein —— 299

Translated by Evan Clarke
Edith Stein. Concerning Heinrich Gustav Steinmann's Paper "On the Systematic Position of Phenomenology" —— 301

Jerome Veith
Paul Natorp —— 317

Translated by Jerome Veith
Paul Natorp. Husserl's Ideas Pertaining to a Pure Phenomenology —— 319

Translated by Jacob Rump, Evan Clarke, and Andrea Staiti
Theodor Elsenhans. Phenomenology, Psychology, Epistemology —— 339

Rodney Parker
Paul F. Linke —— 383

Translated by Evan Clarke
Paul F. Linke. The Legitimacy of Phenomenology: A Disagreement with Theodor Elsenhans —— 385

Translated by Andrea Staiti
Theodor Elsenhans. Phenomenology and the Empirical —— 433

Translated by Evan Clarke
Edmund Husserl and Edith Stein. Critique of Theodor Elsenhans and August Messer (1917) (Edith Stein's Draft) —— 449

Contributors —— 469

Index: author2 —— 471

Andrea Staiti and Evan Clarke
Introduction

After decades of neglect, the first book of Husserl's Ideen zu einer reinen Phänomenologie und phänomenologischen Philosophie, published in 1913 as the opening essay for the newly founded Jahrbuch für Philosophie und phänomenologische Forschung, is slowly being recognized as one of "the great philosophical works of the twentieth century" (Moran 2012, xiv).[1] That this recognition comes more than a century after the initial publication of *Ideas* (as we will henceforth abbreviate the work in question) has something to do, we suspect, with its considerable conceptual novelty and its equally considerable density of exposition. No doubt it also has much do with the damning judgment of Husserl's philosophical contemporaries. Heidegger famously argued that Ideas represents a relapse into early modern subjectivism after the promising new start of the Logical Investigations. Munich phenomenologists rejected the transcendental idealistic thesis that the world is essentially dependent on consciousness and developed a realistic version of phenomenology in response. The Neo-Kantians criticized Husserl's eidetic method as a form of intuitionism lacking any philosophical justification. Empirical psychologists lamented the absence of an experimental basis for Husserl's claims about consciousness. The list could continue, but the attacks coming from otherwise dramatically divergent philosophical camps are clear evidence of the originality of Ideas, an essay that cannot be easily categorized under any of the available rubrics of early twentieth century German philosophy.

Although he allegedly wrote it in a rush ("six weeks – as if in a trance": Husserl 1994, p. 413), Husserl's personal investment in *Ideas* is unquestionable and remained steadfast for the rest of his life. He considered *Ideas* a significant advance vis-à-vis the *Logical Investigations* and held it up as the first work to represent phenomenology as a foundational science, that is, as a form of *transcen-*

---

[1] This new wave of scholarly interest arguably started in 2012 with the reprint of the Routledge Classics edition of the first English translation of *Ideas* with an illuminating foreword by Dermot Moran. In 2013, the centennial anniversary of publication, Lester Embree and Tom Nenon edited a wide-ranging volume devoted to the continuing impact of *Ideas I* (Embree/Nenon 2013). A new translation by Daniel Dahlstrom followed in 2014 (Husserl 2014) and in 2015 the first complete commentary of *Ideas* appeared (Staiti 2015). Tellingly, five out of six contributions in the recently published special issue of the journal *Research in Phenomenology* 46/2 (2016) on "The New Husserl" discuss topics from *Ideas* (Majolino 2016, Pradelle 2016, Hopkins 2016, Jacobs 2016, Staiti 2016).

DOI 10.1515/9783110551594-001

dental inquiry. While the *Logical Investigations* focused on the problems of logical validity and the ways in which contingent acts of thought can instantiate ideal meanings, *Ideas* tackles the problems of transcendence in general and analyzes the structure of conscious acts intending transcendent objects at the most basic level of experience: sensory perception and its manifold modifications. Whether this recalibration and expansion of focus should be interpreted as a turn or as a natural evolution of Husserl's earlier project has been the object of considerable scholarly debate. Be that as it may, one can state with confidence that Husserl's contemporaries perceived *Ideas* as an extremely ambitious shift in direction. *Ideas* presents phenomenology as a unique philosophical discipline: it investigates consciousness and yet is distinct from psychology; it sets out to unearth a priori necessities ("essences") and yet appeals to intuition and direct experience to grasp such necessities. Husserl was well aware that his philosophical project didn't square with received demarcations within philosophy or *between* philosophy and the empirical sciences. No wonder, as he writes in §63, that phenomenology "has to reckon with a basic mood of skepticism" (*Ideen* 121/117).

The debate sparked by *Ideas*, however, went well beyond a generic mood of skepticism. It prompted a whole cohort of philosophers to take a stance on the ambitions of Husserl's new transcendental phenomenology. The present volume offers the Anglophone reader a comprehensive selection of contributions to this debate, including works that Husserl quotes in *Ideas*, responses to *Ideas* that appeared in philosophical and psychological journals after its publication, and Husserl's own attempts to counter criticism and to clarify his position in the ensuing years.

While this volume will be illuminating for those interested in the history of twentieth century European philosophy, these texts are also extremely instructive as commentaries on Husserl's thought. All of them approach Husserl's *Ideas* on its own terms, rather than using it as a foil or springboard for other philosophical concerns. As such, they are much more helpful as a means to assess the merits and shortcomings of the *Ideas* than the writings of a Heidegger or a Sartre, both of whom read Husserl through the (often distorting) lens of their own philosophical agenda.

What's more, these texts tackle issues that are still hotly debated today. Virtually all of the texts in this collection, for example, raise the question about phenomenology's relationship to empirical psychological research and the conditions for a fruitful cooperation between the two disciplines. This issue reappeared on the philosophical scene around the turn of the millennium, when it took the form of a debate on the possibility of naturalizing phenomenology (Petitot/Varela/Pachoud/Roy 1999). As the reader will discover, many of the positions expressed by contemporary philosophers on these matters can be found *in nuce* in these early materials.

Another theme that arises here concerns the possibility of an intuitive grasp of eidetic necessities. This theme resonates with contemporary discussions of phenomenology and fallibilism,[2] and with the recent rehabilitation of intuition associated with Anglo-American philosophers such as Robert Hanna and Elijah Chudnoff. It is also bears on a centrally important issue for phenomenology: the issue of the epistemic status of phenomenological discourse. Is phenomenology empirical, i.e., is it based on observation and inductive generalization? Is it a kind of conceptual analysis, i.e., is it beholden solely to semantic and formal-logical constraints? Husserl's eidetic method offers a third alternative, according to which phenomenology sets out to grasp substantive structures of various regions of objects and yet does not rely on empirical generalization. The texts included in this collection all duly recognize the centrality of this issue, thereby posing an urgent question to contemporary phenomenologists who find Husserl's eidetics unpalatable. If phenomenology is not fundamentally eidetic in nature, then what kind of philosophical discourse can it possibly be?

Conversely, it is noteworthy that a number of the issues that take center stage in contemporary scholarship on Husserl are not as prominent in the texts reproduced here. For example, neither the noema, the epoché, nor the phenomenological reduction receive very much attention here. Part of the reason for this could be the widespread perception of Husserl as the spearhead of a movement, as the leading voice in an effort to articulate a new understanding of philosophy under the rubric "phenomenology." Seeing him in these terms, critics and enthusiasts alike tend to focus not so much on the technicalities of Husserl's thought, but on issues pertaining to the phenomenological movement as a whole.

Husserl's particular version of transcendental idealism, and his particular method of securing an idealist standpoint (through the *epoché* and the reduction), also receive comparatively little attention here. This likely reflects the fact that idealism was a widely adopted position at the time. In spite of the broad differences between Husserl's phenomenological idealism and, say, Neo-Kantian idealism (which is secured not through a redirection of interest or a shift in attitude, but by reference to 'consciousness in general' as the idealized subject of epistemological inquiry) Husserl's novel variant thus failed to generate any philosophical headlines.

---

[2] See, for instance, the instructive exchange between Hopp (2009a, 2009b) and Heffernan (2009a, 2009b) on this important issue.

The Intuition of Essence

Probably the most discussion generated in these texts surrounds Husserl's claim that essences can be grasped intuitively, meaning that there is an intuitive consciousness not merely of particularity, as most philosophers accept, but of generality. This claim gives rise to a variety of reactions. Steinmann, for his part, finds no fault in the idea of an intuitive grasp of material essences, but rejects the idea that these can be characterized as pure or a priori. Empirical experience is the source of our knowledge of different material regions of objects and therefore the essences governing them must be considered empirical as well. Empirically-minded psychologists such as Ziehen and Maier, on the other hand, insist that intuition is unreliable, since different people may have significantly different intuitions.[3] Kantian-trained philosophers such as Elsenhans, finally, insist that every description of the intuitive must operate with the linguistically inflected concepts at hand. This means that our descriptions cannot be understood as purely neutral reports on the content of intuition. It also means that our descriptions are inevitably provisional. Having framed some region of experience conceptually, we can always refine our concept on the basis of subsequent investigation.

Responding to Elsenhans on behalf of Husserl, Edith Stein first challenges the view that phenomenology must avail itself of essentially linguistic concepts. She insists that phenomenology does not admit ready-to-hand linguistic 'precipitates', but forms concepts on the basis of an originally giving intuition. Her more substantial response to Elsenhans amounts to a change in perspective of what a concept *is*. From Elsenhans' perspective, a concept is a kind of cracked mirror, one in which reality can be imperfectly glimpsed. This is why our concepts are ultimately provisional. Since they never quite capture reality, they are always subject to replacement by a substitute that does a slightly better job. According to Stein, however, the concepts that are at issue here have an entirely different status. Phenomenological concepts do not simply reflect our experience as it is given; they prescribe a structure to which experience must conform. Pursuing a parallel drawn by Husserl in the *Ideas*, Stein argues that phenomenological concepts are similar in this regard to geometrical concepts. The geometer might derive the concept of a certain topological structure from various sensible experiences. In subjecting those experiences to scrutiny however, she draws out an essential structure that does more than simply generalize the initial experien-

---

[3] For a recent and wide-ranging reformulation of this position see Deutsch 2015.

ces. She draws out a structure that describes the parameters within which subsequent instantiations of that structure will be given.

This line of argument can be met with the objection that there simply are no essences to be met with in the domain of inner experience. Perhaps inner experience, unlike space, is simply a discontinuous flux, having no overarching, continuous features. Stein responds to this concern by appealing to the manifest stability of certain basic experiential categories. "It is unthinkable," she says, "that through some continual transformation the perception of a thing would change into the perception of a sensory datum, a feeling of rage, or a predicative judgment" (p. 456). In other words, there is something that it is like to perceive a thing, just as there is something it is like to experience rage. These phenomena cannot be made to shade gradually into one another.

Phenomenology and Psychology

Another important area of controversy in these texts arises from Husserl's claim that phenomenology is entirely distinct from psychology. This claim is predicated both on phenomenology's preoccupation with essences, rather than facts about consciousness, and on Husserl's understanding of the phenomenological *epoché* and reduction as methods to disclose a non-empirical dimension of consciousness that cannot be interpreted as a segment of nature. As to the first claim, critics such as Maier and Elsenhans argue that the idea of intuiting essences of conscious phenomena without the aid of empirical observation and induction is entirely based on the supposed analogy between the mathematical disciplines and the study of consciousness. As noted above, Husserl draws on geometry as a means of explaining his conception. He notes that the geometer regards the empirical shapes drawn on the board not as intrinsically significant objects of inquiry, but merely as instances of pure essences. Maier and Elsenhans, however, consider this analogy misconceived. They suggest that consciousness is not a mathematical field, and that it requires empirical, rather than a priori research. August Messer is more amenable to the idea of a purely descriptive approach to the essences of conscious phenomena, but he does not think that this necessarily creates a gulf between phenomenology and psychology. Isn't it possible to conceive of a *pure* descriptive psychology that would form the basis of the other branches of psychological research? Husserl's later conception of a phenomenological psychology concerned with the essences of psychologically construed experiences bears witness to the viability, at least in principle, of Messer's proposal. As for the other source for Husserl's claim of a gulf between psychology and phenomenology, i.e., the non-empirical dimension of consciousness disclosed by the *epoché* and the reduction, Messer is more dismissive. He argues that the performance of the reduction does not have a real bearing on the concrete phenomenological analyses and can therefore be left aside in order to facilitate the exchange with researchers working in other areas of psychology. Steinmann is even less conciliatory. He argues: "[o]ne should remember [...] that there is only one consciousness and that it is *either* absolute *or* bound up with the real world" (p. 280). He then goes to criticize "the exaggeration that tries to attribute metaphysical truth to the basic methodological fiction at the foundation of phenomenology" (p. 281). Like Messer, Steinmann opts for a philosophically less ambitious understanding of phenomenology—one that locates it at the center of psychology.

Again responding on Husserl's behalf, Stein looks to shore up the essential difference between consciousness as such, meaning consciousness as disclosed by the phenomenological reduction, and consciousness as an object of psychological inquiry. She does so by invoking Husserl's now quite famous rumination on the 'annihilation of the world', from Sec. 49 of the *Ideas*. According to Stein, the fact that we can imaginatively detach consciousness from any relation to a transcendent, physical world, demonstrates that "the being of consciousness has nothing to do with reality" (p. 306). The fact that consciousness in the form of a chaotic "stream of immanent data" would still be consciousness, in other words, means that consciousness must stand apart from the world in some essential sense. According to Husserl and Stein, it falls to phenomenology to investigate consciousness in its absolute, non-worldly aspect. The role of psychology is quite different: to investigate consciousness insofar as it is a *part* of the transcendent world.

This solution of course might give rise to problems of its own. If phenomenology really is principally occupied with an absolute, non-worldly reality, then it becomes difficult to understand how phenomenology can tell us anything *about* the world. Steinmann himself raises this concern, suggesting that a "consistent implementation of the phenomenological reduction" effectively traps us within the immanence of consciousness (p. 287). In her response to Steinmann, Stein suggests that this concern betrays a misunderstanding of the immanent "phenomenological sphere." According to Stein, the phenomenological sphere includes both the qualitative and the ontological, or noematic aspects of objects. Thus, it includes the shape, size, and color of objects, as well as the quality of being a *real* object. Being real is not a quality that an object possesses in an absolute, extra-mental sense; it is quality that is constituted *within* consciousness. As such, phenomenology *can* tell us about real objects in the real world. It is in fact the first place we should look in order to understand such objects.

Selection of Material

As a glance at the table of contents quickly reveals, most of the thinkers included in this collection are not very well known. With the exception of Paul Natorp and Carl Stumpf (whose names may sound familiar to specialists of early twentieth century European philosophy, but whose works are for the most part unavailable in English translation), the authors included in this volume have never received attention in the scholarly debate on Husserlian phenomenology. It is therefore appropriate to spell out our selection criteria.

First, we decided to include in this collection only writings that pertain directly to *Ideas I*, rather than Husserlian phenomenology more generally. This led to the exclusion of classic essays such as Eugen Fink's "Die phänomenologische Philosophie Edmund Husserls in der gegenwärtigen Kritik" (Fink 1933) and book-chapters by celebrated post-Husserlian phenomenologists in which *Ideas* is quoted, but which are focussed on Husserl's phenomenology writ large (e.g. Heidegger 1985, §§9b-12; Sartre 1960, 37f.). The reason for this restriction is the desire to revive scholarly engagement with the *Ideas* in particular, a book that is still largely underappreciated and sometimes misrepresented even among Husserl scholars.

Second, only texts Husserl actually read (or could have read) are part of this collection. All of these texts are quoted in *Ideas* or were published shortly after *Ideas*, and all of them are texts of which Husserl was aware. This criterion has led to the exclusion, for instance, of Alexius Meinong's notes for a planned, but never written review of *Ideas* (Meinong 1978)[4], and of Carl Stumpf's critical remarks on *Ideas* in the posthumously published *Erkenntnislehre* (1939/1940).

Third, we only included German texts, thus leaving out, for instance, a set of interesting reviews of *Ideas* that appeared in English after the publication of Boyce Gibson's translation (1931), as well a rich review by Emmanuel Levinas (1929), one of the very first writings on phenomenology to appear in French. The decision to consider only sources in German of which Husserl was aware is motivated by a desire to reconstruct a debate that actually happened, instead of tracing the ways in which Husserl's *Ideas* influenced other thinkers and philosophical communities.

Finally, we excluded sources that, while fitting all of the above criteria, are either too voluminous, such as Stumpf's *Zur Eintheilung der Wissenschaften*, which is complementary to the essay *Erscheinungen und Psychische Funktionen*,

---

[4] Thankfully, Meinong's notes are already available in English translation in Schubert Kalsi 1978 (209–248).

included in this volume, or in which Husserl's ideas are not taken up in a direct, sustained fashion. This criterion rules out the first volume of Külpe's major work *Die Realisierung* (1912), in which references to Husserl's categorial intuition are scattered cursorily in a variety of chapters.

Read together, these pieces offer a vivid picture of the philosophical debate of Husserl's time, which saw philosophers and psychologists belonging to different schools engaged in serious and fruitful intellectual exchange. We hope they can be inspiring for contemporary philosophy in its efforts to overcome old divides and re-establish itself as a choral discipline.

References

Deutsch, Max (2015): *The Myth of the Intuitive. Experimental Philosophy and Philosophical Method.* Cambridge: MIT Press.
Embree, Lester/Nenon, Tom (Eds.) (2013): *Husserl's Ideen.* Dordrecht: Springer.
Fink, Eugen (1933): "Die phänomenologische Philosophie Edmund Husserls in der gegenwärtigen Kritik. In: *Kant-Studien* 38, pp. 319–383.
Heffernan, George (2009a): "On Husserl's Remark that '[s]elbst eine sich als apodiktisch ausgebende Evidenz kann sich als Täuschung enthüllen …' (XVII 164:32–33): Does the Phenomenological Method Yield Any Epistemic Infallibility?" *Husserl Studies* 25/1, pp. 15–43.
Heffernan, George (2009b): "An Addendum to the Exchange with Walter Hopp on Phenomenology and Fallibility." *Husserl Studies* 25/1, pp. 51–55.
Hopkins, Burt (2016): "Numerical Identity and the Constitution of Transcendence in Transcendental Phenomenology". *Research in Phenomenology* 46/2, pp. 205–220.
Hopp, Walter (2009a): "Phenomenology and Fallibility." *Husserl Studies* 25/1, pp. 1–14.
Hopp, Walter (2009b): "Reply to Heffernan". *Husserl Studies* 25/1, pp. 45–49.
Husserl, Edmund (2014): *Ideas for a Pure Phenomenology and Phenomenological Philosophy: First Book: General Introduction to Pure Phenomenology.* Daniel Dahlstrom (Trans.). Indianapolis/Cambridge: Hackett.
Jacobs, Hanne (2016): "Husserl on Reason, Reflection, and Attention". *Research in Phenomenology* 46/2, pp. 257–276.
Külpe, Oswald (1912): *Die Realisierung: Ein Beitrag zur Grundlegung der Realwissenschaften.* Erster Band. Leipzig: Hirzel.
Lévinas, Emmanuel (1929): "Sur les 'Ideen' de M. E. Husserl". *Revue philosophique de la France et de l'Etranger* 107. No. 3–4, pp. 230–265.
Majolino, Claudio (2016): "'Until the End of the World': Eidetic Variation and Absolute Being of Consciousness—A Reconsideration." *Research in Phenomenology* 46/2, pp. 157–183.
Moran, Dermot (2012): "Foreword to the Routledge Classics Edition". In Husserl, Edmund. *Ideas: General Introduction to Pure Phenomenology.* London/New York: Routledge, pp. xiii-xxxiii.
Meinong, Alexius (1978): "Bemerkungen zu 'Ideen einer reinen Phänomenologie und phänomenologischen Philosophie'." In: *Ergänzungsband zur Gesamtausgabe.*

Marie-Luise Schubert Kalsi (Trans.). Graz: Akademische Druck- und Verlagsanstalt, pp. 287–324.
Pradelle, Dominique (2016): "On the Notion of Sense in Phenomenology: Noematic Sense and Ideal Meaning." Research in Phenomenology 46/2, pp. 184–204.
Staiti, Andrea (ed.) (2015): *Commentary on Husserl's* Ideas I. Berlin: De Gruyter.
Staiti, Andrea (2016): "Positionality and Consciousness in Husserl's *Ideas I*." Research in Phenomenology 46/2, pp. 277–295.
Stumpf, Carl (1939/1940): *Erkenntnislehre*, 2 vol. Leipzig: J. A. Barth.

Acknowledgments

Work on this volume began in 2011, thanks to a generous research expense grant from the Office of the Provost and Dean of Faculties at Boston College. The grant supported an extended visit at the library of the Albert-Ludwigs-Universität Freiburg, where the relevant sources of *Ideas I* were first collected. The editors want to express their gratitude to all the translators for their engagement and patience. We want to thank Christoph Schirmer at DeGruyter for his support and expert guidance. We would also like to thank Julia Jansen, head of the Husserl Archive in Leuven, for her assistance in the preparation of the Husserl/Stein translations and for permission to reproduce the image featured on the cover of this volume. Additionally, we are grateful to Springer Publishing for their permission to translate material published in *Husserliana*. Finally, we are deeply indebted to Michaela Sobrak-Seaton, who took on the demanding job of editing the final manuscript.

Part I **Background (1905 – 1913)**

Rodney Parker
Theodor Elsenhans

Theodor Elsenhans (1862–1918) began his career studying theology in Tübingen, but became deeply interested in philosophy, receiving his doctorate in 1885. In the years immediately following, he published a number of pieces, including *Wesen und Entstehung des Gewissens* (Elsenhans 1894), "Das Verhältnis der Logik zur Psychologie" (Elsenhans 1896),[1] and *Selbstbeobachtung und Experiment in der Psychologie* (Elsenhans 1897). In 1902, Elsenhans completed his Habilitationsschrift, *Das Kant-Friesische Problem* (Elsenhans 1902), in Heidelberg. In 1908 he accepted a professorship in Dresden – where he lived out his career – and continued to develop his work on Kant and Fries concerning epistemology. In addition to his work on the theory of knowledge, Elsenhans was interested in the relationship between psychology and other areas of philosophy as well (Elsenhans 1912).

In January 1917, Max Frischeisen-Köhler, then the editor of *Kant-Studien*, sent Husserl a copy of Elsenhans' forthcoming article "Phänomenologie und Empirie" (Elsenhans 1918). This paper was the third installment in the Elsenhans-Linke debate (Elsenhans 1915; Linke 1917), and Frischeisen-Köhler implored Husserl to write a response of his own, suggesting the title "Begriff und Tragweite der Phänomenologie," perhaps being able to finish it over the Easter holidays (Husserl 1994b, 49–50). In April of that year, Edith Stein wrote to Roman Ingarden concerning Husserl's promised contribution to the debate:

> During the holidays...[Husserl] wrote *Einleitung in die Phänomenologie* (Introduction to Phenomenology) divided into two sections *Phänomenologie u. Psychologie* (Phenomenology and Psychology) and *Phän. u. Erkenntnistheorie* (Phen. and Epistemology)...I am trying to get him to see that he should dress up the piece, use it as an answer to Elsenhans, and then submit it for publication in *Kant-Studien*. At the moment, however, he is not con-

---

[1] Husserl published a review of this (Husserl 1903, 395–401), and is discussed in his correspondence with Natorp from 1897 (Husserl 1994a, 49–56). In the *Logical Investigations*, Husserl quotes this text in a footnote: "'If contemporary logic has increased its success in grappling with logical problems, it above all owes such success to its psychological immersion in its subject' (Elsenhans 1896, p. 203). I should probably have said exactly the same before beginning my present investigations, or before realizing the insoluble difficulties in which I was plunged by a psychologistic view of the philosophy of mathematics. Now, however, having the best reasons to see the error of such a view" (Husserl 2001, 319). For more on Husserl's confrontation with Elsenhans in the *Logical Investigations*, see Farber (1967, 137, 181–184) and Fisette (2010, 248–51).

DOI 10.1515/9783110551594-002

vinced. He is indeed committed to an answer but intends to prepare a special reply (Stein 2014, 57–58).

Husserl did not end up publishing these two treatises in the *Kant-Studien*, nor any other response to Elsenhans – perhaps due to Elsenhans' death on 3 January 1918 – though Frischeisen-Köhler had begun announcing that a volume by Husserl titled *Das Wesen der Phänomenologie* would be forthcoming in the *Ergänzungsheft* series. "Phänomenologie und Psychologie" and "Phänomenologie und Erkenntnistheorie", along with the draft of the "special reply" to Elsenhans, "Zur Kritik an Theodor Elsenhans und August Messer. Edith Steins Ausarbeitung" (also included in this volume p. 449–468), can be found in (Husserl 1987).

References

Elsenhans, Theodor (1894): *Wesen und Entstehung des Gewissens: Eine Psychologie der Ethik*. Leipzig: Engelmann.
Elsenhans, Theodor (1896): "Das Verhältnis der Logik zur Psychologie." In: *Zeitschrift für Philosophie und philosophische Kritik* 109, pp. 195–212.
Elsenhans, Theodor (1897): *Selbstbeobachtung und Experiment in der Psychologie: Ihre Tragweite und ihre Grenzen*. Tübingen: Mohr.
Elsenhans, Theodor (1902): *Das Kant-Friesische Problem*. Heidelberg: Hörning.
Elsenhans, Theodor (1912): *Lehrbuch der Psychologie*. Tübingen: Mohr.
Elsenhans, Theodor (1915): "Phänomenologie, Psychologie, Erkenntnistheorie." In: *Kant-Studien* 20, pp. 224–75.
Elsenhans, Theodor (1918): "Phänomenologie und Empirie." In: *Kant-Studien* 22, pp. 243–61.
Farber, Marvin (1967): *The Foundation of Phenomenology: Edmund Husserl and the Quest for a Rigorous Science of Philosophy*. Albany: SUNY Press.
Fisette, Denis (2010): "Descriptive Psychology and Natural Sciences: Husserl's early Criticism of Brentano." In: *Philosophy, Phenomenology, Sciences: Essays in Commemoration of Edmund Husserl*. Carlo Ierna, Hanne Jacobs, and Filip Mattens (Eds.). Dordrecht: Springer, pp. 221–53.
Husserl, Edmund (1903): "Bericht über deutsche Schriften zur Logik aus den Jahren 1895–1899 (III)." In: *Archiv für systematische Philosophie* 9 (3), pp. 393–408.
Husserl, Edmund (1987): "Zur Kritik an Theodor Elsenhans und August Messer. Edith Steins Ausarbeitung ." In: *Husserliana XXV: Aufsätze und Vorträge (1911–1921)*. Thomas Nenon and Hans Rainer Sepp (Eds.). Dordrecht: Martinus Nijhoff, pp. 226–248
Husserl, Edmund (1994a): *Husserliana Dokumente III. Briefwechsel: Band 5. Die Neukantianer*. Karl Schuhmann (Ed.). Dordrecht: Kluwer.
Husserl, Edmund (1994b): *Husserliana Dokumente III. Briefwechsel: Band 8. Institutionelle Schreiben*. Karl Schuhmann (Ed.). Dordrecht: Kluwer.
Husserl, Edmund (2001): *Logical Investigations* I. J. N. Findlay (Trans.). London/New York: Routledge.

Linke, Paul Ferdinand (1917): "Das Recht der Phänomenologie: Eine Auseinandersetzung mit Th. Elsenhans." In: *Kant-Studien* 21, pp. 163–221.
Stein, Edith (2014): *Letters to Roman Ingarden*. Hugh Candler Hunt (Trans.). Washington: ICS Publications.

Translated by Erin Stackle
Theodor Elsenhans.
Selections from *Textbook of Psychology*

Lehrbuch der Psychologie
Tübingen: Mohr (1912)

Chapter One: *Psychology as Science*
Section Four: The Method of Psychology

B *The Method of the Treatment of Material*

[48] It seems hardly possible to separate the method of treatment of the material of psychology from the method of acquiring it. Now, were it the case that concepts were already made available in observation with which to classify the psychological object, and were a distinct experimental design already to correspond to the distinctly scientific posing of a question, then the beginning of a 'treatment' would seem to be already given just with these. But actually, instead, the entire classification by concepts allows itself, almost without difficulty, to be distinguished from the 'making available' of concepts, and the acquisition of the experimental results to be distinguished from their processing; our further survey concerning the method of psychology will show that it is expedient to address particular consideration to the treatment of the material.

I The Idea of a Merely 'Descriptive' Psychology

In *one* case, however, every fundamental would escape this distinction. This would be the case, were psychology required to '*describe*' what is readily available, without mediation. This idea of a 'describing' or 'descriptive psychology' has, in various forms, until the most recent time,[1] found its adherents: These approximate more or less to the first extensive justification we have of this standpoint, given by *Wilhelm Dilthey*. Dilthey's justification is thus best for evaluating the standing of this method.

---

[1] Particularly from *Husserl* and Th. *Lipps*. For more information, see the discussion of the relationships of psychology and epistemology [later in] Section Four.

Explanatory psychology, Dilthey claims, gives itself the task corresponding to 'explanation' in the natural sciences, "to subordinate [the phenomena of its realm] to a vast all-embracing causal coherence by means of a limited number of unambiguously determined elements." Psychology can only reach this, its goal, if it transfers onto mental life the way of forming hypotheses characteristic of the natural sciences, through which a causal coherence is supplementarily added to what is given. Psychology is not, however, entitled to make this transfer.

So, psychology is 'spellbound in a fog of hypotheses'—for example, its teaching of the parallelism between the nervous operations and the mental operations—for which "the possibility for testing them against the mental [*psychischen*] facts is in no way apparent" (Dilthey 1894, p. 1309). In the inner-world, the living nexus was given, rather, in consciousness, and did not need to be introduced only subsequently through hypotheses as is the case with the physical phenomena. Psychology, on this model, has only the inner facts to describe and to analyze, and the gaps to fill in.

II Describing and Explaining

To gainsay the psychologists opposed to this model, H. Ebbinghaus, in particular, lent words. "Explanatory psychology," he says, "does not only somehow explain and construct [49] out of merely hypothetical assumptions, but rather, the vast majority of its adherents in the past, and the entirety of its independent adherents in the present, employ it to first prepare the resources for its explanations through the most careful study of what is given. It thus practices for a long time precisely the procedure that Dilthey holds as advisable" (Ebbinghaus 1896, p. 195).

Mere description could simply not be the task of a science. Descriptive psychology itself does not even content itself with the mere describing, analyzing, and generalizing of what is given, but rather, it recognizes that 'what is given' features gaping holes, which our thinking urgently demands we fill. In filling these holes, however, it proceeds exactly as explanatory psychology.

This instructive back and forth of the two opposing standpoints sufficiently designates the weakness of a psychology that wants to only 'describe'. We further complete what has been said through reference to the nature of the 'describing'.

What happens while we describe that 'sensory world'? We designate the mental processes *with words, which are, however, themselves taken from the psy-*

chological language. We speak of 'sensations', 'ideas'[2] [*Vorstellungen*], 'feelings', 'drives', and with these [words] we subordinate the relevant processes under certain psychological concepts.

We can then either content ourselves with the vague popular word meaning, which confuses, for example, sensation and feeling, or we can strive for scientific clarity and exactness. We will probably prefer the latter.

Then, however, we stand already in the realm of 'explanatory psychology', to whose main task such an exact classification belongs, and which, through the disclosure of the causal nexus, itself first makes possible complete classification.

III The Inevitable Deduction from Innate Capabilities

In addition, there is a further point. Especially for the 'most exact' psychologists, those psychological concepts are collective names for the reactions to stimuli of psychophysical organisms. While such a psychologist speaks in this way about sensation, attention, pitch memory, weariness, etc., with these he makes his own the inevitable explanation of *innate capabilities*, which cannot be avoided in the whole organic world. He thereby lapses hopelessly into a standpoint which concerningly evokes the old 'psychology of faculties'.[3]

In fact, this way of explanation is in no way to be avoided. We can do nothing other than presume such dispositions, whose unfolding in the interplay with the outer world first makes mental life possible. Psychology has, until now, neglected these concepts all-too much, and we will try, in a later segment, to make up for this omission.

Here, our task is only to indicate that the use of such concepts in modern psychology only differentiates it from the old 'psychology of faculties' through the fact that it builds onto the established knowledge with critical diligence the realization that, within certain boundaries, an examination through experiments is possible and that—this is the most important point—the main principle holds: *to reduce, if possible, the number of hypotheses. Every psychological collective name has the tendency to the designation of a 'faculty', or to become an innate capability,* since, as a process in a psychophysical organism, it points to its overall conditions of living.

The important thing is to simplify, if possible, the explanatory process based on it, i.e., *to reduce to a minimum* the application of those concepts of innate

---

2 I translate '*Vorstellung*' with the English 'idea', since Elsenhans uses this term much more like Descartes and Locke do, and the relevant English term in those cases is 'idea'.—Tr.
3 Elsenhans refers here to Wolff's and Kant's (and Herbart's) conception of empirical psychology, the 'psychology of the faculties'. –Tr.

capabilities. There can be no talk of the complete elimination of the same—for this the fight between Locke and Leibniz about innate ideas, discussed earlier, is a telling example. [50]

IV The General Method in the Treatment of the Material

Psychology, thus, can go no other way in the treatment of its material than can science in general. Our desire for understanding is satisfied whenever it is permitted us to ascertain the spatial and temporal characteristics of an object, to classify it in a system of clear and distinct concepts, and to survey completely its causal relationships to other objects.

Spatial characteristics come into consideration in psychology only for the bodily organs and processes, which stand in relation to the mental. So the task of psychology is fulfilled whenever it is permitted to investigate the temporal relationships of the mental operations, to apprehend the individual components of the mental life in clear and distinct concepts, to make clear their development and causal relationships, and, in the context of this knowledge, to learn to understand the mental life as a coherent whole.

Literature:[4]

Kant, Immanuel (1839a): *Metaphysische Anfangsgründe der Naturwissenschaft*. In: *Sämtliche Werke* V, Friedrich Schubert und Karl Rosenkranz (eds.). Leipzig: Leopold Voss.
Kant, Immanuel (1839b): *Anthropologie in pragmatischer Hinsicht*. In: *Sämtliche Werke* VII, Friedrich Schubert und Karl Rosenkranz Wilhelm (eds.). Leipzig: Leopold Voss.
Comte, Auguste (1880): *Einleitung in die positive Philosophie*. Leipzig: Fues's Verlag.
Brentano, Franz (1874). *Psychologie vom empirischen Standpunkte I*. Leipzig: Duncker und Humblot.
Wundt, Wilhelm (1883): "Die Aufgaben der experimentellen Psychologie." In: *Essays*. Leipzig: Engelmann, pp. 127–154.
Wundt, Wilhelm (1887): "Selbstbeobachtung und innere Wahrnehmung." In: *Philosophische Studien* 1, pp. 615–617.
Volkelt, Johannes (1887): "Selbstbeobachtung und psychologische Analyse". In: *Zeitschrift für Philosophie und philosophische Kritik* 90, p. 1f.
Münsterberg, Hugo (1891): "Über Aufgaben und Methoden der Psychologie". In: *Schriften der Gesellschaft für psychologische Forschung* 1, pp. 93–272.
Külpe, Oswald (1893): "Anfänge und Aussichten der experimentellen Psychologie". In: *Archiv für Geschichte der Philosophie* VI, pp. 170–189.

---

[4] This list of works cited, and the one following on pages 29–30, is presented in the non-alphabetical order in which it appears in the German original. The citation format has been updated.

Dilthey, Wilhelm (1894): "Ideen über eine beschreibende und zergliedernde Psychologie." In: *Sitzungsberichte der Kgl. preuss. Akad. Der Wissenschaften zu Berlin*, pp. 1309–1407.
Ebbinghaus, Hermann (1896): "Über erklärende und beschreibende Psychologie". In: *Zeitschrift für Psychologie und Physiologie der Sinnesorgane* 9, pp. 161–205.
Erdmann, Benno (1895): "Zur Theorie der Beobachtung". In: *Archiv für systematische Philosophie* 1, pp. 14–33, 145–164.
Elsenhans, Theodor (1897): *Selbstbeobachtung und Experiment in der Psychologie: Ihre Tragweite und ihre Grenzen.* Tübingen: Mohr.
Elsenhans, Theodor (1904): *Die Aufgabe einer Psychologie der Deutung als Vorareit für die Geisteswissenschaften.* Gießen: J. Rickersche Verlagsbuchhandlung.
Narziß, Ach (1905): *Über die Willenstätigkeit und das Denken.* Göttingen: Vandenhoeck und Ruprecht (esp. Ch. 1).
Lipps, Theodor (1905a): *Bewußtsein und Gegenstände.* Leipzig: Engelmann..
Lipps, Theodor (1905b): "Die Wege der Psychologie." In: *Archiv für das gesammelte Psychologie* 6, pp. 1–21.
Reybekiel-Schapiro, Helena (1906): "Die introspektive Methode in der modernen Psychologie". In: *Viertel jahrsschrift für wissenschaftliche Philosophie* 30, pp. 73–114.
Watt, Henry J. (1906): "Sammelbericht über die neuere Forschung in der Gedächtnis- und Assoziationspsychologie aus den Jahren 1903/4." In: *Archiv für die gesamte Psychologie* 7, pp. 1–48.
Dürr, Ernst (1907): *Die Lehre von der Aufmerksamkeit.* Leipzig: Quelle & Meyer (esp. p. 90).
Bühler, Karl (1907): "Tatsachen und Probleme zu einer Psychologie der Denkvorgänge I: Über Gedanken." In: *Archiv für die gesamte Psychologie* 9, pp. 297–365.
Meumann, Ernst (1908): *Intelligenz und Wille.* Leipzig: Quelle und Meyer.
Wundt, Wilhelm (1907): "Über die Ausfrageexperimente und über die Methoden zur Psychologie des Denkens." In: *Psychologische Studien* 3, pp. 301–360.
Bühler, Karl (1908): "Antwort auf die von W. Wundt erhobenen Einwände gegen die Methode der Selbstbeobachtung an experimentell erzeugten Erlebnissen". In: *Archiv für die Gesamte Psychologie* 12, pp. 93–122.
Wundt, Wilhelm (1908): "Kritische Nachlese zur Ausfragemethode". In: *Archiv für die gesamte Psychologie* 9, pp. 445–59.
Wundt, Wilhelm (1910): "Über reine und angewandte Psychologie". In: *Psychologische Studien* 10, pp. 571–2.

Section Five: The Position of Psychology in the System of the Sciences

[51] In the present, there is hardly a field of study whose position in the system of science is so contested and so unclear as that of psychology. And yet its entire enterprise of research, the understanding of its task, and the specificity of its method, are largely determined by its very position in this system of science.

A *Psychology and Natural Science*

The close contact modern psychology has with natural science has frequently led to it simply being straightforwardly assigned to the realm of natural science, or, at least, to its methods being identified with those of *natural science*. In the latter case, were its research method considered decisive for the *concept* of natural science, psychology would likewise be subordinated under this concept.

A kind of tracing back to natural science happens whenever no scientifically comprehensible reality whatsoever is conceded to mental processes. Such are replaced, then, by the physiological processes corresponding to them in the nervous system, in particular, those in the brain. One believes he has 'explained' the mental [*psychische*] processes whenever he has accounted for the course of the nerve impulse that accompanies it. Such a person holds this treatment of psychology as natural science to be the only possible way of treating it.

Clearly this conception stems from the dogma of materialism (which will not be further discussed here), according to which the mental process *is* absolutely nothing other than a brain process. Were the independent reality of mental [*seelische*] life once acknowledged, however—and precisely the unbiased appreciation of the facts that stems from natural science demands this acknowledgement—then the physiological explanation could never be identical with the psychological.

The physiological explanation can perhaps be the most important tool for the psychological explanation, but the mental process, which is an independent fact and coheres with other independent facts of a similar kind, is not completely explained by the claim that other facts, completely different by their nature, are demonstrated in their coherence with facts of the same kind. Such a "physiologically directed psychology", which turns psychology into a natural science, treats, without further consideration, the given bodily-mental world as a merely bodily world, and thereby makes itself guilty of the same metaphysical bias with which materialism approaches psychological problems.

The justification which is given from the *philosophical* standpoint of this conception of psychology as natural science goes deeper. The most detailed is from Heinrich Rickert in connection with an investigation of "natural scientific concept formation" in general.[5]

The task of a concept of natural science would be the conquest of the unsurveyable manifold in which the bodily world is given to us for the purpose of scientific knowledge. This is to be accomplished through the simplification taking place in conceptual processing. Nature is "reality with regard for what is general".[6]

Everywhere, thus, natural science "goes" "to the general", and the more perfectly the natural scientific concept is formed, the more it loses its proximity to intuition.[7] In this way, natural science fundamentally distinguishes itself as a

---

[5] Rickert wrote his doctoral dissertation (*Zur Lehre der Definition*-1888) on the theory of scientific concept formation. I quote his preface from the first edition of his text, *Die Grenzen der naturawissenschaftlichen Begriffsbildung: eine logische Einleitung in die historischen Wissenschaften* (*The Limits of Concept Formation in Natural Science: a Logical Introduction to the Historical Sciences*), the first volume of which was published in 1896, and the second volume of which was published in 1901: "I have been working on a theory of scientific concept formation since my doctoral dissertation, *Zur Lehre der Definition* (1888). Even then I opposed the idea of a universal method based on natural science, and I tried to demonstrate the emptiness of the doctrine according to which the common elements of things are the same as the essential features of concepts. It had become clear to me both that we always need a specific purpose with reference to which the essential features are distinguished from the inessential, and also that methodology is obliged to identify the diversity of these purposes in order to understand the variety of scientific methods and do justice to it. In my book *Der Gegenstand der Erkenntnis* [*The Object of Knowledge*] (1892), I attempted to establish both a general epistemological 'standpoint' for my further work and a theoretical basis for the primacy of practical reason. Thereafter I returned to methodological investigations. Very soon, however, I saw that the attempt to develop a theory of concept formation embracing all the sciences posed incalculable difficulties owing to the immense body of specialized scientific knowledge that would be required. So I tried to limit myself, above all attempting to understand the nature of *historical* concept formation—first, because this is the area to which logic has thus far contributed least; in addition, because an insight in to the fundamental difference between historical thought and thought in the natural sciences proved to be the most important point for understanding all specialized scientific activity; and finally, because it also seemed to me that this insight was an essential condition for the treatment of most philosophical problems or questions of weltanschauung. Here logical theory is employed to oppose naturalism and also to ground a historically oriented philosophical idealism."

Rickert, Heinrich. *The Limits of Concept Formation in Natural Science*. Edited and Translated by Guy Oakes. Cambridge University Press, Cambridge: 1986, p.3. –Tr.

[6] I think Elsenhans has in mind the following quotation from Rickert's book: "Empirical reality becomes nature when we conceive it with reference to the general. It becomes history when we conceive it with reference to the distinctive and the individual" (Rickert 1986: 54). –Tr.

[7] Elsenhans expresses here, throughout this section, and in the following section, a concern quite similar to the one Husserl, much later, articulates in his *Crisis of the European Sciences*,

"science of concepts" from history, the 'science of reality', which is explicitly concerned with intuitive, individual formations. Even the mental life, furthermore, would be such an unsurveyable manifold, supposed to be conquered through concepts.

In addition to the unsurveyability of the individual processes, we have to address here the restriction to one's own mental life, which alone is accessible without mediation. Already [52] for this reason, "in a psychology that is not supposed to merely represent the individual mental life of a single person," it would be completely impossible "to assume the mental [*psychischen*] processes as we experience them."[8] Psychology, too, would be geared toward the general. Psychology would be a 'natural science', too, because it sets out to understand mental life as a whole, with reference to what is general.

This question of method as such need not occupy us here.[9] It need only be emphasized that we consider the actual goal of natural science to be, not the formation of general concepts or laws, but rather the explanation of reality with the help of such universal concepts and laws.

Reality itself, however, as much the natural scientific as the historical, is *always individual*, so that quite a number of such concepts and laws always cooperate in the explanation of a single phenomenon. The mental [*seelische*] life is also such a reality, and genuine psychology thus does not proceed otherwise.

It is not, thus, a question of using the method of natural science in psychology, but rather of processing the reality of mental life allotted to psychology according to the universal laws of scientific thinking. The universal essential features of the scientific method modify themselves, however, according to the objects—here, according to what is characteristic of mental [*psychische*] life.[10]

Because of these modifications, however, it is even less possible for the method taken from the one field and shaped according to it, to be transferred to the other field. The danger of making psychology into natural science in

---

in his explanation of what precisely is the crisis he designates in the European sciences, namely, that we have lost track of the reality we seek through the mathematical natural scientific systems by which we seek it. Husserl. *The Crisis of the European Sciences and Transcendental Phenomenology.* Evanston: Northwestern University Press, 1970. –Tr.

8 Rickert, *The Limits of Concept Formation in Natural Science*, Cambridge University Press, 1986; p. 187. (*Die Grenzen der naturwissenschaftlichen Begriffsbildung: eine logische Einleitung in die historischen Wissenschaften*, J.C.B. Mohr: Tübingen und Leipzig, 1902, S. 187) The English translation of Rickert's book, edited and translated by Guy Oakes, excludes the entirety of the first two chapters of Rickert's original text, and thus excludes this section of text. –Tr.

9 Compare to this Th. *Elsenhans*, Fries and Kant. Gießen 1906. II, p.177 ff.

10 More information can be seen in the last chapter of this [Elsenhans's] book. [Not included in this translation. –Tr.]

this way is even greater since the modern development of science is completely shot through with natural scientific concepts, and psychology as a science is only preparing itself to gain the right of its own legislation.

B *Psychology and the 'Human Sciences'*

In close connection with these attempts to allocate to psychology its place in the wide realm of natural science, stand the attempts *to separate it from the 'human sciences'*. These are not identical attempts, because there remains the possibility to allocate to psychology a more or less independent position alongside natural science and to allow it to appear as nonetheless insignificant for the 'human sciences'.

According to one of the main proponents of the latter position, Hugo *Münsterberg*, whose physiological standpoint is already known to us, psychology belongs to the 'objectifying sciences', i.e., to those that set themselves the goal of describing and explaining objects apart from their relationship to the real, i.e., to the 'actual' subject.

These encountered objects are thereby completely detached from connection with the real subject and its self-experiences and, as a result, from connection with original reality itself, with which the 'subjectifying' sciences, i.e., the historical and legal sciences, occupy themselves. The concepts of psychology are thus most strictly to be divided from the concepts of real life, and psychology has absolutely nothing to do with the 'subjectifying sciences', i.e., with the otherwise so-called 'human sciences'.

This sharp separation between an unreal world of readily available objects and the real world of 'actual' subjects makes it possible to unify materialistic with idealistic inclinations in the same overall view. This is, however, ultimately, an intolerable dualism.

It is indisputable that those objects, as mental [*psychische*], are, *at least at the same time*, self-experiences of the subject, and likewise, [53] that this subject can become an object of the inner perception, and thereby of psychological research. The meaninglessness of psychology for all branches of knowledge that hang together with this original subject can thus only be maintained through an extremely artificial abstraction.

Something similar holds against other attempts to release empirical psychology from its connection with the 'human sciences'. One recognizes, it is true, that psychological concepts are indispensable for logic, ethics, aesthetics, epistemology, etc., but one believes that he must avoid empirical psychology to ensure for their results an importance transcending the individual.

One thus constructs, as Edmund *Husserl* in particular does, a purely descriptive "phenomenology of the lived-experiences of thinking and knowing" completely separate from empirical psychology, or, with Theodor *Lipps*, a phenomenology of "pure consciousness, transcending the individual," or, finally, with *Rickert*, one distinguishes from empirical psychology, which already, as a 'science of being', is indifferent to an ought and to values, a 'transcendental psychology', which teaches us to understand the realm "of the logical", which transcends the empirical, as "a world of theoretical values". It will be shown later that the interest in justifying valid standards that underlies such theories can also be satisfied in other ways.

In all these cases, however, there necessarily arises a duality of consciousness that cannot be reconciled with the unity of the mental life. There can be no disagreement that the single components of that consciousness which transcends the individual can, *in addition to* bearing the importance of transcending the empirical, nevertheless also be experienced by the individual consciousness. It is consequently unclear why they should not be rendered as such when made the object of scientific investigation, instead of being rendered only in a form that is conceived alongside their empirical existence. This is even more self-evident since we can have awareness of all of our conscious processes only through inner, thus 'empirical', perception.

Were this point conceded, however, the 'empirical' would inevitably become the yardstick of 'what transcends the empirical' (obviously, not with respect to the 'importance' of individual norms, which cannot at all be demonstrated, but only with respect to our knowledge of them).

Indeed, the actual implementation of that 'phenomenology' or 'transcendental psychology' would show, if one does not want to lapse completely into mysticism, that the single psychological concepts used in the course of this implementation cannot finally have any essentially different sense that they do not also have in empirical psychology.[11]

---

[11] The difficulty of a satisfying 'putting out of play' of empirical psychology shows itself particularly with *Husserl*, who, according to the opinion of other proponents of this direction, comes all too close to empirical psychology. It is interesting, for example, what *Rickert* says about it (*Zwei Wege der Erkenntnistheorie*, Halle 1909, p. 61): "Now, precisely Husserl, on the other hand, shows that even the 'pure' logic has still not completely come to a definitive differentiation from psychology. The concept of his "phenomenology" still includes serious problems, and, if Husserl says that even transcendental psychology is psychology, so will one be permitted to add that even phenomenology is transcendental psychology, and can only as such, i.e., through logical value relationship, accomplish anything." [Rickert also published this piece in *Kant-Studien*, Vol. 14 (1909), pp. 169–228. In this latter version, the relevant section of text can be found on p. 277. –Tr.]

With the indispensability of these concepts for the 'human sciences', psychology as a science of experience has, therefore, constitutive meaning for the 'human sciences', and, as we hope to show, a rich variety of fruitful contributions to aesthetics, ethics, logic, philosophy of religion, jurisprudence, history, etc., have arisen (and can still arise) from psychology.

C Psychology and Philosophy

Whoever considers psychology as a natural science, and as completely detached from the 'human sciences', has thereby simultaneously cut the old tie that bound it [54] with philosophy.

But also, many contemporary researchers who do not go so far are still inclined to consider it as a specialized science that has nothing more to do with philosophy than physics, chemistry, history, or any other specialized field of science. Psychology would count, then, as the last of the specialized sciences that have removed themselves from the service of philosophy, which once encompassed all specific areas of knowledge.

The standpoint represented here is completely different. We consider psychology to still belong to philosophy.

First, it may be emphasized that the close relationship that persists of old between these two sciences does not move in the same vein as the relationship between philosophy and any arbitrary specialized science. It could easily be shown that psychological concepts themselves extend much deeper even into the foundations of the great systems, which believe themselves able to do without psychology, than could be the case for any specialized science.

One would, moreover, need to point out that this commonality of the subject and the research activity has on the whole been preserved with remarkable tenacity. It is hardly a coincidence, and hardly to be explained by the original organization of the scientific enterprise that, despite the extensive specialization of psychological work (leaving aside a few exceptions), a close union still persists today between experimental psychology and philosophy.

But these historical matters of fact also always ultimately allow of another explanation or interpretation. They would prove nothing toward philosophy and psychology belonging together if they did not, in principle, give reasons for accepting it.

One reason of this sort could, for example, arise from a conceptual definition of philosophy, to show that it includes psychology. Since, however the true definition of philosophy is contested almost even more than even our question is, we would thus, by this approach, without thorough proof, move on very uncertain ground.

Instead, we single out that characteristic, its 'trade tool', as it were, through which the scientific enterprise of philosophy is most clearly distinguished from the specialized sciences, so we can then ask whether, in this characteristic, somehow philosophy is equivalent to psychology, or not.

It may hardly be disputed that psychology employs itself with abstract concepts to a completely different degree than is the case with the specialized sciences. If we look in the way of scientific thinking, then it is the *degree of abstraction* through which philosophy differentiates itself from the individual sciences. It refrains from distinctions, which are essential for specialized sciences, and it makes use of concepts which encompass a great number of specialized fields of scientific research.

But, exactly this *holds for psychology as well*. It is not correct to say that psychology comports itself to the mental world somewhat as physics comports itself to the physical world, and thus is an individual science, like physics. If one absolutely wants to draw such a parallel, he would encompass not merely physics, but rather *simultaneously* physics, chemistry, biology, and developmental history of the mental life.

The one discipline in the physical world approximately corresponding to it would be only, perhaps, natural philosophy. Psychology 'abstracts' from the differences of content of the specialized 'human sciences', from the special features according to which their objects differ, e. g., philology, jurisprudence, art history, economics, etc., and searches to explain the mental processes as such.

This abstract character of the discipline is still further increased as a result of the fact that the most clear means of differentiating individual entities, one of the great principles of individuation [*principia individuationes*], space, is completely absent for the objects of psychology. The representation of a square is not itself in turn a representation with four angles. [55] The individual mental processes allow themselves to be quite well differentiated in time and according to quality, but the lack of spatial characteristics requires a power of abstraction, which alone already makes comprehensible to us that psychology has preserved its cohesion with philosophy even until today.

The value of psychology for philosophy and, in turn, the necessity of a philosophical approach for a fruitful practice of psychology cannot be thoroughly discussed here. These can only come to light in the work of psychology itself.

There is no lack of evidence for the fact that the direction of our work here proceeds to allow this fruitful interaction between psychology and philosophy to emerge more than previously. As a symptom of this, may the words of one of the first foreign psychologists, who certainly cannot come under the suspicion of practicing psychology too philosophically, close this section:

> "At present Psychology is on the materialistic track, and ought, in the interests of ultimate success, to be allowed full headway even by those who are certain she will never fetch the port without putting down the helm once more. The only thing that is perfectly certain is that when taken up into the total body of Philosophy, the formulas of Psychology will appear with a very different meaning from that which they suggest so long as they are studied from the point of view of an abstract and truncated 'natural science', however practically necessary and indispensible their study from such a provisional point of view may be." [12]

Literature:

Windelband, Wilhelm (1904): *Geschichte und Naturwissenschaft.* Strassbourg: Heitz & Mündel.
Husserl, Edmund (1900): *Logische Untersuchungen I.* Leipzig: Veit & Co.
Husserl, Edmund (1901): *Logische Untersuchungen II.* Leipzig: Veit & Co
Münsterberg, Hugo (1900): *Grundzüge der Psychologie.* Leipzig: Barth.
Münsterberg, Hugo (1903): "The Position of Psychology in the System of Knowledge". In: *Psychological Monographs* 4(1), pp. 641–654.
Rickert, Heinrich (1986 [1902]): *The Limits of Concept Formation in Natural Science.* Guy Oakes (ed. and trans.). Cambridge: Cambridge University Press.
Rickert, Heinrich (1910): *Kulturwissenschaft und Naturwissenschaft.* Tübingen: Mohr.
Rickert, Heinrich (1909): "Zwei Wege der Erkenntnistheorie. Transcendentalpsychologie und Transcendentallogik". In: *Kant-Studien* 14, pp. 169–228.
Elsenhans, Theodor (1906a): *Fries und Kant: Ein Beitrag zur Geschichte und zur systematischen Grundlegung der Erkenntnistheorie.* Band I. Gießen: Töpelmann.
Elsenhans, Theodor (1906b): *Fries und Kant: Ein Beitrag zur Geschichte und zur systematischen Grundlegung der Erkenntnistheorie.* Band II. Gießen: Töpelmann.
Thilly, Frank (1906): "Psychology, Natural Science and Philosophy". In: *Philosophical Review* 15(2), pp. 130–144.
Lipps, Theodor (1905): "Inhalt und Gegenstand, Psychologie und Logik". In: *Sitzungsberichte der philosophisch-philologischen und der historischen Klasse der Königlich Bayerischen Akademie der Wissenschaften* 4, pp. 511–669.
Lipps, Theodor (1905b): "Die Wege der Psychologie." In: *Archiv für das gesammelte Psychologie* 6, pp. 1–21.
Lipps, Theodor (1907): "Bewußtsein und Gegenstände". In: *Psychologische Untersuchungen.* Leipzig: Engelmann, pp. 1–203.
Maier, Heinrich (1908): *Psychologie des emotionalen Denkens.* Tübingen: Barth (esp. p. 53f.)

---

[12] James, *Psychologie* 1909, p. 7. [German Translation of James, *Psychology* (*Briefer Course*) New York: Henry Holt and Co., 1892, p. 7]

Wundt, Wilhelm (1910): *Psychologismus und Logizismus. Kleine Schriften.* Leipzig: Engelmann, 1910, pp. 511–635.
Husserl, Edmund (1911): "Psychologie als strenge Wissenschaft". In: *Logos, Internationale Zeitschrift für Philosophie der Kultur*, pp. 289–341.
Heymans, Geradus (1911): *Das künftige Jahrhundert der Psychologie.* Leipzig: Barth.

Section Forty: The Intellectual Feelings[13]

[289] By the 'intellectual feelings', we understand all feelings that are tied up with the course of ideas, insofar as it serves the purpose of *knowledge*. Here, thus belong, to start with, the feelings of *intellectual satisfaction in general*, which are bound with the successful exercise of thinking. Such feelings likewise emerge where the thirst for knowledge of the investigator in a certain field arrives at its goal, as also where the curiosity of the child who orients himself to the new as such finds its satisfaction.

These feelings can discover a peculiar reinforcement through the fact that determinate regions of the individual's life, by virtue of his disposition or his experiences, are themselves already preferred as pleasurable. They thus become 'interesting' for the individual; because *interest* is nothing other than pleasure in one's intellectual engagement with objects of a specific kind.[14]

Where the task consists in arousing 'interest', as, e.g., in the lecture of the teacher, this goal will best be achieved there if both cooperate: the value the object has for the pupil, or at least its connection to objects valuable to him, and some method of treatment that allows him to find satisfaction in his intellectual engagement with them.

Completely detached from every relationship to individual advantages are the feelings of intellectual satisfaction in 'pure contemplation', most perfectly realized in 'the intellectual love of God' [*amor Dei intellectualis*] Spinoza describes, but also in the playful engagement of the desire for knowledge, one type of which is the solution of *riddles*. Here, in particular, we can talk of one's dissatisfaction growing with the tension [of inquiry].

---

13 In his *Ideas*, Husserl specifically identifies these pages of Elsenhans in a footnote on p. 39 (Section 21): "Presentations, such as, for example, those of Elsenhans (pp. 289 ff) in the textbook of psychology that has just appeared [This is, naturally, *Lehrbuch der Psychologie*. Tübingen: Mohr Siebech, 1912, the text translated here.] are in my estimation psychological fictions without the slightest foundation in the phenomenal" (Husserl. *Ideas for a Pure Phenomenology and Phenomenological Philosophy*. Tr. Daniel Dahlstrom. Indianapolis: Hackett, 2014.) This footnote can be found on p. 47 of the German text. (*Husserliana*, Bd. III, 1950). –Tr.

14 This psychologically and pedagogically so-defined, or similarly defined, concept of the *intellectual interest* is not to be confused with that of *material interest*. The linguistic use of language gives good clues here. With intellectual engagement, the emphasis lies on the object: we *interest* ourselves in something, *it* is interesting to us; the material relationship expresses itself in a condition of the subject: *we are* interested in it. *Kant* means the latter concept whenever he says: The judgment of taste is "without all interest". The material interest, however, can, as was given above, be the cause of the intellectual interest.

We have already encountered one other group of intellectual feelings. They are those through which recurring ideas announce themselves as already having once been there, the *feelings of familiarity*. They are little noticed, since they, as a rule, underlie significant neutralization and mostly are received as ancillary components of more encompassing intellectual feelings.

More important are the *logical feelings*, or the feelings of evidence in the narrower sense. Clear concepts, properly executed judgments and conclusions, the unifying thought of a logical system, are all accompanied by pleasurable feelings.

It would not be understandable why we prefer certain forms of thinking to others, were it not that some feeling of satisfaction is bound with their execution that fails to appear in other cases. Every dispute ultimately boils down to this inner feeling of evidence in conjunction with the common recognition of facts.

We must trust that the thinking of others, guided by this feeling of evidence,[15] also moves itself in the same forms as ours does. "The belief in the justice of this feeling and its reliability is the last anchor of all certainty in general; whoever does not acknowledge this, for him there is no science, but rather only contingent opining."[16] Since these [290] logical feelings first accompany simple, then complex, operations of thinking, and last, the formulation of laws of thinking, and since the simpler are received into the complex as partial feelings, so we have to distinguish lower, higher, and highest orders of logical feelings.

With the logical feelings, it is only a matter of the correct execution of the operations of thinking, regardless of whether the facts from which they originated are correct or the results at which one arrives are matter for knowledge. Where, however, the goal of thinking is *knowledge of truth*, there emerges a broader feeling, in which, again the logical feelings, but also the feelings of familiarity, enter as components, and which we may designate as an '*objective truth feeling*', or even as a feeling of evidence in the broader sense.

Were, for example, an object that we observe to be taken up into our conceptual system, 'determined' to be, e.g., a 'plant', so this procedure would be accompanied by an immediate feeling of the truth of the judgment expressed there-

---

[15] By 'evidence' here, Elsenhans means the just-mentioned pleasurable feelings that accompany clear concepts, properly executed judgments and conclusions, the unifying thought of a logical system, etc. This feeling of satisfaction that is bound into the execution of these forms of thinking explains why we prefer them to other forms that lack them. –Tr.

[16] *Sigwart*, Logik I, 2nd ed., pp. 15ff. [Available also in English translation: Sigwart. *Logic.* 2nd ed. Vol.1. Tr. Helen Dendy. New York: Macmillan, 1895. The relevant material can be found in the English translation in Section Three, on pp. 14ff. –Tr.] Compare also *Schleiermacher*, Dialektik, Section 88, p. 44ff.—Th. *Ziegler*, Das Gefühl, p. 160. For the epistemological meaning of ‚Evidenzgefühls', compare Th. *Elsenhans*, Fries and Kant II, p. 95ff.

in. Where facts stand against facts, and reasons against reasons, there arises a fluctuation between different possibilities, which is reflected in the ambivalent feeling of *doubt*.

The influence of this objective feeling of truth is, however, particularly clearly evident where it is a matter of exceptionally involved creative acts of cognition. The investigator who is able, with a new hypothesis, to light up a previously dark region, is less guided in doing so by executed conclusions and demonstrations as he is by an immediate feeling of truth.[17]

Only later does he [the investigator] unfold the process of his scientific discovery in a complete chain of proof. From the teleological point of view, the objective feeling of truth thus appears as the directing factor in the progress of science.

The psychological justification for finding a judgment true does not, however, always lie in the perception and logical processing of the object, but rather, it can also lie exclusively in the <u>subject</u>. We speak then of *trust* or of a *subjective feeling of truth*, in contrast to an objective feeling of truth, and call this result '*conviction*', in distinction from knowledge.[18] The subjective justifications of holding something for true can either lie in the influence of other subjects or in one's own native desire.

In the first case, we accept what others say, because we 'trust them'. This *trust in authority*, or the heteronomous subjective feeling of truth, is first exercised by children toward their parents, and is based primarily on the sympathy that, according to the laws of feeling expansion, extends to all that emanates from sympathetic people.

As a rule, however, the prospect of reward or the fear of punishment, which consequently form the main elements of *obedience*, join with the feeling complex that accompanies the authority. The authorities—of teachers, of the Church, of the state—appear then as powers, whom the individual is responsible to obey through inner affirmation and outer commitment to the teachings they proclaim.

The feeling complex closely linked with the idea of these authorities extends, through feeling expansion, to everything that is linked to them, and makes the thinking and desire of the individual dependent upon them by virtue of its significant motivating force.

---

17 The essence of this operation will, on the occasion of teaching about the scientific fantasy, become still more apparent.
18 Compare *Kant*, Kritik der reinen Vernunft. Methodenlehre, Ii. Hauptstück, III. Abschnitt. Ausgabe von *Kehrbach*, p. 620 ff. [Also available in English: Kant. *Critique of Pure Reason*. Tr. Norman Kemp Smith. Basingstoke: Palgrave MacMillan, 2003. –Tr.]

The autonomous subjective feeling of truth, or the trust in one's native desire is, on the other hand, based on the universal law that the subject affirms what supports his life, and negates what obstructs it, and, where corresponding ideas are not [291] available, it generates pictures of what is appropriate to the satisfaction of its desires.

This can be seen both in theoretical[19] and in practical fields. The individual is inclined to trust what fits with his own views and what satisfies his claim to life. The psychological confirmation for this is that "the wish" is "father to the thought". Trust in authority and trust in one's native desire, however, frequently cooperate to make the personal opinion into a conviction that cannot be shattered, either through facts, or through logical argumentation.

It is one of the most difficult tasks, and simultaneously one of the most urgent duties, of scientific investigators to let themselves be guided exclusively by the objective feeling of truth. Even, however, after the individual has progressed beyond dependence on the authority of the parental home, the school and the community to the formation of independent views, he never completely gets away from trust in authorities. The circle of what we can perceive ourselves and ascertain through sure inference is too small for us not to rely for a great part of our knowledge upon the statements and work of others whom we trust; and this dependency grows all the greater the more the specialization of science progresses.

Since, however, this kind of trust in authorities is finally based on the fact that we entrust to others our guidance by the objective feeling of truth and by the thinking properly controlling this guidance, so it is here, in a way, only a matter of an expansion of the objective factors of one's own view, in the sense of a working group of science.

The challenge is the more urgent, however, to eliminate from scientific work as such the falsifying influences of a trust in authority [that is] ossified in dogma, and of a trust in one's native desire that, for the sake of the rounding off of one's own view, does not want to accept even the irrefutable, and lets the objective feeling of truth be overgrown by the emotional influences of practical life challenges. It is the self-liberation from this confusion of objective research with egoistic wishes and the disinterested devotion of the 'I' to the truth which makes scientific work such a valuable tool for character formation.

---

19 Compare E. *Adickes*, Charakter und Weltanschauung. 2. Tausend. Tübingen, 1911

Will Britt
Henry Jackson Watt

Born in Aberdeen, Scotland, Watt received his Master of Arts in Philosophy from the University of Aberdeen in 1900, the same year that Husserl's *Logical Investigations* began to appear. He then spent 1901 and part of the following year in Berlin, studying psychology under Carl Stumpf, after which he went to the University of Würzburg to earn his doctorate with Oswald Külpe. After completing his thesis, entitled "Experimental Contribution to a Theory of Thinking," Watt returned in 1907 to teach at the University of Liverpool for a year, during which time the literature review translated here appeared in the *Archiv für die gesamte Psychologie*, edited by E. Meumann and W. Wirth. Watt then moved to the University of Glasgow, where he was professor from 1908 until his death, publishing four books on psychology in that time (with two more appearing posthumously). He died young, his health having been ruined by internment during a visit to Würzburg in 1914 (Murray 2000, 235-6).

Despite working in the tradition of experimental psychology inaugurated by Wilhelm Wundt, Watt and his colleagues in Würzburg thought it possible to pursue higher psychological functions, like thinking and willing, experimentally (Spiegelberg 1972, 57). Watt's work thus stakes out a middle position between Husserlian phenomenology, in which research is carried out entirely through direct first-personal description—which Watt takes to mean self-observation or introspection (*Selbstbeobachtung*)—and the Wundtian experimental method, which is conducted entirely in the third person, as a matter of statistical correlations between (sensory) stimuli and (oral) responses. As is evident in the literature review, Watt is thus methodologically opposed not to self-observation as such, but only to phenomenology's reliance on intuitive rather than inductive *arguments*. He puts it this way in the closing lines of the English abstract of his Ph.D. thesis: "The *great advantage of the experimental method* is that it enables us, by grouping of data and by a more exact knowledge of the elementary factors of experience [i. e., by limited variables], to overcome the insufficiency of our direct introspection." (Watt 1905-06, 266).

In reading this literature review, it will help substantially to have an idea of what kinds of experiments are under discussion, so let me briefly outline Watt's thesis work. His principal claim is that thinking is directed by the particular *task* presented to it, rather than being governed only by the otherwise closed system of associative bonds that are presumed to link up a stimulus with a response. To demonstrate this, Watt performs experiments similar to those of Narziss Ach, showing the subject a card with a noun on it and timing with some precision the (oral) associative response. The experimental subject then notes down whatever she has observed about the content or process of her own response (whether

DOI 10.1515/9783110551594-004

it followed one line of thought, whether she said what she meant to say, whether the process involved a visual or a verbal representation or no representation, etc.), and general inferences are made on the basis of many such experiments.

Watt's crucial development is to assign a particular task to the subject, e.g., *Classify the noun*; *Name an example*; *Name a part*. This gives a determinate shape (or 'determining tendency') to the response by producing a certain *focal engagement* or *attitude* (*Einstellung*) in the experimental subject. The changing of the task then turns out to influence decisively both the nature of the experience (whether it involves a visual representation, say) and the duration of the reaction (at least in some simple kinds of cases). By manipulating the variables, Watt carefully sorts out the differences in influence between task (which instruction is given) and stimulus (which word is on the card). His conclusion is that "the influences which determine every event in our mental experience fall into two large groups, [namely,] the operating task and the individual strength of the reproductions," (Watt 1905-06, 261), i.e., of the associations called up by the stimulus under the influence of that task. (He also refers to the associative strength as the 'tendency to reproduction'). Watt takes this to mean that the response is adequately determined by these two kinds of factors, without need for some further thing called *choice*.

With this background in mind, it is possible to recognize a particular drift of argument in the literature review. The opening section on self-observation criticizes claims to the intuitive transparency of thinking, but it does not seek to dismiss self-observation completely. In the section on the task, Watt unearths from others' research various aliases for his pet function: the determining tendency is shown to correspond to the ability to concentrate (*Fixierbarkeit*), to awareness (*Bewusstheit*), and to one meaning of adherence (*Haftenbleiben*) (but it is *not* the dynamic unconscious). The sections on perseveration, on miscellaneous papers, and on the diagnosis of a state of affairs are then discussions about the determinism of thought. Can ideas occur freely (i.e., non-determinedly)? Should we abandon the term 'tendency'? What is happening when 'free' association betrays itself by looking thoroughly determined? Finally, in the section on psychopathology, Watt returns to the question of self-observation from an odd perspective. Since it seems as though the task continues to function as a determining tendency even in psychotic thinking, and indeed may be the *only* thing still functioning in it, a psychotic person could very nearly outsource his self-observation, as it were, to a third party.

As we learn from his later *Psychology*, Watt (like Husserl) was seeking a science of experience. What Watt meant by 'experience,' however, was something like 'any mental state within the individual's consciousness.' The field of psychology would then include the conditions and means of expression of those experiences. But psychological research, like the phenomenological *epokhē*, would begin from a sort of dualism, trying to understand experience on its own terms, as a closed system, even if that system were taken to be in part dependent upon another (physical) system. Hence, Watt claims that "it would be folly to point to a complicated brain-process as explanation of some complicated, and as yet inexplicable, mental process." (Watt 1913, 14).

Husserl has no complaint with this latter claim, but he *does* feel obliged to respond to Watt's critique of self-observation, which is clearly aimed at first-personal description. In §79 of *Ideas I*, just after developing the central role of reflection in phenomenology, he pauses to deal with skeptical concerns about the general reliability and intuitive clarity of self-observation. Here I will sketch the three major moves that constitute Husserl's reply.

The first response is of a *logical* nature. Husserl begins by displacing the skeptical concern from reflection on something immanent – *Are the observed experiences identical with our real experiences?* – to reflection taken universally – *Can we acquire absolutely valid knowledge that is true for any experience? Or can we only have knowledge about experiences as reflected upon?* The formulation in terms of identity is in fact a question of existence and so should be bracketed phenomenologically; the latter formulation, however, since it asks about essential possibilities, remains an appropriate objection (Husserl 2014, 147-9).

Having marked out the legitimately pertinent version of skepticism, Husserl then claims that all genuine skepticism undermines itself, and this particular concern does so for two reasons. First, doubt is also a variety of reflection, so any serious doubt trades on the legitimacy of at least one sort of reflection. Second, any positive claims about the relation between reflection, on one hand, and unknown, merely lived experiences, on the other, presuppose reflective knowledge about both the acts of reflection and the unknown experiences in question (Husserl 2014, 149-51).

The remaining two responses are more *methodological* in character. First, Husserl accuses Watt of a kind of "pious belief in the omnipotence of the inductive method" (Husserl 2014, 147). Even Watt, he points out, acknowledges that such a method has its limits – but those limits themselves could not have been discovered via the inductive method.

Finally, Husserl pulls scientific rank on Watt, claiming that it is eidetic description (i.e., phenomenology), not experimental psychology, that deals with the conditions for the possibility of objects of knowledge, including such objects as one's own experiences. Watt's general empirical attempt, then, would be similar to a physicist trying "to overturn through experimental physics" something like Descartes's hyperbolic doubt about "whether or not, in the end, every external perception might be deceptive" (Husserl 2014, 153).

To put it quite simply, we could say that Watt is just operating on the wrong level, according to Husserl. If he wants to work out a genuine *critique* of self-observation (in the technical sense of setting out its limits), he must think more like Kant and less like Wundt.

References

Husserl, Edmund (2014): *Ideas for a Pure Phenomenology and Phenomenological Philosophy.* Daniel Dahlstrom (Trans.). Indianapolis/Cambridge: Hackett.
Murray, David J. (2000): "Henry Jackson Watt." In: Alan E. Kazdin (ed.), *Encyclopedia of Psychology, Vol. 8.* Washington, DC: American Psychological Association.
Spiegelberg, Herbert (1972): *Phenomenology in Psychology and Psychiatry: A Historical Introduction.* Evanston, IL: Northwestern University Press.
Watt, Henry J. (1913): *Psychology.* London: T. C. & E. C. Jack.

Translated by Will Britt
Henry J. Watt.
Literature Review: Second General Review On New Research in the Psychology of Memory and Association from the Year 1905

Literaturbericht. Sammelbericht (II.) über die neuere Forschung in der Gedächtnis- und Assoziationspsychologie aus dem Jahre 1905
Archiv für die Gesamte Psychologie 9, pp. 1–34 (1906)

[3] A synopsis of the literature from a single year concerning the currently active research into the psychology of thinking may not be wholly without interest, even if it remains somewhat fragmentary. I have attempted to bring together everything connected to the problems of the psychology of thinking, in the course of which I have also taken into account some heterogeneous points of view. I only hope that my effort will not be without its uses for my colleagues. Of course, there are some essays, mostly minor, that I have not taken up.

The Problem of Self-Observation

It is generally recognized that self-observation is the sole real and immediate source of psychological knowledge. To be sure, the immediacy of this knowledge has at various times been called into question. Nevertheless, we were not in general content to yield to negative conclusions, even when these counterarguments could only be incompletely and unsatisfactorily refuted. With this lack of critical insight and of a reliable method, we have long let ourselves be dominated by various presuppositions that – though they contributed much that is useful to the analysis of the most elementary psychological observations – were not adequate for more fine-grained questions, and in regard to such questions, mostly led to unsustainable consequences. The insufficiency of such presuppositions was more and more openly announced along with psychology's advance; we tried in part to correct it through appendices and additional discoveries of new elementary objects of self-observation, in part to bring it into a more innocuous form through suppressing every consideration of the presuppositions. In the actual formulation of the results, the main point was agreed upon, as it still is, even if some may yet call vigorously for the use of other basic concepts. [4] At present, one such conflict reigns concerning the merits of the concepts 'disposition,' 'tendency,' and so forth, in which epistemological observations about the reception of realities of a mental kind occupy a great deal of space. Yet for the content of specifically psychological knowledge, such observations amount to absolutely nothing. For psychology, the issue at first must be achieving the most general inductions, not proving or deducing universal properties of the elementary constituents of thought processes from universal points of view. Thus the shock that impels us toward a new investigation of the most general facts arose just as much from philosophy as from psychology. These facts pertain to the character of momentary and singular knowing. Philosophy – and especially its logical propaedeutic – no longer wanted to try to deduce this knowing from other facts, while psychology discovered it *as fact* in a peculiar manner and almost to its own astonishment. These two accomplishments now lead toward a renewed intensive investigation of self-observation in its principal significance for psychology. The year 1905 brings a whole series of contributions to this task.

It is in the clearest and most thorough manner that "this most difficult of tasks that can be asked of the human mind" is treated by Theodor Lipps (Lipps 1905b, p. 1). Experiences of consciousness, he says, are the object of psychology. But what are experiences of consciousness? Is blue perhaps one of them? No. The most general concept under which we can subsume blue is that of the object. Blue is in itself always an object, and it can become for me an object at any time. In other words, blue can be experienced [*erlebt*] by me at any time, although it need not always be. Never, however, is blue an experience [*Erlebnis*] in the sense of an experienc*ing* [*Erleben*]. We can designate it correctly if we say, 'Blue can be the content of an experience.' Psychology now concerns itself neither with any blue at all as object, nor with blue as intelligible or sensible object, but rather with blue as it is when it is the content of an experience. Therefore, in the object of psychology – in experience – there are two different things to be noticed: one, the content of the experience [*Erlebnis*]; the other, the experiencing of the content. "I can direct my interest at one time to the content that is experienced, at another time to the experiencing of that content . . . After all, this difference is only such in abstracting thought. The experiencing lies always implicit in the 'contents' of the experiencing, since their being-content [*das Inhaltsein*] just is my experiencing of the content" (Lipps 1905b, p. 5ff). "But whenever I have or experience contents of sensation or representation, not only these contents but also the experiencing itself is in turn experienced" (Lipps 1905b, p. 6). That is precisely what is characteristic of experiences of consciousness: one does not only experience something, but one also experiences consciousness, or one experiences the experiencing itself. Nonetheless, one will not call this experiencing in turn a content of consciousness. Being a content of consciousness, like being-blue, is something wholly other than being-experienced. The former is "simple existing or taking-place [*Dasein oder Stattfinden*]," which is not being-content. In this way, there are thus two sides to be distinguished in the unified experience, the content and the experiencing.

Now this distinction is not somehow the result of certain transformations of the object of cognition, transformations of the momentary experience, i.e., a cognitive process. [5] It is not that every experience has its content as well as a second side, the experiencing, which steps forth whenever the experience itself becomes the content of a second experience. It is not the product of certain cognitive processes that Lipps wants to adduce here, but rather the matter itself. To experience a content and simultaneously to experience this experiencing does not mean to know both.

The discussion becomes enormously complicated here, so one can hardly expect great clarity. It is, however, evidently easy in other areas to make the assumption that for us the cognitive process at last brings to knowledge its object as it is in itself. For one can both presuppose and obtain the result that the cognitive process and the scientific devices compensate for or suspend those blurrings which the effects of the object undergo, until the former call forth in us a cognition concerning the object. But if one always understands in cognition some extant process or other, indeed one cannot at all presuppose that knowing [*Wissen*] can be known as it is in itself, still less a mental state like experiencing, which is not knowing. Consequently, there must be a mental state that, even if it is not knowing, presents something identical, as if it were a cognition without a cognitive process.

Of course, with the above I do not want to say that Lipps followed this or similar paths of thought. Indeed, one can scarcely even conjecture about how one comes to knowledge of immediately experiencing anything, since it is neither knowing nor the object of knowing but instead something else. It is impossible to see how a report about the experiencing of experiencing, even if it exists, can be put down on paper. That difficulty can be heard even in the characteristic words of Lipps: "this strangeness adheres directly to experiences of consciousness." This is, however, always the ultimate question of the basic problem of self-observation, from which one has often set off, indeed with all self-evidence. Today one designates this absolute description as 'phenomenology' (Lipps 1905b, p. 8), and thus avoids the word 'knowing.'

To the experiencing of experiencing we must further add that every experiencing or having of a content of consciousness is simultaneously experienced as *mine*, and moreover that experiencing is *mine* of which I have the content. Here is meant "the immediately experienced I," "the conscious I," the "I-phenomenon." The conscious I is not experienced as the content of sensation and representation, but rather "the experiencing or having of the content is experienced as simultaneous with the content." "One may well wonder about that; consciousness simply is this wondrous thing." Just as in the case of experiencing, one tries in vain to describe this I. "It is what is immediately present in consciousness and at any time available, which everyone means when he says: 'I' sense, represent, think, 'I' am pleased, displeased, and so on" (Lipps 1905b, pp. 9, 10). But it is not the same with pleasure and displeasure. Pleasure is not merely the content of experiencing or a characteristic of experiencing, but rather both. It is both something that I feel and a way of feeling. This, in turn, is not grounded; rather, it is "finally nothing more than self-evident."

We can follow Lipps' further remarks somewhat more closely. He returns to the point from which he had set off. Blue is not only a sensory content, even if it can at any time become such for me. [6] "I can detach in my attention and consideration what is sensed from its existing as sensory content; I can posit and consider for itself what is sensed" (Lipps 1905a, p. 19). Thus it becomes the object of a science other than psychology, e.g., the geometry of colors. Blue is the object of psychology *only* as sensory content. But the fact that the content blue can cease to be merely my sensory content and can occupy in thought the proper place of an object, in which it is not merely had by me, but is also there for my consciousness – this is also important for psychology. Every mental activity, all thought, is directed toward some object or other. The 'blue itself' that is brought forth from out of the sense-content blue must have lain there beforehand, "only precisely not as brought forth, but rather implicitly." The content is not thereby transformed into an object, however; "rather, the content remains, or can remain, as precisely that which it is." This is no mere side-by-side, but an exact identity from the perspective of the 'what.' This is only possible because a content is for me always potentially an object. "(In this way) content and object may be covered over, yet in such a way that the content *is* beforehand precisely not the object, but rather both belong to different worlds" (Lipps 1905a, p. 29). "In the representational content, I think an object that is in fact qualitatively different from this content." "Should content and object be two different things for my consciousness, then I must also think the content. And this I can of course do. In retrospective consideration, I can place over against one another the content (or the image) and the object intended in it. Then precisely the content..., this experience of consciousness likewise becomes the object for me" (Lipps 1905a, p. 30). "The objects thought are therefore independent, whether they are thought in sensory or perceptual content, or in mere representational content." "Now instead of saying: 'I think the object in the content,' we could also say: 'the content represents the object to me... or is for me the symbol of it.'" "With this we must immediately distinguish the symbolic relation's taking place from my cognition concerning it. That this relation occurs means that it is experienced consciously." "I am only able to know of the symbolic relation as I think it and thoughtfully consider it," as I make it into an object for myself (Lipps 1905a, p. 34). Inner perception is in this case consideration of the experiences of consciousness as they become objects for me. "It is at the same time a consciousness of my own reality" (Lipps 1905a, p. 40). But "an experiencing cannot be thought while, or in the moment in which, it takes place." Inner perception is at every moment retrospective consideration. The I lurks in every experience of consciousness, and I can make no experience into an object without making myself into an object of my own consideration. An I stands to the other as object. But one moment does not contain two 'I's. "All self-perception or all perception of one's own conscious experiences therefore necessarily has as an object something which is past" (Lipps 1905a, p. 42). "Present conscious experiences are, to be sure, *conscious*, but they are not *known*. I have no cognition of them" (Lipps 1905a, p. 43). All self-consideration is recollection , not in the sense of recalling, of course, but in the sense of immediate recollection, of retention. "The operation that I have performed does not immediately dwindle while I consider it; it does not vanish while I inspect it, precisely *because* I do so" (Lipps 1905a, p. 45). [7] Self-consideration is the tendency toward present experiencing of what is past; it is most quickly possible and "takes place in a natural way when I have just now experienced this past thing." The reality of the present I and of the present conscious experience stands opposite the known reality of the objects of self-observation. This reality is experienced. "It is, precisely thereby, the absolute reality."

People may initially be of very different opinions about what can be made of this absolute reality. Undoubtedly, however, Lipps pulls together the main properties of mental life in an ordered presentation and with characteristic clarity. Moreover, it is a matter here only of the results of self-observation. Now if this ever-retrospective consideration is always a knowing of experiences that one has just *had*, where they are known as objects, how is one supposed to be able to set up conditions of which one can have no knowledge, conditions that are only conscious? The importance of the entire discussion turns, indeed, precisely on this; namely, on the derivation of a concept of immediate experience that is not a knowing. One must be able to observe. But experiencing is, ultimately, something everyone does – only without *knowing* this. And if he were to know it, how could he know that his experiencing is really absolute in the way that he thinks of it for himself? From whose head is phenomenology permitted to spring fully armed? Is a phenomenology possible, and in what sense? All of these questions become pressing. Perhaps a discussion of the question of self-observation, from the standpoint of experimental psychology, will throw new light on the field. For the problem of phenomenology is one that necessarily arises for experimental psychology, as well. Its answer will perhaps be even more careful, since it lacks the zeal of phenomenology's discoverer. In any case, it is in itself more dependent on an inductive method.

With the thorough implementation of systematic self-observation in the experiments of Ach, it was no longer a distant task to make more precise calculations about self-observation than had previously been done (Ach 1905). Already at the beginning of his book he applies to it some of his major results. Initially, for the purpose of easier analysis, he distinguishes three parts of individual psychological experiments: the initial period, which contains the time between signal and stimulation; the main period, which contains the actual reaction; and the subsequent period, which follows immediately upon the completion of the reaction. "The subject's instructions with respect to self-observation call for a thorough description, in the subsequent period, of the processes experienced in the initial period and the main period." Now in consequence of these instructions, typically no self-observation takes place during the initial period and the subsequent period. If it nonetheless occurs during this time, it usually disturbs the processes of the actual reaction, especially if the experiment is as yet little rehearsed. As the findings of Ach's experiments showed, this is because the so-called "'determining tendencies' of different contents that refer to the same experience exclude one another. The determination can only result in *one* determinate direction" (Ach 1905, p. 9). Now this direction for the reaction is conditioned by the actual instructions for the experiment, given while the intention of self-observation in the meantime remains latent, although this intention was relinquished prior to the beginning of the experiments. [8] But with practice, the determination that is realized in the reaction retreats, the reaction is determined more and more by mere tendencies to reproduction, "and the subject can now turn his attention to this content just as well as to enduring experiences, recollection-images, and external perceptions" (Ach 1905, p. 10). But now with Ach's experiments, there can be no talk of a lengthy practice of the mental process in the experiment. Besides, the procedure of self-observation would also have to be practiced. But that is not so crucial for Ach. He lays the greatest stress on the fact "that an attentively experienced content of consciousness has the tendency to persist as such longer in consciousness." He also believes this fact to be useful in the execution of self-observation. What he wants to indicate thereby is not hard to recognize. It is the same thing that Lipps means when he says that self-observation is the tendency toward present experiencing of what is past, i.e., immediate recollection. The content remains clear and almost sensibly alive. At the conclusion of the experiment, the subject has a peculiar consciousness of what was just experienced. "It is as if the whole experience has been given at once, but without specific differentiation of the contents." "Self-observation now occurs in relation to this enduring representation, in the same way as in relation to an external natural process. It can be observed without the direction of attention that takes place in observation disrupting the experience" (Ach 1905, p. 12). One can in general assign to this perseveration a duration of several minutes.

With the term "determining tendency," Ach wants to designate what was thoroughly reported on in the first of these general reviews under the name 'task' (Watt 1906). The next representative of that regard which, for Lipps, makes a content of consciousness into the symbol of an object (whereby the role that it plays in various cases and especially its relation over against the experience of a content has still been little researched) – the next representative is arguably also well within functional-analytic, causal-explanatory psychology. The older psychology and its successors call this tendency the residues of a prior experience, and in part are even quite right to do so. Herbart highlighted a very important aspect in his concept of 'apperception,' in which he emphasized that grasping some impression is essentially dependent on the multitude of aspects of the experience that are heaped up in the immediately preceding moment. One may indeed locate the influence of the determining tendency in mere aspects of determination, since the determining tendency joins itself purely mechanically to one of the tendencies toward reproduction that proceed from the representation of the stimulus, and thus determines the emergence of that representation which 'suits it' or which is 'required by it,' to put it popularly. Thus, one can consider perseveration as a property of all of the more-elementary constituents of the thought processes, such that any representation that is to be observed later persists in the mind, in gradually fading strength. Considered in such a way, perseveration would be an essential factor in the occurrence of self-observation. One must only remember that with self-observation, a determining tendency other than the one pertaining to the reaction has to affect the corresponding representation that is to be observed. [9] Now, whereas the availability of the representation that is to be observed (as representation of a stimulus) may be secured for a certain period by perseveration, the internal relation between the representation thereby occurring as reaction and the representation of the stimulus is completely different than the relation obtaining between this (observed) representation and the one following it in the reaction process. This intrinsic relation is, however, in this functional-analytic psychology, precisely the foundation of that with which self-observation, as knowing about something, is acquainted [*kennt*]. In the reaction, this relation need not always be a knowing; in self-observation, it almost always is. Now it is *possible* that the change of the determining tendency is not at all constituted functionally, but it is not likely. In any case, this is an important problem that cannot be passed over. To this extent, Ach's functional theory of self-observation must be considered incomplete. Moreover, the strength of the perseveration is known to decline quite precipitously with time, and at different rates for different levels of strength. And the kind of experimental procedure that Ach employed is quite extensive: it highlights one aspect of the reaction process after another, stimulates by questions from the experimenters as well as from the subjects themselves, and thereby brings into play the whole array of tendencies to reproduction and determining tendencies. Here the theory will thus have to wait upon further developments.

In a clearly written essay, Judd presents a theory that is now quite widespread in America. It is of a psychophysical character but often suffers from great impurity of expression, in that consciousness and movement are mixed up together without any order. Now this theory has not been without influence on opinions about self-observation. "Perception is to be described again as a process which is at once a process including sensory content and determined by motor tensions" (Judd 1905, p. 202). "The characteristics which must be especially referred to the motor ends for their explanation, are the relational or unifying characteristics. The characteristics which must be referred to sensory impulses are the diversified elementary characteristics. What the sensation-theory lacked was an adequate explanation of the unity of processes: this the coordination-theory supplies in definite form by a reference to motor ends" (Judd 1905, p. 208). "The motor process in the central nervous system is the end toward which the whole equilibrium is moving. The subject will not be specifically conscious of this end as distinct from the factors which are coordinated towards the end, but he will have in his consciousness just so much unity as there is unity in his coordination" (Judd 1905, p. 213). If one draws somewhat nearer to this theory in its proper sense, the result is manifestly the same as that of our investigation of Ach's theory. For the end toward which the whole mental activity strives is determined by the prevailing instruction, whether this be an authentic experimental instruction or the task of self-observation. Accordingly, the characteristic unity of the mental states is completely altered by the change of this end.

The appearances of Müller-Lyer illusions may be further explained by this theory of motor factors, e.g.: "movement reflects this neglect of the obliques in that the eye-movement is now executed primarily with reference to the comparison of the long lines" (Judd 1905, p. 219). [10] But explanation by these means hovers indeterminately between the effect of an instruction and the effect of the characteristics of the stimulus. To that extent, this manner of explanation may be compared with that of Lipps in his contribution "Toward the Understanding of Geometric Optical Illusions" (Lipps 1905c). This work wants to be phenomenological, purely descriptive. "Like the line, every 'object' is a dovetailing of something given and the activity through which the object becomes for me this object. But then reflection comes along and separates them. For the reflecting I, the activity and its object are set apart from one another and over against each other. And now I indicate the activity with the name 'activity of apperception,' which I exercise on an object or over against it. I do not thereby characterize the activity itself, i.e., I do not ascribe to it thereby a new qualitative determinacy; rather, I only recognize what stands 'over against' me in my separating. Now we are dealing here with that alone which, like the 'apperceptive' activity, is immediately experienced, not with that as which the activity is presented for the subsequent reflection" (Lipps 1905c, p. 247). "Now, instead of saying that such activities 'lie' in the line, and in the same way in all spatial forms, I can also say that the activities in question are empathically understood [eingefühlt] in the spatial forms" (Lipps 1905c, p. 248). It is surely evident that empathic understanding [Einfühlung] here is not to be heard in the sense of associative empathy [assoziative Einfühlung], but rather only as "something wholly peculiar, which bears the name empathy." "The compulsion toward continual expansion of the act of apprehension, or toward magnifying the line's length – a compulsion that lies in the angled lines 'going' forward or outward – becomes an augmentation of the line itself or a relative cancellation of its boundedness, and this has the same significance as a corresponding augmentation of the impression of magnitude that we have from the main lines." Lipps welcomes Benussi's results as a confirmation of his views (Benussi 1904). "That every accentuation of the main lines in the Müller-Lyer illusion lessens the illusion is self-evident, according to my theory, for which everything depends on the unitary grasping of the system of lines" (Lipps 1905c, p. 255). "Wundt calls the impulses 'impulses to eye-movements.' And this will indeed be correct. But it does not have to do with what the impulses *are*; it has rather to do with how I feel them, or, like I already said, what I experience them as in a conscious manner" (Lipps 1905c, p. 256).

It is, of course, unclear whether eye-movements (by regularly accompanying certain judgments) or the apperceptive activity (which is empathically understood in the objects in such a peculiar manner) are most important for the explanation. Certainly that is not to be decided without further work, perhaps not until a dependence between conditions of apperception and eye-movements is established. This apperceptive empathic understanding is nonetheless a highly tempting rationale, especially in the cases where one is already accustomed to its manner of expression – the line appears shorter because it is so constricted by the other one. But one may rightly ask why a vertical line, which is directed against 'gravity,' lays claim to greater apperceptive activity, and because of this should appear larger than and not similar to the constricted main line, which should perhaps appear smaller due to being apparently pinched. This new style of explanation, 'empathic understanding,' as splendid as the idea may be, stands in such cases on very shaky legs. [11] But crucial in these deliberations is the concession that the activity of apprehending lets the contents appear thus altered. Does this also carry over to the alteration of apprehension that takes place in the transition to self-observation? And if not, why? Furthermore, a large role in all of this is ascribed to the constituents of what is sensibly given, namely to the lines branching from the figures, even though everything is apparently chalked up to apperception. We are surely thereby lacking some theory that would mediate between the effects of stimulus-characteristics and those of the task, just as this also seems to be lacking in the above-mentioned achievements of Benussi (Benussi 1904, p. 31).

Finally, there are still some opinions to mention from the remaining literature on the question of self-observation. Gibson says: "My contention is simply this, that if we lay it down as a canon of observation that we can observe nothing except as an object, then we are logically cut off from self-knowledge in any true sense of the term" (Gibson 1905, p. 42). The more important point of view of the experiencing self, however, observes the subjective activities in their own nature, namely, *as* subjective activities. "And the form of observation characteristic of this point of view is simply self-consciousness in its immediacy. Such self-consciousness is the consciousness of self as self" (Gibson 1905, p. 44). Here we have again the point of view of absolutely immediate reality and of absolute certainty with regard to it.

James expresses himself with characteristic openness: "As for me, after many years of hesitation I have ended by making my choice squarely. I believe that consciousness (as it is commonly represented, either as an entity, or as pure activity, but in any case as being fluid, unextended, diaphanous, devoid of content of its own, but directly self-knowing – spiritual, in short), I believe, I say, that this sort of consciousness is pure fancy, and that the sum of concrete realities which the word '*consciousness*' should cover deserves quite a different description. Besides, this deserved description is one which a philosophy attentive to facts and capable of a little analysis should be henceforth capable of providing, or, rather, capable of beginning to provide" (James 1976, p. 267). He also does not shy from saying: "It is, therefore, by the addition of other phenomena that a given phenomenon becomes conscious or known, and not by a having of interior stuff. Knowledge of things *supervenes*; it is not immanent in them. It is a fact neither of a transcendental ego nor of a *Bewusstheit* [awareness] or act of consciousness which would animate each one of them. *They know each other*, or rather, there are some that know the others" (James 1976, p. 270). That means that quite manifold relations can obtain between contents of consciousness, which need not always be relations of cognition of one another, except perhaps whenever such relations are privileged to a great extent by the task of self-observation.

The work of Kiesow belongs almost entirely to this question of self-observation (Kiesow 1906). He wants to establish universally the presence of a reproductive intermediary in those cases of sudden, spontaneous reproduction that could be seen as examples of "freely occurring representations." For this purpose, his wife made many observations and carefully analyzed them. [12] So often was a reproductive intermediary found, that Kiesow feels himself justified in the universal claim: no reproduction without association. For the relation of this intermediary to attention, he favors the designation 'unnoticed' over another such as 'unconscious'. These observations, gathered together in such a way, now clarify many of our remarks, namely, those about the change of task in the transition to self-observation. They are so much the more beautiful, since for the most part certain objects were only naively thought about during the relevant experience, while the task of self-observation was neither effectively nor latently present, but rather was for the most part only summoned in recollection by the surprisingly sudden exchange of the object of thought. A beautiful example is on page 376: "This morning, after admiring the beautiful brown color of the coffee beans I had just finished roasting, I was turning away from the contemplation of them to go on with the roasting of another lot of beans, when suddenly a walk taken 15 years ago with M.H. and T.M. came into my mind. I immediately tried hard to find the connecting link and was just acknowledging to myself that the effort was hopeless, when I remembered (with the usual accompanying mental picture) that when I went for that walk I wore a brown dress of the color of the roasted coffee beans." Here the first object of thought was the beautiful color of the coffee beans, the second was the walk, the third was the two people, and so on. The brown dress was not thought of as an object. The representation of it was, nevertheless, very likely the mental element that effected the transition from one thought of an object to another. It is clear, however, that through self-observation not much is decided about how this intermediary looked to the psyche in the real experience. For otherwise, how could conflict about the concepts 'unconscious,' 'unnoticed,' 'perceived,' and so on continue to crop up?

Thus, there is evidently no lack of variety of opinions. In general, it is recognized that self-observation rests on immediate recollection, in which the vividness of the conditions to be observed quickly diminishes, and therewith also the possibility of their observation. But psychology must make clear to itself that, with self-observation, the objective relation of the experiences that are to be described is altered. Maybe this alteration has a much greater significance than one would at first be inclined to believe, and maybe not. That can be set aside here. But in relation to the I and to the self, psychology seems to be at a dead end. Some authorities affirm that, others deny it, and all are convinced that things are just as they claim. Above all, it must be emphasized that a functional-analytic psychology will never be able to explain the fact of knowing – i.e., of the relation of one elementary constituent of the thought processes to another with regard to content – if it also reveals and must seek to reveal a psychological or psychophysical foundation of that fact. In this respect, James's claim that one representation knows the others is quite innocuous for the theory of self-observation. Furthermore, it is a very important fact that tendencies toward reaction and tendencies in the form of tasks become conscious. If there are classes of categories, then functionally there will be certain groups of tasks or determining tendencies that constitute their genuine psychological foundations. [13] Even now, we will be unable to explain these and their functional relations. They must simply be discovered. Of course, it is another question whether they alter the states to whose determination they contribute. This can surely be investigated. Now, if the knowledge of experiences is not essentially blurred with the transformation of the object relation, then one may safely continue with self-observation. Or better: every advance in the psychology of thinking will contribute to the refinement of self-observation and to the greater exactness of our knowledge won thereby, just as the subject of the experiment becomes more proficient through practice. But one may talk of the I and of immediate experiencing (or the experiencing of experiencing) only with great caution. The word 'I' surely creates more difficulties in this matter than the concept of immediate experiencing. Nevertheless, the claim of Lipps and others that thereby the I of the sensory body should not be the core, the axis of mental life, would also involve the crassest "sensualistic psychology" if it did not turn upon precisely the word 'I'. It is entirely possible that the functional unity of consciousness – the unity of the field of consciousness, in consciousness, etc. – which unity is recognized by all, may receive its designation in this expression 'I,' while its presence is accentuated by some cases of a splitting of this function into multiple personalities. I am convinced, at least for myself, that behind the I of Lipps hides nothing other than just this functional unity. Only most people do not want to build a metaphysics on that. A being [Wesen] could hardly be more shadowy. Those who see it can tell us nothing more about it than that it exists. They are not permitted to know anything more about it. The question of the emergence of this concept of the I or of consciousness is of course something else again, and it need not be able to be led back to an evident assertion of immediate experiencing. For it has been variously maintained that this concept was formed in its genesis as a counter to the concept of the thing [*Ding*], or to that of material [*Materie*].

Nevertheless, since "immediate experiencing" is continually insisted upon, there is no defense against it. Yet the enormous role of mental reaction in our knowing is misjudged. One can recall the motor theory of the Americans; yet here we do not deal at all with movement, but only with what is mental. Considered in terms of the psyche, every cognition encompasses in itself an infinite number of elaborations of mental reactions. Every concept is created only to indicate a never-finalized series of objects. States of consciousness and thoughts are not at all described in themselves by Ach's 'awareness'; they are only fixable in those terms to which their mental elaboration leads certain tasks at hand. They are in fact simply breaks [*Pausen*] (cf. Taylor 1905; Wertheimer 1904), which are only recognizable in themselves and as important because certain experiences, whose psychical-mechanical meaning can easily be imitated in words, precede and follow them. Such breaks arise just as surely in the receptive understanding as in reproductive knowing (Taylor 1905, p. 228). In any case, I believe that we deceive ourselves if we ascribe to our experiences a great continuity or order – perhaps the order into which objects of every kind want to be brought. Our mental life is our own peculiar fabric of representations (images) and feelings, of "breaks" and intentional states, which, even if we have mostly found momentarily arresting signs for them in words, are endlessly referential. [14] It is a land where the practiced travelers content themselves with reading the brief details on innumerable signposts. It is obvious that under such circumstances, a purely descriptive psychology has a much more difficult and less fruitful task than a functional psychology that mainly occupies itself with the relations of temporality and dependence for distinguishable states.

It is also a very important task to fix distinctly the manner of intending, the intending of a group of objects, and the intending of a general or of an individual object. Psychology has long overlooked this in its engagement with the images and sensations of psychological mechanics. One group of such facts is now designated with the term "phenomenology." But if the logic of psychology wants to be independent, and if its phenomenological propaedeutic wants to be more than a synopsis of important results of typical psychological self-observation, then a group of facts must be intended by the term "phenomenology" that as such has nothing to do with the individual particulars and inductive generalizations of the special sciences, even of psychology. I mean that kind of generalization that is also contained in the evident propositions of logic, without recurring to anything more than the consistent meaning of words. Logical phenomenology rests therefore on generalizations that are already, from their proper foundation, found to be independent of individual particulars. But an immediate experiencing in the psychological sense, which knows and expresses itself, and is everything in and for itself, and so on – this is either only a name for what is mentally real as such, without relation to any of its qualities, or it is a non-thing. The history of philosophy is full of caprices that have been ascribed to this self. One must be trained in this self-observation, they say. Does this not then mean, as already indicated, that familiarity with mental conditions can come to expression only in mental reactions, i.e., mediately? And further, that the latter, in that they constitute or strengthen determining tendencies, affect the processes to be observed, and therefore can lead to a more complete expression? And that here, as in all sciences, knowledge only accumulates gradually and itself leads always to more precise knowledge?

General Questions

As recounted in the first review, Semon's attempt, in his book *The Mneme*, to demonstrate the identity of the basis of reproduction of organisms and of conscious memory has naturally occasioned just as much agreement as objection (Semon 1904). Thus Forel accepts Semon's doctrine outright and applies it straightforwardly to matters of detail (Forel 1905). On the other hand, Detto marshals an outstandingly thorough critique, which bears repeating here. He claims that it can in general only be a matter of a purely formal comparison, an analogy, "therefore only of the process of repetition [*Wiederholung*], in which memory in the psychological sense consists" (Detto 1905, p. 661). Detto understands memory purely psychologically. It is not the lasting disposition in the brain that forms memory, but it is rather the repeated emergence in consciousness. [15] Identification of the two would be identification of consciousness and movement. "It is not ambiguity that makes a concept valuable, i.e., applicable and advantageous, but rather the rigor of its definition . . . But if one declares the applicability of the concept 'memory' to nature, to the biological phenomenon, one therefore works with the concept of disposition, and not with that from which one began. Or should someone seriously believe that it is the repetitions of representation that the ontological recurrence (egg–organism–egg) evokes? In which part of the egg cell are these representations to be found? Are they recollections of the kidneys, teeth, and brain of ancestors?" (Detto 1905, p. 661–2) Detto wants to ascribe no proper rhythm to memory. Whatever periodicity there seems to be does not lie in the essence of representations or of consciousness; it is rather conditioned by the periodicity of perceptions, i.e., of the appearances of nature. "The *tertium comparationis*, the repetition, is in no way what is being sought, however. For precisely the repetition, e.g., in the generational exchange, in the manifestations of heredity, should indeed be explained. On the other hand, the repeatability of the representations, as what needs explanation, had likewise been perceived precisely in the memory; one had tried to explain them by a material arrangement; what light shall the fact of the repetition of representations now cast on the material processes of repetition, if the fact itself must first be made intelligible from out of such processes? . . . It remains fruitless under any circumstances to employ mental appearances for the clarification of physiological processes" (Detto 1905, p. 662–3). Detto considers Semon's analysis to be physiological. Its ostensibly psychological origin would be only seeming, even in its implementation. "That which the concept of 'mnemic appearances' contains would have been obtainable just as well solely on physiological grounds alone, e.g., from the analysis of the visible reactions of the higher animals" (Detto 1905, p. 665). The mneme is therefore no recollecting of what was earlier and at one time experienced, but rather simply "the total stock of so-called 'inner causes,' the 'specific constitution,' which in every way conditions one's particular nature and is passed along from generation to generation with the germplasm" (Detto 1905, p. 666). Along with this critique grounded in purely psychological concepts, Detto recognizes "that in the subtlety of his analysis, Semon has surpassed *Hering* and *Haeckel*, and . . . has expressed some thoughts that merit thorough consideration for physiological psychology and the theory of stimulation effects" (Detto 1905, p. 666). One cannot but concur with the leading ideas of this critique.

The Task

The investigation of this very important factor of thinking has been particularly undertaken and developed by Ach. He let his subject perform very extensive and thorough self-observations with regard to it, took note at every moment even of the slightest detail, and conducted his experiment only up to the moment when no change in experience could be detected. In this respect he distinguishes himself from many others who, with great skepticism, oppose the implementation and application of extensive self-observation in psychological experiments. [16] These others would prefer to rely upon presenting the dependence between the particulars of data, which correspond on one side to reactions, on the other side to experimental conditions introduced with the assumption that consistent experimental conditions follow from consistent behavior from the subject. But this assumption need not be valid, if an investigation of the real mental conduct of the subject has not taken place. Thus even regular numerical relations are no univocal criterion of a constant mental conduct, even if the working up of experimental results without self-observation can nonetheless be of great value under certain presuppositions. Aliotta claims in this respect "that if an explanation of numerical relations is to be achieved, this can only be founded upon introspective analysis. One must interrogate the subject from experiment to experiment about what is going on in her consciousness" (Aliotta 1905, p. 150). Now in his investigations, Ach would "value only those observations which are found to correspond in different subjects" (Ach 1905, p. 20). At first, simple reactions would be produced under the guidance of two instructions: to react muscularly and sensorily. It is emphasized that the muscular kind of reactions in the experience take the form of striving to react as quickly as possible, without thereby necessarily attending especially to the means or to the effectiveness of the reaction. The sensory focal engagement [*Einstellung*] is directed in a similar way to the complete grasping of the stimulus. The one form of reaction precludes the other. For "it is not possible for the subject simultaneously to engage focally and to perform two determinations that in their meaning and up to a certain point contradict each other, namely, under all circumstances to react as quickly as possible and to completely apprehend the white card [displayed as stimulus]" (Ach 1905, p. 69). Furthermore, the second task, to completely apprehend the stimulus, is indeterminate insofar as a subject may have difficulty being sure about when the comprehending [*Erkennung*] is complete. This doubt substantially prolongs the reaction times. Ach distinguishes five forms of sensory and four forms of muscular engagement, without claiming the list of possible forms to be complete. The result is "that, as is known, the engagement with the upcoming stimulus and with the movement to be performed can happen in various ways, that for example even a muscular engagement is possible through only inner speech, without intentional sensation of movement and without visual images, and with this engagement time-values are preserved, which are aligned to the order of magnitude that is characteristic for the muscular kind of reactions" (Ach 1905, p. 107). Now this is a confirmation that with constant numerical relations the mental conduct in its specifics does not need to remain constant.

The intent to react as quickly as possible, present in all the experiments, effects a gradual abstraction in apprehending the impression. With increasing practice, the sensory kind of reaction can thus cross over into the muscular kind, without essential boundaries in the content of the reaction's course being thereby transgressed. The typically longer duration of the sensory reaction rests merely on the apperception of the impression, which apperception is typically more complicated in sensory reactions and therefore lasts longer. Only certain behavioral measures can hinder the abbreviation of this apperception process. But precisely in such measures consists the opposition between the sensory and the muscular focal engagements. The latter engagement always inclines toward clearing the former out of the way, whenever it is not restrained. [17] The conduct of the subject also becomes more complicated in that she is able to establish no determinate boundary for the complete apperception of the impression, to which she can adhere. What is essential above all, as was already brought up, is that in the abbreviated muscular form of reaction, the focal engagement is *to react as fast as possible*, while in the lengthier sensorial form, it is *simply to have fully apprehended* the white card. These two instances should really be common to all occurrences of the two engagements in consciousness, and in fact should be effective in all of them. Furthermore, they set themselves in opposition to each other. Therefore, how the focal engagement is represented in consciousness is an inessential aspect, whether it is through so-called intentional sensations of movement, visual images, acoustic word-representations, or the like.

This outcome, which is based, to be sure, only on the data of self-observation, awakens hopes of a sizeable field for new research and of further important results. It is indeed probable that there are many tasks that mutually preclude one another, and that there are others that all contain something common in their effectiveness by which they can be grouped, as they seem to be in practical life. As an objection to Ach's remarks, however, we could well raise the question whether the muscular kind of reaction does not preclude the sensory merely because one is the negation of the other, rather than because the effectiveness of the one is incompatible with the effectiveness of the other at a purely psychological level, i.e., in a manner that we could be familiar with or understand only on the basis of actual analysis. If I should apprehend an impression as *completely* as possible, then I cannot react as *quickly* as possible, in the sense that I react faster when I apprehend the card as quickly as possible. The effort of this analysis on the basis of extensive self-observation is nevertheless richly rewarded with conclusive proof of the inadequacy of the earlier distinction between sensory and muscular kinds of reaction.

"We can accordingly also comprehend the two kinds of reaction as two different focal engagements of the task" (Ach 1905, p. 114). Instead of distinguishing them, along with L. Lange, as sensory and muscular forms, Ach would prefer (with Wundt) to designate them as extended and abbreviated forms of a single reaction, both of which are then "aligned with the natural form of reaction, in which no special instruction is given with regard to the speed of the movement, nor with regard to the apprehension of the stimulus" (Ach 1905, p. 115). "But in the abbreviated form of reaction, we have to do not with a perception of the stimulus, as Wundt assumes, but rather with an *apperception*" not of the stimulus but of the shift (Ach 1905, p. 116). Also, no particular conscious act (which embodies the voluntary action, the determining of the stimulation toward the achievement of a certain movement) needs to be present in the course of the reaction. The determination has already come about through the preparatory focal engagement.

It follows for Ach from all his investigations that, alongside the usual associative tendencies to reproduction and the aspect of perseveration highlighted by Müller and Pilzecker, *determining tendencies* are still to be posited. [18] These "form the foundation of those mental phenomena that in their unfolding have long been consolidated under the concept of act of the will" (Ach 1905, p. 187). Under the influence of suggestion, these determinations of the possible reactions to a stimulus arise with startling awareness, as Ach shows on the basis of interesting experiments. The determination can assert itself in various ways; Ach distinguishes five groups. But common to all of them is "the circumstance that the implementation always happens in a way corresponding to the meaning or the significance of the goal-presentation [*Zielvorstellung*], whether it be that an apperceptive confusion enters in, or that the intended outcome is immediately lifted over the threshold of consciousness by the reference-presentation [*Bezugsvorstellung*]. Only a few experiments constitute an exception, insofar as a reappearance of the goal-presentation occurs. The results up to this point indicate that here the necessary thoroughgoing intention is not present" (Ach 1905, p. 193). Even the comprehension of the stimulus, the properly decisive 'impression,' and its valuation are conditioned throughout by the goal-presentation. This determination can come into effect in the most various forms: suggestion, task, command, intent, and the like.

Ach's results stand in gratifying accord with the works discussed in the section entitled "The Task" in the first of these general reviews. I must refer the reader for many particulars to Ach's book itself and to my more detailed discussion of it in this archive.

In a long essay, Bleuler takes up the task of showing "that, and in what sense, there are unconscious mental phenomena, and in which various ways they may express themselves" (Bleuler 1905, 128). His remarks almost exclusively concern the factor of the task or determining tendency. The author, however, shows himself heavily inclined to construction and thus easily overcomes every difficulty. He brings up, among others, the well-known example of the man on the street, who, though preoccupied by a problem, nevertheless fortunately avoids all obstacles, arrives successfully at his destination, and does not notice most of what goes on around him. "Here we are dealing with *unconscious recognition* as opposed to conscious recognition. But it must be added that this unconscious phenomenon also governs conscious feeling, motor reaction, and even deliberation" (Bleuler 1905, p. 131). The cited examples, however, are all either comparatively long processes that take place under the influence of one task, which needs only to remain in effect, not also to be observed; or reactions like avoiding things on the street, which proceed merely associatively, without explicit knowledge, self-observation, or a struggle between various tendencies taking place; or, finally, such uncritically accepted cases as unconscious deliberations, solutions to mathematical problems in the unconscious that spring into consciousness fully formed, and the like. But it is not by any means required that every mental process be observed, or that it rest on decisions secured with symbolic designations. One can certainly judge according to a "hunch," in that one relies on those associative connections that have developed within one. [19] One can also in this way be quite conscious of the objects of one's consideration and one's respective actions and pronouncements, without knowing to which part of an object or elementary sensory aspect of one's experiences every part of one's general pronouncement pertains, how one's judgment is motivated, or how it is founded. But one does not therefore call a judgment unconscious. Besides, among the examples given by Bleuler are very many cases where self-observation has been, at the least, incomplete and insufficient.

Summarizing everything into a theory, Bleuler claims "that all our conscious mental functions can also proceed unconsciously, without thereby changing anything in their character . . . The conscious quality, the becoming-conscious of a mental process, is therefore something wholly incidental to the consideration of our psyche" (Bleuler 1905, p. 140). Of all the differences between conscious and unconscious processes, only the *focal engagement* plays an essential role. "But what this is, on what it is based, we do not know." "What (hitherto) has been understood as the focal engagement, as attention, uniquely facilitates determinate associations and inhibits all others" (Bleuler 1905, p. 141). One can suggest only that in unconscious acts of thought, considerations, etc., a certain connection with the conscious I or I-complex is lacking. "What is new in our conception is therefore only that it assumes that the distinction constantly to be observed between a present or missing connection with the I suffices to ground the presence or lack of the quality of being-conscious." Bleuler feels unable to give a strict proof for the correctness of this hypothesis, even though it "explains without remainder every pertinent fact that he has observed for 26 years concerning people both healthy and ill" (Bleuler 1905, p. 256).

Since neither a definition of the I or the I-complex nor of consciousness is forthcoming, we need not enter further into this hypothesis. It certainly does not hold for the I-complex of the sensation-psychologists, the bodily and personal I, in which sense indeed it comes to be meant also by Bleuler. It is not clear why this complex should be especially endowed with consciousness, unless that means merely that most people are more interested in themselves and better retain everything concerning themselves. There is much that is correct in Bleuler's essay. But a functional analysis of the given examples, with the aid of self-observation, is missing. Even the effects of mental mechanisms whose first moments of determination were conscious have often been confused with the unconscious. Bleuler has not grasped the full significance and difficulty of the problem of the unconscious and of the conscious, especially this one: that the questions about the details of the mechanism in almost all of his examples are not on the same level. Consciousness can signify various things: the apperceptive judgment 'this is thus and so' or 'I have experienced this and that'; being present as the object of a statement of self-observation; the status of a representation that has not become the object of a self-observation, but could have; and so on. Still, insofar as he attributes to the focal engagement, to the task, a very important role in our conscious life, we can only agree with him.

[20] Ability to concentrate [*Fixierbarkeit*] is a concept that has been established in psychiatry and that corresponds to the one functionally specified here. "We designate a sick person as able to concentrate whenever he reacts to questions or prompts either correctly, or at least in a manner that manifests the reaction unambiguously as belonging to the circle of representations that was stimulated by the question or prompt. The latter case appears whenever the sick person, when asked about the date, for example, provides the wrong one" (Heilbronner 1905a, p. 431). There are differences in this ability, which are correlated with the difficulty of the question posed and of the recollections necessary for concentration. Considered in such a way, distractibility and concentration are essentially identical processes, rather than, as so many consider them, directly opposed aspects. The adherence [*Haftenbleiben*] thoroughly discussed by Heilbronner is quite similar to those processes, but only adherence in the sense of ability to concentrate, of sustaining a line of thought, not in the sense of the role that a concentrating or adhering element plays within the train of thought itself. In this context, Heilbronner also brings to our attention the fact that "it is not settled *a priori* which representation is the point of departure for a train of thought and which representation is the goal; one will not go wrong in the assumption that, in itself, any representation can just as easily be the point of departure as the goal; the two can change places according to circumstance" (Heilbronner 1905c, p. 197).

Ach attempts to provide a theory of the effect of determining tendencies (Ach 1905, p. 223 f.). He links it with his remarks on 'awareness,' with which he has dealt extensively. With this word he designates the presence of a knowing that is not given in intuition, and by which awareness is characterized in its particularity. If an awareness arises often, it gradually fades, becomes less intense – just as do those that embody expectation and knowing, in the initial period of the experiment, concerning what is coming. There are also differences of intensity with regard to various parts of the knowledge contained in awareness. Now this aspect, now that one arises more vividly. Therefore, one would be entitled to differentiate levels of the intensity of awareness. Nevertheless, we might here remember a comment by Lipps: "We still attend especially to the opposition between this 'activity of turning towards' [a content] and the 'act of thought.' This opposition is clearly expressed above all in that the turning towards or the activity of apprehending can be more or less *complete*; in short, that it has *degrees*. By contrast, thinking has no degrees. Something is either thought, or it is not. Something is an object for me, or it is not" (Lipps 1905b, p. 25). Now Ach maintains that, simultaneously or immediately beforehand, a sensation is constantly given along with awareness – a visual, acoustic, kinaesthetic, or muscular sensation, or a recollection of the same. "These sensations thereby form the intuitive conscious representation of the content that is non-intuitively present as knowing. They are signs of meaningful content" (Ach 1905, p. 213). But Ach is of course also not wishing to maintain that what is known as contained in awareness has degrees. It is either known or not known, specifiable or not. It is therefore perhaps not the meaningful content of awareness that has degrees, but awareness itself. These degrees of awareness, however, have as yet only been described through their meaningful content. Ach is the first person who has ascribed any texture to the pure state of awareness. Certainly one says of the *objects* of degrees of awareness, 'I was dimly aware of this or that'. [21] But this can mean that it was simply unclear, or that the one who encountered it could only with difficulty verbalize his knowledge, or that a certain part of the object played a different role in the logical complex than it did in another case, or something similar. At any rate, it may be that Ach is right, and it is to be hoped that future research will also contribute to the description of the state of the degrees of awareness.

The foundation of awareness has now been located in the piecemeal stimulation of the tendencies to reproduction, which are bound to the intuitive element that is linked with awareness. As a condition capable of intensification, awareness is a growing function of just such a stimulation of the tendencies to reproduction. Among these tendencies, the varied strength of the stimulation uniquely explains the various shades of meaning that the same symbol, e. g., the word 'Glocke' [bell], often has. It is thus also understandable how awareness can develop into intuitive aspects, and how one can, through connected levels of awareness, achieve various intuitive aspects and reactions from the same symbol. That the preparation determines the reaction proceeding from a stimulus is also to be thought in this way.

Now this theory of awareness may be quite plausible. But it also veils precisely some of the difficulties of the problem of self-observation. For in what way can we consider as evidence of a certain mental state the continuation of tendencies whose mere resonance is the foundation of this state? Is the cognition that develops out of this mental state not simply a product of this development? How could one in each case achieve certainty in the claim that what results from the state was present in the state itself as cognition? For it is evident that, under the influence of the task of obtaining clearer cognition or observation, one could in no way abandon oneself to this state without immediately developing it into cognition. In the course of naïve, direct thinking, however, the state could certainly have a functional significance and nonetheless, when directly considered as mental, be a mere emptiness – an aspect having the highest importance, but one that we could in no way lay hold of without developing cognition out of it. The aspect would indeed exist only for this purpose, to unfold into cognition, whether this unfolding be wished or necessary. But only as an actual mental state, a complex of mental possibilities, would it itself have an existence. Thus the greatest part of our mental life would not be at all experienced or conscious. Only meager and few representations – in comparison with the degrees of awareness – would drift past us. Considered purely psychologically, most would be only possibilities for the unfolding of cognition, possibilities that would be given in actual, not 'phenomenological' states of our minds, possibilities that hence are really incapable of completely unfolding. I do not thereby mean to say that Ach's theory, in that it is an attempt to discover a foundation for awareness and its functions that would be in line with *Realpsychologie*, is unjustified or unacceptable. With these remarks, I only want to suggest that the state and its functions are hard to distinguish from one another via 'awareness', and that these functions are not necessarily represented in the qualitative texture of the state, but that perhaps the qualities ascribed to the state would have to be more correctly ascribed wholly to the function. [22]

Perseveration

No small amount of work was done on perseveration in 1905. Heilbronner has contributed a very clear overview of the whole relevant psychiatric literature and a thorough discussion of the question. "It is first a matter of deciding whether adherence [*Haftenbleiben*] is to be apprehended as a *primary*, self-standing symptom, arising independently of other elementary disturbances; i.e., whether the adhering representation ('representation' in the widest sense) receives, as it were, a dominant position by its own power, or whether the same only accrues to it *secondarily*, from the (equally conditioned) retreat of another" (Heilbronner 1905b, 293f.). Both perspectives are now represented in the literature. For the experimental test, there arises from the same source the *posing of the question:* "If the adherence were in fact conditioned by an active overvaluation of the adhering representation, by the special intensity with which it imposes itself (in *von Solder's* sense), then the style of the question or the task, or the greater or lesser difficulty of the required performance, would be permitted to exert no essential influence on its occurrence. But the reaction in the sense of adherence generally follows, as with aphasic states, subsidiarily, as it were, because when the correct solution for the task is impossible, the frequency of the perseveratory reaction must be independent of the difficulties of the task imposed" (Heilbronner 1905b, 308f.).

Now Heilbronner conducted experiments with his series of images on a patient in an epileptic state of 'stupor' (Heilbronner 1898). Several times in succession, images of varying objects and complexity were laid before the subject for naming. From these experiments, the conclusion was drawn "that adherence runs parallel to the relative difficulty of the task and that between the two exists an inner connection" (Heilbronner 1905b, 312). Here, however, it would certainly be more correct to refer to the difficulty or complexity of the *stimulus*, since, in fact, the task was identical in every case. It is therefore almost self-explanatory: with complex stimuli that either are unfamiliar or – by the inhibition of many stimulated tendencies to reproduction – nevertheless offer only a slow reproduction, greater opportunity is provided for perseverating reactions. Further, it is impossible to see how the alternative conclusion would be justified in posing the question, since a given representation with a certain intensity is to be thought equivalent to a representation that arises as the result of a deficit of other factors and is subject to a certain, albeit variably strong, stimulation. A dependence of the intensity of stimulation on other factors would therefore be presupposed in both cases. To strengthen his conclusion, Heilbronner adduces the very consideration that one would have to expect, assuming a repression of the correct reaction by the perseverating representation: namely, that in the the case of perseveration, the reproduction times would be shorter, although that was not the case in his experiments. The reproduction times have, however, indeed been shorter than those of the correct reactions would have been, if the latter had been able to appear at all. This is in order to emphasize all the more that when Heilbronner's stimuli were not equally challenging, the experiments were therefore not directly comparable with one another (cf. the principle of determination of a reproduction by the tendencies to reproduction that are in themselves the strongest) (Müller, Pilzecker 1900, p. 103f.). [23]

Heilbronner summarizes the results of his remaining experiments and his conclusions very clearly: "All other things being equal, there exists the least probability of achieving adherence reactions whenever one allows the patient to name simple objects in nature or in fully worked out pictures; the probability becomes greater, if one instead gives the patient schematic images, and in fact more so the less this schema contains. The task of associating continuous sequences leads to repetitions of such minimal frequency that adherence could only be spoken of in a very few cases. Associating stimulus words presents the surest method for inducing adherence. Thereby a gradual transition is accomplished: from resorting at first to already used verbal associations – ones that still make sense – to senseless adherence reactions. The repetitions generally, and most especially the senseless ones, appear sooner with abstract than with concrete stimulus words. The relation of the simple repetition of a stimulus word to adherence requires still more precise investigation" (Heilbronner 1905b, p. 337 f.). The frequency of adherence is thus wholly and essentially dependent on the level of difficulty, the unusualness, of the stimulus. "By contrast, experiments have yielded nothing that would speak for the overvaluation of a single representation that actively makes the occurrence of a correct reaction impossible. The manner in which the repetitions of adherent words are spread, often at great distance, over a single sequence, already speaks against the assumption" (Heilbronner 1905b, p. 338). "A couple of things anticipatorily seem to me to warrant caution: first, the question how, from the beginning or over the course of the investigation, the tendency steps into the foreground to produce, in place of the solution to the task, simply *any* reaction at all. Second, and intimately connected to the first, how far the one being tested still judges and can judge about the difficulty and possible insolubility of the task" (Heilbronner 1905b, p. 339), i.e., the point at which the answer "I can't do that" (or something like it) is encountered as the better output, as responding to the lack of reaction.

The greatest difficulty for Heilbronner remains the irregular and delayed succession of a second appearance of the perseverating reaction-word after the first such appearance. Thus he also takes it as counting against von Solder that brief duration and continuity with the initial occurrence of the relevant representation do not emerge as essential markers of perseveration, but that instead the perseverating representations appear once again after some days, completely discontinuously (Heilbronner 1905a, p. 431). He finds himself convinced, on the contrary, "that adherence can stretch its effect out over much greater intervals of time than would before have been willingly accepted" (Heilbronner 1905c, p. 177). All this leads him to the general claim that perseveration is a matter not of the strength of a certain (perseverating) representation, but of the deficit of other factors, or a matter of a "secondary appearance that enters in place of an absent, correct outcome" (Heilbronner 1905b, p. 345). 'Deficit' here might be understood as, for example, the absence of an appropriate tendency to reproduction upon the introduction of a new stimulus. But in his superb analyses, Heilbronner does add that it is not a matter of an absolute deficit, since the possibility or task of reacting at all remains. [24] Now either he has to admit the possibility (against which he struggles) of the effect of a representation due to the (relative or absolute) increase of its strength through perseveration, or he has to offer a theory of mistaken reactions in general. For, so long as a task is still present, or whatever factors involved have not absolutely disappeared – in other words, in the transition from an easier to a harder task (in Heilbronner's sense) – one must presuppose that a perseverating representation is then holding sway. This is because the task now has little force, i.e., either because the perseverating representation is now stronger in relation to the task, or because the representation has become absolutely stronger through the increase of its perseveration, without any change of task or of stimulus. In fact, the psychological result of Heilbronner's whole discussion is the question: "which general conditions have to be fulfilled, so that the deficient reaction ensues precisely in the form of adherence?" (Heilbronner 1905b, p. 345) Heilbronner additionally draws attention to the fact that much larger complexes adhere as single representations (Heilbronner 1905a, p. 430). This may be compared with the opinion expressed in the first review (Watt 1906, p. 19), that perseveration is an aspect that effectively can appear alongside all the constituent parts of the thinking processes. Some observations of perseveration in a case of epileptic seizures are found especially in Isserlin (1905).

Stransky offers a peculiar method for manufacturing conditions of language confusion in normal subjects. He had already earlier brought attention to the fact that one can encounter expressed language confusion in oneself in a state of drowsiness, if one only allows one's thoughts to run aimlessly, without especially guiding them. He then allowed the subject in his experiment to let loose, so to speak, by talking into a phonograph about whatever was connected to a given keyword, allowing in each case one minute per experiment, and only instructing the subject to relax his attention, i.e., not to monitor what was said (Stransky 1905, p. 13). This resulted in "a mixture of flights of ideas and perseveration in a genuine muddle, leading to wholly singular verbal formations. At the same time, associations of contrast clearly arise and, above all, verbal manifestations that are designated as contamination" (Stransky 1905, p. 15). Now if the treatment of this stream of words is quite difficult and, in Stransky's book, somewhat lacking, the method in itself is brilliant. We will have to return to it later. With reference to perseveration, Stransky is with Heilbronner in the opinion that it is to be considered a deficit manifestation (Stransky, 99). Even Ranschburg assumes a tendency of perseveration belonging to representations, and indeed on the basis of correct reproductions that arise after a delay (Ranschburg 1905, p. 122). Interesting considerations about perseveration are also to be found in Wertheimer (Wertheimer, Klein 1904, p. 123 f.).

The work of Kiesow is devoted not to questions of detail concerning perseveration, but to the principal question, whether there are "freely occurring" representations, reproductions without association (Kiesow 1905). He relies for this on a number of very interesting observations made and collected by *Frau Professor Kiesow*. These are mostly related to sudden intrusions in thought, to unusual memories of experiences long past and seldom recalled, and other such things. In total, there were 892 observations taken down. [25] One can now subscribe without hesitation to Kiesow's conviction that in almost all of these cases, a reproducing middle term was present, even where none could be discovered. That is to say, these same cases are doubtless just as much the most improbable cases of perseveration, in the sense of Müller and Pilzecker, as they are cases of freely occurring representations. For such intrusions presuppose an entirely peculiar, seldom-realized tendency to reproduction, such that the question concerning a peculiar regularity that above all pertains to the individual coefficient of consciousness (e. g., the representation) is not touched by Kiesow's analysis. At least on the basis of his analysis, Kiesow is not justified in his slogan: no reproduction without association (Kiesow 1905, p. 370) – or, as it could be better expressed in Külpe's terminology so as to avoid a tautology: no centrally activated sensation without association. Kiesow speaks additionally of a representation that has persisted for some time unnoticed in consciousness, in order then to reproduce a second representation in turn (Kiesow 1905, p. 375). I think that a problem lies in this possibility of effective persistence in consciousness, one that Kiesow has overlooked: the real problem of the tendency to perseveration. The question of what is unconscious or unnoticed does not belong to this functional question of the duration of an effectiveness. In treating the question of perseveration, often even genuine psychologists conflate different questions: that of the actual existence of the representation, that of what is conscious and what is unconscious, or really that of self-observation, and the question concerning the regularities that are valid for representations. But these are questions that do not stand on the same level. Indeed, the question of perseveration does not at all enter into the sphere of self-observation.

Miscellany

Aliotta has given us an interesting and insightful critique of the narrower psychologies of memory and association and of their methods. His critique harmonizes in all essential points with the intent of this review. In relation to the question of subtraction, e. g., he maintains: "A mental phenomenon that is isolated in its original simplicity is one thing; it is another thing entirely if it has become a member of a complex system. It is not at all evident, much less a postulate, that the phenomenon lasts equally long in both cases" (Aliotta 1905, p. 121). The process of willing precedes, as it also brings about, the reaction itself; hence its duration falls outside the time of the reaction.

Lobsien returns to his earlier essay (cf. Lobsien 1904, pp. 28–29; 1905, p. 21). Namely, he had tried to show there that for the relevant experiments "in the overwhelming majority of cases, a repetition after 24 and then after 48 hours provided a richer rendition than the first observation... There remains, at any rate, one source of error: that the students consult with one another after the lecture hour. But according to my experience, this circumstance is in no way as risky to experimental technique as it might well seem at first glance. It is possible that the danger is greater on the first day of the experiment, but the experiments took place at the beginning of the lecture hour, so that the subsequent lecture had a strong erasing effect" (Lobsien 1905, 17). This justification, however, runs directly counter to the the "fact" of improvement over time. [26] Thereby also in many cases the frequency of a single pair of terms (e. g., inkwell/shoe) greatly increases as the days pass. The most blatant example is 0, 8, 8, 15 times. That means that the children arrive on their own at a harmony in the sequence of designations for an object seen at an earlier time! In consideration of such cases and of the fact that the tables produced by Lobsien do not at all eliminate the possibility of a source of major error – indeed, another treatment of the numbers would have been necessary in order to achieve this – it is generally ill-advised to want to argue away such sources of error, especially where the whole of prior research screams against the new "regularity."

To this direction belongs the work of Wessely, who nevertheless contributes nothing new and is mostly guided by pedagogical perspectives (Wessely 1905). Bernstein and Bogdanoff again confirm an advance in retentiveness with the age of the students (Bernstein, Bogdanoff, 1905). Alexander-Schäfer found that although primary memory images, under the influence of pistol shots occurring nearby, were somewhat unfavorable to immediate recollection, nonetheless the intended progression of familiar memories was not noticeably affected (Alexander-Schäfer 1905). One soon grows accustomed to being an eagerly-learning experimental subject, while remaining calm amidst pistol shots

Ranschburg has already drawn attention to the significance of resemblance for reproduction: "With equal intensity and equal emotional value, out of a simultaneously (or nearly simultaneously) influencing crowd of stimuli, those that are dissimilar to one another are preferred, while those that are similar or identical have an inhibiting influence on each other" (Ranschburg 1905, p. 66). Now learning experiments with rows of syllables, which contain syllables and groups of syllables that are in part heterogeneous throughout and in part repetitive, show that learning of the latter sort of rows is greatly hindered, in contrast to that of the rows with thoroughly varied syllables. The "homogeneous" rows were formed such "that within each six component rows, the first and last consonants of the first component row repeated themselves in identical combination and sequence; yet within every component row, the same consonant pair is connected by a different vowel. For example, if the first syllable of the first component row was 'ber', then that of the second was 'bir', of the third 'bar', of the fourth 'bur', etc. If the second syllable of the first row was 'tef', then that of the second row was 'tif', of the third 'töf', etc." (Ranschburg 1905, p. 96). Ranschburg's results are as follows:

> 1) Homogeneous double rows of eight pairs of syllables – whose consonant pairs are identical in four-to-four pairs – result in fewer correct answers and a significantly longer period of reproduction than the rows of equal lengths that are heterogeneous throughout. Learning of the former sort of rows is therefore mostly more difficult, and their reproduction is more inhibited. Time also has a most decisive weakening influence that is greater on the homogeneous rows than on the heterogeneous. Under repeated interrogation and after a fairly long latency, this influence of time makes itself apparent through a rather heavy decrease in the number of correct answers and a lengthening of reproduction times, as well as a relatively meager strengthening effect of the same number of repetitions and a fairly large amount of effort required to employ methods of re-learning, as the case may be. Thus the retention of learned homogeneous rows for a rather long duration turns out to be less favorable than the retention of heterogeneous rows. [27]
>
> 2) If several short homogeneous component rows (of the construction described above) are learned – split up by intervening breaks – and individually asked about, then, with a growing number of repetitions, the learnability of the individual similar component group increases along with the time, since fewer repetitions are required for completely learning the homogeneous rows than for the continually heterogeneous ones. If the exercise with the identical consonant pairs is then revealed, these are rarely or no longer mistaken and are mostly reproduced mechanically; even the vowels belonging to them are correctly recalled with fairly brief latency times. By contrast, despite a somewhat greater number of correct answers, the reproduction time is shown to be for the most part at least as long as for the heterogeneous rows, and in the overwhelming number of cases significantly longer [...]

3) If they have already been learned individually, several component rows of heterogeneous parts can be learned as a whole without difficulty by means of a determinate – usually not high – number of repetitions (*Rn*). Already-learned component rows of homogeneous construction, consolidated as a whole by this same number of repetitions, are learned, retained, and reproduced with extreme difficulty. The number of correct answers does not increase through the application of *Rn*, nor even sometimes through *R2n* or *R3n*, but decreases, and the scanty reproductions demand a very considerable amount of time, one that almost always expands itself by several seconds.

4) The subjective conduct of the experiment's subjects attests to certainty of the reproductions, continuing practice, and with this a growing feeling of pleasure concerning the heterogeneous rows; concerning the homogeneous rows, it attests to increasing uncertainty, effectiveness that initially grows, then diminishes with the growing accumulation of merely partial identity, and feelings of confusion, of discomfort, of displeasure, of exhaustion. (Ranschburg 1905, p. 119 f.)

The scope of memory is thus broader, the grip of memory stronger, and the reproduction time shorter for contents that are heterogeneous than for those that are homogeneous. Contents of consciousness that are similar to one another, or their mental foundations, are inhibited to a high degree. In connection with the work of the Pavlovian school, Meisl draws attention to very interesting appearances of inhibition (Meisl 1905).

In his critique of Ranschburg, Aliotta betrays a generally widespread prejudice against the concept of 'tendencies' and the mechanical explanation of such psychological results (Aliotta 1905, p. 197). The increase in errors does not come from a dynamic inhibition of the representations of individual numbers in the field of consciousness, but much more from the fact that perception becomes more difficult and requires more time the more complex and unclear is the object to be perceived. Notwithstanding that similar rows are not more difficult to learn under all circumstances (see section 2 of Ranschburg's results above), according to Aliotta, the ground for inferring the greater difficulty of a complex object is lacking. With the homogeneous rows, it is also not a matter of *the* more complex object but of *groups* of objects that are similar or dissimilar to one another. Aliotta calls the inhibition explanation a relic of Herbart's metaphysics. "Empirically, we can determine merely the objective and subjective conditions of such phenomena, without wanting to give a mechanical explanation, which distorts the mental phenomenon in that it ascribes to the phenomenon physical properties and provides no account of the processes of consciousness in their factual course" (Aliotta 1905, p. 197). [28] Now we should notice additionally that both psychology and Ranschburg, with the incorporation of extensive self-observation, strive to accomplish this latter task. Even a pure 'phenomenological' explanation of the course of mental life still hardly exists, to put it cautiously. The use of the word 'tendency' for the presentation of psychological experiments like

Ranschburg's proves itself to be quite expedient and helpful. One can grasp for oneself the concept 'tendency' however one wants: as a mere expression for probabilities, as the energy level of a mentally enduring essence, of representation, or of the physiological basis of something mental that only exists for a moment. In any case, such epistemological objections may not be brought forward against the manner of presentation of a work on particulars. It makes a great difference whether one seeks with *Herbart* to deduce the regularities of mental life from mechanical presuppositions, or whether one seeks with mechanical concepts to present results that precisely *look* as if they depended on mechanisms. The latter approach also says nothing about the nature of these mechanisms, but only that the results show up in numerical determinations, in the manner which we are accustomed to see with mechanisms.

In his habilitation, Jung provides the reaction times belonging to work of his that I have already dealt with (in the earlier review) (Jung 1905b). The measurements were made with a clock specified to fifths of a second. The overall mean value for the length of time of an association comes to 1.8 seconds. But how conditional the significance of this value is "may be illuminated on the basis of the composition of its foundations. The variability of the mean is most easily shown if we arrange the subjects according to certain simple perspectives and compare the numbers of the individual groups with one another" (Jung 1905b, p. 5). Thus, e.g., the duration of association for women is longer than for men. The experimental subject also betrays a clear inclination to provide in the reaction the grammatical form of the stimulus word. This tendency fits under the restrictive influence of the laws of frequency. "Adjectives and verbs occur in speech roughly half as often as nouns. The noun thus has a higher frequency-value, which is why the probability of reproduction of a noun is greater than for adjectives and verbs." In Jung's experiments, what followed noun stimulus words averaged out to 73% nouns; what followed verbs was 33% verbs; what followed adjectives was 52% adjectives. Accordingly, the reactions to verbs and adjectives also show a longer time than the reactions to stimulus words that are concrete nouns. The reactions to general concepts require the longest time. Educated men form an exception, insofar as they have their longest reaction time with concrete stimulus words. Jung does not give an explanation for that. A longer period of time accompanies interior association than exterior. Reactions to sound lie occasionally between or above these two. They are never shorter, although one would expect the shortest time for them. "But evidently in practice the relationships are not as simple as one could believe theoretically . . . Investigating the reaction times in association experiments for themselves, apart from the analysis of the content of the associations, cannot be recommended, since the reaction times are dependent in the highest degree on the momentary content of consciousness"

(Jung 1905a, p. 79). We gladly express our agreement with this thought, with one caveat: that self-observation and the analysis of the content of the association were missing in the earlier works of Jung and Riklin (Jung, Riklin 1904/5). [29] Aliotta, too, emphasizes that the analysis of experiences and the grounding of the reaction times undergird one another in turn.

Diagnosis of a State of Affairs

Under the name "psychological diagnosis of a state of affairs," the following very interesting question had been raised by Wertheimer and Klein: can experimental methods not be found that would distinguish whether someone knows of a particular state of affairs, or whether this is unfamiliar to him? Wertheimer is now striving for this in an extensive investigation (Wertheimer and Klein, 1904). On the way to discovering suitable methods, it is presupposed that the manifold combinations of the genuine circumstances of a deed normally posit a series of mental conditions in the author, namely, determinate associations of individual representations with one another and combinations with emotions and judgments. The methods therefore must be of such kind that they highlight this and allow it to be known, even in the case of the investigated person's willful deception, i.e., without employing this person's direct testimony about the relevant facts. Now in order to obtain an explicit symptomatology, the impressions included in the experiment were not permitted to be too elementary, lest their effects be too much inhibited or blurred by the same kind of impressions or by earlier effects of the same impressions. Quite large complexes, therefore, as for example the history of a home invasion robbery with a plan of the house, were made familiar to the subject with some precision. In order to direct the subject's will in a wholly general way upon producing something in connection with a stimulus or upon hindering as much as possible the reproduction of certain contents, the method of free association was used in the investigation.

Now the experiments were conducted with the usual apparatus for the more exact kind of association experiments. First came 1) initial sequences of free associations, which were supposed to make manifest the effect of prior indifferent impressions on the person under investigation. Then 2) main sequences with the underlying complex, in which the complex was unfamiliar to the subject. 3) Main sequences in which the subject was familiar with the complex and had the task of not letting on (a deception experiment). Next, 4) main sequences like (3), in which, however, no instructions were given to the subject. 5) Sequences with self-observation that correspond to (3) and are meant to further that investigation. For sequences (2) and (3), in each case a complex was used whereby a cyclical distribution to the subject was arranged. For the construction of the sequences of words, I must refer the reader to the work itself (Wertheimer and Klein 1904, 72f.). This construction employed in part (and especially at the beginning) irrelevant words, in part contents of the complex, in part the complex itself, yet contained contents alien to the complex, etc., for the purpose of removing every mental distraction of the person under investigation except that coming from the relevant complex.

Self-observation revealed that with the stimulus words obtained from the complex, the nexus of the complex mostly became effective immediately. Either a particular word intruded from the complex, or this complex was made effective in a visual image, in a general, indeterminate way, or in the the form of an awareness of the relation of what was experienced to the complex. [30] Additionally, the inclination to speak out the intrusive word was generally quite strong, even though the word was, of course, often rejected in favor of another. Sometimes this suppressed word nevertheless won through later in the course of the experiment. Along with this suppression of words, sometimes the word intruding upon it was spoken out straightaway, through which qualitatively abnormal reactions came about. Or a hesitation from embarrassment followed the rejection of the first word, a moment in which nothing arose in consciousness. This is brought to an end by a search for a word, or else either the initially rejected word or another word arises by itself. The word that is spoken out is thus sometimes a complex-word and sometimes irrelevant to the complex. It is not rare for the stimulus word to be mechanically repeated. With one subject, a very strong, distressing feeling of displeasure was usually present along with a complex-sequence. This feeling was stronger, the more clearly the optical image developed in consciousness.

Indeed, one can also perceive the affinity to the complex in the reaction-words themselves. The word appears garbled at times, or no reaction follows it. Other reaction words appear sought-after: they are senseless, sound-associations, repetitions of earlier words of the sequence, or auxiliary words. Only in a few cases do some subjects succeed in reacting to a complex-word with a completely irrelevant word. The reaction times are almost always longer in those cases than the average. In general, the result arises that reactions to complex-stimuli are characterized in all cases by a very high percentage of long and qualitatively abnormal reactions. This is also strengthened by the data of self-observation. Even where the self-observation referred to no thoughts of the complex, with complex-stimuli, the nexus of the complex still appears to have been effective, as the long times and qualitative peculiarities of most long reactions allow us to assume. This is also how the effectiveness of a complex that is not explicitly expressed in consciousness would be surmised. Even where a subject knew nothing beforehand of the experiment's purpose, nor of the connection between the complex and the association-sequence on the test, and had no instruction to deceive, the effectiveness of familiarity with the complex was verifiable. An investigation into very simple complexes and sequences of words confirmed it. The less pronounced effects of these simple complexes nevertheless allow us to surmise that in errors of quite firm associations or in errors of excitation the characteristic effects at first fail to appear, or escape evaluation by these methods. In general, therefore, by common, long (compared to the average for association-sequences relevant to the test), and qualitatively abnormal reactions to the complex-stimuli that are interspersed in the sequences, we can perceive that the subject under investigation is familiar with the relevant complexes.

The following are to be emphasized as conditions that ground this abnormality of the critical reactions: 1) The associative reactions, which are quite stirred up by the repeated 'infringement' of the complex into the test-sequence. 2) The influx of various thoughts and tendencies, and the inhibition that these exercise on one another. 3) The perseveration of various states that hinder the appearance of other contents and obtrude themselves at every favorable moment, and further all kinds of focal engagements. [31] Types of the latter that are characteristic for the experiments are: the focus on any reaction at all, the focus on certain critical words that then appear again and again, the focus on reaction with critical words and on criticality as such, and the like. Finally, the emotional accent of many states plays an important role during the course of the reaction.

Jung lays the greatest weight on emotion in his investigations (Jung 1905a, 1905b). The role of the complex in the context of mental effectiveness struck him during the association experiments discussed earlier (Jung and Riklin, 1904–5). Jung takes "the excessively long reaction times" as his point of departure and finds, as supported by the indications of the subject, that in the specific grasping of the reaction-word, a complex is stirred up during the reaction. "The association in which the complex is stirred up has an excessively long reaction time ... Aside from those associations with a longer reaction time, complex-constellations contain still numerous other associations ... A consistent behavior with regard to becoming aware of the significance of the association could at most be found in this: merely that consciousness of the complex awoke a very heavy and differentiated emotional shading or a very distinctive grasping of the reaction ... In all other reactions, the emotional shading or specific grasping of the reaction merely formed the signals of subsequent recognition of the complex" (Jung 1905b, 19). Jung recalls the results of Mayer and Orth, that the occurrence of an emotionally fraught content of consciousness lengthens the reaction. Ultimately, after an investigation of the objective character of the reaction and of the self-observation (which was not methodically carried through), he summarizes as follows: "1) On the basis of the communicated numbers, it turns out that very long reaction times are caused almost without exception by the interposition of a heavy emotional shading. 2) Heavy emotional shadings belong, as a rule, to broad and personally important complexes of representations. 3) The reaction can be an association that belongs to such a complex and have in itself the emotional shading of this complex without the complex needing to be present to consciousness" (Jung 1905b, 30).

The accord with Wertheimer's results here is quite gratifying, even though Jung's results are not so well-grounded in terms of method as those of Wertheimer. A consideration of the other possible causes for a lengthening of the reaction time is also missing, although Jung ultimately comes back to ascribing to the emotions a role in every longer reaction. Also interesting is his observation that "the emotional shading can unconsciously influence even the reaction next in line, by which various phenomena are to be observed: a. The reaction influenced by the perseverating emotional shading has an excessively long reaction time. b. The reaction is still an association that belongs to the circle of representations of the preceding complex. c. The reaction has an abnormal character, etc" (Jung 1905a, 30). The various kinds of focal engagement mentioned by Wertheimer (e. g., the focus on criticality that arises with the infringement of a complex) could indeed also contribute here to the lengthening of the reaction time.

[32] Wertheimer has delivered an interesting continuation of his investigations, most recently in the *Archive for Criminal Anthropology* (Wertheimer 1905). A certain *state of affairs* was presented to particular subjects. This formed the complex, familiarity with which was supposed to be diagnosed later in the test. The motive to reproduction then formed a history similar to the complex, a history which was composed somewhat like a magazine story. A group of subjects that was not wholly identical to the first group received this history, which was to be read at the same rate. The investigation consisted in a fairly long sequence of questions that pertained to the history they had read, but it also contained more general questions that would allow knowledge of the first state of affairs to be recognized. Lastly, the will to deception was aroused by telling the subjects, before they read the history, that they were under suspicion. "Now in all cases the results let us clearly recognize which subjects were familiar with the state of affairs and which were not, and indeed this happened mainly: a. through materially characteristic mistaken indications in the meaning of the state of affairs (distortions, additions); b. through the relation of irrelevant mistakes to inductions that moved from the state of affairs to the indications that were supposed to be valid for the 'history.' Mistaken indications mostly occurred in the complete conviction that there was no mistake: thus the subjects, without

noticing it, offered facts on the basis of the state of affairs" (Wertheimer 1905, p. 297). There were various other experiments conducted, including some with genuine complexes, that all confirmed and supported what has been reported so far. With the genuine processes, he hit upon the following device: the director of the experiment "knew only so much as in a given case the real examining magistrate would know. He had merely visited the workshops and gathered a 'report on the state of affairs.' Sometimes 'suspects' were presented to him individually; he did not know which subjects really were familiar with the state of affairs" (Wertheimer 1905, p. 315f.). The results overall yielded the solution to the puzzle: the subjects who were familiar with the complex were almost always clearly distinguished from the 'innocent', without the former knowing that they had betrayed themselves.

The Psychopathological

In this section I do not want to interfere in an area that is unfamiliar to me, but only to mention and summarize some work that seems to me to be of inspiring value in the investigation of thinking – an investigation that has now become so active. It is a very difficult area, one that nonetheless seems to depend essentially upon advances in the analysis of normal thought, which is supported by self-observation that is here much more reliable. While psychopathologists handle their material through other objectives and terms, accordance of the results of their research and that of psychologists is thereby all the more worthwhile and important. Bleuler says: "There is no better touchstone for the value of a psychological theory than its usefulness in psychopathology" (Bleuler 1905, 128).

We have an interesting psychological discussion of symbolic appearances from *Heilbronner* (Heilbronner 1905c), whose work on adherence and stereotypy has already been referenced (Heilbronner 1905b). [33] This same work attends extensively to perseveration and its relation to the task of the naming of images. The concept of 'personal contributions' highlights an important aspect in the course of mental processes. "To the sick person (possibly to the healthy person) who 'in the course of conversation' uses without any difficulty a word that is required and sought but that he absolutely wanted not to appear, corresponds the apraxic person, who eats neatly with others at the common lunch table, while attempting to take an exam by writing in the vegetables with a spoon." Here the difference between a stimulus conditioned by a task, a stimulus that mainly appeals momentarily, and the situation for associatively inspired action seems to be clear. If the difference between tendencies to reproduction and determining tendencies is also valid for the physiological foundations of mental processes, then one has to expect that the effect of all kinds of tasks in various dimensions and measures would be suspended in traumatic psychoses, while the possibility of mere reproduction could still exist. Thus, the determination that is brought about by the spoken address could still be effective: while certain stimuli in such cases remain without effect, others affect reactions along with the task as usual, and still others, while they cannot be reached by the effectiveness of a particular task, under favorable circumstances attain a reaction merely associatively. "One can, of course without thereby explaining much, refer to the fact that the customary mistaken reactions of the apraxic person – reactions that are both organized and not conditioned by perseveration – correspond almost without exception to very frequently practiced and thereby favored movements. I have never seen female patients try to 'smoke' all possible objects, as is reported of male patients in nearly every record" (Heilbronner 1905c, p. 177). Maybe even new, unique tasks are cultivated in ill people, as for example speech compulsion, which seems to be something autonomous. Heilbronner has "referred on previous occasions to the fact that it can only be of service in detection of the essence of a flight of ideas, if the *content* of the speech compulsion that involves the flight of ideas is at least initially considered separately from the speech compulsion as such ... With regard to the verbigeration, it is within reach, on the other hand, to make the perseverating of a representation responsible for the arising of the speech compulsion" (Heilbronner 1905b, p. 366). Stransky's method for artificially generating a speech compulsion – letting the subject speak into a phonograph as fast as possible for a minute, in connection to a prompt-word – is quite interesting in this context (Stransky 1905). His results only support the suggestion that the content of the speech compulsion is to be separated from the speech compulsion itself. Which regularities determine this content of the speech compulsion, of course, still remains to be investigated more closely. One finds in Stransky detailed renditions of the speech compulsion so generated; his theoretical treatment of the same unfortunately leaves something to be desired.

"But if we now consider that even normal subjects, when allowed to carry on or to voice aloud their verbal associations without the influence of attention and through a guiding representation that was strong in emotion, presented speech samples that came within a hair's-breadth of presenting in the analysis the same elementary properties as the hebephrenic-catatonic subjects, then we will conceive that it must appear quite plausible to consider even these latter as conditioned by the lack of attention" (Stransky 1905, p. 93). This conclusion from normal subjects to ill ones is methodologically important. [34] Of course it cannot be logically compelling, but it is of great value with regard to hindrances in the path of self-observation in mental illness. In this way, one could, so to speak, consign self-observation to another person. The goal of this is to call forth, by the alteration of familiar experimental conditions, the same manifestations as are observed in sick people. Now if these manifestations are the same, then we may assume, as cause of the same symptoms in the sick person, that which – or a group of conditions related to that which – in the normal subject brought about the alteration of the experimental conditions. Even in those cases where only a very distant resemblance to the form of manifestation of the mental illness can be reached with normal subjects, such artificial "mental disturbance" could perform very useful work.

A very interesting case for psychologists is described by Reich. The patient received a blow to the head from a small stone. Thereafter he had a very short memory, did not know what he had done shortly before; finally, it went so far that by the next moment he had forgotten everything. "If I said, 'Get me the scissors,' or 'Get me the spoon,' then he was at a loss, but if I said, 'Get me that thing there,' then he gave it to me" (Reich 1905, 827). Until his admission to the hospital, he was familiar with a quantity of things that served daily needs and was even able to use them more or less correctly. He still washed himself, in the beginning; then only if his wife gave him sugar and cigars for it; finally, he no longer washed himself at all. The circle of paths familiar to him had gradually shrunk so much, that he only walked around a water tower situated near his residence. It struck his wife that he only found these paths if he came on his own upon the idea to walk there. His memory was, according to his wife, "purely mechanical." Everything stood in its place; if he once skipped something, he never did the thing again. He sought to join conversations with his neighbors, in which it apparently did not trouble him that no understanding came about. His whole reserve of speech, to which he spontaneously returned again and again with greater liveliness and in ever new variations, consisted of some adjectives, verbs, and expletives, along with markedly few nouns, which were used quite senselessly. He responded to questions with an attempt to answer in the manner of the question. The patient correctly counted to 30. On occasion, he also spontaneously hit upon memorized sequences, without the beginning of the sequence being said to him. Questions were not answered in a way that makes sense. He often singled out words contained in the question and put them into the form of a sentence, but without relation to the meaning of the question. The first long, continuous test yielded the result that he correctly recognized and used a few individual objects. But one constantly must first allow him a long time before the correct use occurred to him. Here, various tasks show up as effective in few and occasional ways, only with oft-repeated exposure, or else not at all.

It is very easy to speculate. Nevertheless, only when psychology will have somewhat mastered and organized the manifold of tasks and the regularities belonging to them will such cases admit of treatment with somewhat greater certainty.

References

Ach, Narziß (1905): *Über die Willenstätigkeit und das Denken: Eine Experimentelle Untersuchung.* Göttingen: Vanderhoeck und Ruprecht.
Alexander-Schäfer, Gisela (1905): "Zur Frage der Beeinflussung des Gedächtnisses durch Tuschreize." In: *Zeitschrift für Psychologie und Physiologie der Sinnesorgane* 39. 206–215.
Aliotta, Antonio (1905): *La misura in psicologia sperimentale.* Firenze: Galetti e Cocci.
Benussi, Vittorio (1904): "Zur Psychologie des Gestalterfassens." In: *Untersuchungen zur Gegenstandstheorie und Psychologie.* Alexius Meinong (Ed.). Leipzig: Barth. 303–448.
Bernstein, A. and Bogdanoff, T. (1905): "Experimente über das Verhalten der Merkfähigkeit bei Schulkindern." In: *Beiträge zur Psychologie der Aussage* 2/2, pp. 115–131.
Bleuler, Eugen (1905): "Diagnostische Assoziationsstudien V." In: *Journal für Psychologie und Neurologie* 6, pp. 126–154.
Detto, Carl (1905): "Über den Begriff des Gedächtnisses in seiner Bedeutung für die Biologie." In: *Naturwissenschaftliche Wochenschrift* 20, pp. 657–667.
Forel, Auguste (1905): "Eine Konsequenz der Semonschen Lehre der Mneme." In: *Journal für Psychologie und Neurologie* 5, pp. 200–201
Gibson, William Ralph Boyce (1905): "Self-Introspection." In: *Proceedings of the Aristotelian Society.* New Series, Vol. 5, pp. 38–52
Heilbronner, Karl (1898): "Zur klinisch-psychologischen Untersuchungstechnik." In: *Monatsschrift für Psychiatrie und Neurologie* 17, pp. 115–132.
Heilbronner, Karl (1905a): "Studien über eine eklamptische Psychose." In: *Monatsschrift für Psychiatrie und Neurologie* 17, pp. 277–286, 367–383, 425–460.
Heilbronner, Karl (1905b): "Über Haftenbleiben und Stereotypie." In: *Monatsschrift für Psychiatrie und Neurologie* 18, pp. 293–371.
Heilbronner, Karl (1905c): "Zur Frage der motorischen Asymbolie (Apraxie)." In: *Zeitschrift für Psychologie und Physiologie der Sinnesorgane* 39, pp. 161–205.
Isserlin, Max (1905): "Assoziationsversuche bei einem forensisch begutachteten Fall von epileptischer Störung." In: *Monatsschrift für Psychiatrie und Neurologie* 18, pp. 419–446.
James, William (1905): "La notion de conscience." In: *Archives de Psychologie* 5.17, pp. 1–12
Judd, Charles Hubbard (1905): "Movement and Consciousness." In: *Psychological Review Monograph Supplement* 29, pp. 199–226.
Jung, Carl (1905a): "Diagnostische Assoziationsstudien III. Analyse der Assoziationen eines Epileptikers." In: *Journal für Psychologie und Neurologie* 6, pp. 73–90.
Jung, Carl (1905b): "Über das Verhalten der Reaktionszeit beim Assoziationsexperimente. Diagnostische Assoziationsstudien IV." In: *Journal für Psychologie und Neurologie* 6, pp. 1–36.
Jung, Carl and Riklin, Franz (1904/5): "Diagnostische Assoziationsstudien." In: *Journal für Psychologie und Neurologie* 3: 55–83, 145–169, 193–215; 4, pp. 24–67.

Kiesow, Federico (1906): "Über sogenannte 'frei steigende' Vorstellungen und plötzlich auftretende Änderungen des Gemütszustandes. Sind die Verbindungsglieder, welche hierbei in Frage kommen, unbewusst oder unbemerkt?" In: *Archiv für die gesamte Psychologie* 7, pp. 357–390.

Lipps, Theodor (1905a): *Bewußtsein und Gegenstände*. Leipzig: Engelmann.

Lipps, Theodor (1905b): "Die Wege der Psychologie." In: *Archiv für das gesammelte Psychologie* 6, pp. 1–21.

Lipps, Theodor (1905c): "Zur Verständigung über die geometrisch-optischen Täuschungen." In: *Zeitschrift für Psychologie und Physiologie der Sinnesorgane* 38, pp. 241–258.

Lobsien, Marx (1904): "Aussage und Wirklichkeit bei Schulkindern." In: *Sterns Beiträge zur Psychologie der Aussage* 1/2, pp. 28–89

Lobsien, Marx (1905): "Über das Gedächtnis für bildlich dargestellte Dinge in seiner Abhängigkeit von der Zwischenzeit." In: *Sterns Beiträge zur Psychologie der Aussage* 2/2, pp. 147–160.

Meisl, Alfred (1905): "Die Erfahrungen der Pawlowschen Schule über die Tätigkeiten der Speicheldrüsen und die Psychologie." In: *Journal für Psychologie und Neurologie* 6, pp. 192–203.

Müller, Georg Elias and Pilzecker, Alfons (1900): "Experimentelle Beiträge zur Lehre vom Gedächtnis." In: *Zeitschrift für Psychologie und Physiologie der Sinnesorgane*, Ergänzungsband 1, pp. 1–288

Ranschburg, Pál (1905): "Über die Bedeutung der Ähnlichkeit beim Erlernen, Behalten und bei der Reproduktion." In: *Journal für Psychologie und Neurologie* 5, pp. 93–127.

Reich, S. (1905): "Krankenvorstellung: Ein Fall von alogischer Aphasie und Asymbolie." In: *Allgemeiner Zeitschrift für Psychiatrie* 62, pp. 825–837.

Semon, Richard (1904): *Die Mneme als erhaltendes Prinzip im Wechsel des organischen Geschehens*. Leipzig: Engelmann.

Stransky, Erwin (1905): *Über Sprachverwirrtheit. Beiträge zur Kenntnis derselben bei Geisteskranken und Geistesgesunden*. Halle an der Saale: Marhold.

Taylor, Clifton (1905): "Über das Verstehen von Worten und Sätzen." In: *Zeitschrift für Psychologie und Physiologie der Sinnesorgane* 50, pp. 225–251.

Wertheimer, Max and Klein, Julius (1904): "Experimentelle Untersuchungen zur Tatbestandsdiagnostik." In: *Archiv für die gesamte Psychologie* 4, pp. 72–76

Wertheimer, Max (1905): "Über die Assoziationsmethoden." In: *Archiv für Kriminalanthropologie und Kriminalistik* 22, pp. 293–319.

Wessely, Rudolf (1905): "Zur Frage des Auswendiglernens." In: *Neue Jahrbücher für das klassische Altertum und für Pädagogik* 16, pp. 297–309.

Watt, Henry J. (1906): "Sammelbericht über die neuere Forschung in der Gedächtnis- und Assoziationspsychologie aus den Jahren 1903/4." In: *Archiv für die gesamte Psychologie* 7, pp. 1–48.

R. Brian Tracz
Carl Stumpf

Carl Stumpf (1848–1936) was both Edmund Husserl's habilitation supervisor in 1887 and the man to whom Husserl dedicated his *Logical Investigations*. In the Third Investigation of the latter, Husserl drew heavily upon Stumpf's analyses the dependence relations between visual quality and extension in *Über den psychologischen Ursprung der Raumvorstellung*. (Husserl 2001, p. 7 f.) Stumpf was impressed with the *Investigations*, according it praise in his posthumous *Erkenntnislehre*, though he also registered some critical remarks in the same work regarding the transcendental turn Husserl initiated in *Ideas I*. That said, in Husserl's estimation, Stumpf made a great deal of progress in the terrain of phenomenology that Husserl christens "pure hyletics" in *Ideas I*. (*Ideen* 178/171) It is clear here too that Husserl regarded Stumpf as a fellow phenomenologist.

Stumpf's career was greatly informed by Franz Brentano's philosophy, theology, aesthetics, and science lectures in the 1860s. Brentano encouraged him to attend Hermann Lotze's lectures on psychology and philosophy in 1867 in Göttingen, where he received his doctorate in 1868. Stumpf's dissertation, *Verhältnis des Platonischen Gottes zur Idee des Guten*, was praised by Lotze as "a very successful dissertation by a future master." Stumpf finished his habilitation work *Über die Grundsätze der Mathematik* in 1870 in Würzburg and during the following thirty years held positions in Würzburg, Halle, and Munich. During the 1880s, Stumpf completed the two volumes of his *Tonpsychologie*—one of the foundational texts in the psychology of audition. Stumpf finally moved to Berlin in 1892, where he stayed until 1922 after receiving an appointment as professor in 1894. In Berlin, aside from his ongoing involvement in the establishment of phenomenology, Stumpf had a profound impact on the fields of musicology, ethnomusicology, epistemology, and psychology, founding the Institute of Psychology in Berlin in 1900, the eventual birthplace of Gestalt psychology. He was a lifelong friend of William James, who praised him in his *Principles of Psychology* as "the most philosophical and profound of all writers." (James 1983, p. 911) In 1927, Stumpf began work on his philosophically ambitious *Erkenntnislehre*, which appeared after his death.

"Erscheinungen und psychische Funktionen" ("Appearances and Psychic Functions") was published in 1906, the same year that Stumpf published two other important works, "Zur Einteilung der Wissenschaften" ("On the Classification of the Sciences") and "Über Gefühlsempfindungen" ("On Affective Sensations"). "Appearances and Psychic Functions" can be viewed as an interdisciplinary synthesis of Brentano's descriptive psychology and Husserl's newly published *Logical Investigations* with Stumpf's own work on the psychology of sound and the developments in psychophysics and "new psychology" at the time. Particularly, Stumpf makes a strict distinction between functions and appearances, which he believes can be conceptually distinguished through abstraction, even though they might always occur together. Additionally, Stumpf carves out the concept of a configuration (*Gebilde*), which is a structure that *is* logically dependent upon functions. Stumpf's attention to the multimodal nature of appearances—his phenomenological garden is populated with tones and textures as much as visual sensations—is characteristic of the eventual stress that post-Husserlian phenomenology places on *lived* experience.

I should note some novelties in the present translation. (1) I have opted to translate *Erscheinung* as "appearance" (instead of "phenomenon"). (2) Stumpf's technical use of *Gebilde* is often translated "formation," whereas I have opted for "configuration." This is to avoid confusion since Stumpf explicitly contrasts *Gebilde* with "form" and adds a note of caution about the traditional philosophical use of that word. *Gebilde* and configuration also have an appropriate semantic overlap (Ge*bilde* contains *Bild*, which can be translated "figure" or "image"), and it avoids the undertones of "construction" in the sense of something that is artificial or unreal. (3) I have translated substantivized infinitives such as *Wahrnehmen* and *Bemerken* most often as gerunds (e. g. "perceiving" and "noticing"), though I occasionally have inserted "act of" (e. g. "act of perceiving" and "act of noticing") depending on context.

Finally, I would like to thank Eric Watkins, Florian Marwede, and Andrea Staiti for their kind assistance. Of course, all errors are mine alone.

References

Husserl, Edmund (2001): *Logical Investigations* II. J. N. Findlay (Trans.) London/New York: Routledge.
Husserl, Edmund (2014): *Ideas for a Pure Phenomenology and Phenomenological Philosophy.* Daniel Dahlstrom (Trans.). Indianapolis/Cambridge: Hackett.
James, William (1983): *The Principles of Psychology.* Cambridge: Harvard University Press.

Translated by R. Brian Tracz
Carl Stumpf.
Appearances and Psychic Functions

Erscheinungen und psychische Funktionen
Berlin: Königliche Akademie der Wissenschaften (1907)

[3] The epistemological appreciation of sense appearance has undergone a peculiar transformation in recent philosophy. For the rationalists up to the Wolffians, sensory qualities were regarded as tainted in themselves with obscurity and, therefore, unreal. Even spatial extension, which Descartes accepted as a clear and distinct idea, was construed by Leibniz and (yet more decisively) Wolff, as confused perception, because of the sensory difference threshold of spatial extension. In contrast, Kant saw in appearances formed by space and time the true object of scientific knowledge and assigned to them an empirical reality. Finally, influential modern thinkers such as Mach recognize no other being at all more than that of appearances. These appearances themselves are the sought-after realities, the sole 'elements' of the universe. There is nothing behind appearances, in front of them, or over them—nothing physical or psychic—that does not arise without remainder in them. 'Atoms', as with 'energy' in mathematical physics, are themselves helpful conceptual constructions without any real meaning. The old realism, which takes things actually to be as they appear, is thus basically rehabilitated, and the latest wisdom in the theory of knowledge coincides with this primitive starting point of all reflection on the matter.

The fundamental question that will be dealt with here, and in which all further differences are rooted, concerns the relationship of appearances to psychic functions. This question leads us to the area of psychology. Since the opinions among psychologists too are still split into different camps, in what follows, I want to elucidate the opposition of their views and to justify the position of functional psychology opposite appearance psychology, insofar as it is possible in a general overview. Such principal differences will indeed be settled completely, if at all, only through a centuries-long "struggle for existence"—through the fruitfulness of such views for the progress of science. [4]

I Elucidation of the Terms and Standpoints

We use the word 'appearance' below, completely disregarding at first the question of its reality, only as a common designation for the following:

a) For the contents of sensation. Recent psychology also rightly counts among these contents spatial extension and the distribution of visual and tactile impressions, since the quantitative aspects of these contents of sensation are given in the same way as the qualitative aspects. Most of the time, temporal duration and succession are regarded as sensory contents as well. Although difficulties still exist regarding time, we want to assign it here to sensory contents, since all the following considerations will prove to be applicable in much the same way to both temporal qualities and sensory contents.[1] In contrast, we put aside here the so-called 'pain component' and 'pleasure component' of sensations, since theoretical views of pure sensory agreeableness or unpleasantness are subject to still greater differences. However, I have no objections if one simply assigns them to appearances, not as attributes, but rather as a particular class (Stumpf 1907a, p. 1 f.).

b) For the memory images of the same name, the "merely represented" tones, colors, etc. In order not to prejudice somewhat the relationship of this class to the first class, we will distinguish them as appearances of the *second order* from appearances of the first order.

Certain *relationships* obtain among appearances. Relationships are given in and with every two appearances; they are not inserted by us but, rather, are perceived in and among the appearances. They belong to the material of intellectual functions but are not themselves functions, or even products of such.

We designate as *psychic functions* (acts, states, experiences) the noticing of appearances and their relationships, the synthesizing of appearances into complexes, the formation of concepts, apprehending and judging, affects, desiring and willing. [5] This is not meant to be a sharp and exhaustive classification, but rather only an overview of the most important examples. If we separate intellectual and emotional functions, we also make use of this old and convenient distinction without prejudice in respect to its definitive accuracy.

---

[1] The spatial and temporal distribution of sense appearances can by no means be defined as mere relationships. The difference between 'right and left' and 'now and earlier' is an absolute one for our consciousness. However, there are relationships based on this difference of absolute locations or times, just as with differences of pitch, color brightness, and other absolute qualities.

"Function" is thus not understood here as a *consequence* attained through a process, as one might perhaps designate blood circulation as the function of the heart beat, but as an activity, process or experience *itself*, in the way that the contraction of the heart itself is designated as an organic function. I emphasize this because occasionally an issue worded similarly or identically to ours is understood in a completely different sense from our own.[2]

The question of how we have knowledge of psychic functions is answered in different ways. For one person, only appearances are given immediately. For a second person, however, consciousness in general, which itself can become an object if need be, finds in itself no differentiation. [6] All of the allegedly different functions are defined either as differences in appearances or as unconscious functions that we can only infer from appearances. For the third, emotional functions are immediately given, whereas intellectual functions are only inferred.[3] For the fourth, functions of both sorts are immediately given.

The first position represents the whole of association psychology, though not it alone. The claim that everything capable of psychic experience, aside from sensations, can be explained by the rules of association is only a particular form of the general doctrine that everything capable of psychic experience con-

---

[2] As in the essay by D.S. Miller, "The Confusion of Function and Content in Mental Analysis" (Miller 1895, p. 535). Here, functions are differentiated from contents in that functions are consequences linked to the presence of certain contents. These consequences, however, emerge only in changes in content or in the influence on our practical behavior [*Verhalten*]. As an example, according to Miller, a concept or a judgment has its whole existence only in such consequent appearances tied to sensory contents ("what it does" p. 540). The result of his investigations leads him to deny functions as we understand them, indeed directly because everything that ultimately relies upon their reckoning is disintegrated into functions as *he* understands them. If he indeed takes the will as something available for the analysis of judgment, then it seems that he has definitely implemented his intention only very incompletely at this juncture.

Also the opposing view, which Mary Whiton Calkins emphasized in her German manuscript "Der doppelte Standpunkt in der Psychologie" (Calkins 1905), does not coincide (so far as I understand) with the above, but rather more with what Miller and other Americans have in mind. This came particularly out of her later essay, "A Reconciliation Between Structural and Functional Psychology" (Calkins 1906, 61 f.), where on page 73 "function" is defined according to Dewey's usage as a "*part* played with reference *to reaching or maintaining an end*," and where functional psychology is made to appear as an application of the modern so-called "pragmatism" in philosophy.

I.M. Bentley grasped the opposing view in a similar way (Bentley 1906, p. 293 f.). His essay is particularly informative about the formulation of these questions of principle among American psychologists.

[3] This is what, for instance, David Hume argues in *A Treatise of Human Nature*, B.1, P. 1, Sect. 2 (Hume 1978, p. 29 f.). The reverse point of view is not likely to find serious support.

sists in appearances. There could be yet other laws than the laws of association for appearances of the second order. Most present-day psychiatrists and physiologists, especially among experimental psychologists, revere this purely phenomenal view concerning what is immediately given.

The three latter opinions lead to a functional psychology, but the first of them is very close to pure appearance psychology, since there is not much to say of this general and undifferentiated consciousness. From there on, an investigation of psychic functions would be allowable only in the form of a psychology of the unconscious. Therefore, if there is to be further talk of appearance psychology and functional psychology, then the two extreme points of view (the first and the fourth), in which the contrast takes shape sharpest and purest, are meant in preference to the others. Since I intend to support the fourth, I will now add some explanation about this.

We call *immediately given* what is immediately evident as a matter of fact. That there can be argument over immediate givenness ought not be astonishing, since the existence of a thing can stand beyond all doubt, and yet describing its exact details can create difficulties. So, too, is it with the general laws, the logical axioms, which are also immediately evident. The description of immediate givenness seems possible now with exhaustive completeness only if one counts three things among it: appearances, functions, and finally relationships between the elements within each one of these kinds and between the elements of one kind and the other. [7] It is, for example, surely an incomplete description if one says that all "judging" consists of the mere presence of a sum of appearances regularly connected or standing in various relationships. If one wants to describe what we experience inwardly in judging, then the mere enumeration of appearances (even of second order appearances) and of their mutual relationships leaves a remainder, though one may process them exhaustively. This is of course not comparable to an arithmetical remainder insofar as it cannot be experienced and produced separately from the appearances. In general, we find functions tightly interwoven with appearances and related to them. We also find specific and general differences in functions: analyzing, synthesizing, affirming and negating, desiring and refusing are qualitative differences in psychic behavior, in the manner that the minded organism works.

In this sense, philosophers have frequently discussed the perception and observation of psychic functions since Locke and Leibniz (to say nothing of less recent thinkers). More recently among the Germans, Sigwart, Lotze, Fr. Brentano, and all who stem from them,[4] including Dilthey, Volkelt, B. Erdmann, and Th. Lipps,[5] have expressly taken this position. They are not convinced by the objection that we do not see our own seeing; rather, they conclude from just this circumstance that we must be acquainted with seeing through an orientation of consciousness other than that toward colors. They deny that the consciousness of seeing reduces to remembered appearances that occur simultaneously with color appearances and that show us the image of our organ of sight and the like. Even less do they hold such interpretations as possible in the face of the consciousness of judgment or the will. They believe they are grasping the psychic "living and moving" in itself, with colors and tones only as the contents of acts of perception, thus of a particular class of psychic functions. [8] According to this theory, content and act are connected to each other in a way that calls for further description, but they are not reducible to each other.

The numerous present-day psychologists who claim that there is an essential difference between sensations and mere representation at least admit at this point that a functional difference is given. For since the seen color should not be distinguished from the color merely represented via color tone, brightness, intensity, or another feature of the content, what can be meant by the essential, qualitative, or specific difference other than a "functional difference," a different kind of psychic behavior towards the same appearance? And since this dissimilarity is counted among the facts of consciousness, one thus accepts at this point, so far as I can tell, that functional differences are immediately given.

It should be expressly noted that the claim that there exists a perception of psychic functions as such does not necessarily imply the denial of unconscious psychic functions. Indeed, the third of the four viewpoints above allows intellectual functions to take place unconsciously. The fourth also does not preclude a priori the occurrence of unconscious states and activities that are equal to perceived psychic activities, with the exception of the characteristic of awareness. Nothing should be decided here regarding this point.

We also leave unaddressed the doctrine of voluntarism as well as the question regarding the "feeling of activity" [*Tätigkeitsgefühl*] and concept of the ego. The will may or may not be the basic psychic function, and the ambiguous feeling of activity may be interpreted as one prefers—the question here involves only the *consciousness* of willing and of doing, and this question is independent of the way one positions himself regarding these issues. The same is true of the con-

---

4 Most emphatically, Husserl recently represented the doctrine of "experiential acts" in his *Logical Investigations* (Husserl 2001, p. 216 f., 280 – 1).
5 In his newer writings; if I understand his explanation correctly, Lipps had earlier denied the consciousness of psychic functions as such.

cept of the ego. Consciousness of psychic functions is not necessarily consciousness of a substance behind the functions. Functional psychology is compatible with the view that the mind is to be conceived of as a whole of functions and dispositions in which the body is considered, of course, only as a whole of physical processes, properties, powers and dispositions. However, function psychology can also view the relationship of these two complexes to one another as initially completely undetermined.[6] [9] Nevertheless, if one thinks he has reason to add to the understanding of that whole of psychic functions and dispositions, which we call the "mind", a constant not given to us, or to consider such a constant as a part of that whole that is indeed co-given but cannot be observed separately, it remains the case that the constant is always inferred, not immediately given in the above sense. What ought to be evident immediately as a fact must be perceivable.[7]

The question occupying us here relates to the problem of free will only insofar as appearance psychology cannot construe the will as anything but deterministic (appearance psychology must look, say, for "freedom" in unconscious psychic acts). In contrast, the functional psychologist is not as such necessarily an indeterminist. If the most essential thing in psychic life is psychic functions, and if appearances are merely their material, then the functions can indeed be strictly and lawfully connected with appearances, both amongst themselves and with extra-conscious and extra-psychic conditions. The recognition of functions as facts of consciousness means nothing further than the recognition of a number of variables that, excluding what is given in the appearances themselves (quality, intensity, etc.), one considers to be necessary in a description of the immediate matters of fact regarding the content of consciousness and its changes. The formulas in which these variables belong can be of diverse kinds and can also altogether evade quantitative determinations. Nevertheless, the claim that under exactly the same circumstances the exactly same result must occur can also be valid here; at least, the concept of psychic functions introduced contains in itself no impetus to contest it.

---

[6] The "actuality theory," so named by Wundt, has already been advocated emphatically by Lotze and Fechner. Going back further, one will naturally name Hume, who falsely asserted a merely associative unification instead of a "whole." At base, however, Leibniz already had this conception of the mind [Seele], and in fact in a more correct and more profound form than Hume.

[7] If in the previously mentioned writings by M.W. Calkins, functional psychology is designated as an ego psychology [Ichpsychologie], and my name is cited for such a notion, then this is a misunderstanding. I have never thought to base psychology on an ego-consciousness [Ichbewußtsein].

I add briefly how I conceive of the relationship of immediate givenness to the concept of reality, not because this would be of positive significance for the following train of thought, but only to prevent any misunderstandings:

[10] The totality of the immediately given is *real*. Through this totality, we attain the concept of the "real" in order to then apply it to other things.[8] Appearances are real as contents to which functions refer, the functions are real as functions that act on appearances, the relationships are real as relationships between appearances or between functions, etc. We cannot speak of "mere appearances" as if they were nothing at all without reference to an external reality. Appearances simply do not belong to *the* reality to which naïve thinking at first ascribes them, namely, to a reality independent of consciousness (Husserl 2001b, 347–8).

However, appearances and functions are not merely real, each in its own manner and position towards the other; rather, they form among themselves a real *unity*. They are given in a very close connection with one another, and it is this indefinable consciousness itself in which appearances and functions are given.

We will now investigate whether psychic functions can be determined by some predicate pertaining to the sphere of appearance itself, whether conversely something about psychic functions is immanent to appearances or connected by logical necessity to them, then finally whether appearances and functions, at least within certain limits, independently vary from one another.

II Non-transferability of Predicates and Logical Separability

We can surely assume here that functions are not completely dissolvable into appearances, since all efforts in this regard since Hobbes constituted subreption to an almost grotesque degree. Such efforts rank next to efforts to make gold and to invent the perpetual motion machine, if they are not considerably more profound. Each attempt only exposed anew the characteristic differences of both spheres against one another. Even those who do not consider functions as something directly conscious are, at least on this count, in agreement with the functional psychologists.

[11] However, the difference is also the strictest that we admit. Psychic functions receive none of the predicates of the world of appearances (with the excep-

---

8 Beneke highlighted this point correctly, it seems to me, in his metaphysics. Contrariwise, I would not consider it compelling if one followed Beneke and deduced from this circumstance the conclusion that everything real must be psychic. (Beneke 1845).

tion of time). In any case, functions also do not possess an intensity in the same sense as tones or smells. What we can differentiate in functions are attributes of their own kind, like the clarity of perception, the evidence of judgment, and the level of universality of concepts. One need not deny for this reason that an analogue to the intensity of sensory impressions can be present in emotional functions; we are then simply dealing with an analogy, not with intensity in the identical sense of the word.[9]

Likewise, the psychic functions exhibit among themselves their own diverse kinds of relationships, different from all the types of relationships found between appearances (e.g., the peculiar linkage of intellectual with emotional functions, and again within the first domain the relationship of judgments to concepts, of concepts to intuitions, and within the second domain the relationship of willing means to willing ends, of the will generally to its motives, and so on).

Conversely, however, no functional predicate can be conferred to appearances. If I visualize a red color, a figure, or a motion, surely the perceiving and the entire actual-psychic state present is thereby conscious to me, but I grasp the state only *with* the color, not *in* it. It is not an attribute of appearances like brightness or extension.

The concept of psychic functions is *not* at all connected with that of appearances *through logical necessity.* No conceptual bond is to be discovered here. Appearances without their respective functions or functions without their respective appearances are thinkable without contradiction (if not also functions without any content at all). The only attributes that belong to a tone with conceptual necessity are pitch, intensity, and such things that are absolutely required for a complete description of the appearance. [12] The tone does not include the attribute of "being perceived." This attribute does not differentiate one tone from the other. It reaches beyond the appearances and encroaches into a totally different sphere.

Berkeley's claim that we can think of extension only as perceived extension is thus a misunderstanding. Phenomenalism cannot be justified in this way. Neither the realism of the physicist nor that of the common understanding is in itself contradictory in principle (cf. Brentano 1973, 92). Only indirectly, in conclusions from the detailed facts of appearance, can one prove such assumptions to be in-

---

[9] Indeed, the question of intensity is also not yet solved in the case of appearances, especially in the case of visual sensations. If one allows, with H. Bergson (1889, Ch. 1) and F. Brentano (1897, p. 110 f.), differences in intensity neither for functions nor for appearances, then of course the question regarding common properties in this respect falls away altogether. But then we are indeed left with one distinction fewer.

feasible. Clues for such conclusions also lie, of course, in the nature of our spatial and temporal representations themselves, if not in the ones emphasized by Kant then indeed by more compelling ones. However, the mere general fact that we are acquainted with appearances only as sensory and representational contents still does not provide in itself a forceful conclusion in this direction. From this, it would at most follow that appearances, which exist objectively, independent of every consciousness,[10] still would have to cohere in an analogous way with a function x perhaps completely unknown to us, in the way that sensed colors cohere with the function of sensation. [13] However, a *psychic* function, related in type to what we are experientially acquainted under these names, need not be this transcendent x itself.

We have *within* this sphere of appearances itself a case that can serve well as a clarification. Colors and extension form among themselves a whole in which they can only be distinguished through abstraction. If one were then to conclude: "Extension thus cannot occur without color," this would nevertheless be an error. In fact, the sense of touch shows us that extension without color occurs, albeit not without any qualitative aspect at all. And that this extension could perhaps be an extension in a completely different sense cannot by any means be proven. Saunderson – born blind – composed a geometry textbook. No matter how slowly (for understandable reasons) the transference of specific spatial concepts and names from tactile to optical space occurs in people born blind who undergo surgery, such transference is completely possible and it finally occurs. The nature of the representations at issue does not at any point pose an insurmountable obstacle. By no means, thus, does it deal with something completely incomparable. Therefore, the conclusion that there could be no extension that is not bound to optical qualities is by no means a compelling one.

The situation is entirely analogous, it seems, to the argument that what we summarize under the name of "appearances" could not exist without being a

---

10 One ought not take exception to this expression. If one holds that the word "appearance" already contains, according to its normal linguistic use, a relationship to a consciousness, then we must point to the initially provided explanation of the sense in which the word should be taken *here*. In this sense, it contains a relationship neither to a being nor to a consciousness, and it also contains no philosophical theory; rather, it combines that which one could less conveniently list separately as colors, tones, and so forth.

Also, the expressions "sensory contents" and "memory images," whereby we designated the two main groups of appearances, are only abbreviations in the same way. In this respect, we can say: "The tones (colors) of the upper and the lower intensity zone," if one otherwise finds therein the essential difference between heard and merely presented tones. It seems certain to me that this difference does not lie in the function but rather, primarily at least, in the appearance itself.

content of psychic functions. I do not want to say that the relationship between appearance and psychic function is identical to that between extension and color. The relationship is surely a rather more peculiar one. It is, however, common to both relationships that, in one case as in the other, both constituents can be distinguished only through abstraction. And thus that relationship perceivable within the appearances can likely be held as an explanation for what one can and cannot conclude in such a case. Just as little as a colorless extension implies a logical contradiction despite the deep interrelation of extension and color, so little too is it the case with the concept of appearances that are not contents of psychic functions.

[14] If Kant insists rightly that being is not an attribute of any concept, then an analogy applies here: being represented and being thought are not attributes of any appearance. This is why Spinoza observed the matter better than Berkeley when he argued that each of both attributes, extension and thought, "*must be grasped in themselves.*"[11] Instead of extension and thought, we simply say more generally (though corresponding to the intentions of Spinoza and Descartes) appearances and psychic functions. On this point, in fact, neither Spinoza nor any of the later thinkers actually got beyond the dualism of Descartes. The factual material given to us already shows its two faces at the root, and regardless of what is said further about the unity of substance and reality, about panpsychism, or universal idealism, *this* double-sidedness is not to be taken away.

One can even add the following. Let us concede, for the sake of argument, that the attribute of being presented or being thought is contained as such in all thought-material [*Denkmaterial*]. Even so, our distinction would not vanish. The attribute would then be contained in the psychic functions and the appearances alike, since thinking also directs itself towards psychic functions. Thus, we would have, so to speak, the same factor on the left and right sides of the equation, or the top and bottom of the fraction, and could divide it out for a simplification of these considerations.

So much for the clarification and corroboration of the thesis that no logical necessity connects appearances to psychic functions. This unquestionable detachability is, however, the only thing that immediately interests us at this point. No metaphysical claims should be bound to it. [15]

---

11 Ethica I prop. 10: "*Unumquodque unius substantiae attributum per se concipi debet* [Each attribute of one substance must be conceived through itself]." (Spinoza 2002, p. 221) We can disregard here the unitary character of substance; this, for Spinoza himself, is not a condition for this proposition, since he indeed recognized only *one* substance in general.

III Mutually Independent Variability

Within certain limits, appearances and functions are variable in a mutually independent way. This means that different functions can occur with the same appearances, and that different appearances can occur with the same functions. In other words: nothing in an individual appearance necessarily need be altered through a change in functional behavior, and something in an individual appearance can conversely be altered without a change of function. Of course, such an independent change is not being claimed for all cases. I would like to maintain only that such a change *could* occur, not that it always and necessarily occurs, or that it occurs under the usual, complicated circumstances of psychic processes. By no means do both parts of this claim need to be together false or together true. Finally, I do not maintain them as surely demonstrable propositions, but rather as theses and hypotheses to whose proof psychology (as I understand it) is progressively approaching. Too many subtle, in part experimental investigations are also required in order to test them. In the following, I am trying to state only what can be briefly, though preliminarily, said, and I hope at least to designate exactly the relevant questions and problems.

From the outset let it be noted, however, that a position opposed to our own on the following matters would not amount to a negation of psychic functions as contents of consciousness in general. For example, if under no circumstances an analysis [*Zergliederung*] or synthesis [*Zusammenfassung*] of given appearances were possible without something changing in the analyzed or synthesized appearances or in the entire sphere of momentarily given appearances, it would still not follow that the analyzing or the synthesizing *consisted* in these unavoidable phenomenal alterations. Those who believe that the function itself is experienced would, in this case, only conclude that its occurrence is necessarily and generally accompanied by particular alterations in the appearances.

Conversely, however, an affirmative position on the following questions indeed carries with it, at the same time, a recognition of psychic functions as facts of consciousness in general. [16]

1 Psychic Functions Can Be Altered Without Changing the Appearances

If we subsequently go through the most important functions, we can lay to rest questions regarding classification. If one groups such functions differently, then questions will also recur at different places. Their meaning and the attempt to answer them ought not depend essentially on issues of classification.

I consider *perceiving* or *noticing* (i.e., taking note) a primitive function.[12] The perceiving of appearances of the first order, sense perception in the ordinary sense, we also call sensing; the perceiving of appearances of the second order we call representing. The mere representing of colors or tones is also a kind of seeing or hearing, a noticing of emerging appearances of these groups (eventually also emerging under the influence of the will).

Every sense perception is concerned with the noticing of parts in a whole as well as of relationships between these parts. Let us consider at first only the noticing of parts. Since parts are noticed within the whole to which they belong, every perceiving involves necessarily the differentiation of the perceived part from the unperceived parts of appearances, much like the differentiation of the foreground from the background. That part which stays in the background we call also "merely sensed" or perceived as opposed to what is apperceived. Through the addition of "merely," the meaning of the expression "sensed" is thus essentially altered here. However, we will still have to ask whether the distinction can be considered a completely strict one.

[17] Now applied to sensory perceptions, our thesis firstly indicates that a change in the appearance itself need not occur during the transition of something unnoticed into something noticed. What changes is essentially of a functional sort only. Figuratively speaking, the transition consists of an accumulation of consciousness with respect to some part of the appearances.

If, for instance, a tone is noticed in a chord, then nothing needs to happen to the chord as an appearance. I apprehend the sound first unanalyzed and then analyzed. Likewise, I apprehend the initially unitary impression of a fine meal and subsequently notice something sweet and something sour in it as well as,

---

12 With Brentano, I previously considered every perceiving and noticing already to be a judging (Stumpf 1883, p. 96). However, I now take perceiving and noticing to be the underlying function preceding judgment, through which parts or relationships are lifted out of the undifferentiated chaos of appearances. In any case, an instinctive positing of what has been highlighted regularly attaches to perception. Subsequently, a conceptual judgment about the presence of the part or relation often follows.

What we call "just noticeable" in psychophysical experiments are the smallest parts or differences (particularly: similarity, increase, or other gradually tiered relationships) that are alleged to be present due to a perception. Of course, the concept of a judgment process obviously comes into play in the concept of what is "just noticeable."

It is recognized that the expressions 'sensation', 'representation', and 'perception', besides referring to acts, are also used for the perceived (sensed or represented) appearances. We will also not avoid this convenient usage when misunderstandings are precluded by context.

perhaps, a smell and a quality of warmth, or the skin sensations that are deconstructed into pressure, cool, or pain sensations: they remain what they were. Indeed, not only can the objective stimuli and the psychological processes remain the same but, as I think, also the subjective appearances.[13]

A variety of changes, at least in associative representations and thus in appearances of the second order can certainly be shown in the majority of the more complicated cases in which we say of a sense impression that it now appears clearer, more distinct, and more transparent in its structure to us than before. Thus, when we see a painting for the second or third time, whereby all that was viewed individually before appears jointly as a representation, what was already represented earlier is now reproduced so quickly and vividly that it coalesces, as it were, with what is perceived sensibly. The wandering glance perhaps goes lighter and faster over the picture, with short stops between different focal points, since its task is made easier: thus, the muscle sensations are also modified, at least temporally, compared to the first time.

[18] But not all cases plainly permit such explanations. This was mentioned above. One would not instead invoke the addition of verbal representations like "sour, sweet" or "tone $c, e, g,$" since it is obviously first the consequence of the analysis already performed, and furthermore by no means always joined to the analysis. Likewise: if someone absorbed in his thoughts has seen lanterns in an illuminated street or heard the striking of church bells while coming out of a theater, and then turns his attention to the row of lights itself or to the further striking of the bells, he will have to say to himself that just a moment ago there were already lights and acoustic impressions of the same kind and of the same spatial and temporal intervals (sometimes also of the same intensity as one now perceives them) and not an ineffable, unified something. Of course, one can escape this interpretation through certain artificial hypotheses, perhaps through the assumption that, with the reproduction of what was directly seen and heard in the past (for the purposes of comparison to the present), a transformation or assimilation occurs in the present. However, to those who are impartial, such hypotheses appear hardly believable to begin with.

---

13 Cf. Stumpf (1883, p. 107), and the remarks by A. Marty (1892, p. 324, in contrast to W. James, who maintains a strict simplicity of the appearance before the act of differentiation and, as a result, a real conversion, a kind of transubstantiation of the content of sensation via its decomposition. See also Meinong's detailed examination of this issue in *Zeitschrift für Psychologie* VI (Meinong 1894a, p. 340 f.) The result of Meinong's inquiry stands in agreement with Marty's and my own conception. Cornelius and Krueger recently defended James' position. Incidentally, what it should mean for visual intuitions to be "completely simple" before an act of differentiation occurs is completely unintelligible to me.

If one wanted to deny the evidentiary power of such experiences because they do not involve a transition from something altogether unnoticed to something perceived, but only from a lower to a higher degree of perception, we would reply with the following questions: why should what takes place here become something completely different, if we increase the distance in the degrees of noticeability? And at what point in this increase should the sudden change occur?

One can designate experiences of just the characteristic kind as evidence through direct comparison. We ought not merely mention the comparison of a present element with another present element (although, too, both elements are self-given during the act of comparison), but also the comparison of a present element with a just-past element or of a just-past element with one immediately preceding it, yet retained in consciousness. Every so-called successive comparison presupposes the possibility of comparing a just past element with a present element. [19] We would have no common ground for discussion at this point, in fact, with someone who would deny this possibility in general.

Aside from the evidence of direct comparison, two different things seem to support our thesis.

First is the impossibility or extraordinary difficulty of any descriptive theory of appearances otherwise. If a chord c-e-g is in fact a simple appearance so long as listeners do not disassemble it into its constituent parts, then the chord must be a simple tone that does not coincide with either the c, the e, or the g. Therefore, the chord cannot at all be placed in the line of tones from low to high. We obtain new dimensions of the acoustic realm aside from those dimensions by which the pure phenomenal description of the domain of sound otherwise operates. The complication thus arising is hardly foreseeable. The understanding of acoustic timbre as arising out of tonal timbre becomes illusory, and so forth. The same goes for other sensory domains in which mixtures occur. Indeed, how would one want to classify and characterize the fundamental classes of appearances from a phenomenal perspective? If we name the simple appearance that exists ahead of any kind of differentiation or that comes about through an initial differentiation, the "x-quality," then every further analysis, every (even completely spontaneous) emergence of a particular appearance (temperature or light according to *our* designation) would cause transformations of that x into new, simple qualities. Still, it would also be incorrect to say that one hears a tone if one does not perceive it for itself, alone, without any other accompanying phenomenon (organic sensations and the like), which in fact neither is nor can be the case.

One could perhaps propose to designate the sensations before the analysis as *potential* smells, colors, and so forth, the three-part tone before the analysis as a potential *c, e, g*, and, through this to motivate the usual classification of sensations, such that that one would thereby tally up the potential sensations with the actual sensations. With this differentiation and tally, the theory could at best be satisfied if one takes only the potential smells as *smells* or the potential *c* as *c*, that is, if the quality is acknowledged as the same. Then, however, the situation is exactly as we say, except the style of expression is obscured by dubious Aristotelian terminology.

[20] Secondly, it also seems to me that the existence of intermediate stages between entirely unnoticed and very clearly noticed elements leads to our way of portraying the matter. If the completely unanalyzed triad is a simple subjective quality for itself, but the distinctly analyzed triad exhibits three simultaneous qualities distinct from that initial quality: which quality does the same objective triad have for my sensation when I believe that I am hearing the three tones, or else one or two of them, only *indistinctly?* Where does the difference lie if not in the function of noticing? If there were only the two extremes—the distinct grasping of all simultaneous tones, which are generally distinguishable with the utmost attention and training under the objectively given circumstances, and, on the other hand, the completely unanalyzed grasping of the sense impression— then it could be handled by the theory of qualitative transformation. But the intermediate stages of noticing can hardly be interpreted as changes of appearance with such simple appearances.

Generally, it can easily be said that it would be a fallacy or an impermissible "reification" to assume that what we subsequently differentiate already existed before the differentiation. But would it really be a mere assumption? Why should it be impermissible? As of late, some have also charged the chemist with a fallacy of reification since he "reads" into carbon dioxide two substances, carbon and oxygen, that he subsequently obtains out of it. Now, the psychologist is better off in this respect, since he can appeal to evidence from direct comparison. However, the chemist need not be accused of an erroneous way of thinking either. One can maintain this atomistic hypothesis, and one can also attempt to hold the opposite hypothesis—the doctrine of consistency and transformation [*Stetigkeits- und Umwandlungslehre*]—in which one will provisionally have a steadfast position with respect to chemical processes. In any event, however, the chemist and the psychologist who distinguish perception and apperception are entitled to have their position considered not as a product of childishly erroneous habits of thinking but, rather, as a *theory* drawn up with full consciousness of the rules of scientific research, and a theory that must be evaluated according to the same rules.

[21] We claim, thus, that differences and parts can also be present in appearances when we do not immediately notice them as such. Consequently, in prin-

ciple, nothing seems to stand in the way of the assumption that there might be completely *unnoticeable* parts of appearances, in the sense of Leibniz's "petites perceptions," of Helmhotz's unconscious local signs [*Lokalzeichnen*], of Mach's dull and bright elements of tone sensations, or of other hypothetical components (Spencer, Taine, Brentano). Volkelt designated such appearances that are assumed only in favor of theory as "invented sensations." (Volkelt 1883) However, if the assumption of such parts of the content follows by logical necessity from the nature of the perceived appearances or, at least, offers great advantages for the establishment of regularities, and if besides this it can be shown why these parts can or must evade our perception, then the assumption is at least likewise permissible and possesses the same epistemic value as the assumption of hidden particles and motions on the part of the physicist. Indeed, the criteria named must also not be handled less rigorously. A hypothesis that is not directly verifiable must produce a meaningful theoretical simplification, an abundance of verifiable consequences, or else some profit for advancing knowledge. This is the point at which most are lacking.[14]

As with quantitative and qualitative parts, *attributive parts* are also present in the appearances before they are perceived. A tone as a content of appearance (I am not speaking of the tone stimulus) doubtlessly has, at any given time, a certain pitch and intensity independently of whether consciousness keeps these two aspects apart. Pitch and intensity are not first granted to the tone through the perceptual act. Long ago I tried to show the origin of such differences in the experience of multiple variability of otherwise completely unified sensations,[15] and similar ideas have subsequently been maintained by Münsterberg, Cornelius, and G.E. Müller (Stumpf 1873, p. 135). [22] But with this hypothesis (so I denote it expressly), it is at best shown how we come to the formation of the concepts pitch, intensity, and so forth, which we then use, after they are formed, for an exact description of the individual appearance. It is not shown how the tone-appearance itself comes to have its pitch and intensity. A tone followed by others is not afterwards *provided* with a pitch and intensity through these following tones; it must have possessed pitch and intensity during its own lifespan and in isolation. The objection that the pitch of a tone in general *consists* only in its relationship to other tones would become tangled in the absurdities of the

---

14 Compare Volkelt with Münsterberg's interesting explanation, *Grundzüge der Psychologie* I (1900, p. 369f.; also p. 312).

15 The expression "psychological part" is replaced above with "attributive part." Incidentally, back then I also referred to the habit of hypostatization (Stump 1883, p. 136) as an explanatory device, through which is made clear that the "fallacy of reification" is not completely unknown to me.

doctrine of relativity, which I have sufficiently indicated elsewhere (Stumpf, 1883).

Hitherto we dealt with the perception of absolute contents, of appearances themselves. However, the act of perception can also be directed at *relationships*. In this case we do not speak of a "sensing." The function as such, though, is the very same, while only the content is different. And, just as with the perception of a partial tone, this partial tone does not enter into the appearance first through the act of perception but was already present, so the perceived relationship also cannot arise from the act of perception to begin with but, rather, was already immanent in the appearances. Perhaps some are rather inclined here to concede this thesis or to consider it self-evident. However, the same treatment is necessary in both cases for the sake of consistency, and so they may be mutually illuminating.

Lotze particularly has strongly emphasized that through the perception of relationships (he calls it referring knowledge [*beziehendes Wissen*]) nothing in the material is altered (Lotze 1881, p. 23). Also clear, then, is that all comparison would be senseless if it *eo ipso* caused a change in what is to be compared. Only the way this is expressed, as if the relationship itself was "instituted" first through the comparison (a turn of phrase that recurs with others later on), appears dangerous to me. The relationships are not produced through the functions, but only detected, none differently from the absolute contents.

The correct interpretation of my doctrine on the fusion of tones and consonance is closely connected with this separation of relations (which belong to the material of thought) from "referential acts" (which are acts of thought, i.e., the perceptions of relations). [23] Almost all objections against this doctrine rest on the conflation of the concepts of "fusion" and "absence of an act of differentiation." However, these two do not, in fact, absolutely coincide with each other, although under quite special circumstances one can serve as a mark for recognizing the other. As with similarity, fusion (as I understand the word) is also a relationship that is immanent in the tone-appearances themselves, independent of all intellectual functions. Fusion is to the judgment of unity as similarity is to the capacity for substitution. The similarity of two objects can be the reason that they are taken for the other. Under certain circumstances (if, namely, all other reasons are excluded), judgments of substitution can be used as evidence for the presence of similarity. However, one ought not for this reason *define* similarity in terms of the substitution of two objects. A strong similarity of two impressions can be present without substitution taking place, and vice-versa. Fusion stands to the judgment of unity in exactly the same way. Perhaps I may hope that, through its insertion into the general considerations currently at hand, the salient point of this view, which I constantly hinted at earlier, is brought yet more to light.

Since Plato, synthesis has often been considered a basic function of our intellectual life. As a matter of fact, it seems to me that neither a mere perception of relationships nor a mere transfer of the abstract concept "whole" to the given elements takes place in synthesis, but rather that a function of a particular kind is added. A number of different single contents, tactile impressions, lines, and tones can be combined into a whole, a figure, a rhythm, or a melody.

Now the question again is whether, through such combinations, the appearances themselves are somehow modified. With this it should be noted that spatial size and arrangement also belong to appearances according to our definition, as well as the determinate sequence of time and duration, determinate rhythmic character (distribution of intensity) – in short, everything that characterizes the figure or rhythm as such. It thus does not have to do with the synthesis of an unordered sum of impressions; what we call "intellectual combinations" does not consist in this. [24] Everything named still belongs to the material. The question is rather this: whether the tones, which the listener already finds in a certain sequence, a certain tempo, and certain relationships of intensity, can still be combined in thought by him in various ways, and whether, if this occurs, something is thereby necessarily changed in the material, particularly whether new material (e.g. of muscle sensations) is added.

One sees that the question is less simple than one would initially like to believe. Very minute differences in appearances could come into consideration. It is nevertheless likely that, as the question is understood, the same material is apprehended by one individual as a unitary whole, whereas it is not combined by another individual into a unity at all, or only to a certain degree or with an altered grouping (phrasing). The same material can also be joined by the same subject first this way, then that way. The common occurrence of accompanying muscle actions, already with the mere representation of a rhythm, cannot be denied; however, they ought not be completely essential. Eye movements ought to be just as inessential for visual impressions if, under a number of points distributed completely regularly, every four or every six is synthesized into a group. At any rate, experimental psychology must have the last word, and it has hardly spoken its first.[16]

---

16 Schumann extensively investigated the influence of synthesis on geometric-optical illusions. (Schumann 1904) The influence of synthesis ought also to play a role with the inversion of figures. The laws of synthesis will be obtained through careful study of single sensory domains, which could also become significant for the theory of conceptual synthesis [*Synthese*].

We may consider closely the formation of *universal concepts* as another intellectual function. However one also might otherwise think about the essence of concepts—the question is still the most difficult of all those that concern the psychology of the activities of the understanding—it is at least certain that they can be dissolved into neither a mere sum nor a mere average of single representations. And concerning their origin, it is clear enough that it occurs without consumption or production of single representations and without alteration of their content. Under certain circumstances, a concept occurs (I speak here initially of the simplest concepts, such as color or identity) aside from the present appearances and relations, a concept that is arranged or supported by them, but not composed of them. [25] Or perhaps more correctly said: a judgment containing concepts. A child's first sentence or first word with sentential meaning (not just the transference of a word from one object to another one) ought to count as an outer sign of completed concept formation. Among the essential circumstances is, in particular, the perception of a number of appearances different in terms of species but the same in terms of genus. Besides this, however, certain conditions are satisfied in normal human children in the course of the second or third year and, according to all indications, are completely missing in animals. However, we are currently unable to spell out these conditions. Concepts are added to appearances, sensations, and representations as a "plus," of course not as a new element in the former sense in which the given material would be either increased or decreased.

Conceptual thought proves to be in all its operations (analytic, synthetic, etc.) much more independent of appearances (images) than was believed and taught for a long time in association psychology. Even so-called inner speech is not at every moment an indispensable component of intellectual processes. Logical operations can take place under circumstances without any change in appearances or the representation of words. Though these logical operations may be passing moments of elevated concentration, recent psychologists and epistemologists (O. Liebmann, A. Riehl, W. James, B. Erdmann, Husserl, etc.) are correct in the fact that they occur.[17]

As for *judging*, no matter how one otherwise characterizes and classifies this function, most will admit that the occurrence of this function need not necessarily be linked with a change in the material or an addition or falling away of representations, and that the same material can be judged differently: for instance,

---

[17] Experimental psychology, which on the whole is indeed nothing other than a method that encourages self-observation systematically under objective determination of its conditions, has also lent a hand here. Cf. A. Binet (1903), C.O. Taylor (1905/6), and also other new work from Külpe's school, particularly N. Ach (1905).

once affirmatively, another time negatively, once with discernment, another time with blind acceptance as true. [26] Of course, opposing attempts are also not lacking in the theory of judgment. Evidence is occasionally attributed to accessory representations, while negation is attributed to peculiar relationships within the material of representation. Or, the judgment is even interpreted with respect to the innervating sensation of bending and stretching (why not instead prefer bowing and shaking of the head?). Not every attempt in this direction is so obviously amiss as the latter. However, that an essentially new functional behavior occurs with the judgment can hardly be denied.[18]

"Mere illusions in judgment" in the sphere of sense perception, to which most geometrical-optical illusions belong, along with certain achievements of conceptual subsumption designated as recognition, have led experimental psychology to differentiate between cases in which actual changes take place in the material of appearance, and others in which such change is missing. But we may pass over this since it deals only with the fact that changes of functions are possible without such changes of the material, not with the fact that they occur in all cases.

Finally, investigation has been slightly more productive with *emotional functions*. So much, however, appears also to be certain here: affects and desires admit at least the distinguishing of positive and negative states of joy and sorrow, of pursuing and fleeing, without the representational content necessarily having to be altered somehow (even if alteration were the norm in other cases). One certainly must require differences in the conditioning moments if positive and negative affects occur. [27] But they do not absolutely need to consist in present, current contents of sensations or representational content. In every individual, dispositions towards positive and negative affects are stored up, and it is easily thinkable that a circumstance vanishing immediately again from consciousness (if the circumstance was present to it at all) realizes one of these dispositions. The intuitive element to which the affect refers or which the affect accompanies in consciousness can fail to participate in it.

---

18 Ebbinghaus finds the distinctive trait of judgment in the adding of "a very abstract representation of reality or actuality, which gradually develops as a necessary precipitate [*Niederschlag*] out of certain experiences of sensory life." (Ebbinghaus 1902, p. 168) One will have to wait for the promised upcoming completion of Volume II in order to understand how this could be applicable, say, to mathematical knowledge. (Ebbinghaus 1912) One will always have to give Brentano considerable credit, since, opposing the casual attitude of the old association psychology, he emphatically pointed to the difference between a judgment and an ever so strong connection of representations. Yet I also hold his positive conception as perfectly plausible in principle; only in the more specific elaborations of his theory of judgment I cannot totally agree with him.

It can further be maintained that, except for those two basic contrasts, a large number of variations among affects within both groups is based mainly on alterations of the underlying intellectual functions, and therefore, in turn, not necessarily on alterations of appearances.[19] The whole variegation of this sphere certainly comes about with the cooperation of organic sensations.

The same goes for the will. Here, the meaning of sensation, especially muscle sensations, has also been strongly exaggerated. The occurrences, differences, and alterations of the will are not absolutely bound to alterations in appearances of the first or the second order. It seems to me that an opposite stance can nonetheless take place on the basis of the same continued presence of concrete-intuitive contents in consciousness—a willing or rejecting (negative willing) can occur. This is not to defend an indeterministic conception of the will. For between appearances and the functions of the will, there are still at least the intellectual processes and the passive affects. Indeterminism would imply that when there is equality not merely of appearances of the first and second order, but also of intellectual states and of states of mind and, moreover, of all the associated intellectual and emotional dispositions (which as such are unconscious), different volitions would still be possible. [28] The controversy about this can (as was already noted above) be detached from the discussion of our main question.

Digression Regarding the Configuration of Psychic Functions

As a supplement to the preceding, however, an observation must now be inserted regarding what in psychic functions I would like to label as "configurations [*Gebilde*]." Every function, except the basic one of perception, has a correlate whose general nature, like that of function itself, can only be elucidated through examples.

---

19 In the essay about affects (Stumpf 1899, p.56), I emphasized the presence of a judgment immanent in affects [*Affekten*] as essential for the definition of those affects. One might be afraid of something whose admission appears to be sure, probable, possible, etc. I did not believe or claim to thereby say something totally new, but rather to defend an old truth against more recent purely sensualistic conceptions. Meinong has pointed out that he himself already spoke of "feelings of judgment" [*Urteilsgefühlen*] in the same sense and that he defined value-feelings as such feelings of judgment (with the constraint of existence judgments). (Meinong 1905, p. 27) In fact, I had not yet been aware of his [*Psychologisch-ethische*] *Untersuchungen zur Werttheorie* (1894) at the time, otherwise I would have happily cited it as an endorsement, since every partial coincidence of opinion must be desired in these contentious questions.

Let us take as a propitious starting point what Ehrenfels called "Gestalt qualities" (Ehrenfels 1890). This can be understood as follows: that which distinguishes a melody, a spatial figure or another multiplicity of appearances as a coherent whole from a multiplicity of otherwise identical or identically arranged appearances that are *not*, however, synthesized by consciousness.[20] Husserl speaks in the same sense regarding moments of unity [*Einheitsmomenten*] (Husserl 2001b, pp. 230, 274). One can indeed also employ the old expression "forms [*Formen*]" instead, which definitely remains in far closer accordance with everyday language use than is otherwise the case with the different uses of the term "form" in philosophy.

[29] There are also, however, syntheses in which no objective coherence or joint binding relationship of parts obtains. We can bind the most heterogeneous materials through an "and" in our thoughts. For this reason, in considering these cases, I would like to denote with the general expression "*set* [*Inbegriff*]" everything that occurs as a specific result of a synthesis in consciousness.[21] The set is not the synthesizing function itself, or even the synthesized material. It is the necessary correlate of the synthesizing function. *Forms* (Gestalt qualities) are then special cases of sets, to which are added the objectively binding relationships of the constituents.

Such a third item aside from appearance and function can now be distinguished with respect to all other intellectual functions, as well as with respect to conceptual thinking. The grasping of the simplest concepts is a function,

---

[20] Meinong (1902, p. 245 f.) and Schumann (1898, p. 28; 1900, p. 128, 135) have already pointed to gaps in Ehrenfels' reasoning. (1890, p. 249 f.) Particularly, Ehrenfels relied mainly on the unjustified claim that one might describe two melodies with different absolute pitch simply as the same melody. This can certainly be conditioned by the same tonal and rhythmical relationships along with the associative representations and feelings linked to those relationships. I also cannot entirely agree with Ehrenfels as with Meinong in his grasp of the concept itself and its usage. The timbre and the concurrent appearance of color and extension do not fall under this concept if it is otherwise to receive a clear demarcation. These elements have to stand over and against consciousness as independent and separate from one another while it synthesizes them into a whole.

In the further elaboration of the concept, it is particularly important to note that a uniformly intended melody psychologically disintegrates initially into a series of individual Gestalt qualities for the individual apprehending it. These *Gestalt* qualities are only linked into a unity through conceptual thinking with the help of reproduced fragments of the parts already heard. Very complicated processes occur here, an analog with our conception of large and rich spatial shapes.

[21] In agreement with Husserl, who rightfully refuses to apply the concept of "whole" in the pregnant sense (as he argued in a previous work) to mere sets. (2001b, 38–9; also 2003, p. 74 f.) Only in a broader sense can both expressions be employed synonymously.

and the *concepts* themselves are its correlate. I have previously called them "configurations" in this sense (Stumpf 1902). The expression is, of course, not an analytic or genetic explanation, but it suggests that this problem is analogous to other problems. Additionally, it suggests that one is compelled to acknowledge ultimate facts whose coordination is likewise the only possible "explanation" in the same manner as with other configurations.[22]

Brentano keenly highlighted three decades ago in his logic lectures that a specific content of judgment corresponds to the judgment, and that such content can be divided from representational content (the matter) and can be linguistically expressed in "*that*-clauses" or substantivized infinitives, Even earlier, Bernard Bolzano had already spoken of the "proposition in itself" in the same sense (Bolzano 1972, 20 f.). [30] I employ for this the expression *state of affairs*.[23]

---

22 At any rate, here I am referring exclusively to the origin of the simplest concepts. The manifold operations involving them fall under other functional aspects (analysis, synthesis, judgments, etc.). It should also not be said that we could ever find concepts removed from all connection with other intellectual functions in consciousness.

23 From in an 1888 Introduction to Logic course lithographed for listeners. – Meinong suggested in his paper "Über Annahmen" the expression "objective." I would also find this expression equally useful, but I find it more characteristic as a synonym for "configurations" in general (even more characteristic, perhaps, for that which we will call "invariants of configurations" below). Since configurations are also the content of psychic functions, they all thus naturally bear an objective character and contain in their concept nothing of the momentarily individual act. In the same general sense, Husserl has spoken of "objectivities" of different acts of consciousness (Husserl 2001b, 281 ff.]).

With respect to "assumptions," I already have concerns with the idea of considering them a special class of functions besides judgments, as Meinong does, because otherwise a special class of configurations corresponds to a special class of functions in all cases, which would not apply to this case.

It actually seems to me that the considerations cited against this by Anton Marty, particularly the logical difficulties (Marty 1905, p. 7 f.), were not adequately rebutted through Meinong's reply (1906a, p. 1 f.). Of course, we are not dealing here with a special system of logic, but with the general, indispensable conditions of logical understanding [*Verständigung*]. Whether assumptions are subordinate or coordinate to judgments is a basic and essential distinction for every clear conception on the matter, and the two alternatives cannot obtain concurrently. At most, one can leave undetermined which of the two obtains. Meinong also did this recently by conceding to those who prefer to subsume assumptions under judgments rather than to grasp them as "judgments of phantasy." (1906b, p. 60 f.)

In any case, I do not want to claim that the positive interpretation of the cases combined by Meinong under the expression "assumption" is an easy and thoroughly satisfactorily dissolved task. What he calls "feelings of phantasy" without a doubt also creates a difficulty for a doctrine of feelings, as though we did not yet have enough.

We can also find the same element in the emotional functions. What we call *values* or goods, with all of their classes and opposites (the pleasing, the desirable, the frightening, the agreeable and the unpleasant, means and ends, what has to be preferred and what has to be rejected), fall under the concept of configuration. The specific contents of feeling and willing are to be distinguished from both the functions themselves and from appearances (and furthermore the objects) to which they refer.

Confusing configurations with the functions is, at any rate, not a less serious error than confusing them with appearances (as with objects). The set is not the act of synthesis, the bundle is not the single strand, and substantiality and causality are not *functions* of thought. One must thereby mainly object to the Neo-Kantians, no matter whether they are correct or incorrect with regard to the historical interpretation of the Kantian "forms of thought" in the spirit of Kant.

[31] Without entering further into the epistemological meaning of configurations,[24] we want to turn from there to the above question regarding the changing of appearances via functions. It now appears that indeed something always enters in addition. However, that which is added is not itself an appearance, it is not a content in the original sense but, rather, in a quite different sense of the word. Perhaps this observation serves as a further clarification and a solution to concerns that might still be present.

The fact that no content in the original sense is added must be emphasized particularly with respect to the synthesizing function, in order to distinguish the view developed here from the claim of a "psychic chemistry" or a "creative synthesis [*Synthese*]." A new material should allegedly be produced through these processes; spatial representation should, for example, arise through a creative synthesis out of the linkage of optical qualities with muscle sensations or unknown local signs. This is a process for which no examples are to be found in the whole area of sense perception and representational life. If one wants to be allegorical, one can say: the synthesis sets certain digits of the sense material in a bracket, but the bracket is not itself a digit. However, this comparison itself would still be insufficient and dangerous, since the bracket is indeed still a sensory appearance, even of the same (optical) type, even if it is of dissimilar meaning. We are dealing here, however, with a reach beyond the sphere of appearan-

---

24 In the treatise "Psychologie und Erkenntnistheorie" (Stumpf 1892, p. 31–2), I have already mentioned that the key to the most important problem in the doctrine of the origin of concepts lies in this point. Concepts like "being," "necessity," etc., do not at all originate in inner perception in the old Lockean sense or in the consciousness of function, but in the visualization of particular properties of configurations. One could say they originate in the *innermost* perception. Husserl treats this extensively (Husserl 2001b, 278 f.).

ces in general. It comes down not to the brackets but to their meaning, and so, finally, the brackets would be elucidated through the synthesis, but not the synthesis through the brackets.

One can also attempt from here on a new solution to the question regarding *immediate givens*. What is given to us with psychic functions besides appearances—one could say—is not the function itself but rather only the configuration. [32] We notice, as it were, how much has been going on internally, but we notice nothing of the workings of the machine. This middle way will at least appear tempting for the intellectual functions; the presence of a functional consciousness will indeed be more easily acknowledged with feeling and willing.

However, a fortunate solution ought not lie herein. What should it mean, for example, that instead of thinking of size or motion or wickedness, the generality that is denoted by these expressions is itself given immediately? If I see it correctly, the generality would also have to be able then, as with the appearances, to be acknowledged as being for itself, and we would have to accept all the consequences of the old conceptual realism. Or what should it mean to discover a state of affairs, such as the non-being of the Cyclops, as a fact of consciousness in us? What I can discover and observe is an act of judgment that has this non-being as its content, as with the statement: "There is no Cyclops." We can likely think a configuration conceptually without it being momentarily the content of the corresponding function, e. g. a state of affairs without a judgment being momentarily present whose content is formed by that state of affairs. This manifests itself in the fact that we understand the meaning of a *that*-clause when it is uttered alone for itself, although in this case it does not render a claim but, rather, only the content of a possible claim—true or false. But the state of affairs cannot be given on its own, independent of any immediately given function, and thereby also be real. It can only be real as the content of a judgment that actually takes place. Rather, any state of affairs, and also ones that are surely false or, indeed, absurd, would not only be true but indeed real. Functions (indeed, of course, only the conscious, distinct, and present functions) are thus immediately recognized facts; the configurations, however, are facts in general only as contents of functions.

I think things are quite different regarding appearances. Appearances are indeed only given to us with the functions, but—now the expression will no longer be ambiguous—*next* to the functions, as one of the two elements to which consciousness is simultaneously directed, if in dissimilar ways. They are given to us as logically independent of functions, while configurations are logically dependent on functions. [33] Configurations cannot be grasped without functions, and vice-versa. Here, Spinoza's formula "unumquodque [...] per se concipi debet" would not be valid (Spinoza 2002, p. 221). If we think a configuration conceptually, roughly a state of affairs with the expression of an isolated *that*-clause, then the respective function (in this case: judging) must necessarily be co-thought according to its general concept; only the function need not actually take place, and we need not co-think the *individual* act.

A further question can finally be raised from here on concerning *relationships*. We did not count them among the appearances, but also not among the functions. One could try at this point to bring them under the concept of configurations. I do not maintain that this is possible, though the rationale would lead us unnecessarily off course.[25] [34]

2 Changes in Appearances Are Possible Without Changes in Functions.

That something can change in the visual field without our noticing it appears to be an everyday experience. However, the opponents of the distinction between

---

[25] The above explanations agree in many respects with the diverse investigations of Meinong and his school regarding complexions [*Komplexionen*], objects of a higher order, and ideal objects, while they depart from them in other ways. The same goes with regard to Ebbinghaus' concept of "intuitions." The need manifests itself at many points in recent psychology to separate from the appearances yet something else that, nevertheless, is a content of consciousness. cf. the conclusion of this treatise.

For precision, another differentiation is required here with regard to the so-called "configurations" that we do not want to pass over completely. Husserl correctly points out the fact that the concepts "equilateral triangle" and "equiangular triangle" are different but nevertheless mean [*meinen*] the same thing. He speaks from there of a difference in "meaning" ["*Bedeutung*"] with respect to the same "object." The judgment "$a > b$" as opposed to "$b < a$" has a different meaning as well, but expresses the same state of affairs (Husserl 2001a, 196f.). Sets also behave similarly: $a + b$ and $b + a$ are the same sum, a transposed melody the same melody, but the sets, treated as configurations, are not identical. Similar things ought to be said regarding values (I prefer a to b, I reject b in favor of a). However, it will not be necessary for this reason to introduce a completely new concept vis-à-vis that of configurations, but rather only to separate the essentials in a configuration from the inessential modifications. In this context, we call everything "inessential" that makes no difference for the application of thought (or, with respect to values, for all subsequent feelings, volitional acts, and actions). It is the concept of "equivalence" known in logic that arises here. One can just as well conclude the same from $a > b$ as from $b < a$. We thus further differentiate within the configuration itself what is essential, the invariant, which is expressed as well through one sentence as through another, though it cannot be expressed and singled out for itself.

The epistemological concept of "object" vigorously discussed recently would itself require a special treatment. One names "object," as it seems, everything that is thought under a general concept or is itself such a concept. However, we need not go into this in the present context.

appearances and functions tend to point out that, in fact, the appearances do not thereby also change. Only the external occurrence and, at most, the peripheral nervous process might change, but not the central process to which the sensation (appearance) is bound. If a person completely immersed in thought with his eyes open does not notice the gradual dimming of the room, nothing in the slightest in fact occurs, according to this view, in his individual optical image of the appearances. In the moment where he first becomes attentive, a sudden transition from brightness to darkness takes place for him. Or should we say: from nothing to darkness? Since he did not attend to the appearances within the visual field, according to this view, these appearances could not have been at all and in any way present for him. As a matter of fact, it will require such a consequence.

Against this, we claim that it might very well be conceivable that in such a case, the sensory appearance itself gradually changes (along with the underlying central nervous process). Indeed, we claim that changes in appearances that remain unnoticed can occur even when the highest attention is turned directly to an appearance, in other words, that there could be not only *unnoticed* but also *unnoticeable* changes in appearance. This possibility follows from the concepts without further ado as soon as one discriminates them in the way that we find necessary. The assumption then contains no elements logically contradictory to one another.

Obviously, a lot here depends on definitions and the precise upholding of their sense. Those impressed by terminology will quickly concede that unnoticed appearances are appearances that do not appear, or sensations that are not sensed—thus, contradictory concepts. To such a person, we would suggest leaving the word "appearances" aside and replacing it with such concepts as "elements" (Mach) or "material of thought."[26]

[35] This independent variability of appearances in contrast to functions reaches, however, further into the sphere of the *liminal* [*Ebenmerklichen*]. It

---

26 In *Tonpsychologie* I (Stumpf 1883, p.222), I attempted to prove through a simple consideration that imperceptible changes in appearances (or, as I called them at the time, "changes in sensation") really occur. This proof was received with much agreement, but also with some opposition. Some suspected me, completely incorrectly, of thereby confusing changes in stimulus with changes in sensation. Nevertheless, I admit that this thesis needs a renewed meticulous examination, for in the meantime, G.E. Müller has also defended it. (Müller 1896) This thesis coincides with the claim of *steady* changes in sensation. If one exclusively assumes unsteady changes in sensation and then adds to this assumption, which is already extremely implausible in itself, further hypotheses that are likewise very improbable, one could avoid those conclusions. It is sufficient here to emphasize the possibility, not the actual or necessary occurrence, of imperceptible changes in appearance.

was considered earlier as self-evident that all liminal in sensation differences contents of sensation are the same as one another. Fechner based the deduction of his law on this fact. Yet this self-evidence does not exist. Brentano first pointed to the fact that, with regularly maximal attention, even perceivable differences themselves could possess a varying degree of appearance. Külpe concluded from a series of experiments carried out under his leadership that such a discrepancy really takes place in various sensory fields, that in fact the liminal differences in the comparison of brightness increased with increasing absolute brightness, and likewise in the comparison of stretches of time with increasing duration of the compared stretches of time (Külpe 1902). Though the experimental foundation of this astute conclusion indeed needs to be worked through again according to newer experiments, the way pursued is quite promising. That liminal differences become smaller with increasing pitch (thus larger with increasing wavelength), I believe ought to be expressed observationally according to the same line of thought. The very least of differences still attainable through direct observation could thus become accessible by indirect means as much as by measured comparisons; indeed, it does not thereby involve differences in stimuli but, rather, differences in the appearances themselves.

Thus, it is true not only of external things and occurrences that they possess properties and relationships to one another which we are not able to recognize even with very attentive direct observation and which can only be revealed more or less probably by complex lines of inference; these are also true of the behavior of immediately given appearances. [36] Our own sensory contents are not directly transparent to us down to the last subtlety. In a certain sense, we must make the separation between the thing in itself and the appearance a second time with respect to the appearances themselves. If the distinction between actual appearances and appearances of appearances were pointless because just an immediate given is available here, this would mean only that our knowledge of appearances is adequate to the general nature of its objects. It is not thereby said that all properties, differentiations, and relationships within the appearances would be noticeable at every moment, or that properties, differentiations, and relationships that are not noticeable would be *eo ipso* not present. Such a discrepancy between appearances and the intellectual functions directed toward them (including the judgments based on perception) does not contradict the "evidence of inner perception"; or rather, the notion of evidence must be understood such that it is compatible with this discrepancy. A consistent psychology of the senses seems to require this.

The appearances of the second order, the mere representations, also lead an independent existence to a large extent: this happens in all cases of so-called mechanical memory or of habitual association, where representations roll off exactly as impressions of outer events proceeding in front of our eyes independent of us. In accordance with the experimental memory studies that were inaugurated by Ebbinghaus and, particularly, were continued by G.E. Müller and his school, these processes of merely mechanical association and reproduction are subject to an inner and detailed lawfulness, a lawfulness displaying a close kinship with the laws of physiological processes.[27] [37] Most curious, even if they have to be assumed for the time being with a certain probability, are the consequences of the occurrence of association in the unconscious. Under particular circumstances, representations appear that are not present at all at that moment in consciousness, and thus are present either only as appearances under the threshold of noticeability or as processes completely external to consciousness. Such representations enter into associations among themselves in the same manner as representations in the usual sense do.

Finally, as regards emotional life and the functions of willing, we can also maintain that changes in appearances—in the comprehensive sense defined at the beginning also including visceral sensations—do not necessarily and immediately prove to be changes of emotional functions. Usual experience already indicates that inclination and repulsion, desiring and detesting, and a strong will can remain unaltered when directed toward an object, even while the appearances, which constitute the fundamental intuitions in consciousness, change considerably (as with the other sense perceptions underlying or accompanying the feeling). Thus, an exact analysis should not overturn this fundamentally but, rather, grasp it more exactly and lead us back to the bottom layers of our emo-

---

[27] Cf. the formulas for numerical relationships between what is retained and what is forgotten, the regularity of the speed of forgetting under certain circumstances, the so-called "tendency of perseveration" of representations, the analogy of "attitude [*Einstellung*]" to the motor and the representational spheres (Steffens 1900), the inhibition ensuing from the same constituents of the elements to be memorized (Ranschburg 1902), the experiences of slips of the pen or of the tongue, and so much else.

A very general and always surprising experience with memory experiments is the contradiction of the subjective feeling of correctness with objective correctness of the results, in which the independent unwinding of appearances of the second order is brought particularly markedly to consciousness for the experimental subject. "A series unwinds, as it were, as if one had no part in it, and one is very surprised to hear afterwards from the conductor of the experiment that this series was completely right. The reverse also happens frequently: the pleasurable consciousness of having repeated the series correctly is clouded by the subsequent perception of this or that mistake." (Ebbinghaus 1902, p. 650).

The investigations of the reaction to "stimulus words" also supply a lot of evidence for the automatism of memories. With the aid of such series of experiments, this led to the thought of unearthing experiences [*Erlebnisse*] that are removed from what the test subjects can remember voluntarily or that are deliberately kept secret by them.

tional life that reach far beyond the appearances. In general, of course, it is also true here that the emotional state itself undergoes a change at the same time with a change in underlying sensations and representations. What matters is only whether this parallelism of changes is an absolute and exceptionless parallelism or not.

Deciding this question also comes down to what one counts among the concept of an "affect." In a broad sense (that is, when it comes to a description of the overall conditions labeled with the names "melancholy," "rage," etc.), an affect also encompasses the respective visceral sensations.[28] [38] If we understand the expression in this sense, then we cannot retain our current thesis. However, in a narrower sense, if a definition via the essential distinctions is intended, then an affect is delimited from other affects through the presence of particular intellectual functions.[29] In this narrower sense, affects are grasped just as the underlying intellectual functions, and within the same limits as these, independent of the dissimilarity of appearances.

* * *

It seems that we have answered the questions raised, insofar as this could happen in the setting of a general overview of the relevant relationships according to the present status of psychological investigation. Here, it is most notably important during every individual investigation to keep in mind impartially the different possible positions and to pursue their consequences in order to test them. Individual investigations do not exist in order further to confirm pre-established convictions. Whoever feels the exceeding difficulty of problems in psychology—and further contemplates the modifications and concessions that have been necessary not only on the part of the old association psychology and modern appearance psychology, but also on the part of functional psychology, its doctrine of intensity, its doctrine of inner perception, and so forth—will not be at risk of exchanging a sensualistic dogmatism with a functional one. I hold only this as established: that the description of the immediately given, apart from all that must be added in thought for the production of a causal connection, does not make do with appearances, even if one takes the appearances of the second order in the widest extent. James' doctrine of the "fringes," the younger psychologists' doctrine of "conditions of consciousness," "states of consciousness," and

---

[28] See Carl Lange (1887, 93f.).
[29] Of course, it does not consist in these intellectual functions themselves, which only form its indispensable basis, but rather it builds upon intellectual functions as a new, unique function over them. The expression "intellectualism" is thus completely wrong for this conception.

the like rest on the same acknowledgment that appearances do not suffice.[30] [39] Indeed, one may also say that it is important here to keep in mind not so much the differences of functions but, rather, the sundry concealed, half-conscious, hard-to-describe appearances—appearances of the third order. One could argue over individual cases. It could apply one time but not the next. It is enough if it is conceded (1) that the analysis of immediately given psychic life remains incomplete if one confines oneself to the elements enumerated as appearances at the beginning of this paper, (2) that what is added is of a different type, and (3) that what is added accounts for the core of psychic life. The appearances, however, along with all their stretches and bends, are only the outer rind.

Let us mention just a few consequences. It naturally makes a large difference for the question regarding the localization of psychic function in the brain whether one identifies the psychic completely with appearances and their linkages, or whether functions with all of their "configurations" account for the actual essence of psychic life. For the supporter of functional theory, the question arises here whether functions are not localized in a totally different sense from appearances, and whether or not all that, as yet, is proven about the *special* localized areas in the brain boils down to localization of appearances and their associations (cf. Meumann 1903, pp. 21–36.).

In another direction, consequences arise for the classification of the sciences. It becomes apparent that the description of appearances as such and the exploration of their structural laws taken theoretically belong neither to the tasks of natural science nor to those of psychology in the narrower sense of the word; instead, such a description makes up a particular field of knowledge. Since the completion of these thoughts correlates with more general questions about the appropriate classification of the complete fields of science, I think it ought to be dealt with in a separate presentation.[31]

References

Ach, Narziß (1905): *Über die Willenstätigkeit und das Denken*. Göttingen: Vandenhoeck & Ruprecht.

---

[30] Upon closer inspection, what James summarizes under the collective name of "fringes" should certainly be resolved at first into elements of content, namely into relationships that are co-thought in an indeterminate way with certain expressions and turns of phrase. However, conceptual thought, which is here added to intuitive acts of representation, indeed leads then to the functional component (cf. Marty 1892, p. 327).

[31] [See C. Stumpf, "Zur Einteilung der Wissenschaften."]

Beneke, Friedrich Eduard (1845): *Die neue Psychologie*. Berlin: Posen and Bromberg.
Bentley, Isaac Madison (1906): The Psychology of Organic Movements. *American Journal of Psychology* 17:3, pp. 293–305.
Bergmann, Julius (1870): *Grundlinien einer Theorie des Bewußtseins*. Berlin: Otto Loewenstein.
Bergmann, Julius (1886): *Vorlesungen über Metaphysik*. Berlin: Ernst Siegfried Mittler.
Bergson, Henri (1889): *Essai sur les données immédiates de la conscience*. Paris: Ancienne Librairie Germer- Baillière.
Binet, Alfred (1903): *L'Étude expérimentale de l'Intelligence*. Paris: Schleicher, Frères, and Co.
Bolzano, Bernard (1972): *Theory of Science* 1. Rolf George (Trans.). Berkeley/Los Angeles: University of California Press. 1972.
Brentano, Franz (1897): Zur Lehre von der Empfindung. In *Dritter Internationaler Kongreß für Psychologie*. München: Lehmann.
Brentano, Franz (1973): *Psychology from an Empirical Standpoint*. A.C. Rancurello, D.B. Terrell, and L.L. McAlister (Trans.). New York: Routledge.
Calkins, Mary Whiton (1905): *Der doppelte Standpunkt in der Psychologie*. Leipzig: Verlag von Veit.
Calkins, Mary Whiton (1906): "A Reconciliation between Structural and Functional Psychology." In: *Psychological Review* 13. 61–81.
Ebbinghaus, Hermann (1902): *Grundzüge der Psychologie*, vol. I. Leipzig: Verlag von Veit.
Ebbinghaus, Hermann (1912): *Grundzüge der Psychologie*, vol. II. Leipzig: Verlag von Veit.
von Ehrenfels, Christian (1890): "Über Gestaltqualitäten." *Vierteljahrsschrift für wissenschaftliche Philosophie* 14. 242–92.
Hume, David (1978): *A Treatise of Human Nature*. Oxford: Oxford University Press.
Husserl, Edmund (2001a): *Logical Investigations*. Vol. I. Trans. J. N. Findlay. London/New York: Routledge.
Husserl, Edmund (2001b): *Logical Investigations*. Vol. II. Trans. J. N. Findlay. London/New York: Routledge.
Husserl, Edmund (2003): *Philosophy of Arithmetic*. Trans. Dallas Willard. Dordrecht: Kluwer.
Külpe, Oswald (1902): "Zur Frage nach der Beziehung der ebenmerklichen zu den übermerklichen Unterschieden." In: *Philosophische Studien* 18:2, pp. 328–346.
Lange, Carl (1887): *Über Gemütsbewegungen. Ihr Wesen und ihr Einfluß auf körperliche, besonders auf krankenhafte Lebenserscheinungen. Ein medizinisch-psychologische Studie*. Leipzig: Thomas.
Lotze, Hermann (1881): *Grundzüge der Psychologie*. Leipzig: Hirzel.
Marty, Anton (1892): "Anzeige von William James' Werk 'Principles of Psychology'." In: *Zeitschrift für Psychologie und Physiologie der Sinnesorgane* 3, pp. 297–333.
Marty, Anton (1905): "Über Annahmen." In: *Zeitschrift für Psychologie und Physiologie der Sinnesorgane* 40, pp. 1–54.
Meinong, Alexius (1894a): "Beiträge zur Theorie der psychischen Analyse." In: *Zeitschrift für Psychologie und Physiologie der Sinnesorgane* 6, pp. 340–385.
Meinong, Alexius (1894b): *Psychologisch-ethische Untersuchungen zur Werttheorie*. Verlag Dr. Müller.
Meinong, Alexius (1902): "Über Annahmen." In: *Zeitschrift für Psychologie und Physiologie der Sinnesorgane* 2.

Meinong, Alexius (1905): "Über Urteilsgefühle: was sie sind und was sie nicht sind." In: *Archiv für die gesamte Psychologie* 6, pp. 21–58.

Meinong, Alexius (1906a): "In Sachen der Annahmen." In: *Zeitschrift für Psychologie und Physiologie der Sinnesorgane* 41, pp. 1–14.

Meinong, Alexius (1906b): "Über die Erfahrungsgrundlagen unseres Wissens." In: *Abhandlung zur Didaktik und Philosophie der Naturwissenschaft*, Band 1, Heft 6.

Meumann, Ernst (1903): "Naturwissenschaft und Psychologie." In: *Archive für die gesamte Psychologie* 2, pp. 21–36.

Miller, Dickinson S. (1895): "The Confusion of Function and Content in Mental Analysis." In: *Psychological Review* 2, pp. 535–550.

Müller, Georg Elias (1896): "Zur Psychophysik der Gesichtsempfindungen." In: *Zeitschrift für Psychologie und Physiologie der Sinnesorgane* 10, pp. 1–82.

Münsterberg, Hugo (1900): *Grundzüge der Psychologie*, vol. 1. Leipzig: Johann Ambrosius Barth.

Ranschburg, Pál (1902): "Über Hemmungen gleichzeitiger Reizwirkungen. Experimenteller Beitrag zur Lehre von den Bedingungen der Aufmerksamkeit." In: *Zeitschrift für Psychologie und Physiologie der Sinnesorgane* 30, pp. 39–86.

Schumann, Friedrich (1898): "Zur Psychologie der Zeitanschauung." In: *Zeitschrift für Psychologie und Physiologie der Sinnesorgane* 17, pp. 106–148.

Schumann, Friedrich (1900): "Beiträge zur Analyse der Gesichtswahrnehmungen." In: *Zeitschrift für Psychologie und Physiologie der Sinnesorgane* 23, pp. 1–32.

Schumann, Friedrich (1904): *Psychologische Studien*, part I, book I. Leipzig, J.A. Barth.

Spinoza, Benedict (2002): *Complete Works*. Trans. Samuel Shirley. Indianapolis: Hackett.

Steffens, Laura (1900): "Über die motorische Einstellung." In: *Zeitschrift für Psychologie und Physiologie der Sinnesorgane* 23, pp. 241–308.

Stumpf, Carl (1873): *Über den psychologischen Ursprung der Raumvorstellung*. Leipzig: Hirzel.

Stumpf, Carl (1883): *Tonpsychologie*. Vol. I. Leipzig: Hirzel.

Stumpf, Carl (1890): *Tonpsychologie*. Vol. II. Leipzig: Hirzel.

Stumpf, Carl (1892): "Psychologie und Erkenntnistheorie." In: *Abhandlungen der Philosophisch-Philologischen Classe der Königlichen Bayerischen Akademie der Wissenschaften* 19, pp. 467–516.

Stumpf, Carl (1899): "Über den Begriff der Gemütsbewegung." In: *Zeitschrift für Psychologie und Physiologie der Sinnesorgane* 21, pp. 47–99.

Stumpf, Carl (1902): "Abstraktion und Generalisation." In: *Sitzungsberichte der Königlich-Preußischen Akademie der Wissenschaften*, pp. 593.

Stumpf, Carl (1907a): "Über Gefühlsempfindungen." In: *Zeitschrift für Psychologie und Philosophie der Sinnesorgane* 44, pp. 1–49.

Stumpf, Carl (1907b): "Zur Einteilung der Wissenschaften." In: *Abhandlungen der Königlich-Preußischen Akademie der Wissenschaften*, pp. 3–40.

Taylor, Clifton O. (1905/6): "Über das Verstehen von Worten und Sätzen." In: *Zeitschrift für Psychologie und Physiologie der Sinnesorgane* 40, pp. 225–51.

Volkelt, Johannes (1883): "Erfundene Empfindungen." In: *Philosophische Monatshefte* 19, pp. 513–524.

Adam Knowles
Jonas Cohn

Jonas Cohn's systematic approach to both philosophy and psychology reflects his training in the natural sciences. From 1888 to 1892 Cohn pursued a varied course of studies in Leipzig, Heidelberg and Berlin, culminating in a doctoral dissertation on plant physiology entitled *Beiträge zur Physiologie des Kollenchyms*. During his time in Berlin, Cohn also pursued the study of philosophy, attending lectures by Friedrich Paulsen and Wilhelm Dilthey. In the following years Cohn furthered his studies in the field of experimental psychology under Wilhlem Wundt in Leipzig, engaging in the sort of empirical psychological research [*empirische Einzelarbeit*] which he repeatedly refers to in this article. In 1897 Cohn completed his habilitation in philosophy, under the neo-Kantian Wilhelm Windelband, with a work entitled *Beiträge zur Lehre von den Wertungen*. In the same year he received a position as *Privatdozent* at the University of Freiburg, where he would remain until his forced retirement in 1933 upon the implementation of anti-Jewish laws. Cohn eventually fled from Germany in 1939, and died in England in 1947.

Cohn's philosophical perspective was deeply influenced by the Marburg school of Neo-Kantians, and the problem of finitude decisively informed his various contributions in the fields of psychology, epistemology, religion and aesthetics, beginning with his early work *Geschichte des Unendlichkeitsproblems im abendländischen Denken bis Kant*. He characterized his own philosophical approach as utraquism, a term which he appropriated and reformulated to designate the form of cognition and the content of cognition as equally primordial elements, neither of which ought to be privileged over the other. Cohn's utraquism stands in the background of his critique of Husserl's phenomenology.

Cohn's *Grundfragen der Psychologie*, published in 1913 in the inaugural edition of the *Jahrbücher der Philosophie* (edited by Max Frischeisen-Köhler), can be regarded as a review essay that seeks to reveal two shortcomings in the predominant strains of psychology at this time: the lack of a fundamental grounding, and disregard for the work of individual empirical researchers. As a whole, Cohn identifies a lack of correspondence between, on the one hand, the results of fruitful scientific experiments carried out by psychologists pursuing and presumably solving individual questions and, on the other hand, the philosophers and psychologists who seek to offer systematic theories of psychology. Husserl falls into the latter category, and Cohn's primary dissatisfaction with Husserlian phenomenology focuses on the conception of intuition. Cohn thinks that Husserl's phenomenology presupposes epistemological investigations that are overlooked in Husserl's assumption of essential intuition, thus calling into question the immediacy of intuition. In the *Ideas* Husserl offers little in the way of response to Cohn's critique, dismissing the critiques by Cohn and August Messer (published in the *Jahrbücher der Philosophie*) in a footnote from § 79, stating that "the doctrines which are opposed there as mine are simply not mine at all." (*Ideen* 157/152) Like many of the thinkers he reviews in his essay, Cohn regards Husserl's phenomenology as being incapable of responding to the research of empirical psychologists, whose work, he argues, must be considered in any systematic account of "*das Psychische.*"

References

Cohn, Jonas (1896): *Geschichte des Unendlichkeitsproblems im abendländischen Denken bis Kant.* Leipzig: W. Engelmann.

Husserl, Edmund (2014): *Ideas for a Pure Phenomenology and Phenomenological Philosophy.* Daniel Dahlstrom (Trans.). Indianapolis/Cambridge: Hackett.

Translated by Adam Knowles
Jonas Cohn.
The Fundamental Questions of Psychology

Grundfragen der Psychologie
Jahrbücher der Philosophie 1, pp. 200–235 (1913)

[200] The primary goal of our psychology is to discover confirmed facts, exact descriptions and empirical laws of psychic occurrences. It is possible to increase the quantity of this factual knowledge to a certain degree without having clarity about the fundamental questions of this science. The much-maligned insufficiency of psychological terminology, however, already indicates the limits of this possibility; and these limits become even more clearly evident once one seeks to explain the relevant empirical laws based on more developed theories. This difficulty, in turn, has an effect on empirical research: due to the lack of properly developed theories, the highest form of experiment, namely a decisive result achieved through experimentation on a disjunctively posed question, is extremely rare in psychology. Indeed, there has been no lack of attempts at grounding the psychological science more thoroughly, but unfortunately these attempts only reveal—in contrast to the constancy of individual empirical work—a chaotic confusion and disparity of viewpoints and departure points. Hardly any of the schools of thought which are catalogued in the history of psychology are completely absent today. Nevertheless, the productive friction and conflict between different schools of thought recedes conspicuously into the background. Only the psycho-physical problem constitutes an exception, for it is indeed the most common concern for psychologists pursuing individual research. Given this state of affairs, it would not be fitting to restrict this overview to the most recent publications, for these would represent nothing more than an entirely random sample. One must instead look back at the most recent valuable formulations of each school of thought.[1]

[201] Despite this state of affairs, there are some indications pointing towards more systematic work on the primary questions. Evidence of the need

---

[1] Unfortunately, I must mention the following restriction: I do so to the extent that I am aware of these works. This restriction especially applies to foreign literature, the acquisition of which is not entirely easy. I therefore must rely more strongly on a random selection of articles from journals (of which our library has a more complete collection) in places where the use of books certainly would have been called for.

for clarity and orientation can indeed be found when one turns more closely to the history of the science. The fact that the years 1910 and 1911 each brought us a new history of psychology can be regarded as a symptom of this need (Dessoir 1911; Klemm 1911). However, only Dessoir's book will be of any use. With regard to Otto Klemm's history of psychology, its historical problem-oriented disposition is at first quite captivating; however, it is not only insufficient because the content of the book hardly stands on its own, but it is also lacking in the fundamental guiding thoughts and principles of selection. Moreover, the book is not always reliable. Dessoir's book does not interest us here due to its mastery of a great amount of historical material, rather due to one point of view which dominates its descriptions. This point of view delineates three roots of psychology. The first root is religious in nature, begins with the experiences of dreams and death, and moves through the ancient cult of the soul to the metaphysical doctrines of an immortal god-like soul-substance. The second root has as its basis the fundamental experience that there is a principle of action at work within the human body, leading from there to a mortal soul which is simultaneously the basis of manifestations of life, and, finally, produces from itself the scientific doctrine of the soul. Lastly, the third school of thought begins from practical human knowledge and manifests itself in idiomatic phrases, poetic depictions, and later in collections and observations of characteristics. Dessoir calls the first school of thought psychosophy, the second psychology in the proper sense, and the third psychognosis. Since psychognostic efforts have only very recently sought an alliance with scientific psychology, Dessoir deals with psychognosis in a separate section unto itself, while he concludes his historical work around the time of Fechner and Lotze. In contrast, psychosophy and psychology had to be dealt with together since they have consistently been connected with one another, and it is only very recently that one has generally sought to separate them. Perhaps Dessoir would have fostered the necessary clarification of the problem more thoroughly had he emphasized even more strongly that the epistemological and axiological motifs within "psychosophy," which in turn lead to the concept of the "spirit" and lend to the "I" its rich problematic, have increasingly become dominant in the science. Engaging with the concepts of "I" and "spirit" is the task of the separate sciences of psychology and philosophy. [202] However, the energetic emphasis on the distinct tasks of psychology, which relies in part on Dilthey, is in itself fruitful and prepares the absolutely necessary scientific-theoretical grounding of psychology.

The urgency of this need is shown by difficulties which have already confronted many of those who have attempted to determine the *object of psychology*. The frequently occurring appeals to the actually present appearances of perception, thought, and feeling can only be justified on propaedeutic and didactical grounds. According to the dominant views, the attempts to determine the object of psychology can be classified as ontological and epistemological. The ontological school of thought is present in its purest form in Rehmke, whose views are presented in the most detailed fashion in the second edition of his textbook of general psychology (Rehmke 1905). He separates everything that is given into the intuitively and non-intuitively given. By intuitively given he means what is given in space or what is constantly conjoined with a spatial determination, and he assumes without any further investigation that all sense perceptions possess a spatial determination.[2] A second division into what is immediately and what is mediately given or accessible is especially important for us because it is linked to the basic principle that under no circumstances can we have access to something conceptually novel, i.e. to something which is by nature distinct from the immediately given. What is immediately and non-intuitively given is restricted to what "I think, feel and want." Furthermore, Rehmke transposes the ancient distinction between substance and accident onto the distinction between individual beings and determination. He avoids using the word substance to designate particular objects because he limits its use to what has its subsistence in itself and through itself. Determinations can only be found on individual entities; non-intuitive determinations are non-spatial in their immediate givenness. What is not in a place in its immediate givenness can also not be in a place as something which is given as accessible. [203] For things given intuitively (e. g. color and shape), the determination of place is the ground of unity or the unifying determination. A common unifying ground for intuitive and non-intuitive determinations is thus lacking. However, since there can be no determination without an accompanying individual entity, the existence of non-intuitive individual entities is also thereby determined, which Rehmke characterizes as subject-determination.

It is precisely because Rehmke's system excels in the precision of its formulations that it serves as a particularly good example for demonstrating the difficulties of an objective ontological determination. The contrast between the intuitive and non-intuitive seems to be very clear. However, the completeness with which this contrast covers the entire range of the "given" is based solely upon the assumption that spatial determination and the act of being perceived are

---

[2] Those familiar with Wundt's psychology or contemporary epistemology will notice that Rehmke characterizes the physical as "intuitive." This opposition is primarily terminological. Since Kant it has been customary to use the word "intuition" for the immediate apprehension of an individual object. French philosophers among others have taken on this use of the term. (cf. the article "Intuition" in the "Vocabulaire philosophique," Xavier 1909, p. 273). Here Rehmke is indulging in confusing terminological eccentricities.

necessarily linked to one another. Rehmke does not prove this necessity, though it is subject to serious objections. The spatial determinateness of a sound, for example, does not seem to me to be something that belongs to it by necessity.[3] I can experience sounds without necessarily connecting them to any sort of spatial determination. Yet even if I do take sounds to be spatial, this spatiality is essentially given to me as a direction, and not as a place. The idea of assigning sounds to the place from which they are emitted is a result of experience and is in no way unambiguous—for what place is to be assigned to an echo? The reverberating surface or the mass of air between me and the surface? Moreover, such questions are not precise enough when posed in such a general fashion. One must also ask whether it is a matter of the classification of sounds in the experience of a single person, or in a unified conception of the world, and, furthermore, in which world. If, for example, a mechanistic physics is assumed, then the sound is broken down into the motion of waves in which a large number of bodies participate. In such a case, the sound can never be assigned a unity (and it is given to me as a unity) by means of a spatial determination. If, however, a sound is not in a place in its immediate givenness, then, assuming that Rehmke's proposition cited above is correct, it can also not be in a place in its accessible givenness. Thus there are two possibilities: either Rehmke's sentence is correct, and then sounds (and likewise scents, tastes, sensations of temperature and general sensations) also belong among the "non-intuitive" in Rehmke's sense; or sounds can be assigned a place, and then the reason why physical things cannot be assigned a place falls away—and in that case Rehmke's proposition is no longer correct. [204]

It is sufficient to criticize Rehmke's line of thought on a *single* point, for the artful weave of his sentences is spun from a single thread; if one can loosen a single stitch, then the entirety comes undone. In contrast, it will be necessary to move backwards from the critique of individual sentences to the fundamental error of the system. This error consists in Rehmke's assumption of certain distinctions (such as "singularity" and "determination" or "intuitive" and "non-intuitive") as givens. By drawing these distinctions he does not want simply to say that these distinctions can be found, but rather that they account for the entire terrain of what is discoverable. This is only possible a priori in opposing contradictory pairs. The pairs "intuitive" and "non-intuitive," or with and without spatial determination, appear to be contradictory pairs; but if one looks more closely, Rehmke actually means by intuitive that it is necessarily conjoined with a

---

[3] Rehmke is aware of this objection (cf. p. 179), but he brushes it off with nothing more than an ungrounded assertion of the spatiality of sound.

place, while non-intuitive means being excluded from any possible spatial determination. Then a third possibility between these two arises: not necessarily conjoined with a place, but assignable to a place. Rehmke, however, intends to exclude this possibility through the proposition about which we have been raising doubts. Moreover, the distinctions which are taken to be given are simply accepted and are not analyzed further. It seems clear, however, that spatiality and spatial determination are in no way necessarily connected to one another. When one conceives of a triangle in order to prove a geometrical proposition with it, it has spatiality, but it is not at all necessary that it has a spatial determination; and the same goes for fantasies. The classification of everything spatial into *one single* concept of space is far from being genetically primordial. If, however, a priori validity rather than genetic primordiality is intended, then it is possible to raise the question whether the postulate of classification into the spatial whole is not valid for everything which is part of our world, or which is a part of—as Rehmke quite pointedly describes it—the unified nexus of effects. The dogmatic certainty of Rehmke's rationalized derivations is coupled with a simple positing of fundamental principles. We, however, demand that precisely the fundamental principles demonstrate their validity; be it by showing that a single science can be constructed only with—or at best by means of—such principles, or by deriving them teleologically from a system of sciences. It should not scare us that the dialectic of beginning ingeniously developed by Hegel accompanies any particular determination of this sort. Rehmke seems to be fleeing precisely this uncertainty and thus seeks a rigid preservation of his concepts to a degree that achieves not only a pre-Kantian, but even almost a pre-Socratic dogmatism, [205] although *Philosophy as Fundamental Science* proves how seriously Rehmke has grappled with the problems of critique (Rehmke 1910). In accordance with the limitations of this essay, we must be granted and can also be warranted the necessity of restricting ourselves to Rehmke's psychology. Yet it should be emphasized that we have not done complete justice to the motivations of such a thoroughly systematic thinker.

Even the numerous psychologists who characterize the function of the soul as the object of their science, in contrast to the objects grasped through these functions, tend to consider their delineation of the science to be ontological. Most recently Samuel Alexander has expressed this explicitly (Alexander 1911). In the perception of a tree, for example, he distinguishes between the perceived object and the act of perception. "That these things, the act of consciousness and the object of which it is conscious, are present together and distinct from one another is not a theory or a philosophical postulate, but a description of the event which is the perception of the tree in its simplest terms" (Alexander 1911, p. 239). Likewise, in the act of imagining there is a distinction between act and object, and Alexander correctly concludes from his own doctrines that the object of an act of imagination is non-psychic. The psychic act is lived through and enjoyed, while the non-psychic object is contemplated. German readers ought to be very familiar with this type of distinction from Brentano's psychology. Everything psychic is distinguished by being directed towards an (non-psychic) object, or, as Brentano expresses it in conjunction with the scholastics, it is distinguished by intentionally containing an object within it. Even Brentano then differentiates between the manner of perception of the psychic as "internal" and "solely evident," and the "external" perception of the object. Now, since this function and object refer to one another and can only be defined in correlation to one another, this manner of demarcation of the psychic is not as purely ontological as Rehmke's, which deals with the traits of spatiality and non-spatiality; much to the contrary, for the unified complex of act and object are divided up into their components by the different manners of being experienced. What is decisive, therefore, is the point of view of the analysis, which is not brought to the given, but is instead modeled by it. Stumpf above all approaches the epistemological manner of analysis, though he seems to do so almost against his own will. [206] I select him as representative of the functionalistic conception of the psychic because he formulates its fundamental concepts most precisely and offers the most detailed discussion of its shortcomings. In his treatise "Appearances and Psychic Functions," he starts from the point of the "immediately given," or, as he explains it, from "what is immediately evident as a matter of fact" (Stumpf 1907a, p. 6; incl. in this volume p. 84). That there is disagreement about this immediately given is not to be attributed to the given itself, rather to the difficulty of correctly describing it. "The description of immediate givenness seems possible now with exhaustive completeness only if one counts three things among it: appearances, functions, and finally relationships between the elements within each one of these kinds and between the elements of one kind and the other" (Stumpf 1907a, p. 6 – 7; incl. in this volume, p. 84). The meaning of the word "appearance" is thereby released from any opposition to "a being in itself," and Stumpf, who uses the word "at first completely disregarding the question of reality," employs it as a common designation for the contents of sense impressions (including all their spatial and temporal characteristics), as well as for their images in memory, which he calls "appearances of the second order." "We designate as *psychic functions* (acts, states, experiences) the noticing of appearances and their relationships, the synthesizing of appearances into a complex, the formation of concepts, apprehending and judging, affects, desiring and willing. This is not meant to be a sharp and exhaustive classification, but rather only an overview of the most important examples." (Stumpf 1907a, p. 4- 5; incl. in this volume, p. 82). Appearances and functions are entirely separate from one another. "Psychic functions receive none of the predicates of the world of appearances (with the exception of time) . . . Conversely, however, no functional predicate can be conferred to appearances" (Stumpf 1907a, p. 11; incl. in this volume, p. 88). It is clear, however, as Stumpf details in his second treatise, that what is immediately given is only the starting point of research and the material of conceptual formation, and is never itself the object of science (Stumpf 1907b). Appearances especially are not the object of physics (and of the other natural sciences erected upon it). Stumpf intends to define the type of modern physics which searches for laws and is dominated by mathematics. Thus, he says, "physical objects, or the object of the natural sciences through which these sciences are defined, are neither appearances nor complexes of appearances, but rather *the bearers of change, according to laws demanded by temporal and spatial relations, which have been apprehended through appearances*." (Stumpf 1907b, p. 16). Psychology immediately relates to functions. [207] Furthermore, even its objects are largely accessed and not given; for one can neither characterize one's own psychic functions as given, nor can one do so for the psychic functions of others. In contrast, however, to the objects of the natural sciences, the objects of psychology are qualitatively the same as the immediately given objects. "Political science and sociology, as well as the study of language, religion, art, etc. are sciences of *complex* psychic functions, while psychology is the science of *elementary* psychic functions" (Stumpf 1907b, p. 21). If one defines the natural and human sciences in this way, then a gap remains: a science is lacking which engages with the appearances as such. The peculiarities of our perception of color, for example, the three-dimensional nature of our system of color, the receding series of bright colors, etc., would find a place neither in psychology nor in the natural sciences. Meinong, who first called attention to this gap (Meinong 1903, p. 3), attempted to fill it with a "theory of objects" (Meinong 1904, p. 13 f.). Stumpf calls the science being sought "phenomenology."

If one compares the definitions of physics and psychology offered by Stumpf to one another, their vastly different relation to the actually existing science is conspicuous. While the conceptual determination of physics is chosen so as to encompass the research of modern physics, the conceptual determination of psychology presupposes—as Stumpf himself emphasizes—a controversial theory. According to this presupposition, associationist psychology, which attempts to explain the life of the soul from the connections of individual impressions and conceptions, would not at all be psychology, though even its harshest critics characterize it at worst as false or bad psychology. Indeed, even the question of whether individual aspects of the science even belong to psychology depends—if one accepts Stumpf's definition—upon a controversial theoretical interpretation. If one considers "seeing" and "hearing" to be different functions, then for that person the question of their differences belongs to psychology; if one regards their difference as only being grounded in appearances, then one must assign the question to phenomenology. The same goes for emotions—it is an object of controversy whether desire and aversion are appearances or functions. Now, if one were to ask what the basis of this difference between the definitions is, one would see that the definition of physics contains the end of the science within itself. The essential element of what is said of the objects of physics is, namely, that they are "bearers of changes in accordance with laws," and from this context it clearly follows that Stumpf is thinking of quantitative, mathematically formulated laws. [208] "What is not contained in the formulas of mathematical physics, hence what is not absolutely necessary for the predetermination of the appearances, may be useful as a conceptual aid, model, or access point, yet does not belong to the essential and lasting objects of the natural sciences by which one can define the sciences." (Stumpf 1907b, p. 13–14). The goal of the science thus determines what its "essential and lasting" object is. In psychology, this description lacks an end. In the case of physics, Stumpf recognized precisely the teleological delineation only reluctantly and under pressure from the facts of the history of the science; he did not recognize it on principle. Thus, it remains unclear in his work whether the differentiation of objects which supposedly characterizes the sciences has its roots in the origin of the sciences, or whether it has its origin in the changing points of view of the sciences. This indecision can perhaps be explained by Stumpf's aversion to the word "method." "Those who have never carried out a single objective analysis themselves are especially fond of speaking of method. Thoroughgoing differences of method are ultimately always rooted in differences of objects" (Stumpf 1907b, p. 4). The second sentence is correct if one adds that the end of a science decides what the object of a science is. "Methodos" comes from "path," and whether a path is "right" is determined by its end.[4] If one would like to label the manner of conceptual determination more closely, which I have called "theory of science" up until now with intentional indecisiveness, one would be more apt to call it "teleological" than to call it "methodological." Why, then, has "method" become such a beloved term for many of the representatives of the teleological theory of science? One could see it as a symptom of that carefulness and guardedness which characterizes German philosophy since the collapse of the Hegelian school. But, of course, such a characterization would not be fair to the rep-

---

[4] Of course, it is no less determined by the rough patches that lie along the way and by the means of transport that are available (to stick with the image). But when the theory of science speaks of method, it is not referring to these aspects, though they are often decisive for actual research.

resentatives of Cohen's school of neo-Kantianism. In contrast, one must add that the "telos" of the sciences is mostly unknown to the scientist. It is the philosopher who discovers this telos through a consideration of the sciences' procedures. The goal is revealed to the philosopher along the path and through its direction. Precisely because psychology is only now searching for its path, its end is also that much more difficult to determine than the end of physics. [209] It is remarkable that the most cautious representative of the ontological definition of the object of psychology must make such great concessions to the teleological definition, and that his conceptual definition of the science of psychology conflicts with the actual performance of research due to the fact that he remains stubbornly insistent on his ontology.

All delineations of the theory of science must begin from a point at which the psychic and the physical are not yet divided. Genetically, the early conceptions of a "soul ghost [Seelengespenst]" that still reverberate everywhere contain a reference to this stage. However, what is more important is that, in our experience, we take our own personhood, and likewise the personhood of others, to be a whole in which we cannot separate the corporeal elements from the psychic. In this regard, we cannot speak of a psycho-physical whole; for this expression posits the previously divided sides as conjoined. Thus, it would be more appropriate to speak of a pre-psycho-physical whole. Even the historian proceeds, as Rickert emphasizes, "regardless of whether [the] real existence [of what he depicts] is physical or psychic" (Rickert 1986, p. 143). All delineations in the theory of science must begin from that point, not from the point of an experiential whole broken down into the physical and the psychic. Of course, both this whole and the motives for dividing it (which of course already take effect in pre-scientific thought), are determined differently by different people. With regard to the whole of experience, Dilthey essentially has in mind the object of the human sciences. He expressed this clearly in his final work. The human sciences contain the psychic and physical in an undivided form. Where they must make use of this distinction, they must keep in mind "that they are working with abstractions, not with entities, and that these abstractions are only valid within the limits of the point of view within which they are projected" (Dilthey 2002, p. 102). Just as the material which Dilthey takes as his point of departure is concrete, so too do his concepts of the psychic and physical—even if their emergence from abstraction is recognized—also maintain something which at least calls to mind real and concrete contexts. The psychic is the acquired life nexus of our conceptions, value judgments and goals. Physical objects are the elements that —for the sake of practical ends—underlie the "impressions" and "images," the components of our experiences, through the positing of which the impressions are capable of being constructed. [210] The semi-concrete character contained within Dilthey's conception of the psychic appears even more clearly in another passage. He gives the following "explanation of nomenclature" there: "by 'psychic life-units' I mean the constituents of the socio-historical world; by 'psychic structure' I designate the nexus in which various functions are connected within the psychic life-unit" (Dilthey 2002, p. 153). Dilthey, the historian and theoretician of history, also sees historical formations in the fundamental concepts— or, better said, the fundamental concepts and distinctions are not of interest to him in their strict and bare simplicity, rather they are of interest to him as the roots of systems of derived terms that branch out far and wide and then, in turn, insert themselves into a highly intricate historical life. He urgently warns us not to favor analysis over life and not to favor separate concepts over the problem of unification, yet he sacrifices the exact account of the logical nature of the fundamental concepts to this concern for the living present. And it is worth mentioning that with the term "psychology," Dilthey essential refers to what he calls "descriptive" psychology and to a depiction of the psychic life free of theory, which he believes ought to serve as the basis of the human sciences.

Wundt shares with Dilthey both the opposition to the constructions of physics and the appeal to the immediate, although they significantly diverge from one another in other regards. Wundt has re-published his treatise on the definition of psychology, first published in 1895, in the second volume of his shorter works (Wundt 1911). The changes to the second volume are not significant, and at the most they reveal an even more careful conception of his voluntarism. Wundt has not taken the more recent works by Münsterberg, Rickert, Dilthey and Stumpf into account. Psychology, according to Wundt, is not defined by a particular object of concern, rather by the standpoint of analysis. This is because any lived experience can be the object of psychological research. Lived experience itself—and here Wundt agrees with Dilthey—is initially prior to a psychophysical distinction. However, it is then broken down in a very abstract conceptual manner. All experience is unified, yet in reality it contains two factors that are indivisibly conjoined: the object of experience and the experiencing subject. To the extent that it is possible, natural science abstracts itself from the subject. It wants to determine the connections between objects and can only do that through an abstract-conceptual construction. [211] "Psychology once again undoes those distinctions carried out by the natural sciences in order to examine experience in its *immediate reality*" (Wundt 1896, p. 12). Psychology does not put an abstract-conceptual construction in the place of lived experiences, rather it works with the lived experiences themselves; it is therefore an *intuitive* science. The necessity of such a supplement could only be appreciated once physics recognized its abstract-conceptual character. But this is what occurred in modern, mechanistic physics, and, thus, "the self-sufficiency of psychology is a postulate of the mechanistic conception of nature" (Wundt 1903, p. 103). Time and again, attention has been drawn to the fact that the entire content of psychology certainly cannot be "intuitive" in this sense because it contains universal laws and concepts, and because the universal, even where it brings out moments of the intuitive, cannot be given individually as the universal, and thus is not intuitive. But even with regard to its content, the concept of the psychic exceeds intuition insofar as the "simplicity" it demands can no longer be intuitive. Besides, it is still a matter of controversy whether or not psychology can do without the assistance of concepts whose content can never be demonstrated in an intuition. This is the only thing from Wundt's conception of the intuitiveness of the physic which remains indubitably true: that it is the task of psychology to deal with the manifoldness of lived experiences in their unique form, and it therefore cannot, as physics does, abstract from the experienced side of the intuitions. Nowhere has Wundt shown that a systematic science can remain "intuitive"; everywhere his own interpretations contain conceptual operations. For example, he cannot do without "association," which Dilthey entirely correctly uses as an example of the method employed by the type of explanatory psychology which operates on the basis of natural science. If Wundt presents his theory of actuality—that is to say, if he presents his doctrine that everything psychic is a process and that there are no fixed things in the psychic—as an example of the intuitive conception of the psychic, then a fitting response is that the characteristics of a process and of a change in time are both just as much abstract traits as constancy over time is. Thus Wundt is lacking a positive concept of the end of psychology; fundamentally, he only offers a negative definition in contrast to physics.

Wundt shares this lack of a positive concept of psychology with one point of view that he attacks, the "psychological materialism," or, as one would more appropriately name it in accordance with Wundt's own teaching, "methodological materialism." The only problem is that the representatives of this point of view are aware of this lack and they therefore establish psychology as being in a relationship of dependence [212] vis-à-vis physics and physiology. Among the main representatives of this school of thought, Külpe has said almost nothing regarding these questions of principle since the appearance of Wundt's essay, while Münsterberg has laid out his theory in detail and justified it from an epistemological perspective (Munsterberg 1900). Münsterberg's methodological materialism is built into an idealistic philosophy. With a turn from the metaphysical into the critical, he would agree with Lotze's statement: "The true vital point of the science" lies therein "that we prove how *the meaning of the mission which materialism has to fulfill in the construction of the world* is, without exception, both *universal* and *completely subservient*" (Lotze 1880, p. 15). Much like Lotze, Münsterberg also transposes the mechanistic conception onto psychology. However, and once again following Lotze, he assigns the "exegetical" point of view, a point of view which he demands alongside and above the mechanistic conception, even more decisively than his predecessor, to a different group of sciences, namely history and the normative philosophical sciences. Münsterberg also starts from a description of "pure experience." In pure experience, we have things which constitute unities, things which we cannot be permitted to confuse with the theoretical assumptions of physics, the atoms. In opposition to these things, we find ourselves as an I, not already as a merely representing I, or as a passive point of reference, rather as an I which is actively taking a stance. "The I which stands over and against my representations of things is the stance-taking subject, the subject as which I know and enact myself in every lived experience. Only by taking a stance in opposition to my object do I know about myself as subject; only by taking that stance in opposition to objects do those objects have reality for me. These acts of taking a stance are, as acts of self-positing, distinct from the representations" (Münsterberg 1900, p. 50). The value-neutral observation of things that is carried out by the natural sciences, and by extension by psychology, is secondary with regard to this world of lived experiences; indeed, it is even more so the case that, within this general disregard for all values, a (theoretical) value asserts itself. "To conceive of a world of value-neutral objects is valuable to the freely deciding subject, and this evaluated thought is therefore valid: the things are; but even in this case, the concept of a value-neutral thing is itself an evaluated object" (Münsterberg 1900, p. 53). The subject needs this value neutral thing in order to precisely determine its expectations regarding what is not yet real. [213] It wants to know how the future would be structured if it only depended on the present state of objects. Thus it dismisses its own effect and turns itself into a passive spectator. This subject stands in opposition to a world of objects in which its own activity no longer intervenes. Within this world, however, Münsterberg draws an essential distinction. "In the object as we find it at hand, we call psychic that which *can only be experienced by a subject*; we call physical that which *can be thought in common by multiple subjects*" (Münsterberg 1900, p. 72). The world of objects which can be thought to be open to experience by multiple subjects must, as Münsterberg draws out in detail, be a world of things that are equally durable, and the mutual effects that these things exercise upon one another must be dominated by causal equations. Now it is clear that the entire manifold of present objects will not submit itself to such a transformation. "The psychic is to a certain degree *what remains when we abstract and extract whatever is identifiable in different experiences, and thus whatever is causally connected*" (Münsterberg 1900, p. 88). Even this remainder must still be described, classified, simplified and explained. But that is a paradoxical task, because everything that can be communicated and explained is extracted from the objects by physics. Nothing remains other than to indirectly master the objects belonging to only a single subject (principally even to a single subjective act) by classifying them as physical objects. This occurs in a twofold manner: for the sake of description by assigning the sensations to their stimuli, and for the sake of explanation by assigning the physical occurrences to the processes in the brain. From Münsterberg's presuppositions one can therefore conclude: 1) sensations are the only physical elements 2) there is no psychic causality, and the entire causal nexus belongs to the physical side. In this context, psycho-physical parallelism is therefore not, as is the case for Wundt, a mere auxiliary principle for the cooperation of the science concerned with physical bodies and psychology, rather it is the fundamental principle of psychological explanation. It is conceivable that there is a state of natural science in which we could do without psychology, but we are infinitely far away from such a state. The psychic connection is "the provisional answer to the provisional questions of a provisional science, which, of course, we will not be able to do without in the foreseeable future" (Münsterberg 1900, p. 486–7). Münsterberg's conception of psychology is based upon a methodological rationalism which fundamentally only recognizes the rationalizing tendency of the science, a rationalism which simultaneously traces causality to identity in a genuinely rationalistic fashion. [214] In an earlier publication I attempted to refute the presuppositions of this rationalism, and it is necessary to call attention to that exposition at this time (Cohn 1900; 1902).

Given the incompleteness of the psychological conceptual system, it is not surprising that, wherever one is convinced of its scientific-theoretical nature, the determination of the object of psychology occurs by means of the contrast to physics. For Münsterberg meanwhile, the relationship to physics is much more positive; his concept of an objectivizing science is derived from physics, and he measures psychology against this ideal concept, which then of course does not meet the demands of this ideal. However, in the research of individual psychologists, a great number of very different tendencies assert themselves. It is therefore understandable if this one-sided physical orientation does not lead to a satisfying positive objective. However, in their execution the attempts to go further all fall far behind Münsterberg's systematic hermeticism. There is a widespread assumption, an assumption that also underpins Dessoir's history of psychology, that psychology harbors within itself a multiplicity of sciences. George M. Stratton has given voice to this assumption in a discourse to American psychologists: "What we call psychology is really a writhing brood of young sciences, and he can have no feeling for the future who would try to stifle any of them" (Stratton 1909, p. 68). It can remain an open question whether a unity of these "sciences" or fields of research exists, and, moreover, what the principle of this unity is. Many will be apt to find it in a universal concept of life or concept the organism. Yet, since the foundation of *biology* itself is a matter of dispute, hitherto there has been little reason to expect anything in the way of clarity from this way of thinking. Indeed, the *biological school of thought* plays a much greater role in psychological research than it does in the discussion of the principles.[5] This comes out very clearly in Wundt, whose definition of psychology does not take the biological point of view into account, even while one can characterize his psychology as a biological science. This is because the psychic phenomena can be assigned to the physical-psychic nexus, but also because the act of the will (for Wundt the basic form of psychic occurrence) [215] can be regarded as the preservation and assertion of life against the environment. Indeed, the status of the will for Wundt is most clearly illuminated from this perspective. The will for Wundt should not be regarded as an element or primordial material of the psychic, rather it should be regarded as the typical fundamental form of the psychic, out of which all other psychic process can be regarded as its parts, variations, and condensations. This is a process characteristic of biology, and the concept of "typical" employed here is proper to biology. Of course, one cannot claim that this biological psychology judges the psychic life of the soul according to an external or foreign standard. Wundt is far from making the observation of lower, simpler stages of the life of the soul, such as in the observation of children or animals, into the foundation of his theories, or even from using a purely physiological process such as reflex as the standard for the life of the soul. It is much more plausible to say that Wundt's conception of life is determined by psychology, since he is indeed quite fond of conceptualizing instinct and reflex as the inherited outcomes of mechanized acts of the will.

The researcher becomes conscious of the biological nature of psychology most strongly when it becomes necessary to refer individual traits to the whole of the human being. But that is always the case when one intends to characterize individual human types, whether with regard to ethnic groups, ages, races, tribes, or with regard to any other groups. It is certainly no coincidence that, in his great work on adolescence, Stanley Hall posits the basic dictum: "*nemo psychologus, nisi biologus*" (Hall 1905, p. 55). Stern's differential psychology is likewise dominated in many ways by a consciously biological approach (Stern 1911). This is the case with his definitions of normality and typology, and is also especially the case in his collapsing of the partition between body and soul in his recognition of psycho-physical neutral traits. Responses, for ex-

---

5 It is remarkable that Hellpach, who constantly takes his cues from research, emphasizes the connection between biology and psychology. (1908, p. 377.)

ample, are for Stern reactions of either acceptance or defense which can just as easily be expressed psychically or physically. "A defensive reaction or flight is thus just as much a negative response as the negative answer to a question or the disapproval of an action; in both examples, the action expresses that the individual excludes the object from his individual striving" (Stern 1911, p. 23).

The tendency to assimilate the psychic into the nexus of life fights against the mechanistic conception of life on all fronts. This fact is also of special interest historically if one is convinced that both opposing points of view can be united through clearly formulated questions and precise terminological formulations. [216] Thus, one can clearly distinguish two schools of thought among specialized researchers in the field of animal psychology. The first school of thought attempts to divide the psychic and the physical as sharply as possible, and, thus, because the psychic is only accessible to us in analogy to the human being, seeks to avoid the psychic altogether in the description and explanation of forms of animal behavior (Beth, H.E. Ziegler, etc.). The second school of thought assumes that the psychic intervenes in the general life process, and it therefore tends towards a psychological explanation of animal motions (Wasmann, Forel, etc.). August Franken recently defended the correctness of a psychological interpretation of animal movements in a work which can also be recommended as an overview to these disputes: "Possibilities and Foundations of a General Psychology, especially Animal Psychology" (Franken 1910, p. 413). It is unfortunate, though also understandable, that these problems are almost never clearly developed, even while these fundamental contrasts of principle constantly play into the elucidations of individual problems. This unfortunate state of affairs marks the interesting debate between Charles S. Myers, C. Lloyd Morgan, Wildon Carr, G.F. Stout and William McDougall, which took place in a common session of the Aristotelian Society, the British Psychological Society and the Mind Association in 1910 in London (Myers 1910, p. 209). In this debate, Carr represents Bergson's idea that instinct is an immediate intuition which has developed in arthropods, especially in bees and ants, while it has been suppressed by discursive thinking in mammals, especially in humans. Our intellect cannot help us understand the instinct, but instead only the remains of intuitive thinking which we still possess. While a unified conception of life, indeed even a vitalistic metaphysics dominates here, Myers represents the view that instinct and intelligence contain two different views of the same process. Instinct refers to the mechanical-physiological view, while intellect refers to the teleological-psychological of the same process. As a spiritualist metaphysician, Myers assesses both views differently: the psychic as a manner of capturing reality, the physical as an abstract view. The three other participants in the debate represent, with varying degrees of nuance, a unified evolutionary conception which has no inclination to sharply divide either the physical from the psychic, nor intellectual cognition [217] from intuition. Instinct is an inherited disposition to forms of action, intellect, on the other hand, is a modification in forms of action developed through individual experience. Wherever both are in action, they behave towards one another like real components of a whole, not like different ways of observing the same object. One might be inclined to assume that Myers is simply using the word "instinct" in an unconventional manner. Yet his portrayal suffers from an ambiguity since he does not renounce the common equation of instinct with an inherited disposition. It thus seems that mechanical explanation is to be equated with explanation based on morphological disposition, though even the morphological explanation must take into account the effect of the environment. Conversely, genetic psychology must rely on the predispositions as much as on experiences.

Judd comprehends consciousness as a real potency in the development of life (Judd 1910, p. 77). Edward M. Weyer, who relies upon and follows Judd, seeks to form a concept of an elementary psychic unit containing consciousness, sensations and feelings. He intends for this concept to have the same meaning for psychology as does the cell for psychology (Weyer 1910, p. 301). The soul thus becomes a biological reality. Here there are obvious resonances with related concerns among the contemporary vitalists (psychovitalism). As a biological factor, the soul will constantly approach the ancient "life force," and thus the relation to Aristotle, which is especially emphasized by Driesch, becomes clear. The whole field of contemporary physiological-psychological research can indeed be rethought through a form of Aristotelianism. It is thus no coincidence that in this regard links with modern science have more easily been made within neo-Scholastic philosophy than is the case within the properly philosophical disciplines. Mercier is especially informative regarding this relation. The human is not broken down into two separate beings: "*Il et un être un, qui vit, qui sent et qui pense*" (Mercier 1899, p. 3). The division of the work into vegetative, sensing and rational life is also completely Aristotelian. Much like Mercier's book, Hagemann's textbook, a book popular in German catholic circles, also has a detailed treatment of contemporary physiological and experimental research, especially in the new version edited by Dyroff (Hagemann 1911). However, with regard to metaphysics [218], it reserves a careful reticence and is therefore a rather drab work; it is content with a general theory of the soul-substance.

Ancient systems of psychology were mostly oriented through the normative philosophical sciences or through the great cultural fields or science, ethical life and art; the vast majority of living psychologists reject such an orientation. The modern psychologist's analysis does not evaluate, not even where it has values as its object; and what is more, the psychologist as such does not choose what is valuable from among the manifold objects of the life of the soul, rather every psychic appearance is for him an object of analysis in the same way, the babbling of the maniac as much as the revelation of the genius. In contrast, the aforementioned ancient conception has once again found proponents who, not surprisingly, differ essentially from their predecessors. For while the influence of the norm was often unconscious and a given, today it is for the most part a conscious influence and thus is accompanied by the conviction that it is not the case that the normative sciences must be built upon the foundation of psychology, rather that psychology must be built upon the foundation of the normative sciences. Drawing on the work of Bradley, Harold H. Joachim has represented this point of view in England (Joachim 1909, p. 65). He denies the possibility that the soul conceives of itself or that it conceives of its process of conceiving. "In making this 'psychic process' an object of study, we have disengaged it from the mind whose process it was. We have removed it from the atmosphere in which it drew the breath of its life: and 'it'—the real object of our search—has ceased to be....*That* has slipped away: —only to revive, in a mocking repudiation of itself, as the process of our studying" (Joachim 1909, p. 70). One could of course levy the following objection against Joachim's subtle and learned proof, namely, that it only applies to the unified basic characteristic of the subjective functions, and not to the manifold psychic content, and also not to the differences in subjective functions lodged in the memory. Joachim, however, draws the conclusion that one can only grasp the mind in objective functions, as Plato and Hegel did (Joachim 1909, p. 82f.). This English conception of the mind originates from German Idealism, and it is likewise related to a flourishing school of Idealism among us, which one refers to as the Marburg School—a term which it has recently begun to apply to itself. Recently the leading figures of this school have provided some especially concise evidence for their work. Paul Natorp states: [219] "To give logos to the psyche, language to the soul is not the primary task of philosophy, rather it is precisely the final task of philosophy. One cannot access the immediate aspects of psychic lived experience immediately, rather only by going back from its objectivizations, which in turn therefore must be guaranteed a purely objective ground in themselves" (Natorp 1912, p. 198). The schematic plan of such a science can be explained even more clearly based on some preliminary hints that Hermann Cohen gives in "Aesthetic of Pure Feeling," the still unpublished fourth part of his system of psychology. That section purports to be a unification of the separate fields in a unified cultural consciousness. This consciousness can only ever represent a specific stage in the development of spirit (Cohen 1912; cf. esp. Vol. II, pp. 426f.). The close affinity to Hegel's doctrine of objective spirit is notable, however it is without the claim of grasping the creative god himself in objective spirit. It is perhaps best to learn about the feasibility of carrying out such a schematic plan through the actual attempt to carry it out. In any case, it is clear that this science no longer shares any field in common with what we otherwise call psychology, according to even the broadest definition of psychology.

The psychology of Theodor Lipps has always been oriented on logical, ethical and aesthetic interests. However, for a brief period of time it seemed that he recognized the necessity of a more rigorous manner of engagement. In the second edition of his guidebook, he differentiated between the "pure science of consciousness" which deals with the "intersubjective I" and the "psychology in the common and narrower sense of the word" (Lipps 1909, p. 32). Given this distinction, his psychology remained oriented on the pure science of consciousness, which it ought to comport itself towards "like physics to geometry." In the third edition of his guidebook, Lipps abandoned this position, though at the very beginning of the book he still assigned logic, ethics and aesthetics to descriptive and classificatory psychology. "Even the dictates of theoretical, practical and aesthetic reason, that is to say the logical, ethical and aesthetic laws, can only be found in the individual consciousness, even if these laws are by their nature intersubjective, that is to say, they are not merely for this or that individual, rather they are absolutely valid. Their description and classification therefore belongs to descriptive and classificatory psychology." It is curious that this thinker, whose continuously progressing self-criticism is worthy of the highest praise, has never managed to thoroughly think through the difficulties involved in the "discovery" of a structured whole, or even the difficulties involved in the discovery of what is intersubjectively valid. [220] The tendency to take everything to be immediate, a tendency which is reinforced by "phenomenology," proves to be dangerous for the clear engagement with the tasks and points of view.

Whether we are analyzing the attempts at a delineation or determination of the object of psychology, or whether we are observing the efforts to establish the task of psychology by means of different sciences, we continuously encounter a coexistence of different schools of thought which all have different ends in mind. In individual research these schools of thought constantly encounter one another, while they hardly seem to be concerned with one another when investigating the fundamental questions. Given this state of affairs, it is remarkable that Hans Ehrenberg attempts to grant equal status to multiple tasks within psychology in his "Critique of Psychology as Science." Admittedly, Ehrenberg does indeed characterize the meaning of his work as "philosophical-historical" (Ehrenberg 1910, p. 6); the subtitle "Investigations in Accord with the Systematic Principles of Kant's Epistemology" reveals what was at stake for him: he wanted to investigate whether, and with which reformulations, the systematic of the critique of pure reason allows for an epistemological grounding of psychology. In the course of this investigation he keeps close to the path of Kant's work, which he nonetheless starkly reformulates in the individual details. As is well known, Kant denied the possibility of a scientific psychology. If one wanted, in the spirit of his system (which of course did not remain restricted to the critique of pure reason), to do justice to psychology, then one would have to build upon the theory of the organism in the critique of judgment. In Ehrenberg, any relation to a theory of biology is lacking—the lack which we found almost everywhere in contemporary work thus recurs in him: the close affinity between psychology and biology which is revealed everywhere in the work of individual researchers is ignored by the logical grounding. If one builds upon Kant, and thus if one has a theory of biological science at one's disposal, that at first seems doubly strange, though it will nonetheless become comprehensible from Ehrenberg's "philosophical-historical" position. He wants to criticize Kant by claiming that he measures his system against a task that Kant did not even posit for himself. In itself that is not unthinkable, but this would require dismantling a structure as historically involved as the *Critique of Pure Reason* into its individual elements, and then saying which of those elements one takes to be essential (or ranking the elements in their essentiality according to the demands of the new task). [221] But basing one's own system on a closed system that is simultaneously the whole and depriving that system of its characteristic unity by building it into one's own system (not by "building it upon" according to Ehrenberg's mitigating phrase) cannot lead to valid results. It would hardly be doing the book an injustice to regard it as being intended ironically: under the guise of developing it further, Kant's system is in fact undermined. But is Kant, and is the logic of psychology a *corpus vile*, that is to say, is it just good enough for Ehrenburg to cut his intellectual teeth on it, or to use it to playfully demonstrate his capacity for irony? It cannot be our task here to judge Ehrenberg's book as a depiction and critique of Kant; we thus admittedly deprive ourselves of the possibility to offer a picture of the book's structure and manner of reasoning, which by and large follows Kant's systematic approach. Above all, one cannot at all detach from Kant's doctrine of the principles Ehrenberg's attempted proof for the claim that the differentiation between the psychic and the physical is not "methodological," that is to say, that physical and psychic are not "concepts a priori" (Ehrenberg 1910, p. 71). To do so, one would have to elucidate the famous fundamental question of the principles according to the a priori methods of proof, and simultaneously one would have to clearly demonstrate whether, and in which sense, a relative a priori can be accepted. The epistemological presuppositions necessary for such a task cannot be laid out here. However, entirely distinct from this deduction of principles, it must be emphasized that Ehrenberg's tendency to ground a priori as much of the actual content of the science as possible starkly diverges from Kant's limitation of the a priori to the categories and forms of intuition. Thus, regarding the law of specific sense energies, the following is stated: "The principle as such enables psycho-physical experiences as such by positing the isolation of the psycho-physical elements according to the modalities of sensation as a task (ideal, regulative principle) for psycho-physics" (Ehrenberg 1901, p. 130). Now it is certainly correct that psycho-physiological research is only possible if every difference of sensation corresponds to a variation in physiological processes. However, if it must be a localized variation, such as is posited by the "law of specific energies," then could there not just as well be a variation in the chemistry of the nerves, or in the tempo and rhythm in the processes of the nervous system? Certainly one could not discover anything about that a priori. Therefore, the claim that there is only a distinction between adequate and inadequate stimuli for the "higher" senses (hearing, sight, smell, taste) (Ehrenberg 1910, p. 143) is entirely misguided. In contrast, no example serves to demonstrate the realities of inadequate sensation more easily and without objection than the example of cold spots on the skin. The deduction of Weber's law is thoroughly dubious (Ehrenberg 1910, p. 152). It is supposedly a priori impossible that there is a mathematical relation between a constant stimulus and an inconstant change in sensation. [222] "Weber's law is not wrong with respect to its original content, rather it is simply not a law, but instead the transcendental expression of the impossibility of such a law; for it seeks to translate precisely the non-parallel nature of sensation and increment of stimulus in a universal formula. Thus, the mathematical formulation which Fechner gave to Weber's law is unacceptable. As a result, we have understood what is expressed in Weber's law as an a priori legislation of reason for psycho-physics." If no "law" is supposed to be possible for the relation between the increment of stimulus and sensation, then how is a "formula" for it possible? The difference between Weber and Fechner consists in the following: Weber set the increment of stimulus in relation only with the equal noticeability in the increment of sensation, while Fechner sought to measure sensation by means of the stimulus. Furthermore, if all of this were as clear and correct as it is unclear and problematic, then it would be simply a logical consequence that there is no proportionality between equally noticeable differences of sensations and increment of stimulus.; however, this would not at all offer support for the possibility that the precise relation discovered by Weber is valid. If those who seek to revive Hegel's philosophy (among whose numbers Ehrenberg could be counted, at least in 1910) do not build upon Hegel's great guiding thoughts, but instead build upon the most dubious tendencies of his natural philosophy, then they will be reminiscent of those banished to political exile, who, during a long period of suffering, neither learn anything nor forget anything. Under these conditions, the systematic gain for the logic of psychology, which Ehrenberg expected to emerge as a byproduct of his work in the history of philosophy, did not turn out to be as rich as he had hoped. Here it is not a matter of insights, but instead of suggestions, some of which can become quite important. If one considers the contrast between the completed system of a science and the never-ending research, and if one keeps in mind that, fundamentally, no single scientific proposition can be completely articulated without being placed within a complete system of science, and that, in turn, the system of every science can only be constructed from the propositions drawn from individual and specialized research, then one understands the solid good sense of Ehrenberg's claim that the "transcendental site of all empirical sciences, namely, their doctrine of method" is the dialectic of pure reason, especially antithetic dialectic (Ehrenberg 1910, p. 157). In individual cases, this internal antinomy always reveals itself as two contrary principles, each connected to the other, attempt to assert themselves in science, yet they can never do without one another, and thus manage nothing more than to mutually restrict one another time and again. [223] Ehrenberg observes four antinomies in psychology: 1) the antinomy between the subjective and objective universal validity of sensations. With this he means that the totality of every sensation is a lived experience of unrepeatable uniqueness, which nonetheless can be broken down into repeatable elements of sensation. 2) The antinomy between empiricism and nativism. 3) The antinomy between the doctrine of association and the doctrine of apperception. 4) The antinomy between the sensible and the trans-sensible nature of the psychic, i.e. the soul is, on the one hand, the bearer of cognition and all values, but, on the other hand, it is a sum of accidental empirical facts. It is the task of a special psychological science to resolve each of these antinomies: the first through "psychological morphology" (conceptual analysis), the second through the "genetic history of the soul" (genetic nativism), the third—by virtue of the fact that it takes the individual as the center of apperception, the empirical I as the dominant principle of apperception—through the "doctrine of associative apperception of consciousness" (characterology), and the fourth, certainly not (as Münsterberg intends) through a cooperative effort of psychology and the science of values, rather through a science that tries to understand the forms under which the psychic realizes values, that is to say, through phenomenology. There are thoughts here which are still in need of further development; but, unfortunately, nowhere does Ehrenberg think his flashes of insight through to the end, and this is why a completely different systematic can be found at the end of his book, a systematic in which characterology is completely lacking and apperception is assigned to phenomenology (Ehrenberg 1910, p. 230). All these sciences are to some degree "shaky structures," and if it is true that, as Ehrenberg says, "what *mathematics* means in our relation to the external world, *poetry* gives us as a united inner intuition for the internal world" (Ehrenberg 1910, p. 78), it therefore seems that for him the logical foundation of psychology has an especially close relation to the fairy tale in which frogs turn to princes and giants turn to mice. Unfortunately, since we cannot set aside the pedantic habit of earnestness in scientific matters, we must therefore say that the correct or at least suggestive thoughts in Ehrenberg only appear as it were fleetingly, only to be hidden under all sorts of uncontrollable flashes of insight. It is sad that the mind of the author confuses us more than he enlightens us; he should leave that to the type of mindlessness which there is never too little of in this world.

It is customary to divide the tasks of psychology into the rubrics of *description* and *explanation*. Regardless of whether or not one could raise doubts about this division, we want to preserve it for the moment due to its usefulness for orienting us in the contemporary discussions. The description of psychic states must initially always be the description of a single lived experience. [224] Here, in the course of creating the raw material for all further psychological work, the old question emerges of the possibility and the limits of self-perception and self-observation. In recent years, the question has once again firmly entered the foreground of interest through experimental works in the psychology of thinking and desiring, about which more is said in another part of this volume. K. Oesterreich offers an overview of these older and more recent discussions (Oesterreich 1910). Oesterreich defends a concept of immediate perception, even for the psychic functions, while Th. Lipps and H. Maier, for example, both deny any perception of the psychic act during the course of the act (Maier 1908). Messer also considers self-observation to be a retrospective form of regard (Messer 1906). In the case of certain sensations, Groos considers self-perception to be possible (Groos 1910), likewise with individual emotions which do not overwhelm one's entire internal being, and also with habitual judgments. In contrast, he does not think that this is not possible in the case of emotions that "fulfill me," nor in the case of new judgments. Here the retrospective regard is possible; but even this has its limits: the "I-subject" cannot withstand the retrospective regard, and in the resulting objectivized I, Groos finds only sensations and representations. Simultaneously, he clearly also has in mind "that the observing "I-subject" is *more* than what I discover in the attempt to observe it." Nonetheless, I can only describe this excess through images such as "center" and "gathering place." I know that "such a thing was there, but it does not stand firm in me as an object" (Groos 1910, p. 78). In the most recent contemporary work, the problem is also differentiated along these lines for the psychic processes. With regard to G.E. Müller's excellent treatise on the methods appropriate to this analysis, one must always keep in mind that Müller is carrying out research on memory, and thus the work essentially deals with the type of psychic contents which are more distant from the I-center (Müller 1911). In this work, the main question is no longer whether or not one can observe oneself while doing something. Instead, the main question is: does self-perception deliver judgments which can be proven scientifically? Yet by framing the question in this way, the stress is put on the linguistic formulation and communication of the results of self-perception, and thus what one could call their "description." [225] Two fundamentally different processes are possible here, processes which one ought to keep separated, no matter how often they influence one another in the actual praxis of research. The first process takes as its starting point the very "understanding" which we earlier determined to be the decisive comportment of the human sciences in Dilthey and Simmel. In order to transfer his understanding to the reader, the historiographer makes us of all the means which are at his disposal. Given that psychology is a systematic science, such an operation will not be satisfactory in psychology. However, the fact that it can have a justified role in psychology has been proven in fact by James. Groethuysen provides an excellent assessment of James' procedure in a discussion of James' shorter psychology. "We can characterize it as a fundamental tendency of James' psychology to make psychological processes comprehensible . . . It is the expressions for lived experience, visualizations, images, and manners of characterization which one would call 'apt.' These are expressions according which the object that is intended can achieve a certain concise consciousness, even if the psychological process is interpreted without regard for certain real qualities" (Groethuysen 1911, p. 130). In contrast, the second path is the path of exact analysis which clearly describes all the components of a process. Such an analysis requires unambiguous terminology and it cannot indulge in the freedoms of an artistic use of language. However, since the terminology cannot (as is the case with physical objects) be kept in check through the comparison with demonstrable things, it can only be created with the help of classifications; however, classifications of processes such as these, processes namely in which many different aspects can be differentiated, require dominant points of view.

The first of these two differentiated processes makes use, with full consciousness, of Bergson, whose goal of course is metaphysics, not psychology. For Bergson, the "intuition" of philosophers corresponds to a free, artistic form of communication. Fixed concepts are only practical orders of the will, incapable of grasping the eternal flowing reality. Nonetheless, we also need such concepts in this flowing reality, but we must remain conscious of the necessary incompleteness of the expedient nature of such concepts. Some aspects of the outline of phenomenology, the science which is supposed to be the basis of psychology and epistemology alike, as proposed by Husserl are unquestionably reminiscent of Bergson's intuition (Husserl 1981). The psychic is not "experienced as something that appears," it is instead "vital experience," and "appears as itself through itself." (Husserl 1981, p. 180) [226] The psychic is completely lacking the determination of place not only in space, but also in time. Psychic time is (like Bergson's "durée") unmeasurable. The psychic "is a flow of phenomena, unlimited on both ends, traversed by an intentional line, that is, as it were, the index of the all-pervading unity. It is the line of an immanent 'time' without beginning or end, a time that no chronometers measure" (Husserl 1981, p. 180). Phenomenology is supposed to investigate "pure consciousness," but for that it must begin from empirical consciousness and must (since an exact terminology can only emerge from itself) build on the distinctions that are established in language. However, the "phenomenological analyst" does not accept the meanings of words as the scholastics did, and he also does not deduce analytical judgments from them, thereby assuming that he has gained knowledge of facts. He instead peers into the phenomena elicited by the words. The phenomena are not a form of "nature," i.e. not fixed objects with a spatio-temporal place, but they do have an essence that is "an adequately intuited one, an absolutely given one" (Husserl 1981, p. 181). This essence is universal; in this way Husserl overcomes the difficulties that impede an intuition of the universal. Since, namely, all placement in particular places, and thus all individuality belongs to nature, a pure essential intuition free from any reliance on nature is necessarily intuition of a universal. If I am interpreting Husserl correctly here, then there is an equivocation that is concealed by the conflation of the universal with what is not determined by an individual place. If, namely, the phenomenon flows in the unmeasurable stream of occurrence mentioned above, then a part of that stream is certainly not determined by a chronometrical place; but this lack of determination does not necessarily carry with it the advantage that what is now flowing in the stream is not essentially identical with what is flowing in other streams or identical with what is flowing in different parts of the same stream. As far as I can see, Husserl has not yet demonstrated that the validity, let alone the completeness, of his essential intuition can be proven. Even the mediacy of the results poses a difficult problem, particularly since it is supposed to stimulate empathy in an exact conceptual manner, and is not, as is the case with Bergson, supposed to do so artistically. Here one could raise the objection that the exact description demands the dissection of the lived experience into individual moments, but that such a dissection is possible in different ways from different points of view. Thus, the necessary preliminary work of phenomenology would be to clearly develop and justify these points of view. [227] From this it would follow that phenomenology presupposes epistemological investigations, or at least that it is not prior to epistemology as a whole. Georg Anschütz raises a similar objection to Husserl by emphasizing (along with Paul Stern) the impossibility of pure description, i.e. description without any presuppositions (Anschütz 1911).

Wherever a strict classification is attempted, a principle of division must be clear. For Brentano, whose psychology is a functional psychology, this principle of division is the manner of relation of the act towards the object (Brentano 1911, p. 29). It is entirely indubitable that the unity of Brentano's psychology depends quite closely upon this clear knowledge of the principle of division. But, of course, one could still raise the further question of how the individual types of relation are decided, whether through analysis of the content of consciousness, or through logical inferences about that which is posited alongside consciousness if the act is to be logically complete and valid. As soon as one has made these possibilities clear to oneself, one immediately recognizes that Brentano always realizes the second one. Thus, for example, if he says perception always contains a judgment, then that means that the judgment on the existence of what is perceived is logically posited alongside the perception. It does not mean that in the lived experience of the one perceiving, the judgment is contained as an identifiable component. Brentano also follows the same method in the appendices which he added to the (unmodified) new edition of the book. In the last of these appendices he defends himself against the objection of psychologism levied against him by Husserl. He states that he always differentiated between the "logical validity" and "genetic necessity" of a thought (Brentano 1911, p. 166), But of course by saying this he recognizes that psychology can have something to say in epistemology and logic. This is because cognition is a judgment, and judgment in turn belongs to the psychic fields (Brentano 1911, p. 167). The last claim is certainly correct and nobody calls it into question. But not every concept of the psychic is a psychological concept, as little as the concept of a poisonous plant or a pet are botanical or zoological concepts, despite the fact that they are concepts concerning plants and animals. Wundt rightfully says that the interpretation of the (logically delimited) judgment as an original psychic activity in Brentano turns psychology into logicism and logic into psychologism. (Wundt 1911, p. 256) "Psychologism and Logicism," the essay from which this quote is drawn, deals for the most part with logic, but it does contain a curious formulation of the principles of a self-sufficient logic in opposition to the principles of "logicism." (Wundt 1911, p. 581) [228] Doubtless Husserl, against whom the accusation of logicism is directed, would object to the claim that he abides by the principles which Wundt characterizes as logicistic.

"Description" and "explanation" cannot be as easily divided as one often assumes, for all scientific description already demands analysis, and hence classificatory principles of dissection, and hence it not only establishes the parts, but also the relations between those parts. Thus, as soon as description makes a claim to be universal, it includes the assertion of necessary relations (e.g. every color is associated with an extended body). The links between description and explanation would be better noted if one did not equate all explanation with causal explanation. Stumpf, who avoids this one-sided approach and assumes "structural laws" alongside the causal laws, assigns the structural laws to phenomenology. Thus, the fundamental question of psychological explanation in general remains whether there is a psychic causality, and how it relates to physical causality. At the moment, this problem is very closely related to the mind-body problem. Hence, both problems are closely connected in Sigwart, Wundt, Münsterberg, and Rickert. That the fundamental questions of psychology are also epistemological problems is something that continuously emerges in these works. Questions like these are elaborated upon and variously answered by these thinkers: what causality is, whether causality is necessarily accompanied by the preservation of an identical factor in the occurrence, how the conceptual structure of physics relates to reality, and how the distinction between the psychic and the physical relates to reality. This accounts for their differing perspectives on the problem of psycho-physical parallelism. Erich Becher, the most recent entrant into this field, takes a different path (Becher 1911). He begins from the point of individual research (and thus he is also worth mentioning in an overview of individual research), depicts the anatomical and physiological facts and assumptions, and explains in detail the attempts to interpret psychic phenomena physiologically. Becher doubts this parallelism based on the difficulties which arise essentially when one assigns the qualitatively changing composite in the soul (Wundt's "creative synthesis") to the physical processes which perdure alongside one another. The fact that the theories of parallelism are criticized more for the conclusions they lead to than for their presuppositions corresponds to the book's focus on individual research. But that cannot be a reason to critique this detailed book, for every author is the master over the delimitation of his topic; [229] but what it does reveal is that here, where epistemological considerations cannot be dismissed in the least, the lack of an epistemological substructure leaves some discussions (e.g. the discussion of phenomenalism) suspended in the air. One could perhaps regard it as an unspoken consequence of Becher's work that a strictly logical orientation must precede a thorough discussion of the concluding questions. What is said regarding the mind-body problem could likewise be said for the closely related problem of the unconscious.

If one intends to define what is given in consciousness as a cohesive nexus, then supplementary elements are also required. All psychologists would likely concede to that claim. However, there is disagreement about the following two things: firstly, there is disagreement about whether these supplemental elements are physical or psychic. Secondly, there is disagreement about whether they can only be postulated universally, or whether they can be determined more closely. In the second case, whether it is only possible to find distinctions and relations to and among the supplemental elements which have direct analogs in consciousness, or whether it is possible to go so far as to find distinctions and relations which are fundamentally different from all consciousness (and still not physical). Thirdly (and closely related to the second), there is disagreement about whether it is merely a matter of "supplementary elements" of the conscious cohesive nexus, or whether the true psychic nexus is unconscious and nothing more than a segment—incomprehensible in itself—emerges from it into consciousness. At this point we would be obliged to raise questions about the extent of the necessity for supplementarity which must not concern us in this overview dedicated to the principles of psychology. In recent years, the theories of Freud above all have stimulated discussions of the unconscious (cf. Friedmann 1910, p. 34; Kronfeld 1912, p. 130). Hellpach also offers a good overview of the problematic and the common terminological confusions (Hellpach 1908). In order to avoid equivocations, he proposes to use the term "unconscious" not to designate a state of affairs (for something not remembered, for an action that falls short of its aim, for something overlooked), rather only as an interpretive term that serves to mark the admission of the assumption of third realm of the real beyond the conscious-psychic and the physical (Hellpach 1908, p. 257–8). As a psychologist and neurologist, Hellpach is interested in the interpretation and understanding of special states of affairs. He thus finds that parallelism reverts back into materialism if one does not assume a closed psychic cohesive context, but that an enclosed psychic context can only be constructed with the aid of the unconscious. This accounts for the either-or he proposes: either the unconscious (i.e. parallelism with the supplement of the psychic through the unconscious) or interaction. [230] One of the two must be accepted as a fundamental principle of explanation, but that does not necessarily exclude the possibility that one could combine both principles of explanation as Hartmann does.

Hartmann gave his theories their final form in his "System of Philosophy in Outline." The third volume of his work, "Outline of Psychology," will serve as an effective basis for future discussions of his conception of the unconscious in psychology (Hartmann 1908). The book is a single, well-structured line of argument. Hartmann conceives of consciousness as a unity of the content and form of consciousness. The form of consciousness inheres resolutely in the contents (Hartmann 1908, p. 7), is always the same as itself, but it does not perdure in a stable identity, and is instead marked by gaps (Hartmann 1908, p. 14). Consciousness is completely passive, and all activity is foreign to it (Hartmann 1908, p. 11–12). Now, in the explanation of the psychic there is a methodological demand that one begin from what is known, hence that one begin with consciousness and then to try to see how far one comes with it. The "pure standpoint of consciousness" demands "that the psychic is identified with consciousness, from which it immediately follows that everything that is not conscious either does not exist at all, or—if it is outside consciousness—it is non-psychic" (Hartmann 1908, p. 54). At this point the attempt is made to prove that from this standpoint neither sensation, emotion, desire, reproduction association, nor even the I, nor the relation between soul and body can be rendered comprehensible. With regard to the mind-body problem, the proof is admittedly carried out by shifting the concept of consciousness; for the pure standpoint of consciousness demands that nothing external to consciousness exists, and that even the physical world is only the content of consciousness. But that only makes sense if one posits the equation consciousness = thinkability, not if one takes consciousness to be a quality of lived experience. Hence, the entire division of physical and psychic occurs within the most general concept of consciousness; and the form of consciousness which characterizes the psychic must be distinguished from the most general concept of consciousness, though Hartmann equates the two (Hartmann 1908, p. 64f.). Otherwise, Hartmann relies on the gaps which are revealed in the attempt to construct the psychic nexus exclusively from conscious elements. One could make an initial attempt to fill in these gaps by assuming that there is a "subconscious" peculiar not only to the lower regions of the brain, but also the individual cells, and even the molecules and atoms. [231] Through a weakening of the superconsciousness (e.g. in dreams) some elements of the subconscious become open to lived experience. This "relative unconscious" is capable of explaining dreams and related phenomena, and even sensations and feeling running below the surface, but it leaves the remaining gaps unfilled. Since it is passive like the superconsciousness, it cannot explain any psychic activity. One can attempt to explain what is left unexplained either through corporeal occurrences or (following Hartmann's terminology) in the "physiological unconscious." Of course, such an explanation only makes sense, according to Hartmann, if one assumes the physical to be independent in reality, not if one posits it as dependent on consciousness. Otherwise, one would be explaining what is primary through something dependent on it. Here we can see the same ambiguity in the concept of consciousness noted above. If I call the psychic ψ and the physical φ, then ψ can definitely not be dependent upon φ if φ is a product of ψ. But whether or not φ and ψ are dependent upon an encompassing "consciousness" β is a matter of indifference with regards to the mutual relation between φ and ψ. This, however, is what Kant's idealism assumes in order to avoid any conflict with the type of physiological explanation of the psychic asserted by Hartmann. The "physiological unconscious" is in fact capable of filling the gaps in the conscious nexus—but only in a way that thereby completely shuts out the psychic. For all activity must then be shifted to the physical if the psychic is passive. "Psychic phenomena become passive subsidiary functions of the material process without therefore being components of the material process or without somehow being able to influence it retroactively" (Hartmann 1908, p. 135). One can only escape this consequence by assuming psychic activity. However, this activity can only be unconscious and reveals itself to be the true essence of even the body, such that only now is the expression "physiological unconscious" justified. Hartmann thus proves the necessity of the assumption of an unconscious psychic activity through a type of process of elimination: he shows that all other assumptions are unsatisfactory. He then engages with the objection that an unconscious psychic activity is unthinkable for us. "'Activity' is a clear concept, just as 'psychic' is clear. The connection of the two does not imply a contradiction, and is thus thinkable" (Hartmann 1908, p. 142). Most of those who oppose this view and consider the concept to be contradictory do so only "because they do not distinguish between psychic phenomena and psychic activity and because they errantly transpose the contradiction contained in 'unconscious psychic phenomena' onto 'unconscious psychic activity'" (Hartmann 1908, p. 143). [232] One can in fact avoid the contradiction implied by the conception of the unconscious psychic by defining 'psychic' as everything which, firstly, must be assumed in order to explain conscious processes and, secondly, everything which is not physical. The concept of the psychic formed in this manner is hypothetical, and is only defined through a relation to something known, i.e. to something conscious, and is thus free of contradiction. The only problem is that it has no positive content emerging from out of itself, but only receives this content from something conscious or from something otherwise known. For Hartmann, "activity" counts as something that is otherwise known—and thus we come to the point which, if refuted, causes Hartmann's proof to become invalid: the passivity of consciousness. Much like the content psychologists, Hartmann interprets consciousness as a sum of merely describable states. Nonetheless, none other than Münsterberg, the unwavering representative of content psychology, proves the passivity of consciousness by claiming that it is only possible through an "objectivation" of the psychic, while the actually lived life is precisely activity and self-positing. In actuality, pure content psychology can only be supported in a scientific-theoretical manner, if it can be supported at all; hence, even Brentano, Stumpf, and almost all of the others who define the object of psychology ontologically are functional psychologists. Yet the "conscious" cannot be equated with the "scientifically determinable," but it must instead be equated with what can be a matter of lived experience. Regarded purely for its own sake, what can be a matter of lived experience corresponds less to a sum of passive states and more closely either to the Bergsonian creative activity[6] or to the nexus of self-positing as described by Munsterberg.

In his understanding of both the unconscious and psychic reality, Theodor Lipps has affinities to both Herbart and Hartmann, however, he distinguishes himself from Hartmann through the claim that all assumptions about the unconscious can only derive their content from consciousness. This is closely related to the division between explanatory and descriptive psychology. An individual, real, and psychic life is posited as the foundation of the life of consciousness, the elements of which are processes (Lipps 1909, p. 76). These processes can cross the "threshold of consciousness" to a greater or lesser degree, but they can also remain below it. In the second case, we speak of unconscious sensations or ideas. An "unconscious" sensation or "unconscious" idea is not an unconscious *lived experience* of the sensation or the idea, thus it is also not the unconscious existence of a *content of consciousness*. [233] That would be a contradiction in itself. Rather, only the process is unconscious. This process, however, is in and of itself not unconscious with regard to "unconscious sensations and ideas," rather it is unconscious at all times. It is precisely the psychically "real" (Lipps 1909, p. 83f.) element which is posited as the foundation of a content of consciousness. One must therefore strictly separate the unconscious from the unnoticed, for the unnoticed indeed belongs to the conscious. We can only speak of the unconscious where the psychic phenomena justify it. Everything unconscious is an "auxiliary concept," it is "the process of making exemplary an occurrence that is completely unknown in itself which serves to fill gaps in the causal nexus of psychic occurrences, a nexus which we must take as the basis for the immediately experienced nexus of the lived experiences of consciousness of the individual" (Lipps 1909, p. 85). Lived experiences are "after all what is actually most important for us." The unconscious psychic processes ought to contribute to nothing more than the "simplest possible explanation" of the lived experiences (Lipps 1909, p. 86). The detractors of the unconscious must above all engage with this careful interpretation of the unconscious. Herbertz does just this (Herbertz 1908).[7] He does indeed recognize an unconscious, but he recognizes it—in agreement with Bruno Erdmann—solely as a postulated x, as a supplementary element that is undifferentiated and without characteristics, and as something that is introduced only to rescue the hermetic nature of the psychic that is demanded by parallelism. Admittedly it is not easy to see

---

[6] It is telling that for Bergson consciousness is effective action and activity, while the unconscious remains passive—precisely the opposite of Hartmann.
[7] cf. the detailed critical note by Oesterreich (1909). For a defense of Hartmann's position, see Drews (1909).

what use a supplementary element is for the explanation if one does not attribute any sort of traits to it. Herbertz is overly insistent on using his own terminology as a norm for judging the theories of others. This terminology, however, is not unambiguous. He defines consciousness, for example, as the "sum total of all psychic realities, which are either shown to be real to us in one's own immediate experience, or disclosed to us in its reality through indubitable scientific proofs" (Herbertz 1908, p. 102). Nonetheless, it once again seems that consciousness is taken to be an unchanging trait of every single psychic reality. Moreover, if consciousness is the sum total of all psychic realities, then can the unconscious not belong to the "psychic"? Does it thus form a third realm alongside the psychic and the physical? 'Psychic' and 'psychic,' after all, seem to mean the same thing for Herbertz.

The opposing schools of thought in psychology can be observed most clearly [234] with regard to the treatment of the individual I. But it is precisely with regard to the *individual I* that one all too often encounters the insufficient organization of the problem and opposing voices talking past one another. In what sense an "I" is the final precondition for all cognition, in what sense it is an object of psychology, and whether it should be interpreted as a process—these are all problems that point to epistemological investigations. But one cannot overlook the fact that the empirical state of affairs must also be precisely determined, and examined with regard to its compatibility with different theories. Oesterreich chose this manner of approach (Oesterreich 1910). Oesterreich sees the I in the functions and feelings, and he disputes all theories which discover structural elements of the I in contents (Oesterreich 1910, p. 209). That I is what has immediate consciousness of its own accord, and only the I can have immediate consciousness of its own accord. It is merely a lax use of language if I interpret the I as something else, or equate it with a complex of states, bodily sensations, or the organism. The dispositions prove that more can be attributed to the I than what is discovered in it; Oesterreich excludes these observable traits of the I from his book and therefore speaks of a "phenomenology of the I" (Oesterreich 1910, p. 260). He deals with the processes of the "splitting of consciousness" in an especially detailed manner and in the process comes to the result that: "In none of the cases that we encountered did the unity of the I suffer in the least. Either it is a matter of alternating states of the one, enduring I that remains identical to itself through all changes in affect, or it is the case that necessary abnormal processes force themselves upon the I, which still in part finds itself in its normal form. The theory of the subject even remains valid in these states" (Oesterreich 1910, p. 500). It is more the case that Oesterreich works upon the foundation of certain theories than that he grounds theories. But important addenda to these issues are surely to be expected from the second volume of his work.

Gustav Kafka, in contrast, calls for an epistemological treatment of the I-problem, and he attempts, by means of the most immanent critique possible, to lay the groundwork for that critique in his careful work "Attempt at a Critical Presentation of the Contemporary Opinions on the I-Problem" (Kafka 1910). He regards the subject as nothing more than "the necessary common point of reference of all content which is concentrated in a consciousness" (Kafka 1910, p. 223). Moreover, since he declares the concept of a relation to oneself as contradictory, he also cannot concede any self-conception of the I. At this stage, Kafka has only provided a critical foundation for these propositions, and before we can pass judgment on them, we still must await their positive, systematic grounding, as well as the expansion of his ideas into a theory based upon that systematic grounding. It would be useless to try to offer a critique of his critique since up until now he has only presented an isolated analysis, not a fundamental, systematic treatment. As a supplement to the treatment of the concept of the trans-individual I in Kafka, a treatment that is hardly justified, it is worth calling attention to Christiansen's critique of Kantian epistemology; in Christiansen's critique, the concept of the epistemological subject is developed in an astute fashion (Christiansen 1911).

At the moment, the treatment of the principles of psychology is richer in questions than it is in answers. There is still a need for an epistemological, and especially scientifically theoretical examination that offers greater clarity and more certain results, yet one that is simultaneously always oriented toward the actual work of modern psychologists, while also taking into account their manifold tasks and relations.

References

Alexander, Samuel (1911): "Foundation and Sketch-Plan of a Conational Psychology." In: *British Journal of Psychology* 4, pp. 239–267.
Anschütz, Georg (1911): "Über die Methoden der Psychologie." In: *Archiv für die allgemeine Psychologie* 20, pp. 443f.
Becher, Erich (1911): *Gehirn und Seele*. Heidelberg: Winter.
Brentano, Franz (1911): *Klassifikation der psychischen Phänomene*. Leipzig: Duncker and Humblot.
Christiansen, Broder (1911): *Kritik der Kantischen Erkenntnislehre*. Hanau: Clauss and Feddersen.
Cohen, Hermann (1912): *Ästhetik des reinen Gefühls*. Berlin: Cassirer.
Cohn, Jonas (1900): "Münsterbergs Versuch einer erkenntnistheoretischen Begründung der Psychologie." In: *Vierteljahrsschrift für wissenschaftliche Philosophie* 24, pp. 1–22.
Cohn, Jonas (1902): "Der psychische Zusammenhang bei Münsterberg." In: *Vierteljahrsschrift für wissenschaftliche Philosophie* 26, pp. 1–20.

Dessoir, Max (1911): *Abriß einer Geschichte der Psychologie*. Heidelberg: Winter.
Dilthey, Wilhelm (1910): *Der Aufbau der geschichtlichen Welt in der Geisteswissenschaften*. Berlin: Abhandlung der Preußischen Akademie der Wissenschaften.
Dilthey, Wilhelm (2002): *The Formation of the Historical World in the Human Sciences*. Rudolf A. Makkreel and Frithjof Rodi (Trans.). Princeton: Princeton University Press.
Drews, Arthur (1909): "Das Unbewußte in der modernen Psychologie." In: *Zeitschrift für Philosophie* 134, p. 1 f.
Ehrenberg, Hans (1910): *Kritik der Psychologie als Wissenschaft*. Tübingen: Mohr.
Franken, August (1910): *Möglichkeiten und Grundlagen einer allgemeinen Psychologie, im besonderen der Tierpsychologie*. Langensalza: Mann.
Friedmann, Hugo (1910): "Bewußtsein und bewußtseinverwandte Erscheinungen." In: *Zeitschrift für Philosophie* 139, pp. 34.
Groethuysen, Bernhard (1911): "Rezension von W. James' The Principles of Psychology." In: *Zeitschrift für Psychologie und Physiologie der Sinnesorgane* 59, pp. 130–132.
Groos, Karl (1910): "Bemerkungen zum Problem der Selbstbeobachtung." In: *Zeitschrift für Philosophie* 137, pp. 76 f.
Hall, G. Stanley (1904): *Adolescence: Its Psychology and Its Relation to Physiology, Anthropology, Sociology, Sex, Crime, Religion and Education* vol. 2. New York: D. Appleton and Co.
von Hartmann, Karl Robert Eduard (1908): *Grundriß der Psychologie*. Bad Sachsa: Haacke.
Hellpach, Willy (1908): "Unbewusstes oder Wechselwirkung." In: *Zeitschrift für Psychologie und Physiologie der Sinnesorgane* 48, pp. 321–384.
Herbertz, Richard (1908): *Bewußtsein und Unbewußtes. Untersuchung über eine Grenzfrage der Psychologie mit historischer Einleitung*. Köln: Du Mont-Schauberg.
Husserl, Edmund (1981): "Philosophy as a Rigorous Science." Quentin Lauer (Trans.). In: *Husserl: Shorter Works*. Notre Dame: University of Notre Dame Press, pp. 161–197
Joachim, Harold H. (1909): "Psychical Process." In: *Mind* 18, pp. 65–83.
Judd, Charles Hubbard (1910): "Evolution and Consciousness." In: *Psychological Review* 17, pp. 77–97.
Kafka, Gustav (1910): "Versuch einer kritischen Darstellung der neueren Anschauungen über das Ich-Problem." In: *Archiv für die gesamte Psychologie* 29, pp. 1–15.
Klemm, Otto (1911): *Geschichte der Psychologie*. Leipzig: Teubner.
Kronfeld, Arthur (1912): "Über die psychologische Theorien Freuds und verwandte Anschauungen." In: *Archiv für die allgemeine Physiologie* 22, pp. 130–248.
Léon, M. Xavier (Ed.) (1909): "Intuition." In: *Bulletin de la Société française de Philosophie*, pp. 273–274.
Lipps, Theodor (1909): *Leitfaden der Psychologie*. Leipzig: Engelmann.
Lotze, Hermann (1880): *Mikrokosmos* vol. 3. Leipzig: Hirzel.
Maier, Heinrich (1908): *Psychologie des emotionalen Denkens*. Tübingen: Barth.
Meinong, Alexius (1903): "Bemerkungen über den Farbenkörper und das Mischungsgesetz," *Zeitschrift für Psychologie und Psychologie der Sinnesorgane* 33.
Meinong, Alexius (1904): *Untersuchungen zur Gegenstandstheorie und Psychologie*. Leipzig: Barth.
Mercier, Désiré (1899): *Psychologie*. Louvain: Institut supérieur de philosophie.
Messer, August (1906): "Experimentell-psychologische Untersuchung über das Denken." In: *Archiv für die gesamte Psychologie* 8, pp. 1–224.

Messer, August (1912): "Husserls Phänomenologie in ihrem Verhältnis zur Psychologie." In: *Archiv für die gesamte Psychologie* 22, pp. 117–129

Messer, August (1914): "Husserls Phänomenologie in ihrem Verhältnis zur Psychologie." In: *Archiv für die gesamte Psychologie* 32, pp. 52–67.

Müller, G.E. (1911): Zur Analyse der Gedächtnistätigkeit und des Vorstellungsverlaufes." In: *Zeitschrift für Psychologie und Physiologie der Sinnesorgane* Ergänzungsband 5.

Münsterberg, Hugo (1900): Grundzüge der Psychologie vol. 1. Leipzig: Barth.

Myers, Charles S. (1910): "Instinct and Intelligence." In: *British Journal of Psychology* 3/3, pp. 209–218.

Natorp, Paul (1912): "Kant und die Marburger Schule." In: *Kant-Studien* 17, pp. 193–221.

Oesterreich, Traugott Konstantin (1910): *Die Phänomenologie des Ich in ihren Grundproblemen*. Leipzig: Barth.

Rehmke, Johannes (1905): *Lehrbuch der allgemeinen Psychologie*. Leipzig, Frankfurt am Main: Mayer.

Rehmke, Johannes (1910): *Philosophie als Grundwissenschaft*. Leipzig, Frankfurt am Main: Mayer.

Rickert, Heinrich (1986): *The Limits of Concept Formation in Natural Science: A Logical Introduction to the Historical Sciences*. Trans. and ed. Guy Oakes. Cambridge: Cambridge University Press.

Stern, William (1911): *Die differentielle Psychologie in ihren methodischen Grundlagen*. Leipzig: Barth.

Stratton, George M. (1909): "Toward the Correction of Some Rival Methods in Psychology." In: *Psychology Review* 16, pp. 67–84.

Stumpf, Carl (1907a): *Erscheinungen und psychische Funktionen*. Berlin: Verlag der Königlichen Akademie der Wissenschaften.

Stumpf, Carl (1907b): *Zur Einteilung der Wissenschaften*. Berlin: Verlag der Königlichen Akademie der Wissenschaften.

Weyer, Edward M. (1910): "Unit-Concept of Consciousness." In: *Psychological Review* 17, pp. 301–318.

Wundt, Wilhelm (1896): "Über die Definition der Psychologie." In: *Philosophische Studien* 12, pp. 1–66.

Wundt, Wilhelm (1903): *Gründzuge der physiologischen Psychologie* vol. 3. Leipzig: Engelmann.

Wundt, Wilhelm (1911): *Kleine Schriften* vol. 2. Leipzig: Engelmann.

Rodney Parker
Theodor Ziehen

The name of Georg Theodor Ziehen (1862–1950) is perhaps most well-known today among scholars of early analytic philosophy, particularly those interested in the work of Rudolf Carnap. Ziehen's book *Erkenntnistheorie auf psychophysiologischer und physikalischer Grundlage* (Ziehen 1913), from which the selection translated here is derived, was an influence on Carnap's *Aufbau* (Carnap 1928).[1] He is also known for being one of the psychiatrists who treated Friedrich Nietzsche at Otto Binswanger's clinic in Jena in 1889.

Ziehen studied medicine in Würzburg and Berlin, receiving a doctorate in psychiatry in 1885. He then moved to Jena, where he completed his habilitation, *Sphygmographische Untersuchungen an Geisteskranken* (Ziehen 1887). Over the course of his career he was Professor of Psychiatry in Utrecht (1900–1903), Halle (1903–1904), and Berlin (1904–1912), and Professor of Philosophy in Halle (1917–1930). His primary philosophical interest was the relationship between psychology, logic, and epistemology. Ziehen was a psychologicist and positivist, and was associated with the "immanence philosophy" of Wilhelm Schuppe. His major works were *Psychophysiologische Erkenntnistheorie* (Ziehen 1889) and his two volume *Die Grundlagen der Psychologie* (Ziehen 1915a, 1915b).

In a long note at §79 of *Ideas I* (*Ideen* 157/151–2), Husserl writes that, while his book was in press, he had read Ziehen's *Erkenntnistheorie auf psychophysiologischer und physikalischer Grundlage*, and comments on one of the critical remarks Ziehen makes against the *Logical Investigations*, namely, its reliance on "intuition" as a means of grasping "absolute Begriffe," "Existenzformen," "überempirische Einheiten" or "ideale Spezies," i.e., ideal essences. He quotes Ziehen, who writes:

> that suspicious 'intuition' or 'inner evidence'...has two main characteristics: first, it changes from philosopher to philosopher, and respectively from philosophical school to philosophical school; and second, it appears especially readily whenever the author has just expressed a rather dubious point of his teaching. We are supposed, then, to be preserved from doubt through a bluff. To differentiate these 'empirical' concepts still somewhat more sharply from the common mob of ordinary concepts, the *'logicist'* often even ascribes to them a particular universality, absolute exactness, and so forth. I hold all this [to be] only human presumption[.] (Ziehen 1913, pp. 413; incl. in this volume p. 117–178)

---

[1] See Ziche 2016, pp. 88–90; Mormann 2016.

While Husserl admits that at times the concept of intuition might be used as a mere hand-wave to gloss over points that lack sufficient evidence, he does not agree that it should be taken universally a mere "bluff," at least as no more so than appeals to experience. The concept of "categorial intuition" or the "intuition of essences" [*Wesensanschauung*], must, therefore, be properly defined. Ziehen remains critical of Husserl's position even after the publication of *Ideas I*, writing that the intuition of essences in phenomenology is nothing more than a new version of Schelling's "intellectual intuition" [*intellektuelle Anschauung*] (Ziehen 1920, 306–7).[2]

References

Carnap, Rudolf (1928): *Der logische Aufbau der Welt*. Berlin: Weltkreis.
Cassirer, Ernst (1913): "Erkenntnistheorie nebst den Grenzfragen der Logik." In: *Jahrbücher der Philosophie* 1, pp. 1–59.
Husserl, Edmund (2014): *Ideas for a Pure Phenomenology and Phenomenological Philosophy: First Book: General Introduction to Pure Phenomenology*. Daniel Dahlstrom (Trans.). Indianapolis/Cambridge: Hackett.
Mormann, Thomas (2016): "Carnap's Aufbau in the Weimar Context." In: *Influences on the Aufbau*. Christian Damböck (ed.). Dordrecht: Springer, pp. 115–36.
Ziche, Paul (2016): "Theories of Order in Carnap's Aufbau." In: *Influences on the Aufbau*. Christian Damböck (ed.). Dordrecht: Springer, pp. 77–97.
Ziehen, Theodor (1887): *Sphygmographische Untersuchungen an Geisteskranken*. Jena: Fischer.
Ziehen, Theodor (1889): *Psychophysiologische Erkenntnistheorie*. Jena: Fischer.
Ziehen, Theodor (1913): *Erkenntnistheorie auf psychophysiologischer und physikalischer Grundlage*. Jena: Fischer.
Ziehen, Theodor (1915a): *Die Grundlagen der Psychologie. I. Buch: Erkenntnistheoretische Grundlegung der Psychologie*. Leipzig: Teubner.
Ziehen, Theodor (1915b): *Die Grundlagen der Psychologie II. Buch: Prinzipielle Grundlegung der Psychologie*. Leipzig: Teubner.
Ziehen, Theodor (1920): Lehrbuch der Logik auf positivistischer Grundlage mit Berücksichtigung der Geschichte der Logik. Bonn: Marcus & Weber.

---

[2] A more detailed account of Ziehen's interpretation of Husserl in this later work can be found at Ziehen 1920, 172–88. See also Ziehen's remarks on Husserl in *Die Grundlagen der Psychologie*, especially Ziehen 1915a, 69–97, 1915b, 2. A discussion of Ziehen 1913 can be found in Cassirer 1913.

Translated by Erin Stackle
Theodor Ziehen. Selections from *Epistemology on the Basis of Psychophysiological and Physical Grounds*

Erkenntnistheorie auf psychophysiologischer und physikalischer Grundlage
Jena: Fischer (1913)

Book One: *The Epistemological Fundamental State of Affairs. Epistemology of Sensations.*

Chapter One: *The Epistemological Fundamental State of Affairs. The Raw Data and their First Classification.*

Section One: The Raw Data [*die Gignomene*]

[1] Epistemology must start from a clear declaration of what lies at the basis of its development and a description thereof. It stands to reason that epistemology has neither a cause, nor a right, to exclude any facts whatsoever from its foundation. Everything we experience, or, more specifically, everything experienced by those who think this line of thought through, must be situated in the foundation of epistemology. To define this 'everything' we experience by a common characteristic is not possible, because no 'other' exists. We are left only with the possibility of designating this 'everything' with some name. Countless philosophical systems, in fact, press themselves forward at once with suspicious eagerness, offering us names for the given facts of experience. Unfortunately, all of these names prejudice any further investigations.

If we speak with Kant of the 'appearances' [*Erscheinungen*], we basically grant already that there is something that appears and is itself different from these appearances. If we speak of 'sensations' [*Empfindungen*] and 'representations' [*Vorstellungen*], we then seem duty bound to the doctrine of a sensing and representing subject. Likewise, the designations, 'the real' [*das Reale*], 'that which has being' [*Seiende*], the 'given' [*Gegebene*], the 'already available' [*Vorge-*

fundende], the 'experiences' [*Erlebnisse*], the 'phenomena' [*Phänomene*], the 'actual' [*Wirkliche*], etc., more or less directly involve some prejudicing assumptions.

[2] We could help ourselves with this, by selecting one of these designations, despite its accompanying meanings, and explicitly explaining that we should disregard all such accompanying meanings. This is the course I have pursued, e.g., in my psychophysiological epistemology, in which I selected the designation, 'sensations' (Ziehen 1907). With this approach, however, is bound the disadvantage that the relevant word, here 'sensation', will either elude its ordinary use or receive a double meaning. Concerning this situation, one could simply choose no word at all, but instead select a simple letter, e.g., 'g'. This would, however, introduce an uncomfortable awkwardness in the construction of sentences.

It thus appears expedient and justified to introduce an entirely new designation. I select for this designation '*Gignomena*' or '*Gignomene*',[1] which, according to its word meaning—'*that which is becoming*' [*Werdendes*][2] or, as I like to say, '*moments in the process of becoming*' [*Werdnisse*][3]—can scarcely introduce prejudice (Ziehen 1907, p. 105; also 1901, p. 305; 1903, p. 91; 1906 p. 241).

In principle, the naïve person, whenever he speaks of 'things', means nothing other than this *Gignomene*, as will later be explained. This discussion cannot, thus, be of a '*natural belief*' in things (Jacobi 1787) that is supposed to somehow be the origin of the *Gignomene*.[4] Neither, then, all the more, can the discussion be of some self-evident authority for such a natural belief.

---

1 '*Gignomena*' is the Greek neuter plural present middle participle from the Greek verb, 'γίγνομαι', which verb means, standardly, 'I become'. The neuter plural participle thus means roughly, 'things in the process of becoming'. To Germanize the term, Ziehen has switched the neuter plural ending, '-a' for the German neuter plural ending, '-e', thus, '**Gignomene**', which is the version of the term he uses throughout the work. When Ziehen wants a singular version, he uses '*Gignomen*' (see pp.26 and 444). I am grateful to Matt Dillon, of the LMU Classics department, for his generous help with this analysis. –Tr.

2 '*Werdendes*' is the neuter singular participle of the German verb, '*werden*', and means 'becoming' in the sense that something is in the process of becoming, or of turning into being, of being formed, shaped, etc. –Tr.

3 '*Werdnisse*' is Ziehen's neologism, based on the same verb (see previous note), and would seem to indicate something like 'the events of becoming' or, as I have chosen to translate it, 'moments in the process of becoming'. I am grateful to Mike Herzog, of the Gonzaga English department, for the insight of a native German speaker on this. –Tr.

4 While I have left Ziehen's term untranslated in this section to allow him to explicitly clarify what it means, all future instances of '*Gignomene*' will be translated 'raw data'. This is for the purpose of smoother reading. When the term is combined with another, as, for example, in *Emp-*

Section Two: The Classification Principle. Categorial Representation of Identity/Non-Identity

[3] Having, first of all, accepted the general state of affairs to be thus the raw data, epistemology must then *classify* or *organize* this state of affairs. To prevent this classification from falling into the just-now censured error, we must first of all, using clear words, articulate and justify our principle of classification. We must also, in doing so, avoid introducing any hypotheses, e.g., the 'I'-hypothesis, etc. This classification is supposed to be only an *organized description*.

There is only one single principle of classification, that of *difference* and *similarity*.[5] The representation of difference and identity, or, as it were, similarity, is the single general and original relational representation. [4] This is irrespective of the spatial and temporal relational representations, which cannot be used *with respect to classification*, but are, rather, only *descriptive*, and can only be used, to some extent, in geographical and historical senses.

Insofar as this principle has been applied to the general state of affairs of epistemology, I have designated it '***categorial representation.***' This designation should, on the one hand, remind us of the categories of Kant; on the other hand, it should point toward the classificatory meaning of this relational representation. The application of the categorial representation in our thought should be designated briefly '***categorial function.***'

Its epistemological meaning, as well as its influence on the content and value of the representations we deduce, will be discussed in detail later. I will also come back only later to the relationship of this categorial representation to the 'categories', or 'pure concepts of the understanding', of Kant, and to the categories of Aristotle, and to others. It will be shown through this discussion that the differences in meaning are great enough to justify an alteration of the name.

The categorial representation of difference and similarity, or, as it were, identity, can obviously be considered a single representation insofar as complete difference and complete identity are considered only as limit cases of 'difference' and 'similarity'. In the following, all these cases shall be collected in the designation '*identity/non-identity.*'

---

findungsgignomene, I translate it in conjunction with the other term, e.g., 'the raw data of sensation'. –Tr.

5 With this first positive step, epistemology immediately establishes for itself, naturally, manifold doubts and divergences; these will be carefully considered only when we get to Section Four.

There are four main cases of the application of the general categorial representation to the individual instances of raw data:

In the first case, two or more identical raw data are given at the same time, or quite without a particular temporal relation. With this is presented the simple categorial representation of *identity*.

In the second case, two or more non-identical raw data are given at the same time, or quite without a particular temporal relation. With this is presented the simple categorial representation of *difference*.

In the third case, two or more identical sensations follow each other. With this is presented the simple categorial representation of *remaining identical*.

In the fourth case, two or more non-identical sensations follow each other. With this is presented the simple categorial representation of *change*.

To this must explicitly be added that the representation of 'remaining identical' or that of 'change' in no way somehow implies the representation of an 'object' [*Gegenstandes*] (a 'substance' in the sense of scholastic philosophy) remaining the same or changing. Such a representation of an object is not a representation of a given fact, but rather a hypothesis in serious need of examination (compare Sections 63 and 75).[6]

With those four simple categorial representations, the activity of the identity/non-identity representation is still not exhausted.

There can also, fifthly, be a case in which there are two or more series of raw data, either remaining-identical or changing at the same time, or, quite without a particular temporal relation, remaining identical or changing in the same ways. With this is presented the simple categorial representation of *synchronous identity*.

It will be shown later that this last representation forms the essential content of the so-called *causal representation* [*Kausalvorstellung*] and the foundation of all knowledge of *laws* [*Gesetzen*]. Here, in the beginning of [5] our epistemological investigation, however, it is only a question of the *classification* of the raw data, and for that, the categorial representations of identity and non-identity suffice. With the help of these categorial representations, we arrange the raw data according to their identity, or, as the case may be, their similarity.

---

6 These sections are not included in this translation. –Tr.

Section Three: Sensations and Representations. Fundamental State of Affairs.

The auxiliary science which has undertaken this organization of the *Gignomene* according to their identity, or, as the case may be, their similarity, is psychology.[7] The psychological investigation now shows that the raw data fall into two main classes, namely, into *sensations* and into *representations*.[8] It is further shown that the latter always originate from the former. Each representation originates from *one* or more, or, as the case may be, from many, *foundational sensations* [*Grundempfindungen*]. To this extent, the representations can also be designated as *memory forms* [*Erinnerungsbilder*]. The difference between sensations and representations is indefinable, and can, rather, only be experienced. As the word for this difference, the designation '*sensible animation*' [*sinnliche Lebhaftigkeit*] shall be used.

Since the representations are derived from the sensations, the latter are considered to be the actual material of epistemology. The general state of affairs, which, as epistemology, is under discussion, falls under a primary and under a secondary head. The primary, the *raw data of sensation*, forms the *epistemologically fundamental state of affairs*.[9] All representations, thus even the epistemological representations themselves, belong to the derivative, secondary raw data.

With these determinations, the task of epistemology is also somewhat more closely designated: the treatment of the epistemologically fundamental state of affairs, i.e., the derivation of the representations from this epistemologically fundamental state of affairs, and, of course, treatment of the general representations in contrast to the special representations derived from the other sciences.

---

7 Up until epistemology was "*vacua ab omni scientia*" (Geulinx, Metaphys. vera introd. II, 1), it rested only on the most general experience; it was 'pure' experiential science in the sense of Benecke. The more it progressed, the more it relied, here and there, upon the special experiences of psychology and natural science. Kant believed, as is well known, to be able to do without both. How much the renunciation of psychology has taken revenge in his system, has been everywhere demonstrated. He permitted psychology, "as an episode only", out of the "economical motives," [...] "some sort of a place" in metaphysics, not for the sake of the latter, but rather out of pity for psychology, which is still not rich enough to alone constitute a discipline, and yet, is too important to be discharged to a less related science (Kant 1998, B 664.)

8 Also here and in the following, many doubts and divergences are raised, whose discussion similarly has been pushed off to Section Four and what follows. –The word 'representation' I use everywhere in the sense of my physiological psychology (Ziehen 1911, p. 146).

9 One compares with this, e.g., the fundamental state of affairs, which Spinoza laid down in the psychic realm (Eth., P. 2, Prop.11): ("*Primum, quod actuale mentis humanae esse constituit, nihil aliud est quam idea rei alicuisu singularis actu existentis.*") Obviously, countless hypotheses are slipped in with this, quite irrespective of the implicit postulate that there is still an essence outside of the human mind (*mens humana*).

Certainly, these determinations themselves must first be secured. Already here, many objections raise themselves; already here, many philosophical systems branch off. [6] In the following paragraphs, these objections and divergences shall be individually discussed. [...]

Chapter Two: *The Koinaden. The Changes of Sensation and Their Classification. ξ-and v-Complexes. ρ- and v- Components*

Section Seven: Characteristics of the Raw Data of Sensation. Repelling of False Hypotheses.

[13] Epistemology starts with the treatment of sensations, because psychology establishes that all our representations come from these. At the same time, it does not simply take this psychological claim on faith, but rather itself tests whether, in the epistemological investigation of representations, there are not still established some representations, or, as the case may be, structures [*Gebilde*] characteristic of representations that cannot be traced back to sensations. Thus, it is in no way the case that the epistemology of sensations is simply thereby placed ahead of innate representations, *a priori* representational forms, etc., the entrance for these somehow blocked from the beginning.

Epistemology must, rather, just begin *somewhere* with its work, and, with the selection of its first theme, be guided by that psychological principle. I must only add to this that, as my own faulty attempt has shown, that it only establishes this order of work for epistemology, i.e., beginning with the sensations, so that it can accomplish results. Were it to begin its work, instead, with the representations, it would soon helplessly come to a standstill, and then, either bury itself, or have to make a metaphysical break-neck leap. [...]

Section Eight: Spatial and Qualitative Differences at the Same Time. Koinaden. Self-Sameness

[...]

[15] If one considers 'space' as an independent variable, it then follows, in all respects, that the coordination of the *qualities* is *discontinuous*. The visual sensation of the moon in the night sky that corresponds to the moon's periphery passes suddenly from one quality into another quite different quality. 'Boundaries' are thereby given in the raw data of sensation. 'Space', which, in the first place, shows itself to be a characteristic of the sensations, just as indefinable

and universal as 'quality', and which, for this reason, can also only be quite vaguely articulated through a word like 'localization' or 'position' or 'spatial order', discloses itself now as 'form' or 'shape'.[10]

Mathematical forms without qualities do not exist among the raw data of sensation, and will, thus, confront us only much later. For the epistemology of the sensations, the delimitation of the forms is bound to the *discreteness* of the quality. The delimitation can be comprehensive, but does not need to be. The delimited quality region [i.e., the sensation complex] can, inside its boundaries, contain still further boundaries, thus further qualitative discontinuities. One might think, e.g., again of the chess board, or of the moon with its 'man'. Also, the delimited quality region [16] can harbor simultaneously more than one quality in its entire extension or in its individual parts. One might think, as an example, of a fragrant rose, or of a harmony.

It is advisable to designate such delimited *sensation complexes* with a name. Scholastic philosophy is, naturally, immediately ready with scholastic concepts, like 'object', or even 'substance', or, if it is more critical, it awaits only the smuggling in of such a scholastic concept in order to pounce upon this 'uncritical' epistemology with the well-known set of tools of 'critical' philosophy.

We, on the contrary, refuse to mix up our delimited sensation complex with such scholastic concepts. We still do not yet here have anything to do with the evaluation of complicated thought processes. On the contrary, it is still exclusively a question of representations, which we connect with the raw data of sensation with the help of the categorial representation of identity/non-identity. Even the most strict examination will show that the feared smuggling in of a substance is not attempted anywhere in the following text.

But with this also arises the need for a new designation. I suggest the designation '*Koinade*',[11] for the first-order complexes, those, i.e., inside whose boundaries no discontinuities exist. The single chess board square would be such a '*Koinade*' of the first order, thus, a '*Koinade*' in the strict sense, while the

---

10 This, naturally, has nothing to do with the Kantian 'form'. It concerns, instead, the quite popular meaning of the word.

11 '*Koinade*', which here indicates these spatially/qualitatively delimited sensation complexes, which are demarcated at boundaries of qualitative discontinuity, is another Ziehen neologism. This one seems to be a combination of the Greek, 'κοινός', which means 'common' or 'shared', and the noun stem, '-ad', as in 'dyad', 'triad', 'Olympiad', etc. This combination means literally something like 'commonness' or 'commonality', or the concept of such. (The word '*koinos*' is also the root of '*Koine*', which became the common Greek language after Alexander.) I am grateful to Matt Dillon, of the LMU Classics department, of his help in this analysis. –Tr.

whole chess board would appear to be a higher-order '*Koinade*' (Compare also section 74.).[12]

With this, the first step is made to a delimitation, and thereby, also to a clarification, within the raw data of sensation. The further steps will be discovered only later.

One can now easily reverse the consideration, and say: Whenever the quality does not change *at all* with the space, or only changes *continuously*, so we employ the concept of the '*Koinade*' over the entire region of the continuous change, so long as, with the differences of the sensations, the points of view not hanging together remain disconnected. This is, then, the *Koinade of the first order*, as we have just defined it. Consider a black surface to be a spectrum. Since, within the spectrum, the qualities change continuously, so we will be able to represent the entire spectrum as *one Koinade*. The *Koinade* demarcation is always simply dependent upon a qualitative discontinuity.

It is thereby obvious that these *Koinaden* representations are quite variable. Epistemology still does not at all here depend on the demarcation of the *individual Koinade* as such, but rather only on the *universal* demarcation in general. It must now be especially emphasized that the representation of a *Koinade* is grasped even whenever *small* discontinuities appear. It must further be added that, through discovery, we reach ever further boundaries to ever-higher superordinated *Koinaden*. There can, thus, in no way, be talk about a single division, or subdivision, of the world into *Koinaden*. Only the '*principle of Koinaden*' is essential for the world of the raw data of sensation given to us.

Within the region of *one Koinade*, we employ now a name and concept that comes directly from the categorial representations, [17] but unfortunately is quite ambiguous:[13] the concept of '*self-sameness*'. We say: "it is still the same object," or "that belongs still to the same object," just so long as the qualitative continuity is not at all, or not substantially,[14] interrupted. This 'self-sameness' is thus, nothing other than "belonging to *one Koinade*".

One may here object that, already with this classification of the *Koinaden*, the synthetic function, or the unifying function, of the 'I'-consciousness, or

---

[12] This section is not included in this translation. –Tr.
[13] The principle of identity has the same ambiguity as soon as it is taken to be more than a mere word game.
[14] This addendum, "or not substantially," corresponds to similarity [*Ähnlichkeit*] in relationship to identity [*Gleichheit*].

the unity of the synthesis of the manifolds,[15] and so forth, is already hard at work. On the contrary, it is to be observed that the qualitative discontinuity at the boundaries of the *Koinaden* is a fact of the raw data of sensation, and that our representations as memory forms simply give back again this fact of the raw data of sensation and bind it with words. Some mysterious unity, in the sense of a hypothetical object or substance, is not thought of. The name '*Koinade*' is supposed to designate nothing other than that demarcation.

There remains, then, from the epistemological viewpoint, only the interesting fact, to be discussed at length later, that our representations do not always connect singly to single sensations, but rather, often, one single representation includes several sensations. To exaggerate this fact into some unifying function of an 'I'-consciousness—using words a foot-and-a-half long that lack precise content—is not permitted to epistemology.

The next fact of sensation consists in the fact that, sometimes, two or more identical or similar *Koinaden* are given. Select, as an example, two identical red balls or two identical tones. The categorial representation of identity also applies here. Even here, we use the concept of 'self-sameness', but in quite a different sense. 'Self-sameness' here means the identity, or, as the case may be, the similarity of two *Koinaden* given simultaneously (or also at different times) in different places. As the first 'self-sameness' does not demand an absolute continuity, so also this second 'self-sameness' demands no absolute identity, as our definition already articulates through the addendum, 'or, as the case may be, the similarity'.

Even here, only one fact is delineated of the raw data of sensation from our representations. Here, too, the interesting characteristic of our representations, which we already encountered above,[16] namely, the collection of several sensations in *one* representation, becomes important, albeit in a somewhat divergent manner. This collecting characteristic of our representations will also be more fully discussed in our epistemology of representations and judgments.

[18] With this, a further, and much more essential, step in the classification of the raw data of sensation simultaneously occurs. We collect identical, or, as the case may be, similar, *Koinaden* under one representation. So, the representations of the types [*Arten*] and classes [*Gattungen*] originate from the representations of individual *Koinaden*. These are able to develop, thus, even without any

---

15 According to Kant, this unity is already given conjointly with the intuitions "*a priori*, as the condition of the synthesis of all apperception". ("*a priori als Bedingung der Synthesis aller Apprehension*"). (Kant 1998, B 171)

16 In this way, the principle of Hamilton also makes sense: "Philosophy is only a systematic evolution of the contents of consciousness by the instrumentality of consciousness." (Hamilton 1861, p. 186)

succession of sensations. Theoretically, the identity, or, as the case may be, the similarity, in what is adjacent suffices.

It is obvious that the qualitative-spatial connection to *Koinaden* and the connection of identical *Koinaden* to types and classes conceal themselves with the two main processes of forming representations: composition (aggregation) and generalization (Ziehen 1911, p. 159). Such a coinciding *must* plainly be anticipated. For false epistemologies, e.g., even for Kant's, it is very indicative that they quite lose touch with psychology, or even violate psychology in favor of their epistemologies.[17]

Finally, I call attention to the fact that the second connection is accomplished through the fact that one apprehends 'quality' as an independent variable and seeks its spatial coordination. Even with this, the picture of the raw data of sensation is still being completed. At the same time, it certainly ought not be overlooked that the apprehension of 'quality' as an independent variable furnishes a much less unified picture. This is because the qualities do not form *one* continuous series of manifolds, and because, besides many qualities, very many spatial points are being coordinated. To each spatial point, however, only *one* quality, or at least only a very limited number of qualities, is coordinated in the individual moment.[18] The world picture appears therefore much 'clearer' if I select 'space' as the independent variable.

Section Nine: Changes and their Similarities. Laws Arise Only with the Analysis of the Raw Data of Sensation in Reducible- and v-Components. Parallel-and Causal-Laws. Letter Designations.

But now, what else does epistemology have to do with the sensations? The following work of epistemology hangs together entirely with the *temporal* characteristics of sensations. Were the sensations merely raw data remaining identical, all the work of their description and classification would be done by science. Were the sensations in fact changeable, but these changes *absolutely* dissimilar among themselves, so science could still, if it thought it worth the effort, at least describe these rule-less changes, and the threshold of scientific progress would

---

[17] This need to responsibly keep in touch with psychology when engaged in epistemology comes up as a theme in the first main section of Ziehen's text that is explicitly relevant to our Husserlian interests, 'Digression concerning logic and epistemology'. See p. 411 ff. [174].–Tr.

[18] One could, naturally, very well also imagine a world which only contained continuously graduated quality-series, to which clear or less clear space elements are coordinated, e.g., a graduated grey from a center to all the sides, or the double cone of my system of color qualities.

again be achieved. Were the sensations changeable, and all these changes, directly as such, similar among each other in groups, without exception, so science would have to identify these similar changes and would, with the identification of these boundaries, once more have finished its work.

But, in fact, however, none of these three possible worlds is actual. The sensations do not remain the same, [19] *but rather, they change.* These changes are not absolutely dissimilar among themselves, but rather, significantly resemble each other. These similarities are not directly as such given without exception, but rather, they give themselves without exception—to which degree will be discussed later—only if we reconsider or transform the sensations in quite specific ways. Still more precisely articulated: we must divide the sensations into two parts, which I want to designate now as the ρ-component and the v-component.

It is thus:
$$E = f\,(^\rho E,\, ^v E)$$
or:
$$E = {}^\rho E \,\#\, {}^v E,$$

where E designates the sensations [*Empfindungen*], $^\rho E$ designates the ρ-component of the sensations, and $^v E$ designates the v-component of the sensations. 'f' is the function sign. Since this becomes very tedious for the illustration, however, I have introduced the sign, '#', which, in contradistinction to the '+' sign, is not supposed to indicate the *additive* combination, but rather *some* (for the moment unknown) thinking combination, in the sense of the function sign. It is not at all necessary that this function be one of the familiar mathematical functions.

What does not fit into universal natural-scientific regularity, we accept into the v-component. The ρ-component includes, then, that which lets itself be brought under the universal laws of the character of natural science. If we reduce the sensations to their ρ-component, the changes of the raw data of sensation obey universal laws. I thus designate the ρ-component as the *reducible component*. The universal laws by which the reducible components are governed, are, as the analysis shows, nothing other than the natural laws, as natural science has, for the most part, determined them.

The v-components, which natural science, for the time being, handles (and must handle) almost as weeds, prove themselves, by a careful analysis, to be dependent upon the reducible components in quite regular ways, and, indeed, upon quite particular raw data of sensation, or, as the case may be, their reducible components, which data we, in general, designate as the nervous system. The laws which govern the v-components are, however, in principle, completely different from those ruling amongst the reducible components.

The latter laws, those that hold, in general, among the reducible components, should already be designated as *causal laws*; the laws that hold for the v-components should be designated as *parallel laws*.

[…]

[20] Before the following discussions, I must establish alphabetical symbols, which are not only necessary for the abbreviation of all the later explanations, but also even to hold tight to what clear concepts we already have.[19]

I designate the raw data of sensation, as I already have above, with E [*Empfindungsgignomene*]. I designate the raw data of representation with V [*Vorstellungsgignomene*]. Among the modalities of sensation [*Empfindung*], I will chiefly consider the tactile and the optical. I designate these specifically as E_t [*taktile*] and E_o [*optische*], and the corresponding representations [*Vorstellungen*], I designate as V_t and V_o.

When it is a matter of the combination of a tactile and an optical sensation, I name this combination E_{ot}; the corresponding representation would be called, V_{ot}. [21] The remaining modalities of sensation will occasionally be identified through particular indices, so far as it is necessary. It should, however, in general, be established that the index $_{ot}$ designates by abbreviation, on the whole, the combination of various—without here specifying which—modalities of sensation.

Whenever the opposition between the raw data of sensation [E] and the raw data of representation [V] does not come under consideration—as, e.g., during almost the entire second chapter,—I will write by abbreviation:

o instead of E_o;
t instead of E_t;
ot instead of E_{ot}.

I distinguish the indices ρ and v from the indices of modality, o and t, by, as I have already shown above, placing these *above* and *before* the E, rather than, as with the indices of modality, *below* and *after* it.

---

[19] In the first and second editions of my *Psychophysiologische Erkenntnistheorie* (1898 and 1907) I used less appropriate labels. To facilitate comparison, I would like to briefly cite the old terminology. E_o or O stood for $^\rho E_o$; E_T or T for $^\rho E_t$; $(E_o)^v$ for $^v E_o$; (E_t) for $^v E_t$ (cf. p. 24, 32, and 63 of the first edition).

Section Ten: Foundational Example. Continuous, Discontinuous, and Paired Changes

[...] We can classify the changes of the raw data of sensation, according to the analogy of the considerations of Section Eight, into spatial and qualitative *Koinaden* changes. Also here, 'intensity', and with it, 'emotional tone', should be provisionally contained under 'quality'.[20] [22] Furthermore, time can be considered here, as space was there, either as a dependent or an independent variable. If the sensation complex of a *Koinade* is, in the sense of Section Eight, identical, or almost identical, in two directly successive points in time, we say with the same right and in the same sense, that in both points in time it is a matter of "the self-same" *Koinade*, as we have previously shown for such a sensation complex that is identical in two or more directly adjacent points in space.

We must, however, here also guard against smuggling a unity or a self-sameness into the concept of the *Koinade* that goes beyond the simple fact of the sensational identity. I want next to designate this self-sameness in connection to p.17[21] also as the *"third self-sameness"*.[22]

For the case of non-identity, there arises again the fact that the two directly successive points in time that are coordinated qualitatively, and likewise also the two directly successive points in time that are coordinated spatially, can be continuous or discontinuous, i.e., now continuous, now discontinuous.

---

20 The spatial changes correspond entirely to the φορά, the qualitative changes (including the quantitative) to the ἀλλοίωσις, including to the αὔξησις and φθίσις of Aristotle, who, as is well known, was the first to try a classification of changes. (*Physica*, 225a f.).

He classified the changes first of all into:
1. ἐξ ὑποκειμένου εἰς ὑποκείμενον = κίνησις
2. ἐξ ὑποκειμένου εἰς μὴ ὑποκείμενον = φθορά
3. ἐξ μὴ ὑποκειμένου εἰς ὑποκείμενον = γένεσις

The κίνησις, which consequently actually corresponds to change in our sense and may not be rendered with 'motion' [*Bewegung*], is either,

κατὰ τὸ ποιόν = ἀλλοίωσις

or, κατὰ τὸ ποσόν = αὔξησις and φθίσις

or, κατὰ τόπον = φορά

Incidentally, Aristotle did not always entirely rigorously follow this classification and this word-usage.

21 See, Ziehen, p.17 (section 9), this translation. –Tr.

22 The identity of two successive, widely temporally separated (not following each other directly) *Koinaden*, produces a '*fourth self-sameness*', which corresponds to the second self-sameness (by *spatial* separation) in the case of temporal separation. The second and the fourth self-sameness are often bound. –Tr.

It is advisable, first of all, to turn away from a combination of spatial and qualitative change, and to consider each in isolation. For an example of a continuous[23] qualitative change without spatial change, let us consider a rectangle that does not change in place or in shape, whose coloring, over time, runs through all colors of the spectrum without any leap. A discontinuous qualitative change, by comparison, would be without an accompanying spatial change if in a rectangular field, the coloring changed over in a leap from red to yellow, from yellow to blue, etc., without change of place or of shape.

On the other hand, a continuous spatial change with no qualitative change takes place if a white rectangle, without changing its color, would move itself in the visual field, e.g., in a straight line *abc*, up and to the right (whereby *a* designates the start point, *b* somewhere in the middle, and *c* the end point). If, on the contrary, in the first second, a white rectangle would appear at *a*, in the second second, a similarly sized and similarly white rectangle would appear at *b*, and in the third second, the same would appear at *c*, it would then be a matter of a discontinuous spatial change, with no qualitative change.[24]

[23] It is obvious that the representation of the *Koinade* in the earlier given sense only holds in the case of a *continuous* change. To be sure, auxiliary observations and auxiliary considerations occasionally reveal the continuity or discontinuity to be only *apparent*—one thinks, e.g., of the magic wand of a magician— but the *Koinaden* concept has nothing at all to do with this subsequent revision. It is only supposed to describe one sensation complex as it is given as raw data: that sensation complex, in fact, that exhibits, within a region of space, no, or only continuous, qualitative differences, and, within a stretch of time, no, or only continuous, qualitative or spatial differences.

As in the analogous consideration of Section Eight, one can inversely also consider time as a dependent variable and ask to which point in time the appearance of a particular quality at a particular place corresponds, e.g., of the meridian passage of a star or the turning yellow of the leaves of a tree. For analogous reasons, as was shown at the conclusion of Section Eight, there arises from this inverse consideration, however, a less unambiguous world picture.

According to these discussions, we can briefly articulate the first observational principle thusly: The sensation complex ot ($= E_{ot}$) changes qualitatively and spatially with time. These changes are continuous or discontinuous. So long as

---

23 This continuity approximately aligns itself with Hume's "coherence in the changes of external objects." (Hume 1738).
24 Interestingly, this case seems to involve the supposition that in *b*, or, as the case may be, in *c*, no quality at all was given in the first second. From the peculiarity of the spatial and qualitative, an understanding for this supposition will later be given.

they are continuous, we speak of changes within the *Koinade*, or also, for short, of 'changes of the *Koinade*'.

And the most perfunctory consideration shows us still further that the sensational changes are often *paired*, i.e., the changes of a *Koinade* follow simultaneously with or directly after the changes of another *Koinade*.

Section Eleven: The Main Classification of the Changes of Sensations. Main Groupings. Disappearance of the *E*'s for the Null Value of the Parallel Changes.

[24] It is now a question of selecting the *main epistemological classifications* of the *changes of sensation*. There are many correct selections, but only a few, or, rather, only *one*, that is fruitful for epistemology. This exceptional main classification was already mentioned above (Section Nine, p. 19 [this volume p. 163]) in anticipation. The changes of the raw data of sensation let themselves, i.e., refer to a relatively simple schematic grouping.[25] This reference holds, for the most part, for our preliminary examination, and, entirely for our later definitive examination. The light, the ice cube [*Würfel*], and the optical apparatus of my body (including the visual cortex of the cerebrum), as they were already cited above, give a simple example for this *main grouping* in the optical region. It is designated through the three letters, *L* [*Licht*], *W* [*Würfel*], and *O* [*optische Apparat*]. Of course, *L*, *W*, and *O* do not mean the so-called 'bodies' [25] or 'objects' of physics, or of other philosophical systems, but rather only the sensation complex *E* of Section Nine. In the tactile region, the same main grouping could be designated as *L*, *W* and *T*, where '*T*' designates the tactile apparatus of my body (again including the somatosensory cortex).

Now, within this main grouping, thus, e.g.:

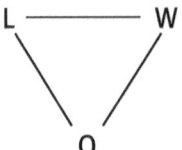

---

25 'Grouping' [*Konstellation*] here indicates a set of *Koinaden* representations, e.g., a light (*L*), an ice cube (*W*), and one's optical (or, as it were, tactile (*T*)) apparatus (*O*). These are used to organize the changes of the raw data of sensation. If one *Koinade* representation of a group is missing, e.g., '*L*' or '*W*', the associated *Koinaden* cannot change. –Tr.

we observe two main classes of changes, which I designate as *causal changes* and as *parallel changes*. The difference between these two classes of changes appears most sharply whenever we pursue, in detail, each complex in the course of its changes. L, as well as W, as well as O, are characterized at a specific point in time through a specific q (qualitative) and r (spatial): L, through $q^l\ r^l$, W, through $q^w\ r^w$, O through $q^o\ r^o$.

With this, let 'quality' retain the sense designated above (Section Eight, p.15 ff, and Section Ten, p. 21 [158 ff., 1664]). Already, the most perfunctory observation now shows that changes of W, and likewise of L and of O, do not occur, so long as the W, the L, and the O, respectively are isolated. Most changes of a *Koinade*, at least of a standard one, presume the presence of other *Koinade*—later it will be shown to hold for *all*.

It is a matter of 'change pairs' [*Veränderungspaare*], or 'paired' changes (compare Section Ten, p.23 [166]). In this respect, we can speak of an 'action' of *Koinaden*, "one on another". Occasionally, this action *seems* to be one-sided: i.e., only one of the two *Koinaden* seems to change, as, e.g., whenever, under the beams of the sun, the ice cube melts. The cooling of the light through the ice is so insignificant that it is invisible to our unmediated observation. Likewise, when a stone falls to earth. The spatial change seems only to concern the stone, and yet we know that the earth is also moved by the stone, albeit to a nearly insignificant degree.

In many cases, the two-sidedness of the change is actually directly perceptible. If we place the ice cube on a metal cube heated to 100°, we do not only notice the change of the ice cube, but also that of the metal cube: the one melting and warming, the other cooling. Physics proves that even where one-sided actions seem to be happening, there is still always alongside the action an opposing action (a reaction), and, thus, that all these changes are two-sided.

Physiology, however, teaches further that through L and W a chemical change, the so-called 'excitation' is evoked in my retina, in my visual nerves and in my visual cortex (O), which change, to be sure, can only be proven with particular auxiliary tools. I designate the relevant changes, thus the actions that W, L, and O encounter, as, W', L', and O', respectively. The causal changes are now, in the first line, characterized through the fact that to the zero value of a *Koinade* corresponds what remains unchanged of the associated *Koinade*.

If L falls away, if $q^l\ r^l$, thus, disappears, W remains unchanged; W' does not occur. If the light [L] is taken away, the ice cube [W] does not melt (always, naturally, presuming that L lacks similarly acting *Koinade*). Likewise, L remains unchanged if W falls away. The same [26] holds also for O, whenever L or W fall away. This state of affairs is characteristic for **causal changes.**[26]

It is quite otherwise, however, whenever O falls away. If my optical apparatus [O] is removed, e.g., by the knife of the surgeon or the destructive process of some illness, so L and W fall away with a single blow: I am blind.[27] The zero values of O, L and W do not remain somehow unchanged, but rather, they entirely disappear.

Still more: L and W disappear not only when O disappears, but rather, they also disappear whenever only O', i.e., the change evoked from L and W in O, fails to take place. Whenever I turn my head to the side or close my eye, or, whenever an opaque object is held before my eye, so that L and W cannot act on my eye, with this, both L and W disappear.

More precisely said: L falls away whenever the change produced by L falls away from O (O'_L), and W falls away whenever the change produced by W falls away from O (O'_W). A quite everyday state of affairs is thereby established that is decisive for epistemology. The disappearance of L and I with the complete disappearance of O is, to be sure, a fictitious example (*exemplum fictum*), inasmuch as I cannot myself observe the destruction of O in my mirror. A complete disappearance of T [tactile apparatus] inside the main sensation grouping is more likely to be realized occasionally. On the other hand, the fact that the absence of O' already suffices to make W and L disappear has been already familiar to us since childhood and is, in each moment, accessible to us.[28]

The characteristic feature of **parallel changes** is thereby given. We will later come to know still other, not less important, nor less interesting, differentiating features between parallel and causal changes, but none of them equally primitive and generally accessible. One would surely not object that, occasionally, also in the region of causal changes, one *Koinade* disappears with the others, e.g., the shadow with the light. This shadow is not to be compared with W, but rather, with W' [changes in W]; it is just exactly the change of the light evoked by a raw datum of sensation.

---

26 Recall the discussion 1913 above of ρ- and v-components. The ρ-components change in a way governed by scientific laws, and the v-components change in a way that depends on the nervous system. Parallel changes, unlike causal changes, can only take place when a member of the changing pair is a part of my nervous system. –Tr.
27 I do not even see, in this case, some 'black'.
28 The case of the so-called 'after-image' forms only an apparent exception, since, in this case, as is generally known, O' does not disappear with the stimulus, but rather, outlasts it.

Section Twelve: ν- and ξ- Complexes

Within the main grouping

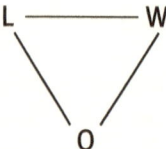

or, as the case may be,

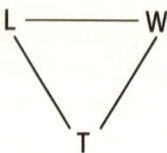

O, or, respectively, T, receives a quite particular position through the facts set forth in Section Eleven p. (24–26 [167–169]). Parallel changes between L and W we do not know; parallel changes are met with only when a member of the 'change pairs' (compare Section Ten, p. 23) is an O, or a T, or another part of my nervous system.

One always considers thereby that O designates always only the sensation complex E_{ot} of my optical nervous apparatus, and that T designates always only the sensation complex E_{ot} of my tactile nervous apparatus. [27] Thus, while parallel changes are bound to the sensation complex of my nervous system, the causal changes take place between all the members of the main grouping: between L and W, between L and O (or T, as the case may be), and between W and O (or, T, as the case may be). The *Koinaden* unification of O + T, etc.,[29] that takes this exceptional position among the raw data, conceals itself with the sensation complex that we designate as our nervous system.

I designate all sensations belonging to it as **ν-sensations** or **ν-complexes**. I designate the changes of the sensation complexes, that do not belong to the ν-complexes and are dependent upon the ν-sensations, e.g., L, W, etc., as ν-

---

[29] With the 'etc.', the other senses of the nervous system are intended; henceforth, they are supposed to be included in O + T.

changes or ***v-actions*** [aka, parallel changes]. And I designate the components traceable back to the *v*-actions as ***v-components*** of these sensation complexes (compare Section Nine, p.19 [163]). Finally, I designate parallel change laws as ***v-relationships***.[30]

I designate the sensation complexes that are not active in the sense of the *v*-complexes as ***ξ-sensations*** or ***ξ-complexes***. What is still contained in the raw data of sensation, besides the *v*-components, (not somehow as the remainder of a subtraction, but rather in the sense of the formula $E == {}^{\rho}E \# {}^{v}E$ of Section Nine, shall be designated as the ***p-component***, or, **reducible component**.[31] [...]

Chapter Seven: *Virtual Reducible Components and Individuation. Permanent Things.*

[256]
Section Sixty-Two: The Self-sameness of the Reducible Components. The Four Self-Samenesses. "Identity" of the Reducible Components.

[257] In Section Eight, it was established that the word 'self-sameness' has four distinct meanings. It means, namely:
1) *first*, the qualitative-intensive identity, or similarity, or, as the case may be, continuous change in what is directly adjacent, i.e., in spatial proximity (contiguity) at the same time (p.17 [160–161]);
2) *second*, the qualitative-intensive identity, or similarity, with spatial separation at the same time, i.e., identity or similarity of spatially separated *Koinaden* (*Koinaden* without spatial proximity, without spatial contiguity) (p.17 [160–161]);
3) *third*, the qualitative-intensive identity, or similarity, or, as the case may be, continuous change in what is directly adjacent, i.e., in temporal proximity (contiguity) in what is adjacent (p.22 [165–166]);

---

[30] Whether for *each* change of O such a change of L, or, as the case may be, W, takes place, is not yet to be discussed here. An exception seems to be making changes of O, which are evoked through stimulus changes situated below the so-called 'threshold of distinction'.

[31] The ***p*-component** (*p-Bestandteil*), or, **reducible component** (*Reduktionsbestandteil*), which was introduced already in Ch. 2, Sec. 9, is that component of a sensation complex that lets itself be brought under the general laws of natural science. If we reduce our sensations to these *p*-components, the changes of the raw data of sensation obey universal laws. This component is thus designated the *reducible component*, and the laws that govern it are designated as '**causal laws**'. –Tr.

4) and *fourth*, the qualitative-intensive identity, or similarity, with temporal separation in what is adjacent, i.e., identity or similarity of temporally separated *Koinaden* (*Koinaden* without temporal proximity, without temporal contiguity) (p.19, fn.1).[32]

[277]
Chapter Eight: *The Plurality of the v-Complexes. Virtual v-Complexes.*

Section Sixty-Five: Transgressive *v*-Complexes[33]

[278] These new *v*-components[34] [presented by others] do not, however, find themselves within my scope [279] of the raw data of sensation. I cover the foreign eye and my optical sensations, e.g., of the light before me, do not change, as they *do change* whenever I cover *my* eye. There must, therefore, also be still other raw data of sensation besides those to which my body, or, as it were, my nervous system, contributes the *v*-components, corresponding to the other *v*-complexes and to the *v*-components that originate from them.

It cannot be emphasized forcibly enough how this class of the raw data of sensation of other *v*-complexes is, in principle, absolutely distinct from the ordinary class of other 'I's'. My classification of other raw data of sensation is *transgressive*, as those virtual reducible components in the previous chapter, that is, it oversteps, in its representation, the boundaries of what is actually given. This classification is not however *transcendent*, i.e., it does not introduce representations that are not derived from what is actually given, but rather, it always still derives its representations exclusively from what is actually given.

The hypothesis of another 'I' (and, likewise, of my own) is, on the other hand, thoroughly transcendent. With the postulation of an 'I', a quite specific, solely unique state of affairs is introduced, to which the postulation of another 'I' is in no way analogous; indeed, it is straightforwardly in opposition. Whoever

---

32 Because of this doubled regularity, I designate the demeanor of the raw data of sensation as also "binomial."
33 Recall that '**v-complexes**' (='**v-sensations**') designates all sensations belonging to the *Koinaden* unification of the various faculties of my nervous system, e.g., optical, tactile, auditory, etc. See Ch.2, Sec.12, p.27 [p. 170–171]. –Tr.
34 Recall that '**v-components**' are components that are traceable back to *v*-actions, e.g., O' from L', and that '**v-actions**' (='**v-changes**') are changes of the sensation complex that do not belong to my nervous system, e.g., L' or W'. See, Ch.2, Sec.12, p.27 [p. 170–171]. –Tr.

places an 'I' at the head of his epistemology has hopelessly surrendered to solipsism. Whoever, on the other hand, with the here-developed epistemology, avoids this 'I'-hypothesis, can, without deliberation, introduce, alongside the v-actions directly given in sensation, still others, on the basis of analogical conclusions, which, in each relationship, agree with what is directly given, just exactly so far as the v-complexes that belong to them agree. Such a representation is exactly just as transgressive and just as entirely justified as the representation of the transgressive reducible components, which—in some form—each epistemology *must* attain; it is also just as justified as each presupposition of conformity in general (Section Nine).

Book Two: *Epistemology of the Representations and of Association*

Chapter Two: *Epistemology of Idea Association*

Digression concerning logic and epistemology

[411] The relationship between logic, psychology and epistemology has repeatedly fluctuated in the history of philosophy. In particular, modern logic has repeatedly endeavored to escape the limits of the purely formal laws that govern it, and instead, to also determine material truths. So far as this has happened in such a way that the *most universal* facts of experience were treated logically, no objection at all should be raised.

It is much more plainly unpardonable that the *simplest* and *most universal* facts are being used in this way for epistemology. The more specific a fact of experience is, the more uninteresting it is to epistemology. Ohm's Law[35] offers effectively no epistemological interest, while more general theorems, as, for example, the theorem of the parallelogram of forces,[36] or that of general gravitation, are of the most far-reaching epistemological importance. Against that way of proceeding, I would therefore raise only terminological objections: that it no longer belongs in the realm of logic, but rather already counts as epistemology.

Some modern logicians have meanwhile gone further and have believed themselves able to establish a special material logic, both independent of psychology and still essentially distinct from epistemology. The proponents of this '*logicis-*

---

[35] Ohm's Law, first formulated by Georg Ohm in his 1827 paper, *The Galvanic Circuit Investigated Mathematically*, is a central theory in the field of electricity. It is formulated as: $\Delta V = IR$, where 'V' = 'voltage', 'I' = 'current', and 'R' = 'resistance'. It articulates that the voltage of an electric circuit is directly proportional to the current of a circuit and to the resistance of the circuit. –Tr.

[36] This theorem of the parallelogram of forces was central to 18th century mechanics. Newton articulates this theorem in his *Mathematical Principles of Natural Philosophy* (1729), p.20: "A body acted on by [two] forces acting jointly describes the diagonal of a parallelogram in the same time in which it would describe the sides if the forces were acting separately". This is then taken up into the work of both Kant and d'Alembert. (Martinez Adame 2012, p. 367) This theorem is used by physicists to calculate the vector that describes the total force applied to an object by two individual force vectors. –Tr.

tic' [*logistischen*] course, as I would like to call it,³⁷ sought, moreover, to discredit the logic and epistemology grounded on psychology as 'psychologistic'.

Their own systems soon seized a bold fantasy as aid, and thereby arrived at pictures of the world which impressed uncritical minds as simply enthralling—I call to mind the Hegelian logic. They were soon lost and losing themselves in exceedingly long drawn-out conceptual investigations. While these probably have accomplishedsomething terminologically useful now and then, they nonetheless cannot thereby obscure the horrifying wasteland of this '*logicism*'.

Since, for all that, this '*logicism*' at least proceeds with scientific thoroughness, and perhaps precisely for that reason, the vacuity of its content is not apparent to many, I want to subject the main propositions of this '*logicism*' to a short critique—prescinding from its numerous individual errors—the more so as this course threatens to lead epistemology onto a completely false path, and to some extent already has.

I hold four main propositions of this '*logicism*'to be particularly characteristic and just as particularly misleading.

Firstly, it is alleged that concepts portray 'ideal unities',³⁸ to which some manner of existence is accorded, even beyond our representations.

I claim, on the contrary, that such ideal conceptual unities are completely meaningless outside of our representations. Sensations and—according to my epistemological theory—also the reducible components³⁹ are similar to each other in many relationships (See Book 1, Ch.1, Sec. 3, and Ch.2, Sec.7.), and our universal representations are grounded on these similarities.

Apart from those similarities and these universal representations, with their 'supra-individual' components (discussed on p. 310; see also, Bk.1, Ch.1, Sec.3), no further 'ideal unities' can exist. [412] Because our concepts, even if they refer themselves to the same raw data of sensation, are subject to small or large variations (both from person to person and, with the same person, from one moment to another), it is correct to say only that we have constructed certain normalizing concepts. This standardization attempt is something like the way we have tried, in bodily realms, to remedy the deviations of linear measure through a 'normal meter' (compare p. 443, fn. 1 [195]). We

---

37 Subsequently I have found that Busse already used the designation 'logicism' [*Logismus*] for this direction. (Busse 1903, p. 153)

38 For example, Husserl, *Logische Untersuchungen* II (1901, p. 42f.) [Translator's note: Ziehen quotes from the 1900/1901 versions of *Logische Untersuchungen* I and II, of which there is no published English translation].

39 These are the components of our sensations that can be subjected to scientific causal laws. See, Ziehen, Bk.1, Ch.2, Sec.9 and Sec.12, this translation. –Tr.

try, then, especially through definitions, which always allow themselves to be easily reproduced and communicated, to prevent such fluctuations, or, at least, to reduce them to a minimum.

Yet, at the same time, we cannot speak of definitions as *absolute* determinations, since each definition still uses divers others for the determination of any one concept. We can, rather, speak only of determinations of *relations*. These definitions are also never finalized, as the discussion in the last paragraph[40] has shown, but always, rather, provisional. In some, certainly rare, cases, they even indicate only a temporary equilibrium in our knowledge.

At the same time, they afford the further advantage that they bind with the 'normalizing concept' a constant unequivocal *word* representation. One can also clarify the meaning of this normalizing concept very well with the help of the concept of 'grouping' [*Konstellation*] (Ziehen 1911, 205f.). Whenever, in the course of our association of ideas, a somehow-composite representation—a composite concept—appears, the grouping specifies which component representations appear in this composite representation, and with what intensity each component representation takes its place in the composite representation.

Now, this grouping, however, changes constantly, and not only, indeed, from person to person, but even also for the same person, since not all representations are always present to him with the same intensity, nor do they always influence his association of ideas with the same intensity. Added to which, the organization of latent representations is often disturbed through individual erroneous representations, in consequence of which, the order of the currently prevailing representations is also disturbed.

The [aforementioned] normalizing concepts are able to remedy all these shortcomings, within certain boundaries. Sigwart altogether rightly characterized this state of affairs for judgment with the words: the normative character of logic rests on the fact that we presuppose "the ideal condition of a thoroughly unchanging present of complete systematic representational content for a single state of consciousness, which [ideal condition] can never be entirely fulfilled empirically." (Sigwart 1873–1878, Vol. 1, p. 383; compare also Sigwart 1889, pp. 84–85).

It is also, indeed, very understandable how we are able to come, despite our fluctuating representations, to such normalizing concepts, through the determination of definitions. We gather our own representations and the foreign representations shared with us by others $a_1', a_1'', a_1'''... a_2', a_2'', a_2'''...$, and so on,

---

[40] Ziehen refers here to the section of text preceding the section here translated, section 98, on the analytic and synthetic judgments in '*logicism*'. This section is not included in this translation.—Tr.

which refer themselves to a determinate sensation complex, A. We bundle the common representations together and exclude those that are not common, or offset for them, so that we finally arrive at a normalizing concept, a, for the sensation complex, A. The various representations, a_1', a_1'', a_1''', and so forth, will certainly recur again and again in my thinking as a result of the grouping and other aspects [*Momente*], [413] but I will still, again and again, be able to correct these variations with the help of the acquired normalizing concept, and the normalizing concept will gradually diminish even these, even if it is never able to completely get rid of them. Logic does nothing other than form these normalizing concepts and teach their use in the operations of thinking.

The '*logicist*' contends, instead, that logic treats of 'absolute concepts', 'forms of existence', 'supra-empirical unities', and so forth. But whence could we know anything about these 'absolute concepts' and 'supra-empirical unities', and so forth?

In response to this question, we will again point out that suspicious 'intuition' or 'inner evidence', which we have already encountered many times, and which has two main characteristics: first, it changes from philosopher to philosopher, and respectively from philosophical school to philosophical school; and second, it appears especially readily whenever the author has just expressed a rather dubious point of his teaching. We are supposed, then, to be preserved from doubt through a bluff.[41]

---

[41] This is one of the sections of Ziehen's text that Husserl cites in a footnote of *Ideas*. I include here Dahlstrom's English translation of this footnote: "During the printing of the present book, I read in a text that has just appeared—Th. Ziehen's *Erkenntnistheorie auf psychophysiologischer und physikalischer Grundlage*—a characteristic utterance about 'that suspicious, so-called Intuition or evidence...that has two chief properties: first, it changes from philosopher to philosopher or from philosophical school to philosophical school, respectively; and second, it tends to be inserted when the *author lectures precisely on a very dubious point of his doctrine*, at that point we are supposed *to be kept from doubting through a bluff.*' In this criticism, as emerges from the context, what is at issue is the doctrine, elaborated in the *Logical investigations*, concerning 'universal objects' or 'essences' and the intuition of essences. Thus Ziehen's work reads further: 'In order to distinguish these supraempirical concepts from the common pack of usual concepts, one often still has to ascribe to them, in addition, a particular universality, absolute exactness, and so forth. I consider all these human pretensions' (Ziehen, p. 413). No less characteristic for this epistemology is the utterance on page 441, related to the intuitive apprehension of the ego (although the utterance is probably universally valid for this author): 'I could think of only one actual attestation of such a primary Intuition, the agreement of all sensing and thinking individuals in the affirmation of such Intuition.'—That such foolishness has often been carried on with the appeal to 'Intuition' should naturally not be denied. The question is simply whether this foolishness with an alleged Intuition could be uncovered other than through *actual* Intuition. Even in the sphere of experience [*Erfahrung*], a great deal of foolishness is carried on

To differentiate these 'empirical' concepts still somewhat more sharply from the common mob of ordinary concepts, the *'logicist'* often even ascribes to them a particular universality, absolute exactness, and so forth. I hold all this [to be] only human presumption and refer to the hypothetical universalization of our universal judgments discussed earlier (compare p. 343).[42]

Secondly, *'logicism'* claims that, in particular, the universal, isolated concepts that Husserl, for example, designated as 'ideal species', lead a quite singular existence, or at least have a quite singular meaning. Whenever I see the same red, i.e., the same qualitative shade of red, in many objects, I form in this way the isolated concept of this 'shade of red'. And from the isolated concepts of many different 'shades of red', I form the universal isolated concept of 'red'.

The genesis of the isolated concept is no more and no less mysterious than the formation of any other universal concepts. The psychological story is the following: I see a red object, M, then an object, N, of the very same red, and so forth. Since, in our association of ideas according to the grouping, now this, now that, partial representation appears with greater intensity, so, at some point, the partial representation that objects M, N, and so forth, share will appear: that quite specific red with its particular intensity.[43] Through this, however, I will attain a comparison of 'M-red', 'N-red', and so forth.

This comparison presupposes only the effectiveness of the categorial function,[44] whose effectiveness we already encounter everywhere. The result of the comparison is the representation of the identity of the 'M-red', 'N-red', and so forth. We recognize for each one of these 'reds' a 'self-sameness in the second sense' and possibly also 'in the fourth sense', as we discussed at length in Sections Eight and Sixty-two (in contrast to the principle of individuation [*Principi-*

---

with the appeal to the latter, and the situation would be quite bad if one for this reason would want to designate experience [*Erfahrung*] altogether as a 'bluff' and to make 'attestation' of it dependent upon 'agreement of all sensing and thinking individuals in the affirming of such an 'experience' [*Erfahrung*].' Compare this with the Second Chapter of the First Section of this [*Ideas*] work" (Husserl 2014, p. 151–152). –Tr.

42 This section is not included in the text translated here. –Tr.

43 In addition, it must be not exactly a question of an *act of attentiveness* in the strict sense (compare also my treatment of attentiveness in *Monattsschrift für Psychiatrie und Neurologie* 24, p.173), as Mill teaches (Mill 1865, p. 394). Also, the linking with a word is not essential to the process.

44 This function is the identity/non-identity function, and is the main principle of classification of our raw data.

um individuationis]). It is a matter of sundry individual, but qualitatively identical reds, as Spencer[45] quite rightly demonstrated against Mill.

[414] To speak of an 'Identity'[*Identität*] or 'unity' [*Einheit*] has absolutely no sense, not to mention no correctness whatsoever. As is always the case with the formation of our representations, we hereby collect many qualitatively identical reds into *one* representation and, after we have become acquainted with other shades of red, universalize this representation, even as we would any other species representation, into the universal representation, 'red'. I would not know in what sense a still further 'unity' might be ascribed, either in the specific case or in the general, to the isolated concept developed in this way.[46]

We are certainly not somehow ignoring the numerical plurality of the qualitatively identical reds, but the categorial function for this concept formation is, rather, simply being restricted to the specific quality of the reds, and is thereby abstracted from place and time.

Third, '*logicism*' claims—naturally in the closest connection with both the previous assertions—that a particular 'object' and a particular 'meaning' correspond to each representation (Husserl 1900, p. 46, 52). The meaning is supposed to be an "ideal, and thus stable unity"[47] (Husserl 1900, p. 89),[48] as opposed to the fluctuating "subjective acts, which grant meaning to the expressions" enacted from case to case.

[Husserl claims] that the essence of meaning is not supposed to lie "in the meaning-granting experience, but rather in its content," "the one identical intentional unity standing firm against the scattered manifold of real or possible events of speaking and thinking." (Husserl 1900, p. 97, 100)[49] The individual

---

45 Spencer surely did not claim that the relevant qualities never completely correspond (one thinks somewhat about the principle of indiscernible identity (*Identitas indiscernibilium*)) but rather, only an individual difference of separate, qualitatively identical reds in the sense of the principle of individuation (*Principium individuationis*). (Spencer 1881, p. 59 ff.)
46 Compare Husserl 1900, 113 ff; on p. 634, Husserl even speaks of a 'perception of the universal'.
47 One thinks of the essences of unchangeable things (*essentiae immutabiles rerum*) of the Scholastics.
48 For Husserl's interpretation and terminology one should further still particularly compare Vol. 2, p. 9, 16, 29 note. 2, 37, 38, 101, 108, 322 ff., 338, 347, 357, 362, 374, 387, 463, 475, 524, 566, 614, 707.
49 I must thoroughly dispute the evidence claimed on p. 100. It is only correct that with the mathematical principles, from the earlier developed reasons, the concepts are very sharp and uniform. With that, however, the mathematical principles still have only a reality, on the one hand, in the raw data of sensations and, respectively, in their reducible components, and, on the other hand, in the individual judgments. An 'ideal being' still different from these, as Husserl has in mind and seems to ascribe to the 'meanings' (p.101, compare also p.124; the expression 'he is absolutely not' on p. 353 is quite heavily relevant, as is p. 388), still requires at least some

"acts of meaning, the meaning intentions" stand over against "the one ideal meaning." Never does the "meaning" coincide with the "object" (Husserl 1900, p. 46).[50]

"Every expression signifies not only something, but rather it refers to some objects." This intentional relationship is not everywhere the same, but rather specifically different. The "intentional meaning" of the "object" is, for example, different in the case of the representation and in the case of the judgment (Husserl 1900, p. 347 f., 364). Husserl designates these differences also along the lines of the "act-character."[51] [415] According to a further discussion [by Husserl], it would remain, then, still to distinguish between "the singular mood of mere understanding and the definiteness that constitutes the 'what' of understanding," ("quality" [in the first case] and "material" [in the second]) (Husserl 1900, p. 428).[52]

What, now, is actually correct about all these claims? Every *representation* has its content (Ziehen 1911, p. 166 f.). This content is derived from the accompanying grounding sensations. The representation relates itself to these grounding sensations, or, whenever it is a question of a fantasized representation, is envisaged with reference to its grounding sensations. This singular root 'relationship', which partly corresponds to the 'intention' of Brentano and of Husserl and to the 'intentional inexistence' (*inexistentia intentionalis*) of the Scholastics, is actually present, albeit only for the representations with reference to the sensations. I have attempted its epistemological explanation in sections 69–72 (compare specifically p. 302).[53]

The relationship of emotional tone to the representation, the relationship of the judgment to a state of affairs, and so forth, have nothing to do with *this* relationship. Furthermore, the relationship of the representation to the sensation is always only a private psychic matter of fact.

This also holds for the representational content: it is always only the experience of an individual (a 'signifying' in Husserl's sense). An ideal unity ('meaning') comes to these private psychic matters of fact solely in the sense of the nor-

---

verification. The same concerns also raise themselves naturally against the assumption of an ideal being for all other species concepts (compare Husserl 1900, p.411).
50 Husserl makes an exception of a "quite exceptional and logically worthless case."
51 Against this act-character, I can only repeat all the concerns which I have already articulated. (Ziehen 1911, p. 164) The interpretation of which Husserl speaks allows itself to be reduced to an influx of other representations (certainly not 'new sensations'). (Husserl 1900, p. 361)
52 On the contrary, I differentiate representational content, root relationship, and specific difference from the sensation.
53 This section is not included in the text translated here. –Tr.

malizing concepts discussed above (p.412f [175]). The meaning exhausts itself thus in the private content of the single representation. Only the sensation (that is, 'the raw data of sensation') comes into consideration as 'object', and the representation relates itself to this sensation.

This object is thus not a mysterious logical entity, but rather is just the sensation that is already so well known to us. Since all representations arise from sensations, the possibility of such a relationship exists for all representations. It is only that this relationship is now direct, now indirect.

We then further come to the fact that we build all manner of representations, like representations of 'things', 'objects', and so forth, onto our raw data of sensation, which, for the time being, we are permitted to think of only as grounding sensations in the sense of that *root* relationship. These explanatory representations are partly right and partly wrong, as has already, in part, been discussed, and, in part, remains still to be discussed (compare also Book Three).

I consider, for example, what I have called the 'reducible components' to be the correct explanatory representation, rather than the things in themselves [*Dinge an sich*], or substances, or objects, etc. The naïve person thinks 'things' in very unclear ways, and ascribes to them this or that characteristic, according to his education.[54] The strong desire for, or—expressed differently—the associative push, or at least the associative tendency, to such explanatory representations puts knowledge into the common man just as into the philosophical one. It is based on the certain need, or, more specifically, inclination, to simplify the given, to classify it, and to bring it under laws (compare Section Nine). This need, or inclination, is in the beginning already induced by the struggle for existence [*Dasein*]; later, however, it has countless other motives. [416]

I unify the quite different sensations that I receive from a die, according to my respective perspective, into an overall representation of a die, whose content, however, is very different—now according to my sensations, now according to my auxiliary representations, and now according to my method of association.

The state of affairs would seem, however, to be immediately inverted, or at least very ambiguously expressed, if the '*logicist*' now claims that we 'intend' this 'object', or our representation 'relates itself to' this 'object', which is only subsequently pushed in by us, and is only held as an 'x' in our raw data of sensation. First of all, therefore, no sort of particular logical existence can be arrogated by this 'object'.

---

54 He stands, moreover, as will later be shown, not even as distant as it appears from the method of my epistemology.

The descriptive phenomenological method that is supposed to disclose such objects with evidence is not so safe as one would expect from the almost scientific-seeming harmlessness of the expression. With the 'description' of a representation, etc., by this approach, that is, all sorts of associated representations[55] introduce themselves, which we then, entirely too lightly, regard as elements of the representation to be described. Whenever we, then, later, as is often the case, bind that explanatory representation ('object', 'thing') with a representation, and 'intend' this object, etc., insofar as we have pushed it into the place of the sensation, so, here, it is still not a matter of a primary epistemological relationship, but rather of a secondary associative linking. The root relationship alone is primary.

The relationship between 'meaning' and 'object' is thereby also clarified. Both are, in fact, different, as the *'logicists'* claim, but not in the sense that they claim (Husserl 1900, p. 49). The 'meaning' is the representational *content* (in the sense of my psychology); the 'object' *is supposed to* be only the grounding sensation, which, among other things,[56] supplied the representational content.[57] Instead of this grounding sensation, however, we often (by no means always) push in one of those explanatory representations ['object', 'thing', etc.] discussed above.

---

[55] Strictly understood, descriptions of representations, judgments and so forth, are absolutely not possible.

[56] They also, that is, confer their emotional tone *directly* onto the representation, not only onto the representational content.

[57] In the content (compare, for example, Husserl 1900, p. 38 and 52), Husserl distinguishes further, aside from the object, also the content as 'intended sense' (which is equal to the meaning purely and simply) and the content as 'fulfilled sense'. I cannot assent even to this distinction. Whenever I have a simple representation, the intended and fulfilled senses coincide. If the representation is composite, the contents of the partial representations blend. This blending is no simple addition, but rather, the sum of physiological partial stimulations is one, up-to-a-certain-degree unified (similar to how it is with sound), physical collective process (compare this work, p. 284)—simply the content of the composite representation, its meaning, Husserl's 'signifying' or 'intended sense' (assigned to the individual case). Through association, I can now subsequently reproduce individually the participating partial representations, and thereby produce the 'fulfilled sense'. Whenever I think 'flower', a psychic process occurs, which, in the first place, is extremely indistinct, just as that up-to-a-certain-degree unified collective process; only if I am somehow compelled to particularize the content of this concept, do single 'fulfilled' partial representations emerge—representations of kinds of flowers and individual flowers, parts of flowers, etc.

Neither the 'specific' nor the 'universal objects' of the logists are any more allowable than are their individual 'objects'.⁵⁸ [417] The atemporal universal objects of Husserl are nothing other than universalized explanatory representations, which are formed from the single individuals, and more or less approximate the reducible components and their characteristics and relationships (Husserl 1900, p. 123). Outside of the de-individualised reducible components and beyond the individual representations, they have no 'sense'.⁵⁹

In my opinion, the main root of all logistic error lies both in the uncritical assumption of intentions and intentional objects (by analogy to the word meanings and pictorial presentations and in the just as uncritical distinguishing of sensations as acts or experiences [*Erlebnissen*] from contents or 'phenomenal determinations'. There is, likewise, an uncritical acceptance of popular or conventional distinctions.

From the '*logistic*' teaching about objects is also missing, then, the teaching about the 'representing objectification' that is supposed to allow us to form representations from representations, to form representations from representations of representations, and so forth (Husserl 1900, p. 452 and 543).⁶⁰

By contrast, I claim that, certainly, in the sense of that root relationship, we form representations of sensations, but that representations of these representations are a fiction.⁶¹ We can form such combinations formally in words, but we cannot realize them, i.e., we cannot bring them forth in representations. *When I speak of the representation of representation 'V' [Vorstellung] , this is just the rep-*

---

58 Husserl conceives the meanings as "ideal unities, thus species" (Husserl 1900, p. 92) and at the same time as "a class of concepts" in the sense of general objects (p.101). Compare also p. 110 ff. About p.113, I should remark that the likeness is completely indefinable, and the species concept is grounded only upon the likeness.

59 Husserl's work shows very clearly and directly the insurmountable difficulties to which the entire '*logistic*' teaching leads. Through the thoroughness and conscientiousness of the author, he himself takes these difficulties into consideration (in particular from p. 403 on). It thereby admits of no doubt for the unbiased reader that his discussion has lost itself in a confused tangle of concepts, out of which the author himself is no longer able to lead us. And the last reason for this miscarriage? Only the untenable teaching about the objects. Ultimately, we would then have to resolve ourselves even to the assumption of 'objects of higher levels' (categorial or ideal objects), that are accessible only to an obviously transcendental perception. (Husserl 1900, p. 617 and 615)

60 The example of the painting, which Husserl gives, is not applicable, because here the continuous reference is given to sensations, not to representations.

61 With them, the confusion conjectured by Husserl (p. 453 and 456) does not come at all into question. –Incidentally, I can also not recognize the homogeneity of modification (Husserl 1900, p. 448).

resentation 'V' without its root relationship. The same holds for judgments. Representations of judgments are a fiction.

I can, to be sure, certainly say: 'The claim that Mars is inhabited has already regularly been made,' and the state of affairs is certainly not the subject of this statement, but rather the claim, i.e., the judgment. It is in no way proven with that, however, that we must form a representation of the judgment, or that we must objectify the judgment in mysterious ways. This representation of judgment 'U' [*Urteil*] is, rather, nothing other than simply this judgment 'U', excluding its root relationship, which grounds itself on the root relationships of the representations unified in the judgment.

[418] It is important to note that everything said holds just as much for *composite* representations (compare Husserl 1900, p. 459f.). These also have their 'object' exclusively in the accompanying grounding sensations. One must not, however, even here, mistake the representational content for the grounding sensations.

Let 'V' be a composite (complex) representation; let v_1, v_2, and v_3 be its component representations; and let e_1, e_2 and e_3 be the grounding sensations [*Empfindungen*] belonging to the latter. There is then given directly also an $E = e_1 + e_2 + e_3$, so that 'V' stands in root relationship to an actually occurring 'E'; in the next moment, however, such an 'E' has never occurred, so that 'V' has the character of a fantasy representation.

It is enough, since the consideration is completely analogous, to here discuss only one of these two cases, e.g., the first. The content[62] of representation 'V', which I shall denote with 'I' [*Inhalt*], is, in this first case, naturally not approximately = $v_1 + v_2 + v_3$; just as little is 'I' approximately = $i_1 + i_2 + i_3$ (where i_1, i_2, and i_3 denote the relevant contents of partial representations). Such a simple addition never becomes possible.

Should one use a sign, only a universal sign, like '#' (compare p. 19),[63] could be considered—naturally in the quite specific sense corresponding to the quite specific blending of the contents.[64] Furthermore, even the following are not approximately equal: $i_1 = e_1$, $i_2 = e_2$, $i_3 = e_3$, but rather the sensation characteristics go over into the representational content in a specific way, neither describable nor definable, but rather only experienceable,[65] and therefore, only to be met

---

62 Obviously in the pure empirical-psychological sense (corresponding somewhat to Husserl's "descriptive content," compare Husserl 1900, p. 470).
63 Ziehen articulates how he intends this sign, #, on his p.19 [163]. He takes it to be an unspecified combinatorial function of thinking. –Tr.
64 Even above, in the formula $E = e_1 + e_2 + e_3$, the sign # is more correct for the majority of cases.
65 See also, Ziehen, Bk.1, Ch.1, Sec.3, p.5 [157]. –Tr.

through experience. $I = i_1 \# i_2 \# i_3$, therefore, coincides in no way with 'E', the 'object' of the representation (if one absolutely must use this misleading expression).

A *fourth* error of the *'logicistic'* author concerns the meaning of the so-called *logical laws*. According to my understanding, the latter have a merely technical meaning for epistemology. They neither have the meaning of epistemological propositions, nor do such arise from their presence.

The so-called 'Principle of Identity' (*Principum identitas*), $a = a$, is often held up as the supreme logical law. That this, taken literally, is empty of content, is now probably generally acknowledged. Only if the 'a' on the right and the 'a' on the left side do not have exactly the same sense does the proposition receive any content at all. Such a difference of sense is then, also, in manifold ways, read into both a's.[66]

Now, obviously, that metaphysical explication and thus, the claim of an identity of being, is quite illegitimate in the face of the fact of changes. An unchanging being, in the sense of the Eleatics or of Plato (an ἀεὶ κατὰ ταὐτὰ ὄν), belongs to mythology.

One can, therefore, merely think about the self-samenesses, as we earlier discussed them, and the substance concept hanging together with them, and, in this sense, claim the Principle of Identity for the reducible components. According, then, to the concept of self-sameness, [419] the right and left 'a' would then be differentiated in temporal, locational, and associational ways, (respectively, temporally, locationally, and associationally), and the agreement would simply be claimed despite this difference.

To what extent such a claim applies is discussed at length in Section 62. According to the discussion there, such a self-sameness is not, in any case, intended with the Principle of Identity. Still less can one attribute to it any kind of agreement between 'thinking' and 'being' (*Sein*) (compare Schleiermacher 1903, Sec. 112). Even if one wanted to concede such a 'being' alongside thinking, the Principle of Identity remains nonetheless, with this apprehension, an unrealizable *desideratum*—the highest proposition of logic a mere wish.[67]

---

[66] In addition, I remember that the Identity principle was originally *metaphysically* conceived (from Parmenides up to the students of Wolff) and that only since Kant did the logical conception appear in the foreground. To be sure, the latter also showed itself now and then in older times (for example, even with Aristotle in particular places, e.g., *Metaphysica* 1051).

[67] Naturally, one may not let himself be misled through the fact that mathematics occasionally writes:

$$\frac{\begin{array}{c} a + b = c + b \\ b = b \end{array}}{a = c}$$

There remains, therefore, only a logical interpretation. This, if one abstains from 'logicistic' fantasies, can only consist in the fact that one understands with 'a' the concept that belongs to some sensation complexes and compares with this concept the a's that appear to the same individual, i.e., by the same v- system,[68] at different times, and to different individuals, in relationship to the same sensation complex. As discussed on p. 412 [175–176], these are subject to manifold variations, and therefore differentiated among themselves.

Through thedefinition of normalizing concepts (compare p. 412ff [175]), we try to balance out these differences. To these normalizing concepts we ascribe hypothetical equality, despite temporal and individual differences, and we articulate this hypothetical constancy through the formula $a = a$. Even with this understanding, a *desideratum* articulates itself, but at least a kind that can be fulfilled by a substantial approximation.

But, in any case, it is a matter of an imperative rule, that is, a *norm*, not some governing law of thinking. The principle supplies no material for epistemology, but rather, a, nonetheless indispensable technical directive.

The *remaining* so-called fundamental laws of logic[69] come together only through the introduction of *negation*. This introduction proffers one of the most interesting problems of psychology and logic. Countless times, it has been claimed that negation is a quite primary, *a priori* function of our intellect, capable of no derivation or explanation.

I claim, on the contrary, that it originates completely secondarily out of the categorial function, i.e., the identity/non-identity function. We see an 'a', a 'red', for example, and beside it a 'b', a 'green', for example, a 'c', a 'd', and so forth, then a second and third 'a', and so forth. The categorial function allows us to recognize the identity of all these a's, just as also their difference from the b, c, d, and so forth. Just as we gather together the identical a's, so we gather to-

---

Here b = b absolutely does not mean the identity principle, but rather means that on both sides of the first equation, the same process, namely, subtraction from *b*, is undertaken. The justification of this process and, with that, of the inference, a = c, lies likewise, not in the identity principle as such, but rather in the categorial function.

68 A *v*-system is a *v*-complex that is both spatially coordinated and linked through multidirectional pathways in its elements. To a single *v*-system belong all the *v*- and *υ*-elements that somehow, directly or indirectly, i.e., through the mediation of other *v*-, or, as the case may be, *υ*-elements, are linked with each other. On this prevailing linkage is based the apparent unity of single I's. See Ziehen, p.452 [207–208] –Tr.

69 I here pass over the so-called 'Principle of Consistency' (*Principium convenientiae*)—'an 'a' which is *b*, is *b* '. It arises from the Principle of Identity (*Principium identitatis*), in which the partial is substituted in the place of total identity. It is thus that the = sign, that is, the copula connection, is also introduced for this partial identity.

gether the non-identical b, c, d, [420] and so forth. Thus, we place opposite to the 'a' a 'not-a'—quite in the sense of the predicate of the so-called 'infinite judgment'.[70] It suffices for this that 'a', for some reason—e.g., because of its more frequent occurrence—excites our attention more than the b, c, d, and so forth.[71]

One surely would also not object that the categorial function, as the identity/non-identity function, already involves negation. This function only involves negation insofar as it includes negation as a special case. The identity/<u>non</u>-identity function is more than negation.

Moreover, this negation, which originally restricted itself to concepts, was transferred to propositions, so that negative judgments came about. Even here, the meaning of the identity/non-identity function remains clearly recognizable.

Through this introduction of negation, further general logical laws reveal themselves: in particular, the principle of contradiction (*Principium contradictionis*) ("it is not possible, that a = non-a"), the principle of contraries ("it is not possible, that at the same time[72] a = b and a = non-b"), and the principle of excluded middle ("one of the two propositions, a = b and a = non-b, must be cor-

---

[70] It would naturally be very interesting in this connection to determine whether in the development of languages the privative words still appear before the sentence negations. Unfortunately, I have been able to obtain no credible information about this. In any case νη (e.g., in νηκερδής) is a very old prefix. It is likewise very interesting that the negative prefix (which contains the same nasal sound) ἀνα (then ἀ)—e.g., in ἀνάεδνος and in the Zend form *ana-zàtha*—is probably identical with the pronominal stem *an* (ἀνα above) (compare Curtius 1879, p. 306 and 317). Perhaps the relationship of ἀνα with the negation and of κατα with the positing κατάφασις (affirmation) is understandable if one reflects that, for the residents of the plains (*Ebene*) and of the coast (*Küste*), mountain (*Berg*) and sea (*Meer*) are remote (I am thinking here about ἀνάπλους in opposition to κατάπλους). In this way, ἀνα coincides with ἀπο, whose relationship to negation is understandable without adding anything further ('remote' = 'not here', compare ἀπόφασις negation). Certainly one must presume with this that language development, especially the Greek language development, was predominantly carried out by coast- and plains-dwellers and did not originate with mountain-dwellers. The French *oc* (= *hoc*) and *oïl* (=*hoc illud*) also contain an indication about proximity as affirmation. Incidentally, affective interjections also appear to have cooperated in the development of affirmative and negative particles. So the 'n' in the negating words of almost all languages could also be construed as a nasal interjection that articulates the emotional state of doubt (in regard to this, see Tylor 1873, p. 193)

[71] I do not therefore agree with Husserl, who, exactly contrary to that, deduces agreement and conflict from "fulfillment and disappointment," and does not understand disappointment as mere privation of fulfillment. (Husserl 1900, p. 514, 519, 584).

[72] In actuality, it should be said "at the same time and in the same place", since 'a' is extended, and, as a consequence, can fall into parts.

rect ").⁷³ All these principles mean only that the identity/non-identity function is an unambiguous function, that its judgment can admittedly be sometimes doubtful between identical and non-identical, but that it can never, for the same individual (for the same spatially and temporally specified raw data), in reference to the same thing, be anything other than *identity* **and** *non-identity*.

No further explanation for this characteristic of the categorial function can be demanded. It is a matter of ultimate fact. The alleged logical laws can, it turns out, be traced back, without further ado, to this ultimate fact.

[421] The raw data of sensation, or, as the case may be, their reducible components, are among themselves partially identical, partially non-identical. Under the influence of this characteristic of the reducible components, the v-systems have so developed that the categorial function (the identity/non-identity function) has also appeared among the parallel functions.⁷⁴

With its appearance, however, the just mentioned logical principles were given. They are, in fact, only verbal explications and variations of the same thing. They are, therefore, in contrast to the claims of most logicians, dependent upon our intellectual organization. (Husserl 1900, p. 668)

These logical laws are completely different from the mathematical laws and even from the principles of the so-called 'doctrine of the manifold', ⁷⁵ with which the logicians would gladly fill the empty coffers of pure logic. Underlying the *geometrical* principles is the entire wealth of the spatial manifold, as it is given to us in the raw data of sensation, and, thanks to determinate characteristics of locality (compare Section 27),⁷⁶ can still be augmented in fantasy almost without limit.

The arithmetical principles, in the older, narrower sense, are, to be sure, dependent upon a more limited empirical material. Accordingly, the number of principles is also very much more limited. They likewise differentiate themselves quite determinately from the logical laws, insofar as they do not take as a basis entirely indeterminate quantities like 'all', 'some', and so forth, but rather, definite numerical quantities, and thus, once more, determinate empirical data.⁷⁷

---

73 Strictly taken, it must be added: "whenever they are supposed to hold at the same time and for the same place".
74 Parallel functions are functions that do not follow scientific natural laws, but rather depend on the nervous system. See Bk.1, Ch.2, Sec.9 and 12. –Tr.
75 I understand this in the universal sense, so that 'number theory' and 'the theory of linear extension' are contained in it. (Compare Grassman 1844, p. 21 ff.)
76 This section is not included in this translation. –Tr.
77 Or at least determinately *thought*, like x, y. Whenever the mathematician speaks of x, it is true, he leaves x unspecified. In general, however, he does mean by this that x can mean some-

Ultimately, the doctrine of the manifold entirely grounds the concept of 'quantity' [*Quantum*] in the most general sense, and, indeed, this doctrine considers the concept of 'quantity' only in its relations, without any backwards glance at the content. The doctrine of the manifold certainly thereby very apparently approximates itself to that so-called pure logic, but it does this only apparently. It can, namely, determinately designate and deductively develop the functional dependency of these *quantities*, since it is not entirely universal, like the pure logic *concepts* and their connections, but, rather, somehow involves measurable or, thought-to-be-measurable, *quantities* (in the widest sense). But this concept of function in its relationship to *quantity* is absent from logic.[78] Moreover, mathematics always presumes the *continuity* of its functions,[79] whereas *continuity* is consistently lacking for the logical concepts.

One could perhaps believe that still, at least in the so-called 'arbitrary' functions of mathematics, [422] the backing would be brought about with formal logic, insofar as the function, $f(x, y, z...) = 0$, establishes merely a reciprocal dependency of several variables, without legitimate quantitative coherence. I could never concede this. To the degree that mathematics has really accomplished synthesized principles for such arbitrary functions, it has been obliged to somehow foist upon the relevant functions nonetheless quantitative, legitimate and continuous relationships.

---

thing like 'some' or 'all', but rather only that it is *unspecified* only insofar as it is *unknown*, i.e., that it can have infinitely many values (in the sense of the *sejunktiven* possibilities (p. 367), depending upon which of the *quantities* standing in relation to him have been selected. This *sejunktive indeterminateness*, which is thus actually a determinateness depending upon laws, ought naturally not be confused with the indeterminateness discussed in the text. [This term, *sejunktive*, is derived from the psychology term, 'sejunction hypothesis'. It stems from the Latin noun *seiunctio*, a term that means 'divorce', 'separation'. The term was introduced by Carl Wernicke, a German neurologist, in his book *Grundriss der Psychiatrie* (1900). According to J.D. Blom, the term 'sejunction' was used to "denote an intracerebral mechanism by means of which regular associative processes are blocked and then shunted into an aberrant direction. In conformity with the 'dissociation model' of hallucinatory experience as formulated by the German hallucinations researcher Edmund Parish (*Hallucinations and Illusions: A Study of the Fallacies of Perception*), Wernicke's sejunction hypothesis postulates that the majority of hallucinatory phenomena arise from aberrant activation of the sensory cortex's projection fields, in the absence of a matching object or stimulus in the outside world" (*Dictionary of Hallucinations*. J.D. Blom. 2010 (http:\\hallucinations.enacademic.com/1700/sejunction_hypothesis) 5 June 2014). –Tr.]

78 In a similar sense, Wundt says "In the logical relationship, therefore, the concept of function can be considered as that reconfiguration which the concept of logical dependency must undergo in its application to the universal concept of quantity" (Wundt 1894, p. 201)

79 Number theory only constitutes an apparent exception, as Wundt has convincingly proven.

There thus remains even here a boundary line, on the other side of which stands formal logic. The *'logicist'*, who always promises us a pure logic in the sense of the doctrine of the manifold, a pure logic which is supposed to contain more than the old logic, ought to share with us at least a few such new laws that are not of a quantitative nature. But we are still fruitlessly waiting.

Of course, the logician may desire to lay claim to the doctrine of those 'arbitrary' functions for logic; he would then, however, annex a region of mathematics which must remain essentially different from the realm of logic.

With all recognition of the use to which the individual *'logicistic'* inquiries have been used for the sharp differentiation of concepts and terms, I must nonetheless still hold the basic standpoint of *'logicism'* to be mistaken. [...]

Chapter Three: The 'I' (*Das Ich*)

Section 102: *The Hypothesis of a Primary 'I'*

[439] The consideration of the raw data of representation would be settled by the epistemological discussion of representations, judgments and conclusions in the two previous chapters,[80] [440] if two representations in the history of philosophy, and even specifically in the history of epistemology, had not demanded and received, probably even until today, a dominant status. This status contrasts glaringly with the almost republican parity of representations that I have taken until now as the basis of the inquiry. The two representations I mean are the representations of 'thing' and of 'I'. Both now require a special inquiry.

The representation of 'thing', and its variant, the representation of 'object', has, however, already been so thoroughly discussed in the previous sections that it needs no further investigation. It is otherwise with the representation of 'I'. In Section 21,[81] the consideration of the representation of 'I', or the representation of 'subject', as part of the given fundamental facts of the matter of the raw data of sensation, was only curtly dismissed.

Now, we must determine how this representation of 'I', which still actually occupies a special status among the raw data of representation, emerges, what it means, and which role it plays in epistemology. An opportunity will thereby also be found to test once more, according to all sides, the arguments in favor of a *primary* 'I'. Furthermore, we will discuss how far, and in which sense, I's

---

80 These chapters are not included in this translation. –Tr.
81 This section is not included in this translation. –Tr.

—and therefore, 'fellow I's' [*Mit-Ich's*]—are to be also taken for the transgressive raw data of sensation, which arose out of the discussion of Section 65.[82]

The first task that arises after these preliminary remarks is to discover the origin of the representation of 'I'. The *first* view that confronts us in undertaking this task supposes that the representation of 'I' flows from sensations, as does every other representation, but from a quite unique sensation, essentially different from the remaining sensations. This 'I-sensation' then gets attributed to the 'inner' sense, thus to the same, quite hypothetical, faculty of the soul that already had been tasked with the 'perception' of the representations, the sensations, etc.

Now, since this inner sense is not somehow authenticated through any single fact, and even lacks every analogy with the outer senses, which are so well known to us, so the first view would be more honest if it relinquished the semblance (lying in the word 'sense') of such an analogy, and instead, disdaining all analogies, attributed the cognizance of the 'I' to an entirely new function, standing alone, which function has now been charged with a wide variety of names.

With this, the first view passes into the *second*, which claims[83] that we recognize the 'I' through an intellectual contemplation [*Anschauung*], intuition, or the like. Naturally, 'inner evidence', [441] 'self-certainty', or a similar self-authentication is attributed to this intuition, etc. With this, people even believe that they have established the 'fundamental fact' of psychology and epistemology. Naturally, the subject of this intuition is again the same 'pure I'. A doubtful x thus

---

82 See, Ziehen, Book I, Ch. 8, Sec. 65, pgs. 278–9 (not including in this translation); By 'transgressive' here, Ziehen means that the classifying the raw data of sensation as an 'I' or an 'accompanying I' oversteps in its representation the boundaries of what is actually given. He contrasts this with 'transcendent' classifications, which introduce representations that are not derived from what is actually given. A 'transgressive' classification, on the other hand, still always derives its representations exclusively from what is actually given. –Tr.

83 One finds examples for this view everywhere in the history of philosophy. In Section 21, I mentioned Fichte and Schuppe. It is also enunciated very clearly in Natorp's *Einleitung in die Psychologie nach kritischer Methode* (1888, p. 11) Besides, the formula of the Cartesian '*cogito, ergo sum*' is already only another expression for the second view. With the '*cogitare*', which, in itself comprises, besides the '*intelligere*', also the '*dubitare, affirmare, negare, velle, nolle, imaginari* and *sentire*,' is bound the distinct and clear '*cognoscere*' of the 'I'. There is no talk of a justification. Descartes invoked only the distinct and clear thinking (*cognoscere*). He says literally, "At last I have discovered it—thought; this alone is inseparable from me. I am, I exist—that is certain." (Descartes 1996, p. 18)

beholds a doubtful *x*. This is what this self-perception, or this self-cognizance, amounts to.⁸⁴

I could only think of *one* possible genuine authentication for such a primary 'I-intuition': the consensus of all sensing and representing individuals in the establishing of such an intuition.⁸⁵ Perhaps one could then disregard the inadequacies of all analogies and simply accept the fact. But such a consensus by no means exists, as I already established on p. 50.⁸⁶ In fact, it seems to me there are just as many who lack such an 'I-intuition'.⁸⁷

---

84 I also assign Schopenhauer's teaching to this second view, however much he himself elsewhere mocks related views. He says explicitly: "…in self-awareness, the 'I' is not absolutely simple, but rather consists of a cognizing, the intellect, and a cognized, the will: the former is not cognized, and the latter is not cognizing, even though both merge in the awareness of *one* 'I'." (Schopenhauer 1891, vol. 2 p. 228; compare also p. 293 and vol. 3, p. 161)

85 This sentence is quoted by Husserl in *Ideas* (Husserl 2014, p. 151–152). The footnote in its entirety cited in the translator's footnote on p. 177–178 of this volume. Here, I include the paragraphs from Husserl's text that immediately precede (and include) this footnote, in the hopes that this will help contextualize Husserl's concerns. The text in question occurs in Section 79, 'Critical excursus: phenomenology and the difficulties of 'self-observation'": "At the same time this entails that the reflection is not entangled in any antinomy-like conflict with the ideal of perfect knowledge. Every kind of being—we have already had to emphasize this many times—essentially has *its* manners of givenness and, together with them, its manners of knowing it methodologically. To treat essential peculiarities of these manners as deficiencies, to attribute them to the kind of contingent, factual deficiency of 'our human' knowledge, is absurd. A different question, however (albeit one that likewise must be weighed in terms of essential insights), is the question of the possible 'scope' of the knowledge in question, thus the question of how to guard against assertions that go beyond what is in each case actually given and needs to be grasped eidetically. Yet another question is the question of the *empirical* methods, namely, how we human beings, perhaps as psychologists, have to proceed under the given psychophysical circumstances in order to lend our human knowledge the highest possible dignity.

It should be stressed, moreover, that our repeated recourse to insight (evidence or, better, Intuition) here as everywhere is not a phrase but instead denotes, in the sense of the introductory section, the path back to what is ultimate in all knowledge, just as is the case in talk of insight with respect to the most primitive logical and arithmetical axioms. [Husserl's footnote is placed here.] Yet whoever has learned to grasp with discerning insight what is given in the sphere of consciousness will only be able to read with astonishment such propositions as the one already cited above: 'One cannot make any conjectures of how one comes to knowledge of immediately experiencing [anything].' The only thing to take from this is how alien to modern psychology the immanent essential analysis still is, although it forms the only possible method for securing the concepts that have to function in every immanent psychological description as the determining description" (Husserl 2014 p. 151–152). –Tr.

86 This page is not included in this translation. –Tr.

87 So professes Husserl, for example, who most certainly cannot be counted an empiricist: "Now, I must admittedly confess that I am utterly unable to find this primitive 'I' as the neces-

Now, admittedly, the 'I'-theorists claim for such cases that this lack is only apparent.[88] They repeat again and again: you *must* notice it. This is something like the hypnotist insisting: you must sleep. Occasionally, they have success with this, but they regularly do not. Where, then, does the consensus abide? In this situation, a single negative instance proves much more than all positive instances. These may be based on easily understandable conflations (see below). But how shall the lack of such an intuition be explained?

One variant of the second view speaks of 'I'-feeling instead of 'I'-intuition. I consider this move not quite honest, since the word 'feeling' once again feigns all kinds of analogies that do not actually exist. Also, the indeterminacy and ambiguity of the expression 'feeling' make it easy for the uncritical mind to then identify as 'primary 'I'-feeling' any indeterminate sensations and representations that properly belong to the secondary 'I'-representation. Finally, we must consider that the 'I'-representation, which is secondary and derivative, is marked by strong emotional tones (in the original sense). This is why a view that speaks of the primary 'I'-*feeling* is so enticing to the layperson. [442]

Exactly this variant thus enjoys particularly great popularity. Critically considered, if 'feeling' is supposed to mean nothing other than a quite unique 'taking note', then this view coincides with the second main view. On the other hand, should the word 'feeling' have one of the meanings that it has elsewhere in psychology, e.g., the meaning of skin- or common-sensations or of emotional tones or affects, so it must then be objected that those probably provide us a representation of our body, rather than of a pure 'I', and thus, that they can absolutely never procure for us any cognizance.

Closely related to the second view is also a *third*, which wants to know absolutely nothing about a cognizing or becoming aware of the 'I', and puts the 'I'

---

sary relationship center." (Husserl 1902, p. 342) It is not quite clear to me what Husserl means by the empirical 'I'.

88 Schelling, who recognizes this non-consensus, has another excuse, and claims that for the recognition of these fundamental facts, a native talent, precisely the gift of inner contemplation, would be required, a talent which only belongs to a few anyway. (Schelling 1978, p. 13) The contradiction is admittedly thereby very comfortably dispatched. Whence, however, does Schelling know that he has the *correct* inner contemplation? Where *is* the 'identification card' of this contemplation? Inasmuch as Schelling teaches besides that the 'I' comes about through the act of self-awareness and consists in it, he approaches the fourth view, which we are about to discuss. (Compare Schelling 1978, p. 42ff.) Also, Schelling differs from most representatives of the second view insofar as the 'I' he means is not individual, but rather, timeless. (Compare to Fichte 1794, p.442, footnote 1.)

down as a fact that is given and that lies beyond all sensing and cognizing.[89] To refute this view, one need merely ask its adherents whence they then know anything at all of this 'I'-fact. They will, then, if they absolutely want to hold onto their view, be forced in some way to give in to one of the other views.

A *fourth* view earns much more consideration. This view derives the 'I'-representation from an *argument*. In its most common form, it runs as follows: In our raw data of sensation or in our raw data of representation[90] or, ultimately, in our association of ideas (judgments, conclusions), facts are given which require the assumption of a primary 'I'. Here is thus renounced a primary immediate cognition of the 'I'. But it *is* nevertheless claimed that the mediately cognized 'I' is, as opposed to the sensations and representations, primary. The 'I'-representation is supposed to be secondary; the 'I' itself primary.

The *'I'-testifying facts*, which the fourth view claims, are quite numerous. They all, however, allow themselves to be reduced to two main [groups of] facts: specifically, first, those which allegedly make necessary the assumption of something *permanent*, and second, those which allegedly force the assumption of a *unity*. One thus proceeds either from [the assumption of] the thorough-going changeability or from the thorough-going local diversity and multiplicity (*diversitas*) of the raw data of sensation, and then sets against these the alleged unchangeability und unity of our representations and judgments. One then claims that this opposition and contradiction in the facts could only be redressed through the acceptance of a permanent, simple 'I'.[91]

It thus becomes a question, first, [443] of proving the claimed facts themselves. There is no doubt about the thorough-going changeability and diversity of the raw data of sensation. But how does it stand with the *unchangeability* and *unity* of our representations and judgments?

---

[89] This view thereby approaches the teaching of Deutinger and others, according to which the recognizing and the recognized coincide in the 'I'. Obviously, specifically through this coinciding, every recognition will be annulled. The same holds also of Fichte's teaching, according to which "the 'I' absolutely posits its own being" and thereby also "posits" the "unity of the subjective and objective."

[90] Among these raw data of sensation and of representation are also included those which refer to our action; likewise also the emotional tones that accompany the sensing and representing.

[91] Herbart explained this line of thought, which coincides with his whole epistemological principle very clearly. (Compare Herbart 1851a and b, *Allgemeine Metaphysik*, section 91 and 310 f. and *Psychologie als Wissenschaft*, sections 13, 15, 24 f. and 132 f; Vol. 3, p. 248, Vol. 4, p. 278 f., Vol. 5, p. 225, 229 and 267 f. and Vol. 6, p. 228 f).

First, how does it stand with their alleged unchangeability? I can nowhere discover this. We must, rather, invent[92] for ourselves ideal, never obtainable, normalizing concepts (compare p. 412 [175–176]), in order to provide some degree of stability for our representations. One could thus, at most, think somewhat on the parallel actions (*v-actions*),[93] which are—corresponding to the approximate constancy of the parts of our nervous system participating in this—at least approximately constant. This *approximate* constancy is obviously, however, of no use in establishing an absolute 'I'.

One could perhaps also refer back to the *Kantian* proof for the permanence of substance, and want to try a similar proof for the permanent 'I'.[94] Even if we grant the conclusiveness of the Kantian argumentation, however, the Kantian proof itself demonstrates that the allegedly proven permanence does not absolutely have to be an 'I', but rather, can equally be located in the appearances of the outer sense.

At first glance, the *unity* of concepts and judgments seems obvious. Every universal concept, as it is said and has been said, gathers different things in a single unity. The same holds for every universal judgment. People want to go still further even and claim that each representation complex (thus the formation of all complex concepts, even if they are individual) already means a unity over against a manifold. All representations of *Koinaden*[95] are, in fact, such unities.

---

92 We do not thus actually form these representations, but rather only fix certain conceptual relations through rules and definitions, and in this way balance out, to a certain degree, the fluctuations of concepts from today to tomorrow with the same individual, as well as from one individual to another. This is like the way a scaffold becomes more stable through the counterbalanced connection of its members (also, we could consider the comparative illustration through astatic double-magnet needles).

93 Parallel actions, also known as *v*-actions, or *v*-changes, indicate those changes of a sensation complex that do not belong to the nervous system, but that are dependent upon the *v*-sensations, e.g., *L, W*. All sensations belonging to the nervous system are ***v-sensations*** (*v-Empfindungen*) or ***v-complexes*** (*v-Komplexe*). So, e.g., in a grouping that involves light, an ice cube, and one's optical apparatus, any changes in the light or the ice-cube would qualify as parallel actions. See Ziehen, Bk.1, Ch.2, Sec.12, p. 26–27 [170–171]. –Tr.

94 Kant himself does not share the fourth view. He much more essentially takes the first view (cf. p. 398; not incl. in this volume). The inner self-perception is for him given in mere apperception: 'I think' (Kant 1998, B 274) In the section of the 'Paralogisms of Pure Reason', Kant treats the inverse question, whether the substance character and the identity of the 'I' follow from the 'I think', and this namely, as is generally known, in a repudiating sense. (Husserl 1900, p. 278 ff.)

95 '*Koinade*' is Ziehen's term for the product of the first step by which we move from sensation to representation. A *Koinade* is the delimitation in both quality and space of the raw data of sensation. A *Koinade* is delimitated by some discontinuity of quality. So, if one were looking across the surface of the moon, one would see, bright surface, bright surface, darkness. The change

People will make the same claim for the secondary individual concept (compare p. 283),[96] which bundles the individual object with all its temporal changes. Quite commonly people will say that the categorial and the synthetic functions,[97] both of which are active in the formation of all these concepts and the corresponding judgments, are unifying functions, i.e., they accomplish unity through their connections.

Unfortunately, however, even this line of reasoning fails. In order to realize its shortcomings, we need only more carefully examine the kind of unity is that appears to be present in these cases. I select as an example a universal concept. This is a unity insofar as, in it, we abstract from individual differences [444] and bundle in it either what is common to all individuals or (*sive*), what is the same for all individuals. The variety does not somehow disappear, but rather it is blended in the sense discussed on page 284.[98] Strictly speaking, our universal concept implies only: n individuals have s constants, i.e., common characteristics, and p-variables, i.e., characteristics that are not common. What we say about identity and unity lies already in the raw data; we extract it from them and need not for our purpose add any further identity or unity to them.

'But the blending!' someone will interject. I answer that: 'does the alloying of two metals somehow mean a unity?' Surely not, and indeed, for this reason: because, in specified ways, both the metals, even in the alloy, are still individually identifiable. The fact that we are again able to isolate the partial representations from the blending of the universal concept also supports this. Even to a chemical bond, no one will ascribe the unity that is ascribed to the 'I', even though here the resolving into the elements only succeeds through particular operations.

Thus, if one could establish analogous psychical [*psychische*] bonds—although, to me, none are known—whose dissection could only succeed through particular operations, so, even with this, no unity would be given for these bonds in the sense that the 'I'-theoreticians use. This unity [ascribed to the 'I'] is without comparison: I contest the claim that any psychical processes whatsoever show the unity under discussion. I find everywhere only connections and blendings, which are again further resolvable and which correspond to analogous connections of the original raw data of sensation.

---

from bright surface to darkness would be the boundary of the *Koinade*. A *Koinade* is a particular kind of representation. See also, Bk.1, Ch.2, Sec.7 and 8, this translation. –Tr.
96 This section is not included in this translation. –Tr.
97 One could also, without difficulty, expand this claim further to the analytic function insofar as this requires a previous synthesis.
98 This page is not included in this translation. –Tr.

One will thus, perhaps, renounce the absolute unity and as a last resort claim that even such a combination and blending, even if it is also resolvable, and even if it also corresponds to the binding of the raw data of sensation, for all that, still implies a unity, and with that, perhaps points to the root relationship of the representation (p. 302 ff)[99] and to the comparison and bundling of what are successive [des Sukzessiven] as particularly demonstrative examples.

I now want to happily concede such a restricted unity and unifying-function, but, as such, it stands in no way in opposition to, or contradiction with, the difference and multiplicity of the raw data of sensation (compare p. 442 [193–194]). Without this contradiction, however, we also lose the claimed necessity of the assumption of a permanent, simple 'I'. The 'I'-testifying facts have thus forfeited their testifying power.

We stand, then, only before the simple fact, which does not warrant any further conclusions, that, through particular parallel processes (more precisely, v-processes), corresponding to the similarities and the bonds of the raw data of sensation, other raw data, particularly the raw data of representation, emerge, which are not always referred only to *one* raw datum of sensation, but rather, frequently to several. Comparisons with brackets, webs, etc., only illustrate this state of affairs in the most crude manner.

The decisive argument against the fourth view lies not in such comparisons, but rather simply in the fact that connection and blending do not involve any unity that stands in contradiction to manifoldness. Furthermore, why should such a restricted unity not exist just as much as universal concepts, universal judgments, etc., appear? We bundle all these unifying acts under the concept of the categorial and synthetic function.

But what entitles us [445] to make one 'I' with a quite nebulous new reality out of this abstract bundling of single acts? The connection of the v-elements (especially of the u-elements)[100] in a v-system,[101] as it serves the brain, suffices to explain the nexus[102] of our universal concepts, i.e., their occasional reciprocal reproduction and unification in the association of ideas. To speak of a 'unity

---

99 These pages are not included in this translation. –Tr.
100 'u-elements' are the elements of judgments (<u>U</u>rteilen). –Tr.
101 A v-system is a v-complex that is both spatially coordinated and linked through multidirectional pathways in its elements. To a single v-system belong all the v- and u-elements that somehow, directly or indirectly, i.e., through the mediation of other v-, or, as the case may be, u-elements, are linked with each other. On this prevailing linkage is based the apparent unity of single I's. See Ziehen, p.452, this translation [207–208]. –Tr.
102 By this, Ziehen means, 'the fact that our universal concepts hang together'; another word to translate this well would be 'coherence'. –Tr.

of consciousness' and to invoke a primary 'I' is just as unnecessary as it is illegitimate. The complete burden of explanation and of proof (*onus explicande et probandi*) weighs on those who introduce into the science such imprecise and groundless concepts, or rather, the mere words for such concepts.

Section 103: *The 'I' Representation Originates Secondarily*

It is common to all the four views just discussed that they consider the 'I', which is supposed to have been cognized through sensation, intuition, argumentation, etc., as a primary, simple, permanent reality [*Reale*], which, above and beyond the raw data of sensation and the raw data of representation, leads a quite peculiar existence.

Against all these views, I now claim that the 'I'-representation only comes about, in multitudinous ways, secondarily and tertiarily, and that the 'I' presented in this 'I'- representation is neither a simple raw datum of sensation, nor a reducible component, and hence also does not possess any distinct reality of content, but rather only sets forth a very composite complex of sensations and sensation relationships, which is bundled into a universal complex concept.

The course of events is thereby, in essence, the following: Among the raw data of sensation, those of my own body play a significant role, due to their *omnipresence*. Whereas all other sensations—clothing, bed, living quarters, neighborhood, etc.—are, at most, relatively constant, the sensations of my body are in every moment plentifully at hand (compare also section 15).[103] Even without a mirror, most parts of my body are given to me again and again as visual sensations.

Tactile skin sensations are never absent, even if they, precisely because of their continuous, roughly uniform presence, only every now and then provide occasion for forming links between representations, i.e., only every now and then arouse my attention. Finally, the so-called kinesthetic sensations, which even in rest position never entirely cease, are quite particularly involved in the sensations of my body (compare p. 109 ff).[104] This omnipresence explains itself very simply by the fact that only my body, with the support of the *v*-elements,[105] is lastingly bonded to my brain.

---

[103] This section is not included in this translation. –Tr.
[104] These pages are not included in this translation. –Tr.
[105] Recall that these indicate the components of one's sensation complexes that depend on one's nervous system. See Ziehen, Ch.2, Sec.9 and Sec.12. –Tr.

Besides the omnipresence, there is still another characteristic of my body that likewise has a special position among the raw data of sensation. Think of a man who, all his life, is shackled to a chain, or his bed, or a machine. Such a man will nevertheless still differentiate his body from the chain, the bed, and the machine. But the visual sensations that he has from the chain, and from his hand, are not, [446] in principle, distinguishable from each other.

By contrast, the tactile sensations *are* essentially distinguishable. If I touch the chain with my right hand, I have only *one* sensation, if I touch my left hand (or another of my body parts) with my right hand, I have a *double* sensation. I have, specifically, both a sensation of the touched left hand in my right hand and also a sensation of the touching right hand in my left hand.[106] This *reciprocal touch sensation*, as I shall call it,[107] designates a raw datum of sensation as belonging to my body.[108] [109] Naturally, an ongoing control of the operation through the visual sense is required. We can supplement the experiences of the reciprocal sensitivity through the further experience that, when complexes that do not belong to my body mutually touch, which phenomena my visual sense helps me articulate, *no* touch-sensation appears for me, generally speaking.[110]

A *third* element[111] that contributes in subordinate ways to the delimitation [*Abgrenzung*] of the sensation complexes of my own body is the conduct of the

---

[106] An exception takes place whenever the respective object, thus, the chain, is in contact, or comes into contact, with two places of my body simultaneously. Such exceptions must simply be excluded through the control of the eyes, i.e., recognized and excluded from use with the formation of the concepts of one's own body.

[107] The same has already long been, at least essentially, recognized. Compare Waitz, *Lehrbuch der Psychologie als Naturwissenschaft* (1849, p. 258).

[108] The inverse of this claim is not always correct. We consider our hair as belonging to our body, although it gives, by careful touching no double sensation, due to its lack of nerve endings, but rather only *one* sensation (specifically the hair in the touching hand). One must only be careful in doing this that the hair is not thereby bent or compressed, since in this case the hair follicle, i.e., the skin wrapped around the hair root, is also irritated. For these further delimitations of our body, the lasting coherence with the body parts in the strict sense, i.e., with the v-supports, is obviously authoritative.

[109] While Husserl is often credited with the 'discovery' of double sensation as the foundation of embodiment, this is here shown to be clearly false. Here Ziehen mentions the same phenomenon, quoting the work of *Waitz* as a precedent. –Tr.

[110] Only by way of exception can a sensation still appear: if, namely, the touching of my self is hereby caused, e.g., through the moving against each other of both the objects.

[111] These are the three elements that allow the demarcation of the particular sensation complex that is my own body. The previous two elements were: 1) the omnipresence of my bodily raw

active *kinesthetic* sensations. Its active character—I say at the outset—becomes cognizable to us once again partly through the control of optical sensations, partly through its peculiar quality.[112] These active kinesthetic sensations[113] come into play whenever it is a question of an exclusive movement of *my own body*, whenever I, thus, e.g., perform a movement of my arm in the air, very often without any tactile skin-sensation, only accompanied by corresponding optical sensations and optical movement representations (compare p. 109 ff).[114] Tactile skin-sensations and, indeed, then, those reciprocal tactile double-sensations are only added by way of an exception whenever I explicitly touch my own body by my movement.

It is otherwise whenever I move *an object*, e.g., throw or shove it. By one such movement of my own body *and* simultaneously of a foreign body, I regularly have tactile sensations besides the optical and active-kinesthetic sensations. [447] To the triad corresponds, thus, the combination of sensation complexes of my own body *and* foreign bodies.

Whenever it is ultimately merely a question of movements of foreign bodies, e.g., other men, animals, clouds, etc., absolutely no active-kinesthetic sensations appear, but rather only optical ones. At most, by way of exception, if the moving foreign body touches me,[115] there are also tactile sensations. The exclusive appearance of *optical* sensations of movements, without active-kinesthetic ones, at most accompanied by tactile sensations, corresponds thus to the appearance of the sensation complex of foreign bodies.

The difference between these three situations becomes more clear in some respects whenever I exclude the optical sensations in some way, e.g., by closing my eyes. The movements of my own body make themselves known to me then *only* through active-kinesthetic sensations (possibly accompanied by reciprocal tactile double-sensations); the movements of foreign bodies moved by my own body, through the combination of tactile and active-kinesthetic sensations, and

---

data of sensation, and 2) the distinguishability by reciprocal tactile sensation of what is my body. See preceding pages, 445–446 [197–199]. –Tr.

112 (Ziehen 1911, p. 61). Among the *passive* kinesthetic sensations. I always comprehend (throughout the following sections), incidentally, the vestibular sensations, but not, however, the mistakenly so-called 'optical movement-sensations'.

113 My presentation of the following facts in the *Leitfaden der physiologischen Psychologie* [See previous note.] (even in the last edition) is not complete. I now also believe that I laid too great a weight on the involvement of the kinesthetic sensations, as such, in the construction of the representation of one's own body.

114 These pages are not included in this translation. –Tr.

115 Whenever the foreign body sets me in motion, kinesthetic sensations are added, but only passive ones.

finally, the exclusive (independent of me) movement of foreign bodies, either not at all or, at most, through tactile sensations.

It is clear that there are, besides the aforementioned, further important indications of the demarcation, for, as it were, the differential diagnosis of one's own body. The fact that therefore the active-kinesthetic sensations already, as such, contain a quite special unambiguous reference to my own body, becomes sufficiently understandable if we consider that the associated stimulus arises *within* our own body through active innervation.[116] And finally, we must consider that, very regularly, the movements of my own body, as they present themselves in my optical and active-kinesthetic sensations, are preceded by corresponding movement- and motive-representations, as whose fulfillment they can, to an extent, be observed to be.

Through the effectiveness of the three enumerated elements—the omnipresence, the reciprocal touch-sensitivity and the particular relationship of the active movements of one's own body to one's kinesthetic sensations and movement representations—the demarcation of a particular sensation complex, that of *my own body*, is thus reached. With this, the *primary 'I'-representation*, i.e., the representation of the primary 'I'-complex, is given.[117] This sensation complex is, furthermore, also exceptional through the fact that strong variations within this complex, such as injuries, hunger, thirst, satiety, are accompanied by strong emotional tones, which are transferred to the primary 'I'-representation.

[448] A further level of my 'I'-representation is characterized through the fact that memory forms of the alterations of my body, thus of my previous bodily experience,[118] are associated with the primary 'I'-representation. Age, name, birth-

---

116 I am also reminded here of the so-called organ sensations (general sensations), which, in this relationship, occupy a similar place and thus also contribute more than negligibly to the representation of our own body. The old teaching of 'the vital sense' or 'inner feeling sense' is partially grounded on this. (Compare, e.g., Drobisch, *Empirische Psychologie nach naturwissenschaftlichen Methoden* (1842, p. 42); [Lindner and] Fröhlich, *Lehrbuch der empirischen Psychologie* (1898, p. 41); M. v. Lenhossek, *Darstellung der menschl Gemüths in seinen Beziehungen zum geistigen und leiblichen Leben*, (1834, p. 83) "From the incitation of the general-feeling and the outer sense follows first and foremost self-consciousness...").

117 Recall that sensation complexes were introduced in Bk.1, Ch.2, Sec.8, when certain characteristics of the raw data of sensations were delimited as *Koinaden*. These sensation complexes are then classified into those that are identical and those that are different. They are delimited by some kind of discontinuity. In this case, the sensations that are exclusive to one's body are grouped together through the effectiveness of the aforementioned three elements, and a representation is formed. –Tr.

118 Fantasy- and speculation-representations of my future experience (my plans) are also regularly involved.

day, and others, as well, also belong here, at least partially. These are joined then by the representations of my bodily relationships, of my earlier and of my current living place, of my surroundings, of my possessions, etc. One can also designate this level as that of the *extended bodily primary* 'I'.

Even more significant is another further development of the 'I'-representation, which refers to my mental property [*Besitzstand*]. Each individual has at his command a certain treasure trove of memory forms and, from these, derives concepts. All these representations have a certain intensity,[119] and many also have a determinate emotional emphasis. The selection, intensity and emotional emphasis of the representations is characteristic for the individual. In particular, a certain number of intensive, strong emotionally-emphasized concepts, that, in part, hang together with personal experiences, specifies the personal individuality.

Out of these dominating representations, I now also gradually form an overall representation. Of course, not in the sense of a representation of a representation. Such representations of representations do not exist. Still less does a self-knowledge in the sense of 'know thyself' (γνῶθι σεαυτόν) come into consideration. It can only be, rather, a question of that combining discussed on p. 436 and 438,[120] which bundles in the sense of a universal representation composed of individual representations, and in the sense of a complex representation composed of partial representations. Also, these can only occur insofar as, on the one hand, the individual representations either have common partial-representations or are similar, and, on the other hand, the partial-representations stand in continuous relationships. Such bundling dominating representational complexes are, e.g., my everyday concerns; my opinions about religions, politics, philosophy, and so forth; my inclinations to certain people (family, friends); certain occupations; certain amusements and more of the like; and, moreover, my most frequent emotional responses (Ziehen 1911, p. 179 ff., 239/109–11 ff., 143–144).

Now, all these representational complexes would be without meaning for my 'I'-representation if they were not present in associative connection, both among themselves, as also with the primary 'I'-representation, thus, with the representation of my bodily 'I'. The *actuality* of such a connection is very easy to demonstrate. One need only once question, in the sense of a psychological experiment,

---

[119] It is here, naturally, primarily a question of the intensity of the latent representations (cf. Ziehen 1911, p. 170/120).

[120] These pages are not included in this translation. –Tr.

fifty people, children and grown-up, educated and uneducated, how they represent their 'I'.¹²¹

To most, even to the educated, their own body first occurs to them, often conjoined with a gestural representation of pointing to the chest or of lowering the head and looking at the chest. Not infrequently, the corresponding gesture is even added. Secondly, the above-stated [449] experience—and relationship—representations (p. 448 [202]) usually join in. Thirdly, then, follow the representations now at issue, of my personality, *and, indeed, in unmistakable connection with the representation of my bodily 'I'*. Whoever has himself performed such experiments in considerable number can have no doubts at all about them.¹²²

The possibility of such a connection on the basis of laws of association is, however, also evident. Precisely the omnipresence, and the frequent appearance of the sensations of one's own body connected with it, favor the realization of extensive simultaneous association with the most diverse representations appearing to me. Naturally, this is particularly true for that so often prominently dominating representational complex that now stands under discussion. Specifically, the kinesthetic sensations and the corresponding gestural representations, which, as above stated, constitute an essential component of the primary 'I'-representation, will also be quite particularly suitable to associatively connect the respective representational complexes with the primary 'I'-representation. This is because they frequently are directly attached to motive representations, among which these dominating representational complexes play the deciding role.¹²³

This *second main level* of the 'I'- representation, which is characterized by the addition of the bundling representation of the dominating complexes of my representational life to the representation of the bodily 'I', I want to describe as *secondary 'I'-representation*. The added representations themselves I describe briefly and concisely as *concretizing representations*.

---

121 Conventionally I ask, e.g., 'on what do you actually think, whenever—?' or 'what occurs to you, whenever you think about your self?'
122 One observes exceptions with philosophically-educated individuals, whose natural 'I'-representation has almost entirely been supplanted by the product of philosophical literary studies or their own philosophical reflections, and they, therefore, answer with some definition.
123 The meaning of the action for the development of the 'I'-representation emerges here clearly. In a unilateral way, Fichte has, as is well known, set the action in the epicenter of the 'I'. The 'I' is supposed to originally discover itself as willing (Fichte 1794, p. 3, 9/93, 97) One finds the consequences of this teaching in Schopenhauer, even if he also disputed the connection of his teaching with that of Fichte. Also, in the metaphysics of Fries, the relationship of the 'I' to action emerges very sharply. (Compare Fries 1824, p. 397)

Even with this second level, the development process of the individual 'I'-representation is still not complete. Even the most naïve and uneducated person instinctively puts forth a quite rudimentary epistemology or metaphysics. He specifically develops, in some form, the representation of a contrast between material and mental [reality].[124] In the most naïve ways, this happens through the fact that material bodies are taken to be the origin of sensations and, by contrast to these, the sensations themselves, even together with the representations, the judgments, and emotional processes are taken to be mental processes.

Through the opposition between 'outer' and 'inner', the uneducated person tries to make this dualism still somewhat clearer. He, moreover, now bundles the mental, or inner, processes once more in the representation 'mind' (somewhat similar to how he bundles material bodies as 'world'). The assignment of these representations [450] to the 'I'-representation now leads to an essential reconfiguration of the latter. Those bundling representations of the dominating complex of my psychic personality, added in the secondary 'I'-representation, must obviously be assigned by the naïve person to his mind. The 'I'-representation now simply consists of the two representations, 'I-body' and 'I-mind'.

With this, however, the relationship of both complexes reconfigures itself somewhat. The most simple observation teaches that my body, to a large extent, carries out its movements on the basis of my sensations, of my representations, and of my thinking. The illusion of 'will' (to be discussed later), and especially of 'free' will, fortifies us in this conviction. The mind emerges, consequently, as the ruler, the body as the subject, in the 'I'-complex. Thus far the naïve further development of the 'I'-representation.[125]

I designate as the *tertiary 'I'-representation* the hereby reached *third* main level of the 'I'-representation, which, in the simplest case, is characterized by the splitting into 'I-mind' and 'I-body'. It is not absent even with the educated or even the most educated. It merely clothes itself, according to education and reflection, in a more or less philosophical and especially, particularly logical, garb. The tertiary 'I'-representation shifts with one's world-view. Every philosophical system puts it together in a different way.[126] Many systems even try to

---

[124] At least the modern person. In antiquity, this contrast was still not distinguished with such acuity. (Compare p.45ff and (not included in this translation) and Ziehen 1912)

[125] I have not somehow constructed this at my desk, but I have, rather, put to use the many answers I have received from uneducated people to the correlated questions.

[126] That many philosophical systems, through fantasy or wrong conclusions, try to reinterpret their actual tertiary 'I'-representation to a primary 'I'-intuition and the like does not need to be proven again here.

reverse the split again in some way (thus, the monistic system), but it emerges in some form despite all these attempts.

I consider only some of the most prevalent among the ways that naïve people think to be varieties of this tertiary 'I'-representation. Many naturalists and physicians, and many lay people who have acquired for themselves scientific knowledge, do not content themselves with the opposition of 'I-body' and 'I-mind', but rather, in addition, construct a special relationship between one part of the 'I-body', namely the brain, and the 'I-mind'. The materialist infers the further monistic claim, that the mental operations of the 'I' are only functions of the brain. The philosopher and the philosophically-trained lay person reinterpret the 'I-mind' as, e.g., the subject of thinking and willing, as the synthetic unity of apperception, etc.

My epistemology likewise knows this third 'I'-representation very well. It avoids, however, as was proven in the first book, the false and content-less opposition between material and mental; instead, it has discovered a fundamental opposition between the reducible components of ξ—complexes,[127] which only presuppose causal changes, and the reducible components of the v-complexes, to which parallel actions also correspond. It uses this latter opposition for its tertiary 'I'-representation.

All my v-complexes, so far as our experience reaches (compare section 54), are located in the reducible component of my body, whereas the ξ-complexes are not connected with my body. Therefore [451] the v-complexes, with their parallel actions, come into a direct relationship to the primary 'I'-representation. For my epistemology, the tertiary 'I'-representation consists almost entirely in the v-com-

---

[127] Sensations can be divided into the ρ-component and the v-component. The former can be brought under natural scientific laws; the latter cannot, but rather depends in regular ways upon the reducible components of particular raw data of sensation, which data we tend to designate as the nervous system. A v-complex, or v-sensation, indicates the raw data of sensation that belongs explicitly to the nervous system. An ξ-complex, or ξ-sensation, on the other hand, indicates the sensation complexes that are not active in the sense of the v-complex. The reducible components of ξ-complexes, thus, are in no way directly dependent upon the nervous system, and thus presuppose only causal changes. The reducible components of the v-complexes, on the other hand, also correspond to parallel changes, which are changes that are exclusively bound to my nervous system. Were I, for example, to lose my sight, the objects that would otherwise provide me with sensations disappear. This is a parallel, rather than a causal, change. The main distinction is between the sensations that belong explicitly to my nervous system and those that do not. So, instead of splitting the 'I'-representation into 'I-body' and 'I-mind', Ziehen discovers that this distinction between sensations that belong to my nervous system and those that do not is already in the data of our sensation, the primary material of epistemology. See Ziehen, Bk.1, Ch.2, Sec.9 and 12. –Tr.

plex, which is both spatially coordinated and linked through multidirectional pathways in its elements; briefly said, it consists in the *v-system*,[128] which is contained in my body, the 'I-body'.

The 'I-mind' has no place in my epistemology; just as little do mental processes, in the narrow sense of something in opposition to material processes. The concept of 'mind' is, rather, an incorrect bundling of my mental processes. The opposition between mental and material processes has proven itself untenable, since only mental processes are given to us. In consequence of the new opposition between ξ-complexes and v-complexes, we find the alleged material [reality], which other systems teach, in the reducible components of ξ-complexes and v-complexes. The alleged mental [reality], however, we find again in the v- and υ-components of the raw data (including, naturally, the differentiating function).[129] The concretizing representations added in the secondary 'I'-representation thus prove themselves as universal concepts for dominating v- and υ-actions (see p. 450 [204–205]).

I must definitely claim, on the basis of all the previous discussions, that, through just such a determination of the tertiary 'I'-representation, is given the sole natural and substantiated delimitation of the tertiary 'I'-representation within the raw data. At the same time, this tertiary 'I'-representation, as it now turns out to be at the bottom of my epistemology, makes both the other 'I'-representations, i.e., the primary and secondary, superfluous, insofar as epistemology is concerned. The delimitation of the 'I-body' is, by contrast with the delimitation of the individual v-systems, of entirely subordinated meaning, and the same holds for the concretizing representations by contrast with the delimitation of the v- and υ-components.[130]

---

128 A v-system is, thus, a v-complex that is both spatially coordinated and linked through multidirectional pathways in its elements. To a single v-system belong all the v- and υ-elements that somehow, directly or indirectly, i.e., through the mediation of other v-, or, as the case may be, υ-elements, are linked with each other. On this prevailing linkage is based the apparent unity of single I's. See Ziehen, p.452, [207–208]. –Tr.

129 Compare also to the concept of individualization, p. 62 [not included in this translation].

130 To summarize: There are three main levels of 'I'-representation. The first main level, the 'primary 'I'-representation, is the demarcation of the particular sensation complex that is one's own body, and it consists of the three elements by which we make this demarcation: 1) the omnipresence of my bodily raw data of sensation; 2) the distinguishability by reciprocal tactile sensation of what is actually my body; and 3) the active kinesthetic sensation that is exclusive to my movements of my own body. The second main level, the secondary 'I'-representation, adds the bundling representation of the dominating complexes of my representational life, e.g., my previous bodily experiences, my age, my home, my mental treasure trove and concepts, my emotional emphases, etc. These, Ziehen calls the 'concretizing' representations. The tertiary 'I'-

A development of the 'I'-representation beyond the tertiary level is not possible. All we can do is bundle the 'I'-representation at all its levels through a convenient *word*. This is the proper name of the person and—universalized—the word 'I'. The *formal conclusion* is thereby reached.

It is perfectly obvious that we also attribute an analogous 'I' and an analogous 'I'-representation to our fellow humans, and—with proportionate restrictions—even to our fellow animals. It was comprehensively discussed in section 65 with what right I equally attribute the nature of v-complexes to certain ξ-complexes that are similar to my body, and change similarly, and are thus designated by me as fellow humans. It is a matter, therefore, of an argument by analogy, which kind of argument is essential to us even in our establishment of the laws of nature.

There it would also be shown that this epistemology escapes solipsism precisely through the rejection of a primary 'I'. Even my own 'I' is no simple, persisting being. Rather, the representation of my 'I' expresses much more a very compiled secondary state of affairs, and comes into being only through a quite complicated, if also, by our arrangements, quite unavoidable, process of association. The deep chasm, which, in other epistemological theories, divides my own [452] 'I' from all 'fellow-I's', is thereby bridged. Both the 'I' and 'fellow-I's' are equally products of a process of association. In the latter case is added only an argument by analogy, which in *this version* is used by us everywhere. The acceptance of 'fellow-I's', in the sense of our now-developed 'I'-representation, thus, in the sense of the v-systems similar to my own, with similar v- and v-actions, is, to repeat the expression of section 65,[131] a *permissible transgressive representation*.

---

representation often manifests itself through the imposition of a rudimentary metaphysics and epistemology that splits the 'I-mind' from the 'I-body'. Ziehen, however, makes his on the basis of a distinction, already present in the raw data of experience, between the v-complexes and the ξ-complexes, between, that is, what belongs to my nervous system, and what is instead governed only by causal laws. He claims that such a tertiary 'I'-representation makes the previous two superfluous by showing that, in the first case, delimiting an 'I-body' is merely subordinate to delimiting the v-system, and, in the second case, delimiting concretizing representations is subordinate to delimiting the v- and v-components. –Tr.

131 See, Ziehen, Book I, Ch. 8, Sec. 65, pgs. 278–9; By 'transgressive' here, Ziehen means that the classifying the raw data of sensation as an 'I' or an 'accompanying I' oversteps in its representation the boundaries of what is actually given. He contrasts this with 'transcendent' classifications, which introduce representations that are not derived from what is actually given. A 'transgressive' classification, on the other hand, still always derives its representations exclusively from what is actually given. –Tr.

Section 104: *The Content of the 'I' Representation. The Unity of the 'I'. Relationship to the v-System and to Individualization.*

With the origin of the 'I'-representation delineated, its *content* is also already characterized. It contains nothing that would not be already known to us from earlier investigations of the raw data of sensation and of representation and of the differentiating functions. The content definitely does not have the central meaning for the construction of our world-view that we so readily attribute to it. As we for a long time erroneously took the earth to be the center of the physical world, so we still readily take, in the philosophical realm, the individual 'I', or the individual I's, to be the center and starting point of all being. For this, *our*, epistemological theory, the 'I' is neither the most central, nor the most certain, nor is it the law-maker, but rather, it is an interesting composite state of affairs that stands midway between the raw data of sensation and of representation.

We can now also briefly formulate the 'I'-representation (including the representation of 'fellow-I's') as the reducible representation of the v-systems, of which each single one consists of a plurality of v-elements and υ-elements diversely linked among themselves,[132] or in other words: the 'I' arises whenever it is reduced to a natural and clearly delimited representation, as such a v-system.

The delimitation of single v-systems, and thereby of single I's, is performed through linking. To *one* v-system belong all v-elements and υ-elements, which somehow, directly or indirectly (i.e., through mediation of other respective v-elements and υ-elements), are linked with each other. The apparent unity of single I's, i.e., of the single v-system,[133] is based on this prevailing linkage. Its apparent invariability and its apparent permanence are based on the relative insignificance of the variations of the single v-elements and υ-elements (except, naturally, for the transitory variations originating through causal stimuli, compare p. 238, footnote 4).[134]

If this now is the content of the 'I'-representation, so the question arises (exactly in the sense of a final objection): 'How does it happen that my 'I' is confined to a spatially and temporally very restricted set of the raw data of sensation and the corresponding raw data of representation, such that we must form trans-

---

[132] It must thereby remain open whether v-systems also occur quite without υ-elements (such as with lower animals, for instance). Furthermore, at least a partial coincidence of the v-elements and υ-elements must at least be recognized as possible. All these are, however, questions that belong more in the realm of physiology and zoology, than in that of epistemology.

[133] Whenever I speak of the '*v-system*', I always include the υ-elements with it. Compare p. 451 [206].

[134] This page is not included in this translation. –Tr.

gressive representations[135] of other raw data of sensation and raw data of representation?'

To this, it can only be answered that, at the bottom of this epistemological theory, [453] this confinement is self-evident. Since the raw data of sensation, and, consequently, also the raw data of representation, of *one v*-system, are dependent on the causal stimuli bringing it about, and since, according to the causal laws, only the causal stimuli of a restricted set of ξ-complexes can bring about *one v*-system, so also *one v*-system can only carry out parallel actions (reflections) on a limited number of ξ-complexes,[136] and, correspondingly, also, only a limited number of raw data of sensation and of representation is given for the single v-system. The *individualization* (compare p. 62 and p. 280)[137] is, as even the name should already express, simply always a restriction.

The further question which one perhaps still would like to connect to this—why my 'I' is bound to *one v*-system—would be, however, entirely inadmissable. Since this 'I' is identical with this v-system, and we only know it, from this system, so the stipulated question has no sense at all. I could just as well ask why a v-system, with all its characteristic v-actions and v-actions is tied to a v-system.

The true meaning of the 'I' for epistemology thus reduces itself to the meaning of the v-system, which, indeed, is a main topic of this entire work.

References:

Aristotle (1837a): *Metaphysica*. In: *Aristotelis opera*. Ed. Immanuel Bekker. Berlin: Königlich-Preußische Akademie der Wissenschaften.
Aristotle (1837b): *Physica*. In: *Aristotelis opera*. Ed. Immanuel Bekker. Berlin: Königlich-Preußische Akademie der Wissenschaften.
Busse, Ludwig (1903): "Rezension von E. Husserl, *Logische Untersuchungen*." In: *Zeitschrift für Psychologie und Physiologie der Sinnesorgane* 33, pp. 153–157.
Curtius, Georg (1879): *Grundzüge der griechischen Etymologie*. Leipzig: Teubner.
Descartes, Rene (1996): *Meditations on First Philosophy*. Trans. and Ed. John Cottingham. Cambridge: Cambridge University Press.
Drobisch, Moritz (1842): *Empirische Psychologie nach naturwissenschaftlichen Methoden*. Leipzig: Voss.
Fichte, Johann (1794): *Grundlage der gesamten Wissenschaftslehre*. Leipzig: Gabler.

---

135 These are representations that go beyond the raw data of sensation, but are still derived exclusively from it. See, Ziehen, Ch.8, Sec.65, this translation. –Tr.
136 We thus have our distinctive, limited points of view. –Tr.
137 These pages are not included in this translation. –Tr.

Fries, Jakob (1824): *System der Metaphysik.* Heidelberg: Winter.
Grassman, Hermann (1844): *Die lineale Ausdehnungslehre ein neuer Zweig der Mathematik.* Leipzig: Wiegand.
Hamilton, William (1861): *The Metaphysics of Sir William Hamilton.* Cambridge: Sever and Francis.
Herbart, Johann (1851a): *Allgemeine Metaphysik nebst den Anfängen der philosophischen Naturlehre.* In: *Sämmtliche Werke.* Leipzig: Leop, Voss.
Herbart, Johann (1851b): *Psychologie als Wissenschaft.* In: *Sämmtliche Werke.* Leipzig: Leop, Voss.
Husserl, Edmund (1900): *Logische Untersuchungen* I. Leipzig: Veit & Co.
Husserl, Edmund (1901): *Logische Untersuchungen* II. Leipzig: Veit & Co
Husserl, Edmund (2014): *Ideas for a Pure Phenomenology and Phenomenological Philosophy: First Book: General Introduction to Pure Phenomenology.* Daniel Dahlstrom (Trans.). Indianapolis/Cambridge: Hackett. Jacobi, Friedrich (1787): *David Hume über den Glauben, oder Idealismus und Realismus. Ein Gespräch.* Breslau: Gottlieb Löwe.
Kant, Immanuel (1998): *Critique of Pure Reason.* Paul Guyer and Allen Wood (Eds.). Cambridge: Cambridge University Press.
von Lenhossék,, Michael (1834): *Darstellung des menschlichen Gemüts in seinen Beziehungen zum geistigen und leiblichen Leben* Vol. 1. Vienna: Gerold.
Lindner, Gustav (1898) *Lehrbuch der empirischen Psychologie als induktiver Wissenschaft.* Revised by Gustav Frölich. Vienna: Gerold.
Martinez Adame, Carmen (2012): "The Parallelogram Law in the Works of d'Alembert and Kant". In: Theoria 75, p. 365–388.
Mill, John Stuart (1865): *An Examination of Sir Hamilton's Philosophy.* London: Longmans, Green, and Co.
Natorp, Paul (1888): *Einleitung in die Psychologie nach kritischer Methode.* Freiburg: Mohr
Schelling, Friedrich (1978): *System of Transcendental Idealism.* Peter Heath (trans.). Charlottesville: University Press of Virginia
Schopenhauer, Arthur (1891a): *Über die vierfache Wurzel des Satzes vom zureichenden Grunde.* In: *Sämtliche Werke in sechs Bänden* Vol. 3. Leipzig: Reclam.
Schopenhauer, Arthur (1891b): *Welt als Wille und Vorstellung.* In: *Sämmtliche Werke in sechs Bänden* Vol. 2. Leipzig: Reclam.
Sigwart, Christoph (1889). *Logik* I. Freiburg: Mohr.
Spencer, Herbert (1881): *Principles of Psychology* Vol. 2. London: Williams and Norgate.
Spinoza, Baruch (1677): *Ethica.*
Tylor, Edward (1873): *Anfänge der Kultur.* Leipzig: Winter.
Waitz, Theodor (1849): *Lehrbuch der Psychologie als Naturwissenschaft.* Braunschweig: Bieweg, Cohn.
Wundt, Wilhelm (1894): *Logik* Vol. 2. Stuttgart: Encke.
Ziehen, Theodor (1901): "Erkenntnistheoretische Auseinandersetzung." In: *Zeitschrift für Psychologie und Physiologie der Sinnesorgane.* Vol. 27, pp. 305–343; 1903 Vol. 33, pp. 91–128; 1906 Vol. 43, pp. 241–267.
Ziehen, Theodor (1907): *Psychophysiologische Erkenntnistheorie.* Jena: Gustav Fischer.
Ziehen, Theodor (1908): "Zur Lehre von der Aufmerksamkeit." In: *Monatsschrift für Psychiatrie and Neurologie* 24, pp.173–178.

Ziehen, Theodor (1911): *Leitfaden der physiologischen Psychologie in 15 Vorlesungen*. Jena: Fischer.

Ziehen, Theodor (1912): *Über die allgemeinen Beziehungen zwischen Gehirn und Seelenleben*. Leipzig: Barth.

Andrea Staiti
August Messer

August Messer (1867–1937) was professor *ordinarius* of philosophy, psychology and pedagogy at the University of Gießen. He began his career as a student of prominent experimental psychologist and philosopher Oswald Külpe in Würzburg. Külpe introduced Messer to the methods and problems of experimental psychology, which he practiced in a non-reductionistic and philosophically informed fashion. The rejection of reductionism and mechanism in psychology motivated Messer's lifelong sympathy for Husserlian phenomenology, which he carefully studied and defended from early on.

Messer's expertise in psychology and his phenomenological inclination are documented in his two major works *Empfindung und Denken* (1908) and *Psychologie* (1914). Külpe's influence on Messer is also reflected in Messer's extensive work on Kant and the theory of knowledge. Like Külpe, Messer defends a version of so-called 'critical realism', that is, a theory of cognition accepting the basic tenets of Kant's transcendental philosophy but rejecting the kind of idealism championed by several Neo-Kantians of his time. Messer's critical realism is presented in his *Einführung in die Erkenntnistheorie* (1909), while his extensive knowledge of Kant is documented in several monographs on various aspects of Kant's thought, including a *Kommentar zu Kants Kritik der reinen Vernunft* (1923) and a *Kommentar zu Kants ethischen und religionsphilosophischen Hauptschriften* (1929). In addition to psychology and the theory of knowledge Messer wrote important essays in pedagogy and a handful of books and articles on philosophical issues in the culture of his time, such as a thought-provoking debate with Jesuit priest Max Pribilla on *Katholisches und modernes Denken* (1924).

The two essays translated in this volume, both entitled "Husserl's Phänomenologie in ihrem Verhältnis zur Psychologie", are particularly relevant in light of Messer's attempt to reconcile Husserl's phenomenology and experimental psychology. The first essay examines Husserl's manifesto "Philosophie als strenge Wissenschaft" and argues that, *pace* Husserl, "insofar as it seeks to clarify psychological concepts with the aid of immanent seeing, phenomenology is psychology, indeed *even the most fundamental part of psychology*" (221). Messer concedes that phenomenology has broader philosophical concerns and cannot be reduced to a fundamental psychological discipline, however, he finds Husserl's forceful rejection of modern experimental psychology unwarranted and lacking sufficient knowledge of the relevant literature. Messer considers the method of eidetic intuition developed in phenomenology a *sine qua non* for a correct understanding of psychical life, rather than a separate project entirely disjointed from psychology. In the second essay Messer turns to *Ideas I*, and while he reasserts the thesis of his first essay, he concedes that Husserl's introduction of the epoché and the discontinuation of the natural attitude do mark a difference between phenomenology and psychology. However, he finds this difference purely of "theoretical significance", since it "fades into the background where the praxis of research is concerned" (251). According to Messer, Husserl's own recognition of a discipline called 'eidetic psychology' partially overlapping with 'phenomenology' in dealing with essential, rather than contingent structures of experience, bears witness to the affinity of intent between Husserl and the best 'descriptive psychology' of his time.

Husserl's draft of a letter to Messer (Husserl 1987, 249–252; incl. in this volume p. 255-259) makes it abundantly clear that he was not prepared to accept Messer's attenuation of the difference between phenomenology and psychology. However, considering Husserl's subsequent re-evaluation of the significance of eidetic psychology as a pedagogical way into transcendental phenomenology, and his lifelong struggle to correctly determine the difference between a psychological and properly phenomenological reduction, it is fair to say that Messer's critique hit upon a central aspect of Husserl's project, and certainly prompted further analyses on the relation between psychology and phenomenology.

References

Husserl, Edmund (1981): "Philosophy as a Rigorous Science." Quentin Lauer (Trans.). In: *Husserl: Shorter Works*. Notre Dame: University of Notre Dame Press, pp. 161–197

Husserl, Edmund (1987): "Entwurf eines Briefes an August Messer." *Husserliana XXV: Aufsätze und Vorträge (1911–1921)*. Thomas Nenon and Hans Rainer Sepp (Eds.). Dordrecht: Martinus Nijhoff, pp. 249–252.

Klamp, Gerhard (1947): "August Messer – Leben und Werk. Ein Nachruf post festum und erste Würdigung." In: *Zeitschrift für philosophische Forschung* 1/2–3, pp. 397–403.

Messer, August (1909): *Einführung in die Erkenntnistheorie*. Leipzig: Dürr'sche Buchhandlung.

Messer, August (1923): *Kommentar zu Kants Kritik der reinen Vernunft*. Stuttgart: Strecker und Schröder.

Messer, August (1929): *Kommentar zu Kants ethischen und religionsphilosophischen Hauptschriften*. Leipzig: Meiner.

Messer, August and Max Pribilla, S.J. (1924): *Katholisches und modernes Denken. Ein Gedankenaustausch über Gotteserkenntnis und Sittlichkeit zwischen August Messer und Max Pribilla*. Stuttgart: Strecker und Schröder.

Translated by Andrea Staiti
August Messer.
Husserl's Phenomenology in Its Relation to Psychology

Husserls Phänomenologie in ihrem Verhältnis zur Psychologie
Archiv für die gesamte Psychologie 22, pp. 117-129 (1912)

[117] In his essay "Philosophy as a Rigorous Science" Husserl subjects experimental psychology to a sharp critique. He fails, however, to support his charges against what he calls "experimental fanatics" with references from the literature. Considering the remarkable breadth of experimental psychological literature and the marked differences between the many scholars involved in experimental psychology, it might appear doubtful at first whether Husserl's quite general remarks are justified.[1] On the other hand, it would be unfair to assume that a scrupulous scholar like Husserl would pass such harsh judgments without compelling reasons. Since it is valuable for a developing scientific discipline to receive substantive criticism honestly and without over-sensitivity (just as it is valuable for the individual who strives to improve their moral character to do so), I want to take the opportunity here to examine what an experimental psychologist can learn from Husserl's criticism. In particular, I want to examine the meaning of Husserl's "phenomenology" for the experimental psychologist.

To begin, Husserl challenges the view that experimental psychology represents the "scientific foundation" of logic, the theory of knowledge, aesthetics, ethics, pedagogy, the human sciences, natural science, and of metaphysics as the general theory of reality (Husserl 1981, p. 171).

[118] In point of fact, empirical psychology (of which experimental psychology counts for us as the most scientifically developed form) is entitled to claim this status with respect to the philological and historical disciplines and with respect to metaphysics. I do not think that Husserl has exposed this claim as unwarranted with regard to these sciences. Things are different, however, with the view that psychology is the foundation of the normative sciences, meaning logic (along with the theory of knowledge), aesthetics, ethics, and pedagogy. It will be difficult to find many supporters of this view among serious psychologists. In

---

[1] It would be easy to show that this is not the case, for instance, by reference to G. Anschütz's informative essay "Über die Methoden der Psychologie" (1911, 414–498).

any case, it is incorrect, as Husserl shows convincingly.² As a science of *facts*, psychology cannot ground the validity of *norms*. From the most comprehensive and exact knowledge of what *is* and *happens*, we cannot draw intrinsically necessary conclusions about what *ought* to be and *ought* to happen.

As regards the relationship of psychologists to the theory of knowledge in particular, Husserl argues as follows (Husserl 1981, p. 171 f.). It is the task of psychology to "explore the psychical scientifically within the psychophysical nexus of nature (the nexus in which, without question, the psychical exists), to determine it in an objectively valid way, to discover the laws according to which it develops and changes, comes into being and disappears. The psychical processes are invariably thought of as belonging to nature, that is, as belonging to human or brute consciousnesses that for their part have an unquestioned and coapprehended connection with human and brute organisms" (Husserl 1981, p. 171–172).³ "[E]very psychological judgment involves the existential positing of physical nature, whether expressly or not" (Husserl 1981, p. 172).⁴ Since this positing of nature in natural science occurs "naively," the scientific attitude of the natural scientist and of the psychologist differs in principle from that of the theorist of knowledge. While natural scientists and psychologists "naively" presuppose a psychophysical reality as given and knowable, the theory of knowledge asks how knowledge based on experience qua consciousness can relate to an object, how processes of consciousness [119] can have objective validity relative to realities existing in themselves, and so forth.

Against this argument, it seems to us doubtful that every psychological judgment does in fact involve the positing of nature and is actually, in this sense, a psychophysical judgment. If this were true, a "pure" psychology that was limited to the determination of conscious experiences would be fundamentally impossible. In what follows, though, we will see that Husserl's own "phenomenology" entails a pure psychology of this kind and that such a pure psychology can therefore be very well developed in its own right. (Naturally, this does not rule out the possibility of *subsequently* inserting conscious processes into the nexus of physical events). In any case, this denial of the possibility of a pure psychology is quite unnecessary in order to prove that psychology cannot be the foundation

---

2 It is appropriate to recall Husserl's thorough critique of "psychologism" in the first volume of his *Logical Investigations* (Husserl 2001).
3 [Translator's note: Messer uses quotation marks, but fails to provide page numbers for this passage. He also does not indicate some minor changes and the omission of two sentences from Husserl's original passage.]
4 [Translator's note: Messer uses quotation marks, but fails to provide page numbers for this passage.]

of the theory of knowledge. For this purpose it suffices to point out that the psychologist (as much as the practitioner of any other specialized discipline) *simply presupposes* the existence and the knowability of his object. The theory of knowledge, on the other hand, asks whether this presupposition is *justified*. For the theory of knowledge, therefore, the specialized sciences, in their entire scope, are themselves problems. These problems obviously cannot be solved on the basis of some specialized discipline.

It is certainly in psychology's best interests to distance itself from all psychologism and thus from an objectively unwarranted extension of its own mode of investigation to problems of a completely different kind. However, psychologism only succeeds in blurring the boundaries between psychology and other disciplines; it does not necessarily discredit psychological inquiry itself. Husserl, on the other hand, believes that he has discovered a fatal flaw within psychological inquiry. He claims that since its beginnings in the eighteenth century empirical psychology has been confused by "the deceptive image of a scientific method modeled on that of the psychochemical method" (Husserl 1981, p. 178). This confusion, he thinks, leads to a "reification of consciousness" (Husserl 1981, p. 178).

To be sure, the temptation to reify consciousness is a serious danger for the psychologist. However, this danger has not gone unnoticed. One thinks for instance of Wundt's energetic fight against the reification of presentations [*Vorstellungen*] in Herbart's psychology. Husserl will find general agreement among psychologists, therefore, when he claims that psychical phenomena are neither appearances of things nor substantial unities standing in a causal nexus [120] but that the psychical, rather, is "lived experience and lived experience seen in reflection, [...] in an absolute flow, as now and already fading away, clearly recognizable as constantly sinking back into a having been." (Husserl 1981, p. 180, translation modified). From Husserl's perspective, the "monadic" unity of consciousness in which everything psychical belongs "in itself has nothing at all to do with nature, with space and time or substantiality and causality" (Husserl 1981, p. 180).[5] However, psychical phenomena, as immediately seen, can be brought into relation with the experienceable things that together constitute "nature."

Husserl identifies a further "ubiquitous fundamental trait" (Husserl 1981, p. 174)[6] of modern exact psychology in the tendency "to set aside any direct

---

5 [Translator's note: Messer uses quotation marks, but fails to provide page numbers for this passage.]
6 [Translator's note: Messer uses quotation marks, but fails to provide page numbers for this passage.]

and pure analysis of consciousness [...] in favor of indirect fixations of all psychological or psychologically relevant facts" (Husserl 1981, p. 174).[7] Modern psychology, he suggests, "passionately combats the method of introspection" (Husserl 1981, p. 174)[8] and expends its energy in trying to overcome the defects of the experimental method by the experimental method itself (Husserl 1981, 303/174).[9]

However, on this point, too, the contrast between Husserl and the modern psychologists is not as sharp as he makes it out to be. Thus, for instance, Anschütz notes that inner perception or self-observation "have maintained their status well into the modern time as a fundamental means for the investigation of the facts of psychical life" in spite of a number of attacks from natural scientifically oriented thinkers (See Anschütz 1911, p. 426 f.; Müller 1911, p. 72 f.). Following a more thorough account of self-observation, Anschütz concludes that self-observation is "the immediate, primary, fundamental, or principal method", and that other methods stand to it as "mediate, secondary, and almost accidental", such that they are only able to "complement, but not to replace self-observation" (Anschütz 1911, p. 427).[10] For the psychologist, the attempt to "set aside" self-observation would indeed mean giving up the main source of his knowledge. But of course, the question of the *extent* to which self-observation requires supplementation and [121] correction from other methods meets with differences of opinion among psychologists.[11] Nonetheless, an excess of critical caution with respect to self-observation would not amount to a methodological error *in principle*. One can agree with Husserl that the psychologist must interpret the statements of test subjects on the basis of his *own* foregoing self-perceptions and that, in like manner, all of the psychophysical facts and regularities garnered from experimentation presuppose an *analysis of consciousness itself*. Only on the basis of such an analysis can these facts and regularities be understood and appraised.

Of course, practitioners of experimental psychology carry out this analysis of consciousness in a completely *insufficient* manner, according to Husserl. They do

---

7 [Translator's note: Messer uses quotation marks, but fails to provide page numbers for this passage.]
8 [Translator's note: Translation modified. Messer uses quotation marks, but fails to provide page numbers for this passage.]
9 [Translator's note: Messer fails to provide quotation marks for this passage.]
10 [Translator's note: Messer uses quotation marks, but fails to provide page numbers for this passage.]
11 It is appropriate to recall here the controversy between Wundt and Bühler about the methods for a psychological investigation of thought, see Psychologische Studien III und Archiv für die gesamte Psychologie IX. (Bühler 1907; Wundt 1907)

not endeavor to attain a "systematic analysis and description of the data that present themselves in the different possible directions of immanent seeing" (Husserl 1981, pp. 303/174)[12]; and when they are compelled by the matter itself to produce such analyses, these analyses are carried out only 'in passing', only with great 'naiveté'. What follows from this is that in posing questions and in formulating results, experimental psychologists operate with "crude class concepts such as perception, imaginative intuition, enunciation, calculation and miscalculation, size appraisal, recognition, expectation, retaining, forgetting, etc." (Husserl 1981, p. 174, translation modified).

Here, though, Husserl may once again be too pessimistic. In particular, he is perhaps overlooking the fact that the "crude class concepts" in question are clarified and enriched in many ways precisely through experimental investigations. On the other hand, it is beyond dispute that Husserl points here to a highly significant, even fundamental, task for psychology, the solution of which still demands much serious work. Husserl himself has taken on this task, approaching it precisely by means of the "phenomenological" method. By coming to grips with this method, and by bringing it to fruition in the way that Husserl intends, psychology stands to profit immensely, in my view. [122] Many misunderstandings still hinder such a development, thus it is necessary above all to resolve them. Thus, *what does Husserl's phenomenology seek to accomplish?*

Husserl characterizes phenomenology as a "systematic science of consciousness that explores the psychic in respect of what is immanent in it," and as the systematic analysis "of the data that present themselves in the different possible directions of immanent seeing" (Husserl 1981, p. 174). He declines, however, to straightforwardly identify phenomenology with "descriptive phenomenology. The reason is that "phenomenological descriptions do not concern experiences or classes of experiences of empirical persons" (See Husserl 1994, p. 251). As a *natural* science of consciousness, psychology must be distinguished from phenomenology, according to Husserl. Both deal with consciousness, but in different "attitudes." Psychology deals with "empirical" consciousness, that is, with experiences belonging to me or to other persons. These experiences are interpreted as "existing within the nexus of nature" (Husserl 1981, p. 174. Translation modified.). The subject matter of phenomenological description is "pure consciousness": "in phenomenological description one views that which, in the strongest of senses, is given: lived experience, just as it is in itself" (Husserl 1994, p. 251). Phenomenological description analyzes, for instance "the lived experiences of

---

12 [Translator's note: Translation modified based on Messer's slight change in wording. Messer uses quotation marks, but fails to provide page numbers for this passage.]

knowing, wherein the origin of the logical ideas lies [...] in removal from all interpretation that goes beyond the immanent [*reell*] content of those lived experiences. And the authentic meaning [*Meinung*] of the logical ideas [...] is brought to evidence" (Husserl 1994, p. 251. Translation modified.).[13] When the phenomenologist "makes use of objectifying expressions, as when he says: '"We find' in direct 'lived experience' this and that" (Husserl 1994, p. 251), these should not be heard as a natural-scientific or metaphysical objectifications. Rather—and here we will supplement Husserl so as to explain what he has in mind—the phenomenologist wants to clarify what is actually meant by psychological expressions such as perception, memory, expectation, supposition, etc. This clarification proceeds by evoking experiences of the corresponding types, or by reconstructing such experiences through memory and immanent contemplation. Subsequently, the object toward which all these kinds of experiences are directed is characterized in terms of [123] the manifold ways in which it is intended – "now clearly, now obscurely, now by presenting or by presentifying, now symbolically or pictorially, now simply, now mediated in though," and so forth (Husserl 1981, p. 173).

From my perspective, it not necessary to separate the phenomenology of consciousness from psychology as carefully as Husserl does. It is true that the phenomenologist is not interested in fixing, analyzing or finally even explaining the determinate experiences of determinate individuals as real occurrences in the nexus of nature; and that the psychologist, on the other hand, can set for himself a task of this kind. But does the psychologist *have* to do so? Is this the only task that naturally belongs to his science? The psychologist strives to achieve *general* cognitions. He wants to grasp regularities from the unfolding stock of psychical experiences. The singular real experience in his own consciousness or in the test subject's consciousness only interests the psychologist as an example, as a singular instance, as something from which a general conclusion can be drawn. The psychologist is not interested in these experiences as *real* events happening with real people, and so does not look to situate them in a determinate place within the greater nexus of natural processes.[14] This tendency characterizes only those who *apply* psychological cognitions, for instance, the historian or the jurist who endeavors to observe determinate psychical processes within determinate people. The fact that a psychologist can occasionally learn something from novelists shows that in his striving toward *general* cognitions

---

13 [Translator's note: Messer uses quotation marks, but fails to provide page numbers for this passage.]

14 Incidentally, this interest is also far removed from the investigator of nature who studies chemical or physical processes.

he has a completely different attitude. Obviously, the psychologist wants to grasp regularities in the psychical occurrences of real people. He does not want to invent or poetize about anything, he wants to cognize reality. But are things essentially different for "phenomenologists"? The concepts that the phenomenologist endeavors to clarify should be applicable to real experiences. Precisely for this reason, the phenomenologist also takes into consideration real experiences with the aim of clarifying them. In so doing, he can abstract from certain issues that are of interest to the psychologist, for instance, the explanation of how experiences come about, individual [124] differences within experiences, the correlation of such differences in multiple classes of experience of the same individual, etc. Most of all, the phenomenologist will abstain from any investigation of the connection of psychical and physical processes. *Thus, Husserl's phenomenology should not be separated from psychology overall, but rather from physiological psychology.* The goal of this separation would be to avoid a naturalistic reification of the psychical. The psychical is not "nature" in the sense of being the bearer of appearances in sensory perception. The psychical is not "objectively" determinable as the substantial unity of real properties that we can grasp and determine over and over again in experience. "[Physics] excludes in principle the phenomenal in order to look for the nature that presents itself in the phenomenal, whereas psychology [wants] precisely to be a science of phenomena themselves" (Husserl 1981, p. 178; cf. Husserl 1981, p. 181).

In this last remark, Husserl professes precisely what we are attempting to show, namely, that insofar as it seeks to clarify psychological concepts with the aid of immanent seeing, phenomenology is psychology, *indeed even the most fundamental part of psychology.* The phenomena have an "essence" that can be grasped in immediate seeing and the concepts through which we describe the phenomena "must permit of being redeemed in an essential intuition" (Husserl 1981, p. 181). In other words, the concepts must prove their validity in an essential intuition. The intuition must contain, as immediately given, what is merely "intended" in the concept. In this way, "the psychical [is made] an object of intuitive investigation from the pure rather than from the psychophysical point of view" (Husserl 1981, p. 181); we carry out "pure" description as opposed to explanatory or physiological description; we do psychology, and to the extent that we clarify our (prescientific) psychological concepts, we deepen and enhance our knowledge of the psychical.

Obviously, one can ask whether immanent seeing really does grasp the "absolute given"[15] "adequately", as [125] Husserl emphasizes (Husserl 1981, p. 181).

---

[15] Presumably, "absolute" has to be interpreted in the sense of immediate given.

His concept of "essential intuition" does not seem to me to necessarily require this. Husserl argues, for instance: "If [...] looking, say, at one perception after another we bring to givenness for ourselves what 'perception' is, perception in itself (this identical character of any number of flowing singular perceptions), then we have intuitively grasped the essence of perception" (Husserl 1981, p. 181. Translation modified.). However, to the extent that, in so doing, we connect the concept with corresponding intuitions, we can indeed "bring to full clarity, to full givenness" what is intended in the concept, without requiring that inner intuition enjoy an unceasingly "adequate" grasp of what is given in consciousness. Such a grasp is made difficult by the flowing character of psychical phenomena (which Husserl also emphasizes) and by the fact that inner perception is mostly a retrospective act (cf. Anschütz 1911, p. 431f.; Müller 1911). But even if we doubt the adequate character of inner intuition, we can nonetheless agree with Husserl when he says that "the field dominated by pure intuition includes the entire sphere that the psychologist reserves to himself as the sphere of 'psychical phenomena', provided that he takes them merely by themselves, in pure immanence" (Husserl 1981, p. 181).

Precisely this statement reinforces our view that Husserl's phenomenology does not have to be distinguished from psychology, but can instead be recognized as its fundamental part. As a further confirmation of this view, we refer to the study "Contributions to the Phenomenology of Perception" by Wilhelm Schapp, a student of Husserl (Schapp 1910). This article is devoted essentially to the psychological description of perception and manages to achieve truly remarkable results in this area.

Carl Stumpf's occasional suggestion to distinguish a discipline that he calls "phenomenology" from the natural and the human sciences (and thus also from psychology) cannot be invoked in support of Husserl's distinction between phenomenology and psychology, since Stumpf and Husserl's respective concepts of phenomenology are very different. [126] By "appearances" or "phenomena" Stumpf means solely the contents of sensation and the images of memory that go by the same name (including the spatial properties as well as spatial and other relations that occur in both classes) (Stumpf 1906a, p. 4; 1906b, p. 26). Phenomenology in Husserl's sense, on the other hand, includes everything that is immediately given (Husserl 1981, p. 174; Schapp 1910, p. 1), "everything that imposes itself immediately as a fact" (in Stumpf's words). In addition to (intuitive) "appearances" this immediate given also entails (non-intuitive) "functions" or "acts", as well as the relations among the elements in each of these species and the relations between the elements of the two species in their connection. Thus, Husserl's concept of phenomenology is much broader than Stumpf's. It encompasses the entire scope of conscious experiences along with the "objects" correlative to these experiences. For this reason, Husserl's phenomenology cannot be characterized as a "special science within the overall field of psychology", as G. Anschütz does. Its characterization as a "special attitude" is perhaps more acceptable, but this does not do justice to phenomenology's *fundamental* character (Anschütz 1911, p. 442). Anschütz's characterization of phenomenology as "a kind of introductory discipline for more specialized psychological research" (Anschütz 1911, p. 443),[16] meanwhile, succeeds in relegating phenomenology to psychology's front porch, whereas phenomenology actually constitutes psychology's ground floor. Incidentally, Anschütz, too, ascribes to Husserl's phenomenology an "*essential meaning*"[17] (Anschütz 1911, p. 443).

Let me acknowledge in passing that the positive assessment that I have offered here differs significantly from the verdict that other psychologists have pronounced concerning Husserl's phenomenological investigations. These investigations are certainly not "merely verbal," "merely grammatical", or "scholastic" analyses. Meaningful and thorough investigations like Husserl's ought not to be devalued with slogans such as "armchair psychology." These manifestations of deficient understanding and superficial rejection may be partly responsible for the harsh judgments that Husserl has passed on experimental psychology. [127] In any case, it would be in the best interests of psychology if mutual understanding rather than animosity arose between the two approaches, which are destined to mutually complement and support each other.

Up to this point we have limited ourselves to considering the relationship between Husserl's phenomenology and psychology. However, we must also briefly address the much broader significance that Husserl attributes to his phenomenology. Husserl calls phenomenology "a great science unparalleled in its fecundity, a science which is on the one hand the fundamental condition for a completely scientific psychology and on the other the field for the genuine critique of reason" (Husserl 1981, p. 181). The task of such a critique of reason consists for Husserl in the following: "[R]endering intelligible the possibility of a knowledge which is delimited by concepts and laws of pure logic, by tracing these back to their 'origin'; the task of resolving, in this way, the profound difficulties which are tied up with the opposition between the subjectivity of the act of knowledge and the objectivity of the content and object of knowledge (or of truth and being)" (Husserl 1994, p. 250). Thus, while abstaining from all metaphysical tendencies, phenomenology has to clarify cognition by bringing to evi-

---

16 [Translator's note: Messer uses quotation marks, but fails to provide page numbers for this passage.]
17 [Translator's note: Messer uses quotation marks, but fails to provide page numbers for this passage.]

dence the authentic meaning of logical ideas. Phenomenology takes its departure from the following fundamental principle: all concepts (that is, word-meanings) "must permit to being redeemed in an essential intuition" (Husserl 1994, p181), they must demonstrate their validity in the immediately given (Schapp 1910, p. 1). This holds for concepts such as thingness and substantiality as much as for concepts such as 'sensory and non-sensory intuition', 'thought and intuition', 'physical and psychical', and so forth (Schapp 1910, p. 3). Thus, the phenomenological method consists in starting from the 'ordinary linguistic characterizations' and then, in living through (*Einleben*) their meanings, asking about the phenomena to which these characterization mostly vaguely and equivocally relate. In so doing, the goal is not to acquire new knowledge of facts via an analysis of word-meanings. [128] This was the error of scholastic ontologism. The intention, rather, is to "[look] into the phenomena that language occasions by means of the words in question or to [penetrate] to the phenomena constituted by fully intuitional realization of experiential concepts, mathematical concepts, etc." (Husserl 1981, p. 175. Translation modified and completed.) What matters above all here is the clarification of equivocal meanings and, along with this, a resolution of the ambiguities that afflict many of the words used in science. The long-term goal is a "definitive fixation of scientific language", which can only happen on the basis of a complete analysis of the relevant phenomena (Husserl 1981, p. 175).

By virtue of these investigations, one of the fundamental principles advanced by thoroughgoing empiricists such as Hume is liberated from an excessively narrow interpretation, acknowledged and implemented for the first time. This is the principle according to which the 'origin', the true meaning and the validity of all concepts, must be exhibited in 'impressions' (*Impressionen*), that is, in intuitive impressions (*Eindrücke*). Unfortunately, the concept of 'impression' is not wide enough to denominate all that which is immediately given and can serve for the verification of concepts. On the other hand, it is legitimate to require that all concepts must find a footing as solid as the one that impression offers for concepts of sensuously perceivable things (Schapp 1910, p. 2).

The phenomenologist will draw a connection between this procedure—the clarification and verification of concepts through the exhibiting of their 'origins'—with the one of illuminating the *relations* between concepts. The task of carefully distinguishing the various meanings of certain words already makes the examination of such conceptual relations necessary. In this process, the phenomenologist comes to notice *a priori valid principles*. This is because at stake in his analyses are not facts—about facts we can only acquire a posteriori valid cognitions—but rather essential, that is, conceptual, nexuses. Since the fixation of conceptual contents is a task for scientific thinking, the relations holding among the concepts that have been fixed can also be known a priori. For this purpose we do not need to consult experience. [129] As Schapp states, very aptly: "A relation is a priori if it is grounded in the 'essence' (i.e. in the concept) of the related objects and with respect to which one abstracts completely from reality or non-reality" (Schapp 1910, p. 12).

With these investigations of a priori conceptual relations, phenomenology enters the terrain in which 'critical' or 'methodological' idealism—as it is presently represented by Cohen, Natorp and the members of the 'Marburg School'—can boast its greatest accomplishments. Phenomenologists should seek allegiance with this current. They could provide it with a more solid foundation by carrying out their foundational idea: *exhibiting the sense and validity of concepts in the intuitive given*. Conversely, phenomenologists could benefit from the thorough work that the Marburg School has done and will continue to do concerning the a priori relations among concepts.

After what has been said, it seems understandable and justified that Husserl attributes to phenomenology – or more accurately, the phenomenological method – a fundamental meaning not only for psychology but also for the theory of knowledge and other disciplines. However, in this article we have only hinted briefly at this second aspect. Our real task was to clarify phenomenology's relation to psychology and to highlight the great value of the phenomenological method for the descriptive task of psychology and for the clarification of psychological concepts and their relations.

References

Anschütz, Georg (1911): "Über die Methoden der Psychologie." In: *Archiv für die gesamte Psychologie* 20, pp. 414–498.
Bühler, Karl (1907): "Tatsachen und Probleme zu einer Psychologie der Denkvorgänge I: Über Gedanken." In: *Archiv für die gesamte Psychologie* 9, pp. 297–365
Husserl, Edmund (1981): "Philosophy as a Rigorous Science." Quentin Lauer (Trans.). In: *Husserl: Shorter Works*. Notre Dame: University of Notre Dame Press, pp. 161–197.
Husserl, Edmund (1994): "Report on German Writings in Logic: from the Years 1895–1899." Dallas Willard (Trans.). In: *Early Writings in the Philosophy of Logic and Mathematics*. Dordrecht: Kluwer, pp. 207–302.
Müller, Georg Elias (1911): *Zur Analyse der Gedächtnistätigkeit* I. Leipzig: Barthes.
Schapp, Wilhelm (1910): *Beiträge zur Phänomologie der Wahrnehmung*. Dissertation: Göttingen.
Stumpf, Carl (1906a): "Erscheinungen und Psychische Funktionen." In: *Abhandlungen der preußischen Akademie der Wissenschaft vom Jahre 1906*, Philosophisch-historische Classe Abhandlung 4, pp. 1–41.

Stumpf, Carl (1906b): "Zur Einteilung der Wissenschaft." In: *Abhandlungen der preußischen Akademie der Wissenschaften vom Jahre 1906*, Philosophisch-historische Classe Abhandlung V, pp. 1–94.

Wundt, Wilhelm (1907): "Über die Ausfrageexperimente und über die Methoden zur Psychologie des Denkens." *Psychologische Studien* 3, pp. 301–360.

Part II Responses (1913 – 1918)

Rodney Parker
Heinrich Maier

Heinrich Maier (1867–1933) began his academic career at the University of Tübingen, where he received his doctorate for the work *Die logische Theorie des deduktiven Schlusses* in 1892, under the supervision of Christoph Sigwart. In 1896, Maier habilitated with the first installment of his three-volume work *Die Syllogistik des Aristoteles* (1896–1900). After four years lecturing as a *Privatdozent* at Tübingen, Maier took up a position as professor of philosophy in Zurich in 1901. In 1902, Maier returned to Tübingen for a professorship and married Anna Sigwart, the daughter of his former mentor. Together they had one child, Anneliese, who would become a philosopher herself. During his time in Tübingen, Maier published a treatise on the *Psychologie des emotionalen Denkens* (1908), wherein he separates thought into emotional thinking and judgmental thinking, attempting to avoid the traditional dichotomy between emotion and reason.[1] Maier notes in the opening chapters of this book that his own investigations are meant to correct the confusions one finds in Husserl's *Logical Investigations*, particularly those related to immediate and reflective consciousness, and judgment.[2]

It might come as no surprise that when Maier took up a position at Göttingen in 1911, he and Husserl did not get along. In a letter to his friend and former student Dietrich Mahnke, Husserl writes that he considered Maier, rather than Müller, to be "the archnemesis" of phenomenology (Husserl 1994a, 475). In a letter to Paul Natorp, Husserl remarks, "Maier is a competent historian, but in my opinion he is *no* philosopher, as his thick and terrible book on emotional thinking all too clearly proves" (Husserl 1994b, p. 102).

What follows is a translation of Maier's essay "Psychology and Philosophy" which was presented at the fourth congress of the Society for Experimental Psychology held in Göttingen in April of 1914, along with the transcription of the discussion that followed. The Society for Experimental Psychology was established by G. E. Müller, Robert Sommer, and Friedrich Schumann, and held its first meeting in Gießen in 1904. At its inception, the Society had roughly 104 members, including psychologists, philosophers, and physicians. While the group included a number of students of Wilhelm Wundt, the Society was decidedly opposed to

---

1 Maier notes at the very beginning of his book that his own investigations are meant to correct the confusions present in Husserl's phenomenology as it is presented in the *Logical Investigations*. (Maier 1908, p. 20). Günter Patzig claims that Maier's *Psychologie des emotionalen Denkens* can be seen as a precursor to deontic logic. (Arndt 2001, p. 362).
2 See also Maier's essay "Logik und Psychologie" (1914).

DOI 10.1515/9783110551594-014

Wundt's version of psychology, particularly his claims that the proper subject of psychology is the "psychical" individual and his insistence on the practical limitations of experimental psychology, namely, that it could not study the phenomena of thought (Ash 1998, pp. 22–27; Kusch 1995, pp. 142–3). Like Müller, Maier was a hardline empiricist when it came to psychology, and advocated for a version of critical realism in philosophy. In "Psychology and Philosophy," Maier enters the debate concerning the proper place of psychology within the academy. At this time in German universities, psychology was primarily subsumed into the Faculty of Philosophy, much to the chagrin of some psychologists. In his presentation and the subsequent discussion, it becomes clear that Maier believes that it is empirical psychology that must inform discussions of lived experience, and takes explicit aim at phenomenology.[3] In addition to attending Maier's talk and participating in the discussion period, Husserl made a number of annotations and marginal notes in the published conference proceedings. These marginalia are included here as well.

References

Arndt, Karl; Gottschalk, G.; Smend, R (2001): *Göttinger Gelehrte* Vol. 1. Göttingen: Wallstein.
Ash, Mitchell G. (1998): *Gestalt Psychology in German Culture, 1890–1967*. Cambridge, New York: Cambridge University Press.
Ehrlich, Walter (1923): *Kant und Husserl*. Halle an der Saale: Niemeyer.
Husserl, Edmund (1994a): *Husserliana Dokumente III: Briefwechsel: Band 3. Die Göttinger Schüler*. Karl Schuhmann (Ed.). Dordrecht: Nijhoff.
Husserl, Edmund (1994a): *Husserliana Dokumente III. Briefwechsel: Band 5. Die Neukantianer*. Karl Schuhmann (Ed.). Dordrecht: Kluwer.
Kusch, Martin (1995): *Psychologism: A Case Study in the Sociology of Philosophical Knowledge*. London, New York: Routledge.
Maier, Heinrich (1908): *Die Psychologie des Denkens*. Tübingen: Mohr.
Maier, Heinrich (1914): "Logik und Psychologie." In: *Festschrift für Alois Riehl, von Freunden und Schülern zu seinem 70. Geburtstage*, pp. 311–378. Halle an der Saale: Niemeyer

---

3 In *Kant und Husserl* (1923), Maier's student Walter Ehrlich raises the problem of objectivity against both phenomenology and transcendental philosophy, two positions which he takes to be, at least in terms of their method and epistemological aims, the same.

Translated by Rodney Parker
Heinrich Maier. Psychology and Philosophy

Psychologie und Philosophie
Bericht über den VI. Kongress für experimentelle Psychologie in Göttingen, vom 15. bis 18. April 1914. Leipzig: Barth, pp. 93–99

[93] The "political" debate within the university concerning psychology has again focused its attention on the factual relationship between psychology and philosophy. The consensus reached today is that psychology is an *empirical science*, and there is prevailing agreement that it is to be counted among the *"human sciences"* [*Geisteswissenschaften*]. The objections against this latter view, at least those that have been raised, cannot be considered valid. Psychology is therefore within the sphere of that academic discipline, thus the last word concerning its relationship to philosophy has not yet been spoken. The significance that psychology in fact has and can have for philosophical work will be revealed, on one side, when we bear in mind *their place within the system of the human sciences*.

There are three points of view from which research in the human sciences looks at the matters of fact pertaining to the mental-life of humans: the genetic-historical, the theoretical, and the normative-critical. Accordingly, each of the specific [94] human sciences—linguistics, history and philosophy of science, religious studies, art history, law, political science, sociology, economics, etc.— divides into three sub-disciplines. They are most closely concerned with these matters of fact in their individual-historical concreteness. Thus, they all have an historical component (history of language, history of religion, history of science, history of law, etc.). Furthermore, from the theoretical point of view—to which the systematic-descriptive interests are subordinated—the theoretical components of the human sciences, which seek the essence of the typical forms and laws governing spiritual realities, are derived. They are, if their means of research are psychological, psychological theories (psycholinguistics, psychology of religion, social-psychology = sociology, psychology of art = theoretical art history, etc.). Finally, the third point of view leads to the normative-critical disciplines (critical science of knowledge, normative philosophy of religion, normative legal theory, normative political theory, normative economics, etc.). Over and against its matters of fact, which are the most recent human activities, the human sciences must, at the same time, return in a systematic-critical manner to the needs or goals that the different types of activities strive toward in order to determine the ideal terms and conditions under which they might be perfectly achieved. The three components of the special human sciences point back, then, to three fundamental human sciences, and these are: first, general history (which includes the natural aspect of the spirit and should contain the developmental history of the psychophysical organization of man), followed by psychology, and finally ethics, the theory of the ideal human life, which encompasses all aspects of individual and social mental life [*Geisteslebens*].

From this we can see *just how closely psychology is related to a number of sciences that are conventionally referred to as philosophical*. First, consider philosophy of language, economics, philosophy of art, philosophy of religion, philosophy of law, and political and economic philosophy. In each of these "philosophical" sciences, two disciplines are blended together: a theoretical psychology and a normative-critical.[1] Clearly, psychological research now stands in immediate interaction with the theoretical psychological disciplines, which in turn find their unity in a comprehensive historical or cultural psychology. [95] Psychology—not merely descriptive psychology, but the whole of its research methods—is the foundation of cultural psychological theories, and on the other hand not only provides the remainder of psychology in general with valuable material, but also an "objective" method (a cultural-psychological method, not an ethno-psychological one) without which, of course, subjective-psychological procedures do not apply.[2] Psychology, providing such an important service—along with normative-critical science[3] and especially the universal normative science, ethics—is likewise still considered a "philosophical" discipline. Knowledge of actual activities and their factual intentions everywhere condition critical normalizing, and ultimately this can be obtained in no other way than by psychological analysis and description. The latter, however, must utilize all tools and results of explanatory psychology for themselves. This is unobjectionable so long as we keep our eyes focused on the descriptive aims themselves.

The "philosophical" disciplines previously touched upon, which in fact belong in the system of the special sciences, can be referred to as "secondary philosophy." *Philosophy proper* is the science of the norms of thought and the essence of being. To it, psychology in fact stands in no different a relationship than any of the other positive sciences. Nevertheless, it has a far greater signifi-

---

[1] [Translator's note: Husserl's marginal note: "Psychology." Husserl thus understood the two sub-disciplines Maier is referring to as being theoretical psychology and normative-critical *psychology*].

[2] [Translator's note: Husserl makes the following note corresponding to what comes after the colon: "Psychology as the foundation of the theoretical parts"].

[3] [Translator's note: Husserl underlines this sentence to here and writes: "Psychology as the foundation of the normative-critical parts"].

cance for philosophical research than all the others. Time will tell if we pursue their relationships to the fundamental philosophical disciplines of logic, epistemology, and metaphysics.

Logic, which immediately goes beyond the science of knowledge, is the critical science of the norms and the ideal forms of valid thinking. However, valid thinking is not the same as true thinking. "Emotional" validity also falls within the normative domain of logic.

The *norms of cognitive thought themselves*, where the absolute being of the "in it-selfness" of valid truths become constituted, do not lead back to the laws of being in an "absolutely" logical manner. The alleged "absolute validity" of truths, which are intended to be eternal, even if there is no thinking individual to grasp them, is based on a hypostatization [96] that stems from the acts of judgement that deal with judgements of striven-after moments of logical necessity and universal validity, such as to attach a "pure", "supra-empirical" I or a pure "rational-consciousness" to the absolute truths as the hypostatization of a subject corresponding to the universally valid judgements. The chief norms of logic, however, are and will remain norms that declare an "ought." The ideal aimed at by them, which is in turn rooted in the moral desires of humans, and by no means in some absolute cosmic "value," is simply a necessity of thought, i.e., simply a transcendent postulate demanded by the functions of thinking. Moreover, the forms themselves, which logic highlights, are ideal forms that are acquired by critical reflection, by comparing the structures of actual thoughts to their corresponding logical ideal. As such they are only norm-objects.

Thus, the role that psychology must play in the context of logic concerning the forms of cognitive thought is sketched out.

Knowledge of actual thoughts and their intentions is a condition for the normative-critical work of logic. There can be no doubt that logical reflection has to seek out the actual thinking of cognition where it is engaged in a relatively perfect way, namely, in scientific cognition. Also important is the form of propositions, like the comparative syntax of the various parts of speech it brings together. But this will only be fruitful, indeed will only become feasible, when both modes of procedure—the forms of thought in scientific cognition and the forms of language—gain psychic life, that is, when we know the functions of thought to which they refer. In other words, the key to applying the objective methods lies here too in psychological research.

The aim of the psychological groundwork of logic is a descriptive analysis; but again, not only descriptive, but also explanatory psychology is to be utilized. The "laws" of the latter define general concepts of dependency relations between psychical lived-experiences and the elements of lived-experience. Without knowledge of these dependency relations (and this applies also to the case of descriptive analysis), [97] we can never reach exhaustive insight into the essence of actual thinking. The risk of "psychologism," however, will again be avoided only if the descriptive aim is maintained. In contrast, the analytic-descriptive groundwork of logic has no equal interest in the whole actual course of cognitive thought. Its attention is directed to the sides of consciousness that are immediately lit up of by the awareness of logical necessity and universal validity. It primarily investigates the final effects of the acts of judgment; the "judgments," rather than the acts of judgment themselves. After all, those are not entirely understood without the latter. The investigation must also go back to the habitual, mechanized thinking that the "psychology of thought [*Denkpsychologie*]" of the Külpean school has almost exclusively taken into account, in the original, in full ostensive evidence of the executive functions of thought—then also will the illusion disappear, as if a "pure," i.e., completely non-representational thought, had existed. But primary thinking offers itself on the merits of psychological observation, and if this is not the case, additional experiential conclusions occur. To what extent experimentation can provide fruitful results here I leave undecided. In any case, the analysis of randomly occurring lived-experiences, if it is done rationally, has its rightful place here.

From here, we can also consider Husserl's phenomenology and its position on "intuition." The "intuition of essences," to the extent that it is scientifically indisputable, is descriptive psychology, but which, insofar as it rejects the help of explanatory psychology, remains one-sided.

Even greater is the importance of psychology for the logical treatment of *emotional thinking*, which logic should finally tackle. Here nearly everything remains to be done. Only when emotional thinking is explored will the logic of cognitive thought fully come to light. The logical ideals themselves, including those of cognitive thought, are emotional objects of thought, and if one would have made clear the nature of these, the absolutist errors would have been avoided. Should it not, however, be particularly obvious today, when one so strongly tends to treat logic as a theory of objects, to also investigate logically the "objects" of emotional thinking, the aesthetic objects of illusion, the religious objects of belief, [98] moral ideals, concepts of rights, etc.? The concept of "values", which is so often misused, would then be quite understandable. Likewise, justice can be done to the logic of the various types of propositions, if one also knows the forms of emotional thinking. The normative-critical theory of knowledge itself will always remain full of gaps so long as this omission is not compensated for.

Psychological research is simply indispensable for knowledge of the actual forms of emotional thinking. Because here the task of preparatory analytical work is not merely the elucidation of the functions of thought, but also the inquiry into the manner in which emotional representational data enter into consciousness: without the psychology of feelings and desires there is nothing here to arrive at.

The *second* fundamental philosophical discipline is *epistemology*. Its central question is the problem of being about which realism and idealism quarrel. Its next object of investigation is the consciousness of reality in our judgements. The task of epistemology is not merely that of logical normalization. A critical appraisal of its value in terms of validity is only the precondition. Epistemology wants, rather, to explain the consciousness of reality—not a psychological, but a transcendental explanation. So long as this moment extends itself over all aspects of the representations of reality, epistemology is a transcendental theory of knowledge. It extends to all "givens", to the "transcendent consciousness" of the given, which are "grasped" in our judgments as "underlying" the representations of physical/objective as well as psychical/subjective reality. And in this way we can hope also to settle the question of the transcendence of the "reality of appearance" and how representations of reality come into appearance.

As little as epistemology is psychological theory, this much is clear: its work is entirely bound up with the psychology of knowledge. It is the critically assessed *actual* knowledge that should be understood transcendentally. And this knowledge must be psychologically examined in all its modes of existence before epistemological work can be done.

Metaphysics is, however, intimately connected to epistemology. [99] It is based entirely on epistemological work. But whereas epistemology strives for a transcendental theory of moments of reality in our representational knowledge, metaphysics seeks to gain a systematic-transcendental theory of the whole of reality. It places the results of the entire complex of theoretical science in the light of epistemological insights. Thus, metaphysics is directly related to psychology, insofar as it is based on epistemology. Moreover, metaphysics utilizes the results of psychology just as much as it does the other theoretical disciplines.

As a result, despite its individual scientific character, psychology is inextricably connected to the most genuine tasks of philosophy. The philosopher who turns away from psychology is left with no other choice than to conform to psychology.[4] The issue is whether or not philosophical work gains anything in this exchange. In the second half of the 19th century, three major tendencies have left their mark on German philosophy: empiricism, critical philosophy, and psychology. They have led to positions that are blatantly one-sided: positivism, agnosti-

---

4 [Translator's note] Husserl inserts an "!" next to these last two sentence.

cism, and psychologism. And certainly, the reaction that has for some time been strongly opposed to these extremes is warranted. But it would be disastrous if the legitimate motives behind these movements were to be forgotten thrown to the wind. It would be a misfortune especially if the tie that binds psychology and philosopher were to be severed—a misfortune for philosophy, and I believe also for psychology.

Discussion [Among the Conference Participants, Following Maier's Lecture]

[144] *Max Wertheimer:* The lecturer has based his criticism of Külpe's *Denkpsychologie* on "readily available" evidence to the contrary. It would have certainly been better to have communicated the evidence in question. We experimental psychologists are surely all of the conviction that a "simple proof," at least, is out of the question.

When the lecturer brings forth the further criticism that, in the work in question, what is being investigated is not that which he calls "primary thinking," it should be mentioned that in another context he himself has said that specific difficulties prevent an investigation directly addressing "primary thinking."

Edmund Husserl:[5] I cannot here give detailed reasons as to why I cannot, in principle, go along with Prof. Maier. I must limit myself to stating that pure phenomenology (in the sense of *my* work) is neither descriptive psychology nor does it contain anything of psychology – as little as pure mathematics of materiality, especially pure geometry, contains anything of physics. Psychology and physics are "factual sciences," sciences of the real world. Pure phenomenology, however, along with geometry and some similar science, are "sciences of essences", sciences of purely ideal possibilities. For these sciences, the existence of reality is not a question, therefore, never and nowhere a theme of assessment. We can equally say they are not based on "experience" in the sense of the word associated with the natural sciences, as that which assess real being and ways of being [*Dasein und Sosein*] through observation and experimentation. Analogous to how pure geometry is the study of the essence of "pure" spaces, or rather the science of the ideal possible spatial forms, pure phenomenology is the study of the essence of "pure" consciousness, the science of the ideal [145] possible forms of consciousness, along with their "immanent correlates." Rather than on experience, such sciences are based on the "intuition of essences," whose simpler and in no

---

5 [Translator's note: the following remarks are reproduced in *Husserliana XXV* (1986, p. 266)].

way mystical sense is illustrated by the essential relationships between the intuition of basic geometrical forms and the axioms we speak of as primitive. Pure mathematics of corporeality finds its *application* to nature as it is experienced, and makes possible "exact" natural science in the highest sense of the word – modern physics. Likewise, pure phenomenology finds its application in psychology and makes possible, or will at some point make possible, an "exact" (descriptive and explanatory) psychology in the highest sense.

Erich Jaensch: The difficulties in finding simple cases of primary thought highlighted by Dr. Wertheimer are without a doubt. But precisely the current state of experimental psychology makes it seem appropriate to warn against overestimating this difficulty. More and more the general psychology of perception, which stands in the foreground of the interests of psychological-philosophical research, shows that very similar generating processes are performed in the cases of sensation and representation. While this area of perceptual psychology is experimental in the strictest sense, it is based on sound methods, and so it would be pointless to doubt their accuracy. That many of us deal extensively with the problem of perception is not due to physiological propensities or to the widespread specialization of the younger generation, but solely due to the fact that, more and more, the method referred to, though slow and painstaking, has also proven an indisputably accurate way for psychology to investigate the higher mental process, and this is knowledge which is indispensable to many areas of philosophy. By a turning away from philosophy here, one can only talk of someone who does not appreciate it.

This remark, the content of which I take, by the way, to be in total agreement with Dr. Wertheimer, is intended to serve first and foremost to simplify the debate.

Wilhelm Jerusalem: The presenter has a limited amount of speaking time for responses, so I cannot justify my stance on the comments made by Prof. Husserl in detail. I will only say that, concerning the statements that Prof. Husserl has made against the remarks of the speaker, I must express my complete disagreement with Prof. Husserl's claims. Geometry is empirical in origin, and evidence of its propositions owes to the continuous confirmation of experience. The possibility of a phenomenology that should have the same meaning for psychology that mathematics has for natural science is something that I must completely deny.

Theodor Elsenhans: The remarks by Prof. Husserl [146] have shown that his theory of the relation of phenomenology to psychology is entirely dependent on the analogy of mathematics and its relationship to natural science. Only by this analogy can we speak of an "intuition of essences" that would not be dependent on the empirical knowledge of reality [*Einzelwirklichkeit*]. But this analogy is entirely tied to mathematical intuition. Where this no longer applies, mathematical knowledge cannot be used as an example, and therefore completely divorcing knowledge of essences from empirical knowledge of individuals is untenable.

Dr. von Hattingberg points out that for the psychology of emotional thinking, a comparison of the experiences of the psychology of animals with those of the mentally disturbed, as well as the observational data obtained through the analysis of neurosis and dreams, can provide very valuable information. It is now already possible to give at least a preliminary formulation of some of the laws of thought, for example, of the exclusive validity of the I-relation. He poses the following question to Prof. Husserl: where in psychology do we find the analogy of the straight line being the shortest distance between two points?

Wilhelm Wirth: We must be grateful to Prof. Maier for providing us with a clear and, I believe, correct representation of the unity of philosophy and psychology. At the same time, within it there is partial acknowledgement of Prof. Husserl's endeavors, insofar as it assumes the *a priori* relationship of conscious states. Prof Maier has therefore offered an olive branch to Prof. Husserl and invited him to collaborate with psychology, as far as this is possible from his position of inquiry. In psychology, after all, we do not want simply to collect individual facts; rather, we want to handle them thoughtfully, that is, to understand them from a general point of view.

Heinrich Maier: (In some brief concluding remarks, the speaker deals with the concerns that have been raised. In particular, against Husserl he claims that there can be no other way of discovering the essential concepts of the lived experiences of the mind than through psychological-descriptive abstraction. In any case, there is no *a priori* method applicable in this area that would be analogous to how mathematical construction can be used in the service of the description of physical reality).

References

Husserl, Edmund (1987): "Beitrag zur Diskussion über den Vortrag "Philosophie und Psychologie" von Heinrich Maier." In: *Husserliana XXV: Aufsätze und Vorträge (1911–1921)*. Thomas Nenon and Hans Rainer Sepp (Eds.). Dordrecht: Martinus Nijhoff, p. 266.

Translated by Andrea Staiti
August Messer.[1]
Husserl's Phenomenology in its Relation to Psychology (Second Essay)

Husserls Phänomenologie in ihrem Verhältnis zur Psychologie (Zweiter Aufsatz)
Archiv für die gesamte Psychologie 32, pp. 52–67 (1914)

[52] I have already expressed my views on this subject in issue 22 of the *Archiv für gesamte Psychologie* (p. 117–129; incl. in this volume p. 215–226). In the meantime, Husserl has produced a very thorough exposition of his thoughts on phenomenology (thoughts that he had previously published only in a concise and rather cursory form) in his *Ideas for a Pure Phenomenology and Phenomenological Philosophy*,[2] of which only the first book, "General Introduction to Pure Phenomenology", has so far appeared. The publication of this book gives me the opportunity to enhance and correct my previous remarks on some points.

Since psychologists are accustomed to using the phrase 'phenomenology' synonymously with 'descriptive psychology', we have to emphasize from the beginning that for Husserl 'phenomenology' has a different and much more comprehensive meaning. For him, phenomenology is the fundamental philosophical discipline, the pre-condition for every metaphysics and for every kind of philosophy "that will be able to come forward as a science" (*Ideen* 5/7).

The scholastics were already familiar with the important distinction between *existentia* and *essentia*. Phenomenology has as its subject matter exclusively the *essentia*, the essence. It is, as Husserl calls it, 'eidetic science'.

So what is this 'essence' ('Eidos')? An example should furnish us with the answer [53]. Consider a sound. Regardless of whether we are perceiving, remembering, or imagining it, we can pay attention exclusively to the *what* of the sound, and in so doing abstract from every thought about its factual existence i.e., about its existence as an individual thing. When we do this, we intend the 'essence'. And when we say of two qualitatively diverse sounds that one is lower and the other higher, we are expressing a relation among 'essences'

---

1 [For biographical information on Messer, see p. 213–214 of this volume.]
2 In the first issue of the *Jahrbuch für Philosophie und phänomenologische Forschung*, Halle 1913. The page numbers in the text refer to this edition. I also consider the other essays in this issue.

(*Ideen* 39/38). The same goes for the statement 'a judgment cannot have a color', or 'a + 1 = 1 + a'.

If by 'concepts' we mean psychical entities, i.e., products of abstraction, then we are guilty of psychologism if we identify 'essence' and 'concept'. The concept of number is not the number, the concept of sensation is not the sensation, the presentation of a centaur is not the centaur.

The clarification of concepts and the determination of their relations with one another—two of phenomenology's principal tasks—is carried out by means of "eidetic intuition" (*Ideen* 10/12).

Eidetic intuition is certainly intuition. It should however be sharply distinguished from all 'experiential' intuition. Through experiential intuition, something individual is given. Through eidetic intuition, the essence is given. Obviously, if we are to direct our gaze toward the what of some individual thing, that thing must somehow become manifest to us. If we are to rise to the level of grasping what is typical, or essential, in the appearance of some singular thing, that singular thing must first be given to us as an example. So, for instance, the geometer needs an actually drawn triangle in order to carry out the eidetic intuition of 'triangle in general'. But eidetic intuition does not require that the individual on whose basis eidetic intuition takes place be grasped as *singular* or posited as "*real*" (*Ideen* 12/13).

Eidetic intuition is a "polymorphic act" (*Ideen* 43/43), which can take place on the basis of outer or inner perception, memory, fantasy, and empathy (*Ideen* 292/279). Eidetic intuition is characterized by evidence. Evidence is not a particular feeling (*Ideen* 39/39) or a mystical voice calling us "Here is the truth" (*Ideen* 300/287). Rather, evidence consists in the fact that what is intended in thought is given intuitively. Husserl considers the following proposition the 'principle of all principles': "that each intuition affording something in an originary way is a legitimate source of knowledge, that whatever presents itself to us in 'intuition' in an originary way (so to speak in its actuality in person) is to be taken simply as what it affords itself as, but only within the limitations in which it affords itself" (*Ideen* 43–44/43). Truth can actually be given only in actual evidential consciousness (*Ideen* 290/277–278).

[54] What is grasped evidently as lying in a given essence holds a priori for every singular thing that bears this essence (*Ideen* 15/17). Something analogous applies in the case of those connections between essences that are grasped with evidence.

As to Husserl's subsequent distinctions between 'adequate' and 'inadequate', 'mediate' and 'immediate' evidence (*Ideen* 286 f./274 f.), I will not delve into these here (in their generality). I will simply make a critical remark. I wholeheartedly support the general tendency of this appeal to 'intuition'. This tendency already expressed itself—albeit insufficiently—in Hume's fundamental principle, according to which every 'idea' has to be traced back to an 'impression' from which it is to receive its legitimation. The intuitive presentation of essence and essential nexuses is bound to be extremely fruitful for the clarification, the enrichment and the correction of conceptual thoughts and for the appraisal of their validity and degree of validity. Husserl underscores that it is not easy to attain eidetic intuition in his sense, owing to a number of prejudices and misunderstandings. "If one has acquired the right attitude and fortified it through practice, but, above all, if one has gathered the courage to draw the consequences in a radically unprejudiced manner, untroubled by all the currently circulating and learned theories, i.e., to draw the consequences from the clear instances of essential givenness, then the immediate result is a number of substantial possibilities, possibilities that are the same for everyone in the same attitude. Among those results are substantial possibilities of communicating to others what one has seen oneself, testing their descriptions, bringing out the unnoticed intrusions of empty verbal meanings, and, through subsequent measuring in intuition, making known and eradicating errors that are possible here as they are in every sphere concerned with validation" (*Ideen* 181/173).[3]

This explanation might, however, be a bit too optimistic. In any case, the confident statement that "substantial results are immediately given" does not really square with the admission that errors are possible here as well.

Generally speaking, it would be necessary to further clarify the central concept of eidetic intuition and to check whether the representatives of the phenomenological method do not perhaps lump together under this concept different modes of cognition having different degrees of reliability. In most cases, eidetic intuition is a matter of clarifying meanings (concepts) and of distinguishing those meanings from related concepts by means of reflection on the sense of the words that are associated with them (and partly through the analysis of individual examples). This occurs, for instance, [55] when Scheler distinguishes the concept of "goal" from the concept of "purpose" (Scheler 1973, p. 30) or when Reinach determines the content of the concepts "claim," "obligation", "promise," and "waiving," or when he distinguishes between "mandate" and "warrant" or between "representative" and "ambassador" (Reinach 1983, p. 8f.). If one considers the numerous unsolved controversies in jurisprudence about the meaning and the relations among juridical concepts, one will have to be cautious with the affirmation of 'evidential' insights into 'essence' and 'essential nexus-

---

3 [Translator's note] Messer uses quotation marks, but fails to provide page numbers for this passage.

es'. Thus, Reinach himself observes correctly in his essay on "The A Priori Foundations of Civil Law": "Fundamental eidetic intuitions, too, must be achieved" (Reinach 1983, p. 133)[4]; we do not receive them effortlessly and free from error.

Since the meaning of many colloquial terms and even many scientific terms is not sharply defined, or is subject to fluctuation, the resolution of the ensuing disputes is frequently a matter of simply proposing a determinate application for a given word. Where such recommendations ought to be presented as useful linguistic conventions, however, they are occasionally put forward as "eidetic intuitions". We see this for example when Scheler states: "the feeling-states belonging to this modality [of spiritual values] range from 'blissfulness' to 'despair' (Scheler 1973, p. 109); "the person exists solely in the pursuance of his acts" (Scheler 1973, p. 29); "the wish *phenomenally* lacks the ought-to-be with regard to reality" (Scheler 1973, p. 40); "there are no 'sensations'" (Scheler 1973, p. 157); "if a value is self-given [...] willing [...] becomes necessary in its being, according to laws of essential interconnections" (Scheler 1973, p. 69) (which actually only means the following: I call a value 'self-given' only when the will is determined by the feeling of the value).

At the end of the day, though, the quest for 'essence' consists for the most part in questions that can only be answered through outer or inner perception, observation, analysis, comparison, etc., i.e., through cognitive tools that have always been employed in natural science and psychology and in no way exclude the possibility of error. Consider, for instance, the way that Scheler analyzes the different modes of striving (Scheler 1973, p. 32) or the way in which Geiger analyzes aesthetic pleasure (Geiger 1913).

We should not forget that the task of conceptually grasping and linguistically formulating what has been seen also harbors great difficulties. Metaphorical turns of phrase are often unavoidable and the risk that such turns of phrase are taken literally is considerable. Perhaps even more ominous is [the suspicion] that with the appeal to 'eidetic intuition', one is guilty of the same kind of abuse that was perpetrated [56] under the heading of 'intellectual intuition' in the heydays of speculative idealism[5].

---

[4] [Translator's note] Messer uses quotation marks, but fails to provide page numbers for this passage.

[5] One should consider from this perspective the grandiose statements Scheler occasionally presents as completely apodictic in his (otherwise very remarkable) essay *Formalism in Ethics and Non-Formal Ethics of Values* (Scheler 1973). Scheler, too, builds his analyses upon eidetic intuition. In Scheler's essay we read (without any further justification) statements like the following: "*all* possible values are 'founded' in the *value of an infinitely personified spirit* and its correlative '*world of values.*' Acts which comprehend values comprehend absolutely objective

Our remarks show at the same time that the reliance on 'eidetic intuition' entails a methodological tool whose use is not at all limited to psychology.

I did not emphasize this point sufficiently in my essay (Messer 1912; incl. in this volume p. 215–226). There, for instance, I wrote (on page 125): "Husserl's phenomenology does not have to be distinguished from psychology, but can instead be recognized as its fundamental part." It was misleading to omit from this sentence the qualification that I introduced on the previous page: phenomenology "insofar as it seeks to clarify psychological concepts with the aid of immanent seeing." Disregard for this qualification lead Anschütz to the view that I consider Husserl to be the representative of a brand of psychology that is exclusively based on self-observation (Anschütz 1912, p. 224).

Such a characterization would certainly fail to recognize the scope of Husserlian phenomenology. According to Husserl, phenomenology should encompass the fundamental formal (in particular: logical) and material (ontological) branches of philosophy. Moreover, phenomenology should not be limited to fundamental *theoretical* truths, but should also include axiological and practical truths (*Ideen* 290/277).

However, phenomenology is not distinguished from psychology solely by virtue of its scope and its fundamental character. Rather, it is distinguished from psychology and from all other sciences of experience by virtue of an essentially different 'attitude'. [57] The sciences of experience are and ought to be 'dogmatic', i.e., directed toward things and unconcerned with skeptical worries and epistemological problems. "On the other side stands scientific research in the epistemological attitude, the *specifically philosophical attitude* that pursues the skeptical problems regarding the possibilities of knowledge and initially resolves them in an intrinsically universal way in order then to apply the attained solutions and draw the consequences for the assessment of the ultimately valid sense and epistemic value of the results of the dogmatic sciences" (*Ideen* 47/46).

Husserl worked out the distinction between the "philosophical" attitude of phenomenology and the "natural" ("dogmatic") attitude of the sciences of experience in a particularly thorough way (*Ideen* 48 f./47 f.).

For a human being in the 'natural attitude', the spatiotemporal world with its things and living organisms is simply there. He directs his inquiring observa-

---

values only if they are executed '*in*' this world of values, and values are absolute values only if they appear in this realm." (Scheler 1973, p. 96) ([Translator's note] Messer uses quotation marks, but fails to provide page numbers for this passage). Scheler's statements about the 'a priori' hierarchy of values, which he presents as 'evident' (Scheler 1973, p. 104 f.), will also give rise to various objections.

tion, his descriptions and explanations—briefly put, his theoretical consciousness—toward this world; but he also directs his practical consciousness toward it: his pleasure and displeasure, his hopes and fears, his will and his actions. He can also turn toward his own I and his experiences in 'reflection', without on this account having to leave the 'natural attitude'. Just as little does he leave the natural attitude when he discovers that here and there the world is other than he thought, when he expunges something from the world as an 'illusion' or 'hallucination'. Even these cases change nothing about the 'general thesis of the natural attitude', a thesis that we simply take for granted (and that does not become conscious for us in any particular act of consciousness): the world that we share with other subjects is always there as reality.

In order to enter into the philosophical attitude of phenomenology it is necessary to radically alter this natural thesis. This alteration does not amount to doubting or disputing the reality of the world. We do not give up our natural belief in it. We change nothing in our conviction. We simply 'put it in brackets', we put it 'out of action', we decline to make use of it. Husserl also characterizes this 'bracketing' as a certain abstinence from judgment (*epoché*), an abstinence from judgment that is perfectly compatible with an unshakeable conviction in the truth of our natural belief in reality, but which means putting this unshakeable conviction to the side. Not only is the existence of this world 'discontinued'. All of the sciences related to the natural world undergo 'bracketing', too, in the sense that [58] we no longer seek to establish the empirical validity of any statements of phenomenology by grounding them in the principles of the natural sciences (even if they have perfect evidence).

By putting the natural, physical and psychophysical world out of action we also put out of action all of the objects constituted through the valuing and practical functions of consciousness, i.e., all kinds of cultural objects, works of technical and fine arts, products of the sciences (as cultural factors), aesthetic and practical values, and, moreover, entities such as the state, customs, right, religion. Accordingly, the bracketing targets all of the natural and human sciences precisely as sciences that require the natural attitude (*Ideen* 108/104).

But the bracketing reaches farther. To each group of sciences belongs an 'eidetic' science, an 'ontology', which deals with the 'general objects', the 'essences' of the corresponding sphere of individual being. All of these disciplines, be they already developed or merely postulated, receive their brackets: geometry, phoronomy, 'pure' physics of matter, eidetic psychology, sociology, etc.

However, it is not merely the material-eidetic sciences that are put out of action, but formal sciences such as formal logic and formal ontology as well. One may think, of course, that a researcher should be able to assume the validity of these formal sciences, since "whatever he investigates, they are always objects, and what holds formally for objects as such (properties, states of affairs in general, and the like), that is his as well. And however he construes concepts and propositions, however he draws conclusions, and so forth, what formal logic establishes about such meanings and genera of meanings (in terms of their formally universal character) applies also in the same way to him as it does to any researcher of a special field. So, too, for the phenomenologist" (*Ideen* 112/108).

But the phenomenologist carries out nothing other than a pure investigation of consciousness, in the form of descriptive analysis, to be executed though the pure intuition of conscious experience. The logical principles to which he appeals are exclusively logical axioms, such as the principle of contradiction, the absolute validity of which he can 'make evident' via examples in his own stock of givenness. Thus, phenomenology "lays claim to nothing other than what we are essentially able to make transparently evident to ourselves in consciousness itself, in pure immanence" (*Ideen* 113/109).

This leads us immediately to the following question: what remains if we 'bracket' all of the sciences and their objects in this way, [59] if we carry out the 'phenomenological reduction', (as Husserl also calls that radical transition from the 'natural' to the 'phenomenological' attitude)? One might almost worry that there would be nothing left for phenomenology. This, however, would be to conflate 'bracketing' with cancellation, or annihilation, from which it should rather be sharply distinguished. In bracketing, we simply put out of action the natural positing ('thesis') of a world of realities and values, a world that presents itself to us as self-evidently distinct from consciousness both in our dogmatic (naïve) comportment in practical life and in the pre-philosophical sciences. This 'putting out of action' means: we 'no longer participate' in these positings, we no longer 'live' in them. When we retreat from them in this way, however, they do not sink back into nothingness. Rather, we hold fast to our positings as objects of reflection, we grasp them in their immanent essence.

What is left, then, as the object of phenomenology? "Pure consciousness in its own absolute being"; this is the "phenomenological residue" sought. Although we have 'put out of action' the whole world with all things, living beings, humans, and ourselves included, "we have actually lost nothing but acquired the complete, absolute being that, correctly understood, contains every instance of worldly transcendence in itself, 'constituting' them in itself" (*Ideen* 94/91). Thus, phenomenology retains as its object the whole content of pre-scientific and of (dogmatically oriented) scientific consciousness with all of its positings of realities and values transcending consciousness. It is simply that these positings are no longer our own position-takings; they are merely our objects of reflection. We leave the validity of all our cognitions, values, and volitions suspended, but we continue to investigate their content, including all of their claims to validity. Thus, 'bracketing' is simply what helps us to turn our gaze toward 'transcendental consciousness'.

Let us clarify this with an example. Assume that we are contemplating a blossoming apple tree with enjoyment. "In the natural attitude, the apple tree is for us something existing in the transcendent actuality of space, and the perception, like the enjoyment, is a mental state belonging to the real human being. Real relations obtain between the one and the other reality, between the real human being or the real perception respectively and the real apple tree" (*Ideen* 182/175). Let us now carry out the 'phenomenological reduction'! Now [60] it remains an open question whether I am real, whether the tree is real, and whether a real relation obtains between us. We do not pursue these questions; we put them out of action. "This thetic actuality is, indeed, not there for us in the way of a judgment. And yet everything remains, so to speak, as it was before. Even the phenomenologically reduced experience of perception is perception of 'this blossoming apple tree, in this garden, and so forth' and likewise the reduced enjoyment is enjoyment of the same thing. The tree has not forfeited the slightest nuance of all the inherent aspects, qualities, characters, with which it appeared in this perception, and with which it was 'beautiful', 'eye-catching', and the like 'in' this enjoyment of it" (*Ideen* 183/176). In the 'reduced perception' we find the perceived as such as part of its essence. But this 'perceived-tree' as such (that is, the 'sense' of the perception) is not the real tree, the thing of nature. The latter can burn up; it can dissolve into its chemical elements. The sense of this perception, on the contrary, cannot burn up.[6]

The 'bracketing' or the 'phenomenological reduction' of perception prohibits any judgment about the perceived reality; but it does not prevent us from judging that perception is consciousness of a reality (albeit a reality that we are not permitted to posit); and it does not prevent us from describing the perceptual experience, including the reality appearing in it as such.

What holds for perception holds likewise for memory, fantasy, thinking, and for all 'intentional', i.e., object-directed, experiences; and of course not merely for theoretical experiences, but for axiological and practical experiences as well.

Now, "it is intentionality that characterizes consciousness in the precise sense of the term and justifies designating the entire stream of experience at

---

6 Husserl correctly avoids calling the sense the 'intentional' or 'immanent' object, since this would easily lead to the mistake of considering this 'mental' object as an inherent element of the perceptual experience. In this case, two realities would stand in front of one another: the 'real' thing, on the one hand, and the 'immanent' thing, which would function as a depiction of the real thing. However, we cannot place a consciousness of images at the basis of perception, since perception, considered descriptively, has a very different structure (*Ideen* 185f./177f.).

the same time as a stream of consciousness and as the unity of one consciousness" (*Ideen* 168/161).

Thus, the object of phenomenology remains the stream of experience in its whole plenitude, with its real components and with all [61] of the object-correlates that are conscious in it. All of this, however, is taken according to its immanent qualities. Nothing external to consciousness is posited. And, of course, phenomenology as an 'eidetic' science is "a doctrine of the essence of the transcendentally purified consciousness" (*Ideen* 114/109), i.e., of consciousness having undergone the phenomenological reduction. Phenomenology seeks to intuitively grasp and describe the essence of 'pure' experiences, no less than it seeks to grasp and describe essential nexuses.

All of these somewhat long-winded considerations were necessary in order to answer the question raised above (page 56): what is the distinction between the 'attitude' of the phenomenologist and that of the (empirical) psychologist, according to Husserl? Both phenomenology and empirical psychology have the stream of consciousness and the experiences constituting it as their object. Whereas the phenomenologist puts the reality of these experiences out of action and considers them solely with regard to their immanent essence, however, the psychologist treats them as real processes. According to Husserl, psychology is a science of realities. "The 'phenomena' that it treats, in its capacity as psychological 'phenomenology', are real occurrences. As such, if they have actual existence, these occurrences fit, together with the real subjects to which they belong, into one spatial-temporal world as the *omnitudo realitatis* [the whole of reality]" (*Ideen* 3–4/5). By means of the 'phenomenological reduction', on the other hand, phenomenology succeeds in purifying these occurrences of anything that might lend them reality, and hence inclusion in the real world (*Ideen* 4/6).

Psychology belongs in the ranks of the sciences of experience, having as their object psychophysical nature in its consciousness-independent reality. Consciousness, as it is given in experience as a human or animal consciousness and in connection with a bodily element, belongs to nature. Human consciousness in particular appears as "a persisting state of consciousness, that of an identical, real ego-subject manifesting its individual, real properties in that state" (*Ideen* 104/100).[7] For the phenomenologist, on the other hand, the human being is 'put out of action', together with the states that characterize the real existence of the human being. The phenomenologist pays attention only to conscious ex-

---

7 [Translator's note] Messer uses quotation marks, but fails to provide page numbers for this passage.

periences as such in their 'purity', conscious experiences that no longer have a natural meaning.

Before making a couple of critical remarks on this *first* mark of distinction between psychology and phenomenology, let me mention the *second* mark of distinction invoked by Husserl. Psychology, as a science of experience, is a science of facts, of matters of facts in Hume's sense. As an eidetic science, on the other hand, phenomenology [62] does not seek out facts as such; rather, it sets out to attain 'eidetic cognitions'. It should be remarked that Husserl limits the concept of 'experience' to knowledge of natural realities (*Ideen* 35/35), and that by 'facts' he means "singular individualities" exclusively (*Ideen* 4/6). Phenomenology does indeed take its departure from singular individualities, but it "lets the individuation fall to the side"; in this way, "it elevates into eidetic consciousness the entire essential content in the fullness of its concreteness and takes it as an ideally identical essence that, like any essence, could be instantiated, not only hic et nunc but in countless exemplars" (*Ideen* 140/134).

Without challenging Husserl's core convictions in any way, we could sum up the situation as follows: to the extent that phenomenology takes its departure from facts rather than theories, and must for this reason begin with the observation of facts, it too can be described as a 'science of facts'. But phenomenology's actual goal is not the cognition of singular facts as such. Rather, phenomenology seeks through observation to determine the essence of facts and the essences of relations holding among facts. Geiger rightly stresses that 'obtaining results through 'induction'' and 'obtaining results by examining the facts' are not simply different expressions for the same procedure (Geiger 1913, p. 570 f.). Induction is actually the narrower concept; it is simply *one* method of obtaining knowledge on the basis of facts. With induction, one begins with the cognition of the singular case and achieves general cognition by means of generalization and probabilistic reasoning. In phenomenological research, by contrast, one grasps the essence on the basis of 'intuition'; one brings a certain lawfulness clearly into view on the basis of the singular case.

Scheler, too, explains that every cognition must be based on "facts" (Scheler 1913, p. 446). He casually identifies eidetic intuition as "phenomenological experience" (Scheler 1913, p. 446) and observes that this kind of experience is distinct from all of other kinds on the basis of two characteristics: 1) phenomenological experience gives the 'facts' themselves, hence in an immediate fashion; 2) phenomenological experience alone is 'purely immanent', i.e., it entails only what is intuitive in the corresponding act of experiencing (Scheler 1913, p. 449 f.).

We saw above (page 58 [244-245]) that Husserl assigns to empirical psychology, as to every other science of experience, a 'material ontology', namely, 'eidetic psychology'. In keeping with its concept, eidetic psychology, too, does not deal with [63] individual facts, but with essences. In this respect, eidetic psychology accords with phenomenology. For eidetic psychology the second mark of distinction does not hold. Let's now consider the significance of the first mark of distinction for the demarcation of 'eidetic psychology' and 'phenomenology'.

Husserl does not carry out this demarcation in this first volume of his 'Ideas' (the only volume published thus far), suggesting that it will be carried out in the second volume. We can safely assume, however, that his first distinction between phenomenology and psychology holds not merely for empirical, but also for 'eidetic' psychology. Husserl thus presupposes that where eidetic psychology is concerned, we again remain in the 'natural attitude', meaning that we live in the belief in psychophysical reality. In phenomenology, on the other hand, we 'bracket' this belief and the thesis that it entails.

I do recognize that phenomenology and psychology can be distinguished along these lines. On the other hand, it does not strike me that this distinction is so important for actual research that it must be constantly borne in mind.

Husserl himself concedes that eidetic psychology is "intimately bound up with" phenomenology (*Ideen* 160/153). And when he assures us in a different passage that "abysses separate" phenomenology from "all psychology" (*Ideen* 184/177), he certainly means only empirical psychology.

Even though the phenomenological manner of consideration is "more encompassing and... radical", nevertheless "every phenomenological determination regarding absolute consciousness can be re-interpreted into an eidetically psychological determination" (*Ideen* 143/138). Just as a mathematical expression is not transformed in its value and in its intrinsic composition by being put between brackets, so the essence of an experience undergoes no modification by virtue of being 'bracketed'. As far as their content is concerned, the phenomenological observations remain unmodified. They are simply marked with a kind of algebraic sign when they are interpreted in terms of eidetic psychology. In this way we remind ourselves that our phenomenological observations concerning the essences of experiences are not mere fabrications. Rather, those essences carry within them real psychical occurrences.

It should be admitted without reservation that psychologists have failed to draw this subtle distinction between 'phenomenology' [64] (in Husserl's sense) and 'eidetic psychology'. We should also admit that what goes under the name of 'phenomenology' (or else 'pure' viz. 'descriptive' psychology) in psychological circles is best characterized as 'eidetic' psychology. However, it does not appear as if the absence of this subtle distinction has had detrimental consequences. Because when the descriptive psychologist wanted to characterize some class of experiences (be it perception, or memory, or volition, etc.) in general terms, he regarded the individual experience from which he took his departure merely as an arbitrary example, as something that would render the sought-after essence intuitive. The existence of the individual experience in the real nexus of nature was of no concern, because the descriptive psychologist was interested not in existence, but essence [*die Essenz, das Wesen*].[8]

As for Husserl's complaint that immanent eidetic analysis is still alien to modern psychology, this claim (*Ideen* 158/152) also fails to find adequate support in his new work. In his essay "On the Psychology of Attitudes", Alexander Pfänder argues much more reasonably that the progress of phenomenological insights contributed to significant progress in modern psychology, regardless of whether the phenomenological insights "were put forward under the heading 'phenomenology' or under a different heading" (Pfänder 1913, p. 329). This holds in particular for the careful qualitative analysis of conscious phenomena envisioned and practiced by the modern psychology of 'thinking'.

The phenomenological method, as it is applied to psychological objects by Husserl, his students, and his followers, is thoroughly consonant with this manner of analysis. As evidence of this, I have already mentioned in my first essay (Messer 1912, p. 125; incl. in this volume p. 222) Wilhelm Schapp's dissertation, "Contributions to the Phenomenology of Perception", which was defended in Göttingen and published in 1910. Further confirmation of my position comes from "Investigations of the Concept of Sensation", an essay by another student of Husserl, Heinrich Hofmann (Hofmann 1912).

It is particularly instructive to compare this essay to a book by an experimental psychologist, David Katz, *The Modes of Appearing of Colors* (Katz 1911). [65] Hofmann himself draws attention to his agreement with Katz (Hofmann, pp. 71, 78).

One will hardly notice here the 'abysses' that, according to Husserl, separate psychology from phenomenology.

One could also consider the examples of phenomenological analysis included in Husserl's *Ideas*. These examples can be taken up without further ado within the context of what empirical psychologists have long referred to as 'descriptive' psychology or 'phenomenology'.

The same goes for Moritz Geiger's essay "Beiträge zur Phänomenologie des ästhetischen Genusses" (Geiger 1913).

Finally, let me mention the essay "On the Psychology of Attitudes" by Alexander Pfänder, which appeared immediately following Husserl's *Ideas* in the first volume of Husserl's yearbook. There, we read the following methodolog-

---

[8] I pointed this out already in my earlier essay (Messer 1912, p. 123; incl. in this volume p. 220–221).

ical preliminary: "Psychological knowledge of attitudes necessarily begins with the phenomenology of attitudes. The phenomenology of the psychical must press forward until it directly grasps the psychical itself. It must then produce a fully accurate description of the psychical material. In so doing phenomenology attains ultimate fundamental knowledge of the psychical. Only when this knowledge has been reached in a psychical domain can one avoid the risk of conflating essentially different facts. On the contrary, if one leaves the 'what' of psychical facts unquestioned and unilluminated, one surely gets a false, merely constructed picture of psychical reality in general. Under these circumstances one wastes a substantial amount of effort on psychological investigations that are bound from the start to be untenable, since they lack a sufficient phenomenological basis. This phenomenological basis alone makes it possible to overcome and to destroy unnoticed false presuppositions concerning psychical reality" (Pfänder 1913, p. 328).

Any levelheaded psychologist would agree with this warning! However, it will hardly appear to him as something new, as something that he has so far failed to notice.

Comparing the present analyses with the ones in my first essay, one will find numerous additions that I hope will aid in the understanding of Husserl's *Ideas*. One will also notice, however, a pair of corrections.

In the first place, I have emphasized here [66] that Husserl's phenomenology has a very comprehensive character, a point which I did not sufficiently highlight in my previous essay. Phenomenology is fundamental not merely for psychology, but for all of the sciences of experience. Not only does phenomenology investigate all of the different kinds intentional experiences; it investigates the objective sense of these experiences (*Ideen* p. 188 f./180 f.). In my first essay I was not concerned with characterizing the scope and significance of phenomenology, but with determining its relations to psychology.

The second correction pertains precisely to these relations. I recognize that in light of its characteristic 'bracketing' of all positing of reality, phenomenology must be distinguished from psychology, including 'eidetic psychology' in Husserl's sense (i.e. a psychology that merely describes psychical experiences according to their immanent essence). We have seen, however, that this distinction has a merely theoretical significance, that it fades into the background where the praxis of research is concerned. Thus, I can retain the main thesis of my previous essay in its essence: "insofar as it seeks to clarify psychological concepts with the aid of immanent seeing, phenomenology is psychology, *indeed even the most fundamental part of psychology*" (Messer 1912, p. 124; incl. in this volume p. 221). To formulate this point more precisely I could say (as Husserl says in one passage): "phenomenology (or eidetic psychology) is the science that lays the groundwork methodologically for empirical psychology" (*Ideen* 159/152). However, how little Husserl himself considers this more precise formulation necessary can be evinced from another passage, where he briefly explains that "phenomenology makes up the essential eidetic foundation of psychology and the humanistic sciences" (*Ideen* 34/34).

After saying this, I can confidently leave it to reader to adjudicate the extent to which Husserl's charge against my first essay, namely, that I "misunderstood the sense of his presentations", is justified (*Ideen* 158fn./152fn.). He added no further explanations to justify this charge, and the same goes for the same charge that he raises against Külpe (*Ideen* 11fn./13fn.) and Cohn (*Ideen* 158fn./152fn.). Husserl [67] limits himself to the remark that the doctrines that are contested are by no means his own doctrines. By contrast, I want to stress that the basic tendency of my first essay was not at all polemical. That I would criticize Husserl's overly broad attacks against experimental psychology was inevitable; however, this was not my main point. What I wanted, rather—and this is also my intention in the present essay—was to point out *the tremendous significance of Husserl's phenomenology for psychology*. In any case, I hope that the "animosity to ideas" (*Ideen* 34/34) that psychologists are guilty of according to Husserl will not be directed toward his *Ideas for a Pure Phenomenology*. I would hazard, incidentally, that this animosity does not really exist.

References

Anschütz, Georg (1912): "Bericht zu A. Messer 'Husserls Phänomenologie in ihrem Verhältnis zur Psychologie.'" In: *Zeitschrift für Psychologie und Physiologie der Sinnesorgane* Vol. 62, pp. 224–225.
Geiger, Moritz (1913): "Beiträge zur Phänomenologie des ästhetischen Genusses." In: *Jahrbuch für Philosophie und phänomenologische Forschung*, Vol. 1, No. 2., pp. 567–684.
Hofmann, Heinrich (1912): "Investigations of the Concept of Sensation." Göttingen dissertation. Also published in: *Archiv für die gesamte Psychologie*, Vol. 26, No. 1/2, pp. 1–136.
Husserl, Edmund (2014): *Ideas for a Pure Phenomenology and Phenomenological Philosophy: First Book: General Introduction to Pure Phenomenology*. Daniel Dahlstrom (Trans.). Indianapolis/Cambridge: Hackett.
Katz, David (1911): "Die Erscheinungsweisen der Farben." In: *Zeitschrift für Psychologie und Physiologie der Sinnesorgane* Ergänzungsband 7, pp. 6–31.
Messer, August (1912): "Husserls Phänomenologie in ihrem Verhältnis zur Psychologie." In: *Archiv für die gesamte Psychologie* 22, pp. 117–129.
Pfänder, Alexander (1913): "Zur Psychologie der Gesinnungen." In: *Jahrbuch für Philosophie und phänomenologische Forschung*, Vol. 1, No. 2, pp. 325–404.

Reinach, Adolf (1983): "The A Priori Foundations of the Civil Law." In: *Aletheia* III, pp. 1-142.
Scheler, Max (1973): *Formalism in Ethics and Non-Formal Ethics of Value*. Evanston: Northwestern University Press.
Schapp, Wilhelm (1910): "Beiträge zur Phänomenologie der Wahrnehmung." Göttingen dissertation.

Translated by Evan Clarke
Edmund Husserl.
Draft of a Letter to August Messer (1914)

Entwurf eines Briefes an August Messer
Husserliana XXV: Aufsätze und Vorträge (1911–1921).
Thomas Nenon, Hans Rainer Sepp (Eds.)
Dordrecht: Martinus Nijhoff, pp. 249–252 (1987)

[249] Dear Colleague. Thank you very much for sending your recent paper on the subject of my phenomenology (Messer 1914; incl. in this volume). It is a very valuable indication of your generous disposition, which is of course also apparent in the paper itself. In fact, upon a comparative reading of your two papers I had to convince myself anew that my (absolutely not angrily intended) comments in the Jahrbuch concerning your earlier paper were justified. The justified nature of my initial response, however, remained concealed to you because, in spite of the much closer approximation to my views that I have already mentioned, residues of misunderstandings still persist. [...] I will address these misunderstandings straightaway. I will continue by considering the misunderstandings that arise in connection with those elements of the *Ideas* that are not yet treated in the *Logos* article (Husserl 1981). Before everything else I must remark that my theories as regards the essence and the necessity of a "pure" or transcendental phenomenology must only be evaluated on the basis of my own presentations of these theories. The researchers with whom I am associated, namely, the contributors to the Jahrbuch, took their point of departure from the *Logical Investigations*, and have developed relatively independently from that point on. Direct or indirect acquaintance with the intuitions that I have developed since that time has likely influenced in them in certain ways, in some cases more, in some cases less (e.g. Pfänder). But what I presented to the general public as results of my work of decades was not known to them in advance. The Jahrbuch is not a journal for orthodox Husserlians, whose contributions would be filtered for purity by its editor. Many contributions follow the thread of pure phenomenology and can do a great service to the promotion of the interests of phenomenology. However, I would not consider these contributions pure and methodologically perfect. In the journal I have to be broad-minded: the incipient science will purify itself, and my own research will help in that regard. If, for example, Pfänder does not take up an eidetic perspective in his work, it is nevertheless easy to see, for one who has been instructed and indeed trained in phenomen-

ology, that what he says acquires its full value when viewed in terms of the eidetic attitude. The work of both Geiger and Reinach is from the outset eidetic; Reinach's work is even [250] essentially ontological. The journal, however, is not just a journal of phenomenology, but of philosophy in general, and even of psychology, to the extent that the latter refers essentially to pure phenomenology (in the same way that mathematical journals include papers that are mathematico-physical in orientation, which is to say, natural scientific papers that are structured methodologically in terms of mathematics). Moreover, supposing that uncertain claims and even errors appear in individual papers, phenomenology itself is no more responsible for those errors than psychology itself is responsible for the errors and undemonstrated claims of the contributors to the *Archivs für Psychologie*.

The main point, however, is that—after having almost grasped this point—you again misconstrue the difference between factual and eidetic science, or between fact and essence. A fact, for me, is equivalent to a *matter of fact* in Hume's sense. All sciences that attend just to individual beings (to individual instances of "this here!") are sciences of fact. The sciences of physical and psychical nature belong (for the most part) in this category (as has been repeatedly explained). The lawful sciences also therefore belong in this category. The opposition between the universal and the individual is not identical to the opposition between the essential and non-essential. Mathematical physics is a factual science, but it does not fix any individualities. In the Humean sense, it is a science of *matters of fact* and not of *relations of ideas* (provided that we understand the concept of idea in my sense and not in a Humean sense. There is a considerable difference between the two conceptions).

A physicist who would invent natural processes purely on the basis of phantasy, and who would establish natural laws on the basis of those phantasied processeses, belongs in a madhouse. On the other hand, the geometer can and indeed must operate in the domain of phantasy, thus with forms generated in free phantasy. Even when he does take something perceived as an example, the empirical thesis of perception does not come into play; it contributes nothing to the process of justification. Experience does not figure here *as* experience. The geometer, moreover, can immediately and freely transform the perceived in phantasy; the result offers just as much to the eidetic grasp as what was originally experienced. The eidetic scientist treats exemplification in a totally different fashion than the natural scientist. The latter must grasp individual existence; he must perceive; he must experience. The eidetic scientist does not base his determinations on individual existence; rather, he conjures for himself an individual existence in a clear manner, or operates with what is perceived *as if* he had conjured it up. That is, he doesn't concern himself with whether the thesis of perception is preserved.

The correct position, therefore, is the opposite of what you argue on page 62, that is to say, my view. Phenomenological reality is not factual reality, but rather essential reality, and the originally given act corresponding to this reality is not experience, but ideation, or eidetic insight. The phenomenologist, therefore, needs to establish nothing less than the existence of his lived experiences, perhaps even the existence of the phantasies that he performs, [251] through which he brings phantasied perceptions, judgments, and so forth, to givenness. Such phantasies offer intuitive aid in his research into perception as such and judgment as such. By no means does he need *memories*, which are a kind of experience. And if he were to attach himself to inner perceptions and memories, then he would get no more out of this, phenomenologically speaking, than would a psychologist who took the same approach. If these differences are not understood, then the radical break between eidetic psychology and empirical psychology will not be understood; nor will one understand the massive and essentially new challenge that lies in the renewal of the idea of a rational psychology (albeit a fundamentally different, phenomenologically-oriented psychology standing in contrast to those of the 18th century). In saying therefore, that "the quest for 'essence' consists for the most part in questions that can only be answered through outer or inner perception, observation, analysis, comparison, etc" (Messer 1914, incl. in this volume p. 242), one has said something that is perhaps as remote as possible from a statement that I can hold true. Rather, it would be absurd if, by such means, one set out to discover even the most trivial eidetic psychology and phenomenology, e.g. that a judgment is not a color.

Pure sciences like phenomenology are similar to logic in the sense that they are independent in principle of all experience as regards their justification. Even if all of the observations and experiments of the psychologists remained unmade, or were completely false, these pure sciences would still be valid. They would be valid even if there were no nature in general, and no kind of singular-phenomenological being (individuation of a phenomenological eidos).

Connected with this is the fact that neither the radical novelty, nor the immense scope of an eidetic psychology (let alone a transcendental phenomenology) has been recognized. Repeatedly in my work I have drawn parallels between phenomenology (or the eidetic psychology that is related to phenomenology) and geometry. If geometry were a mere natural science, then the methodological gains that it generates for natural science in general would be won through observations and experiments carried out in external experience. But this would be as if geometry had not in fact been discovered, and one had to make do with carrying out mere measurements on what is empirically given, with describing shapes just as field-shaped, house-shaped, wall-shaped, etc., and with forming general statements on that basis. In point of fact, this is exactly the situation of contemporary psychology. It describes lived experiences from case to case in inner experience, for example, intentional experience and their intended contents, Admittedly, it is occasionally the case that what is attributed to inner experience actually arises from an eidetic attitude. But even if this occasionally does happen, it makes an enormous difference when we actually recognize that what we have here are infinite fields of eidetic and systematically fulfilled cognition, as I have tried so insistently to show, and as we have long recognized in the case of pure space. As soon as this was recognized, a pure and systematic geometry became possible, one that systematically explored the eidetic possibilities [252] of the geometrical. Only through this (as well as through other pure forms of mathematics) was exact natural science possible. In a precisely parallel sense, if we have an eidetic psychology, then an "*exact*" psychology will be possible. And we will indeed have such an eidetic psychology, because it is possible, and because this possibility demands to be worked through. It is recognized as possible as soon as one sees that a grasp of essence can be realized at any time in the sphere of lived experience, and that possible connections can be pursued through free phantasy. Exactitude does not arise from experiment; the source of exactitude is the founding of a given science in the a priori of its objects, that is, in the eidetic investigation of the object sphere with which it is concerned.

As I have already shown (Husserl 2014, §7), factual sciences are sciences that are grounded in experience. No essence, and no eidetic science can be founded through experience—where by 'experience' we mean in general every perception, memory and every equivalent act that carries out the *thesis* (positing) of individuals. As soon as this thesis comes into play as regards the *grounding* of a given science (be it even in the most universal form of the thesis of nature in general), then the science in question is a factual science. It is likewise a misunderstanding to try to disprove, on the basis of the second chapter of the first part (of the *Ideas*), and many other later passages, that factual sciences are simply those sciences that proceed on the basis of the "cognition of individual facts," or, in your sense, cognition of *certain* particulars. The claims made in your first paper are dominated by this misunderstanding, which completely inverts my conception as it is presented in *Logos* and in the Jahrbuch. (Messer 1912, p. 123; incl. in this volume p. 220–221) In no instance is the determination of an essence or of a universal eidetic cognition grounded in experience. It is never the case, in other words, that the determination of the being of some fact is a presupposition for the determination of the being of an essence or the existence of an eidetically structured state of affairs. The physicist, who is responsible for establishing such universal natural laws (laws of energy, laws of gravity, and so forth), can do so only if he takes his point of departure in observations and experiments; that is, only if he has already inspected individual existence. Drop tests fix individual determinate existence. But they merely fix them: such things actually do occur in nature. If this were uncertain, then there could be no "induction," no forming of hypotheses, no appeal to natural laws that relate to falling, or to gravity in general. In contrast, sciences like pure logic, arithmetic, geometry have no need of observations, experiments, or the inspection of facts when it comes to their foundations; indeed it would be nonsensical to attempt to ground eidetic laws in this way. The geometer operates essentially in phantasy. He can also draw on the blackboard. But this is not an experience and not an observation, because the existence of the triangle on the blackboard is not a necessary condition for the inspection of the same. The geometer "induces" nothing.

References

Husserl, Edmund (1981): "Philosophy as a Rigorous Science." Quentin Lauer (Trans.). In: *Husserl: Shorter Works*. Notre Dame: University of Notre Dame Press, pp. 161–197.

Husserl, Edmund (2014): *Ideas for a Pure Phenomenology and Phenomenological Philosophy: First Book: General Introduction to Pure Phenomenology*. Daniel Dahlstrom (Trans.). Indianapolis/Cambridge: Hackett.

Messer, August (1912): "Husserls Phänomenologie in ihrem Verhältnis zur Psychologie." In: *Archiv für die gesamte Psychologie* Vol. 22, pp. 117–129.

Messer, August (1914): "Husserls Phänomenologie in ihrem Verhältnis zur Psychologie. (Zweiter Aufsatz)." In: *Archiv für die gesamte Psychologie* Vol. 32, pp. 52–67.

Translated by Andrea Staiti
Edmund Husserl. Remark on Messer and Cohn (February/March 1913: First Draft)

Erster Entwurf zur Anmerkung über Messer und Cohn (Februar/März 1913)
Husserliana III: Ideen zu einer reinen Phänomenologie und phänomenologischen Philosophie
2. Halbband: Ergänzende Texte (1912-1929)
Karl Schuhmann (Ed.)
Dordrecht: Martinus Nijhoff, pp. 571-2 (1976)

[571] Messer has simply misread my expositions of the concept 'essence' and of the sense of an essential analysis. Accordingly, he did not understand a single word of all the fundamental inquiries. This is obviously noticeable, once again, in his new essay.

* * *

Cohn accuses me of an equivocation, arising from equating the general with that which is not determined by one individual (spatial and temporal) place. "If, namely, the phenomenon flows in the unmeasurable stream of occurrence mentioned above, then a part of that stream is certainly not determined by a chronometrical place; but this lack of determination does not necessarily carry with it the advantage that what is now flowing in the stream is not essentially identical with what is flowing in other streams or identical with what is flowing in different parts of the same stream" (Cohn 1913, p. 226; incl. in this volume p. 140). My answer to this remark is the following: I do not equate the general (i.e., the essence) with that which is not determined by an individual (i.e., real) place in world-time and world-space just because I emphasize that, as a matter of principle, an essence does not have such place. An essence is given in eidetic intuition. Anyone can grasp directly and without biases what that means. It suffices to bring to givenness the 'clear sense' of 'color in general' and 'tone in general'. There is no need to waste more words on this matter here. The following statement is more important. Obviously, the phenomena in the reduced but not yet eidetic stream do not possess a chronometrical place. However, the fact that they do not have such place plays no role in this context, neither does it play a role in the analyses of the *Logos* essay (Husserl 1981).

What I defend is the possibility of an eidetic knowledge, of the apprehension of essences and of the essences of lived-experiences. Moreover, I defend the cognition of unconditional, universally valid statements [572] on essences, and in particular on essences of lived-experiences. The possibility of eidetic knowledge cannot be proved, it can only be seen in its evidence. This possibility is itself a piece of eidetic knowledge. Asking for a demonstration would amount already to absurdity, since the demonstration would presuppose that which has to be demonstrated and so forth *in infinitum*. If today we had to defend pure arithmetic or pure geometry, someone like Cohn could raise the same objection. Geometry is related to the continuity of the configurations of spatial things, which are empirically inherent in a ceaseless stream. Geometrical eidetic intuition grasps the essence in the empirical and puts forward unconditionally universal geometrical propositions. This is what the idealist argues. However, such eidetic cognition is exposed to the objection raised by the empiricist (whose advocate, in this case, would be Cohn): the pure grasp of the essence, which consists in pulling out the pure idea from the empirically individual spatiotemporal being, does not necessarily imply the fortunate fact that what flows momentarily in the stream is eidetically identical with what flows in other streams, etc. The same goes for arithmetic cognition, to the extent that it relates to the empirical, i.e., to something flowing. Now, would it be wise to argue against the establishment of such disciplines for these reasons and to reject the enormous significance of unconditionally valid pure cognition for the empirical investigation of nature? In Cohn, too, a misunderstanding is at work behind these objections, as if the phenomenological method ought to replace the empirical method. However, the phenomenological method does not contribute to psychology anything more than the a priori of nature (in particular, for instance, the mathematical a priori) contributes to empirical natural science. The a priori of nature does play a role in all rigorously scientific observations of existing being; however, it is no physical method. Thus, the phenomenological method is the foundation of rigorously scientific psychology, and yet it does not stake out any claim about existing being.

Appendix 24

Remark on Messer and Cohn (Second Draft)

February/March 1913

The two essays by A. Messer and J. Cohn, which came while I was completing the correction of the proofs for this book, show anew how little even thorough researchers manage to free themselves from the course of the dominant prejudices and grasp the distinctiveness of a pure doctrine of essence. As for Messer, this is not the place to reply to his repeated objections against my analyses of the psychological method. [573] Let me just say, regretfully, that he completely missed the sense of my presentations, such that (to the extent that he discusses anything fundamental at all) I would have to reverse negatively the meaning of all his expositions of my theories in order to be able to somehow recognize my own actual theories in them. His complete misunderstanding is palpable even in his quotations, in which (obviously without noticing) he leaves out decisive sentences, such that their sense is transformed in precisely the opposite sense (Messer 1912, p. 120; incl. in this volume p. 217–218). All my analyses of the concepts 'essence', 'eidetic analysis', 'pure analysis of consciousness' remain ineffective. Messer understands them as introspection and my phenomenology as a supposedly improved version of introspective psychology. There is nothing else to say about this here. I hope that the detailed presentations of the present work will keep misunderstanding of this sort from coming up anymore in the work of such an esteemed scholar.

J. Cohn accuses me of "an equivocation" flowing from "the equation of the general and that which is not determined by one individual (spatial and temporal) place" (he means real being in world-space and world-time). Cohn adds the following objection: "If, namely, the phenomenon flows in the unmeasurable stream of occurrence mentioned above, then a part of that stream is certainly not determined by a chronometrical place; but this lack of determination does not necessarily carry with it the advantage that what is now flowing in the stream is not essentially identical with what is flowing in other streams or identical with what is flowing in different parts of the same stream" (Cohn 1913, p. 226; incl. in this volume p. 140). The first thing to reply is the following: An equation of the general, i.e. of essence, and that which is not determined by an individual place never crossed my mind. This does not require an argument here. Obviously, in the description of an essence one should not fail to say that an essence does not have spatiotemporal being. However, does that amount to an equation?

Moreover, I gladly admit that so far I have not proved that the validity of the results of my 'eidetic intuition', let alone their completeness, can be demonstrated. What I do not understand is how J. Cohn could attribute to me the intention to provide such demonstration, which would be a complete absurdity. Hence, Cohn, too, failed to understand the whole sense of my analyses or, which amounts to the same thing, he has not grasped the sense of 'essences' and 'eidetic cognitions'. It is incorrect and by no means my position, as it could appear from Cohn's analyses, that, as he says on page 226 (p. 140 in this volume), "phenomenology is supposed to investigate 'pure consciousness,' but for that it must begin from empirical consciousness and must [...] build on the distinctions that are established in language." By contrast, already in the *Logos* essay I have placed a lot of emphasis on the fact that phenomenology, as much as every other eidetic discipline, does not have to begin from empirical consciousness, i.e., from an experiencing consciousness [574] that, as such, posits existing being. See our analyses on phantasy and apprehension of essences. This lack of understanding goes hand in hand with Cohn's expectation that phenomenology should inform us (or better, he speaks as if I attributed to phenomenology the capacity to inform us) as to whether what is currently present in the stream of consciousness is really eidetically identical with what was present at an earlier point. This would amount to expecting from a geometer statements about whether in the stream of empirical sensory givens pertaining to things a spatial configuration, e.g., one given first here and then there, falls under the same geometric essence, that is, whether it is determined in a geometrically identical fashion. Or else, it would amount to expecting from an arithmetician information about how one should go about ascertaining empirically the identity of numbers. Let us imagine that the purely mathematical disciplines had not been established. Would anybody demand (against the new foundation of the postulate of a mathematical eidetic theory of mathematics free from everything empirical and to be developed in pure intuition and pure thinking) a "proof" of the "validity of the results of eidetic intuitions" for the empirical? Or would anybody misunderstand the statement that in this context pure cognition obviously has to be fundamental for the corresponding empirical sciences, as if it meant that the pure sciences as such should produce out of themselves observations about existing beings and the methods for the investigation of being? I cannot consider Cohn's further objection more pertinent. He objects that the exact description would require a dissection of the lived-experience in isolated moments, but that such dissection can be carried out from different perspectives and in different ways. The exact description of factual lived-experiences is the task of empirical psychology, in the same way in which the exact description of a given thing is the task of empirical natural science. However, insofar as in the essence of a thing we find prefigured highly comprehensive eidetic generalities, such as 'spatial configuration, 'temporal configuration', 'configuration of movement', 'substantiality', 'causality', etc., without which a thing is not possible, the corresponding a priori disciplines provide the investigator of nature with a system of 'exact descriptive' concepts, which he employs in experience, but does not derive from experience. Pushing aside this a priori and intending to form all concepts from experience would amount to rendering impossible exact natural science, i.e., natural science of the highest level. The same applies by analogy (*mutatis mutandis*) to our case.

References

Husserl, Edmund (1981): "Philosophy as a Rigorous Science." Quentin Lauer (Trans.). In: *Husserl: Shorter Works*, pp. 161–197. Notre Dame: University of Notre Dame Press.
Messer, August (1912): "Husserls Phänomenologie in ihrem Verhältnis zur Psychologie." In: *Archiv für die gesamte Psychologie* Vol. 22, pp. 117–129.
Cohn, Jonas (1913): "Grundfragen der Psychologie." In: *Jahrbücher der Philosophie* Vol. 1, pp. 200–235.

Andrea Staiti
Heinrich Gustav Steinmann

Heinrich Gustav Steinmann was born in Freiburg in Breisgau on November, 28th 1887. He was the son of leading geologist and paleontologist Johann Heinrich Conrad Gottfried Gustav Steinmann, who taught at the Albert-Ludwigs-Universität Freiburg at the time, and even became rector in 1899. In 1906 Heinrich Gustav Steinmann moved to Bonn, where his father was appointed director of the local institute of geology, which still carries his name. At the University of Bonn Heinrich Gustav Steinmann studied mathematics, philosophy and physics. On July, 27th 1913 he defended a dissertation in philosophy "On Newton's Influence on the Epistemology of His Time" (Steinmann 1913). His dissertation advisor was prominent psychologist and philosopher Oswald Külpe, who had moved to the University of Bonn in 1909, before leaving for Munich later in 1913. After publishing the article that is translated here, "On the Systematic Position of Phenomenology," in 1916, Steinmann left academia and became a teacher in Essen, first at the Krupp-Oberrealschule and then from 1920 until his retirement in 1952 at the Goethegymnasium.[1] He died in Essen on February, 24th 1954.[2]

"On the Systematic Position of Phenomenology" is a particularly interesting reaction to Husserl's *Ideas* for a few reasons. First, it provides a substantial clue as to what a broadly Külpean critique of Husserlian transcendental phenomenology would have looked like. Despite various thematic affinities, Külpe only mentions Husserl tangentially in his works, and his death in 1916 prevented a direct critical confrontation with the new transcendental orientation of phenomenology in *Ideas*. Like his teacher Külpe, Steinmann defends the view that reality and consciousness are only contingently, and not essentially related, thus opposing Husserl's idealistic thesis. Second, "On the Systematic Position of Phenomenology" is virtually the only article that appeared in response to *Ideas* to place some emphasis on the noetic-noematic correlation as a central discovery of Husserl's transcendental phenomenology. Third, Steinmann raises a number of important questions about the relationship between formal and material eidetics, ranging from the status of axiomatic geometry, to the complex issue of distinguishing between *mathesis universalis* and formal logic. Husserl would continue to grapple with these issues in the years following the publication of *Ideas*, ultimately accepting Steinmann's view that in order for the essences of

---

[1] As per the *Personalakte* 141–4205 of the city of Essen.
[2] As per the death certificate Nr. 30/1954 of the registry office Essen-Bredeney.

a material region to be discernible, objects belonging to that material region must be factually, i.e., empirically given in the first place. Fourth, like August Messer, whom he quotes approvingly, Steinmann interprets phenomenology as a special kind of descriptive psychology, and, as Edith Stein recognizes in her draft of a response to Steinmann (Stein 1987; incl. in this volume p. 301–315), in so doing he holds fast to the distinction between the eidetic and the transcendental dimensions of Husserl's approach. Husserl's lifelong struggle with the problem of distinguishing between psychology and phenomenology despite the applicability of the eidetic method in both domains of inquiry bears witness to importance of this issue. Scholars like Steinmann and Messer can be credited for putting their finger on this issue at an early moment, thereby spurring Husserl to further clarify his ideas.

References

Steinmann, Heinrich Gustav (1913): *Über den Einfluss Newtons auf die Erkenntnistheorie seiner Zeit.* Bonn: Cohen.

Steinmann, Heinrich Gustav (1917): "Zur systematischen Stellung der Phänomenologie." In: *Archiv für die gesamte Psychologie* Vol. 36, pp. 391–422.

Stein, Edith (1987): "Zu Heinrich Gustav Steinmanns Aufsatz 'Zur systematischen Stellung der Phänomenologie.'" In: *Husserliana XXV: Aufsätze und Vorträge (1911–1921)*. Thomas Nenon and Hans Rainer Sepp (Eds.). Dordrecht: Martinus Nijhoff, pp. 253–266.

Translated by Andrea Staiti
Heinrich Gustav Steinmann. On the Systematic Position of Phenomenology

Zur systematischen Stellung der Phänomenologie
Archiv für die gesamte Psychologie 36, pp. 391–422 (1917)

I

[391] In the decade that followed the appearance of Husserl's *Logical Investigations*, this work exerted an influence on the philosophical development in Germany like no other. First, a circle of men gathered around the author wanting to do philosophy in his sense. More importantly, even quite distant philosophical tendencies proved unable to escape the influence of the book. This obviously did not indicate general approval; much opposition and many doubts were voiced, in particular, the demand for a methodological clarification of phenomenology. A short essay could not suffice to meet all these demands, and so it happened that people approved and disapproved of many different things under the name of phenomenology.[1] (Husserl 1981) Some praised the new development of psychological research, some condemned a refined and disguised form of psychologism, some extolled the speculative restraint that limited itself to the mere description of what is evidently given, and some criticized the esoteric method with its reliance on a supra-rational intuition inaccessible to ordinary mortals.

Now, in the inaugural edition of the Jahrbuch, a journal devoted to phenomenological research, Husserl has developed the foundations of his method and provided an overview of its full scope. (Husserl 1913) Those who want to evaluate this [392] new method for the foundation of philosophy on the basis of an authentic presentation will have to stick to this new treatise. Certainly this work has resolved many doubts and dispelled many concerns; we are now in a position to look at the more aphoristic *Logical Investigations* of the second volume in their systematic and methodological context. However, the more clearly we discern the essence of phenomenological research, the more strongly fundamental concerns regarding the foundations and alleged scope of this research make themselves heard. Obviously, this criticism cannot affect the pure phenomeno-

---

[1] Back then August Messer already understood phenomenology in keeping with Husserl's later explanations, in spite of Husserl's opposition.

logical results; in the face of the accomplished fact, the question of whether it is possible loses all meaning. If some were still inclined to doubt the legitimacy of phenomenology after the *Logical Investigations*, this is probably no longer possible; one must admit that this method has disclosed a large sphere of important problems. One can have different opinions concerning the details of Husserl's descriptions and classifications; but the fact that a wide field of scientific research has been sighted and successfully grasped cannot be denied. Even Elsenhans, a fierce opponent of Husserl on fundamental theoretical questions, recognizes the development of phenomenology as an "energetic and sharply conducted attempt to secure for a modern descriptive psychology reliable conceptual foundations and a procedure free from the admixture with natural-scientific methods" (Elsenhanns 1915, p. 263; incl. in this volume p. 370).

Obviously, the claim of phenomenology goes much further; it is supposed to be independent of philosophy and psychology and yet to provide the foundations for those sciences to the greatest extent. In his second essay, Messer shows on the basis of examples that phenomenology, as it is described by Husserl in *Ideas*, is not "separated by abysses from all psychology" (Messer 1914, p. 65; incl. in this volume p. 250) he maintains that phenomenology is "also psychology, and even its most fundamental part." On the other hand, he does not dispute the claim of phenomenology to found all of philosophy, and he even concedes, precisely for this reason, that phenomenology goes beyond the scope of descriptive psychology (Messer 1914, p. 52; incl. in this volume p. 239); but Messer abstains from delving into the scope and import of phenomenology. (Messer 1914, p. 56; incl. in this volume p. 243) This question however is extremely [393] pressing, since it touches on the important problem of the relations between philosophy and psychology. In what follows, therefore, this issue will be handled at least for theoretical philosophy, after having established on the basis of Husserl's own characterizations in what sense phenomenology can be rightly considered psychology.

Husserl approaches the distinction between his phenomenology and empirical psychology from two entirely different directions; first, on the basis of the logical distinction between *knowledge of essence* and *knowledge of facts*; second, on the basis of the transcendental distinction between the *phenomenological* and *natural* attitudes.[2] These distinctions have in common the fact that they are not immediately familiar, which is why Husserl seeks to clarify them in an extensive introduction. Apart from that, they belong in entirely different dimensions and

---

2 First introduced in *Ideen* 3f./4f.

must be investigated separately.³ In the first case, what is at issue is the logical structure of certain cognitions and sciences about which it should be possible to reach agreement on the basis of existing disciplines. The second distinction, on the other hand, touches on epistemological and ultimately metaphysical questions. Here, one can probably clarify Husserl's position on individual issues, but neither an overall agreement nor a decisive verdict can be reached overnight. The more fruitful standpoint is thus obviously the first distinction; as far as the position of phenomenology is concerned, however, the second distinction proves to be decisive.

Husserl himself sharply separated the logical and the epistemological introductions from one another and deals with each of them in the first two sections of *Ideas*. The fact that Husserl himself considers such introductions necessary cannot be used as an objection against phenomenology's claim to provide the foundations of philosophy. This is because the ideas developed in these sections do not in turn provide the foundations for phenomenological truths. Rather, they are only supposed to establish the legitimacy of the method against objections flowing from some logical or epistemological standpoint already at hand. The charge of circularity undermines this undertaking just as little as it undermines logic and epistemology in general.

II

[394] Husserl clearly distinguishes between knowledge of facts and knowledge of essence, and on the basis of this distinction he derives the concepts 'region' and 'category'. These analyses may remind the reader of Lask. (Lask 1911; 1912) In particular, Lask disassociates the formal region (Lask calls it the "reflexive region") from all material regions and emphasizes that the subordination of material categories to the formal region cannot be interpreted as if the formal categories were the uppermost genera of material categories. This perspective is very important with respect to the empiricist critique of the doctrine of categories,⁴ which recognizes only one type of subordination: the inclusion of extensions

---

3 Elsenhans does not always seem to make this distinction sharply enough in the aforementioned essay (Elsenhans 1915; incl. in this volume p. 339–381).

4 See recently Külpe (1915, p. 33; p. 72f.), where Wundt's position, in its essence, is approvingly cited. Incidentally, the position I defend here is close to Külpe's and is largely indebted to him. The sudden twist of fate that put an end to his work on his systematic magnum opus, not even half a year after Lask's death, struck a huge blow to the prospect of clarifying the problems touched on here.

in broader extensions. Through this pure extensional logic two distinctions are swept away: on the one hand, the distinction between generalization and formalization; on the other hand, the distinction between the eidetic subsumption of species under genus and the relationship between the τόδε τι [the 'this-here'] and essence, or τόδε τι and empirical genus. To be sure, all these relationships have in common that they correspond to subordinations of extensions, so that the formal logical calculus can be applied. However, this applicability is grounded in entirely distinct logical relationships in each case.

The formal region in Husserl appears to correspond to Lask's reflexive sphere almost exactly, both in terms of its content and its systematic position. We will have to look more closely at this issue in the last section. In contrast to Lask, Husserl expands the number of material regions significantly. Lask acknowledges only three: being, validity, and supra-sensible being [*Übersein*]. Husserl says expressly: "*Every science of facts* (science of experience) *has essential, theoretical foundations in eidetic ontologies.*" (*Ideen* 19/20) And since every ontology corresponds to a region, there are a whole host of Husserlian regions within Lask's sphere of being. Unfortunately, a survey of the material regions [395] and the "hierarchy of the doctrines of essence" (*Ideen* 322/308) is nowhere to be found, not even at the conclusion. The region "thing" (physical nature) assumes a privileged position for all regions of reality; it stands in a foundational relationship with them. In addition to the region of real psychic being, what is meant here are the axiological and practical regions, such as, e. g., those regions containing cultural objects. However, these regions encompass realities (at least in the examples provided on page 318 (*Ideen* 318/304)); hence, following the customary terminology, they encompass *goods*, not values. The conclusion seems obvious that a particular region of values besides the region of things provides the foundations for the region of goods, yet Husserl does not indicate this anywhere. Husserl, too, sharply distinguishes Lask's third region, 'supra-sensible being', from all other kinds of transcendence, but he does not investigate it with respect to its doctrine of essences, as one might expect. (*Ideen* 96f./93f.)

Yet another point is in need of clarification. Eidetic sciences should apprehend their object purely in terms of essence, that is, without considering existence and thus independently of experience. This is the point where Elsenhans, too, launches his criticism. For the aforementioned reasons, however, he fails to recognize the sense of the Husserlian term 'essence' and its relation to the *a priori*. Therefore, he fails to address the essential elements of eidetic research. However, this is absolutely necessary in order to understand to what extent the problem of phenomenological method is influenced by its eidetic character. If our criticism occasionally overlaps with Elsenhans, it is important to note that is only due to a preliminary logical issue, that the main point of contention does not lie in the eidetic, but rather in the authentically "phenomenological" character of Husserl's doctrine.

The formal region is only accessible to eidetic investigation, and therefore the apriority of the formal sciences will not give rise to any objection. The status of material ontology appears more doubtful. Let us dwell on the most pertinent example and the one that Husserl appeals to almost exclusively: the ontology of physical nature. A branch of the ontology of physical nature is, for instance, geometry, since the "thing" is essentially res extensa. Husserl has to argue along these lines: "regardless of whether bodies actually exists or not, the essence of what we call "body" necessarily entails the following: it cuts out a delimited piece from a three dimensional multiplicity, called space, as the content of this space." [396] Obviously, I am free to conceive of a multiplicity of arbitrarily many dimensions, constituted in some manner, and to characterize a clearly delineated piece thereof in some way. To every well-defined multiplicity corresponds a pure *a priori* geometry, and among these geometries we also find physical geometry. But how are we to recognize physical geometry from this multiplicity of geometries? There are two answers to this. Either one admits that the geometry that founds physics does not enjoy any essential priority vis-à-vis all other possible geometries, i.e., that its privileged application to nature is founded on certain experiences (or even: experiments) that have to be carefully verified, or one appeals yet again to the intuition of the pure essences 'body' and 'space'. This path is not viable as it rests on a fallacy of four terms. *Either* one understands by *res extensa* the fulfillment of a segment of some well-defined multiplicity, in which case there is no way to grasp the priority of this multiplicity relative to any other multiplicity; *or*, on the contrary, 'body' means the individual substrate of nature as it appears to us. In that case, it is essentially impossible to determine anything about its properties, including extension, before we become familiar with the fundamental traits of this essence on the basis of experience. The fact that experience in this context assumes a legitimate position within essential knowledge has its basis *precisely in the essence* of the apprehended body, and this fact can itself be recognized in its essential necessity. The essence "body" has necessary relations to the essence ("outer") experience.

If, in opposition to this, one proposes to appeal to the intuition of a space that is pure, yet necessarily valid of nature, this will of course call to mind what has been rightly said since Gauß's time with respect to Kant, whose view of space is the same as the one just described. Insofar as the content of this intuition is not deducible from other parts, it should be described by the *axioms*. If this were the case, then one could very well understand disagreement concerning the *formulation* of the axioms; however, we could not understand how, in the face of a generally acknowledged disjunction of three axioms, one could seriously doubt *which of the three cases corresponds to nature*. This is the case with the so-called Euclidean axiom. Experience, which, undoubtedly, alone can decide, has not yet spoken; however, it is certainly possible to imagine observations from which the physical validity of a "non-Euclidean" geometry would follow. This question is thus far from being resolvable through an intuition of space. Rather, its solution depends on experiences, whose [397] conditions can certainly be conceived, but not produced. In light of the indubitable possibility of such experiences (such as the contemporary appearance of a star in opposite directions or angular measurements of large triangles that result in a spherical excess or hyperbolic defect) the assertion that the Euclidean axiom alone describes the evident content of spatial intuition and is therefore the only axiom relevant to physics proves to be a careless simplification. However, if our supposedly infallible intuition deceives on these points, we have no remaining reason to trust it on other matters. Actually, the experiences on which the validity of the remaining axiom groups for physical geometry is rooted can be exhibited in detail, one by one, even if this is not so simple. So for example, the axioms of congruence (without which pure projective geometry forms only a vast system of important theorems) are only justified in a world in which there are *rigid bodies* that can be moved and rotated.

One can of course say that axiomatics is neither the only, nor the most insightful way toward a foundation of geometry. (Study 1914, p. 125 f.) It is possible to construct analytical geometry from pure set theory with the aid of the arithmetic derivable from it, thereby borrowing as definitions some propositions that academics usually characterize as "synthetic." Let us consider a 'point' an entity that consists of three numbers x_1, x_2, x_3 and let us define identity as the corresponding equality of all three coordinates ($X = Y$, when $x_1 = y_1$, $x_2 = y_2$, $x_3 = y_3$) and as the square of the distance between two points with the following expression $(x_1 - y_1)^2 + (x_2 - y_2)^2 + (x_3 - y_3)^2$. It is easy to then prove the invariance of this function for displacement and rotation. Here too, the difficulty lies in the foundation of the individual steps (e. g., the three-dimensionality, the definition of distance, and so on) through experience. However, this difficulty can be overcome by way of thinking through the problems consistently, whereas, even through the best phenomenological analysis of the constitution of *res extensa* in absolute consciousness, spatial intuition does not gain any demonstrative force in geometrical matters. (*Ideen*, p. 315/301)

The example of geometry shows that material ontologies are not *a priori* in the sense that they allow [398] for knowledge of the real (even if only with regard to the essence of real things) to be grounded without any recourse to experience. Actually, the issue is the same for all material ontologies as it is with geometry; it is simply that this most developed of all material ontologies makes the situation particularly clear. One can define whatever one wants as an *organism*, including in one's definition what biology understands as an organism; *then*, from this definition, certain proposition follow *a priori*. Such inferences are actually used quite often, and presumably it is a thoroughly helpful enterprise for the person researching organic nature to define the concept of organism precisely, using as few fundamental properties as possible, in order to then figure out which additional properties can be deductively inferred from the fundamental properties. For instance, from the fact of reproduction alone, the necessity of nourishment immediately follows; the essentially irreversible process of life requires an energy supply. Even more than in the case of geometry, however, it is a pointless fiction to present these concepts purely *a priori* as *specifications* of all possibilities; as a matter of fact, the realm of the possible (i.e., the realm of non-contradictory concepts) is so immense that no systematic specialization within that realm can lead to the concept of organism. And this is probably not what Husserl means. The *possible* is itself a purely formal object (and thus merely the form of an object), and can just as little be considered the uppermost genus for all kinds of essence (εἴδη) as the object in general can be considered the uppermost genus for the specific regions of objects. Rather, the *specific* essence *itself* should be *intuitable a priori*. It is repeatedly emphasized that the results of empirical sciences must be kept at a distance from eidetic science, since the sharp opposition between apriority and experience corresponds exactly to the opposition between essence and existence. (*Ideen* 18/19) Yet here, as in other passages of the book, Husserl betrays a reversion to Kant in the wrong spot. Today we know that existence is just as much essential property as the qualities. (Selz 1911) The fact that real existence seems to dissolve into particular relations on closer inspection is something that real existence has in common with some other properties. Surely it belongs to the "essential" characteristics of bodies that they belong to nature, that is, to the world of experience. However, if existence can really be attributed to 'essence' (*Essenz*), it follows that, if we want to avoid the error of ontologism, not every essence [399] can be given entirely *a priori*. One can absolutely acknowledge the essence and value of eidetic knowledge while still conceding that material ontology, although itself *not* knowledge of experience, nevertheless is *tightly interwoven* with certain results from associated empirical sciences. This mutual dependence, the passing of the baton from one method to another where the former cannot advance any further, amounts to an extremely intriguing interplay that poses highly rewarding tasks for methodological analysis. This interplay is usually described, though not very precisely, as the cooperation of induction and deduction. What particularly attracts the *logician* here is the problem of how the construction of empirical class concepts is nourished through the anticipation of genuine species and genera. The relationship of genuine species to methodologically regimented induction also deserves consideration. In this context, ontology does not run parallel to empirical science, but stands before it as its methodological ideal. It should also be noted that the originator of ontological disciplines, Christian Wolff, is close to our view as well.[5]

In this way, however, it seems that *a priori* knowledge is reduced to "analytic" knowledge and that the role of intuition[6] is diminished. Intuition does nevertheless have a role. In actual experience its role as sensory intuition is uncontroversial. However, there is also a genuine eidetic intuition. Every *non-sensory evidence*[7] is an example. The entire act presents itself as insight into certain necessary relations between states of affairs, as in the previous example of [400] reproduction and nourishment in organisms. Of course, that is not to say that here we have an insight into the logical dependence of two propositions (as premise and conclusion). Even if one limits evidence to experiences of judging, it is only exceptionally (for the so-called judicative evaluations) that "the truth of a judgment [...] is immediately clear" (Elsenhans 1915, p. 260; incl. in this volume p. 368). What is intuitively seen is rather the obtaining of a state of affairs, an essential state of affairs in this case.[8] The judgment depends on evidence for its claim to validity; how would that be possible, if in this evidence only further judgments, and not the things themselves, came to givenness?[9] We can only see with evidence what lies open to our inquiring gaze. Let us test the correctness of an eidetic judgment, such as 2 x 3 = 6. We will see that this is only properly

---

[5] Cf. my essay on the influence of Newton on epistemology of his time (Steinmann 1913, p. 59f.), and H. Pichler (1910).

[6] Today it is no longer an option to categorically restrict the concept of intuition to the *sensuous* sphere, as Külpe would do (Külpe 1915, p. 50, fn. 2). Since Kant's time we have heard enough of intellectual and other possible or impossible kinds of intuitions that we are prepared to accept a reasonable widening of the concept of intuition. The fact that Lask holds onto the equation "intuition = sensibility" seems to me a restriction inherited from his school that blocks his progress towards an unbiased interpretation of mathematics, just as it did for Rickert (1912, p. 26–78). Kant, however, defined intuition as every mode of givenness of objects, and this continues to be the best meaning of the expression today. The limitation to sensibility is not part of Kant's definition; on the contrary, this limitation is conditioned by his view of the contingent organization of the human cognitive faculty.

[7] "Evidential seeing" as defined in *Ideen* 285f./273f..

[8] Husserl says 'make up of an essence' (*Wesensverhalt*) (*Ideen* 285/273).

[9] For Lask as well (1912), judgment is something derivative, and even doubly so. It justifies its claim to validity only with respect to the original measuring rod, namely, theoretical validity, i.e., with respect to the simple material standing in its category, i.e., with respect to a sphere that is surely accessible to a logical grasp but that stands beyond expressive activity.

speaking possible if one focuses one's gaze on the *state of affairs* itself until the state of affairs, albeit supported by an exemplary substratum, offers itself to our grasp in concrete self-givenness. Only what is *grasped* can be evidently formulated. If the state of affairs is not itself present, but *only intended*, it can indeed also be formulated. In this case, however, the judgment does not possess the original rational legitimacy to which Husserl, for good reasons, restricts the concept of evidence.

Because the sources of evidence lie beyond the sphere of judgment, it is probably advisable to give a broader meaning to this term, one that is detached from judgment. At its core, this is what Husserl's account of evidence does. (*Ideen* 824/272) Even though the customary limitation to non-contradictory judgments is mentioned a few pages later, this limitation is hardly compatible with Husserl's position. (*Ideen* 287/300) By locating evidence in the act of *grasping*, and not in the *expression* of a state of affairs, Husserl also does justice to the conditions of *assertoric* evidence. The possibility of such evidence in external perception or in reflection is often contested, as it is allegedly impossible to formulate the supposedly evident content [401] in a still completely evident judgment.[10] Nonetheless, both perception and reflection actually do typically possess such truly rich evidential content. Even if we bracket all moments of experience, we cannot deny this evidential content. Obviously, the evidential content cannot be *described* without employing general expressions, which can never fully capture the individual sense in which such content is alone evident. The forms of assertion alone already occlude the evident state of affairs in such a way that it loses its unambiguous character.[11]

---

[10] Elsenhans (1915, p. 259; incl. in this volume p. 367) raises his objection against intuitive evidence along the same lines. It need not be added that for us, as for Husserl, *all* evidence is intuitional, provided that intuition retains the Kantian sense of givenness of the object.

[11] The problem of evidence need not be dealt with further here. On the criterion problem, however, the following should still be noted: a criterion is nonetheless a mark, i.e. something that is itself accessible and that, by virtue of a lawful relation, gives me information about something inaccessible (either momentarily or fundamentally). In immediate evidence, however, the thing itself is given, such that the demand for a criterion loses its sense. If one wanted a criterion to determine whether a state of affairs is self-given or not, one would then have to demand a subsequent criterion to determine whether the state of affairs expressed by the first criterion is given, and so on. By contrast, if a state of affairs is inaccessible, an accessible criterion can certainly transpose its own evidence mediately onto that state affairs; this is the criterion's proper function. The appearance of sediment of barium chloride is an excellent criterion to determine the presence of sulfuric acid in an aqueous solution. If I have poured sulfuric acid into the solution myself, however, I can do without the criterion.

Evident insights also harbor completely different formal moments, which, unlike the apophantic moments, do not disappear when we return to consider the state of affairs. Nevertheless, each insight into a material essence entails an element that finds its legitimacy only in the intuition of the essence itself; this element is the applicability of precisely this formal scheme and no other. For instance, before I carry out the formal operation of a syllogism, I must 'see' that the essences at issue stand in the required relations to one another. What is meant here is not the trivial proposition that one must have premises in order to draw a conclusion; rather, the art of making inferences, the actual "insight," consists in one's ability to "*see*" that the familiar states of affairs have the character of premises.[12] Something similar holds for the application of other [402] pure forms. In the example of reproduction and nourishment, for example, we find the pure form of the multiplication of a continuous magnitude with a natural number governing the progression; obviously this is only revealed through logical analysis. In this case too, however, the heart of the inference is the insight that we are dealing with an instance of *this* form. For Kant, this crucial feature of the material intuition of essence is a function of the power of judgment. This allows us to understand his argument that this capacity does not possess general rules, and that "its deficiency cannot be remedied." (Kant 1998, B 172f.) Of course, as with sensuous seeing, intuition cannot be taught, but only exercised, and rules for it should follow the model: something is blue if it is blue.

Both in perception and in reflection on lived experience as *facts*, we saw that evidence is only related to the immediate perceptual content, which cannot be formulated without the aid of eidetic expressions. However, because the inevitable tension between fact and essence, individual and species, and empirical contingency and eidetic necessity entails the imperfection of all formulated knowledge of experience, one has often been tempted to overlook the evidence of sensory intuition. In contrast to sensory intuition, the pure knowledge of essence obviously appears as *necessary*, and in this sense, as *a priori*. However, it must not be forgotten that the realm of εἴδη forms an unsurveyable ocean, in which one can orient oneself only by keeping the islands of experience constantly in view. Obviously, no one reaches the rich treasures of those islands without giving oneself over to the ocean.

---

[12] In simple cases, we move in the sphere of *unexpressed* consciousness of eidetic states of affairs. The terms "premise" and "conclusion," that are typically only used for judgments, must be correspondingly transposed onto this unexpressed sphere.

Let us summarize the results of all these considerations with respect to Husserl's eidetic science of consciousness: no material essence is given *a priori* merely because it is an essence; even if authentic eidetic intuition (i.e., the seeing of what is formal within material essences) is not an experiencing act, the essence must be constituted in some other way, if we want to depart from the sphere of mere possibilities. In particular, the essential feature, "real existence," always points back to a founding experience. Even the exemplary fantasizing of individuals combined with ideation cannot dispense with this foundation. This is because even if ideation is *a priori*, the question of the provenance of the exemplary *tode ti* and how it comes to be given still remains. This question [403] is by no means marginal, since the foundation for the cognition of essence is provided by certain features of the individual, even if indirectly (via ideation). The essential knowledge of *pure consciousness* will also have to be tested on this point.

III

Let us now turn to the second section of *Ideas*. It contains two important claims: (1) by bracketing the "natural thesis" we obtain a domain of *pure consciousness*, which can be investigated on its own terms; (2) the data of this pure consciousness are always self-given, that is, they do not possess the phenomenal character of external experience; consequently, this entire sphere is *absolute*, while everything real is *merely relative*. The correctness of the first claim is easy to prove, as the rest of the book provides sufficient evidence for it by actually carrying out the research. The second claim, however, seems highly dubious, bound up in old philosophical errors.

The absoluteness of self-consciousness in Descartes is famously the point of departure for all modern theory of knowledge, and Husserl himself is well aware of this connection. All subsequent philosophers, including Leibniz and the British empiricists, were influenced by it. Kant worked very hard to free himself from Descartes' thesis, without fully succeeding (Kant 1998, B 422, fn.); the thesis is restored to its former standing by his successors, notably Schelling and Schopenhauer. In explanatory psychology, the need to study the actuality of lived experience, not as an ultimate datum, but as the appearance of psychical reality, created a counterbalance. The Neo-Kantians had a similar effect, only, in the place of psychical reality, they introduced a more or less unknowable X. One sees that we are dealing here with an entirely central issue; the founding principle of the absoluteness of consciousness is the cornerstone of all subjective idealism and phenomenalism [*Konzientialismus*], from Descartes to Mach. Naturally, Husserl is not working towards a phenomenalism in the usual sense; he emphatically stresses that the transcendent "reality" of things should remain untouched. Rather, his analysis pertains only to the supposedly legitimate core of Cartesian and all later idealism, which he locates in the proposition according to which "the world of transcendent 'res' is utterly dependent upon [...] currently actual consciousness." (*Ideen* 92/89, see also 93/90) Precisely this is the authentic, fundamental position of idealism [404] which Kant struggled against. (Kant 1998, B 274 f.) One may want to object to Kant's proof by saying that what is at issue here is not a science of *real* consciousness that is woven into the world, but a science of phenomenologically *reduced* consciousness. One should remember, however, that there is only *one consciousness* and that it is *either* absolute *or* bound up with the world. If justification requires not only *freedom from contradictions*, but also *agreement* with a *state of affairs*, then it is entirely impossible to acknowledge both the realist and the idealist positions as justified from their respective standpoints. Both want to determine the "true" relationship of consciousness and reality. Even if one can *conceptually* disentangle pure lived experience from all connections with the real world, the question remains whether the objects that correspond to this concept, namely, the actual streams of experience of living people, exhibit the same isolation and autonomy in their being. The reasons that prompt us to doubt this view have been put forward often enough by the supporters of realism;[13] a discussion of these reasons is not our task here. What's more, they will hardly be disputed, provided only one admits that they pertain to present consciousness in its authentic being. The only way out, which remains available in order to save the distinctive character of phenomenology, is to interpret the phenomenological reduction as a *methodological aid*, as an abstractive restriction of interest to that segment of reality determined by the concept "pure lived experience." This route appears *quite passable*, but Husserl has to reject it (*Ideen* 91 f./88 f.), because while it may lead to a new *specialized science*, it will not lead to the *founding science of all philosophy*.

Once we have freed ourselves from the compulsion to regard the immediate data of consciousness as something independent and absolute, the argument that lived experiences do not give themselves through "profiles" loses its force. (*Ideen* 89 f./86 f.) Indeed, if one took this last line of thought seriously, the very notion of an eidetic science of lived experiences would be undermined. The anger that I feel now is the same as the anger that I felt two minutes ago, and not merely because it belongs within the same extended duration ("lasting

---

13 For example, see the first chapter of Külpe's *Die Realisierung* (1912), or §17 of his *Einleitung in die Philosophie* (1895) and the fifth chapter of Messer's *Einleitung in die Erkenntnistheorie* (1909).

for two minutes"), but also because of the conscious identity of its intentional object. Nevertheless, it is given to me now in an entirely different profile than before; indeed, the profiles have since that time transformed in exactly the same way as the appearance of a body is transformed when it moves some distance away from me. If we try to deny the reality of this anger, which appears in its own profiles, and explain it as a falsely hypostasized generality, then we have to do the same with the appearing body, and we fall prey to an irredeemable empiricist skepticism. Such skepticism will also be pernicious in the context of phenomenology, even if one leaves aside the comparison with the physical world. The theory that pure lived experiences are not appearances, but are rather something absolutely independent, clearly makes their subsumption under eidetic moments impossible. This would allow at best for a *factual science* of pure lived experiences (*Ideen* 119/114), but not an *eidetic theory* of pure lived experiences. Undoubtedly, the possibility of phenomenology is grounded in the true essence of lived experiences, as the possibility of physics (as eidetic science) is grounded in the true essence of outer appearances. It is irrefutable that what imposes itself on us in the appearance is precisely what appears. To be sure, it is possible to abstract from what appears, but one cannot easily believe that the essence of consciousness is grasped by means of this abstraction. Otherwise, our sensitivity to differences would inform us about all of the sensory qualities and intensities that are possible within one interval, whereas we assume with good reasons that the sensations can vary as steadily as the stimuli themselves, and that small differences simply go unnoticed. *To understand appearances is to go beyond them.*

It will be replied again and again that phenomenology is not touched by these objections. Indeed, these objections do not touch phenomenology, but only the exaggeration that tries to attribute metaphysical truth to the basic methodological fiction at the foundation of phenomenology. Precisely this exaggeration lies in Husserl's analyses. (*Ideen* 106 f./102 f.) One thinks that one is hearing Lask again when one is told that reality and world only exist through meaning-bestowal, that they are grounded in certain nexuses of absolute consciousness. The lamentable philosophical absolutization [405] of the world comes face to face here with a no less philosophically laden absolutization of *consciousness*. The fact that we can think away the world proves nothing at all. A philosophically uncorrupted spirit can think away all conscious beings from the world just as well, perhaps even more easily. This happens, for instance, in considerations regarding the origin of our solar system. Suns and planets come and go without the least concern for their conscious spectators. If this thought is a naturalistic absolutization then at least it is no more misguided than its idealistic counterpart.

Here the first idealistic prejudice intersects with a second prejudice, which Kant's followers already played off against their teacher. One can call it the πρῶτον ψεῦδος (*proton* pseudos) of *objective* idealism, whereas the absoluteness of consciousness originally aims at a *subjective* idealism. The external world, Husserl says, is only accessible to us as the intentional object of our thought. (*Ideen* §49 f.) The external world is thus only mediated by consciousness, and is thereby merely relative. It is astonishing to hear that Husserl, of all people, holds this view. Is it really necessary to point out again that an object is not at all determined by being described as the target of a possible intention? Just about everything is accessible to a meaning *intentio*.[14] To be an intentional correlate is not a special feature of a class of objects; it is not a *feature* of objects at all. Rather, it is a *relation*, and indeed, considered from the side of the object, a merely *ideal* relation. The fact of "being-the-object-of-an-intention" does not determine or influence an object in its essence, nor does it determine its *metaphysical* locus, in the sense that a centaur, the Θ-function, God, the piece of paper before me, and a square circle have different metaphysical loci. I can "intend" all of these objects in this order, they all stand in the relation of being an object for consciousness. But it is thereby left entirely unsaid whether they are real, ideal, absolute, relative, or whatever else they could be. If the world were nothing more than a sum of intentional objects, then it would be nothing at all; everything that the world is, it is independently of this relation. Over and against the bold human endeavor to relativize things through thought, these things stand in complete ataraxia. [407] The whole bias stems from an intellectual milieu from which Husserl is otherwise fairly removed. To the best of my knowledge, Hegel is the originator of the critique of the Kantian concept of the a thing-in-itself which points out that the thing-in-itself, as pure object of thought, does not lead beyond the sphere of consciousness. Husserl has cleared up the confusion of representation and object; thus, Hegel's notion of *belonging to* consciousness becomes a *dependence on* consciousness.

There remains only the claim that consciousness, unlike an intentional object, is given to us immediately and absolutely, while the external world is accessible only as an act-correlate. This claim stands in peculiar opposition to Husserl's subsequent analyses concerning reflection and attentional modifications. (*Ideen* 138/133; 190/182) According to these analyses, that which is not grasped at this moment, but which is nonetheless conscious, is at all times the target of a non-actual intention, one that can be actualized by a redirection of the

---

[14] Lask refers to this accurately in his language with the expression "panarchy of logos, but not panlogism" (Lask 1911, p. 134).

look however. The reflection through which pure consciousness is grasped, though, is itself nothing other than such a redirection of the look. It actualizes something that has hitertho gone unnoticed but which is nonetheless intentionally present. Hence, there is no hint of a fundamentally different manner of givenness of pure consciousness here. And even if consciousness were really *closer to us* than things are, what would this prove as regards the *intrinsic* autonomy of things? Perhaps our position in the totality of world and consciousness is contingent; perhaps we do not grasp the wellspring of being at its *origin*, but only in its *final products*. Whoever forgets this, whoever seeks the absolute in what is closest to him, is taking what is first for us as what is first per se.[15] He elevates the conventions by which Mephistopheles recognizes the learned gentlemen to the level of a metaphysical principle.

IV

Let us briefly summarize our results so far. The possibility of an eidetic science is always given evidentially when the path by which we reach an intuition of the essences that are at issue lies open. As the domain that is thereby opened is larger and smaller, we are more or less independent from other sources of knowledge. There are numerous gradations here, for which the eidetic natural sciences provide examples. [408] The scope of pure eidetics narrows progressively from the *a priori* disciplines of pure mathematics to the succinct lines of reasoning incorporated into the determination of facts.[16] Let us now consider the status of phenomenology in this regard. Deduction in the broad mathematical sense is denied to phenomenology (*Ideen* 140/134); it is obliged to return continuously to a new ideational intuition. To begin with, however, this is always a singular intuition (*Ideen* 124 f./119 f.), and even if the choice of the highlighted moments is determined by the eidetic-scientific objective at hand, the content of what is seen is nevertheless supplied by this individual intuition. Here, in fact, we have a case that is distinguished from the abstract eidetic sciences. The eidetic task here is not deduction, but rather is simply the highlighting and description of essential characteristics.[17] Having set aside deduction, however, phenomenology cannot

---

15 See *Ideen* 93/90, beginning of §50. One becomes aware that "the game that idealism play has with greater justice been turned against it" (Kant 1998, B 276).
16 Several levels may serve as examples: theoretical mechanics, electrostatic, thermodynamics, chemical structural formulae.
17 Also, therefore, the seeing of something in its essence, as we found in *Ideen* (40 f./39 f.) to be the core of eidetic research in general.

generate essences on the basis of a few elements through eidetic work alone, as is done in mathematics; rather, the essences must be given to phenomenology from the outside. Before anything is elevated to the level of full intuitiveness and clarity, it must be given always anew by novel individual intuitions, upon which ideation builds. The act through which these intuitions can alone be given is reflection, and Husserl's fine discussions of reflection and inner perception indicate that we do not have to understand this term in a fundamentally different sense than psychology does. The procedure described hereby would thus be the entirely legitimate method of a *descriptive eidetic psychology*.

The phenomenological reduction remains as a fundamental difference. The psychologist also has to carry out the reduction, albeit in the only form that the reduction can have according to the account given in the foregoing sections: as a methodological fiction, as a redirection of interest from the objects of intentional lived experiences towards these lived experiences themselves. In so doing, the psychologist is guided by a double interest. *First*, he wants to reach an attitude that is especially appropriate for reflection on lived experiences. Through the reduction, he methodologically forecloses the possibility of straying from the path of pure description [409] to the all too proximate pathways of causal explanation of physical or real psychical kinds. The phenomenological reduction does not find its justification in an *idealistic theory of knowledge*, but rather in the *requirements of descriptive psychology*.

In this way, the partition that Husserl erects between phenomenology and eidetic psychology[18] falls down, both for us and for Messer. (Messer 1914, p. 32; 62f.) The method described does not fundamentally differ from a psychological method, and phenomenology seems to sink to the level of a special discipline of psychology.[19] This does not affect the value of Husserl's fine analyses in the third and fourth sections; indeed, the author himself repeatedly emphasizes their close relationship to eidetic psychology. Phenomenology need only give up its claim to be the fundamental philosophical science from which logic and the theory of knowledge must draw.

But precisely here one can raise some concerns; because in fact, in Husserl's sketchy analyses in the fourth section, there exists a substantive connection between the *phenomenological* findings and the *rational-theoretical* problems that are addressed there. If one concedes that the solution to these problems can only be expected from phenomenology, then, having claimed that phenomenol-

---

[18] Whether there can also be a non-descriptive eidetic psychology remains to be seen. Cf. *Ideen* 141/135f.

[19] Elsenhans reaches similar results in an entirely different manner (1915, p. 240f.; incl. in this volume p. 351f.).

ogy is a branch of psychology, we can rightly be accused of psychologism. This buzzword has of course gradually been discredited, since it has been used to oppose almost all modern theories of knowledge. This already tempts one to think that—no matter how justified the general argument against psychologism may be—there must be something obscure in the thing itself, something that casts an ugly shadow over all attempts to address the issue.

Since we are concerned here with the scope of phenomenology, only a few remarks with respect to this very controversial problem can be given. For the sake of expediency, we will take our point of departure from Husserl's fundamental distinction between noesis and noema. (*Ideen* 191/183) [410] The distinction between noesis and noema does not coincide with the customary distinction between act and object, but rather separates real and intentional components within the act itself. As Husserl understands these concepts, the distinction cuts across the act so sharply that every modification (attentional, doxic, and so on) unfolds on both sides as noetic and as noematic. All of the ensuing analyses, therefore, are dominated by the strict correlation between noesis and noema, and it can hardly be denied that this descriptive determination is correct. One must ask oneself, however, whether it is necessary or appropriate to keep a pair of concepts in the foreground which all further objects of investigation duplicate and which therefore, precisely because of this thoroughgoing correlation between noesis and noema, obstruct the possibility of an appropriate classification. And is it really impossible to classify different moments in terms of whether they pertain *originally* to the act itself or to its intentional correlate? For example, let us consider *attentional* modifications. It can easily be proved that they are originally *noetic*. Of course, the noema is different, depending on whether it is situated in the focal point of consciousness or "to the side"; but Husserl himself must recognize that this is merely a change in illumination and not in the actual meaning content. (*Ideen* 191) A change in the *object*, on the other hand, pertains originally to the *noema*, specifically, to its "core stratum"; only in relation to such change in the object can the simultaneous change in the noesis be understood. The noesis that is directed toward the blooming tree certainly differs for essential reasons from the noesis that is directed towards the house; however, the two noeses only differ insofar as the tree-noema and house-noema are different. The fact that the noematic differences are the original ones is already clear from the fact that the noetic differences are not at all comprehensible without reference to the noematic.

It is not our goal to work through this distinction of act structures between *originally-noetic* and *originally-noematic* in detail; what has to be shown is merely that such a distinction is possible. The Husserlian partition between noesis and noema thus resembles a half-transparent mirror: one can look into it from whichever side one wants, but one will always behold the same totality of things. He who looks closely enough, however, will notice that each time only some of those things are seen in the original, while the others are mirrored, and that the ones that are mirrored are precisely the ones that appear in the original on the other side. We therefore form [411] the concept of the originally-noetic and then originally-noematic, and in so doing we believe that we remain within the descriptive sphere, since those characteristics announce themselves in the pure givenness of the corresponding essence.

What is originally noematic is everything that is determined by the object itself; this is precisely what Husserl designates as the noematic *core*.[20] The *object itself* is not the theme of phenomenological investigation. Phenomenology's theme, rather, is the object's *mode of presentation* in the intending consciousness. This is true not only of real objects,[21] but of all other kinds of objects as well. Of course, the specific objects of phenomenology fall into this category as well, but there is no contradiction in this: when we phenomenologically investigate the acts that are directed towards phenomenological objects, this investigation presupposes none of the phenomenological truths that hold of those objects. Rather, such investigation neutralizes, or "parenthesizes," all of these truths. In the noematic-core, then, we are presented with an element that, phenomenologically speaking, is *not graspable* with respect to its proper content, even though its surrounding elements and its position with regard to these surrounding elements belong to phenomenology's innermost field of research. This peculiar state of affairs is grounded in the particular essence of the consciousness of objects. This form of consciousness encompasses its correlate along with its forms, but does not, however, dissolve or transform the correlate into something internal.

Husserl himself, however, did not observe this point consistently. The exaggerated pretensions of phenomenology flow precisely from this oversight. The phenomenological reduction is supposed to encompass the formal and material doctrines of essence (*Ideen* 111f./112f.); later, however, it turns out that phenomenology is supposed to have fundamental importance for precisely these disciplines as well. (*Ideen* 307–319/293–305) Obviously, this entails no intrinsic contradiction, since the reduction determines only the independence of phenomenology from those other sciences and not the reverse, the independ-

---

[20] In his use of this and other terms, Husserl himself takes into account the point made here to a certain extent. He has surely noted it on occasion, but he has not systematically expanded on it.

[21] For the terminological distinction between "Gegenstand," "Objekt," and so forth, see Külpe, (1912, p. 11), even if the departure from signs does not seem appropriate to me.

ence of those other sciences from phenomenology. Once one becomes clear on the state of affairs that is described above [412], namely, that the objective determinations of the noematic-core are not at all on the same level as the fundamental noetic modifications, it is apparent that the consistent implementation of the phenomenological reduction in no way allows us to emerge from the specifically phenomenological sphere. Thus, it makes no difference whether the originally excluded and now no longer accessible object is itself a fact or an essence. Concerning the sphere of fact, this is entirely clear, and Husserl concedes this as well. The phenomenological investigation of an act directed toward facts, for instance, the perception of this blossoming tree, does not include any claim related to the fact itself (the tree in the garden). For the phenomenologist, there is really no way from this sphere to the thing itself. The only possibility, that of inferring from the content of the noematic-core back to the object that is presented in it, is ruled out by the reduction. If one holds fast to the reduction (but at the same time gives up the directedness to what is essential) it would certainly be possible to determine the factual content of the lived experience, including its noematic side. However, this would not enable us to learn anything about the object intended in the lived experience and would be of no interest whatsoever.

Apparently, Husserl thinks that the situation with respect to *essences* as act-objects is different than the situation with respect to facts. His analyses in the last chapter of *Ideas* allow us to recognize the difference that he sees. Facts cannot be adequately given, but essences can. We have seen in section II how adequate eidetic intuition is structured. But eidetic intuition must be sharply distinguished from the givenness of lived experiences in reflection. This givenness is also fundamentally adequate, but it is structured in a completely different way. We saw that an essence is only graspable intuitively when one has secured its material components beforehand by some other means. When it comes to the *essence of lived experience*, the material components can be secured within the framework of the phenomenological reduction. Even the ideation that is built upon it, as a purely logical operation, does not take us beyond this framework. However, if *other essences* come to be intuited (let us disregard the purely formal essences for now), then their material components are just as *inaccessible* to phenomenological observation as the *facts* of the corresponding region. To deny this would be to transform all eidetic sciences into phenomenology. It would mean, for instance [413], that one could learn everything there is to know about the essence "body" through precise analysis of the consciousness in which this essence presents itself. This, in fact, is the meaning of Husserl's above-mentioned analyses. We have already seen, however, that this is impossible. It belongs to the essence "body" in all instances to be a member of nature, that is, to be transcendent and fundamentally *not* graspable phenomenologically.

Naturally, the content of the actual lived experience can be established phenomenologically, which is also the case with respect to facts. This is true even if the lived experience in question is, for instance, the most adequate possible intuition of a material essence. Nothing will be gained here through the reduction, however, just as nothing is gained through the reduction with respect to thing perception. To be sure, we will learn nothing through phenomenology that we did not already know or could have known through simple eidetic intuition. Eidetic intuition, however, has its ultimate sources in material components that are given from somewhere else, on the one hand, and in the purely formal essences on the other hand. To conclude, we want to consider these formal essences one more time.

V

Husserl introduces formal ontology as a kind of redirection of the interpretation of formal logic and apophantics, although it exceeds even this framework. (*Ideen* 307 f./293 f.) Of course, the inner relation between the two domains cannot be denied, but the preeminence of formal logic in Husserl's account is clearly conditioned by the fact that he approaches this issue from a phenomenological direction. *Pure mathesis*, at its highest level of formalization, is objectively primary, and also clearly independent of phenomenology. Within pure mathesis, almost everything can be understood as an "element" (or however one wants to refer to the simplest object of investigation). All of the constraints that determine an element more specifically (e. g., that it is distinguishable from others) are introduced as preconditions for special disciplines. Such conditions, which are put forward not just for one proposition but for an entire system of propositions, should be called *axioms*, although this expression obviously has another meaning when we speak for example about the axioms of physical geometry. We do not operate here only in an eidetic region, but rather in a purely formal region, that is, in a world of mere possibilities, in which the question of the "real" validity of an axiom makes no sense. [414] We first become acquainted with the specific features of the objects on the basis of the axioms alone; there are no specific "productive definitions." The definitions are only explanations for abbreviated expressions. The research proceeds deductively from the axioms to individual propositions. This is the case also in that peculiar reversal of the deductive process, which we may call regressive, and which goes from some formal state of affairs contingently known to us back to the axiomatic system that conditions it. A connection between the two methods can be found in the inquiries concerning the compatibility of axioms.

Like the realm of possibilities, the scope of this discipline is fundamentally unbounded.[22] But an approximately exhaustive treatment of the possible cases can only be carried out with respect to the most general part. The widespread attention that is paid to *particular* axioms and axiom systems, by set theory for instance, is due on the one hand to their broader theoretical fruitfulness, for example, where the well-definedness of sets is concerned. On the other hand, it is due to the fact that they are realized within specific *materially* determined regions. This makes possible the application of formal mathesis within material ontologies. The development of so-called pure mathematics has also therefore been guided primarily by perspectives that are oriented towards the application of formal mathesis. The validity of its doctrinal content is left unaffected; since formal mathesis introduces the axioms purely as preconditions, it need not worry whether and where these axioms are fulfilled.

Nonetheless, the question of the origin and the areas of application of the axioms is a question of interest. We already saw in section II how one must approach the answer to this question in the context of geometry. Similarly, one can ask why set theory has a general validity within a wide domain of the objects that we otherwise busy ourselves with, and how in particular it is possible that such an apparently formal discipline as syllogistic logic can be presented as an area of application for set theory.

The answer to the last question is: the extensions of concepts are sets, namely well-defined sets, therefore the syllogisms operating with the extensions of concepts must be presentable as applications of set theoretical operations. The so-called *logical calculus* does nothing other than this,[23] and one will gladly concede that, of all presentations of syllogistic logic, [415] logical calculus is the only formally satisfactory one, since it sharply distinguishes the axioms from what is demonstrable, whereas in the customary presentations exhibition [Aufweisung] and proof are blended together in a colorful mess. It is certainly the most striking, but definitely not the only case in which mathematical deduction is applied to logical problems. Peano and Russell have attempted to present the logic of relations in the same manner; indeed, the axiom of well-definedness already indicates by its name that it is to be fulfilled in the domain of logical objects. One can say in general that formal logic and pure mathesis overlap to a

---

[22] Husserl also shares this wide concept of meaning (cf. Husserl 2001, p. 154f.)
[23] Let me refer here only to Couturat's compact presentation: *L'algèbre de la logique* (Couturat 1905).

large extent, namely, to the extent that logic offers domains in which the axioms of mathesis can be fulfilled. This extends far enough that many axioms are grasped not in their full abstractness, but according to their logical form, such that that the meaning of these axioms can only be fully elucidated through logical investigation.

Within its domain of operation, in any case, pure mathesis can expect no clarification from phenomenology. Its deductive steps are performed in complete clarity, a clarity that is not capable of any increase. The phenomenology of acts of adequate eidetic intuition is certainly of great general interest, but it cannot found or strengthen the self-certitude of truth; it can only bring it to light. Things are different as regards the question of the *origin of axioms* and the legitimacy of attributing specific *areas of application* to them. A glance at the essence of material ontologies already showed us that the basic material features of the essences (i.e., that which fulfills the axioms) cannot be located mathematically in turn. Of course, this also applies to their fulfillment with formal-logical material. The axioms are situated as far back as mathematical methods in general can be; the facts that determine their fulfillment can only be grasped *descriptively*. Thus, formal logic maintains a peculiar middle position; it supplies material for certain branches of pure mathesis, while in its ontological reformulation, as the doctrine of the pure form of a region, it stands over against the material ontologies. In both cases, clearly, we are dealing with different meanings of the terms "form" and "material." *Mathematical* formalization (one of the most fruitful principles of modern mathematics) presents the pure, deductive framework of an applied mathematical discipline, freed from restrictions arising from particular meanings. For *natural* geometry [416], for example, mathematical formalization forms the broadened concept of an *abstract* geometry that is bound neither to a definite number of dimensions nor to certain other restrictions. *Logical* formalization, on the other hand, does not produce a *broadening*, but rather only a *thinning* of the object; its entire content is reflexive. This is the content that one usually ascribes to formal logic, and since we already know that this content is not to be found in the area of formal mathematics, we must exhibit the material sphere which creates such content and which thereby lends it that characteristic "reflexive" formality that distinguishes it from other, actually material regions.

If one keeps both dimensions of this problem in mind, namely, that the material content of formal logic must stem from a determined region and that this region, in contrast to all other regions, must be formally reflexive, then the solution cannot be in doubt. Lask has presented the solution with the utmost clarity.[24] It is the *activity of the subject* that creates this world of reflexive forms. Whereas all other types of objects, including ideal objects, are independent in their specific essence from the acts of a subject, the objects of formal logic obtain their sense from a cognizing mind, one that continues to display the traits of a human mind in spite of its generality. This applies particularly to the *forms belonging to the expressive sphere*, which only have meaning with reference to an understanding subject; it is also true of *the concept*, both in the general sense of meaning as such, or in the more specific sense of the meaning of a genus; it is also true of *judgment*, whose wealth of forms Lask correctly refers back to the activity of the subject; finally it is true of *inference*, whose forms of justification indeed arise from the knowledge of the subject and not from objective foundational relations. The criticism of the Kantian deduction of the categories from the table of judgments has constantly pointed to the radical gap that exists between the (constitutive) categories as components of the object and the reflexive determinations that serve as the foundation for the traditional table of judgments.

Something further ought to be said about the reflexive categories. In modern logic, *identity* is often considered the general fundamental characteristic, even the *constituens* of objects. This is true if, by object, one means act-correlate. In view of the different acts in which it is graspled, [417] the object can rightfully be considered as the single, identically present object;[25] without considering such relation, this makes no sense at all. It is not appropriate to posit identity as the constitutive fundamental characteristic of all objects, in the same way in which, for example, *temporal* determination is constitutive of *real* objects and *spatio-temporal* determination is constitutive of *material* objects. One can no more describe 'being yellow' and 'being identical with itself' as properties of this rose than one can describe Caesar's crossing of the Rubicon as a decisive deed and as the content of a judgment. If one does not want to falsely ascribe a temporal meaning to identity,[26] then identity has no tangible content that pertains to the objects themselves independently of their being grasped. The same applies to all other reflexive forms.

It is important at this point to draw out the necessary consequences of what has been said for the treatment of formal logic. It will ultimately be shown, with the highest degree of clarity, that logical structures are the spheres of fulfillment

---

24 See the whole of "Lehre vom Urteil" (Lask 1912), and "Logik der Philosophie" (Lask 1911, p. 138 ff), where Lotze and Windelband are indicated as predecessors.
25 Külpe also gives this meaning to identity, but he limits it to acts of thought (Külpe 1912, p. 92 f.).
26 Kant already objects to this with respect to the principle of contradiction (Kant 1998, B 191 f.).

of certain axioms, and that the subsequent treatment of mathematical deduction falls to these logical structures. But how should the investigation be carried out up until this point? It is important to become familiar with the essence of that act whereby the subject adopts a theoretical position toward objects, so as to grasp in this position-taking the foundational structure of formal logic. *This task falls obviously to phenomenology.* Husserl is in the right here when he expects the clarification of the logical problems to come from his new approach. Yet it is only new in its consistency and methodological awareness; at base, formal logic has always been done in this manner. Obscurity with regard to the method, however, has led not only to the previously mentioned confusion of the phenomenological and the deductive parts of logic. It has also caused the ongoing conflicts that are today connected with the slogan "psychologism." It has always been felt that the validity of logical truths has more in common with the validity of mathematical truths than it does with that of psychological truths; nevertheless, the sentiment prevails that logic should receive some sort of instruction from psychology. In order to get to know the different kinds of positions that a thinking subject can take with respect to the object, the various acts of theoretical [418] apprehension must indeed undergo eidetic analysis; in addition, it is specifically the acts of meaning that are important for a logical theory of forms. In fact, a broad domain of inquiry opens itself up here to phenomenology, one in which it can practice a purely descriptive study of essence; not of course entirely independently of experience, but nevertheless with an ideational direction towards what is purely essential. The eidetic direction of research secures the essential generality of the described structures and allows, ultimately, for the proof of the fulfillment of certain purely formal axioms and the transition to deductive logic as a sub-discipline of general mathematics.

It is therefore apropos to confront the charge of psychologism and to sharply distinguish between the idea of founding formal logic on the essential traits of acts of thought, on the one hand, and an illegitimate generic empiricism, on the other. It is obviously not our purpose to make the validity of the principle of contradiction dependent on psychological observations; only its *meaning* is to be clarified through phenomenological (and so, in a certain sense, from our perspective, psychological) analysis. If one has taken into consideration the essence of the act-correlate in question, meaning reflexive objectivity, then the principle of contradiction itself can be obtained in its strict generality through insight into the essential state of affairs. The task of phenomenology is this alone: to learn to understand the logical structures, whereupon the laws that are valid within those structures will reveal themselves in their full rigor.

However, it is not only the *apriority* of formal logic that appears to contradict its foundation in experience, but also its alleged character as a *normative sci-*

ence. Psychology, it is sometimes said, can at best study how one actually thinks, whereas logic should establish norms for how one *ought to* think.[27] Husserl has already dealt with logic as a normative science and as the art of thinking. (Husserl 1900, chapters 1 and 2) The only question is that of the "theoretical foundations" of this normative science. This alone is what we are looking for here. To be sure, a second foundational discipline appears alongside the phenomenological exhibiting of the meaning of logical objects—a pure logic. This is precisely *mathesis universalis* in the broadest sense. Each deductive step [419], even the smallest one, is based on such pure logic. Its scope and importance for all thinking is so seldom recognized only because it is almost impossible to work out all of the deductive elements in a train of thought. One can indeed point to a place in a supposedly rigorous proof at which an unproven point has been taken from experience, even though this is difficult when it comes to everyday experiences;[28] one must abstract thereby only from one's *experiential knowledge*. To abstract from the simple forms of deduction has almost never been seriously attempted; hence, there is certainly a purely deductive, yet no purely deductionless, ideal of science. We also never feel the need for such abstraction, and so it is that we usually have no idea how deeply the domain of validity of mathematical form extends into what is apparently purely material. Once one makes this explicit, however, one will no longer shy away from recognizing in pure mathesis the theoretical foundations for logic that are sought after, the theoretical foundations that are completely independent of all psychology.

In addition to the psychological foundation, there is a further point that may make people balk at this conception of formal logic: the *division of its domain of operation* between phenomenology and mathematics. What remains of actual philosophical work within logic? Now, we believe that it is no disgrace to philosophy to hand over a certain area of inquiry to the special sciences after it has been fully clarified that these sciences can work in this area. In this way, philosophy fulfills the task that has always been its most beautiful and fruitful: to bring about new specialized disciplines, to encourage new directions of research, and to instruct them as to their fields of inquiry. And we need not fear an impoverishment of the philosophical domain. After all, this is only about *formal* logic; both the doctrine of categories and the entire domain that is commonly called "transcendental logic," or "theory of knowledge," remain unaffected. Philosophical inquiry should continue to deal with the formal region as with all other re-

---

27 See August Messer in the *Archiv für die gesamte Psychologie* 22 (Messer 1912, p. 118; incl. In this volume p. 215–216).
28 As, for example, the controversy concerning the foundations of geometry demonstrates.

gions: as the theory of formal-logical knowledge, as its theory of categories and methodology. The region "nature", too, is substantively divided between natural science and mathematics; nevertheless, theoretical philosophy draws abundantly from its problems. The same goes for the formal region.

[420] The comparison between formal logic and the ontology of nature should not be exaggerated, of course, but it can give us a pointer in a particular direction. We saw that *mathematical* logic, even at its greatest possible extension, cannot exhaust its domain of problems, but is rather supplemented by a *descriptive* discipline (in this case, a branch of phenomenology), which provides the material foundations for the mathematical schema. It is the same for the ontology of nature. For example, as we already argued in section II, physical geometry does not have purely mathematical foundations. If one wishes to found physical geometry axiomatically or analytically, one must exhibit the validity of the axioms or the simple steps of the analytical construction in the essence of *res extensa*. It will therefore be necessary provide, on an empirical basis, a *description*[29] of those essential characteristics of physical space that are absolutely necessary for the construction of geometry. We meet here the same conditions as in the formal region: the foundation of *mathematical* eidetics is provided by *descriptive* eidetics, which is clearly not accessible without recourse to experience. The "rigid body," without which it is impossible to found physical geometry, is just as little given purely *a priori* as the "doxic noeses" that we study in logical phenomenology. The comparison thus helps to insulate our position from the charge of psychologism. Gauss's conception of the problem of space subtracts geometry's deductive force just as little as the movement back to the constitutive acts of a subject makes logical structures dependent on psychological frivolities. The person who would prop up the validity of syllogistic figures with psychological experiments can only be compared to the person who would check the higher, analytically calculable decimals of π by drawing large, maximally precise radii.[30] Such attempts are certainly possible, but they are pointless and methodologically flawed because they disregard the limits between exhibition [*Aufweis*] and demonstration [*Beweis*], and between description and [421] deduction—these limits lie in the very nature of the objects. Such attempts make the same mistake that one would rightly deride in the following case. Suppose someone arranges 1000 counted small stones in piles of 27, and then, having 1 stone

---

[29] Even Hilbert—who clearly does not want to call in experience, but rather only the intuition of space—assigns the axioms the task of *describing* the mutual relations between points, straight lines, and planes. He does so right at the beginning of his *Foundations of Geometry*.

[30] Thereby, obviously, the validity of the Euclidean axioms is presupposed.

left over after producing the 37th pile, argues that they have demonstrated what was until then a prematurely accepted hypothesis, that 37 x 27 = 1000 – 1.

One could object against the whole comparison that the formal region is *all-encompassing* and therefore not comparable to a specific region, such as nature, which only embraces a specific part of the formal region. Against this objection, we must remember what was said above about the *reflexive* character of the formal logical region. The objects of natural science are not *essentially* act-correlates, even though they are *accidentally* act-correlates in all acts of cognition directed towards them, in passing, as it were. Natural science never needs to reflect on the acts in which natural science itself lives. Nowhere does natural science base its lines of reasoning on the fact that its objects must be graspable by thinking beings. In the face of the unbounded universality of the logical, such an argument would have no probative force at all. Once again we see here the radical gap, which, considered phenomenologically, lies between the objective core and the noematic appendage [*Beiwerk*]. Only in this noematic appendage do we find the formal determinations that, being its very core, are also valid for the material object. They all find their ground in noetic structures, and only the above-acknowledged perfection of the noetic-noematic mirror transfers the formal determinations into the noematic sphere, thus enabling the objective interpretation of the fundamental principles of logic and converting formal *logic* into a formal *ontology.*

On the other hand, it would be wrong to interpret the above-developed *analogy* between two regions in terms of the full *equality* of the relations internal to them. The foundations of the ontology of nature, like those of the formal region, must be descriptive; but this does not mean that they are both phenomenological. If one understands phenomenology as a science of consciousness, then phenomenology contributes nothing to the doctrine of objects that, in their essence, contain nothing related to consciousness. Already in the previous section, we rejected Husserl's attempt to ground the material ontologies phenomenologically as well. If one decides not to extend the concept of phenomenology to cover all descriptive eidetics—an extension that was perhaps possible after the *Logical Investigations*, but is no longer possible after *Ideas*—one must concede that there are yet other descriptive [422] eidetic sciences alongside of and independent from phenomenology.[31] The essence "nature" cannot therefore be understood as having been derived from the essence "nature-meaning act," be-

---

[31] Messer also claimed in his second essay (Messer 1914, p. 56; incl. In this volume p. 243) that the method of eidetic intuition extends over the sphere of consciousness. However, he seems inclined to expand the concept of phenomenology accordingly.

cause in order to understand it in these terms, one would first have to show that this act, with its intention, grasps real nature. This can happen only if one already knows the essence of real nature and can compare it with something else; in that case, however, one already has what one wants, and the detour through the act is superfluous.

Nonetheless, Husserl has clearly recognized that the mathematical-deductive type of eidetic knowledge is not the only type, but must rather be completed by a descriptive type. One of the great merits of the *Ideas* is to have highlighted this descriptive type and distinguished it from the mathematical type. (*Ideen* p. 132f./127f.) This methodological achievement is enhanced by a substantive achievement: these fundamental outlines of phenomenology already delineate a portion of descriptive eidetics. Thereby, Husserl has grasped his problem exactly in its full extent: next to the *theoretical* acts stand the *evaluative* and the *volitional* acts; by investigating these, Husserl seeks the foundation of "axiology" and "praxis." We have limited ourselves to the theoretical as the foundational dimension. Here the yield was already rich: even if the limits of phenomenology had to be drawn a little more narrowly than its founder would prefer, we preserved its essential content, and at the same time, we opened up a perspective onto new problems and the methods that can be used to solve them.

References

Couturat, Louis (1914): *L'algèbre de la logique*. Paris: Gauthier-Villars.
Elsenhans, Theodor (1915): "Phänomenologie, Psychologie, Erkenntnistheorie." In: *Kant-Studien* 20, p. 224–275.
Husserl, Edmund (1981): "Philosophy as a Rigorous Science." Quentin Lauer (Trans.). In: *Husserl: Shorter Works*. Notre Dame: University of Notre Dame Press, pp. 161-197.
Husserl, Edmund (2001): *Logical Investigations* I. J. N. Findlay (Trans.). London/New York: Routledge.
Kant, Immanuel (1998): *Critique of Pure Reason*. Paul Guyer and Allen Wood (Eds.). Cambridge: Cambridge University Press.
Külpe, Oswald (1895): *Einleitung in die Philosophie*. Leipzig: Hirzel.
Külpe, Oswald (1912) *Die Realisierung* Vol. I. Leipzig: Hirzel.
Külpe, Oswald (1915): *Zur Kategorienlehre*. Munich: Verlag der Königlichen Bazerischen Akademie der Wissenschaften.
Lask, Emil (1911): *Die Logik der Philosophie und die Kategorienlehre; eine Studie über den Herrschaftsbereich der logischen Form*. Tübigen: Mohr.
Lask, Emil (1912): *Die Lehre vom Urteil*. Tübigen: Mohr.
Messer, August (1909): *Einführung in die Erkenntnistheorie*. Leipzig: Verlag der Dürr'schen Buchhandlung.
Messer, August (1912): "Husserls Phänomenologie in ihrem Verhältnis zur Psychologie." In: *Archiv für die gesamte Psychologie* 22, pp. 117–129.

Messer, August (1914): "Husserls Phänomenologie in ihrem Verhältnis zur Psychologie (zweiter Aufsatz)." In: *Archiv für die gesamte Psychologie* 32, pp. 52–67.

Pichler, Hans (1910): *Über Christian Wolffs Ontologie*. Leipzeig: Verlag der Dürr'schen Buchhandlung.

Rickert, Heinrich (1912): "Das Eine, die Einheit und die Eins. Bemerkungen zur Logik des Zahlbegriffs." In: *Logos* 2, pp. 26–78.

Selz, Otto (1911): "Existenz als Gegenstandsbestimmtheit." In: *Theodor Lipps: zu sinem sechzigsten Geburtstag*. Leipzig: Barth.

Steinmann, Heinrich Gustav (1913): *Über den Einfluss Newtons auf die Erkenntnistheorie seiner Zeit*. Bonn: Cohen.

Study, Eduard (1914): *Die realistische Weltansicht und die Lehre vom Raume*. Braunschweig: Vieweg und Sohn.

Steinmann, Heinrich Gustav (1913): *Über den Einfluss Newtons auf die Erkenntnistheorie seiner Zeit*. Bonn: Friedrich Cohen.

Michaela Sobrak-Seaton
Edith Stein

Unlike many of the authors included in this volume, Edith Stein (1891–1942) is by no means an obscure figure. As such, her contributions appearing here require little in the way of biographical introduction. She is known to some as a Carmelite nun who converted from Judaism, was killed at Auschwitz, and was canonized as a Catholic saint. To those familiar with the phenomenological tradition, she is known not only as Husserl's private assistant, but also as a creative and prolific philosopher in her own right. Though relatively little attention was paid to Stein's work during her lifetime and for several decades following her death, scholarship on her thought has blossomed in recent years, and continues to develop and flourish.

While the themes Stein explores cover a diverse range (e.g. personhood, community, education, and Christian spirituality, to name a few), her writings bear the unmistakeable mark of her close involvement with Husserl and his followers[1]. As a young student, she left the university in Breslau (Wroclaw) in 1913 to study with Husserl in Göttingen, then went with him to Freiburg and assumed the role of his assistant in 1916. In this capacity, she was responsible for editing Husserl's voluminous and often unstructured manuscripts. Stein's deep familiarity with Husserl's work led her to active engagement in the conversation and controversies surrounding phenomenology, particularly its relation to psychology[2]. During the tumultuous aftermath of *Ideas I*, she defended Husserl against Heinrich Steinmann's criticism in "Zu Heinrich Gustav Steinmanns Aufsatz 'Zur systematischen Stellung der Phänomenologie" (Stein 1917; incl. in this volume p. 301–316) an essay published under her own name in Volume 36 of *Archiv für die gesamte Psychologie*. She also urged Husserl to respond to Theodor Elsenhans, which resulted in Husserl entrusting her with the drafting of a response to Elsenhans and August Messer (Husserl/Stein 1917, incl. in this volume p. 449–468).[3] Although Husserl appeared to be happy with Stein's work on the critique,

---

[1] For insight into Stein's professional and personal relationships with Roman Ingarden, Adolf Reinach, and other students of Husserl, see her letters to Ingarden (Stein 2014).
[2] Sarah Borden notes that Stein's decision to study with Husserl was largely motivated by her dissatisfaction with her studies in psychology, and her fascination with "the claim that Husserl's new philosophical method, phenomenology, could provide a theoretical grounding for the sciences—something Stein thought psychology needed" (Borden 2003, p. 3).
[3] For a summary of the positions put forth by Stein in both her own article and her draft of Husserl's response, see the Introduction to this volume (p. 1–9). For more information about Stein's

this article was never published during the lifetimes of Husserl and Stein, but appeared first in *Husserliana XXV* (1987).

References

Borden, Sarah (2003): *Edith Stein*. London/New York: Continuum.
Stein, Edith (2014): *Letters to Roman Ingarden*. Hugh Candler Hunt (Trans.). Washington: ICS Publications.

---

difficulty in persuading Husserl to publish a response to Elsenhans, see Rodney Parker's introduction to the latter in this volume (p. 13–15).

Translated by Evan Clarke
Edith Stein. Concerning Heinrich Gustav Steinmann's Paper "On the Systematic Position of Phenomenology"

Zu Heinrich Gustav Steinmanns Aufsatz "Zur systematischen Stellung der Phänomenologie"
Husserliana XXV: Aufsätze und Vorträge (1911–1921)
Thomas Nenon and Rainer Sepp (Eds.)
Dordrecht: Martinus Nijhoff, pp. 253–266 (1987)

[253] Among the many critical discussions that have so far taken a position on the theme of "phenomenology and psychology," Steimann's paper has distinguished itself in having clearly recognized *both characteristics* that distinguish phenomenology from psychology, according to Husserl, and in having stayed close in his polemic to these two principal points (Steinmann 1917, p. 393; incl. in this volume p. 270–271):

1. *Phenomenology is an eidetic science; psychology is a factual science.*
2. *Phenomenology is a transcendentally pure science; psychology is a science of transcendents.*

I The Possibility of a Material Ontology without "Appeal to Experience"

Steinmann's doubts are directed initially toward the first point. "The formal region" is indeed "only accessible to eidetic investigation" (Steinmann sets this down without demonstration), "The status of material ontology appears more doubtful" (Steinmann 1917, p. 395; incl. in this volume p. 273). *Geometry*, an already established branch of the ontology of physical nature that Husserl calls for, serves as an example for Steinmann. It looks to him as if geometry could not get by without experience. Because, "*either* one understands by *res extensa* the fulfillment of a segment of some well-defined multiplicity, in which case there is no way to grasp the priority of this multiplicity relative to any other multiplicity" (after all, "I am free to conceive of a multiplicity of arbitrarily many dimensions," to which *eo ipso* "a pure *a priori* geometry" would belong); "*or*, on the contrary, 'body' means the individual substrate of nature as it appears to us. In that case, it is essentially impossible to determine anything about its properties, including extension, before we become familiar with the fundamental traits of this essence on the basis of experience" (Steinmann 1917, p. 396; incl. in this volume p. 273).

Clearly, this objection to the possibility of a pure eidetic method has its basis in Steinmann's concept of *experience*. It seems that he includes under this heading every *intuition of a full concretion*, and opposes to it "*authentic eidetic intuition*," or "the *seeing of what is formal* [254] *within material essences*" (Steinmann 1917, p. 402; incl. in this volume p. 279). This, however, does not agree at all with Husserl's conception of experience or eidetic intuition. Experience is the positing of objects given *here and now* in the actual world. Essence, on the other hand, principally designates "what is to be found in the being that is proper to an individual as its *what*. Each such "what," however, can be '*put into [the form of] an idea*'", and correlatively, every "*experiential* or *individual intuition* can be transformed into an instance of *seeing the essence (ideation)*" (*Ideen* 10/11). The full concretion, therefore, already belongs in the domain of the eidetic; we do not find here just the universal species-ideas or formal categories to which the concretion is subordinated. A closer analysis, of course, makes clear the necessity of distinguishing between different kinds of essence [*Wesenheiten*]; such an analysis shows, for example, that in the construction of a concrete eidos, there are moments that can be freely varied, and other moments that cannot be omitted from its total content, at least insofar as one wants to retain the same eidos.[1] But all such distinctions are made within the eidetic sphere, and one is correct in applying the overarching term "essence" to the whole domain. Everything which can come to givenness in an exemplary intuition belongs in this domain: every intuitive content represents an a priori relative to the empirical givenness in which it is actually realized. "The essence," Steinmann says, must "be constituted in some other way" (namely, through eidetic investigation) "if we want to depart from the sphere of mere possibilities" (Steinmann 1917, p. 402; incl. in this volume p. 279). But we do not actually want this. Because everything that is "*possible*" exists in the realm of the eidetic, and we need experience just for the positing of something real. Of course, "possibility" here does not mean logical possibility (i.e. freedom from contradiction), but is equivalent rather to intuitability, or unifiability in an intuition. Thus, from each intuition of an individual (be it an experience or a phantasy) I can "extract" an essence; every intuition entails not merely that "this is real" or "I am aware of this," but also "such a thing is possible," or "such a thing *exists* in an ideal sense." I can then "experi-

---

[1] Johannes Hering has investigated these themes in a work that has unfortunately not yet appeared (Hering 1921).

ment" with the concrete, intuitive essence in complete freedom (as was already indicated). Drawing on a multiplicity of intuitions, I can "test" the essence, and determine those moments of its total content that are variable. What's more, I can do this at different levels of generality (for example, the level of the completely intuitive *what* of this stone, the level of stones in general, or material things in general). What emerges in this process as *necessary* content will serve as a basis for concept formation: I am bound absolutely to what is discovered intuitively, and am absolutely not allowed, for example, [255] "to define whatever I want as an *organism*" (Steinmann 1917, p. 398; incl. in this volume p. 275) —supposing, that is, that I am interested in acquiring scientifically valuable concepts.

Let's apply these observations to geometry. A material nature having determinate intuitive content is given to us. We ascertain this content "in idea" and now look to see what belongs necessarily to its structure. Among other things, we find that a material thing is not possible without a spatial form (it would not change anything in the eidetic analysis if we restricted ourselves to the type "rigid body"). The basic properties of such spatial forms can be "described" in a series of "axioms," as Steinmann himself indicates: "the foundation of *mathematical* eidetics is provided by *descriptive* eidetics" (Steinmann 1917, p. P. 420; incl. in this volume p. 294)[2]. These axioms are characterized by the fact that they can become part of a formal system, that is, they can be grasped in formal-mathematical concepts; and from these formal laws, further propositions can be deduced purely deductively, by the laws of formal logic. *In these formal systems neither space nor spatial intuition plays any further role*: "Mathematical formalization [...] presents the pure, deductive framework of an applied mathematical discipline, freed from restrictions arising from particular meanings." It is now possible, through the formal variation of these systems—for example, through the abandonment of some axiom—to develop different systems; or, expressing the same point with Steinmann, to form "for *natural geometry* [...] the broadened concept of an *abstract* geometry that is bound neither to a definite number of dimensions nor to certain other restrictions" (Steinmann 1917, p. 415 f.; incl. in this volume p. 290). But are we justified in calling such multiplicities, which correspond to Euclidean geometry as regards their *form*, geometries? As it turns out, one is justified in doing so only when spatial forms can be intuited that correspond to these formal definitions (if only on the basis of exemplifying phantasy)—insofar, that is, as one still understands geometry as the science of the spatial. Supposing that a Riemannian geometry, or some other geom-

---

2 What he means, of course, is that they are "not accessible to us except through experience."

etry, were intuitively given, how would things stand with the question posed by Steinmann? Which of the different possible geometries "*corresponds to nature*" (Steinmann 1917, p. 396; incl. in this volume p. 274)? Here, we must have the essence of (pure) geometrical and empirical spatial intuition clearly before our eyes. *Pure* geometrical forms (like the *pure* straight line, or the *pure* circle) are visible in empirical-intuitive bodies as "*boundaries*" or "limit ideas." The *experienced* body is given intuitively as a "realization" of these ideas; not as a "complete" realization, but as an "approximation." Now, it is possible that we are deceived by our *empirical* spatial intuition, that "in reality" the [256] physical bodies presented to us in nature are not realizations of Euclidean forms—as they seem to be—but of some other forms. In that case, we would do well to base our physical calculations on non-Euclidean axioms. But the validity of Euclidean geometry as a pure *theory of space* would not in this way suffer the least damage. It is precisely here that the pure a priori character of Euclidean geometry (and correspondingly, the pure character of geometrical intuition) becomes apparent: in the fact that it is not affected when the experiences that it takes as examples turn out to be deceptive. The "*axioms of congruence*," says Steinmann, are "only justified in a world in which there are *rigid bodies* that can be moved and rotated" (Steinmann 1917, p. 397; incl. in this volume p. 274). Rather, they can only be *applied* where this is the case (and *whether* it is the case is something that only experience can teach us); as regards the *existence* or the truth of these axioms it is entirely irrelevant whether there or not there is something factical to which they can apply.

The doubts concerning the possibility of material-eidetic intuition and pure material-eidetic science seem at this point to be resolved. That they do not make possible "knowledge of the real [that is] grounded without any recourse to experience" (Steinmann 1917, p. 398; incl. in this volume p. 274) is Husserl's position as well: "*pure truths of essences do not contain any claim about facts at all.* Hence, from truths of essences *alone* not even the slightest truth of facts is to be inferred" (*Ideen* 13/15). Steinmann's amendment to this, according to which we are unable to learn anything "concerning the *essence of the real*" without recourse to experience, cannot be conceded. The essence of the real (as well as the essence of reality itself, and the fact that both essences can only be given through experience) is only to be won from pure eidetic cognition; that an example of a given essence factically exists is only to be determined on the basis of experience.

Steinmann wants to support the claim that eidetic cognition contains elements of experience within it by showing that existence itself—which can only be *experienced*—belongs together with "essence" (Steinmann 1917, p. 398; incl. in this volume p. 274). This, however, is not correct. I can of course include the way of being of an object and its corresponding manners of givenness within its essential content, but not its factical existence. I can say: it belongs to the essence of the real that it can only be established through experience. This is valid even if there is nothing real and no experience; and it does not imply *that* there are such things.

The independence of eidetic cognition is not qualified by the fact that "the development of material ontology [...] is *tightly interwoven* with certain results from associated empirical sciences" (Steinmann 1917, p. 399; incl. in this volume p. 275); nor by the fact "that the realm of εἴδη forms an unsurveyable ocean, in which one can orient oneself only by keeping the islands of experience constantly in view" (Steinmann 1917, p. 402; incl. in this volume p. 278). [257] There may be empirical motives, perhaps even interests stemming from practical life that prompt me to take up investigation of essence. The necessity of engaging with physical bodies may excite in me a desire to make clear the essences of these objects. The illusions to which I have been subject in experience may lead me to an eidetic analysis of perception. But that there are factical motives underlying my theoretical engagement with these objectivities entails neither that these objectivities, nor the ideal system of sciences corresponding to them, are dependent on this facticity.

II The Absoluteness of Pure Consciousness and the Meaning of the Phenomenological Reduction

Steinmann's second objection concerns the *absoluteness of pure consciousness*, which is secured by the phenomenological reduction (the elimination of all positing of transcendent objects). There is "only *one consciousness*," he says; and that consciousness is "*either* absolute *or* bound up with the world" (Steinmann 1917, p. 404; incl. in this volume p. 280). If one acknowledges that embodied consciousness exists in the real world, then the phenomenological reduction will represent merely a "*methodological tool*" (or a "fiction")—an "abstractive restriction of interest to that segment of reality determined by the concept 'pure lived experience'." What one acquires through this restriction of interest is "an attitude that is especially appropriate for reflection on lived experiences"; moreover, one manages to block the "possibility of straying from the path of pure description to the all too proximate pathways of causal explanation of physical or real psychical kinds." But we do not in this way succeed in separating phenomenological and psychological reflections, let alone the sciences themselves: the method portrayed here is rather "the entirely legitimate method of a *descriptive eidetic psychology*" (Steinmann 1917, p. 408–409; incl. in this volume p. 284).

This would of course completely invalidate the *transcendental* meaning of the reduction. Indeed, the task of the reduction is to provide an *absolute* ground of investigation, a being that allows of no doubt, that can suffer no cancellation, which, for any transcendent thing, is always possible in principle. One may be an "idealist" or a "realist"; that is, one may view the claim of experience, that of delivering to us a being that is independent of consciousness, as justified or not: but even the realist cannot deny that every experience can be invalidated by another experience, that there is no being that is simply indubitable. And it is just as certain that reduced consciousness, as it is posited in pure reflexion, cannot suffer any cancellation, that what we have with reduced consciousness is an indubitable being. Indeed, there is a cardinal difference between [258] *psychological experience*, which posits consciousness as being in the transcendent world, and *immanent reflection*, which posits pure consciousness as absolute. We are not dealing here with a mere difference in the direction of attention. The possibility of the reduction—the possibility of crossing-out the entire world, along with human bodies and souls, and retaining just pure consciousness as a remainder that cannot be crossed out—indicates that the being of consciousness has nothing to do with reality. From this, it follows that: 1) The possibility of a consciousness that exists independently of the existence of a real world is thinkable. This consciousness could have a world of appearances set against it; but the latter, like the fever-dream of someone in a state of delirium, would exist "by the grace of" consciousness itself. This might also amount just to a stream of immanent data, one that would never come to be constituted in terms of appearing objects. 2) If a real world exists, and along with it an animal consciousness, then this real consciousness conceals within itself an ontological element that is *independent* of its reality, an element that independent of the real relations in which it involved. Steinmann's disjunction—either absolute consciousness or real consciousness—is therefore incomplete.

In this way, it seems, we have eliminated both objections against the separation of phenomenology and psychology, and have once again determined the character of phenomenology as a *material-eidetic science of transcendentally pure consciousness*.

But there still remains to consider several important problems that Steinmann raises in connection with these two points.

A first objection concerns the *ways of givenness of pure consciousness*. Husserl gives rise to this objection in claiming that it is "evident and something that is to be gathered from the essence of being a thing in space [...] that a being of this kind can intrinsically be given only through various profiles with their different shadings, just as it is evident and something to be gathered from the essence of cogitationes (the experiences in general) that they exclude anything like" (*Ideen* 77/75). Steinmann is of the view that lived experiences are also given as profiles: "the anger that I feel now is the same as the anger that I felt two minutes ago, and not merely because it belongs within the same extended duration ('lasting for two minutes'), but also because of the conscious identity of its intentional object. Nevertheless, it is given to me now in an entirely different profile than before; indeed, the profiles have since that time transformed in exactly the same way as the appearance of a body is transformed when it moves some distance away from me" (Steinmann 1917, p. 404 f.; incl. in this volume p. 280–281).

We can leave aside the fact that Steinmann situates lived experience in transcendent time, which is obviously not correct. The argument retains its meaning even if we substitute immanent for transcendent time. Lived experience extends across a duration, it "becomes" in this duration and constantly takes new moments into itself—but it is nevertheless *one and the same lived experience*. In this connection, we are able to see something that Husserl only occasionally gestured to in *Ideen*, [259] and which is more closely investigated in still-unpublished texts: namely, that the pure lived experiences that we grasp in the reduction are already "*constituted*" *unities* of immanent time. It is clear, however, that this "constitution" in immanence is essentially different from the constitution of the transcendent. Every appearance of a transcendent thing has a meaning that is predelineated by empirical consciousness—the meaning, namely, of being the appearance of an objective unity, an objective unity that "expresses" itself in the appearance, but which can never itself be intuitively given, except insofar as it is mediated by profiles. The *lived experience*, on the other hand, gives itself as something that has only *become* a unity, in which guise it stands—as it were, frozen—before the gaze of reflection. But this unity does not "express" itself in "appearances"; it is itself intuitively given, along with its constituent moments. Here, there are no immanent data that would be "interpreted" as "expressions" of a transcendent thing (like, for example, the sensory data of external perception), such that the interpretation could turn out to be false; rather, the immanent data join together to form *immanent* unities, which are likewise entirely absolute and not subject to cancellation. "The theory that pure lived experiences are not appearances, but are rather something absolutely independent"—Steinmann argues—"clearly makes their subsumption under eidetic moments impossible. This would allow at best for a *factual science* of pure lived experiences, but not an *eidetic theory* of pure lived experiences" (Steinmann 1917, p. 405; incl. in this volume p. 281). If we now substitute "constituted" for "appearing" unities of lived experience, we can go further and say the following: if it did not lie in the essence of consciousness to form such unities, then *every* science of consciousness would be impossible, since the constant flowing of consciousness is ungraspable. This does not, however, nullify the difference between immanence and transcendence in any way.

III The Transcendental Meaning of Phenomenological Claims

A wider circle of objections is directed toward the meaning of phenomenological claims for the world of objective things, culminating in the assertion "that the consistent implementation of the phenomenological reduction in no way allows us to emerge from the specifically phenomenological sphere," that "for the phenomenologist, there is really no way from this sphere to the thing itself." And this is supposedly valid not just for facts, but also for essences.

Here, we once again encounter a lack of clarity as regards the ultimate meaning of the phenomenological method. Steinmann objects to Husserl's "idealist" turn, according to which "the external world is only accessible to us as the intentional object of our thought" (Steinmann 1917, p. 406; incl. in this volume p. 283) [260] (If we do not want to distort Husserl's standpoint, we should substitute "consciousness" for "thought." This will become clear momentarily). But "to be an intentional correlate is not a special feature of a class of objects; it is not a *feature* of objects at all. Rather, it is a *relation*, and indeed, considered from the side of the object, a merely *ideal* relation. The fact of 'being-the-object-of-an-intention' does not determine or influence an object in its essence, nor does it determine its *metaphysical* locus, in the sense that a centaur, the Θ-function, God, the piece of paper before me, and a square circle have different metaphysical loci. I can "intend" all of these objects in this order, they all stand in the relation of being an object for consciousness. But it is thereby left entirely unsaid whether they are real, ideal, absolute, relative, or whatever else they could be. If the world were nothing more than a sum of intentional objects, then it would be nothing at all; everything that the world is, it is independently of this relation" (Steinmann 1917, p. 406; incl. in this volume p. 282)—Now, one may share the standpoint of "idealism" or not: the phenomenological method is not in the least affected by this (as already indicated). Even the committed realist —for whom the existence of objects independently of their correlation with consciousness represents an unshakeable dogma—cannot deny that he owes his ability to make statements concerning objects to this correlation, that he is absolutely unable to say what those objects might be outside of the correlation. To be sure, one can investigate and speak about objects without investigating and speaking about the correlation; in so doing, however, one has not succeeded in eliminating the question of the correlation; rather, one is simply practicing "self-forgetfulness" (as Husserl is wont to say): this is a method to which the "dogmatic" scientist can allow himself to appeal; the philosopher, who seeks ultimate clarity, cannot do so. Now, the fact of this correlation in no way implies an indiscriminate "relation of being-an-object," and correspondingly, an "intending" or "thinking" that would be the same for all objects; rather, it amounts to a multiplicity of modes of consciousness, in which such objectivities come to givenness (what Husserl has said in the *Ideas* concerning noetic-noematic structures in general, and specifically as regards the analysis of object-perception, already makes this adequately clear). Because *as correlates of consciousness* all objects are included in the phenomenological sphere: "Thus, phenomenology actually encompasses the entire natural world and all the ideal worlds that it suspends. It encompasses them as 'the sense of the world' through the kinds of essential legitimacy that connect the sense of the object and the noema in general with the closed system of noeses, and specifically, through the rationally legitimate, essential connections, whose correlate is the 'actual object' that thus, for its part, respectively presents a marker for entirely determinate systems of teleologically unified configurations of consciousness" (*Ideen* 302–303/290). As the foregoing shows, [261] it is not merely the complete qualitative content of the respective objects that enters into the phenomenal sphere, but also the *ontological character* of those objects ("real," "ideal," "fictitious," etc.). These determinations, however, do not appear as "metaphysical locations" (which would mean that the objects had been completely posited, a scenario that is ruled out); they come to light, rather, as "noematic" characters, as characters that can be exhibited as such in the intentional correlates. "*To every region and category* of alleged objects there corresponds not only a *basic kind of senses or posits*" (or in other words, certain noematic contents in terms of which those objects can be given: this object here, for instance, can be given in different possible "apprehensions" as "wooden thing," "brown thing," "writing table," "material thing in general," or "useful object in general"—a list that already brings in the "senses" corresponding to different regions) "but also a *basic kind of consciousness originally affording* such senses and, inherent to it, a *basic type of originary evidence*, that is essentially motivated by the originary givenness of the specified kind" (*Ideen* 280/276).

The question of the "absoluteness and relativity" of objects must also be decided on these grounds, if indeed the pronouncements that we make on these themes are to be *grounded*, if they are not to amount to mere blind dogma. Steinmann himself sees a means of deciding this question in the separation of a "noematic kernel" from the complete noema, that is, in the grasping of an identical content from amidst the manifold modes of appearance in which the complete noema is represented. (It is the "same thing" that stands before me now as "clear" that stood before me earlier as "obscure," the same thing that I merely remembered, or "had in mind," that now imposes itself on me in its full "physicality," the same thing that earlier had the meaning "a piece of agate" and which now has the meaning "paperweight").[3] Of course, he does not see that this path leads to the goal, because "the only possibility, that of inferring from the content of the noematic-core back to the object that is presented in it, is ruled out by the reduction" (Steinmann 1917, p. 412; incl. in this volume p. 287). This is not terribly unlucky from the perspective of the phenomenologist, since this allegedly unique path forms a circle: the inference from the noematic kernel to the object is indeed conceived as a causal inference, leading ostensibly from what is immanent to its transcendent "cause." This inference, however, presupposes that there is some transcendent thing, which is precisely what is in question. On the other hand, if this "representing" means only that "something" is discoverable in the noema, something that—although necessarily appearing in some manner or another—maintains its identity across all changes in its mode of appearance, then I do not need any inference whatsoever, but remain in the space of phenomenological givenness. It is obvious that Steinmann has not become adequately clear as to the consequences of divorcing the noesis and noema. Otherwise he could not raise the question of "whether is it is necessary or appropriate to keep a pair of concepts in the foreground which all further objects of investigation [262] duplicate and which therefore, precisely because of this thoroughgoing correlation between noesis and noema, obstruct the possibility of an appropriate classification" (Steinmann 1917, p. 410; incl. in this volume p. 285). Indeed, what could it be for a science of consciousness to be "necessary and appropriate," if not to determine the *most essential characteristic of consciousness*, and to make careful observations in all of its investigations? This characteristic consists in nothing other than the fact that consciousness is *consciousness of something*, that it has, according to its own essence, an intentional correlate, a noema, that belongs "as such" in the phenomenological sphere, and does not fall to the reduction.

That different layers of this noema can be brought to light has already been shown: the modes of attention, the different perceptual and reproductive modes of givenness, the "sense content" that remains constant across these changing noematic characteristics, and in turn, the central kernel, or "object," that per-

---

[3] On the "*noematic kernen*," or the "central point" contained therein, see the treatment of these themes in *Ideen*, §§ 91, 99, 128 f.

sists across different "senses." The distinction between these noematic layers (which is somewhat crude in comparison to the distinction already carried out by Husserl) correctly expresses the distinction between the "original noetic" and the "original noematic" sought by Steinmann (Steinmann 1917, p. 410f.; incl. in this volume p. 285–286). The characteristics of the first species (say, for example, the attentional modes) would correspond to the correlate only as a correlate of its particular noesis; the characteristics of the second species would concern the fundamental layer of the noema and only subsequently the correlative noeses (thus, for example, the differences between house- and tree-perception). Should this difference express *more* than the distinction between different noematic layers (for instance, the fact that the attentional modes are only "accidentally" related to the noema) then it is absolutely to be rejected. Indeed, every object about which we can say something is necessarily an object for a consciousness and must necessarily therefore appear in some mode of attention. This level can no more fall away than the fundamental layer. Of course, this does mean that different noematic layers—which can, again, be brought to light phenomenologically—do not correspond to difference transcendental meanings. Even the sense corresponding to "real being" and of "cognition of reality" must be determined through an investigation of consciousness. "*Reality*" and "*true being*"—though they are not posited—appear nevertheless in the phenomenological sphere as noematic characteristics, indeed as the correlates of certain conscious processes falling under the title of "*reason.*" "Correct" positings of being are just those that are rational. "*The character of positing has, however, a specific rational character of its own* (as a *distinction* that *essentially* pertains to it) *when and only when* it posits something, not on the basis merely of any sense at all, but on the basis of a replete fulfilled sense, affording something in an originary way […] Here and in every kind of rational consciousness, the talk of 'being inherent to' takes on a meaning of its own. [263] For example, positing a thing *is inherent to* every case of it appearing in person. It is not simply one with this appearing in general (as if it were somehow a mere universal factum —which is out of the question here); it is one with it in a sui generis manner. That is to say, it is '*motivated*' by the appearance and once again not merely in general, but '*rationally.*' The following says the same thing: Positing has its *original ground of legitimacy* in originary givenness" (*Ideen* 283–4/271–2).

In the phenomenological sphere, therefore, we can pose the question of the possibility of transcendent objects, or rather, the question of the lawful basis for the positing of transcendental objects. Indeed, it is only in the phenomenological sphere that we can pose this question, since absolute consciousness is the *only* terrain in which the possibility that is in question is not already presupposed. To really posit such objects of course, the act of experience must be released from the fetters of the reduction, meaning that the phenomenological attitude must be overcome. After all, one would not claim on the basis of the foregoing that the clarification of transcendent objects as regards their meaning and possibility accomplishes nothing; one would not claim that such clarification is "of no interest whatsoever" (Steinmann 1917, p. 412; incl. in this volume p. 287).

There is still a word to be said as to why "the situation with respect to *essences* as act-objects is different than the situation with respect to facts" (which remains unclear from Steinmann's perspective), as to why it is incorrect to say that transcendent essences are "just as *inaccessible* to phenomenological observation as the *facts* of the corresponding region" (Steinmann 1917, p. 412; incl. in this volume p. 287). Actual experience is required for the identification of facts; since this is "put out of action" in the reduction, phenomenology cannot make any factual claims. Any intuition (even an intuition that is not posited) suffices for the grounding of an essential truth. For that reason, all statements concerning essence are possible in the reduction; what is necessary is just that these statements be understood purely, and not, as is always possible, as statements concerning possible real individuations of essence, since this means introducing a transcendental thesis.

In this sense, it is possible to "transform all eidetic sciences into phenomenology" (Steinmann 1917, p. 413; incl. in this volume p. 287), and thus to describe all ontological investigations that are purely objectively possible as phenomenological. Husserl, however, has never denied that they can be detached from this context, that "there are yet other descriptive eidetic sciences alongside of and independent from phenomenology" (Steinmann 1917, p. 421f.; incl. in this volume p. 295). On the contrary, this is clearly and distinctly expressed in his call for material-ontological disciplines in the style of geometry for all object regions. One must simply be clear as to the sense of this "independence." This does not affect phenomenology's status as *"foundational science"* in the least. Being a foundational science, indeed, does not mean that phenomenology generates presuppositional statements for all other sciences, from which the latter would be able to logically derive their own theorems. [264] Rather, by removing the "self-forgetfulness" of the dogmatic scientist, phenomenology reveals the dimension of unclarity that attaches to *every* dogmatic science, and transforms "naive" science, which does not inquire into the meaning and justification of its methodology, into a science that has been clarified by critical reason. Steinmann himself remarks correctly that "The phenomenology of acts of adequate eidetic intuition… cannot found or strengthen the self-certitude of truth; it can only bring it to light" (Steinmann 1917, p. 415; incl. in this volume p. 290).

This clarificatory work is to be afforded to all objective sciences, even to *formal ontology*, or *mathesis universalis*, whose "independence" from phenomenology is particularly important for Steinmann (Steinmann 1917, p. 413 f.). The theory of the pure forms of all possible objects in general is certainly an objectively oriented discipline, and can expect no help from phenomenology *"within its domain of operation."* Husserl has already stressed this quality of *mathesis universalis*, and he has long emphasized that the largest part of logic belongs to mathematics rather than philosophy, which Steinmann himself appears to regard as a new discovery (cf. Husserl 2001, p. 158 f.). But in spite of—or rather because of—its "dogmatic" character, formal ontology also requires a phenomenological "grounding or clarification." Even formal-categorical objectivities are consciously constituted, and the eidetic structure of this constitution must be explored. Only on the ground of such investigations can a clean distinction be made between *"formal ontology"* in the broadest sense, as a theory of the forms of objects in general, and *apophantic logic*, the theory of the pure forms of propositions—a distinction on which Steinmann places so much weight, but which has almost never been taken into account in traditional logic, and which, before Husserl's *Logical Investigations*, had hardly even been seen. Steinmann sees the difference between pure apophantic logic and pure *mathesis* as consisting in the fact that the *"forms belonging to the expressive sphere"* (such as concepts, judgments, inferences, and so forth) "only have meaning with reference to an understanding subject," that such forms are "reflexive" and that it is "the *activity of the subject*" that "creates this world of reflexive forms." In treating of these forms, therefore, it is necessary to "become familiar with the essence of that act whereby the subject adopts a theoretical position toward objects, so as to grasp in this position-taking the foundational structure of formal logic. *This task falls obviously to phenomenology*" (Steinmann 1917, p. 416 f.; incl. in this volume p. 292).

In pure phenomenological analysis, however, the situation turns out to be somewhat different. Every logical discipline deals with "objects," and we can say with respect to each discipline how their objects come to givenness, how they are originally constituted. In this way, we will be lead back to the different acts, or the different, essentially possible [265] "attitudes" corresponding to the different disciplines. "Whereas the primary attitude is directed at something objective, the noematic reflection leads to the noematic components, the noetic to the noetic components. The disciplines of interest to us here extract pure forms from these components by way of abstraction; the formal apophantic discipline extracts the noematic forms, the parallel noetic discipline the noetic forms. Just as these forms are connected with one another, so both are connected, in an essentially legitimate manner, with ontic forms that can be apprehended by turning back and focusing on the ontic components" (*Ideen* 307/294). The objects of the apophantic sphere point back, therefore, as regards their original constitution, to reflective acts. This does not mean, however, that they are "objects" in any less sense than objects that have their being independently of the acts of the subjects that are engaged with them. Being "objects" of a special kind, they fall under the formal category of "object in general," and in accordance with the formal apophantics of formal ontology (as Steinmann rightly stresses) (Steinmann 1917, p. 414 f.; incl. in this volume p. 288 f.). As objects, however, they can also be investigated from within a purely objective attitude. The logician, who studies the forms of true sentences and valid connections, can proceed without considering the reflexive acts in which such objects are constituted; just as the researcher who is occupied with formal ontology can proceed without reflecting on the acts in which his categorial objectivities (objects, attribute, quantity, etc.) are constituted; and just as the natural scientist has no need to reflect on nature-constituting consciousness. Formal logic is possible as a purely objective science, and thus has traditionally been developed in this way; it is absolutely incorrect to say, however, that "formal logic has always" been driven by a reflection on logical acts (Steinmann 1917, p. 417; incl. in this volume p. 292). Occasional noetic phrases like "I am not allowed to entertain two contradictory judgments" are merely applications of a noematic insight concerning the incompatibility of the sentences in question. This does not represent the discovery of logical rational consciousness as a unique domain of investigation; the leading interest is absolutely the noematic.

The work that phenomenology does on behalf of formal logic, therefore, is different in principle from that work that it does on behalf of every other science. If the relationship between phenomenology and formal logic appears to be particularly close, this is probably due to the historical fact that phenomenology first arises as an effort to clarify logical problems, and to the fact that the tangible results of the *Logical Investigations* have shown what can be accomplished in this domain. That the significance of phenomenology goes beyond this is already apparent from the fact that it is only with the help of phenomenological clarification that the idea of a formal ontology emerges and is distinguished from formal apophantics (in the first volume of the *Logical Investigations*, §67; in §10 ff., §133 f., and §147 f. of *Ideen*); in addition, the analyses of the constitution of nature in the first part of *Ideen* have already offered several clues as to the [266] importance of phenomenology for the clarification of natural science. The concrete analyses of the second part, however, will contribute still more significantly to the facilitation of understanding: "*in the face of the accomplished fact, the question of whether it is possible loses all meaning*" (Steinmann 1917, p. 392; incl. in this volume p. 270).

References

Hering, Johannes (1921): "Bemerkungen über das Wesen, die Wesenheit und die Idee." In: *Jahrbuch für Philosophie und phänomenologische Forschung* 4, pp. 495–543.

Husserl, Edmund (2001): *Logical Investigations* Vol. 1. J. N. Findlay (Trans.). London/New York: Routledge.

Husserl, Edmund (2014): Ideas for a Pure Phenomenology and Phenomenological Philosophy. First Book: General Introduction to Pure Phenomenology. Daniel Dahlstrom (Trans.). Indianapolis: Hackett.

Steinmann, Heinrich Gustav (1917): "Zur systematischen Stellung der Phänomenologie." In: *Archiv für die gesamte Psychologie* 36, pp. 391–422.

Jerome Veith
Paul Natorp

Paul Natorp (1854–1924) occupied a significant yet still underappreciated nodal position in German philosophy during the first quarter of the twentieth century. Having studied under Hermann Cohen, then teaching such figures as Ernst Cassirer and Hans-Georg Gadamer, and finally appointing Martin Heidegger to a chair shortly before his own death, Natorp's influence from his seat in Marburg spans philosophical eras as well as disciplinary and scholarly boundaries. While trained early on as a classical philologist, Natorp was concerned for much of his career both with the clarification of Platonic *eidē*, and with fleshing out (historically and conceptually) the neo-Kantian system developed earlier by Cohen. These endeavors drew sustenance from a fervent dedication to the notion of "philosophy as science" (Cassirer 1925, p. 275) and this commitment widened to include engagement with the social sciences and psychology, phenomenology and *Lebensphilosophie*.

Natorp's review of Husserl's *Ideas I*, appearing here in English for the first time, bears evidence of all of these directions. In a way, it represents his attempt to locate and assess Husserl's developing phenomenology both within the context of the history of philosophy, and among contemporary discourses in the philosophy of science and the burgeoning empirical science of psychology. First published in 1914 (in *Die Geisteswissenschaften*), then again in 1917 (in *Logos*) when the previous journal went defunct, the essay draws explicitly on Natorp's earlier work in psychology in order to highlight ongoing parallels with Husserl's philosophy (Natorp 1888; 1912). Natorp had already been occupied with this philosophy from as early as 1901, and found himself "in line with Husserl from the start" (Natorp 1917, p. 224; incl. in this volume p. 319). This alignment forms the overall backdrop to Natorp's review, and takes the shape of a general agreement in method and aims. Natorp takes his own work, for instance, to share Husserl's goal of uncovering pure consciousness through a phenomenological reduction, and sees in the *epochē* a direct correlate to his own concept of 'reconstruction.'[1]

However, the review is not an uncritical tribute to Husserl's *Ideas*. Having announced at the outset that an engagement with Husserl's thought is unavoidable, the essay unfolds as an almost sequential reading of Husserl's text, continually holding in suspense whether the latter will end up being congruous with Natorp's own position or not. Along the way, we witness Natorp's expertise

---

[1] For a detailed examination of this parallel, see Luft (2010).

come to bear on phenomenological concepts, as when he criticizes Husserl's "pointillistic" grasp of cognitive acts and stresses that this remains caught up in a fixed conception of *eidē* that fails to follow Plato to their infinitely fluid *kinēsis*. Indeed, this infinite fluidity is a pervasive theme in Natorp's review, representing the flow of consciousness that, in his view, can never be captured by any higher-level objectivizing act or experience. One of the deepest impulses of Natorp's review is to trace in Husserl's *Ideas* a compatible yet underdeveloped concern with the infinite, localizable in Husserl's appeal to the 'idea in the Kantian sense.' It is here that Natorp detects the common ground of a critical project.

Natorp's sense here is quite accurate, though perhaps it comes as no surprise. Through decade-long exchanges with Husserl, he was well-acquainted with his trajectory and saw a common direction in the turn to concrete subjectivity. Little could he know, however, that Husserl would eventually develop a notion of subjectivity that mirrors Natorp's fluid infinity. Whether this review bore any direct influence on that development is unclear. It nevertheless stands as a pointillistic snapshot of Husserl on the way to his foundations, an outside view of a phenomenology in fluid genesis.

References

Cassirer, Ernst (1925): "Paul Natorp." In: *Kant-Studien* 30, pp. 273–298.
Luft, Sebastian (2010): "Reconstruction and Reduction: Natorp and Husserl on Method and the Question of Subjectivity." In: *Neo-Kantianism in Contemporary Philosophy*. Rudolf A. Makkreel and Sebastian Luft (Eds.). Bloomington: Indiana University Press, pp. 59–91.
Natorp, Paul (1888): *Einleitung in die Psychologie nach kritischer Methode*. Freiburg: Mohr.
Natorp, Paul (1901): "Zur Frage der logischen Methode. Mit Beziehung auf Edmund Husserls 'Prolegomena zur reinen Logik.'" In: *Kant Studien* 6, pp. 270–283.
Natorp, Paul (1912): *Allgemeine Psychologie nach kritischer Methode*. Tübingen: Mohr.
Natorp, Paul (1914): "Husserls *Ideen zu einer reinen Phänomenologie*." In: *Die Geisteswissenschaften*, pp. 426–448.

Translated by Jerome Veith
Paul Natorp. Husserl's Ideas Pertaining to a Pure Phenomenology

Husserls „Ideen zu einer reinen Phänomenologie"
Logos: Internationale Zeitschrift für Philosophie der Kultur 7, pp. 224–246 (1917–18)

I

[224] An engagement with Husserl's stance of "phenomenology" is a necessity for anyone seeking progress in the basic questions of philosophy; it is doubly so for someone who, in a series of fundamental presuppositions, finds himself in line with Husserl from the start. Thus, even my first volume of *General Psychology*, in its critical survey of others' related and fundamental presentations, had to dedicate a discussion to E. Husserl (Natorp 1912, pp. 280–290). There, in addition to the *Logical Investigations*, I was also already able to make note of the systematic treatise *Philosophy as a Rigorous Science* (Husserl 1981, pp. 289 f.). However, now that the *Ideas Pertaining to a Pure Phenomenology and Phenomenological Philosophy* (Husserl 2014) presents a new, foundational display of phenomenology's principles, it is my task to test my erstwhile critique upon this new elucidation and expand the critique in light of it. The question for me is as follows: How does Husserl's phenomenology relate to my *General Psychology*—his method of "phenomenological reduction" to my method of "reconstruction"? Which ultimate assumptions are common to both of us, and to what extent do we arrive at the same conclusions from the same premises? What, conversely, is the point at which our paths diverge? [225] My critique begins with the first section of Husserl's text, "Essence and Knowledge of Essence" [*Wesen und Wesenserkenntnis*] which brings to light not only the clear congruence of our ultimate aims, but precisely the fundamental difference between our basic stances.

"Phenomenology" demands a completely new "attitude" of thinking. This attitude rests upon a twofold "reduction": (1) from the singular, individually experienced, spatio-temporally determined *factum* to the necessary and general *eidos* ("essence" [*Wesen*], also "essence" [*Essenz*]) (in old terminology: to the *a priori* of the presupposition, of the principle, pure in the objective sense of the logically prior); (2) from the "*real*" [*realen*], i.e., that which is inserted into the *world*-construction in a singularly determined manner, to the *irreal* [*Irrealen*], which is actually the pre- and super-real: to *pure consciousness*.

Both of these characteristics of the pure "phenomenon" pertain exactly to the pure consciousness or the ultimate subjective [stage] sought by *General Psychology*. It lies on this side of all *objectification*, be it toward the naturally real, or toward some practical or artistic *object* that presents itself in reality; and it also entirely eschews the character of being *merely factual*—which is just the final conclusion of the aforementioned demand. I did not see the latter as clearly before, even though I already stated its decisive premise—the *exclusion of temporal determinacy* from pure consciousness—in the *Introduction to Psychology* (Natorp 1888); in *General Psychology* I draw the conclusion explicitly (Natorp 1912, pp. 29, 32, 58 f., 228 f., and esp. chapter 10, §§10 – 15, pp. 250 f.). The dual task that I assign myself in *General Psychology* is (1) that of a general (in Husserl's terms: eidetic) description of the *constituents* of consciousness according to their types, which I also call a "phenomenology" of consciousness; (2) that of a "distinction of lived experiential units," which, over against the "ontic," represents the "genetic" side of investigating consciousness; this, however, does not pertain to genesis within a presupposed time, but instead to the temporal form of lived experience itself, and thus intends to first *ground* all *possibilities* of temporal arrangement of lived experiences, as *discretion* [*Diskretion*], upon the originary *continuity* of consciousness. It thereby first leads over to psychology as a pure *science of fact*, in relation to which it stands as the general *doctrine of principles*, the *doctrine of categories*; which itself is no longer philosophy, [226] but returns entirely into the empirical sciences. Yet Husserl's phenomenology takes a very similar stance toward psychology as pure investigation of facts (p. 2/3, 5/6, 34/ 34 etc.). There is only brief allusion to a "phenomenological science of facts" (§62, Remark), which, according to at least one main section, is to be the "'phenomenological transformation' of the ordinary sciences of facts," and made possible by eidetic phenomenology. In another passage (p. 103/99), Husserl speaks of a peculiar instantiation of consciousness that is in itself super-real, pre-real, and absolute; an instantiation through which consciousness first becomes human, animal, etc., namely by virtue of the experiential relation to the organic body. This is how the peculiarly "psychological" attitude first arises. In any case, our points of view are very close on this; almost all that remains is the terminological difference that I, on the one hand, call the pure doctrine of consciousness "psychology"—but general, pure psychology, since after all, only it provides the *logos* of the psyche, whereas the other mode of observation, which as it were translates psyche into *physis*, should really be called *psycho-physics*—while Husserl on the other hand, in a traditional way, takes "psychology" to be only this naturalistic kind, and introduces the distinguishing name "phenomenology" for the pure doctrine of consciousness.

As we thus agree on the demand for a *foundational, pure doctrine of consciousness*, we move on to assess the exact sense of this *purity*. In Husserl, the *facts* and the *essences* stand in stark opposition to each other. "From facts only facts follow" (p. 18/20). Even general judgments of facts (causal propositions) are not, as such, judgments of essences (§2 and §6). Yet every cognition of facts includes cognition of essences, is dependent on the latter, and has the latter as a logical presupposition (§2 and §8); the opposite is not the case at all (§7). To be sure, the positing of essences can be typified in experience or fantasy, but does not in itself imply any positing on the part of an individual, and does not contain any claims about facts (§4). However, positing of essences does pertain necessarily (essentially-necessarily [*wesensnotwendig*]) to the facts to which it is applied, as mathematics for natural science. Phenomenology also therefore contains the theoretical foundations for all sciences of facts, the conditions of *possibility* of their *objects* as such (§8 and §9); it is thus also called "*transcendental*."

Up to here, this is just a basic clarification of the *sense of the a priori*. In this respect, Husserl is fully in the clear. [227] He convincingly refutes empiricism, which does not recognize principles independent of factual observations, and yet constantly needs to support itself upon premises that could not possibly be grounded through experience (§20 and §25). One then seeks to interpret these premises as products abstracted from experience, by which logic even fantastical experiments (in mathematics) could lead to inductive proofs, a notion that any natural scientist would certainly reject as evidence in his field of research. But mathematical axioms, for instance, do not contain the least positing of experiential facts, and can therefore also not be grounded by the latter (§25; Kant says of pure thought-positing: it *abstracts*, but *is not abstracted* from the sensible (Kant 1992, §6)).

If the knowledge of essence is thus *not to be grounded through experience*, what is the basis of its certainty?

Husserl answers this strictly in line with Descartes: through *intuition* and *deduction*. Knowledge of essences is grounded, first and foremost, through intuition: an immediate seeing, looking-at, "visibility" (§3), "intuition of essences" [*Wesensanschauung*], "apprehension" in immediate insight. To this comes the second aspect: *mediated* insight through apodictic *proof*, according to the example of mathematics (§7). Everything that phenomenology sets up arrives with the demand of ultimately being directly *presented* in "intuition" (§18), without any hypothetical or interpretive laying-out or imposition. The "*principle of all principles*" is that "each intuition affording [something] in an originary way is a legitimate source of knowledge" (§24) or, still closer to Descartes, that *"perfect clarity is the measure of all truth"* (§78). Empiricism is entirely correct in that vision is decisive; but there is not only *one* seeing, namely that of experience (§19, cf. §24). Phenomenology replaces this with the more *general* "intuition" as such; it is founded upon *all* types of intuition. Every judging insight falls under the concept of "affording intuition," and is a matter of its "evidence" that is not just a mere feeling but a kind of seeing (§21). There is pure intuiting as a "kind of givenness in which *essences are given as|objects in an originary way just as much as* individual realities are given in experiential intuition" (§21). For instance, the fact that a + 1 = 1 + a is *something given by* eidetic intuition, but is not the expression of a fact of experience (§20). If one takes the "positive" as *that which is originarily to be grasped*, [228] then the stance of phenomenology is true positivism (§20, p. 38/38).

This is the first point at which concerns arise for us; and based on the extraordinary weight that Husserl places on this "principle of principles," it might appear that an unbridgeable gap opens up here within the most fundamental of presuppositions.

However, one immediately realizes that there is no mention of a straightforward *being*-given, but of an originarily *affording act* or *consciousness* (§23), of *affording* intuition, etc. Is that just an involuntarily inserted variation of expression, or is this insight perhaps reached that there is no given in the sense of mere *receptivity*, that "giving" itself must have the sense of a completely peculiar "act"—the fundamental act of knowing, the act of *positing*?

The expression "*Anschauung,*" "*Intuition*" points back to Plato who, just like the entire army of rationalists that followed, speaks of a "look" [*Schau*], a pure seeing *of* [Er*schauen*] the pure "beings." The "*eidos,*" the "idea," also indicates a "mode of seeing," just as in our word "*insight*"; additionally (and this is also since Plato), there is the equally common sensible analogy of reaching, grasping, taking a hold of (one might think of Descartes' *percipere, perceptio*), as in "grasping conceptually" [*Begreifen*], "concept" [*Begriff*] (*conceptus*), etc. As much as these differ from sensation in terms of objects, do they really differ *in terms of type*—be it vision or tactile sense—i.e., from a merely *passive taking-in?* Or are they supposed to represent, in contrast, a pure *act*-character of thoughtful knowing?

If the latter, wherein does the *analogy* to sensible vision or grasping lie? Certainly in the fact that whatever one sees and grasps *exists* in any case. What is to be seen must be *there*, must be *before one's eyes*; and what is to be grasped must, as our language puts it so well, be "*ready-to-hand.*"

But must it also be there *in advance*? That is what is at stake here. There is an *original* acquisition (Kant says) of that which *was not even there before*, and thus *did not belong to any matter* [*Sache*]. If that is the sense of the "giving" act of "knowledge of essences," then such a "giving" is just as inoffensive as the "giving" in Kant, which he elucidates as [229] *exhibiting* in intuition, and *presenting* to experience (actual or possible; Kant 1998, B 195).

Yet the language of *actio* and *passio* needs a lot of clarification. In the final analysis, what is the impulse that one takes from the "given"? Why did Plato himself, who especially in his mythical passages describes the intelligible "looking" in such sensual and lively terms, not rest with this, but instead demand a strictly *logical* account of his "ideas" (a λόγον διδόναι); namely, the evidence of their *accomplishment* as ὑποθέσεις, "foundations" for firm *knowledge—sciences?* Or why is Kant so emphatically opposed to taking some propositions "*without justification and proof, as directly certain*. For, if we were to grant this for synthetic propositions, no matter how *evident* they may be, viz., that *without providing a deduction* one may on the strength of their own pronouncement commit them to unconditional approval, then *all critique of understanding is lost.* [...] Our understanding will then be open to every delusion" (Kant 1998, B285–286)? If this demand for "justification" (through proof or "deduction") simply intends to refer from *immediate* "intuition" to *mediation* by means of an Aristotelian "*apodeixis*," then this would merely mean positing a seeing-*together* [*Zusammenschau*] in place of a seeing-*alone* [*Einzelschau*] – yet the seeing-together would thereby be just another mere "seeing." It would need (1) to take in every individual thing "clearly and distinctly"; for how else would the context be seen clearly? And it would need (2) to grasp the context itself in an individual "sight" – regardless of how "logical" the context is; just as Descartes expressly teaches: the single steps of *mediating* deduction must themselves be grasped in *immediate* intuition, such that deduction is just a chain of intuitions whose connections are themselves a matter of intuition, albeit an intuition of a second order.

Yet the demand for a *context* of the individual thought-positings [*Denksetzungen*], be it in the successive ordering of the logical according to the relation of conditioning and conditioned, or in the simultaneous order of mutual conditioning, conceals the decisive moment: the retreat to the original *continuity* of thought, in which and through which the single instances of knowing [*Einzelerkenntnisse*]—isolatable in abstraction (and *only* in abstraction)—gain a hold and permanence. For this reason and in this sense, all *being*-determined—which is the only acceptable sense of being-given—is only to be thought [230] as a result and as an expression of an *act of determining*. The "act" of giving ultimately may not—and cannot—mean anything other than the grounding of the initially isolated single positing of thought *from* the continuity of thinking, *out of* it and *by virtue of* it.

Put differently: the *rigidity*, the *pointilistic* character of the "insight" taken in isolation must be suspended, overcome, and in this overcoming also be explained. Thinking is *movement*, not fixation; the stases can only be passages, just as the point can only be part of the drawn line, not present for itself prior to it, and not "determined" through itself. This is what the διαλέγεσθαι, logic as dialectics, understanding as *discursus* means: that thinking is movement, that one is to inquire about the *fieri*, and only on the basis of the *fieri* can one recognize the *factum*.

That is the offensiveness of every and all *ready-made* givenness, every *tout-fait*, be it called a priori or empirical: the purported "fixed stars" of thinking are to be recognized as "wandering stars of a higher order"; the purported *fixed points* of thinking must be dissolved, made fluid within the continuity of the thought-*process*. Thus nothing *is*, but rather something *becomes* in its being "given." Every *discrete* positing that is "rational" in the bad sense must return to the irrational, i.e., the pre- and super-rational of a logical continuity, which constantly *develops* the finite determinacies from out of the infinite into the infinite. Even a + 1 = 1 + a is *not* automatically valid by virtue of immediate evidence; it is not valid, for instance, if 'a' is a Cantorian 'ω'; the "commutative" addition thus becomes a special case of a further concept of addition; thus Euclidian geometry, in all of its evidence, becomes a special case in the eightfold infinite (according to Wellstein) system of "possible" geometries. Therefore, no "synthetic" positing of thought can ever be viewed as *absolutely* and *finally* given, but is instead only "given" in and through the process of thinking. *The process itself is that which "gives"* for the (*always* only relative, *never* absolute) "principles"; only in this way "is" there [*"gibt" es*] a given, and only in this way does the given "give itself" (as other languages put it), even in the pure, but especially in the empirical. In analogy to Husserl's statement that his apriorism is the true positivism, one could say: true apriorism, for which no statement is valid "a priori" as something final and absolute, corresponds to true empiricism, for which no statement of experience can be plainly valid as something final and absolute. This is what the *"generation"* [*Erzeugung*] of the a priori tells us, which has nothing to do with psychologism; and this is all that the "giving" act can mean, [231] if it is to mean anything sustainable. Even the "intuitus," the insight or inner sight, can only signify the seeing-into [*Hineinsehen*] of things discretely posited by virtue of arbitrary delimitation into the original continuity, out of which and in which it first arises for positing thought; the *inclusion* in the ultimately all-encompassing infinity of mutual relations in which only the single positing of thought can firmly ground itself. The demand of the *"ground"* is ultimately this: that of Cohen's *"origin,"* the expression of primordiality that no theory of thought can circumvent, the groundedness of thought within itself; "in itself" can only mean: in the process. Only in this way can there be a truly *independent method* of philosophy.

This was already intimated in Pythagoreanism, which allowed the finite to determine itself by the infinite or super-finite as the undetermined or *predetermined*. It is first securely reached, however, in Plato's deepest discovery: that of the *kinesis* of the *eidē*. Yet it was the fate of Aristotelianism, holding philosophy back for thousands of years, to have seemingly taken over completely the Platonic rationalism of "proving," while precisely missing Plato's deepest insight; or rather, whenever Aristotelianism encountered this insight in Plato or in the Pythagoreans, more in its consequences than in its principle itself, it consciously denied the insight, in a truly old-Hellenic flinching before the infinite. If the Aristotelian finitism was finally burst by the cosmology and mechanics of Copernicus and Galilei, and if mathematics first found in the infinitesimal method the secure handle of a strict, scientific procedure upon the infinite, then the logic of this great turning has only hesitantly followed. Leibniz recognized something of this, and it slumbers as the deepest theme in Kant's claim concerning the "synthetic" character of real knowledge; we are just now coming to work it out in full rigor and purity.

Perhaps it is the case that Husserl will come closer, or has come closer, to this insight in the further development of his thought; but at the moment, as the sentences stand here, it appears that while he advanced to Plato's *eidos*, he remained standing on the *first step* of Platonism, that of the rigid *eidē* that stand immobile "in Being"; that he did not follow the final step of Plato's that was his greatest and most properly his own: to bring the *eidē* into movement, to make them fluid within the ultimate *continuity* of thought.

[232] In many ways, Husserl appears all too readily to stand firm on the ground of *Aristotelianism*; thus, the Aristotelian concept of substance seems to have been taken over completely in the purely analytically grounded postulate of the final, absolutely individual "this-here" [*Dies-da*] (§§11, 14). For Husserl, things are *prior* to relations, instead of relations being (logically) prior to things, which recent research has discovered to be the specific difference between Plato and Aristotle. In this way, the old system of genus and species can reappear without debate (§12); for which purpose the entirely Aristotelian demand for *amesa*, for ultimate principles that are "not freely variable" but rigid (§16), seems all too well-suited. And so the final conclusion of eidetics is a *"classification"* of sciences according to ultimate "regions of being" (§17) that are decisively bounded off against each other, and to which there are correspondingly many "regional *ontologies*"; one need instead demand logical *genealogies*.

Thus, one could naturally speak of a *being*-given without a giving *process*, especially a process of thought. But precisely this is why it is wrong. If Husserl did not supercede this, then the accusation that he returns to *scholasticism*, that he wishes to immortalize the hurdle that Aristotle could not surmount, would not be groundless (a claim that he defeats reasonably in other respects).

But one knows Husserl to be one who restlessly strives forward. And thus one will not stop with such an initial judgment and aim to decide prematurely over the whole. Rather, one will need to test further whether the error corrects itself in the development, either in whole or in part.

II

Pure consciousness is to be presented in stark *contrast* to *experienceable reality* [*erfahrbaren Wirklichkeit*], but at the same time by *starting* from the latter. Thus, it is of initial importance how one conceives of the *experienced reality* itself. This can be answered with one word: essential, *in the critical sense*. "Givenness" here entirely loses its character of the *absolutely* given; all experienced reality only acquires "profiles [...] *never affording itself absolutely*" (§49, p. 93/90). "An absolute reality is no more or less valid than a round square" (§55, p. 106). This is demonstrated extensively through many convolutions (esp. §§40, 41, 44, 49). For the natural attitude, [233] things in perception are plainly given. They are also "*present*" in perception in a certain sense, and not merely *represented* or symbolized, as in a depiction or sign (§43). Nevertheless, for the scientific attitude this "given" of perception is merely an "appearance," an indication towards an entirely different world, one that is foreign to consciousness and *transcendent* of consciousness; this world is only "given" as X, in progressively more detailed identification, but never exhausted, *determinable*, or *determined*. The "transcendence" of the object therefore has nothing to do with absoluteness, but rather just indicates the X-character, that of the more-and-more, but never complete, and thus that which is *only relatively* determinable. Conversely, [transcendence] also does not mean an extension over the world *for consciousness*. For concepts such as force, acceleration, energy, atom, ion, etc. *determine* nothing other than the perceived processes and contexts of which one is conscious. In this, one does not reveal an unknown world of thing-realities "in themselves," which would somehow take the place of appearances for the sake of their *causal explanation*. It makes no sense to think of sensible lived experiences as connected to physical things through causality, a causality that moreover only has its place in the context of the constant intentional world. The transcendence of physical things is only the transcendence of a *being that constitutes itself in consciousness and is connected to consciousness* (§52). And it is one of the main tasks of phenomenology to show how reality constitutes itself for consciousness, i. e., makes itself possible through *functions* of *"synthetic unity"* (esp. §86, p. 176/169): not through "replication"—that would presuppose two realities standing over against each other, whereas only one is present and possible (§90, p. 186)—but rather on account of "intentional" functions—and that can now no longer mean direction toward object *given from the outside*, but only functions directed *toward constitution* of an objectivity [*Gegenständlichkeit*] *as such* (*in* consciousness and *for* it) (§§86, 90, 146, 117; on "constituting" cf. §§50, 52, 150, 153). The object, as X, is understood in Kant's sense as expression of the identity that is always first to be presented, and never absolutely, but always in an infinite process from determination to determination (§131; on the X "*that comes to a synthetic unity*" cf. p. 273/261; cf. also §41, p. 75/72–73). A real thing [*Dingreales*] *can* fundamentally only ever be inadequately presented, [234] can never exhaustively and ultimately be the rational positing on the basis of the appearance (§138); adequate givenness of things is only "*prefigured* [...] as a system absolutely determined in terms of its *type of essence*, a system of endless processes of continuous appearing," as "*idea*" in the Kantian sense (of the "endless" process, §149); the field of these processes is *determined a priori*, but is a continuum of appearance that is *infinite in all directions*, with various yet determined dimensions, pervaded by *fixed essential lawfulness* [*Wesensgesetzlichkeit*] – but because of its infinity can never be given in complete (determining) unity (§143). So the object is never adequately given, but only the *idea* of such objectivity, and thereby the *a priori rule* for *lawfully determined* infinities of inadequate lived experiences in which the idea realizes itself in stages, but due to its infinity, never adequately (§144; cf. §§149, 150). In this context, *evidence* too undergoes an invasive correction of its features (§145): it does not mean some index of consciousness that, attached to a judgment, calls to us like a mystical voice from a better world: Here is the truth! It is not a content appended somehow to the act, a supplement of whatever sort, but instead a peculiar mode of *positing*. Thus also §49 (p. 93/90): the spatio-temporal world is a merely intentional being, i.e., a being that "consciousness *posits* in its experiences, a being that is in principle only capable of being intuited and *determined* as something identical on the basis of motivated manifolds of appearance–but *beyond this* is a nothing." Husserl repeats and elaborates, albeit briefly, that this is not only the case with objectifications of natural science, but also with axiological and practical ones, and objectifications of all sorts (§§52, 147, 152, 153).

Yet *in distinction* from this merely *ideal* character of experientially lived reality and of all objectivity as such, *pure* phenomena are supposedly *given absolutely*. What does this absoluteness mean, and how is it reached?

It is reached, according to Husserl, by *shutting off* or *bracketing* the character of reality, a kind of transposition of value, an "*epochē*," a refraining, an inhibition, a *setting-out-of-action* of the *thesis*, of the *judgment* by which is "posited;" to be sure, what is bracketed is "still there," but simply placed in parentheses, [235] such that "no use" is made of it (§31). This shutting off (which is comparable to Cartesian doubt) stretches to cover the entire "world," including ourselves and everything mental, insofar as it is taken to occur in the world; what then remains, as a "phenomenological *residuum*" (p. 59/58), is consciousness *in itself*, in its own being, the *pure* or *transcendental consciousness* (§33). What is reached in this manner is not the *psychological* reflection upon the *I and its lived experiences*; that would also be "transcendent," "intentionally" directed, *objective [gegenständlich]* consciousness, but merely directed at a *second objectivity*. There is no such thing as such an objectivity; that is why Husserl also rejects the distinction of *external* and *internal perception* (§38; on the difference between phenomenological and psychological attitudes, cf. §53, 85). Instead, what is at stake here is an *intention that remains in the same stream of lived experience and is immanently directed*. An act can be directed at another act, instead of at a transcendent object. There is precisely not a *second objectness [Dinglichkeit]* (as §§39f. explicitly show), but rather, over against *all* transcendence, the *lived experiencing* itself; this does not in turn "appear," is not given as something identical in various modes of appearance through "adumbration," but is given *in itself* – although Husserl already admits here an *incompleteness* of every *experience* of lived experiencing [*Erfahrung vom Erleben*] (§44), which is still something entirely different than the experience of the transcendent. Every *immanent perception* necessarily guarantees the *existence* of its object. When reflective grasping directs itself at my lived experiencing, then I have grasped an *absolute self* whose existence [*Dasein*] is in principle not negatable (§46; one is reminded of Descartes' *cogito*). What one has in mind may be a fiction, but the being-in-mind itself, the feigning *consciousness* is not something feigned. *My* consciousness is originarily and absolutely given *to me*, not merely according to its essence, but according to existence as well (§46). All actually given objectness could also not exist, [but] no actually given lived experience can fail to exist. This is deemed the "high point" of the observation (p. 87/84). §49: It could be that all apprehension of the world was destroyed through contradiction; [yet] the being of consciousness would be unscathed. The immanent being of consciousness is *absolute being* in the strict sense that it *"nulla re indiget as existendum,"* whereas every *res* is reliant upon real existing consciousness; [236] so between them [there is] an "abyss of sense." The being of consciousness is a "*context of absolute being*" into which nothing can penetrate and from which nothing can escape, which has no spatio-temporal outside and cannot be in any spatio-temporal inside, which cannot experience causality from any thing or exercise causality upon any thing, but contains all of this in the sense of intentionality (p. 93/90). After shutting off the psychic-physical totality of nature, this is what remains as phenomenological residue: the whole field of *absolute consciousness*, to be grasped through *acts of a second order* – acts of *reflection* whose given is the infinite field of *absolute experiences:* the "field of phenomenology" (§50).

One need barely indicate the extensive overlap with *my* position, especially concerning the fact that one here does not suppose a *double objectivity*, to which would correspond a *double mode of appearing and perception*, but rather just the originary, indissoluble opposition of *immanent consciousness to everything objectively posited*; so that on the one hand, *all* consciousness, as "intentional," is directed at the object, and that because of this, on the other hand, there must always be possible a retrospective relation [*Rückbeziehung*], a "reflection" that seeks its way back from objectivities of any sort and order—and the hierarchy of orders is infinite for Husserl, too—to the "pure," that is, simply *pre-objective* consciousness. We also agree that the acts of reflection are "acts *of a second order*," directed at all of the (primary) acts in which the positing of the object occurs.

Up until now, the most radical difference between us seems to be that for Husserl, the pure consciousness is *given* "absolutely," and is thus capable of being delimited as an unquestionable "residue" through a simple "reduction," indeed through the mere *refraining* from an objectively positing act, whereas I claim that to "*reconstruct*" this consciousness is a peculiar and difficult task that demands its own method; a method that stands as a *precise reversal* to that of objectification, and thus also in strict correspondence with that method, and just as that method opens a *path into the infinite*.

Now, it is easy to understand how one arrives at the opposite, [237] absolute conception. All *mediating* positing by thinking requires an *ultimate immediacy*. The "sense-affording" *consciousness* cannot itself in turn be given only through sense-affording (§55). That is doubtlessly how the pure consciousness is *necessarily thought* and inevitably *demanded*; except that would be full *lived experiencing* and not just *experience of* lived experiencing. But the point is not to *experience* our lived experiencing in a *lived* manner. Why would we need a *science*, a *method* for that? Rather, the point is to go beyond the lived experiencing and bring it to cognition, *to hold it fast* in cognition, to *secure* it for cognition. Just as certainly as lived experiencing is not mere experience of lived experiencing, so must the experience of lived experiencing be something other than lived experiencing. The former is "immediate" and "absolute," the latter necessarily *mediating*. Indeed, Husserl presupposes the necessity of its mediation when he speaks of a "perception," an "apprehension," a peculiar type of "experience" of the lived experience, of "reflection," even of a peculiar "intention," of peculiar "acts," specifically acts "of a second order," i.e. those directed at the original acts. Acts and intentions unavoidably direct themselves at "objects;" so if the act of reflection does not direct itself toward transcendent objects, but toward the acts through which the latter are posited, it *makes* these acts into its own objects, it is "intentionally" directed toward them, i.e. directed in a way that is first *questionable* for knowing, to be *established*, not *standing established* in advance. This expression of "establishment" might serve further clarification: after all, Husserl conceives of the nexus of lived experience as a continual *"stream."* Yet the knowledge of this nexus must stop the stream, as it were, must try to *hold it fast* at a determinate point; however, then it is no longer the *streaming* stream, and the difference is not just one of "completeness;" instead, "grasping" *changes* what is grasped *in its very character*; the streaming stream is something other than what is grasped and retained of it in reflection. This is what I have so frequently had occasion to underscore: the "immediate" of pure consciousness is not already *immediately known* or knowable as such. Rather, since the primary "intention" is directed toward the "transcendent" object, the knowledge of that "immediacy" is even more of a "mediated" knowledge than that of the object in the actual sense, Husserl's "transcendent" object. But then it is untenable that this *knowledge* is absolute.

[238] It seems that one confuses the *demand* of presenting pure consciousness with what can be presented *in actual knowing*. It is certainly demanded to present consciousness in its full absoluteness. But that is why it does not present itself in this way in "reflection;" and the closer investigation of how (on what methodical path) such presentation is even possible, i.e. the *transcendental* investigation of the *possibility* of a pure presentation of the pure content of consciousness, results in the fact that it is just as unpresentable in its respective absoluteness as the transcendent object, which is just as absolutely *demanded*, but not therefore *given* or ever capable of being given. But both for the same reason: because, in each case, it is an *infinite* task. If consciousness were not infinite, then the task of objectification, which is only directed at the "given" of consciousness and cannot go beyond it (nor does it seek to), could not be infinite. But if consciousness *is* infinite in every direction, then no finite knowledge of it, no matter what its method, can simply present it; after all, that would mean presenting it in its pervasive, inner and outer infinity.

It is especially implausible that a *mere shutting off*, a *not-participating* in the objectifying act, a *looking away* from the whole world of objectivity, in short, a mere *negative* action should lift out and present consciousness in its purity. To be sure, it is not meant as a simple *abstraction* from components of more comprehensive contexts, be it necessary or factual ones, or a mere *limitation of judgment* to a cohesive piece of total real being (§51, p. 95/92). Objectifying science (mathematics, mechanics, physics, etc.) actually proceeds in an abstracting fashion. Apparently, it would be necessary for the totality of being, *experienced* in an absolutely *lived* manner, to present itself, in its integrity, for questioning cognition, which may be more of a task of *concretion* than abstraction. But precisely this concretion, upon the slightest inspection, turns out to be *conditioned* by *prior abstraction:* one can only become aware of the *infinite interweaving* of consciousness by first dissolving it; and thus only *to the extent* that this dissolution succeeds. If, as infinite, the interweaving of consciousness is *never entirely dissoluble*, then it is also not capable of being presented in its roundedness, i.e. presented "absolutely" in cognition.

[239] Upon immediate general consideration, that is incontestable. Since the *third section* of the treatise is specially dedicated to the question of the *method* of phenomenology, one might here hope to glean decisive information concerning this decisive question. It will be best to adjoin the discussion of *section four* to the third, as it remains in the same context of thought.

III IV

The *object* of phenomenology, says Husserl (§63), has never been seen until now, to say nothing of finding a *method* for it. But how is it that one did not see what is, after all, absolutely given? And why does one need a method at all to uncover it, or in other words, to *give* it? Husserl indeed acknowledges stages of *clarity* in the grasping of essences; but over against the null-limit of total darkness, there is to stand a unified limit [*Einsgrenze*] of *absolutely grasped* essence "completely as it is in itself" (§67). *Perception*, or rather *fantasy*, forms the pathway out. It prefers free *mobility*, by virtue of which it also bears great significance in mathematics. While mathematics is certainly an eidetic science, having to do with *abstract eidē*, phenomenology deals with "essences of experience" (§73) that are not abstract entities but concrete ones, *fluid* ones, *concrete entities flowing in all parts*; here, one cannot conceive of conceptual and terminological *fixities* as one can in mathematics (§75). The *generic essence*, like perception *as such*, memory, empathy, willing *as such*, lived experience, cognition *as such*, may be determinable through strict concepts; but these do not offer leverage for a *deductive theorizing* according to the model of mathematics. Mediated conclusions can at most only have a guiding significance; the *direct viewing of essence* that follows is alone decisive (p. 140/134–5). As we know, this viewing is now to be achieved through *shutting off* all objectification; but this shutting off simultaneously bears the significance of an "*alteration via an operation sign*" by which what is altered is *in turn integrated* back into the phenomenological sphere (§76, cf. §50). Thus, there is a phenomenology of the *consciousness* of natural science and of the human sciences, indeed of *nature* and of *spirit* themselves: everything transcendent (in our terms: objectified), [240] as that which is given and as that which is taken at face value in givenness, is, *according to the consciousness of it*, an object of phenomenological investigation (p. 142/136–7). Husserl (like me) prefers to designate this backward relation of all objectifications into the original pure consciousness with the term "*reflection.*" And here it is expressly explained: by the fact of one's *experiencing*, one does not already have one's experience in view or *apprehend* it; rather, reflection is a second lived experience for which the first *becomes an object* (§74, p. 145/139–40). This does not just occur through remembering *after the fact* (retention), but also through remembering *before the fact* (protention); in such acts, then, the stream of lived experience becomes *graspable* and *analyzable*. They are thus "reflectively *experiencing*" acts (§78, p. 150/144) through which alone we *know* anything about the stream of lived experience. But does this not *stop up* the *flooding stream* of consciousness against its nature, dissolve its *concretion* in a sum of *abstractions*—especially if (according to Husserl) what is individually experienced in a lived way is immediately grasped in "*eidetic universality*"? Basically, this is the old interjection about "self-observation" as such *changing* what is observed. Husserl takes the objection seriously enough (§79): In the "process of forming a new idea" do I not have *something new* before my eyes? How can I claim to have thereby gleaned the essential components of *unreflected experience* (p. 154/149)? But the question is probably not answered radically enough by stating that, even whoever raises the doubt cannot avoid *presupposing* a knowledge, by reflection, of unreflected experience – for this is indeed a *requirement* of the thesis itself; for by doubting the epistemological significance of reflection, one still *reflects* and for *one's own* reflection makes use of the general epistemological significance that one denies. The answer is quite right, but it only confirms that the epistemological status of reflection is a *presupposition*, an *hypothesis*; it is certainly a *necessary* one but, like all hypotheses, it will *first have to prove its correctness in the process*. There is certainly good cause for Husserl to deny *induction* as a *replacement* for reflection, for induction only bears proof if one presumes that there is reliable reflection. But it does not follow from this that it is not necessary to *prove* the "thesis" of reflection through induction. *As* a thesis it *demands* this process; and 'proving the thesis in the process' is the meaning of all true [241] induction; no pure doctrine of consciousness and no science can dispense with this true induction. All that is justified is to eschew an "inductive" proof of such a sort that seeks to magically produce general propositions from singular *facts* (as if those were fixed in advance). Moreover, the sparse indications that are made precisely here about the relation of phenomenology to psychology (§79) give the impression that Husserl does not even want to deny such an inner connection between phenomenology and empirical psychology. When he underscores that knowledge of "possibility" takes precedence over that of reality, this is not intended to mean that the former can exist without the latter, or without relation to it, or that "possibility" can signify anything other than the making-possible of the real; thus (in line with Kant), the proof of reality will be the necessary second stage in the process of cognition, which is only introduced by the first stage, the setting-up of possibility. But then the method of pure research into consciousness obviously steps into a *precise and essential relation to the method of all objectification*, which is "inductive" in no sense other than this one.

Husserl fully approaches this insight, and thereby comes close to my *method* of "*reconstruction*," by continuing to demand above all an "*objective orientation*" for phenomenology. It is precisely the phenomenological attitude that discloses pure consciousness as being *dually oriented* in its original essence: "from the I to there," and "in the *opposite directional ray*" toward the I; or: every lived experience can be differentiated into a *subjectively oriented* and an *objectively oriented side*, to which there corresponds a similarly dual-sided (but not really divisible) investigation, one oriented toward *pure subjectivity*, the other toward that which belongs to *the constitution of objectivity for subjectivity* (§80, p. 161/154–5). *The objective orientation necessarily precedes*, because it is the primary one for the natural attitude. Here it is even more difficult to say what still differentiates Husserl's standpoint from my own than to point out commonalities. In any case, an initial prerequisite for Husserl as well as for me is that *consciousness is objectifying in its essence*, in Husserl's language 'intentional' (cf. esp. §84, §90f., §117, §146). But does this not demand the conclusion that the other, merely inverted "orientation," [242] the subjective one, must stretch out over *all* consciousness, all types and all stages of it, and must thereby *in its inversion thoroughly correspond* to the objective orientation? If objectification is an *infinite* task, in the strict sense of the Kantian "idea," does not this same character of the infinite task apply to subjectively oriented research of consciousness? But then what becomes of the absolute *intuitional* character of phenomenological insight? It is clearly *demanded* as absolute – just as cognition of objects is demanded as absolute; there will also be general, *lawful presuppositions* in the one as in the other direction of cognition, presuppositions that are not liable to justified doubt and which, although they are not *more* than presuppositions, are still necessary *as* such. But the same necessity is not accorded to every statement, which intends and pretends to *immediately bring to cognition* the flooding stream of consciousness, *as it is in itself*, in the middle of its flooding, in its "absolute" concretion and continuity.

Husserl's immediately subsequent elucidations clearly indicate this [conclusion]. He investigates (§81 f.) how the infinite, continually cohesive stream of lived experience "that demands its continuity of content" "constitutes itself" as *singular* for a singular pure I (I have preemptively taken the expression of 'self-constitution' from §118). This cohesion can never be given as a whole through a singular pure look (§83); however, it is *intentionally* graspable in the mode of the *"endless" progress* of immanent intuitions; we grasp the cohesion not as a singular lived experience, but in the way of the *idea* in the Kantian sense! Also, no concrete lived experience can ever count as an *independent* one in the full sense, but instead our perception, for instance, changes according to the respective changes in environing determinacies. That is why it is impossible for any two perceptions, or any two lived experiences in general, to ever be *absolutely* identical. But then it is difficult for every concrete lived experience to be *determinable* in its absolute content, since its determination requires *identification*. Finally, a lived experience's relation to the *whole* stream of lived experience, in the three dimensions of before, after, and simultaneous, belongs to the full content of that lived experience – as Bergson has convincingly shown in detail, and moreover as every serious investigation has certainly found. That is the depth that can never be plumbed, which holds the *logos* of the psyche; that is the "limitlessness of progress" [243] on each of the many paths upon which one might attempt to traverse the field of consciousness – already since old Heraclitus.

We must only wait for the treatment of *functional* problems concerning the *constitution of the objectivities of consciousness* to rise to the peak of Husserl's phenomenological investigation. From the beginning, he conceives the two sides of pure consciousness research (which I distinguish as "construction" and "reconstruction") as lying in close proximity; against which I have no objections, given how I understand the relation of the two. But the *leading* point of view remains the objectifying "function," which is expressly identified as the *central* stance of phenomenology (§86): the observation of individual details under the *teleological* aspect of their capacity *"to make synthetic unity possible"* replaces the analysis, comparison, description, and classification that sticks to *individual lived experiences*; the question of the "material" [*Stoff*] remains *completely subordinated* to this (p. 176/169). Here we find Husserl entirely on the path of critical thought; he himself relies on Kant's "transcendental deduction" as it is presented in the first edition of the *Critique of Pure Reason*, in other words on that which Kant (in the Foreword there) distinguishes as the "subjective" from the "objective deduction," but at the same time sets in the closest possible relation. It is the same Kantian discussion that once gave *me* the impetus to search for a new "psychology" as the study of pure consciousness, according to the method of "reconstruction" (cf. Natorp 1888, p. 128 f.).

The two-sidedness of phenomenological observation expresses itself most determinately in Husserl as *the correlation of noema and noesis*, which dominates the entire remainder of his investigation from here on out (§3, chapter 3). "Noema" names the *sense* of every intentional positing, that which is posited in it insofar as the posited (immanently) belongs to the *intentional lived experience* itself, not insofar as it is (transcendently) present; for example, over against the "real" tree, it would be that which, for instance in perception, is intentionally posited *as* tree. To be sure, the possible "noeses" over against *one* such noema seem to be *many*, as in the case of the various directions and degrees of "attention." But in truth, *the noemata change their content along with the noeses* (§92; whereby it is noted that "attention" is nothing other than a basic type of *intentional* modification, which until now no one has noted). [244] It furthermore especially interests us how the *thorough correspondence* of noesis and noema is achieved: they do not both act as a mirror; and it is not the case that they transition into each other by mere shift of a sign; or that any noema need only be substituted by an *N*: "consciousness of *N*" (§98, p. 206/198); or is it rather the case that the noematic is the field of *unities*, whereas the noetic would be the manifold that constitutes it (p. 207/199)? This, too, turns out to be inaccurate; instead the *parallelism* of noema and noesis is so *pervasive* that noematic manifolds *always* correspond to noetic ones; for example, as the different "conceptions" of the same sensible object have just as many different *orientations* in which the object presents itself. Thus, for example, *remembering* is not a merely different "mode of consciousness" than perception, but also another way that *the thing of which one is conscious presents itself* (§99). Likewise, in the layering of intentionalities upon one another (presentification *of* presentification, etc.), the order extends in the same way to noema and noesis (§100); one presents [*stellt...vor*] the other objectively, as it were; it is not just that *I* present one along with the other; i.e., there is a "noematic intentionality" over against the noetic one, such that the latter always carries the former in itself as a correlate (§101). Thus, there are even noematic correlates for the "doxic modalities" (§104 f.) like possibility, problem, question, affirmation and negation, i.e., there *is* (a noematically thought) possibility, problem, question, (in the noematic correlate) being and non-being, according to the affirming or negating doxa; all of this does not just exist on the act-side (in noesis) but also in its correlate (the noema), and is to be grasped in direct line of sight with the latter (§108). The same goes for the "neutrality-modification," in which [there is] no supposition, no "thinking oneself" [*Sichdenken*] that includes positing, and thus no thinking that could be predicated as correct or false (§110 f.; the neutrality then evinces itself as *potentiality*, §115). All of these considerations lie in the direction of my own mode of observation, and have precise analogies in my reconstructive psychology. However, how does this answer the question above: How do noema and noesis *radically differ*, *if not* through a mere change of sign? There hardly remains anything peculiar for the characterization of "acts" if *every* difference between acts expresses itself in their correlate, [245] and indeed presents itself *primarily* in the correlate. In fact, nothing remains except the difference in the *direction* of observation; the direction of *unification* [*Vereinheitlichung*] (*identification*), [which is] at the same time both the *dissolution* from the infinite concretion of *thorough mutual relations* that distinguishes the full lived experience, as well as *multiplication* and *reintegration* into the full concretion of what is experienced as lived: I have found no other difference, and as far as I can tell, Husserl has not indicated one, either. To him, *every* consciousness is (actually or potentially) "thetic," i.e. all "acts," even mental acts and acts of the will, are objectivating and originally constitute objects; which explains the *universality of the logical* as well as the predicative judgment (§117). Yet the constitution of the object rests in any case on *identification*, on "synthetic unity;" this strictly means that noeses do not join together in a multitude, but that *one* noesis constitutes with *one* noema, which is grounded in the noemata of the connected noeses (§118). This ultimately goes for the *entire stream of lived experience*. As distinct as lived experiences can be in their essence, they ultimately constitute themselves, in a *primordial synthesis*, as *one* temporal stream. Synthesis is thesis of a higher order; just as its correlates build upon each other in stages, so do the theses themselves, as acts. In short, noesis and noema *consistently go together*. The description of *consciousness* in its essence always leads to *that of which it is conscious within itself*; the *correlate* of consciousness is inseparable from consciousness, even if not actually [*reell*] contained in it; every most minute difference on the noematic side eidetically (i.e., according to its concept) points back to the smallest differences of the noetic side, and this applies to all categories and species of each (§128). In the *Logical Investigations*, according to "the natural path from psychology to phenomenology," the immanent study of pure lived experiences was understood self-evidently as the study of their actual [*reellen*] components, which were taken as indices for parallel noeses (p. 266/255). But what one took to be noetic analyses of acts was in truth a description of *noematic* structures!

Accordingly, the final (fourth) section is to treat the object-relation especially from the "noematic" side, and only "conversely" [246] also from the noetic. We have already anticipated some of this above, and for our purposes it is not vital to delve any deeper. In light of everything said here, the whole widely-branched investigation bears a distinct type: in it, the "objective orientation" is kept in view to the end, and is treated as at least *foundational* for all consciousness-research. But this is precisely the essential sense of *my* method of "reconstruction." There will certainly be plenty of differences, even deeply seated ones, that arise in the execution of the program; but the fundamental conception of the task is essentially common to us both. Even the difference that appears so radical at first, namely that Husserl maintains an "absolute" conception of the pure object of consciousness whereas I fundamentally deny such a stance, has virtually dissolved upon closer inspection; according to the subject-matter, and for Husserl as for myself, the task of "subjectivization" (to put it in my terms) is no less an "infinite task" than that of "objectivization;" the absolute (pure, i.e. pre-objective) *consciousness* is no less an "*idea*" in the Kantian sense (of the "limitlessness of progress" from determination to determination) than the absolute (pure, i.e. pre-conscious [*überbewusste*]) *object*. Here as there, it is the *method*, the *lawfulness* of determination that is "absolute;" *if one could succeed* in setting it up with complete certainty, the basic categorial structure upon which both build, and which for both would ultimately be the same, would be absolute; but not the individual positing, insofar as it would claim to present at once both the *determinate object* and the *determinate lived experience* just as they are experienced as lived in the infinite continuity of the stream of consciousness; the "*possibility*" of a double "experience" (directed there "transcendently," and here "immanently," but ultimately just *one* doubly directed experience) is absolute, but not the *actual* experience. Only in this way does [my position] correspond to the sense and solid grounding of "*critical*" philosophy in which Husserl is completely rooted, and the demands of which he would like to fulfill, even if he traverses so freely beyond its classical founder. What remains is a certain semblance of an absolutism that is irreconcilable with the spirit of "critique," but it is a semblance that dissolves upon closer examination; apart from that, it is [a] real and right, extremely thorough and demanding "critical" investigation, before which no attempt may pass unpunished that seeks to ground a doctrine of "pure" consciousness with certainty.

References

Natorp, Paul (1888): *Einleitung in die Psychologie nach kritischer Methode*. Freiburg: Mohr.
Natorp, Paul (1912): *Allgemeine Psychologie nach kritischer Methode*. Tübingen: Mohr.
Husserl, Edmund (1981): "Philosophy as a Rigorous Science." Quentin Lauer (Trans.). In: *Husserl: Shorter Works*. Notre Dame: University of Notre Dame Press, pp. 161-197.
Husserl, Edmund (2014): *Ideas I*. Daniel Dahlstrom (Trans.). Hackett: Indianapolis.

Kant, Immanuel (1992) "On the Form and Principles of the Sensible and the Intelligible World." David Walford (Trans.). In: *Theoretical Philosophy, 1755–1770*. Cambridge: Cambridge University Press, pp. 373–416.

Kant, Immanuel (1998): *Critique of Pure Reason*. Paul Guyer and Allen Wood (Eds.). Cambridge: Cambridge University Press.

Translated by Jacob Rump, Evan Clarke, and Andrea Staiti
Theodor Elsenhans.[1] Phenomenology, Psychology, Epistemology

Phänomenologie, Psychologie, Erkenntnistheorie
Kant-Studien 20, pp. 224–275 (1915)

[224] Phenomenology has entered into the fundamental debates of contemporary psychology with increasing success. In light of its significant achievements and its scientific claims, it is necessary—if the confusion of the current situation is to come to some clarity—that we engage phenomenology in debate. This is a debate in which not just psychology, but the theory of knowledge and logic, have an essential stake. In cases such as this it is advisable to locate those instances, from amidst a multiplicity of possible instances, in which the tendency of inquiry that is at issue finds its most acute specification. Not only do we find such an acute specification with Edmund Husserl, indeed he can be regarded as the original creator of this tendency of inquiry, even if others had made suggestions and attempts of various kinds in this direction prior to Husserl. His newest work, the *Ideas Pertaining to a New Phenomenology and a Phenomenological Philosophy,* contains a complete program on this topic with detailed scientific [225] execution and justification.[2] The journal in which this treatise is published, the *Yearbook*

---

1 [For biographical information on Elsenhans, see p. 13–15 of this volume.]
2 *Jahrbuch für Phänomenologie und phänomenologische Forschung,* edited by Edmund Husserl. Vol. I, Part I. *Ideen zu einer reinen Phänomenologie und phänomenologischen Philosophie.* Introduction. First Book. *Allgemeine Einführung in die reine Phänomenologie* by E. Husserl. *Zur Psychologie der Gesinnungen* by Alexander Pfänder. Part 2. *Der Formalismus in der Ethik und die material Wertethik* by Max Scheler. *Beiträge zur Phänomenologie des aesthetischen Genusses* by Moritz Geiger. *Die a priorischen Grundlagen des bürgerlichen Rechtes* by Adolf Reinach. In addition, the earlier principle work, already appearing in the second edition: Edmund Husserl, *Logische Untersuchungen*, 2 volumes, 2nd Ed. 1913 (cited as: Log. Unt.) Later the following shorter treatises of Husserl are considered: "Bericht über deutsche Schriften zur Logik in den Jahren 1895–99," *Archiv für systematische Philosophie,* Vol. X (1903) pp. 397–400 and "Philosophie als Strenge Wissenschaft," *Logos,* Vol. I (1910–11) pp. 316–318. Finally the following works by earlier researchers, to which Husserl's Phenomenology is closely related, are mentioned: W. Dilthey, *Ideen über eine beschreibende und zergliedernde Psychologie, Sitzungsbericht der Kgl. Preuss. Akad. der Wissensch. Zu Berlin 1894,* pp. 1309–1407. C. Stumpf, *Erscheinungen und psychische Funktionen,* ibid 1906. W. Dilthey, *Studien zur Grundlegung der Geisteswissenschaften 1905.* Th. Lipps, *Inhalt und Gegenstand: Psychologie und Logik. Sitzungsberichte der philosoph. Philol. und der hist. Kl. Der K. bayr. Ak. Der Wissensch. 1905* pp. 511–669. Same author,

DOI 10.1515/9783110551594-025

for Philosophy and Phenomenological Research, wants however above all to meet the widely expressed desire "to get to know the character of the phenomenological method and the consequences of its achievements" (Husserl 1989, p. 63)[3] In the assessment of the latter, we should also bring into consideration the treatises that have so far appeared in this journal by Pfänder, Scheler, Geiger, and Reinach, treatises which deliver a welcome illustration of the application of this method to specific single problems. Husserl's own earlier works, especially his *Logical Investigations,* do not entirely agree throughout with the completely developed "Phenomenology" of the *Ideas.* In view of the impossibility of "elevating" the *Logical Investigations* "wholly and completely to the level of the *Ideas,*" a reworking was chosen that would "consciously lead the reader onward and upward, in such a way that, in the final Investigation the level of the *Ideas* is in essentials reached, so that the previous unclearness and half-truths, [226] that we had to put up with, appear perspicuously clarified" (Husserl 2001, p. 5).[4] In contrast, the treatise *Philosophy as Rigorous Science* already conforms fully to the standpoint of the *Ideas* and has its programmatic significance in the fact that, in keeping with a brusque emphasis on the non-scientific character of all previous philosophy, it assigns to phenomenology the task of accomplishing a strong scientific foundation for philosophy.

A Phenomenology and Psychology.

I General Circumscription [*Umgrenzung*] of Phenomenology

In order to understand phenomenology in Husserl's sense, the first task must be to decisively establish its boundary vis-à-vis descriptive psychology. The difference between the two is already outwardly evident in the fact that phenomenology employs a unique terminology that deviates entirely from the conventional designations of psychology. This makes reading the *Ideas* in particular quite difficult. One might complain that the discussion of these central questions is burdened with a new scholarly language [*Schulsprache*], a language that leans to some extent terminologically on Aristotle and the Scholastics, but as far as its meaning is concerned is a new language. Thus, the effort to reach a unified ter-

---

Bewusstsein und Gegenstände, Psychologische Untersuchungen edited by Theodor Lipps Vol. I 1907 pp. 1–203. Same author, *Die "Erscheinungen,"* ibid. pp. 523 ff.

[3] [Translator's note: Elsenhans uses quotation marks but fails to provide a reference for this quote.]

[4] [Translation slightly modified]

minology is hampered at an important point. Under these circumstances, one may better understand why the author has taken issue with almost every one of his critics over misunderstandings.[5] But one would not contest the right of someone who has something new and valuable to contribute, and who finds no expressions for his concepts in the current conceptual language of science, to shape his thought in an individual manner. We must be all the more stringent in testing whether these conditions are met when we bear in mind that "in phenomenology," as Husserl explains, "all concepts or terms have to remain in flux to a certain extent, always primed to be differentiated in keeping with the progress made in the analysis of consciousness and the recognition of new phenomenological layerings within what is first viewed as an undivided unity" (*Ideen* 170/163). [227] The difficulties that are already implicit in a special terminology are thereby increased considerably.

Phenomenology's deviation from descriptive psychology at the level of external form points to the line of demarcation that separates phenomenology from descriptive psychology at the level of *content*; this brings to light at first a negative determination of the concept of phenomenology. Descriptive psychology, as empirical psychology, is an empirical science [*Erfahrungswissenschaft*], meaning a science of *facts* and *realities*, of real occurrences, which, as such, have their place within a spatiotemporal world, along with the real subjects to which they belong. But phenomenology has nothing to do with particular experiential facts [*Erfahrungstatsachen*]. Although it provides essential foundations for psychology, it is itself as little [a form of] psychology as geometry is a natural science. It does not seek to determine facts, but—and here we are arriving at a positive designation of phenomenology—knowledge of essences [*Wesenserkenntnis*]. It is not a factual science but a science of essences [*Wesenswissenschaft*]. He who completes this movement from psychological fact to pure "essence," that is to say, the "eidetic reduction," is thereby related to this world of facts in the same way that the geometer is related to the natural scientist. "The *geometer* who draws his figures on the board produces by this means factually existing lines on the factually existing board. But his experiencing of what is produced, qua experiencing, no more provides a *justification* for his geometric seeing of essences and thinking of them than his act of physically producing [the figures] does. Thus, it is the same whether he is hallucinating thereby or not and whether, instead of actually drawing, he imagines his lines and constructions in a

---

[5] Thus, against Külpe, A. Messer, J. Cohn, Cf. *Ideen* 11, 158/12, 151. In the first case cited, e.g., the claim is that the misunderstanding is so complete, "that nothing more is left of the sense of one's own determinations."

world of fantasy. Matters are completely different for someone engaged in *research of nature*. He observes and experiments, i.e., he ascertains *existence* empirically, *the experiencing is for him an act that provides justification* and that can never be substituted by a mere imagining" (*Ideen* 3f., 17/ 3f., 18)

Phenomenology is distinguished from phenomenology, secondly, in that its phenomena are *irreal*. As the geometer does not research realities but "ideal possibilities," so phenomenology is not concerned with real, but with "transcendentally reduced phenomena". [228] Thus—and here we assemble the features so far identified together into a positive determination—phenomenology is a *doctrine of the essence of transcendentally pure lived experiences*.

Even as it describes lived experiences, it simultaneously distinguishes itself, as a *descriptive* science, from the exact sciences. While for instance the exact geometrical concepts, as ideal concepts that express something that one cannot "see," have a determination independent of all givenness of things, the descriptive concepts of phenomenology necessarily inhere in a certain indeterminateness. Through this "vagueness," then, which is connected to the fact that phenomenology has its application in flowing domains, phenomenology further distinguishes itself from mathematics (*Ideen* 138f./133f.).

Phenomenology is thus even more precisely determinable as a "*descriptive* eidetics of pure lived experiences."

II Intuition of Essences

But this leads immediately to the further question: what method is this description grounded on? If the essence-contents are "captured in unmediated insight," in what does this capturing consist? Since what is at issue is the essences of the phenomena and not the phenomena as facts, one is at first inclined to look at this "capturing" as a function of thinking that is carried out through concepts, judgments, and inferences. According to Husserl as well, the results of phenomenological knowledge are to be captured in conceptual expressions and are to be given a strict logical grounding through broader scientific reflection; the cognitional content [*Erkenntnisinhalt*] as such, however, is not won through conceptual thinking, but by means of unmediated intuition, the "intuition of essences." The essence-contents designated by genus and species must not be confused with the purely logical subsumption of a lower concept under a higher one. Rather, the general essence is contained in the particular in a determinate sense that is "to be grasped in the eidetic intuition in accordance with its own kind of being" (*Ideen* 25f./26f.).[6]

[229] Thus the method of phenomenology can be summarized in the following way: "It has to place before its eyes pure occurrences of consciousness as exemplars; it has to bring them to ever more perfect clarity; within this clarity it has to make an analysis of them and apprehend their essences, it has to pursue the discernible connections among the essences, and take up what is respectively seen into faithful conceptual expressions that allow them to dictate their sense purely through what is seen or, better, what is generally discerned, and so forth" (*Ideen* 123/119).

Thus the proper source of the knowledge of essences is intuition. In "eidetic intuition" an essence is objectively grasped in the same way that an individual object is grasped in individual or experiential intuition. The essence is in fact a "new type of object" which is captured in an "originally given intuition." Husserl himself sees here a kind of rapprochement with positivism. "If positivism" he says, "means nothing less than an absolutely unprejudiced grounding of all sciences on the 'positive,' that is, on what is to be apprehended in an originary way, then *we* are the genuine positivists. In fact, we do *not* let *any* authority ... curtail the legitimacy of recognizing every sort of intuition as an equally valuable, legitimate source of knowledge" (*Ideen* 10f., 13, 38/11f., 14, 38).

If one seeks to approach the concept of eidetic intuition more closely—this concept that stands at the center of phenomenology, and which should be understood neither as a concept nor as an empirical intuition—one should obviously consider historical connections. Husserl rejects the accusation of Platonic realism as a confusion of the object [*Gegenstand*] and the real [*Realem*], or of actuality [*Wirklichkeit*] and real actuality [*realer Wirklichkeit*] (*Ideen* 40f./39f.; cf. Natorp 1912, p. 288f.). Kant's "*intuitus originarius*" is confined to an "original intuition" [*Urwesen*]. Fichte's intellectual intuition is "an act of intuiting himself while simultaneously performing the act by means of which the I originates for him" (Fichte 1994, p. 46).[7] With Schelling it is not a sensuous intuition, but on the contrary, an intuition in which the producer [230] is one and the same as that which is produced (Schelling 1800, p. 50). The connection is somewhat closer with Schopenhauer's intuitive philosophical recognition of ideas, with his notion of philosophy as a "median between art and science" and as the stuff of in-

---

6 [Translation slightly modified]
7 [Not cited in original.] The most important debate of this concept in the second *Einleitung in die Wissenschaftslehre* (Fichte 1994, p. 46), though, touches upon Husserl's work on the point of the presentation of the relation between intellectual and sensual intuition.

genious thinkers who grasp the essence of things immediately (Schopenhauer 1892, §28 f.).

Husserl's "intuition of essences" is distinguished from all of these historical precedents through the stress placed on its "descriptive" character and on its objects as "pure" or "phenomenological givens" [*Gegebenheiten*]. One probably encounters the fundamental character of this phenomenology and its historical position most directly when one takes its two basic characteristics together: that it wants to be *descriptive* and that it wants to be *non-empirical* at the same time. It has in common with the empirical sciences that it is concerned with "givens," but these are not empirical, but rather "pure" or "phenomenological givens."

III "Pure Givennesses" and the Analogy of Mathematics

Within sense perception, we can very well imagine what it means to describe a given. But it is clear that we are essentially passive in this process, a thought that finds expression in Kantian epistemology in the doctrine of the "affecting Object" [*afficierenden Gegenstand*] (Kant 1998, B 33). The "originally giving" intuition of essence or "ideation" is distinguished from perception as "originally giving experience," however, in that it is not "given" in the same sense as the individual object. Rather, it is absolutely dependent on our "phenomenological attitude." It is a surplus that, coming to a significant extent from us, is dependent for its appearance not on some "affection"—like the individual object—but rather exclusively on our attitude. It belongs to the character of the intuition of essences that an appearance, a "being-visible" [*Sichtigsein*] of individuals underlies it, be it in instances of "experiential givenness" or in mere "phantasy givenness" (*Ideen* 12/13). [231] But it utilizes this individual intuition only for exemplification, without in any way taking the individual as a reality. What sense does mere description have here? Is it really the case that the "pure essence" is there independently of us in order to be "grasped," "described?" The aforementioned expressions seem to point toward this idea, as do the processes of "suspending" or "bracketing" everything that lies in the world as it is posited by the natural attitude and encountered in experience—processes that leave behind only the curious region of being proper to phenomenology (*Ideen* 52 f., 94/51 f., 90). But does this region of being not have reality in the same way as the empirical world? It is a world of "pure givenesses," a world of absolute existences [*Seins*], and it is not we who create them. The activity of essence-researchers is limited to the "phenomenological attitude" through which this world of "pure givenesses" is opened up.

From the consideration of the activity or passivity of the knowing subject, a claim concerning a special "phenomenological knowledge" emerges. The more forcefully this claim appears, however, the more urgently the question arises: upon what, strictly speaking, can it be based? It is characteristic of Husserlian phenomenology in the widest sense that here the analogy with mathematics, particularly geometry, is decisive. Geometry appears as a form of essence-science [*Wesenswissenschaft*] in comparison to factical sciences [*Tatsachenwissenschaften*]. Like geometry, phenomenology investigates essential contents rather than actualities. "Geometry and phenomenology as sciences of pure essence [*Essenz*] make note of no determinations about real existence." This is also connected with [the fact] "that clear fictions serve them not only just as well but to a great extent as even better underpinnings than givennesses of currently actual perception and experience [*Erfahrung*]" (*Ideen* 153/147). For both, therefore, the ultimately foundational act is not experience but the "intuition of essences." It is probably no accident that in the progress from the *Logical Investigations* to the *Ideas*, [232] geometry more and more takes the place of arithmetic as the typical example of the parallelism between mathematics and phenomenology. In its intuitive character, it accords with the stronger emphasis on the *experience* of essence through "ideation" that is found in the *Ideas*. But the particular difficulties of such an intuition of "pure essence" are discovered in part precisely through this analogy with geometry. What is possible here seems to be possible in an entirely different region as well, *without this coincidence being adequately justified through a fundamental agreement of the two regions*. In geometry it seems to us indeed that the problem that was first precisely formulated by Kant has been solved—namely, how non-empirical intuitions are possible. But are we allowed to transfer this possibility to a region where mathematical intuition completely fails? And are we justified in ascribing that particular connection of "irreality" and apodictic (and "eidetic") necessity that is doubtlessly characteristic of mathematics to phenomenology, the objects of which have an entirely different character? Suppose one thinks that the problem of understanding our mathematically grounded knowledge has been solved by the combination—only belatedly worked out clearly by Kant—of a *synthetic* function with intuition. Must the phenomenologically oriented, merely *descriptive* "essence-researcher" reject every foundational analogy of this type?

Of course, Husserl himself in no way misconceives the difference between phenomenology as a descriptive science and mathematics as an exact science. Phenomenology is clearly differentiated from the formal mathematical disciplines, since it evidently belongs to the "material," "essential" or "eidetic" sciences. But it is clearly also to be distinguished from material, "eidetic" disciplines like geometry. It cannot be construed as a "geometry of lived experiences" (*Ideen* 133 f./128 f.).

The method of geometry is specifically characterized by [the fact] that "a finite number of concepts and propositions, to be gathered in any given case from the essence of the respective domain, completely and univocally determine the totality of all possible configurations of the domain in the manner of a purely analytic necessity – so that, consequently, as a matter of principle, nothing more remains open in it" (*Ideen* 135–130).[8] As a descriptive science, phenomenology does not correspond to any such "mathematically definite manifold." [233] Supposing phenomenology has to describe, e.g., an experience of the genus "phantasy of a thing" [*dingliche Phantasy*], what is "phenomenologically singular" is just "this phantasy of the thing, in the entire fullness of its concreteness, precisely as it flows by in the flow of experience, precisely in the determinateness and indeterminateness with which this phantasy brings its thing to appearances, one time from this side, another time from another side, precisely in the distinctness or fuzziness, in the wavering clarity, intermittent obscurity, and so forth that are directly proper to it" (Ideen 139–140/134).[9] In this connection, we at the same time clearly experience how the shift from empirical inner perception to phenomenological intuition of essences takes place. "Phenomenology lets *only the individuation* fall to the side *but* it elevates into eidetic consciousness the entire essential content in the fullness of its concreteness, and takes it as an ideally-identical essence that, like any essence, could be instantiated, not only *hic et nunc*, but in countless exemplars" (*Ideen* 140/134 f).[10] We learn that in subsequent advances to essences of "higher levels of specificity"—e.g., to the description of generic essences of any perception whatever, any memory whatever, any empathy whatever, any willing whatever—the intuition of essences remains dominant. The dependence of accomplishments at higher levels on those of lower levels does not occur, "as though the methodic requirement would be a systematic inductive procedure, ascending step by step up the ladder of levels of universality." To this corresponds the fact that phenomenology rules out "deductive theoretizations." It does reject indirect inferences straightaway, "yet since all of its knowledge is supposed to be descriptive, purely adapted to the immanent sphere, then inferences, all non-intuitive ways of proceeding, have merely the methodical significance of leading us to the matters that a subsequently direct discernment of essence has to bring to the level of being given."

With this remark the all-encompassing dominance of intuition in the realm of phenomenology first emerges with complete clarity. Only that which can be

---

8 [Translator's note: Elsenhans fails to provide a citation for this passage]
9 [Translator's note: Elsenhans fails to provide a citation for this passage]
10 Here the instructive demonstration at Husserl 2001b, p. 439f./135f. is especially relevant.

"brought to givenness" through eidetic intuition counts as real knowledge for phenomenology. [234] Thereby it is also shown with full evidence that the phenomenological intuition of essences is not a positive intuition, one that engenders the essence of the object in the act of observing it. Rather, it is a process that, in its degree of passivity, amounts to mere sensuous intuition. *The "pure essences" are there; it is only a matter of us "seeing" them.* What we contribute to this is only the "attitude"; certainly Husserl himself occasionally emphasizes the spontaneous character of the "originally giving consciousness of an essence," or of "ideation," in contrast to the sensuously giving, experiencing consciousness, for which spontaneity is inessential: the individual object can "appear," can be conscious in the mode of apprehension [*aufassungmäßig bewusst sein*], without a spontaneous "activity" directed toward it. This form of apprehension is better explained, though, by saying that what is created in ideation is not the *essence* but rather the consciousness of it; and the intuition of essences is to be explicitly absolved of the skeptical charge that "essence" is a fiction, as the analogy with sensuous perception rather than "imagination" indicates (*Ideen* 42 f./41 f.). Is it possible to follow this series of ideas without thinking —in spite of the author's caveat, and in spite of the fact that the phenomena of "pure phenomena" are characterized as "irreal"—of Platonic realism? We must leave it at this: they do not have the "reality" of real occurrences, which are arranged with their real being in the spatio-temporal world. But since they are neither produced as "givenesses" from us, nor able to be brought, as true judgments, under the concept of "validity," they must have at least that *measure of reality that makes them able to be discovered*, makes them able to be visibly apprehended. Their "exemplification" in empirical givenesses changes nothing in this regard, since the latter are only "examples" in which each pure givenness is seen. Such a reality of "pure essences"—even though quite diluted—may be understandable to us within the framework of certain systems of the past; but there is hardly a place for it within modern thought that would justify its deployment in this form. And yet, as we have seen, its adoption is an undeniable consequence of phenomenology. [235] The assumptions of this descriptive science lead—since its objects lie beyond experience and yet are also not produced by us—into the thick of a metaphysics[11] so daring that its content is supposed to

---

11 One can compare, for example, the following lines from (*Ideen* p. 94/ 91): "...we direct our focus (the focus that apprehends and investigates things theoretically) on *pure consciousness in its own absolute being.* What is sought is, accordingly, what remains as the "*phenomenological residue,*" what remains, despite the fact that we have "suspended" the entire world with all the things, animate beings, human beings, ourselves included. We have actually lost nothing, but

arise not out of a generally controllable thinking, but out of a likewise non-empirical intuition.

But this last point still demands a special investigation. One could always say: there is in fact a particular way to achieve knowledge of those "pure essences"; he who does not know how to follow this path will naturally also believe that he must reject the knowledge that is discovered along it. In fact, Husserl takes this position. The shift from the natural to the phenomenological attitude is not easy to complete. The new field does not lie "spread out before our view, with an abundance of separate givennesses, such that we could simply grab hold of them, and be certain of the possibility of making them the objects of a science, not to speak of being certain of the method, by which we are supposed to proceed here" (*Ideen* 120/116). In order to "bring the field of the subject matter [*Sachfeld*] – that of the transcendentally pure consciousness – into [the scope of] a focus that apprehends it" at all, it is necessary "to shift focus painstakingly from the kinds of natural givenness of which it is continuously conscious, and which are, as it were, interwoven with the newly intended kinds of givenness," whereby everything is lacking "that works to our advantage for the natural sphere of objects, namely, the familiarity through practiced intuition, the benefit of inherited ways of theorizing and discipline-specific methods," the assurance that follows from manifold applications in science and in praxis (*Ideen* 121/117). But isn't it strange that the possibility of a knowledge that is free from all errors of experience, and which, once at hand, should lead to absolutely necessary and general acceptance of compelling results, [236] was not realized earlier, and has until now borne no fruit whatsoever? Although it is elsewhere employed quite abusively, this argument probably has some evidential force in this context, where it is a matter of adding a new method to the cognitive activities of thought that have been practiced and understood in their particularity for centuries, cognitive activities that are directed toward the essences of things.

In any event, we cannot avoid inquiring into the place of this phenomenological function within the "stream of lived experience" [*Erlebnisstrom*] of the psyche itself. Indeed, the essence of phenomenology as a "pure lived experience" [*reinen Erlebnisses*] must be phenomenologically identified in turn (*Ideen* 122f./118f.). With this backward reflection upon itself, phenomenology is not completely in the same situation as psychology and logic, which likewise apply their method to themselves. For in order to identify the essence of phenomenology, the essence-researcher must first discover and learn to apply this

---

acquired the complete, absolute being that, correctly understood, contains every instance of worldly transcendence in itself, "constituting" them in itself."

method of knowledge. No matter what, therefore, the phenomenological function itself must be empirically discovered in the "flow of lived experience." At the basis of the intuition of essence there is always an individual intuition, whether from experiential- or phantasy-givennesses. Such a point of departure in individual intuition must also be available to phenomenology; indeed it is virtually an indispensable presupposition of phenomenological knowledge. In this light, however, it is not unproblematic for this entire direction of knowledge that so many researchers can discover nothing of this "intuition of essences" on their own; or moreover, that they always find the function that would be ascribed to this "intuition of essences" in the procedures of empirical descriptive psychology instead.

For there is no doubt that one of the weakest points of phenomenology lies in the unification of two claims: the first, that phenomenology grasps "givennesses," and the second, that this procedure itself is dissociated from any kind of experience. In mathematics—the analogy with which is supposed, among other things, to clarify the possibility of such a state of affairs—one cannot talk of "pure givenesses" in the same sense as one does in phenomenology, as Husserl himself admits. There it is a matter of objects, which, as "irreal possibilities", are produced at will in the manner of "pure analytic necessity." [237] Here, it is a matter of objects which are given in the first instance in experience, and which, in the context of phenomenology, are to be grasped "in the complete fullness of their concreteness," albeit not empirically. Where the particularity of a concrete given is concerned, on the other hand, it does not matter which attitude we adopt; we remain with the radical distinction that Kant characterized most keenly for all time as follows: "With regard to the latter (the 'something' that 'contains an existence and corresponds to sensation'),[12] which can never be given in a determinate manner except empirically, we can have nothing *a priori* except indeterminate concepts of the synthesis of possible sensations insofar as they belong to the unity of apperception (in a possible experience). With regard to the former (the form of intuition in space and time)[13] we can determine our concepts *a priori* in intuition, for we create the objects themselves in space and time through homogeneous synthesis, considering them merely as *quanta*" (Kant 1998, B 751). By applying the concept of givenness to something that is concretely present, but that is not discoverable in experience [*Erfahrung*], one pushes that concept into the incomprehensible. Is there really—to speak once again in Kant's language—something intermediate [*Mittleres*] between the "re-

---

12 [Translator's note: Elsenhans' interpolation.]
13 [Translator's note: Elsenhans' interpolation.]

ceptivity of impressions" through which an object is *given* to us, and the "spontaneity of concepts," through which that object is *thought* "in relation to every representation," something to which spontaneity and givenness can be attributed simultaneously?

IV The Relation of Phenomenology to Empirical Psychology, of Description to Conceptual Elaboration [*Bearbeitung*]

To this basic non-unifiability of the two concepts can now be added the difficulty that lies in the relation between "pure" and empirical givennesses and in the reciprocal relation of their conceptual determination. Husserl has dealt with phenomenology's relation to exact empirical psychology in detailed fashion, particularly in the treatise on "Philosophy as a Rigorous Science." [238] Experimental psychology carries out the description of the givennesses of experience. The immanent analysis and conceptual apprehension [*Fassung*] that accompany this description proceed by means of a pool of concepts, the scientific value of which prove decisive for all further methodological steps. A psychology that used the concepts determining its objects (e. g. the words "perception," "memory," "imagined presentation," "fantasy presentation" only in the vague, completely chaotic sense that it had somehow acquired in the "history" of consciousness would have just as little claim to exactitude as a physics that contented itself with everyday concepts of "hard," "warm," "mass," etc. In order to be able describe and determine the "psychic phenomena" with which it is concerned with conceptual precision, psychology must already have appropriated the necessary precise concepts through methodical work. This means that psychology presupposes phenomenological analysis of the conceptual contents that it applies to experience, even though these concepts are "a priori in relation to experience" (Husserl 1981, p. 178.). Allegedly, psychology has lost sight of this basic defect only by virtue of its "naturalistic attitude," as well as its eagerness to emulate the natural sciences and consider the experimental method the most important thing; however, the psychical is only "nature" in a second, completely different sense and can only be grasped according to its essence through immanent seeing.

By no means, however, does Husserl completely repudiate empirical psychology as such. Rather, he accepts its validity as a science of the "psychophysical attitude" in which the "psychic" is correlated in its entire essence with a body and with the unity of physical nature, and is "intersubjectively" determinable "as individual being" by virtue of its "indirect natural objectivity" (Husserl 1981, p. 183–184). In the *Ideas*, there is less emphasis on empirical psychology's dependence on its relation to psychology, on its psychophysical character. Lived experience as such constitutes the experientially given starting point, which is grasped at first in the "natural attitude" and is then passed over to the "phenomenological reduction." In so doing, we "transform" the "determinations" [*Feststellungen*] in "exemplary cases of essential universalities," [239] which we are then able to "make our own in the framework of an unadulterated Intuition [*Intuition*] and to study systematically" (*Ideen* 146/140). Consciousness as "the given of psychological experience" is the object of both types of psychology. In the context of "empirical science" [*erfahrungswissenschaftlicher*], it is the object of empirical psychology; in the context of the "science of essences," it is the object of "eidetic psychology" (*Ideen* 143/137). Hence, the same psychic experience can be the object of both modes of observation. "Essence-scientific" research is the foundation and indispensable precondition of the other.

But mustn't phenomenology itself also experience repercussions and substantive corrections from empirical research? Can the essence-researcher completely avoid utilizing *empirical* results that he establishes in relation to the same object through different means? Indeed: the knowledge of essences is supposed to be fully separated from the knowledge of facts; 'pure truths of essence" should not contain the least claim concerning facts (*Ideen* 13/14). Does this mean that we are dealing with a form of empirical investigation that is focused on real occurrences, and that presupposes an analysis of the essences of those occurrences, but which in its subsequent unfolding leaves those essences impossibly unaffected? Let us hone in on an example! "We transport ourselves, in a lively intuition (even if it be imagined), into any sort of implementation of an act, for instance, into an enjoyment of a sequence of theoretical thoughts [*Gedankengang*], freely and fruitfully elapsing. We carry out all reductions and see what lies in the pure essence of the phenomenological matters. What is first is, accordingly, [the attention] being turned to the elapsing thoughts... and so forth" (*Ideen* 146/140). Undoubtedly associative presentations, feelings of pleasure, and other factors that are readily accessible to experimental and empirical-descriptive research are mixed together in this process, thereby variously conditioning and modifying it in its essence (in the usual sense of the word). At the moment of "immanent intuition," should the essence researcher relinquish all the results of empirical research that are known to him with respect to these objects? And if empirical science has somehow corrected what is intuited phenomenologically, [240] should he ignore this correction? Naturally phenomenology answers this question affirmatively, since according to its fundamental thesis the intuition of essences has more credibility than any experience. But this brings us face to face once again with that *that sharp cleavage between a world of "pure essences" and a world of experiential facts, a cleavage which is supposed to establish the beginnings of all knowledge but is simultaneously the boldest of all metaphysical hypotheses.*

So it is no wonder that Husserlian phenomenology has again and again been confused with empirical descriptive psychology, despite the protests of its originator. It is not only Husserl's own earlier mode of expression that has contributed to this. It has to do, as well, with the reluctance of authors who probed Husserl's overall logical position and his terminology (which is at least in part reminiscent of scholasticism) to follow him in this step toward a conceptual realism that at least comes close to Plato's. Every real implementation of Husserl's program, moreover, shows that where determinate statements concerning lived experience are concerned, it is not possible to maintain a strict barrier against empirical science. It is of course true that empirical-inductive science by no means gains knowledge exclusively through induction as such. Aside from the basic logical presuppositions of all inductive methods (which, contrary to John Stuart Mill, cannot themselves be derived from inductive methods), the empirical description of psychic lived experiences operates necessarily with word meanings that are initially "vague" and that cannot have been achieved inductively, since, after all, such description must begin somewhere. In this context, it is always necessary to keep in mind what the process of "description" depends upon. When we describe a psychic process of perception, memory, imagination, joy, or pain, we are helping ourselves to these and other words in order to indicate what we intend [*meinen*] in a meaning [*Bedeutung*], a meaning that must already somehow be defined, even if only in a provisional and indeterminate manner. *Description is thus always already classification.* Subsequent exact investigation or more penetrating analysis may provide various corrections and may first make possible strict conceptual determination; in order to begin at all, however, [241] we must isolate particular lived experiences from the "stream" of psychic occurrences to be analyzed and described in a definite manner.

Thus one has no right to speak of a "merely descriptive psychology" in the sense of a psychology that could somehow reproduce what is merely factual and that would not already contain scientific assumptions (Dilthey 1894; cf. Elsenhans 1912, p. 48 f.; incl in this volume p. 17 f.). Every denomination that picks out a psychical process from the overall psychical nexus and thereby isolates it *is* already such an assumption. At its prescientific level (which certainly at some point must have predated the scientific level) the denomination itself stems from the inheritance of an individual body of language, which, in turn, has to be considered a sediment of multiple experiences. Subsequently, this preliminary delimitation of the concept gives way to a process of exact scientific concept determination and classification, in which modifications that originate with the investigation of the relevant objects are introduced. Science thereby accomplishes one of its most important cultural tasks, namely, forming the knowledge of reality that is laid down in language such that it is free from error and dependable. This process is thus always an *intertwining of experiences, observations, comparisons, and conceptual work.*

From the standpoint of these considerations, does it not appear impossible that phenomenology could perform its "descriptions" of "essence" completely independently of all conclusions derived from experience? Should we still claim that "everything that is purely immanent to the experience and, once reduced, is peculiar to it," is separated by an abyss from all of nature and physics, and no less from psychology (*Ideen* 184/177)?[14] Every attempt at a description seems to me to demonstrate the opposite. When for example Husserl describes the perceptual experience of a flowering apple tree, [242] and with reference to the "reduced perception," i.e. the "phenomenologically pure experience," determines "which essence it belongs to"—"the perceived as such (expressed as 'material thing'), plant, tree, flowering, etc."—this description depends for Husserl, as for the listener or reader, on his empirical understanding [*Kenntnis*] of plants, trees, and so forth. This understanding is itself modified with the progression of knowledge [*Wissen*], and also modifies the apprehension of the "pure essences" that are described on the basis of that knowledge. It is indeed impossible to understand how the phenomenological knowledge of a lived experience could be independent of the ongoing empirical investigation of its qualities. Once this is admitted, however, then phenomenology is no longer a priori; then the entire edifice of the "pure science" has fallen.

V The Individual Application of Phenomenology as Descriptive Psychology.

In fact all attempts up to the present to apply phenomenology to the area of mental life [*Seelenlebens*] confirm how little it is possible to free the essential knowledge of a lived experience of any grounding in experience. Even the *Yearbook for Philosophy and Phenomenological Research* seems to testify to this in many ways. When, for example, Alexander Pfänder begins a psychology of attitudes [*Gesinnungen*] with a "phenomenology of attitudes," and gives to the latter the task of "penetrating as far as the direct grasping of the psychic self and then

---

14 Cf. here and for the following the entire example on *Ideen* 182 f/174 f. Also at this point we are still refraining from the concept of "intention," for which, in the case of the pages under consideration here, the "description" is not essential and which cannot be dealt with without consideration of the epistemological questions to be posed later.

giving a fully accurate description of the psychic condition itself," it is already apparent on the opening pages that this description is not merely tied to "particular experiences of attitudes," but also that every phenomenological statement concerning the essence of attitudes is conditioned [*mitbedingt*] by experiential observations [*erfahrungsmässige Feststellungen*] (Pfänder 1913, p. 325f.). The essences of these appearances are not disclosed by means of a mysterious intuition of essences; rather—just as in every other inductive-empirical comparison and observation, only with greater concern for conceptual analysis—conclusions are drawn from what is in fact "available" or occurs in attitudinal impulses [*Gesinnungsregungen*]. Max Scheler, [243] in his treatise *Formalism in Ethics and Non-Formal Ethics of Values* (Scheler 1973),[15] also strongly emphasizes the uniqueness of phenomenology vis-à-vis all empirical sciences. He speaks of "phenomenological experience," thus approaching the empirical more closely than Husserl does, at least in expression; but this "phenomenological experience" is then even more sharply distinguished from all other types of experience, e.g., the experience of the "natural worldview of science." In this way, we also learn more about the relation between the "intuition of essence" (which means the same as "phenomenological experience") and the general concept, and likewise about its relation to observation and induction. The essentiality or "whatness" that it offers is "*as such* neither universal nor particular. The essence red, for example, is given in the universal concept as well as in each perceivable nuance of this color." The intuited essence also can[16] be "given to a lesser or greater degree, comparable to a more or less exact 'observation' of an object and its traits. Either this 'what' is intuited and, hence, 'self'-given (totally and without subtraction, neither by way of a 'picture' nor by way of a 'symbol'), or this 'what' is *not* intuited and, hence, not given" (Scheler 1973, p. 48).

The "intuition of essences" is unmistakably depicted here as an *absolute of knowledge*, relative to which all previous and subsequent investigation of the same "given" objects means nothing. We have not yet discussed the question of how this assumption, which would secure a fully unassailable position for any opinion of any "essence researcher" whatever, can be reconciled with the question concerning the criterion of knowledge. Here we seek only to determine in passing how close this doctrine comes to that of Jakob Friedrich Fries, which is otherwise very differently oriented. [244] For the latter as well, there is an "imme-

---

[15] Regarding the following cf. especially the demonstration regarding the a priori and the formal in general (Scheler p. 48f.).
[16] [Note that Scheler actually claims in the passage referenced by Elsenhans that what is intuitively given "*cannot* be given to a lesser or greater degree" (Scheler 1973, p. 48, emphasis added). -eds.]

diate knowledge" of the absolute sort in the realm of intuition. But here it is an immediate intuition through the senses insofar as it "exists in the mind," in which there are neither errors nor degrees of certainty (cf. Elsenhans 1906a, p. 4f.). The motives that lead to this kind of absolute starting point for all knowledge, however, are very similar in nature. Just as for Fries distinctions of certainty and of error are to be attributed simply to "mediated knowledge," to "re-observing [*wiederbeobachtenden*] reflection," so we hear in this case that only "phenomenological experience" gives "facts 'themselves' and, hence, immediately", meaning "not in a way mediated by symbols, signs, or instructions of any kind" (Scheler 1973, p. 50).[17] Phenomenological experience alone gives us the color red, rather than merely some particular determination of red, for example. Intuition—in one case sensory intuition in the other case the intuition of essence—is in both cases immune to correction through activities of relating and comparing. It is simply that "phenomenological experience" lies at the same time beyond "all experience of the natural world-view and of science" and escapes all scrutiny from the latter.

In carrying out this program, it is clearly demonstrated that also in this context, i.e. the attempt to found a "material ethics of values" on the basis of phenomenology, it is impossible to prevent the utilization of experiential observations and comparisons from influencing the results. What Scheler claims against Kantian formalism in ethics is "an *emotive apriorism* [...] and a new division of the false unity of apriorism and rationalism that hitherto has existed. An 'emotive ethics,' as distinct from a 'rational ethics,' is not at all necessarily an 'empiricism that attempts to derive moral values from observation and induction. Feeling, preferring and rejecting, loving and hating, which belongs to the totality of spirit [*des Geistes*], possess their own a priori contents independent of inductive experience and pure laws of thought. Here, as with thought, *there is* the *intuiting of essences* of acts and their correlates, their foundations, and their interconnections. In both cases there is 'evidence' and maximum exactness of phenomenological findings" (Scheler 1973, p. 65). The a priori [245] is thus here a given for intuition, its identifying mark: independence from experience is maintained; however, as a "givenness" it is discovered, and for this reason is thus still a posteriori.[18] When now the "set of facts" upon which such a "value-apriori material ethics" is supposed to be based is discussed in detail, when we hear that values are first given in feelings, that "having values is in

---

17 [Translator's note: Elsenhans erroneously cites *Ideen* 449. In actuality, this quotation is from Scheler, on p. 449 of the original text (there is, in fact, no p. 449 in *Ideen*).]
18 With this thought phenomenology also comes very close to the *Neue oder anthropologische Kritik der Vernunft* by Fries (1828; cf. especially Scheler 1973, p. 449).

no sense dependent on conations," when allusion is made to analogous facts of involuntary striving, when it is claimed that the "preference" [*Vorziehen*] as an act is to be fully separated from the manner of its realization, that the hierarchy of values is only graspable "in" acts of preferring and placing after [*nachsetzen*] (Scheler 1973, p. 34, 37, 43, 91), then we follow this argument about the "facts" [*Tatsachen*] upon which a material ethics "as opposed to arbitrary constructions" (Scheler 1973, p. 47) is supposed to base itself not without constant appreciation of the acuteness of the analysis, but with growing astonishment over the fact that the author thereby believes to find himself beyond all other empirically comparable observations and to practice an "intuition of essences," which through future empirical research directed to the same object will in no way be able to experience any revision. What we read are *penetrating descriptive analyses, which begin from facts of experience* [*Erfahrungstatsachen*] *and lay out the conceptual foundations with particular care.*

This result is also confirmed in the aesthetic treatise of Moritz Geiger and newly illuminated from a particular perspective (Geiger 1913, p. 567 f.). Here, too, we find we find a demarcation in principle from the inductive-empirical method. The inductive method recognized in itself as obvious, according to which "all types of aesthetic pleasure are to be investigated one after the other, all possibilities are to be tested, all aesthetic feelings are to be analyzed [...] in order then to finally attain a positive or a negative result through the consideration of the outcomes", is repudiated. And in response to the objection that would be readily raised—[246] that one would certainly choose the opposite way, i.e., the deductive method—Geiger points out that induction would only be one method—in fact a method that entails very specific presuppositions for its application—for attaining knowledge on the basis of facts. Consider, for example, the proposition "two straight lines intersect each other only at one point," or the proposition "orange lies between red and yellow on the color scale." As certain as it is that one attains such propositions through determination of the given and not through speculation, they are not reached through induction, i.e., through generalization (Geiger 1913, p. 571 f.). The mathematical example is out of the question for us, since its application adheres to the abovementioned analogy between phenomenology and mathematics, an analogy that is particularly liable to criticism in this context. When it comes to such mathematical statements one can speak of an "observation of the given," if at all, only in an entirely different way, in a sense clearly demarcated from all that is "the empirical." By contrast, the second example is extremely instructive for the methodological question of principle. The ordering of orange between red and yellow on the color chart is naturally dependent upon [the fact] that there really is a "color scale" which is itself most certainly discovered by way of inductive-empirical research. The lived experience of the quality "orange," which first makes possible its relation to the lived experience "red" and "yellow," is naturally as little a product of generalization as any other lived experience is. But as soon as we want to say anything at all about this lived experience and its relation to others—and this is what it is always all about in science—there is revealed in every expression—even if we just consider the word-meaning of the supposedly "pure description"—the impossibility of fully abandoning all consideration of earlier similar experiential facts and of artificially excluding everything that looks like inductive method. In our example the conclusion is only possible through the [fact] that empirical results already lie within the "color spectrum," into which a new lived experience is classified. We repeat: it must be conceded throughout that induction holds some presuppositions within itself that it itself cannot demonstrate. We emphasize further that induction [247] helps itself to substantive conceptual elements [*inhaltlich-begrifflicher Elemente*] which are relevant to the outcome, without themselves being derived from individual data as their generalization. This process is more frequent than it may appear from the above description of the inductive method and it happens mostly already in the formulation of the question, but usually also over the course of the investigation. But this does not change the fact that earlier experiences and the outcomes of earlier researches enter into every such "observation" of the given. How little it is possible to keep apart this empirical aspect from a mixing together with the phenomenological description of singular experiences is also shown by Geiger's further analyses.

In the distinction between aesthetic liking [*Gefallen*] and aesthetic pleasure [*Genuss*] he argues that "whoever approaches the facts without bias,"—part of this is that one bring to mind and compare the different facts presented to experience—would not notice the customarily held identity of liking and pleasure (Geiger 1913, p. 573 f.). The difficulty in the conceptual demarcation of aesthetic pleasure from other [types of] pleasure is first of all attributed to [the fact] that two problems are frequently confounded with one another: the value-aesthetic problem of the distinction between justified and unjustified aesthetic pleasure and the descriptive problem of the distinction between aesthetic and non-aesthetic pleasure. The handling of the latter problem as a "purely phenomenological problem" proceeds in almost all cases in the form of a comparative observation. The author recollects some singular experience of pleasure [*Genusserlebnis*] and other lived experiences that stand in contrast to it, e.g., joy; he continues by means of a comparison and observation of them, and seeks through conceptual analysis of that which is observed and that which is compared to arrive at the knowledge of their "essence" (Geiger 1913, p. 584 f.).

The a priori character of phenomenology is emphasized considerably more strongly than in Geiger's work in Reinach's philosophy of law (1983). Nonetheless it seems to me that insofar as it purports to be oriented to the "simple facts" [*schlichten Tatsachen*], [248] here, too, the desired apriority of the propositions holding for legal realities excludes the rigid distinction between the phenomenological and the empirical defended by Husserl. Already the first example derived from the "great realm of the apriori doctrine of law" leaves no question regarding this. The process of "promising" [*Versprechen*] is traced in its essential character, its unfolding, its components, [and] its particular marks [*Sondermerkmalen*]. Reinach talks about the peculiar bond which the promise creates between two people, of the duration of this bond, of the claim contained therein, of the carrier of this claim, etc. (Reinach 1983, p. 8f.). Even readers who do not lose sight of the exceptional position of the "specifically legal foundational concepts", for which the author likewise relies on the analogy with mathematical laws, cannot avoid the impression that they are prompted to call to mind the various cases in which they have themselves experienced or observed promising, in order to derive from these cases their knowledge of the essence of promising and to confirm Reinach's results on the basis of their own experience; however, the sense of the phenomenological method would suggest that just one given instance serve as "exemplification" and the intuition of essences be exercised only on this basis.

But the phenomenological method must nonetheless rely on the reader's ability to re-live the cases exhibited to him, in order to be convinced of the description's correctness. If we recall to ourselves the process going on in the reader, however, it turns out that it is fully impossible to exclude the consideration of the singular cases of the experience at issue that are available in memory; however, a process of generalization of the experience at issue has already taken place by necessity, according to the specificity of human thinking. Just as little is it possible to reject the possibility that the essence, having been once established, could receive a correction through later experiences. In short: at all of the seams of the apparently so tightly sealed structure of the phenomenological method, inductive-empirical elements leak through. It is likewise all-too-bold an undertaking to ground a science on the observation of facts and in so doing to rule out the methods of the factual sciences.

[249] So we arrive from different sides at the result that phenomenology, in the event that it does not want to take a resolute turn toward Platonic metaphysics, despite all protests cannot in fact be divorced, despite all protests, from descriptive psychology in the empirical sense (cf. Messer 1912, p. 117f.; incl. in this volume p. 215f.). This fact should not detract from phenomenology's historical right. It irrupted as a force worthy of consideration into the battle of contemporary science concerning the position of psychology, and its work arises from mo-

tives whose permanent meaning must be recognized. In his treatise on "Philosophy as a Rigorous Science" Husserl has singled out with great clarity the weaknesses of modern exact psychology and emphasized the necessity of a "systematic science of consciousness whose research is immanent to the psyche" (Husserl 1981, p. 174). He rightly disputes the "exactness" of a psychology that, without preceding analyses, works only with rough class concepts such as perception, imaginative intuition [*Phantasieanschauung*], predication, calculation and miscalculation, measure, recognition, anticipation, retention, forgetting, etc., without providing a scientific fixation, a methodological treatment of their object-determining concepts (Husserl 1981, p. 174). He has thereby promoted the effort, growing ever more clearly out of the psychology of the time, to secure (without diminishing the recognition of successful experimental work) the right of an autonomous analysis of psychic phenomena and to set a dam against the imminent transformation of the complete science of psychology into a specialized region of natural science: "the absurdity of naturalizing something whose essence excludes the kind of being that nature has" (Husserl 1981, p. 180). It is thus no wonder that so many psychologists, who recognize certain inadequacies in the ruling enterprise and hold a self-standing psychological analysis to be indispensable alongside experimental methods (especially the school of Lipps, whose lifework lies entirely in this direction) draw nearer to phenomenology or expressly affiliate themselves with it as scholarly representatives. [250] It is only regrettable that the battle against the arch-enemy, i.e. "psychologism," and the conviction that one can only free oneself from its consequences by a complete dissociation from everything empirical, has pushed the leader of this movement in a direction which, by placing itself beyond all experience, sets out to cognize pure givens thorough an 'intuition of essences' that escapes both the control of the experiential sciences and that of conceptual thinking.

Also those who do not identify the empirical and the natural scientific elaboration of psychology will not merely grant their appreciation for the great intellectual work that went into the principled foundation of this line of research; they will also see in phenomenology, as it is exemplified in some already available works, a valuable confederate in the fight for a self-standing position for psychology in the whole of contemporary science.

B Phenomenology and the Theory of Knowledge

I The Ultimate Source of Legitimacy of all Knowledge.

A fundamental clarification of the position of phenomenology vis-à-vis psychology leads with necessity to epistemological questions. Certainly, phenomenology is not itself a theory of knowledge; it expressly ignores "the substantial and multifaceted problems of the possibility of the diverse kinds of knowledge and correlations of knowledge" (*Ideen* 48/47). However, both the grounding of the central position of phenomenology within the realm of science in general and especially the epistemological significance [*Bedeutung*] of the principle of intuition harbor within themselves epistemological problems. According to Husserl, "*[i]mmediately 'seeing' – not merely sensory, empirical seeing* but *seeing in general, i.e., any kind of consciousness that affords* [something] *in an originary fashion –* is the ultimate source of legitimacy of all rational claims." "It has this legitimizing function only because and insofar as it affords [something] in an originary way" (*Ideen* 36 f./36 f.). It is the *principle of all principles: that every originally given* [251] *intuition* is *a source of legitimacy of knowledge,* that "*whatever presents itself to us in 'intuition' in an originary way* (so to speak, in its actuality in person) *is to be taken simply as what it affords itself as, but only within the limitations in which it affords itself there*" (*Ideen* 43 f/ 43 f.). Every statement that does nothing further than deliver such givenesses to the appropriate expression, is therefore really "an *absolute beginning,* called upon to lay the ground in the genuine sense, a *principium*" (*Ideen* 43/51). Naturally one can go further from this beginning, that which is seen can be [further] processed; concepts, judgments, conclusions can be established upon it; but these later steps, all these "non-intuitive methodologies" [*unanschaulichen Verfahrungsweisen*] have, as we heard earlier, only "the methodological significance" [*methodische Bedeutung*] "of leading us toward the things that an ex post facto intuition of essences has brought to givenness" (*Ideen* 140/135). Intuition in the special sense of phenomenology therefore remains here also the ultimate source of legitimacy of knowledge. With this characteristic intuitive knowledge of essences phenomenology is therefore "the essential eidetic foundation of psychology and the humanistic sciences" (*Ideen* 34/34; cf. here and the following: 11f., 121, 179, 282f./12f., 117, 180, 270f.). It encompasses "in the extent of its eidetic generality" all knowledge and science, namely "in regard to everything that is *immediately discernible* in them" (*Ideen* 118/113).[19] As applied phenomenology it accomplishes "for each intrinsically sui generis science the ultimately evaluating [*letztauswertende*] critique, and, along with the latter, in particular the ultimate determination of the sense of "being" of its objects and the intrinsic clarification of its methodology." It is thus understandable, that phenomenology "is the secret longing of all modern philosophy" (*Ideen* 118/113–14). Its traces can be found in Descartes, in Locke and Hume, and in Kant.

With this, the all-encompassing meaning of phenomenology, as it is conceived by its originator, is first brought into its proper light. Phenomenology first delivers the authentic foundation for philosophy and through it for science in general. The principle that rules in it, that of "originally given intuition," establishes a set of certain and originary cognitions, which, independently of fallible logical process or subjective hypotheses, is able to constitute the starting point and at the same time the criterion for all [252] further cognitions [*Erkenntnisse*]. The fact that such originary cognitions can have these functions, however, is based essentially upon two fundamental characteristics [*Grundmerkmalen*] that are peculiar to them: their presuppositionlessness and their unmediated evidence. The two are most intimately connected. That which is to be an absolute beginning, may not be dependent something else, neither for its content nor for its validation.

II Evidence

To begin with let us take a look at "evidence." For the determination of this concept the opposition between thing and lived experience, between "transcendental" and "immanent" perception, is decisive. Every immanent perception should necessarily warrant the existence of its object. "If the reflecting apprehension is directed at my experience, then I have apprehended an absolute self, the existence of which is intrinsically undeniable. In other words, discerning its non-existence is intrinsically impossible [...] The intrinsic possibility of obtaining this evidence is inherent to every stream of experience and every ego as such. Each ego carries within itself the warrant of its absolute existence as an intrinsic possibility" (*Ideen* 85/82). Even if an ego only had phantasies [*Phantasien*], i.e., fictitious intuitions in its stream of experience, the consciousness of these fictitious intuitions would not itself be fictitious; rather it belongs here to its essence,

---

[19] [Translator's note: The quote continues (uncited by Elsenhans) "...or at least would be if they were instances of genuine knowledge."]

as to that of every lived experience, "the possibility of reflection that perceives it and apprehends the absolute existence of it" (*Ideen* 85/82). A more exact determination of the concept of evidence, however, results from the distinction between the "assertoric" seeing of an individual, e.g., the "attentive perceiving" [*Gewahren*] of a thing or an individual state of affairs, and the "apodictic" seeing, the act of insight of an essence or essential relationship [*Wesenesverhalt*], which furthermore, namely in the application of an essential insight to something assertorically seen, can also appear in a modification conditioned by their admixture. Evidence in general can be attributed to both, but only the second has "apodictic evidence" (*Ideen* 85/82). It is strongly emphasized that in the case of evidence it is not just a matter of "a content somehow attached to the act, something added to it, of whatever kind," [253] but rather of "a distinctive mode of positing." Evidence is "not some kind of mark of consciousness that is attached to a judgment [...] like a mystical voice calling us from a better world: Here is the truth!" Otherwise one would have to entertain the worry "that no theory of evidence as a marker of consciousness or a feeling can overturn. Such are doubts about whether or not a deceitful spirit (the Cartesian fiction) or a fatal alteration of the factual course of the world would have been able to bring it about that exactly every false judgment would be outfitted with this marker, this feeling of the necessity of the thought, of the transcendent ought, and the like" (*Ideen* 300/287).

If we begin immediately with this last point, we see ourselves challenged to pose the counter-question: Is then the theory of evidence proposed here, is any such theory in general in the position to overcome skeptical objections of this sort, as they find their most extreme expression in the Cartesian fiction of the deceiving demon? Is then the "eidetic researcher" in a better predicament when another "eidetic researcher" looking at the exemplification of a real or imagined experience [*Erlebnis*] determines the essence of this experience differently from himself? How will he demonstrate the opposite to him who takes the alleged reliability of the "intuition of essence" for a self-delusion? The phenomenologist demands that one attempt to attain the "phenomenological attitude," he emphasizes the difficulties and prejudices that the empiricist [*Empirist*], in particular, has to overcome, in order to grasp the "pure givens" and expects that, so long as he in the right attitude [*ist richtig eingestellt*], the same unmediated evidence of the "intuition of essence" will be accorded to him. The empirical researcher finds himself in precisely the same situation when he presupposes that another observer will be lead to the same correct judgment through the same consciousness of evidence, based on a perception and observation of the same experience. But the empiricist does not thereby require of his opponent a hitherto unknown act of "seeing" or "intuition," but rather the same method of connecting intuition and thinking that has long been enshrined in the practice of science. Rightly understood, the claim of a consciousness of evidence that accompanies valid judgment does not mean that the validity of the judgment must be inferred from an inner perception of the evidence or even derived inductively from the facts of evidence. [254] Rather, speaking of consciousness of evidence,[20] we merely determine on the basis of psychological analysis that psychical component on which the carrying out of correct judgments is based, exactly as Husserl phenomenologically recognizes the "intuition of essence" as the path to attain correct judgments concerning lived experiences. The psychological ascertainment of the available feeling of evidence in a given case is naturally not the reason to evaluate a judgment as correct. It is rather the lived experience of this evidence as such, which as a rule is not presented at all clearly in consciousness to the judging subject. In a dispute, consciousness of evidence stands against consciousness of evidence in exactly the same way that intuition of essence" stands against "intuition of essence."

III Reflection and Self-Observation and the Overcoming of Doubt Concerning Their Outcomes

But no! We can neither leave it at this mere juxtaposition of for and against, since a decision between true and false must be possible, nor at the apparently equal rights of the moments that ground the correctness of the judgment, since a

---

[20] As to the quality to be accorded to this consciousness of evidence, whether at its core it is a feeling or something else, is not the issue here. Cf. on the epistemological side of the question my work on *Fries und Kant* II, (1906b, p. 96f.). On the psychological side of the question see my *Lehrbuch der Psychologie* (1912, p. 289f.; incl. in this volume p. 31f.). Husserl's remarks (Ideen p. 39f./39f.) that the abovementioned presentations from my *Lehrbuch* are "psychological fictions without the least basis in the phenomena" I have read with some astonishment. Should the various feelings mentioned here—the feeling of intellectual satisfaction that Husserl himself refers to as the "enjoyment of a sequence of theoretical thoughts, freely and fruitfully elapsing" (Ideen 146/140.), the much-discussed "feeling of acquaintance" [Bekanntheitsgefuehl], and the "feelings of evidence [Evidenzgefuehl] defended by Sigwart (the belief in the right of this feeling is, according to Sigwart, "the last anchoring point [*Ankergrund*] of all certainty in general")—be mere appearances, the occurrence of which (leaving aside the debate over the quality of feelings, which does not come into play here) is confirmed by various scientific observers, [should such appearances] really not have the "least foundation" in the "phenomena?" It seems to me that here the oft-misused phrase: "He who lives in a glass house should not throw stones" is truly difficult to suppress. Whoever asks us to perceive "pure essences," pure "givens" that present us with an "absolute being" and are neither concepts nor intuitive contents in any received sense, must, I believe, be more cautious with the accusation of fiction.

closer inspection of [255] the supposed "apodictic evidence" of the "intuition of essences" leads us with necessity beyond it. Naturally the mere 'having' of a lived experience does not suffice; it must be viewed with regard to its essence. But even this seeing [*Erschauen*] does not suffice, when somebody wants to convey this knowledge to others, and even when somebody wants to possess it for himself as a clear and complete knowledge. One must grasp it in concepts and name these concepts with words. The essence that has been seen must thereby pass through reflection in the first place. Husserl himself has something to say the difficulties that lie in this process. He brings the difficulty into connection with the difficulties of self-observation, which lie in the identity of the observer and the experiencer. Indeed, phenomenology does not have to make any claim regarding the existence of lived experiences, nor any claim with respect to "experiences" or "observations", in the natural sense in which a factual science must base itself on such things; however, it nonetheless makes "essential determinations regarding unreflected experiences, as an intrinsic condition of their possibility" (*Ideen* 153/148). This it owes, however, to reflection, more specifically the "reflected intuition of essences" [*reflektierten Wesensintuition*]. Here the skeptical objections with regard to self-observation also come into consideration for phenomenology, insofar as these objections "can be extended ... from the immanently undergone reflection to every reflection in general" (*Ideen* 151 f./148 f.). Husserl is of the view, however, that like every genuine skepticism, this skepticism is intrinsically absurd in that it "implicitly presupposes, in its argumentation, as conditions of the possibility of its validity, i.e., just what, in its theses, it denies [...] So, too, anyone who simply says: 'I doubt the epistemic meaning of reflection,' maintains something absurd, since he reflects in making assertions about his doubts, and since setting forth this assertion as valid presupposes that the reflection actually and doubtlessly (namely, for the cases in question) *has* the doubted epistemic value, that it does *not* alter the objective relation, that the unreflected experience does *not* forfeit its essence in the transition into reflection" (*Ideen* 155/149). Since further in their arguments skeptics constantly refer to reflection as a fact and similarly to unreflected experiences [256] as facts, they would in so doing presuppose a knowledge [*Wissen*] of unreflected lived experiences, including unreflected reflections, while at the same time they question the possibility of such knowledge. Not the least ground of justification would then remain for the certainty that there is and could be in general an unreflected lived experience and a reflection. Here as everywhere skepticism loses its power "if we turn from verbal argumentations to the intuition of essences, to the intuition that affords things in an originary way, and to its legitimacy, a legitimacy that is primordially its own" (*Ideen* 156./150).

This sharply articulated stance against skepticism, in whose overcoming lies one of the strongest motifs of phenomenology, as well as the attempt to thereby effectively dissolve the problem of self-observation, is, however, as will now be shown, dependent throughout upon the already-discussed question concerning the relationship of lived experience to statements about lived experience. The analysis of self-observation already leads with necessity to this question.

Observation is not identical with perception and just as little is self-observation identical with inner perception. The zoologist who observes an animal does not merely perceive it like a random person on a nature walk, but rather he directs his attention to the object that interests him. This is the point that especially interests us: the sensory experience is immediately and inextricably brought into connection with all the conceptual presentations [*Vorstellungen*] of similar objects which the observer already possesses and which now "make themselves available" [*bereit stellen*] in order to make possible the scientific grasp of the object, in this case, particularly, its classification. The behavior of the psychological observer is not fundamentally distinct from the situation just described, insofar as he, too, has no choice but, at the moment of observation, to bring to bear the previously acquired concepts pertaining to the object (cf. Elsenhans 1912, p. 36f.; also Elsenhans 1897). But it is precisely in regard to this point that the phenomenological grasp of the essence of lived experiences should distinguish itself in two separate directions. First, it should be a pure seeing characterized by the absence of logical mediation, [257] which is a guarantee of its infallibility. Second, the intuition of essences, which can also help itself to any imagined experiences [*Phantasieerlebnisse*] whatsoever for exemplification, demarcates itself most sharply over against every determination of facts. But with what right, then, is any lived experience in general denominated with a specific name, if the "eidetic researcher" does not already possess concepts of lived experiences, which make it possible for him to place a lived experience directly under this and no other concept and to designate it accordingly? Thus, the "having" of the lived experience as such really means nothing as yet; any value for knowledge first arises in the moment in which the lived experience can be named and thereby is elevated out of the sphere of the mere "having", which in the case of many experiences is shared by humans and animals, into the sphere of knowing.

These considerations also pertain necessarily to the whole argument, through which Husserl strives to overcome skepticism. When he sees the absurdity of a skepticism which doubts the possibility of stating anything at all concerning the content of an unreflected lived experience and the achievement of reflection in the fact that the argumentations of the skeptic constantly refer to reflection and unreflected experiences as facts, and thereby presuppose as possible the knowledge of reflection and unreflected experiences that they call into question, the weakness of such a skepticism has been undoubtedly exposed. But thereby it does not yet follow that this knowledge can only be grounded as "unmediated knowledge" "though reflectively affording intuition" in the Husserlian sense. In fact this view points with necessity beyond itself. It is incontestable that many lived experiences, e. g., joy or anger, are modified under the influence of the reflections directed toward them; however, we must assume, if we do not wish to fall into that untenable skepticism, that it is nonetheless possible to determine their presence and to cognize their essence. This assumption fundamentally implies the presupposition that "the unreflected experience does *not* forfeit its essence in the transition into reflection" (*Ideen* 155/149). But this presupposition [258] refers to an indivisible moment of time; and even for such a moment itself it could never be determined whether the lived experience is joy, anger, reflection, or something else, if the subject of reflection did not possess a criterion stemming from earlier experiences and the concepts of these experiences to establish what joy, anger, and reflection are. Thus, we see that the intuition of essences as supposedly unmediated and absolute knowledge leads always over into thinking and can never be separated from thinking if it aspires to count as knowledge at all. In all cases, if we want to investigate 'givens', and even if we pursue the "essence" of such "givens", we stand on the ground of empirical science, which Kant proved to us is the inseparable conjunction of intuition and thinking.

This demand for a criterion is strengthened even more, however, when we recall that there is no such thing as a function of consciousness that is limited to an indivisible moment in time. Even reflection, which coincides with self-observation as far as scientific knowledge of the psychical is concerned, takes a certain amount of time in order to accomplish its effect; if this is the case, then there always remains the possibility that the quality of that which is observed may have already changed between the moment in which the reflective activity is initiated and the moment in which it manifests its full effect. Here the only help comes from memory and the comparison of the remembered moments under the guidance of an empirical concept of the lived experiences at issue. Let us assume that the quality of an experience was "a" and the complete availability of the same were designated with "aaa." Then the change arising under the influence of the reflection could be symbolically displayed in the series: "aaa, aab, abc, bcd, cde" etc. After it is past, every momentary state can be reproduced in memory and in this respect it does not undergo the modifying influence of reflection. The remembered moment can be compared with other remembered moments and with the experienced moment. It is then possible to establish on the basis of the concept that provides the denomination, e. g., A, that the series from "bcd" on no longer belongs to the lived experience under scrutiny. Thus, insofar as reflection in general is meant to be knowledge, it is never merely "affording intuition," but rather [259] always already application of concepts, an intertwining [*Ineinander*] of intuition and thinking.

It is not difficult to draw the consequences of this point for the concept of evidence. One may apply the word "evidence" also to the particular intuitions, or one may, like Husserl, call evidence the "insight into an essence or essential relationship [*Wesenesverhalt*]". In either case the concept of evidence first achieves cognitive value through [the fact] that it finds application in a judgment formulated as a statement, whether this judgment is grounded in intuition or in other judgments. The "intuitive [*anschauliche*] evidence," in every case in which it is supposed to really convey knowledge, is thus always at the same time "conceptual evidence."[21] It won't do to take some intuited content of knowledge, which refers to some given, and separate it fully from the previously acquired knowledge already available in concepts and judgments. We may perhaps at some time, live in a momentary present [*Gegenwartsaugenblick*] in such a way, that past and future sink away and the lived experience in which we are engrossed appears completely isolated within the complete "stream of experience" [*Erlebnisstroms*]. But for cognitive purposes this isolation, even if it were possible in a developed consciousness, would be worthless insofar as the knowledge of such an experience only becomes knowledge to begin with when the experienced content is set in relation to already available concepts through judgment. For the mystic and the ecstatic, his own ego-consciousness, and thereby also every tie to the further nexus of his thinking, is dissolved in the dedication to the all-one; however, as soon as he speaks of that which fills his whole being, in order to communicate his cognitions to others, he make use of certain concepts, which bring what is said into relation to his other knowledge [*Wissen*] and—despite the fundamental denial of all human diminishment, as it is most sharply and boldly represented in Plotinus' *Enneads*—makes it in some way dependent upon human-conceptual presentations [*Vorstellungen*].

IV The Question of the Criterion and its Relation to Evidence

In order to delve deeper into this problem of evidence it is necessary to bring the relationship between the concepts of evidence and criterion [260] closer into view. We speak of evidence where the truth of a judgment, regardless of whether

---

21 This distinction is especially strong in Wundt's *Psychologismus und Logicismus*, *Kliene Schriften I*, (Wundt 1910, p. 627 f.).

the judgment is derived from intuition or independently of it, is immediately clear [*unmittelbar einleuchtet*]. Naturally, evidence is not truth itself, nor does it coincide with the content of the true judgment. It is rather the *psychological expression for the truth-character of the truth* [*Wahrheitscharakter der Wahrheit*]. The conceptual determination [*Begriffsbestimmung*] of evidence that Husserl provides in the *Logical Investigations* is not so far from this conception as it may seem upon first glance. There the claim is: "*truth is an Idea, whose particular case is an actual experience in the inwardly evident judgment.*" And a proper definition of evidence is given in the proposition: "*the experience of the agreement* between meaning and what is itself present, meant, between the actual *sense of an assertion* and the self-given *state of affairs*, is inward evidence: the *Idea* of this agreement is truth" (Husserl 2001b, p. 121; cf. Elsenhans 1906b, 96 f.). If we set aside the Platonic concept of truth that is here implied and the thesis that the evidence of the judgment can be rooted exclusively in "original givenness," in the unmediated "intuition of essences"—a thesis which we believed we had to reject considering that the formulation of a judgment that alone raises the content of that judgment to the level of evidence necessarily extends the claim to evidence also to the conceptual relations that are thereby expressed and that are dependent upon earlier experience—then it agrees therein with our conception that the truth-character [*Wahrheitscharakter*] of the truth is lived through in a particular lived experience. For Husserl, too, the evidence is not the living-through [*Erleben*] of the content of truth as such, but rather a process in which the very "being truth" [*Wahrheitsein*] of this content is lived through. Which quality one ascribes to this lived experience, whether it is considered as a feeling or as something different, is not essential here. By contrast, the pressing and most radical question here is naturally the following: in what sense is this evidence to be considered as a criterion? If we start with the original meaning of κριτήριον, which signifies "a means to decide," a "decisive marking [*Kennzeichnen*]," we then arrive first at the notion that the criterion is a means to decide between truth [261] and untruth. This is the case first of all for the judging subject himself. We can designate this subjective side of the criterion the "subjective criterion" for short. This "subjective criterion" coincides with evidence; however, as we already mentioned, its effectiveness does not consist in [the fact that] the judging subject detects the experience of evidence within itself and draws the conclusion that the judgment that accompanies this experience is true; rather, for the judging subject the consciousness of evidence [*Evidenzbewusstsein*] functions as a factual motive to carry out the judgment. That is also why as lived experience of one subject, the experience of evidence has no meaning for the agreement of other subjects as regards the same judgment. If other subjects agree, they obviously do not do so because, from the somehow surmised or detected evidential consciousness of others, they draw the conclusion that their judgments are true, but rather because, on the basis of the lawfully— not "accidentally," as Husserl wants—occurring consciousness of evidence, which we admittedly believe is best described psychologically as a feeling, they can do absolutely nothing else than to grant their agreement. Therefore it makes no sense to appeal to this feeling of evidence before others, for either it is there or it is not there. We can *only prompt* other judgers [*Urteilende*] whom we would like to persuade—and that is obviously what matters—*to carry out acts of intuition and acts of thought by which this feeling of evidence arises*. The correctness of the execution of such acts is the "objective criterion" of truth, the only one to which we can appeal when what is at stake is the common quest for truth in the debate with others. Also when the conditions of human knowledge are themselves made into the object of research, as is the case, e. g., in Kant's *Critique of Pure Reason*, things are not essentially different. Beginning from that intertwining of intuition and thinking that we call "experience" [*Erfahrung*], the conditions of possibility of this experience must be derived in a correctly executed regress, and the objective criterion appears here as the principle of the "possibility of experience"; however, since this kind of inquiry, insofar as it itself is cognition [*Erkenntnis*], already presupposes the possibility of cognizing [*Erkennens*], it cannot itself first prove this possibility, but rather it must rely upon [the fact] that the ultimate subjective criterion, which constitutes the background of all [262] recognition of truths, does its part. But here, too, the objective criterion is indispensable here, since the possibility of finding a common ground for the decision between truth and untruth rests exclusively on it.

But right here is the point where the principle of the intuition of essences scarcely allows a satisfactory solution to appear as possible. The communal search for the truth depends upon the possibility of persuading others of the correctness of one's own results. This however once again presupposes the possibility of bringing the other to [the view] that he is subject to certain criteria of truth commonly valid for both parties. Since an external necessitation is not possible, it can only be a matter of an inner psychical necessitation, which as such is at first of the subjective sort, but which is tied to objective components that can be re-lived by any thinker.

For phenomenology *there are basically no such objective criteria at all* (cf. Hönigswald 1913, p. 30). It demands of one who wants to know the essence of the objects under scrutiny [that he adopt] the "phenomenological attitude," and whoever adopts this phenomenological attitude, "grasps" or "sees" without further ado the essence of those objects, i. e., lived experiences. He who believes that he is not able to attain such an intuition of essences, is instructed about the difficulty of the procedure, the necessity of practice and the presupposition of a complete dissociation from all the prejudices of the common empirical method. Such a cognitive method, however, places itself beyond all other criteria of knowledge. Every objection derived from facts known through experience that one may raise against a result of such eidetic research is countered with the reply that it does not stem from the right method. For the moment one conceded the *possibility of a correction of eidetic research through empirical research*, the special right and the foundational meaning of eidetic research would be taken away from it. Such a position seems unassailable but it is at the same time—at least from the standpoint of epistemology—helpless against every attack. For since it claims a special way of knowledge, which cannot be controlled through the hitherto tested methods and is only viable through a special "attitude-taking," [263] it also enables the opponent, on his part, to establish for himself a special procedure to assess the truth, which evades the hitherto tested oversight of science. But even those researchers who assent to such an esoteric doctrine are hardly able to critically confront one another. At the very least the critical adjustment [*Ausgleich*] of inquiries developed on common ground would only refer to something secondary. Since the intuition of essences as such is absolute, it is not subject to any correction through inductive derivation from givens. Contention stands against contention; one views this, the other views that as the essence of a lived experience.

All these difficulties fall away if we remove the scholastic-apriori clothing of Husserl's phenomenology and see in it the energetic and sharply conducted attempt to secure for a modern descriptive psychology reliable conceptual foundations and a procedure free from admixture with natural-scientific methods (cf. Maier 1914, p. 360f.). The work of phenomenology so far and its historical right allows it, as we have just seen, to be considered from this standpoint without difficulty. But there is still a final and fundamentally more important standpoint that speaks against phenomenology's full identification with psychology, one that requires separate treatment.

V The Presuppositionlessness of Phenomenology in its Relation to the Theory of Knowledge.

According to Husserl psychology is an empirical science, which as such already presupposes a philosophical working-out of its domain of experience, namely a "systematic science of consciousness that explores the psychic in respect of what is immanent in it" (Husserl 1981, p. 174). This very science is phenomenology. It is the presuppositionless foundation of all philosophy in general. If one requires from a scientific philosophy an epistemological justification, and on the other hand, from an epistemological investigation which raises earnest claims to scientificity, that it satisfies the principle of presuppositionlessness [264], according to Husserl this principle can mean nothing more than "the strict exclusion of all statements not permitting of a comprehensive phenomenological realization" (Husserl 2001, p. 263). Phenomenology is capable of meeting this requirement since it does not have to put forward some assumptions that require demonstration and merely describes without prejudice "pure givens." It thereby delivers absolute beginnings and authentic descriptive foundations of all knowledge and through this it makes it possible to lead philosophy out of the stage of the non-scientific over to that of "rigorous science" (Husserl 1981, 166 f.).

With this remark we touch on what is perhaps the strongest theoretical motif of phenomenology as a whole. Husserl is aware how near he comes to Descartes' attempt to overcome universal doubt through reflection upon an unmediated certainty, a given in consciousness. Indeed it seems at first to be only a modern version of that very fundamental thought of Cartesianism, when the possibility that an ego [*Ich*] in its stream of experience has "only imaginations," "only fictionalizing intuitions" [*fingierende Anschauungen*] is countered with the statement: "What I have in mind may be a mere figment, but the [act itself of] having it in mind, the fictionalizing consciousness, is not itself fictionalized, and the possibility of reflection that perceives it and apprehends the absolute existence of it belongs essentially to it, as it does to any experience" (*Ideen* 85/82). But two things characterize the essential difference. The universal "suspension" or "bracketing" of the whole world of experience [*Erfahrungswelt*], which leaves only the world of "pure consciousness," the "world as *Eidos*", replaces Cartesian doubt. Secondly, the criterion of knowledge progressing from this point of departure is not found rationalistically in the clearness and distinctness of thinking, but rather intuitionistically, in the "seeing of essences." The second of these distinctive traits has already occupied us in detail, but the first is thoroughly decisive for the type of presuppositionlessness claimed by phenomenology in its relation to the theory of knowledge.

This important point receives new light, when we contrast the standpoint of phenomenology to another modern philosophical [265] attempt to develop the foundations of philosophy from a given standpoint in the most presuppositionless way possible. According to the empirio-criticism founded by R. Avenarius, the "natural concept of the world" [*naturliche Welbegriff*] is—similarly to Husserl's "natural attitude"—the natural starting point of all philosophizing. The world-concepts of philosophy are only variants [*Variationserscheinungen*] of the natural concept of the world. Considered formally, this natural concept of the world is split at once into two logical components of different value: a "manifold of factually present elements" and a "hypothesis." The first, the "empirio-critical material" [*empiriokritische Befund*] further divides into two major parts, the "I" and the "environment," whose reciprocal relation is unresolvable and thus is called "empirio-critical principal coordination." The second component of the natural world-concept consists in [the fact] "that I attribute a more-than-mechanical meaning to the movements of fellow human beings, which, as far as they are considered exclusively as factually present materials from my spatial standpoint, only have a mechanical meaning" (cf. Avenarius 1891, p. 144 f.; 1894, p. 174, 153); however, since the ruling psychology locates this "a-mechanical" element that has to be assumed inside us as a set of "sensations" that have their place in the brain, this "introjection" falsifies the entire natural world-concept, and through this falsification the distinction between an external and an internal world—a distinction which is foreign to the natural world-concept—arises in the first place. The "critique of pure experience" then, is supposed to suspend this introjection, in order to re-establish the unvaried natural world-concept (Avenarius 1888). The path along which this occurs, however, shows that that which is "found as factually present" is already considered in the light of a determinate science (Avenarius 1888). The human individual appears as "highly developed organism" with a "plurality of sub-systems," the "environment–components" as conditions of alteration for the organism, the central nervous sub-system C, correlated with the brain, fully takes the place of that which for natural knowledge is something like an "I" or as self-consciousness, and the [266] whole system stands throughout under the criterion of preservation the entire organism (Avenarius 1888, p. 32 f.).[22]

Thus, what emerges here is not a variant of the natural world-concept, but rather an *abolishment of it in favor of a scientific world-concept of a different type*, namely the biological, which has already determined the manner of the description of that which is factually found as given.

VI The Concept of Intention and the Picture Theory

Now it seems to me that Husserl's phenomenology contains formally the same admixture of a natural and a scientific concept of the world, even though it is oriented in a completely different way as far as the material. "I and environment," the "empirio-critical principal coordination" correspond to Husserl's "in-

---

[22] The question of how far already psychological presuppositions are co-contained [*mitenthalten*] in that which has been discovered, which it seems to me should be answered in the affirmative (cf. Elsenhans 1906b, p. 15 f.), should here be abandoned.

tentionality." This concept follows Franz Brentano's demarcation of "psychic phenomena," that describes every psychical phenomenon as "characterized by what the Scholastics of the Middle Ages called the intentional (or mental) inexistence of an object, and what we might call, though not wholly unambiguously, reference to a content, direction towards an object (which is not to be understood here as meaning a thing), or immanent objectivity" (Brentano 1995, pp. 88–89). For Husserl, too, consciousness is a synthetic designation for "any kind of 'psychic act' or 'intentional lived experience'"; however, this has nothing to do with a real process or a real relation, as Brentano's manner of expression may suggest, between the consciousness or the I and the object "of consciousness". It is also not a matter of a relation between two things equally found as real occurrences in consciousness: "act and intentional object." In the intentional lived experience an object is "meant" [gemeint], it is "targeted" "in the manner of the presentation [Vorstellung] or at the same time the judgment, and so on" and therein lies nothing other than [the fact] "that even certain experiences are present, which have a character of intention and specifically the objectivating [vorstellenden] [267], judging, desiring intention, and so on" (Husserl 2001b, p. 95 f.; translation modified) Such a lived experience can naturally be present with its characteristic intention in consciousness, without the object itself having to exist and perhaps without it even being able to exist at all. "I think of Jupiter as I think of Bismarck, of the tower of Babel as I think of Cologne Cathedral, of a regular thousand-sided polygon as of a regular thousand-faced solid" (Husserl 2001b, 99; cf. Ideen 64/62). Thereby emerges a fundamental and essential distinction between being-as-lived-experience and being-as-thing. It belongs to the essence of the lived experience that it is perceptible in immanent perception, to the essence of a spatial thing, however, that it is not (cf. Ideen 76f./74f.). We therefore designate the thing as "transcendent per se" [schlechthin transzendent]. To this fundamental distinction in the mode of being, the most paramount of all, between consciousness and reality, between immanence and transcendence, belongs however also a "an intrinsic difference in the kind of givenness" (Ideen 77/74). We perceive a thing insofar as it "is given in profiles" [sich abschattet] according to its various determinations. A lived experience, an experience of feeling, for example, does not present itself in profiles. "If I look at it, I have something absolute, it has no sides that could display themselves one time one way, another time another way" (Ideen 81/78).

The epistemological meaning of intentionality becomes even clearer on its negative side in the rejection of any kind of "picture" or "sign-theory." When one says that the thing itself is "outside" and that in consciousness there is a representative picture, one completely overlooks the most important point, namely, "that in a representation by images the *represented* object (the original) is *meant*." The picture theory does not explain what "enables us to go beyond the image which alone is present in consciousness, and to refer to the latter *as* an image to a certain extra conscious object" (Husserl 2001b, p. 125). Even the reciprocal similarity that is attributed to picture and thing does not make the one into the picture of the other. Consciousness itself must first lend to the object appearing to it perceptually the "validity" or "meaning" [*Bedeutung*] of a picture. The apprehension [268] of something as a picture thus itself already presupposes an object intentionally given to consciousness, and would obviously lead to an infinite regress, since that object itself should in turn be constituted through a picture. The sign theory also succumbs to the same objection. For it, too, presupposes a "founded act of consciousness" whereby the sign is connected to the object. It is in general a grave error to "draw a real [*reell*] distinction between 'merely immanent' or 'intentional' objects, on the one hand, and 'transcendent', 'actual' objects, which may correspond to them on the other." It suffices just to state the following and anyone must recognize it: *"that the intentional object of a presentation is the same as its actual object, and on occasion as its external object, and that it is absurd to distinguish between them*. The transcendendent object would not be the object of *this* presentation, if it was not *its* intentional object." (Husserl 2001b, pp. 126–127).

Thereby the epistemological position or—as we would better say in the phenomenological sense—the non-epistemological or pre-epistemological position of phenomenology is designated with all desirable exactness.

If we begin first with the polemic against the picture theory, it would be advisable first and foremost to remember that the view that our perceptions can only reach out to things through mere presentations-in-profile [*Abschattungen*] of the same, while lived experiences do not present themselves in profile, nonetheless has quite a few similarities with the picture theory, insofar as the shadow [*Schatten*] can be considered as a picture reduced to contours of that which is "presented in profile" [*Abgeschatteten*]; however, our interest is primarily directed toward the deeper question, i.e., to what extent phenomenology manages to set up against false presuppositions that have been foisted upon the relationship between thing and perception a presuppositionless grasp of the 'givens'. This question, in turn, is closely connected with the other [question] about the relation between the naïve and the scientific approach, between the "natural" and the "scientific world-concept." It appears, namely, that the objections put forward here only have traction against a correctly understood picture- or sign theory when both approaches are mixed with one another, but they dissolve if the two approaches are purely kept apart. Let us focus on one example. "Before me, in the dim light, lies this white paper. I see it, touch it. This seeing and touching of the paper […] is a cogitatio, an experience of consciousness. The paper itself with its objective make-up, its extension in space, its objective place relative to the spatial thing that is called 'my body' is not a cogitatio but instead a cogitatum, not the experience of perception but instead the perceived. Now, something perceived can itself very well be an experience of consciousness, but it is evident that something like a material thing, for example, this paper given in the experience of perception, is intrinsically not an experience but instead a totally different kind of being" (*Ideen* 61f./60). The fact that this paper that I perceive as a "material thing" is "a being of a totally different kind," a transcendent thing, precisely the way I perceive it, can only be claimed when I put myself in the standpoint of naïve thinking. If I do this, however, I must also do it with complete consistency. For naïve thinking this thing exists "outside" the perceiver. One only speaks of a picture when the thing is no longer perceived, no longer seen, heard, or touched. One can make for oneself a picture of the thing, which is similar to the perceived thing. This similarity, however, does not put the picture and the thing on the same level, so that they would be interchangeable; for the picture is *in* the perceiver. In case the perceiver compares the picture with the thing itself, then the selection of that, which he "means," is given precisely through the similarity of the content that for him coincides with the object; however, the thing itself is thereby sufficiently characterized as being "outside." Moreover, an infinite regress need not be generated; for the picture is only required because the object itself is not there; the picture itself does not demand this mediation.

If we now go from here over to the scientific approach, we thereby set aside the oldest picture theories that explain sensuous perception (as in Empedocles [270] and Democritus) by reference to little pictures coming off of things and migrating into the sense organs. In a clarification that historically presupposes Kant's philosophy we cannot speak of the relation between thing and perception without being aware of the dependence of the "thing" upon us, the perceivers, upon our forms of intuition and thought. *The object of knowledge of necessity becomes a problem.* Nor does the object that we "mean" [*meinen*] escape it. If we speak of "intentional lived experiences" and if all lived experiences are recognized as "conscious" [*bewusst*], then we stand directly upon the ground of the fundamental Kantian thought, and we can no longer speak of the relation to the object contained in any lived experience as if the object thereby "meant" were given independently of our representation and thought. Even the "intuition of essences" cannot elude it; also for it the object must become a problem, after it is once seen as lived-through [*miterlebt*] and thereby drawn into the subjectivating process. Then it can no longer be a matter of a mere description of givens; for the "given," the "object" of perception is known by our mind already with regard to its content as 'mind' [*Geist von unserem Geist*]. As Natorp said in a debate with Husserl, "reconstruction" must replace mere description (Natorp 1912, p. 33 f., 286 f.). To pull out the relation to the object from this implication would only be possible if we remain in the standpoint of the naïve approach, for which content and object of perception together with all sense-data are "outside" our consciousness. With this, however, the entire doctrine of "lived experience" would collapse.

If we turn back once again to picture theory and to sign theory (of which the latter only comes into consideration for the scientific approach), it becomes apparent that even vis-à-vis a consistently conducted scientific-epistemological approach at least the objections mentioned here do not prove to be cogent. Let us adopt, for example, the Kantian standpoint and assume that the unmediated relation of a cognition to its object in intuition is only possible insofar as the "object [271] affects the mind in a certain manner," then at the moment of intuition the "picture" or "sign" of the object coincides with the object itself. In the reproduction, however, the relation to the object lies indeed only in the "picture's" similarity with this [object] itself or in the representing [*Vertretung*] of it through the "sign," which is also proven by the fact that the "picture" or "sign" can be erroneously referred to another similar object. An infinite regress is not the necessary consequence, since the representation of the object through a picture or sign is conditioned by the absence of an outer "affection," but a representation of the representation appears to be superfluous. The other epistemological difficulties that undoubtedly affect such a theory are not at issue here. We only wanted to show that a critical confrontation with the picture theory does not necessarily lead to the doctrine of intention, that rather the difficulties emerging at this juncture stem from a mixing up of the naïve and the scientific-epistemological standpoints, in that on the one hand the "object" is considered to be "something" independent from the presentation of it, and on the other hand the perception of the "object" as a whole is considered to be a lived experience of consciousness.

In this way, however, the *presuppositionlessness* of phenomenology is qualified on an important point. The "absolute being of the immanent," that as such makes possible the unmediated "intuition of essences" as the foundation of all science, borrows its absoluteness from the contrast against the "merely phenomenal being of the transcendent." But the latter is neither as "transcendent," as "thing" in a naive sense, nor as "transcendent" in the epistemological sense something "merely phenomenal." It first receives this character because in the presuppositionless consideration of the "givens" in the transfer from the "natural" to the "phenomenological attitude," a very specific concept of "lived experience" comes into play. Thus we see: in the same way in which in the other excellent attempt to move without prejudice from "that which is factually found as given" [*Vorgefundenen*] (i.e. Avenarius'), a biologizing approach (as one is tempted to call it) mixes itself up with the description, so here it is a psychologizing approach (which is indeed epistemologically possible, but does not, however, coincide with the [272] natural concept of the world[23]) that modifies the description of the immediate given almost imperceptibly in a certain direction.

VII The Necessity of a Presuppositionless Starting Point that is Provided by "Practical Realism"

Here, too, as in phenomenology's abovementioned endorsement of a descriptive psychology independent from natural science, there is a fundamental theoretical motif, whose fulfillment in such a coherent logico-systematic form already secures for phenomenology its meaning [*Bedeutung*] and its historical right. If the theory of knowledge concerns itself with the presuppositions of all knowledge to be found in cognition as such, then the extent to which the theory of knowledge itself can be presuppositionless or can ground itself in presuppositionless beginnings is all the more an important question. Thereby, the theory of knowledge will always have to somehow start with 'givens', at the very least with knowledge and its object as "givens."

This fact clearly emerges even in a theory of knowledge that seeks to avoid any empirical interference in its foundation as carefully as Kant's theory of knowledge does. If Kant seeks to demonstrate the principles of knowledge as conditions of the possibility of experience, or—which amounts to the same thing—of experiential cognition, then this demonstration is only convincing if experience *must* be possible, namely, because it is real. Experience as an "*original fact*" [*Urtatsache*], as Kuno Fischer says,[24] thus forms the starting point of Kantian epistemology (Fischer 1883, pp. 91, 99 f.). "Experience" [*Erfahrung*] here is not taken in a merely empirical sense as the "raw material of sensuous impressions," but rather in the more pregnant sense of the already carried out processing of this raw material through the activity of the understanding, since its availability in this sense is presupposed by the transcendental deduction of the categories; however, since this experience cannot be the philosophically processed experience of the epistemologist without generating an intolerable circle, i.e., [273] since it cannot be an experience already separated into its

---

23 In the widest sense, which also encompasses phenomenology.
24 Similarly, though from a different standpoint, A. Riehl, *Der philosophische Kritizismus* I, (1909, p. 303): "The concept of experience is the constant ground, the sole presupposition of Kantian epistemology."

component parts, then it must, at least as a starting point, coincide with the pre-scientific, or better yet, the pre-epistemological, the "common" [*gemeine*] experience. Hence, as a matter of principle, theoretical reason, too, carries out something of a "transition" from the "common" "knowledge of reason" to the "philosophical,"[25] as "practical reason" does for Kant.

This train of thought, especially the question about how things stand with regard to the a priori character of the principles of knowledge, is one we cannot further pursue here.[26] We only note that it is possible to detect the inevitability of such a starting point even among modern scholars who cannot be suspected of making concessions to empiricism. Let me mention as an example Rickert, who strongly emphasizes the necessity of an object presupposed by the theory of knowledge, namely, cognition itself (Rickert 1909, p. 4 f.; 1904, p. 1 f.). Whether this cognition is the cognition of the specialized sciences or that of practical life makes—at least as a matter of principle for the theory of knowledge—no essential difference. The specialized researcher, too, occupies as such a "naïve" or "natural" standpoint. Even epistemologists like, e.g., Külpe, who expressly put the specialized sciences at the foundation of their inquiry, in order to examine the processes of "realization" at work in them, thereby presuppose as a starting point a cognition that is not yet affected by epistemological reflection (Külpe 1912, p. 2 f.). But also the individual who reflects epistemologically sees himself forced to return to this starting point again and again. Whether he now expressly makes cognition itself into the object of his investigation or goes back in a regressive method to recede behind its conditions: if he does not want permanently ungrounded assumptions [274] to enter into his theory, he must keep bringing to mind what cognition, uninfluenced by his own theory, is. And he is capable of this; for regardless of how far he may have distanced himself in his science from the natural standpoint, in practical life he sees himself always under the spell of the natural outlook, which has also been called "naïve realism," but which is better called practical realism, insofar as it continues to hold sway in practical life also for those who have overcome it scientifically.

In what way this "practical realism as starting point," which thus accompanies not only the beginning, but also the complete epistemological reflection, is developed by such reflection, we cannot further pursue here. We only highlight two consequences, which ensue for the fundamental questions touched upon by our considerations. First, the theory of knowledge cannot be merely psychology,

---

25 Cf. the caption of the first section of the *Grounding for the Metaphysics of Morals:* "Transition from the Ordinary Rational Knowledge of Morality to the Philosophical" [Kant 1993, p. 7].
26 I must also for this purpose make reference to my book on *Fries und Kant* I, (Elsenhans 1906a, p. 30 f.).

since it otherwise would rule out in advance as a possibility the assumption that is always to be found in practical realism of a being independent of the subject and all its representations [*Vorstellungen*]. Second, psychology must have a comprehensive meaning for the theory of knowledge—although it may remain preliminarily undecided whether psychology has to be taken in the form, e.g., of Husserl's phenomenology or Rickert's transcendental psychology or some other empirical psychology—since a theory of knowledge is unthinkable without exact knowledge of the process of cognition which, according to practical realism, goes on "in" the subject. Psychology certainly presupposes epistemology —but only in the systematic order of science, not in its practice, since its most important processes, the presentations, feelings, and desires that attach to practical life, only presuppose the same practical realism which also provides the starting point of epistemology, and in their facticity [*Tatsachlichkeit*] are not touched by any epistemological destruction of this standpoint. In contrast, the right to apply any epistemological results on psychological cognition is retained as much the theory of knowledge itself – which falls into a similar circle – must retain the right to apply its results to its own inquiries.

This retained right, however, once again presupposes that there is a starting point still unaffected by the investigation itself, and thereby confirms the necessity of starting from what we have called practical realism. For an epistemological reflection that wishes to examine itself without reference to a 'given' that hasn't yet been affected by it, that circle would be insurmountable.

The theory of knowledge as a science destroys its own starting point, but it always turns back to it and orients itself toward it. Just as for the astronomer the apparent movement of the heavenly bodies, whose perception he shares with the layman and whose illusory nature he sees through, always again serves as starting point and constant orientation for his scientific measurements of the universe, so the thinker must always turn back again from the height of his abstractions to the "natural concept of the world," which, although he sees through its untenability, does not merely remain as the obvious arena of his actions, but also as the starting point and means of orientation in his deepest research and boldest ideas.

References

Avenarius, Richard (1888): *Kritik der reinen Erfahrung*. Leipzig: Fues.
Avenarius, Richard (1894): *Der menschliche Welbegriff*. Leipzig: Reisland.
Avenarius, Richard (1895): "Bemerkungen zum Begriff des Gegenstandes der Psychologie."
    In: *Vierteljahrsschrift für wissenschaftliche Philosophie* 18, pp. 137-161.

Brentano, Franz (1973): *Psychology from an Empirical Standpoint.* A.C. Rancurello, D.B. Terrell, and L. McAlister (Trans.). London: Routledge.
Dilthey, Wilhelm (1894): "Ideen über eine beschreibende und zergliedernde Psychologie." In: *Sitzungsberichte der Kgl. preuss. Akad. Der Wissenschaften zu Berlin* 1894, pp. 1309–1407
Elsenhans, Theodor (1897): *Selbstbeobachtung und Experiment in der Psychologie.* Leipzig/Tübingen: Mohr.
Elsenhans, Theodor (1906a): *Fries und Kant: Ein Beitrag zur Geschichte und zur systematischen Grundlegung der Erkenntnistheorie.* Band I. Gießen: Töpelmann.
Elsenhans, Theodor (1906b): *Fries und Kant: Ein Beitrag zur Geschichte und zur systematischen Grundlegung der Erkenntnistheorie.* Band II. Gießen: Töpelmann.
Elsenhans, Theodor (1912): *Lehrbuch der Psychologie.* Tübingen: Mohr.
Fichte, Johann Gottlieb (1994): *Introductions to the Wissenschaftslehre and Other Writings (1797-1800).* Daniel Breazeale (Trans.). Indianapolis/Cambridge.
Fischer, Kuno (1883): *Kritik der kantischen philosophie.* Munich: Bassermann
Fries, Jakob Friedrich (1828): *Neue oder anthropologische Kritik der Vernunft.* Heidelberg: Winter.
Geiger, Moritz (1913): "Beiträge zur Phänomenologie des ästhetischen Genusses." In: *Jahrbuch für Philosophie und phänomenologische Forschung* 1, pp. 567-684.
Hönigswald, Richard (1913). "Prinzipien der Denkpsychologie." In: *Kant-Studien* 18, pp. 205-245.
Husserl, Edmund (2014): *Ideas for a Pure Phenomenology and Phenomenological Philosophy. First Book: General Introduction to Pure Phenomenology.* Daniel Dahlstrom (Trans.). Indianapolis/Cambridge: Hackett.
Husserl, Edmund (1981): "Philosophy as a Rigorous Science." Quentin Lauer (Trans.). In: *Husserl: Shorter Works.* Notre Dame: University of Notre Dame Press, pp. 161-197
Husserl, Edmund (1989): "Vorwort zum *Jahrbuch für Philosophie und phänomenologische Forschung I.*" In: *Husserliana XXV: Aufsätze und Vorträge (1911-1921).* Thomas Nenon and Hans Rainer Sepp (Eds.). Dordrecht: Martinus Nijhoff, pp. 63-64.
Husserl, Edmund (2001a): *Logical Investigations* I. J. N. Findlay (Trans.). London/New York: Routledge.
Husserl, Edmund (2001b): *Logical Investigations* II. J. N. Findlay (Trans.). London/New York: Routledge.
Kant, Immanuel (1998): *Critique of Pure Reason.* Paul Guyer and Allen Wood (Eds.). Cambridge: Cambridge University Press.
Külpe, Oswald (1912) *Die Realisierung* Vol. I. Leipzig: Hirzel.
Kant, Immanuel (1993): *Grounding for the Metaphysics of Morals* with *On a supposed Right to Lie Because of Philanthropic Concerns.* James W. Ellington (Trans.). Indianpolis: Hackett.
Maier, Heinrich (1914): "Logik und Psychologie." In: *Festschrift für Alois Riehl, von Freunden und Schülern zu seinem siebzigsten Geburtstage dargebracht.* HalleÖ Niemezer, pp. 311–78.
Messer, August (1912): "Husserls Phänomenologie in ihrem Verhältnis zur Psychologie." In: *Archiv für die gesamte Psychologie* 22, pp. 117-129.
Natorp, Paul (1912): *Allgemeine Psychologie nach kritischer Methode.* Tübingen: Mohr.

Pfänder, Alexander (1913): "Zur Psychologie der Gesinnungen." In: *Jahrbuch für Philosophie und phänomenologische Forschung* 1, pp. 325-404.
Reinach, Adolf (1983): "The Apriori Foundations of the Civil Law." In: *Aletheia* III, pp. 1-142.
Rickert, Heinrich (1904): *Der Gegenstand der Erkenntnis: Einführung in die Transzendentalphilosophie*. Tübingen: Mohr.
Rickert, Heinrich (1909): "Zwei Wege der Erkenntnistheorie." In: *Kant-Studien*, pp. 169-228.
Riehl, Alois (1909): *Der philosophische Kritizismus: Geschichte und system*. Leipzig: Engelmann
Scheler, Max (1973): *Formalism in Ethics and Non-Formal Ethics of Value*. Evanston: Northwestern University Press.
Schelling, Friedrich Wilhelm Joseph (1800): *System des transzendentalen Idealismus*. Tübingen: Cotta.
Schopenhauer, Arthur (1892): *Neue Paralipomena: vereinzelte Gedanken über Vielerlei Gegenstände*. Leipzig: Reclam.
Wundt, Wilhelm (1910): "Psychologismus und Logicismus." In: *Kleine Schriften*. Leipzig: Engelmann.

Rodney Parker
Paul F. Linke

Paul Ferdinand Linke (1876–1955) was labelled by his student Gershom Scholem (2003, pp. 60) as an "unorthodox" pupil of Husserl. There are perhaps two things that make Linke an unorthodox pupil. First, Linke never studied with Husserl. Linke studied with Theodor Lipps and Hans Cornelius at the Ludwig-Maximilians-Universität in Munich in 1897–1898 and participated in the recently founded *Psychologische Verein*. This group would later evolve into the Munich Circle of phenomenologists, but during Linke's tenure as a student of Lipps, Husserl's name was relatively unknown. After leaving Munich, Linke enrolled at the University of Leipzig, where he completed his dissertation, *David Humes Lehre vom Wissen* (Linke 1901), under the supervision of Wilhelm Wundt. His first publication dealing with Husserlian phenomenology appears to be his book *Die phänomenale Sphäre* (Linke 1912), though we know that he had been interested in phenomenology prior to this.

In a letter from Moritz Geiger to Husserl dated February 5th, 1911, we find the first mention of Linke in Husserl's correspondence.[1] We learn from this letter that Scheler, Eucken, and Linke had been arranging for Husserl to give a talk in Jena, where Linke had been teaching since 1907 (Husserl 1994a, 106). Unfortunately, these plans never came to fruition. However, in a letter from Eucken to Husserl (July 9th, 1911), Eucken notes that Linke was extremely disappointed that Husserl would not come, and that Linke was both scientifically and personally faithful to Husserlian phenomenology and had already won a circle of young scholars for Husserl (Husserl 1994b, 91).[2] By all indications, Linke was one of the first professors outside of Göttingen and Munich to lecture on phenomenology. But just how faithful Linke was to Husserl's teachings, having never been a student of the Master, leads into the second point which makes him an unorthodox student.

Following the publication of his article in the second volume of Husserl's *Jahrbuch* (Linke 1916) and his response to Theodor Elsenhans in *Kant-Studien* (Linke 1917)—translated below—Linke began explicitly advocating what he called *Gegenstandsphänomenologie* or "object phenomenology" (Linke 1918,

---

[1] Others include a letter from Reinach to Husserl, 21.VIII.1915 (Husserl 1994a, 199), and from Scheler to Husserl 01.X.1912 (Husserl 1994a, 216).
[2] One of these students was Arnold Metzger, who later studied with Alexander Pfänder in Munich and Husserl in Freiburg.

DOI 10.1515/9783110551594-026

1919, 1926, 1930). This was a strand of realist phenomenology that was also advocated by Geiger, who we might reasonably speculate was a friend of Linke dating back to their time together as students of Wundt in Leipzig.[3] Though Linke continued to consider himself a phenomenologist, he considered himself closer to Brentano and the phenomenological psychologists.

References

Husserl, Edmund (1994a): *Husserliana Dokumente III. Briefwechsel: Band 2. Die Münchener Phänomenologen*. Karl Schuhmann (Ed.). Dordrecht: Kluwer.

Husserl, Edmund (1994b): *Husserliana Dokumente III. Briefwechsel: Band 6. Philosophenbriefe*. Karl Schuhmann (Ed.). Dordrecht: Kluwer.

Linke, Paul Ferdinand (1901): *David Humes Lehre vom Wissen: Ein Beitrag zur Relationstheorie im Anschluss an Locke und Hume*. Leipzig: Engelmann.

Linke, Paul Ferdinand (1912): *Die phänomenale Sphäre und das reale Bewusstsein: Eine Studie zur phänomenologischen Betrachtungsweise*. Halle an der Saale: Niemeyer.

Linke, Paul Ferdinand (1916): "Phänomenologie und Experiment in der Frage der Bewegungsauffassung." In: *Jahrbuch für Philosophie und phänomenologische Forschung* 2, pp. 1–20.

Linke, Paul Ferdinand (1917): "Das Recht der Phänomenologie: Eine Auseinandersetzung mit Th. Elsenhans." In: *Kant-Studien* 21, pp. 163–221.

Linke, Paul Ferdinand (1918): *Grundfragen der Wahrnehmungslehre: Untersuchungen über die Bedeutung der Gegenstandtheorie und Phänomenologie für die experimentelle Psychologie*. Munich: Reinhardt.

Linke, Paul Ferdinand (1919): "Die Minderwertigkeit der Erfahrung in der Theorie der Erkenntnis: Phänomenologische Randglossen zu Hans Cornelius' "Transzendentaler Systematik."" *Kant-Studien* 23, pp. 426–43.

Linke, Paul Ferdinand (1926): "Bild und Erkenntnis: Ein Beitrag zur Gegenstandsphänomenologie in kritischem Anschluss an Nicolai Hartmanns Lehre vom Satz des Bewusstseins." In: *Philosophischer Anzeiger* 1 (2), pp. 299–358.

Linke, Paul Ferdinand (1930): "Gegenstandsphänomenologie." *Philosophische Hefte* 2 (2), pp. 65–90.

Scholem, Gershom (2003): *Walter Benjamin: The Story of a Friendship*. Harry Zohn (trans.). New York: New York Review Books.

---

[3] Unfortunately, Geiger's *Nachlass* does not contain any correspondence with Linke. It would be interesting to know if Geiger and Linke corresponded after Geiger left Leipzig to study with Lipps in Munich.

Translated by Evan Clarke
Paul F. Linke.
The Legitimacy of Phenomenology: A Disagreement with Theodor Elsenhans

Das Recht der Phänomenologie. Eine Auseinandersetzung mit Th. Elsenhans
Kant-Studien 21, pp. 163–221 (1917)

[163] If one wants to highlight the significance of the phenomenological approach for the philosophy and psychology of the present, and to do so objectively and without preconception, then it is perhaps advisable to orient oneself around its history, because even though it is quite young, phenomenology does have a history.

It is undoubtedly correct to trace the birth of phenomenology to 1913, the year that the *Jahrbuch* first appeared—or rather, it is correct in the same sense that one dates the birth of pedagogy or science to the appearance of the first pedagogical manual and first logic, and in the sense that we are able to say that the art of singing was called into life by the first master who was able to *teach* this art *methodically*.

Because there is a massive difference between practically, implicitly, even virtuosically [164] applying a given method—taking the term 'method' in the widest sense—and explicitly singling out that method, gaining insight into all of its parts, presenting it clearly, and communicating it to others—precisely *as* a method. In other words, even if logically speaking, method primarily means method in the sense of what is explicitly grasped; practically speaking, it largely signifies the opposite of this.

It is certainly a matter of merely external accident and thus completely indifferent whether—as in most cases—the explicitly singled-out and systematically presented method is different from its merely practical counterpart, or whether they are bound together in a kind of personal union—which is precisely the case for phenomenology.

One thing at least is certain: any determinate method—or rather, since we prefer to employ the word 'method' in relation to the already abstractively clarified method—any determinate *process* is realized in the moment that it is first applied. In that sense, the birth of phenomenology really happens in 1901: the year in which the second volume of the *Logical Investigations* appears (Husserl 2001b).

We might add: phenomenology at that time was already, in its *decisive* points, the phenomenology of today—even if it has certainly grown in the meantime, both in terms of scope and in terms of its self-consciousness as its inherent possibilities.[1]

Of course, this was generally not seen. For the most part, one did not sense what was special and new in the methodology of the Husserlian investigations.

One small group of researchers formed an exception to this rule, and it is very striking that this group was made up of the students of Theodor Lipps, [165] standing in very close intellectual proximity to that remarkable man—who, for his part, was a fanatic advocate of the universality of empirical psychology and the method of introspection, but whose accomplishments are only properly assessed from a standpoint opposed to this method, a standpoint of which Lipps was quite unconscious. It is no wonder, then, that it is among Lipps' followers that Husserl's slashing critique of the scientific prejudices of his day first found an understanding reception.

In this connection, the following problem presents itself: despite having shown quite clearly that logic could not be grounded in psychology (Husserl 2001b), Husserl undertakes simultaneously—in the second volume of his *Logical Investigations*—to provide logic with a grounding, and to do so by means of analyses that have to be regarded as *psychological*, not only in Lipps' sense, but according to the admittedly rather vague terminology adopted by Husserl himself at that time. Strangely enough, many at that time missed what was perfectly self-evident: that this designation was and could only be a makeshift designation, that it was a designation taken over from the available terminology, because the new word, at least with the significance that it would later come to have, was not yet available. Had it been other than a makeshift designation, Husserl would have counteracted, perhaps even destroyed, the meaning and the goal of his investigations.

But even among those who have recognized the impossibility of a logic grounded purely in psychology, thus, the impossibility of a "psychologistic logic," there exist those who see no contradiction in describing Husserl's investigations as empirical-psychological.[2]

---

1 Alongside Twardowski, Ehrenfels, and others, Alexius Meinong and his associates stand in close proximity to Husserl and his ideas. As near as Meinong's "theory of objects" comes to Husserl's *Logical Investigations* on individual points, however, it remains the case that the ideas that were decisive for the new direction were first articulated by Husserl.

2 This is the case even for a thinker as close to Husserl as August Messer (Messer 1912b; incl. in this volume p. 215–226; moreover Messer 1914; incl. in this volume p. 239–253). I take up Messer's attacks against eidetic phenomenology and Messer's own empirical-descriptive phenomen-

[166] But what kind of investigations were these actually? This is the problem that now arises. Husserl would soon give an answer—not publicly at first, but cautiously, just within the circle of his followers. From the work undertaken in concert with his followers, and from their many discussions, the essential kernel of the new theory would arise, a theory that gradually came to be known as *phenomenology*. Only years later would this theory find its literary expression in *Ideas*, the theoretically rich work of phenomenology's founder.

Of course it was inevitable that this work would be something more than a presentation of the shared views of all phenomenologists, since even today it is unlikely that any such work could emerge from any of those engaged in phenomenological research. Rather, because Husserl tries in his own way to grasp phenomenology at the level of its ultimate foundations, the *Ideas* comes to have a strongly individual imprint. What we learn, above all, is how *Husserl himself* sees phenomenology. This we experience in the most exact and thorough manner.

Husserl himself stressed, of course, that phenomenology, as represented in his work, was only an *incipient* science, and that only the future would show to what extent the results of his analysis would be retained. In other words, he submitted his ideas consciously and as explicitly as possible to discussion. The debates which had unfolded just within a small circle of followers prior to the appearance of the Jahrbuch would now be brought before a broader, scientific public.

Scientific discussion, after all, is tightly connected with the essence of phenomenology. This much is clear from its history.

From this standpoint, the clear and thorough critique that Theodor Elsenhans has recently directed against phenomenology appears even more commendable than it already does (Elsenhans 1915, p. 224 f.; incl. in this volume p. 339 f.).

[167] At the same time, the intrinsic necessity of every objective discussion to shed light on the problems from as many sides as possible may justify the fact that we have here an author who has reached phenomenology starting from empirical-psychological issues, and whose position, therefore, allows some hope of understanding for the empirical investigator.

Of course, we should not obscure the in-principle opposition that exists between these two standpoints, as they are presently configured. The opposite,

---

ology in a separate, larger work, dealing with the issue of 'psychologism' in modern psychology and drawing on examples from the modern, experimental investigation into the perception of movement. See also my essay in the second (as yet unpublished) volume of Husserl's *Jahrbuch* (Linke 1916).

rather, is our objective. What we will do, therefore, is examine the most important of those standpoints that are presently in question. In the process, we will make clear our complete solidarity with Husserl's position.

Our claim is that phenomenology, both in regard to its method and its sphere of theoretical activity, is a *non-empirical* discipline; that within the irreal and real regions of inquiry that are particular to phenomenology, *evident insights having apodictic certainty* are possible; and that these insights allow phenomenology to provide the foundations for empirical psychology.

It is just this series of claims that Elsenhans has thoroughly and staunchly opposed. The following analyses aim exclusively at the defense of this thought. I think that it will greatly facilitate the thoroughness and clarity of our argument if we leave everything that is merely incidental to the side.

I What Is Experience?

Elsenhans locates one of the *undoubtedly weakest* aspects of phenomenology in the union of two claims: "first, that phenomenology grasps 'givennesses,' and the second, that this procedure itself is dissociated from any kind of experience" (Elsenhans 1915, p. 236; incl. in this volume p. 349).

For us, by contrast, this point is actually one of the *strongest* elements of Husserl's position, [168] even *the* strongest element in the whole of phenomenology. Not only does the meaning of phenomenology turn principally on this point, it is also closely bound up with a situation that we must try to understand if we are to come to terms with the phenomenological standpoint.

In this key point lies the possibility of finally overcoming the confusion concerning the use of the words 'empirical reality' [*Empirie*] and 'experience'.

Insight into this confusion, and the need to overcome it, is also present outside of the Husserlian school. I would like to call here on a thinker whose scientific past alone (he is a student of Jodl) need not lead us to suspect that he is prejudiced against phenomenology from the outset, but who has nevertheless made his opposition to Husserl's view quite clear.

In his "analytic psychology," Schmied-Kowarzik emphasizes quite urgently that the word 'experience' is used in two very different ways in the *scientific* literature (Schmied-Kowarzik 1912, p. 38 f.)[3]. On the one hand, it is simply opposed

---

[3] Naturally, we do not share Schmied-Kowarzik's standpoint, according to which the difference between empirical and non-empirical research (which he correctly grasps in many particulars) is merely a methodological difference.

to speculation, meaning unscientific, uncritical speculation. But in its original, and its only authentic sense, it means 'cognition of reality on the basis of perceptions and observations'. Thus understood, however, the original meaning of this term would point to a *knowledge of reality* on the basis of perceptions and observations. While the first, relatively wide meaning has its basis in historical accident, the second does not arise just out of language use, but is the unique, properly scientific meaning—the meaning that can be implemented largely without complications. Namely: in the second third of the previous century, when "the healthy understanding rebelled against the conceptual poetry of the moribund romantic intellectualism, it was the key term 'experience' that all creative minds called into service. We owe this period infinitely much: an awakening of the empirical sciences that was unparalleled in the history of the human sciences. [169] Nevertheless, the theory of knowledge that springs from this key term is one-sided and mistaken: its basic law maintains that all knowledge originates with experience, which is to say, induction. In that time of empiricism, the word 'experience' in the prevailing scholarly language came to imply a dismissal of everything "non-empirical" as extra-sensory, impossible, and thus irrational, so that one understood the opposite of experience as that old, romantic, conceptual play, that excessive speculation" (Schmied-Kowarzik 1912, p. 39). In current German speech, on the other hand, 'experience' always and above all means "a knowledge that has been drawn from the wealth of empirical observation, and that is capable of increase." An older person has more 'experience' than a young person, because they have lived more; but one who has traveled extensively also qualifies as particularly experienced. "Experience" therefore arises from the quantity of perceptions... A proposition of experience can be introduced "to the extent that something has already been perceived" (Schmied-Kowarzik 1912, p. 39).

These analyses (where Kant, incidentally, is given the last word, in keeping with views that Schmied-Kowarzik expresses elsewhere) articulate a distinction that is also drawn by the phenomenologist—a distinction between what is *experientially* given and what is *given* in general. What is given experientially is already something present, "hic et nunc," meaning a part of the concrete world that we accept immediately as real. It is the particular task of the empirical scientist to investigate the real parts or "pieces" [*Stücke*] of the world, whether individual or general (such as types and genera), and to determine those parts and pieces with increasing precision, perhaps even—insofar as their particular character allows for it—in accordance with "exact" laws.

But in order to make such determination possible, what is required in all circumstances is a knowledge of that which determines the *means of determination* [*Bestimmungsmittel*], or, as one says in familiar, but highly vague terms—and thus in terms that should *be dispensed with in all contexts*—a knowledge of that which determines "the concept." This determining element must somehow be "encountered"; it must somehow be discovered or "given." We do not stipulate, however, that this given must be an *experiential* given, meaning a concrete piece of the real [170] world or an *abstract* part of a concrete piece (whether a quality, a process, or a state belonging to that concrete piece).

Because it is perfectly sensible to conceive of a given that—taken just as it is, in and for itself and also for us (to the extent that we have learned to *analyze* it)— would be given immediately, not as a real piece of the world or as a moment that is inseparably bound to some real piece of the world, and thus not as something that would come under consideration as a real fact, but rather as something irreal and ideal ('eidetic' in a Husserlian sense), and as something that would only be concealed by the attitude that is directed toward real facts, the attitude that is common to everyday life and the majority of the sciences. In order to create a place for the phenomenological method of analysis, therefore, what one would call for is an overcoming of this attitude and of these tendencies.

In fact, this is precisely the demand that now resonates. Once one has recognized this, then one has also grasped what phenomenology is about. Of course, in order to recognize this, two things are necessary: first, one cannot foreclose insight by utilizing a one-sided and arbitrary terminology; second, one must be clear above all that an idea in the narrow sense, the Husserlian 'eidos', does not arise from an "abstraction" or indeed from any kind of "thought process" directed at real (physical or psychic) facts, and that ideas are totally different from universals based on empirically real objects, indeed totally different from universals in general.

Since Elsenhans declines to accept either principle, it is necessary to go into more detail on both.

First, therefore, the current use of the words 'empiricism' and 'experience' is anything but clear and unambiguous. That was already Schmied-Kowarzik's point: naturally one can wonder whether the confusion around these terms originates in the second third of the 18th century—in my opinion the confusion begins at an earlier [171] moment—but it is correct that in actual linguistic use (and not merely in the case of the German language) this confusion does not occur. In actual language, to "have experience" is not to grasp or to consciously "have what is 'encountered' or 'given' in the widest sense"[4]; it is to grasp and to consciously

---

4 Naturally, the phrase "to have experiences" [*Erfahrungen machen*] is the only linguistic expression at issue here. We are not concerned with the phrases "to find out" [*in Erfahrung bringen*] or "to learn" [*erfahren*], which tend to designate just the linguistic understanding involved in hearing or reading.

have just what is given *hic et nunc*. At best, we can have experience of the *factual employment* of the number π. We cannot experience the number itself.

II 'Empirical' and 'Given': Historical and Fundamental Remarks on Terminology

One will no doubt affirm the extremely important rule which says that for the purposes of scientific research, one should not depart from natural language use *except* in cases of necessity. One might think, perhaps, that it is more trouble to amend a terminology that has been established and widely disseminated. But supposing that this terminology has real objective reference, then this would be correct only if the terminology in question is consciously held and rationally motivated: in our case quite the opposite is the case. It is a matter, namely, of a certain carelessness, one that only manages to take hold because a direct orientation to what are ultimately the decisive literary sources has not been adequately sought after—much to the detriment of philosophical language use.

As far as our literary orientation is concerned, one figure is decisive above all: John Locke. It is Locke who first tried to show in a decisive way that the problem of knowledge is the problem of experience—appealing to reasoning that would be determinative for subsequent developments.

At first glance, of course, it looks as if this interpretation of Locke's views is consonant with the interpretation that equates "given in general" with "experientially given." Because for Locke all knowledge originates with what is experientially given: he does not acknowledge any other *actual* source.

[172] This is admittedly true: but it is easy to see that where *terminology* alone is concerned, this can in no case come into consideration. Because the problem of knowledge, understood as the problem of the sources of knowledge, is for Locke a pure *quaesto facti*. He tries to prove that there exists no other source of knowledge; by no means does he say, however, that a hypothetically adopted "knowledge" that did not flow from this particular source, or for which the question as to sources would be without meaning, could no longer sensibly be called knowledge. In other words, it is absolutely not Locke's view that nothing whatsoever could be discovered that is not a fact of consciousness, given on the basis of sensation or reflection. He does not think that the notion of such a thing is contradictory. Locke's struggle against innate ideas would otherwise be impossible to understand. Because Locke's objective is solely to show that such ideas, and the *consensus omnium* that characterizes them, do not *factually* exist; or more precisely, that the data of consciousness in which these

ideas would become present, and with reference to which they would be provable, are not actually given. They are not found in children or idiots, and anything that can be cited in defense of them, in Locke's view, is inadequate.[5]

In exactly the same way, a mineralogist might attempt to show that an exact cube shape is not encountered in any actual crystal, and a skeptic of moral history might try to show that sincerity and selfless charity are not actually encountered in real people. Because of course one would not claim that what is meant is that cube shapes, sincerity, and charity are something *contradictory*. On the contrary: only because what is at issue here are meaningful objects does the denial of their real givenness have any interest for us. It is the meaning, rather than the existence, to which the scientist is and must be bound terminologically—whether he is conscious of this or not. The mathematician forms the expression "rotational ellipsoid" quite independently of the question of whether such a shape is anywhere given; [173] likewise, when we coin the terms "sincerity" and "charity," what is decisive is simply that these virtues *could* be given—the terms themselves, again, merely circumscribe an orientation toward meaning.

Only meaningless (or more precisely, nonsensical, contradictory[6]) words must be banished from scientific language use. We need not banish words simply because they correspond to nothing that is factually real. Had Locke or one of his followers provided evidence that the notion of a non-empirical given—meaning something that is not "real," something that does not come forward as a singular-individual fact, or even as a fact of consciousness—is a meaningless notion, then and *only* then would they have the right, even the duty, to identity natural language not just with empirical givenness but with givenness in general.

This, however, cannot be correct. As far as Locke's *positive* claims are concerned, just the opposite is true: as Ernst Cassirer has recently highlighted (Cassirer 1911, p. 185f.), we find in Locke the beginnings of an opposition between experience *qua* sensation and reflection and intuition as the foundation of knowledge *in general* (even if this opposition is not really clear to Locke himself).

But this does not capture Locke's position on the point of interest, because Locke's *terminology*, which is alone of interest here, is as clear as possible with regard to our question. Experience is sensation and reflection; in both, the direct and indirect effects of "things" are presented to consciousness, and with them, singular-individual data of consciousness are fused together in consciousness to become new conscious facts [*Bewusstseinstatsachen*], while remaining just such conscious facts throughout.

---

5 For a particularly representative passage, see Locke 1996, p. 23.
6 Contradiction is not meaninglessness (cf. Husserl 2001b, p. 82).

As regards its *possibility*, however, experience stands in opposition to a different form of perception, a form of perception whose untenability Locke could demonstrate very easily, because it is given only in the form of an innate idea, and indeed, only from the standpoint of a particularly questionable assumption—even if [174] a demonstration would decide nothing as regards the meaning of the conceivability of this form of perception. Locke's opponents claim that a form of perception [*Erfassens*] *actually* exists in which an external fact is encountered or given according to its essence. Locke himself denies this. Both, however, count this manner of givenness as a debatable and meaningful possibility.

One cannot say that the situation has essentially changed when we come to Locke's successors. The denial of the actual existence of a non-empirical given is still held as self-evident—not, however, in the sense in which a generation that has grown up in an aesthetic climate of thought treats the denial of the existence of God as self-evident; and definitely not in the sense in which someone might hold that the very concept 'god' is absurd, and who therefore rules out the use of the corresponding word as invalid. Naturally, one frequently lacks insight into the presuppositions underlying one's own terminology, and this, in point of fact, is by no means easy to achieve, especially for the empiricist: because what is above all characteristic of each brand of empiricism is the tendency to replace questions of meaning with questions of fact. The *quaestio facti* dominates and tries to supplant other kinds of questions, of which the Kantian *quaestio juris* is merely one example. In this way, the wellspring that is decisive for all terminological inquiry is simply buried. In fact, this wellspring has been buried, which means that the carelessness mentioned above must now emerge, the carelessness which—quite understandably, given the enormous influence of empiricism—has lead to the regrettable distortion of linguistic use, and has sown confusion in the sciences.

Perhaps, though, we are exaggerating when we invoke the "sciences." What we are properly referring to is philosophy, psychology, and indeed anywhere that one has occasion to construct *theories* of the sciences. In terms of the *practical* operations of the sciences, the problems that we are concerned with, when they were present at all, were never very serious. Despite the fact that he is often required to appeal to induction, [175] the theoretically unprejudiced mathematician will not for that reason think that he is in the business of making *observations* or having certain kinds of *experiences*, thus of appealing to the scientific strata proper to chemistry, biology, or history. The representatives of the latter disciplines, on the other hand, will not forget the empirical foundations of their investigations, even in those instances where they proceed *deductively*.

Here, therefore, empiricism means a particularly, entirely determinate scientific method. It does not mean each (or each non-deductive) scientific method whatsoever.

Nowadays, though, one does not tend to talk so radically. One readily acknowledges the non-empirical character of several sciences, above all mathematics, seeing this, however, not in the "given"—as Elsenhans does, in a supposedly faithful echo of Kant—but rather in something that one believes can be opposed to all givenness, for instance the form or the "connection of a synthetic function with intuition." As if this connection and this function must not somehow be on hand, must not somehow be detectable or discoverable.

If one takes the word 'given' in the widest sense, therefore, as phenomenology now takes it, and as phenomenology is entitled to take it, then it must be said that the aspect that constitutes the non-empirical character of mathematics is indeed given.

But perhaps one genuinely wants to throw the legitimacy of this word usage into question. That would be a new nuance in the conflict, in any case, because what we tried to show until now was only that it is absolutely within the scope of a reasonable terminology to speak of a something that can be encountered [*Vorfindlichen*] in a non-empirical, non-experiential sense. Henceforth, we must oppose this position to the following claim: that in no case can this something be called a *given*.

Again, therefore, this is a purely terminological matter. Insofar as we count [176] only this terminological standpoint as valid—as indeed our analysis demands—then we must emphasize that there is no scientific tradition that permits the word 'given' to be used in the sense of "what is encountered [*vorfindlich*] in general" and thus no scientific tradition that regards the compound expression 'empirically given' as anything other, or as anything more important, than a mere pleonasm.

Even Kant, who of course tends to speak of the given exclusively in terms of what is empirically given, nevertheless emphasizes that he refers this term not just to real, but also to possible experience (Kant 1998, B 154); subsequently though, his actual statements make clear that for Kant, the given (note that we are speaking just of terminology) applies in a different and wider sense (Kant 1998, B 154, 162). Even just the simple fact that Kant speaks of what is empirically given—for instance, in the passage cited by Elsenhans (Kant 1998, B 555; cited in Elsenhans 1915, p. 237; incl. in this volume p. 349)—instead of what is given per se, is, in my opinion, the best proof that the two are not identical for Kant: because it would surely not otherwise occur to anyone to describe a square that has been defined as equilateral *as* equilateral, or more pleonastically still, as an equilateral square.

One will say perhaps that in Kant's case, it is not correct to place so much emphasis on *terminology:* because one knows well enough that the absence of clear terms is an undeniable weakness of the great man. This is undoubtedly correct: in that case, however, one simply should not rely *terminologically* on Kant.

And materially [*sachlich*]? Materially speaking, Kant certainly does recognize a non-empirical 'given' in the wide sense that we give to that term, because he takes the idea of apriority not just in the sense of a something about which valid statements can be made, but speaks explicitly and without reservation of what can be encountered in pure, non-empirical intuition (Kant 1998, B 53).[7]

[177] Naturally, we are not thinking here of identifying the non-empirical given in the phenomenological sense with the a priori of the transcendental aesthetic, or of placing both at the same level. *The non-empirical given of phenomenology appears to us as a significantly wider concept than the a priori of pure intuition and the Kantian a priori overall.*

This does not mean, however, that there do not exist highly important relations between the two concepts: and it is an important and even urgent task to investigate these relations individually[8]—because we are of the opinion that the phenomenological method of analysis is not only consistent with many of the most fruitful and valuable insights of Kantian philosophy, but that phenomenology is even capable of providing these insights with a new and deeper foundation, albeit on the basis of different presuppositions. It will not succeed without shifts in the prevailing views—and shifts that, to be sure, are often very substantial; but only the scientific philistine who is convinced that he alone is in possession of the truth could wish otherwise in the final equation.[9]

For these reasons it would be good in every case not to paint phenomenology from the outset with a Kantian brush, but to try to see it, rather, in terms of what it wants to be at the level of its method and its appointed task: to see it, in other words, as phenomenology.

---

[7] Naturally, we do not subscribe to what else is contained in this passage.

[8] A. Metzger's *Untersuchung zur Frage der Differenz der Phanomenologie und des Kantianismus* (Metzger 1915) represents a beginning in this regard. This thorough study—a dissertation produced in Jena that is concerned, in part, with my own ideas—deals principally with the standpoints taken by Rickert and Lask, and underlines the contrast between the two major philosophical directions very sharply; somewhat too sharply, it now seems to me.

[9] Insofar as it is a matter of *distinguishing* between a non-empirical and empirical scientific method, then the Kantian and the phenomenologist can and must *already* run in tandem for a considerable distance: compare the remarks of Bruno Bauch in "Zum Problem der allgemeinen Erfahrung" (Bauch 1911, p. 76f.) with those of the present text.

III False Theories of Abstraction of the "Universality of the Idea"[10]

[178] We come now to the second, incomparably important point: one closes off access to phenomenology through false empirical theories of abstraction.

As is well known, the objective of such theories is to make the universal comprehensible, and to do so by grasping it as an empirical-individual that has been modified in some way; to do so, in other words, by nullifying the particular essence of the universal. While for the phenomenologist all universals are grounded in the eidetic-ideal, they rest, for the empiricist, on singular-individual facts, or more precisely, on the data of consciousness. Indeed, the universal even *arises* genetically from such data—through a particular "process of generalization" (Elsenhans 1912, p. 205).[11]

Initially, then, one holds to the Lockean view according to which everything that exists can only exist as an individual fact, as a singular-individual something (Locke 1996, p. 181), while that which we *call* universal is called this for two reasons: first, because it belongs to the region of 'representations' [*Vorstellungen*], which are also singular-individual in essence; and second, because by singling out and giving exclusive attention to the plurality of constituents that these representations have in common (Locke 1996, p. 182) it is possible to draw singular-individual objects together into particular groups ("as it were in bundles" (Locke 1996, p. 187).

[179] These Lockean notions resonate more or less with the Berkeleyan-Humean theory of representation, which is, at bottom, simply a critical extension of Locke—unified by, and to be explained in terms of, the results of modern psychology.

---

10 Compare this whole section to Husserl's *Logical Investigations*, particularly Investigation II: "The Ideal Unity of the Species and Modern Theories of Abstraction." It is worth emphasizing, however, that Husserl, according to his own remarks (Husserl 2001a, p. 237 f.) no longer regards the views that are represented there as entirely correct (this judgment would certainly apply, for instance, to his conception of the identify of meaning as an identity of species). For this reason, I have felt compelled to independently pursue several, perhaps quite important elements of Husserl's research, the results of which I hope to be able to communicate on another occasion (cf. Linke 1912).

11 [Translator's note: the text cited here is found in this volume (p. 17–34), but the section quoted is not included]

A The Theory of Vagueness [*Verschwommenheitstheorie*]

Let's listen for a moment to the author himself. We read in Elsenhans' *Lehrbuch der Psychologie* that "observation suggests, in the first place, that the role of 'representative' impression [*Einzelvorstellung*] is never filled by a completely determinate, object-related impression [*Vorstellung*]; any such impression, rather, is inevitably marked with a striking indeterminacy...Once the vivid experience of perception has passed, the train of images has already begun to become unclear, and herein lies the first germ of generalization. The greater the distance from perception, the further this unclarity extends, and if our memory is not supported by new perceptions, then it is only by virtue of language and thought that it is possible to grasp individual differences. The principle of generalization, which is a part of this process, can thus be observed most clearly in children and primitive peoples [*Naturvolk*], where language and thought are in a less developed state. What the child associates with an individual, visually perceived object at the beginning of the language learning process can only be a 'raw and blurry image of the thing, in which only the most prominent features appear, as in a crude drawing; so that for the most part we cannot know what picture the child actually brings to mind upon hearing a particular word'" (Elsenhans 1912, p. 201; section not incl. in this volume).[12]

At this point, therefore, the universal is characterized by indeterminacy, and —as Elsenhans remarks explicitly in the same place—by the lack of individual differentiation [*Abgrenzung*] that is characteristic of this indeterminacy. This indeterminacy can now be characterized further as an indeterminacy of the *presentations* [*Vorstellungen*]. However, as with all words ending in –ung, the word 'presentation' [*Vorstellung*] is ambiguous: [180] as is often remarked, it can mean many things. Certainly, the word has the following two meanings: first, what is presented, the presented object; second, however, the change in the conscious state of the experiencing subject through which the givenness [*Gegebensein*] of the object in question is enacted; in other words, the act of the experience of what is presented. Which of the two meanings is intended here? The act? As far as the act of presentation of a rose is concerned, though, there is no sense in which we can speak of a fading or a lack of individual determinacy; this is more likely true of the rose itself. But of course it is not the *real* rose that is in question here, but rather the 'merely' presented rose. No reference is made to a possibly existing real correlate. This would still be something essentially differ-

---

[12] The citation included within this is from Sigwart (1889, p. 52). Sigwart, incidentally, is generally much less psychologistic.

ent than a mere *mental picture* [*Vorstellungsbild*], because a picture [*Bild*] would naturally presuppose the existence of a real correlate, to which it would have to stand in a particular kind of relation, which we would capture with the words 'depiction' or 'being a picture of'. This extraordinary, mystical mental picture [*Vorstellungbild*], however, appears for Elsenhans to be the basis of the word 'presentation' [*Vorstellung*][13], since he speaks in many places of 'pictures'. Nevertheless, one can again be in error on this point. Since it is essential to a picture that it refer to a depicted object—whether the object is real or not—the functionally universal picture must be recognizable on the basis of this reference; with the caveat that the picture does not refer just to an individual object, but rather to a *group:* to a species of a genus of 'similar' objects. But this means that the 'imaging', representing function must be extended to every case of generalization: employing the same logic that the theory in question does when it takes up the problem of universals, we must require that a picture not only represent an *individual*, but several objects, and that we note this fact explicitly. It appears to us, however, that the fading and the indeterminacy of the picture changes nothing in this regard. Certainly one can say that the mental picture—just like any other picture—loses clarity and individual differentiation over time. [181] What is alone important, however, is the loss of *individuality:* this has precisely as much to do with the loss of individual *differentiation* as a change in national boundaries has to do with nationality. The nearsighted person sees the trees of a nearby forest blurrily. The individual tree is not clearly distinguished from its environment (thus, for instance, from a neighboring tree). The tree, however, has certainly not lost individuality in the process; nothing non-individual has appeared in the place of an individual. Naturally, the same is true of pictures of any kind. A picture with very blurry contours is nevertheless in each case a representation of something individual—even if the picture does not allow us to grasp *what* kind of individual is represented, or where *one* represented thing stops and another one starts. Perhaps the blurriness is so extreme that I am unable to identify any determinate thing in the picture; I perceive only colors, in which case the 'picture' has naturally ceased to be a picture. On the other hand, it is not yet something *universal* or non-material, because the colors are none the less individual. In itself, each one is a particular something persisting in time, and the same is true naturally of the background on which they are presented.

And further, given a thoroughly vague 'presentation', a presentation from which all conceivable "individual" determinacy is lacking, I can nevertheless

---

[13] We will come back to this point below, p. 219f. [this volume p. 428].

speak about that presentation in general terms. I can do so, namely, because I can speak of such a presentation in general, rather than this or that particular presentation. How is such a generalization framed? In terms of a vagueness of a higher order? I see no other possible recourse. And indeed there is no other recourse for a theory that can in all seriousness invoke the "fortunate gift of forgetfulness" (to cite Ernst Cassirer's characterization (Cassirer 2004, p. 18)) as the basis for universal objects. Such theories are as unsuited as possible to making comprehensible the *true* nature of universal and ideal objects and the important role that such objects play in all consciousness life. Where thought in particular is concerned, such theories lead to "the strange result that all the logical labor which we apply to a given sensuous intuition serves only to separate us more and more from it. [182] Instead of reaching a deeper comprehension of its import and structure, we reach only a superficial schema from which all peculiar traits of the particular case have vanished" (Cassirer 2003, p. 19).

B The Theory of Compression and the Theory of Attention

Nevertheless, Elsenhans has still another theory of generalization, one that is quite differently oriented, even if consists just in the introduction of a further "moment in the process of generalization as it bears on presentation"—namely, "the progressive intensification (or "compression" [*Verdichtung*]) of similar features in the presented object, along with the progressive weakening of dissimilar features. Proceeding through repeated perception, this is a process that we can illustrate with reference to so-called "composite photography" [*Durchschnittphotographie*]. The faces of a company of soldiers of the same background [*Volkstamm*] are photographed sequentially on the same plate, so that the outlines of their faces coincide as closely as possible. In the resulting composite image the common features are preserved, and the differences dissolve" (Elsenhans 1912, p. 202; section not incl. in this volume).

Without a doubt, this theory has an advantage over the first: the presenting function is brought into relation with a *group* of individual objects. The "universal" mental picture appears as a summation phenomenon: it represents the totality of features that several individuals have in common. Quite obviously, then, we have to understand the mental picture itself as a presented individual, only as a typical individual—typical of a number of other individuals that it 'represents' and that it binds together as a unity.

Evidently, this theory is tied up with essentially Lockean principles. Berkeley, however, also comes into consideration.

At first, of course, we might think that Berkeley could be brought in here for purposes of contrast. Since the universal (as everyone recognizes) often requires a unification of features that cannot be present together in any concrete individual, [183] a contradiction results when we suppose that the universal is visible in an individual, be it the most 'typical' representative individual. Even the soldier, taken as a universal type, will nevertheless be blond, brown-haired, or black-haired; he will not be a fusion of all three (as for example we see in the composite photograph). He stands in this sense on the same level as the universal triangle.

Elsenhans recognizes the justice of this objection, and probably in the interests of meeting it, speaks of a third "factor of generalization": the isolation of particular features through interest and attention. It is possible to examine particular soldiers just in terms of *the* feature that does not differ from soldier to soldier. My respective perceptions of soldiers convey certain pictures, albeit pictures that are not *exactly* the same across perceptions; when they are taken together, what is similar in them is strengthened, and what is dissimilar is weakened. Here, then, the inclusion in a common presentation is possible: "the selection through attention and interest restricts itself from the outset of the whole process to certain integral parts of individual presentations" (Elsenhans 1912, p. 202; section not incl. in this volume).

According to Elsenhans, therefore, we have to see the actual factor of generalization in the *second* moment: in the process of typification. And it is true: supposing that this is correct, then the Husserlian objection that I have explicitly mentioned cuts no ice. The exclusive attention to a particular feature of some thing does not nullify [*aufheben*] the individuality of that thing. Certainly!—as long as it is still there. If, however, the individuality of the thing is eliminated —as indeed happens as part of the typification process in question—then one can allow that the attention to particular features has a role to play in universalization; not of course for universalization in general (which is accomplished by typification!), but for the occurrence of universals that would otherwise remain problematic.

C The 'First' Universal; Lotze's Error; The Basis of Similarity in Identity

The question on which everything rests, therefore, is whether the typification process or something [184] analogous to it really renders universalization comprehensible. Before one tries to give an answer to this question, one must be clear as to what the universal stands in contrast to, and thus, what the process of universalization is supposed to extend. We call it the factual [*Tatsächliche*]. We mean by this term what is factual in the pregnant sense: the singular-individual.

If one wants to view the problem of *universals* correctly, however, it essential that one does not inadvertently incorporate moments that are essential to the universal in one's examples of what is individual and factual.

Language makes it extraordinarily difficult to arrive at clarity on this matter.

Take for example the following expression: 'this determinate shade of red, as I find it on the blotting paper that I have just used'. It is tempting to see in this expression an unambiguous and entirely typical example of something that is palpably opposed to any universal. A dangerous error!

No less a figure than Lotze falls into this error, even if his strong logical interests prevent him from subscribing to the usual, empirical theories of abstraction.

As is well known, Lotze recognizes those things that are referred to linguistically as 'red', 'sweet', and 'warm', etc., as the "first" universals. For the purpose of comparison, he brings these universals into essential relation with one another; and he quite explicitly opposes them to the particular shade of red, the individual quality of sweetness, and the determinate degree of warmth.

This is obviously false. The wide gap separating what is individual from what is not individual turns up earlier than this and has nothing to do with comparison. The words "this determinate shade of red" is possibly already something universal, or something ideal, to put this in better, less ambiguous terms.

[185] Language can help us to clarify this somewhat. I can speak of the shade of red that is *on* my blotting paper, and I will be for most part directed toward a genuinely individual red, toward the shade of red that is characteristic of just this particular blotting paper, which is an *exclusive* "moment" of that blotting paper. It shares in the fate of the paper: should I burn the paper, then everything that is a quality of the paper in this sense will be destroyed: its form, its magnitude, its color—hence, also the consciousness of the shade of red in question.

On the other hand, I can speak of the red that is like the red on my blotting paper here, I can speak of the shade of red as this shade of red here, and I can underline the *as*. Then, in however varied a way this color is determined, and however intuitively clear it may be, it is no longer intended as an individual. Quite the opposite: it is what this *particular* blotting paper *can* and often really does have in common with many similar objects. Right now I bring three other sheets of paper out of my desk that are colored in the same way; three sheets of paper, in other words, that "have" *the same* color. Obviously, the same considerations apply to form, magnitude, and all other qualities.

One cannot reply that it is not identity but equality that is in question here, because equality "is" identity, meaning that equality always and necessarily includes identity. Equality is a relation and relates, like every relation, to several members: different objects are equal in a certain *respect:* they are equal or agree *in or in relation to* something: that something with respect to which they are equal is—when they are taken in a certain way—*common to them*. It is given with them as one and the same thing.

And this commonality and identity signifies nothing more than it usually does. It means just what it does when we say, for example, that two houses have a connecting wall in common, that two pieces of land have an owner in common, or that two lands have a king or government in common. [186] The difference is just that the 'features' [*Merkmale*] or non-independent moments in our case are abstract parts (or at least appear to be at first), of which commonality is predicated. On the other hand, this predication is beyond any doubt: it is simply nonsensical to speak of an equality that does not presuppose the commonality of a "moment" or of a unified group of moments. What could it mean to say categorically, and without further specification, that two men, two mountains, two books, or two individual objects of any kind are equal? I must of course specify whether they are equal as regards their form, their size, their color, or some other characteristic or group of characteristics. *In that case*, I have a right to claim that they are characterized by the same property, one that is intuitable at the level of the perceptual object itself, just as two pieces of blotting paper agree with respect to their color when they are determined in exactly the same way just with respect to their color.

One then sees immediately that the characteristics or moments of which commonality is predicated cannot possibly coincide with the *individual* moments of the *individual* object. These individual moments exist as two-ness, three-ness, four-ness, and so forth. The two, three, four factually existing colors are two *individual colors*; they can be the same, but not identical. Insofar as they are the same, however, they presuppose the identity of the one non-individual *color-determination* that they both have in common.[14]

---

14 Even prior to the publication of the *Logical Investigations*, I emphasized in my doctoral dissertation—contra Meinong—that sameness has its foundation in identity (Linke 1901, p. 668): this, however, was still framed in very psychological terms. Nevertheless, this was an important result: because from here on out one sees the indispensability of the "idea." Theodor Ziehen disputes this, and believes that he can derive the pure idea (or species) from sameness (Ziehen 1913, p. 417; incl. in this volume p. 183). I ask—does Ziehen know of a sameness that would be something other than sameness *in a certain aspect*? And if not, what does he understand by such an aspect, if not a pure idea or an *ideal* moment or quale. I know that Ziehen is concerned about the "mystical" quality of such ideas. However, he will certainly not be able to raise this objection in relation to my own presentation of things, and may be especially interested in p. 201f. [in this volume p. 413f.].

[187] In these non-individual determinations or moments, clearly, we have the only genuine "first" universal before us, the universal in which everything that is otherwise called general is grounded: the ideal. This is opposed to the temporal-singular [*Zeitlich-Einmalige*], for which it is essential to be located at some temporal point. For *idealities* [*Ideelen*], by contrast, the notion of fixed temporal determinations is nonsensical (since this would make an ideal into a singular thing, thus negating the very essence of the ideal): the shade of red that several red individuals can have in common as an ideal determination can no more be thought of as arising and passing away than the number π or the truth.[15]

One now sees clearly what every theory of *generalization* must actually accomplish: starting from the individual, they have to show how the individual is to be *transcended* [*überwinden*]; the individual-singular gap that divides the temporal-factual from the non-individual "timeless" ideal is to be overcome.

Must it be said explicitly that the typification process in question is not up to this task? Only those who confuse the "universality" of the type, of the average individual, with the genuine universality of the idea—which is much more appropriately called 'ideal'—can hold this opinion, because the average individual is naturally just as much an individual as every non-average individual something. It makes no difference whether I think of this as a "picture" or not. A picture is individual in a double sense: first, insofar as it represents an individual, or also, of course, a plurality of individuals; second, to the extent that it belongs, as this *particular* determinate picture, to the world of individuals.

The average typical individual, and—what by no means coincides with this— the normal[16] typical individual can both be called [188] universal, admittedly, to the extent that both unify the characteristics of a series of more or less similar individuals: but this unification [*Vereinigung*] of characteristics has only a secondary relation to *universality in the sense of the idea*, which for us is of fundamental logical and philosophical importance; because the unification of a series of qualities through combination and comparison does not belong essentially to the idea, to the eidos, to the ideal "characteristic" or "determination," as we

---

[15] W. Schuppe was probably the first to have seen the genuinely primary "universal" for the first time (cf. Schuppe 1878, p. 169 f.).

[16] cf. William Stern's significant investigations, which reach far beyond the issues of normality and type (Stern 1911, p. 155 f.). I happily take the opportunity to refer to these analyses because they constitute a good example of the following fact: provided that they are clear and thoroughly executed, principled investigations—even in the area of *applied* psychology—lead entirely on their own to issues having just as little to do with empirical psychology as with logic, and all the more to do with phenomenology: the way in which Stern tries to delineate psychic normality can be made clear to anyone.

have called it. Not the unity itself, but rather the *impossibility* of *meaningfully applying* an essentially temporal predicate to it—this is the true characteristic of all ideal determinations as well as all combinations of these; i.e. all ideas in general and thus the root of all those that can alone bear the name of a general idea.

This shows very clearly that a unity of characteristics is the exact opposite of a universalization: a square, for instance, is obviously the unification of the equilateral and right-angled parallelogram, but is precisely therefore less general than each of these individual geometrical ideas.

Above all, our analysis has shown that the way that leads to idealities is not, in general, the way of unification and comparison. My blotting paper is ideally determined by the conscious shade of red and remains so determined, whether or not other pieces of blotting paper or other objects characterized by the same color determination are present at some time and place. Just as a wall common to two houses can already exist before the second house is built, so a color determination common to two objects does not presuppose the existence of a second object from the outset; and the second object is invoked just so that we can prove the ideal nature of that determination, precisely through an analysis of the "commonality" that is here in question. [189] The secret to understanding this commonality lies precisely in its independence from the existence of each individual (which, as we will see, is not equivalent in meaning with 'concretion')[17].

On the other hand, the reverse is also true: if we have correctly seen the particularity of all ideal determinations, then, on their basis, we can make comprehensible the formation of species and genera. Through the idea of our particular shade of red, the totality of all objects (be they real objects or not) that are characterized by that shade of red is clearly circumscribed; only now can it be described as a *genuine* universal, as a totality of real, that is, empirically given individuals.

The fundamental difference between ideality and individuality, and simultaneously, the impossibility of leading ideality back to individuality, has become clear: the path towards securing idealities does not lead through the grasping of the individual-factual: in other words, it does not require the *empirical* as a presupposition.

In this way, the path toward phenomenology has been made free.

---

17 As Elsenhans appears to recognize (Elsenhans 1912, p. 233 [not included in this volume]). See also below, p. 208 f. [this volume p. 418 f.].

IV The "Copernican Turn" of Phenomenology

But if indeed ideality and universality *cannot* be understood on the basis of individuals, and stubbornly resist all efforts at reduction, we should not dismiss the suspicion that we are dealing here with a mere *pseudo-problem*. Ultimately, it is in the nature of the ideal to be *given just as immediately* as the individual.

And it can now be shown that the ideal does in fact behave in this way: indeed, we claim still more: what is actually *immediately* given is, in the main, only the ideal: more precisely, *nothing individual-factual is immediately given* [190] apart from the intention [*Vorfinden*] itself, apart from the act in which or through which something is given.[18]

Thus, we entirely reverse the usual opinion and proceed as Copernicus did in the area of astronomy, and as Kant—in a conscious echo of Copernicus, according to his well-known remark—would later do in the philosophic arena. It is indeed obvious that the relations between our method and Kant's "Copernican" turn are much closer than they need to be for the purposes of a common point of comparison. What is at issue is in any case something more than a *mere* analogy, and we should not refrain from emphasizing that fact. At the same time, we must stress that we are far from wanting to interpret the sense of the Kantian turn through the lens of phenomenology, or indeed of correcting it. Above all, *our* Copernican turn is not oriented around the problem of knowledge *alone*—for while it belongs to the essence of phenomenology to strive toward constructing a foundation for epistemological endeavors, this is not its only task. If we take the word 'epistemology' generically in terms of the totality of prevailing or superseded epistemologies, then phenomenology is *pre-epistemological*—also (and not least) in the sense that it can help the epistemologist of any school in the necessary task[19] of avoiding unclarity and ambiguity in the *presentation* of his thoughts.

In this connection, we want to highlight also the following point: phenomenology will always appear as a pre- and therefore non-epistemological science most extremely to those who want to attribute to epistemology a relationship to the appraisal of the reality-content of the naïve world-picture,[20] [191] be it in the sense of a correction or of a justification. Their conception, in the most extreme case, is the following:

---

[18] This thought is already expressed in principle in my "Die phänomenale Sphäre und das reale Bewusstsein" (Linke 1912), which complements the present text on many important points.
[19] This is in relation to the observation of August Messer (Messer 1915, p. 302).
[20] Elsenhans belongs within this group (cf. Elsenhans 1915, p. 270; incl. in this volume p. 375–376).

The world, which is represented in the naïve attitude [*Auffassung*] as a totality of colorful, resonant objects, formed and arranged in many different ways, is gradually understood as "subjectively" conditioned: first, in respect of so-called secondary qualities, and then, later, in respect to other elements, which, however, must be conceived by analogy to secondary qualities.

We will not investigate to what extent such an analysis can legitimately be called an epistemological (let alone a philosophical) analysis. It is certain, in any case, that it is characterized as *empirical*; it exploits the results of a multitude of perceptions and observations so as to show, on their basis, that certain determinations, that we refer at first to the individual-factual things and events that *surround* us, must rather be credited to something different, something that is also individual-factual in nature. Ultimately, therefore, this analysis does not proceed any differently than the naïve world-view itself. This analysis too encloses the *individual-factual* world in all manner of determinations; that it is a matter of determinations of a somewhat different kind does not, naturally, make any essential difference.

Surely, however, it is clear that I must in some way "have" things if I am to attach determinations to them; and, insofar as I have them, they must acquire a meaning, a *sense*. This "having" of sense-bearing [*sinnhaltiger*] determinations is the primary, essentially necessary presupposition for other, *empirical* forms of analysis—be they naïve or scientific. If I attach the determinations *red* and *rectangular* to the individual-factual something that now lies before me, then, from the perspective of the *sense* that I thereby attach to these determinations, it is all the same whether what is characterized as red and rectangular is "there" merely for my consciousness, or whether it really exists, independently of my consciousness (thus, in a [192] "transcendent" world).[21] Still further, from this perspective

---

[21] This transcendence is naturally entirely distinct from the one that August Messer invokes in his dispute with Bruno Bauch (Messer 1915, p. 300). In another passage, Messer emphasizes the "evidence" of belief in the reality of an external world (Messer 1915, p. 76 f.): self-evidently, this is meaningful just from the standpoint of practical knowledge; certainly not in a properly epistemological sense. Here, *methodological* doubt makes possible an opening to a singular layer of insights, namely, those of phenomenology. *Without falling into absurdity*, I can imagine that the perceptual qualities of the paper on which I write do not correspond to any "really" present, verifiable paper *individuum*; but I cannot meaningfully doubt the existence of *the qualities themselves as mere* qualities (forming a concrete whole). Does Messer propose to dispute this? Then he can no longer seriously speak of all those things that one is accustomed to calling "hallucinations." See also the section concerning illusions from the work mentioned on page 165 [386] above (Messer 1914; incl. in this volume p. 239–253), as well as sections 5 and 7 of this work, and finally Geyser's remarks about Messer (Geyser 1909, p. 23).

it is irrelevant whether a "transcendent" world exists, indeed whether speaking of such a transcendental world has any *sense* or not.

Here then is the point at which the new perspective is put into play. Over and against the individual-factual something that is to be determined in some way or another appears the non-individual determination itself; the means of determination [*Bestimmungsmittel*] as a sense-bearing, 'timeless' 'moment', as an ideal 'quality' [*Beschaffenheit*], if one wants to invoke that word in this context.

Earlier, one tended to bypass or even to blur the fundamental opposition between these two perspectives, indeed in a surprisingly causal manner. One interpreted the means of determination in question as *"general"* [*allgemein*] in the sense of empirical species and genera, and hence, on the basis of the prevailing theory, as *general presentations* [*Allgemeinvorstellung*] and concepts, which one should therefore obtain through the likewise empirical means of generalizing abstraction. One believed, therefore, that it was possible to dismiss all of the problems that are here in question as problems of an alternately logically and psychologically conceived process of concept formation (or even a causal-genetic process of concept emergence). Whoever, on the other hand, is convinced of the instability of empirical theories of abstraction will necessarily reach a different result: *above all, he will be on guard to divide everything about which meaningful statements can be made into* [193] *two regions: physical and psychical realities.*[22] Before today, in fact, this distinction was made almost universally: one recognized that the "logical" was something special, and so grouped it together with that vaguely defined group of possibilities that are related to logic just insofar as they are not *really* present, either in a physical or a psychical sense.

The Reduction

The characteristic feature of the phenomenological approach [*Betrachtungsweise*] can perhaps best be clarified in the following way.

We will proceed on the basis of an example lying close at hand: At 5:10PM yesterday, I saw the sun going down in a somewhat cloudy sky. Today, I think back to what I perceived yesterday: with the aid of memory, I *imagine* the setting sun, and indeed—as we will assume for simplicity's sake—just as I perceived it yesterday. Now, I can experience ever-renewed acts of imagination, in which I

---

[22] We can see in what sense this is inadequate by looking at anything fictional: as soon as I decide to take a character from a fairly tale, say, Puss in Boots, just as I strictly intend that character, it is obvious that it is nothing real. Even as non-real, however, Puss in Boots is a tomcat having paws, fur, and indeed all predicates of a cat (cf. Linke 1912, especially section 2).

am directed in the same way to the sun that I *perceived yesterday:* the object itself is always *the same*—entirely *one and the same*, not merely "*identical*." Provided only that our presupposition is correct, the object in front of us has not changed in the slightest: it remains precisely the setting sun of yesterday, even if the act and the "illustrative images" that perhaps accompany the act have changed to a considerable extent. Now we perform the phenomenological reduction: the ἐποχή. We exclude everything that in any way presupposes the correctness of the results of empirical inquiry: we add a *question mark* to every *truth* that is given as bearing exclusively on the *individual, particular case* (or on a generalization from particular cases), and to every truth that *can* only be given in this way according to its essential character. Of course, this does not mean that we [194] *assume* that such truths are false, but rather that we regard the results of these kinds of investigations as indifferent from the standpoint of our particular problem. From the outset, we ignore all methods of investigation in this particular area: we behave "as if"[23] empirical reality could somehow not be present, as if it could be thought that the whole empirically given world, which we regard as "real" from the perspective of the natural attitude (and hence, as arranged in the form of our *one, individual, unique,* spatio-temporally existing world) might not actually be entitled to this predicate: the "thesis of existence" [*Daseinsthesis*], which can in this sense be called the "general thesis of the natural attitude," is "placed in brackets" (*Ideen* 53f./52f.).[24]

It seems to me that the meaning of this bracketing or cancellation [*Ausschaltung*] emerges most clearly when we distinguish between two levels.

The real world is generally regarded as the "*hic et nunc*" existing world, as the spatially and temporally extended individual world. In the first instance, therefore, we can exclude *spatial* reality. That does not mean, however, that we exclude the *spatial* determinations of the objects of interest; rather, it means that we regard the spatially determined object as an object that does not necessarily exist in the *individual-singular spatial world* (and hence, as an object that can in no case be discovered in the spatial world): in this way, we exclude that "kind" of transcendence that one tends to think of in association with this questionable, ambiguous term, namely, transcendence in the sense of spatial reality, or the reality of the "external world." Since this applies well to the example of the hallucinated object, we can also say that we regard yesterday's setting sun as if it were a hallucination. Obviously, for *our immediate con-*

---

[23] As for the relations between Vaihingers as-if perspective (which comes into question for us, of course, only with respect to those aspects that are independent of the pragmatic standpoint of its author) and phenomenology, see the work that is cited on page 165 [386–387].

[24] Our reductions, however, are performed in a somewhat different manner than Husserl's.

sciousness, the hallucinated sun remains just as "external" [195] as the sun of astronomy: indeed, the fact that it is and remains external is precisely what is characteristic and peculiar about hallucinations. The hallucinated sun is only distinguished from the sun that is presupposed by those empirical sciences that investigate the spatial world to the extent that it does *not* exist in the world of "real" space. It does not serve as a point of departure for the investigations of those sciences.

It is essential, however, that we exclude *all* of the points of departure for empirical research, because it is our goal to carve out a special region of the non-individual, hence non-empirical. That leads immediately to the second level of the reduction. Because the sun that does not exist in the real world, but nevertheless "exists" in *some* sense—not as a mere nothing of thought, possibly as a hallucination—is still something individual: it is *fixed* at an entirely determinate temporal point, namely at just that point at which it is hallucinated. Speaking more generally: everything perceived is individually determined to the extent that it is *perceived* at a determinate time. As I think back today to the setting sun that I perceived yesterday, that setting sun is individually determined by virtue of being bound to that particular moment of perceptual apprehension: even if it turns out to be a hallucination, indeed if I am conscious in the moment of apprehension that I am subject to hallucinations, nevertheless it is always intended as a *unique* occurrence, as an occurrence that is temporally fixed or that is an individual. *It is a unique, fixed moment of change in the external world, one that presents itself to me subjectively, beginning in this particular, individual, never-to-be-revisited moment and terminating at another such moment.* As it showed itself to me, and still shows itself, it is determined in the flux of time: because naturally it would be grasped in a perceptual act having a fixed place in the chain of my experiences, and having fixed boundaries determined by preceding, following, and simultaneous experiences: it is these experiences, and from our temporal perspective *these experiences alone* that temporally determine the setting sun. All later, more precise determinations must somehow be tied in with these experiences and with the perceptual act itself— [196] with the sensation [*Empfindung*], in Kant's terms. We even exclude this kind of individuality; hence, we no longer take any interest in the *act* in which the setting sun was for the first time experienced, neither in its psychophysical nor its psychological conditions. I regard even the experience of the act as if it did not exist.

What remains then? Obviously, what remains is the setting sun. I absolutely still imagine the *setting sun*, even if I do not regard it as existing in the real world, as something perceived *yesterday*, or as something that co-exists with certain of my other experiences. What I imagine remains a red, round something that is sinking below the horizon: *a unified complex of imagined qualities.*

Our insight into this basically simple state affairs stands in opposition to all kinds of traditional prejudices. As soon as one invokes "content" [*Inhalte*] in place of what we have described as imagined qualities, one comes very quickly to these prejudices. Because contents are "naturally" psychic contents, thus, *facts* of consciousness. Thus, a complex of qualities that is entirely unreal (and *given* only in real acts) is transformed unexpectedly into a real state of affair of consciousness [*Bewusstseinstatbestand*].

But do we not identify the complex itself as unreal, thus as mere appearance [*Schein*], finally as nothing? Our investigations cannot possibly be directed at a nothing. But this nothing is only a nothing from the perspective of the natural, empirical attitude. Nothing means nothing real, nothing existing in the individual-singular spatial and temporal world, and it is precisely what this way of speaking systematically overlooks that phenomenology seeks to investigate. What this way of speaking overlooks, however, ultimately exists for it as well. What it describes as "nothing" is, in the final analysis, a something. According to Husserl, "what appears as such is the obvious subject of the predication, and we ascribe to it (a thing-noema that is, however, anything but a thing) what we find as a characteristic in it, precisely, this nothingness. Here as everywhere else in phenomenology, one must simply have the courage [197] to take up what is actually to be detected in the phenomenon, as it affords itself, and to describe it *honestly*, instead of reinterpreting" (*Ideen* 221/212–13).

The ambiguity of the word 'real' (like the words 'actually' and 'really') also makes itself disturbingly noticeable here. At times, it refers to what is *truly* present, what is given in an immediately accessible manner; at other times, it refers to what is given sometime and perhaps somewhere in the factual-unique world of individuals. Our mere complex of qualities—one says—cannot be found in this "real" world of individuals, thus it is nothing "real," nothing truly existing and immediately given, but rather only a collection of sensations that have been interpreted in a certain way. As indubitable facts of consciousness, we must hold onto these. But we have no *immediate* knowledge of these sensations whatsoever; only a red, round, thingly [*dingliche*] unity is given to us. And it is certainly not a collection of impressions: "red" is a thingly quality, meaning a quality that occurs only in things (or in things and thing-noemata)[25]; in no real sense is it a sensation, as "round," "dual" [*doppelt*] and so forth, are sensations. Evi-

---

25 Only when one takes the thing from the outset as the *real* (meaning *genuinely* individual) thing, as Husserl appears to do, is it necessary to distinguish between thing and thing-noema: in my opinion, this distinction is neither appropriate nor permissible. It is highly artificial, perhaps simply incorrect to say that when a fairy-tale tells us that Little Red Riding Hood holds a basket in her hand, what we have is in fact a basket-noema.

dently, therefore, one should give the name "sensations" to certain obviously thingly qualities (as Hering has in fact done), merely because they are "subjective,"[26] from a physiological (or psychophysical) standpoint: a terminology that is at the very least misleading.

Let us then direct our attention to the sun that is now a merely imagined *unity of qualities*. We still have an entirely determined setting sun before us. It is no longer yesterday's sun, indeed it is no longer at any temporal location, [198] but otherwise—taken always in its pure immediacy—it remains *unchanged:* it is now a setting sun of the same "kind" as that of yesterday. It is the kind, the species, "setting sun like the one that I saw yesterday". Better still, it is what underlies such a speciation, a pure idea; in the new Husserlian terminology, it is an eidos, an essence. We have in fact fulfilled an eidetic intuition: each individual setting sun—even one that is hallucinated or given in a distorted memory—is a mere "individuation" of this essence or this idea.

But is it therefore true that what we have secured as an idea has no place in individual-singular or real time? In the final analysis, couldn't this be a mere abstraction?

Perhaps we abstract from the one determinate temporal moment only in the sense that we abstract from the determinate intensity of the color that confronts us, in which case the color nevertheless retains *some* degree of intensity. In this case, our supposedly "ideal" setting sun would also have some kind of location in real time. Only the question of *which* temporal location it had would have become indifferent for us. In just the same way, we are also occasionally persuaded that an event whose temporal location we have forgotten, but which is in all other respects perfectly "present," must have had some kind of temporal location. However, *that is certainly not the case here*. At first, of course, it looks very plausible: an event without a fixed temporal location—that is, simply an event that, viewed correctly, has *some* fixed temporal location. It is just that the location is arbitrary: within a given, temporally determinate whole, I can ascribe the event arbitrarily either to this moment or that moment. The unvarying "part" of this whole that I retain is then just the event "without" a fixed temporal location, just as the unvaryingly retained red, which always has some degree of intensity, and which I can always arbitrarily vary, becomes in this process a red "without" intensity.

---

26 Max Frischeisen-Köhler is apparently misled by this terminology, when, in his *Wissenschaft und Wirklichkeit*, he denies the subjectivity of sensations (Frischeisen-Köhler 1912, p. 219f., cf. Oesterreich 1910, p. 32f.).

But this beautiful analogy does not work. Certainly the red, to which I can attribute arbitrarily many degrees of intensity, can be thought of throughout this whole process as a real red: for instance, as the red of this disc that is now in front of me. [199] I can *effect* the variations of intensity *experimentally* on the disc; nevertheless, the red remains an individual. It remains temporally fixed for the duration of the process, and can be determined without thereby cancelling the process as such. Things are much different in the case of an event. An event cannot be treated in an analogous fashion. It passes and—as in our case—is finally gone, but I cannot experiment on what has passed by. If I want to do it anyway, however, if I want to carry out some kind of modification on it (even just a modification that affects the temporal location), then I must somehow make it "present" beforehand, I must somewhat isolate it from a rapidly vanishing time; from its absorption in the flow of time, I must have it as temporally isolated. In order to be able to "look back" on it, while in reality it has already disappeared, I must literally "present" it, meaning that I must place it *before* myself mentally.

In order to be able to carry out the process in question, however, it is presupposed that I have already managed to completely detach the event from the fixed temporal location that it occupies. The apparently so enlightening mental process rests, therefore, on a veritable *vicious circle*. The process which was to *lead* to de-individualization *already presupposes it:* from the outset, it is necessarily temporally indifferent to the object that was to be *made* indifferent vis-à-vis its particular temporal location, namely, by means of abstraction. The fact, embarrassing in itself, that I am driven away from the object in the flux of time must somehow be overcome. I must isolate it from the temporal flow; I must *present* it—but already from the outset, the essence of presentation implies *de-individualization*. The true analog of the object "without" fixed temporal location is not the red that (to the extent that the red "itself" is given directly, and not indirectly, by means of mere symbols) always has *some* degree of intensity, even though I do not know which; perhaps, rather, it is the red without an external casing [*Umhüllung*] or the roof without a house; just as the red can be given without an external casing, the roof can be given without the house. The perceived (and also the remembered) object is not freed from its temporal location merely through abstraction, but rather through authentic omission [*Weglassung*], or separation [*Trennung*]: this naturally presupposes that what is to be separated is "unified" beforehand; or better—since we cannot speak of an active [200] process of unification—that it has been *given* as "united," as a composite of independent entities, just as the house and roof, mountain and forest are in this sense *given together*—in contrast to the togetherness of a house and its front, or a mountain and a valley.

This corresponds precisely to our earlier results (p. 195; this volume p. 409): the fact that a certain given appears as an individual (i.e. singular, real) or is individually determined in its manner of givenness owes, in the really decisive cases, just to the circumstance that it is temporally bound to an act of apprehension and to its fixed place in the stream of experiences; it co-exists with a determinate, concrete experience and gets a fixed temporal location only by virtue of that concrete experience—and hence accidentally, one might say. In the absence of this temporal co-existence, a given object would be temporally indifferent, a mere quale that could just as well exist now, earlier, or even later. Without this temporal co-existence, it is merely such a quale[27], and it can be factually situated at this or that temporal location.[28] Examples of this can always be given. Often enough we know a previously perceived thing quite well in terms of its "content," but we are not in a position to assign it a fixed temporal location. Perhaps, though, we nevertheless give it *some* temporal location, just as we generally think of a roof as bound to *some* house or another. Or we let go of every relation to a coinciding experience, along with every relation to a temporal location—just as we can imagine the roof as quite distant from any corresponding house (and [201] so deprived of its function as a roof). In this case we have penetrated to the "timeless" or ideal *content* [*Gehalt*] of the perceived object, toward its "eidos" or "essence." The phenomenologist has to put this content, in its full purity, in his "line of sight." In thousands of cases in everyday life this line of sight is already appropriately directed, but it is continually mixed in with the natural attitude. One can recall, for example, the painter who clings, and only can cling, to the ideal content of the perceived landscape, but who does so in an attitude of "learning."

I choose this example because it lies particularly close to the experimental psychologist. When he is clear regarding the meaning of his experiments in the area of learning, he cannot possibly fail to recognize that a perceived object that is present in the manner of *something learned* has an entirely different meaning

---

27 Hans Driesch speaks, in an *essentially narrower sense*, of a "pure suchness" [*reine Solchheit*] (Driesch 1912, p. 84f.). On another occasion, I hope to be able to take up Driesch's interesting line of thinking, which relates to my investigations in many ways. The old term "idea" still seems to be the most suitable way of expressing this "suchness." Husserl's term "essence" [*Wesen*] is awkward in that it coincides with natural language use, which is oriented around *empirical* essences. For the unprejudiced, the *essence* of the color red is what is essential for the empirical red. Similarly in the case of electricity, warmth, etc.

28 More exactly: it can be regarded as a member of this or that sequence of events. The term 'temporal index' above means precisely this quality of being a member of a determinate sequence of events.

than it has in recollection. I recall the sequence of syllables that I learned yesterday: that means that the sequence of syllables as I learned it yesterday is present, wrapped in yesterday's act of learning,[29] "situated in a historical context of particular experiences," and thus individual, temporally determined, real. The opposite holds for the sequence of syllables that one knows "by heart," that are grasped in the manner of learning. When these have only just been learned, then it is entirely indifferent when, how often, and in what way these have been impressed on us. The question of whether the sequence of syllables is given uniquely or multiply is not relevant; we can completely *forget* the givenness of the sequences of syllables without forgetting the sequence "itself"—understandably enough, because it is the ideal, identical content that is intended in all acts, "without temporal designation," or, if one prefers, "timelessly."

Of course, these things are not lost on empirical researchers—even Elsenhans recognizes them. In the last paragraph, I have indeed quoted him almost verbatim (Elsenhans 1912, p. 358 f.; not incl. in this volume).

It is with a certain degree of joyful astonishment, therefore, that we find that our author himself is not a phenomenologist. [202] He nevertheless bears within him a seed, and doubtlessly the most important seed. In order to become a phenomenologist, he must of course draw the *consequences* of the just mentioned insight, namely, that his other opinions are incompatible with it. In this regard, I am thinking in particular of his theory of abstraction, which would then prove tobe not merely false, but superfluous.

For example, the syllable that is grasped in the "learning attitude," for instance the syllable "vil," already entirely suffices to allow us to grasp the factually given, individually perceived, read, and heard syllable "vil" as the "instantiation" (given sometimes with this temporal index, and sometimes with that) of an idea, namely, the idea "vil". In the same way, different, mutually identical sunsets can be regarded as differently temporally indexed instantiations of a single idea, the idea of a "thus and thus determined sunset," and which can be seen as such already on the basis of a single case—perhaps yesterday's sunset.

In this case, of course, Elsenhans would not have accused Husserl's theory of eidetic intuition of being an ill-advised metaphysics. It is in truth the exact opposite.

We must only be clear that each perceived or imagined individual, every *empirically given* object is already ideal from the outset, if not purely ideal then nevertheless ideal in an essential respect; that it can be viewed as the result of two

---

[29] Because I can only remember experiences [*Erlebnisse*] (cf. the thorough investigations of Gallinger 1914, pp. 11 f).

components, or—by way of an appropriate comparison—as the intersection point of two coordinates: a mere "what" or "quale," the "timeless" idea and an individualizing, temporally determining factor.

If one has made this clear, then one has also seen that the ideal and the universal cannot be developed or derived from the given empirical-individual, as had earlier been universally assumed. One sees, rather, that the ideal (and mediately, therefore, the universal) is already on-hand from the outset. It is literally true: "the 'pure essence' is there; we need merely to see it" (Elsenhans 1915, p. 234; incl. in this volume p. 347). *The whole real world is given to us in "timeless" ideas. That is the sense of what we described above as phenomenology's* [203] *"Copernican turn".*[30]

V Empirical and Phenomenological Questioning: The Fiction

With the foregoing remarks, we are conscious of having gone beyond Husserl on many essential points—hopefully not to the detriment of the matters at hand. Above all we have tried to avoid anything that could draw the popular accusation of 'Platonism'. Perhaps we will be branded instead as Aristotelian. This may indeed happen, but one should at least concede that we have managed to avoid the problem which makes the word 'Aristotelian' into an accusation in the first place, namely, the failure to do justice to the essence of empirical investigation by virtue of a "theory of ideas." We hope that we have done precisely the opposite, insofar as it is at least *a* task of phenomenological science to illuminate the *meaning* of the empirical method, to bring to clarity the conditions that "first make experience possible."[31]

---

30 Emil Lask (1911) invokes the Copernican turn in connection with Kant; his understanding of the Copernican turn stands relatively close to ours, only our procedure is much more radical. Ours is also a "two-element-theory", but we oppose idea and individuality rather than form and 'sensuous' content. In this way we not only achieve greater contact with empirical research, but also with those views of Lotze that Lask disapproves of (Lask 1911, p. 35). Concerning the meaning of the Kantian Copernican turn, see also the thorough investigations of Fritz Münch (1913, p. 6f.)

31 I must refrain from entering further into the many problems that arise here. One, however, is obvious: precisely as an *idealistic* philosophy, phenomenology does justice to empiricism and to the realism immanent within phenomenology itself. As a genuine idealism, it "assimilates" realism within itself—as Bruno Bauch has recently emphasized with respect to *transcendental* idealism (Bauch 1915, p. 116).

This becomes clear from a problem that seems at first to constitute a serious objection to our views.

We say that an individually presented (and thus perceived) object is a *divisible* collection of two things: its *ideal* content and [204] its *individualizing* determination. That would mean, then, that individuality does not belong *essentially* to the object. If however the object is presented as an individual, then it is obviously presented as something for which individuality is essential. Consequently, our claim leads to an absurdity and must be judged false.

This is a fallacy based on the inaccuracy of the expression. *Of course* the object is presented as something for which individuality is essential. This, however, only allows us to draw an entirely self-evident conclusion, namely, that the object that is characterized as individual in our presentation exhibits the characteristic feature that determines something for us as an individual—just as the object that is presented as a sphere exhibits the characteristic feature that determines something for us as spherical. It cannot mean, however, that it is *essential* to the object presented as an individual that it be an individual. Even the object that is presented (and perceived) as spherical does not always need to be a sphere.

It is well known enough: the individual and the presented individual are by no means the same. In nothing that is given as an individual do we find individuality as an *essential* determination, and we can never therefore specify with *absolute* certainty whether a determinate given that is characterized as temporally fixed (an eidos encountered in a determinate individuation) is in fact an individual or not. In order to determine this with *relative* certainty, i.e. with a reasonable degree of probability, a special method is necessary—namely, empiricism.

One generally regards the following question as typical for any empirical method: through which qualities (determinations) is this individually appearing something—perhaps the one that is now before me—characterized? It is certain that every such individually appearing something is characterized in some way from the outset. I already ascribe all kinds of qualities to it: for me, it is a *given complex of qualities* bound to an individualizing factor. Therefore it must necessarily first be asked: do these [205] *given qualities*, which are bound to this individualizing factor from my perspective, really correspond to this individualizing factor in truth? Or must they be regarded in whole or in part as *mere* ideas, floating together in the phenomenological air? By answering this question, we learn whether that "what" which looks to us like an individual actually is an individual—in agreement with our above formulation. Supposing that the answer is yes, then a given individual would be empirically determined. Supposing that the answer is no, then I must say that the so-constituted "individual" that was given to me was actually no individual at all, and I must place individuals of perhaps an entirely different constitution in its place (in the case of the hallucinated sun, psychophysical processes). I must bind the relevant individualizing factor in a different way.

All empiricism, however, is directed toward the binding of the ideal 'complex of qualities' to the individual. It asks: through which ideas is the individual given determined? Which ideas go hand in hand with it? It asks whether the "individuals" that appear for us as bound to determinate ideas are *in fact* individuals, i.e. whether they reveal themselves in all experiences as being individuals.

In any case, empiricism is always directed in some way toward the individuals for their own sake, toward individual reality as such. But it is absolutely reliant on the ideas.[32] [206] in order to determine the individual through the ideas (and how else could I possibly determine them?) I must already have grasped the ideas with completely clarity; I must everywhere attach a completely clear sense to them.

In this clarification of the meaning of ideas, which is nothing other than a precise exposition of qualities and the laws that attach to those qualities, and in the investigation into the possible syntheses of those qualities, we find the task of phenomenology. This task, which belongs to phenomenology rather than empiricism, has never clearly been seen before, because it has been confused with the inquiry into the formation and the analysis of *concepts* taken in an empirical-psychological sense.

Perhaps it would be wise to clarify this task *without appealing to any phenomenological terminology whatsoever*; thus, in language that is *incorrect, but immediately understandable*. No one doubts that the empirical world is given to us in a great abundance of possible combinations of extraordinarily few "features" or "qualities." In all of his determinations, the empiricist is inevitably brought back to something analogous to Locke's primary and secondary qualities. Remaining at first with the external world, geometrical-mechanical data come into question for us. Later, colors, tones, smells, and ultimately certain categorial "features" like thing, cause, etc., come into question for us.

All of these "qualities"—this word is of course taken here in an exaggeratedly wide sense—are set apart in a region that is entirely independent of empiri-

---

[32] So, if Rickert says that "we recognize the real precisely insofar as we acknowledge the unreal" (Rickert 1915a, p. 223), then we can agree with this in principle and at the level of its bare verbal signification. In spite of this, there naturally exists a huge difference: as we hope to show in this work, it appears to us above all that the proof of the ideal factors in knowledge must be carried out well in advance of a theory of judgment. Rickert makes concessions to traditional positivism much too early (cf. the remarks on p. 203 of this work; incl. in this volume p. 415). Rickert seems to me to have come closest to phenomenology at several places in his *Zur Lehre von der Definition* (Rickert 1915b). I intend to take this up in greater detail elsewhere.

cism (because, as presented ideas, they are entirely *independent* of the individuals that they determine, as we have seen).[33] Determining whether the crystal lying before me is an octahedron or not—that is the empirical task. Determining what qualities the octahedron has *as an idea*—that is the *extra-empirical* task that is presupposed by the empirical task. [207] This is a *phenomenological* task to the extent that it does not subject the spatial relations characteristic of the octahedron to a method that operates *principally* with conceptual symbols —namely, the *mathematical* method. While the mathematical method allows for a significantly simpler solution of the problem at hand, it leads back in its ultimate foundations to phenomenology.[34]

Determining whether the crystal lying before me is yellow or not—that is the *empirical* task. Determining what qualities the yellow has as an idea—for example, that it is bound on the one hand to a particular degree of brightness, and on the other hand to extension—is the corresponding phenomenological task.

Determining whether ideas like "contact," "order," "combination," "separation," "sequence," "freedom," "cause," etc., can be applied to this or that actually given fact or process—that is the empirical task. [208] Determining what is *meant* by these ideas: whether they have any meaning whatsoever (i.e. whether their "concepts" correspond to a genuinely ideal object, or are simply empty)

---

[33] We come back, therefore, to the "content," which is of course entirely ideal. Julius Guttmann's position on this matter, as it is developed in the sixth part of his *Kants Begriff der objektiven Erkenntnis* (1911) would come much closer to ours if Guttmann had taken his concept of content determinacy somewhat further.

[34] Like everything methodological, mathematics is of course rooted in *objectivities:* mathematical objects, however, are peculiar in that we can operate creatively with them without referring back to an ultimately foundational concrete intuition. This does not mean that this intuition is not in the final analysis important for the full *understanding* of mathematics as science; while mathematics per se does not form a branch of phenomenology, "foundational research" into mathematics does.

Incidentally, it is only on the basis of such a viewpoint that it is possible to explain how "Spielregelmathematik" theories can be established (for instance, in the work of Johannes Thomae; cf. Frege 2013, p. 96, §88 f). On the other hand, this view makes it equally possible to explain why *philosophically* inclined mathematicians are lead necessarily toward phenomenology. In my opinion, therefore, Frege's "realm of the objective, non-actual" is nothing other than the realm of phenomenology (Frege 2013, p. xviii). Perhaps a more detailed engagement with the penetrating investigations of these remarkable thinkers would convince figures such as Elsenhans (1915, p. 230 f.) and Messer (who, in rather positivistic fashion, curtly identifies the "ideal" objects of mathematics as objects that are "merely thought" (see for example Messer 1912a, p. 132) that the problems lies elsewhere than they think they lie. Compare this with Husserl, who does seem to conceive of the relationship between phenomenology and mathematics in the way that we do (*Ideen* 196/188 fn.).

and if so, which meaning they have—that is the phenomenological task. Because it is highly incorrect to say of a chemist, for example, that he learns the meaning of the concept "atomic bond" on the basis of *empirical* investigations: he must at least *believe* that he knows the meanings of "atom" and "bond" independently of these investigations. What he tries to grasp is just the *infinitely important* fact corresponding to the ideas that these concepts realize—just as all empiricism is directed toward determining that element from the realm of the possible that is present in the real world. The realm of the possible, however, falls under the jurisdiction of phenomenology.[35]

We occasionally call ideas "complexes of qualities," and we do so intentionally, in spite of the fact that this is an *incorrect* way of speaking: ideas can only be understood as complexes of qualities to the extent that the individualizations of ideas can be thought of as "qualities" of the corresponding *individuals*. Instead of the *far too widely used word* 'quality', it would be better to speak of "non-independent moments": non-independent—namely, with respect to the *individuals* to which they would therefore belong essentially, just as the natural world-view indeed presupposes. In truth, though, these moments do not belong *essentially* to the corresponding individuals (as we have said).

At this point, everything becomes quite simple: every given whole, even when it is only "posited in idea" (i.e. even when it is deprived of the moment of individualization) is, phenomenologically speaking, independent: an independent "essence," as Husserl says, an [ideal] concretum (*Ideen* 28f.).

[209] The non-independent moment—that can form a whole with only so many other non-independent moments, namely, the ones that are necessary for the independent givenness of the whole—therefore forms a *simple* ideal concretum, a phenomenological "ultimate" [*Letztheit*] (of which a homogeneously red ball would be an example).

Provided that it is given as it is, which is to say intuitively, in its "self," then I can analyze such a simple concretum: I can compare it with other ideas and I can bring to givenness the moments and relations that are "founded" in it

---

[35] Nicolai Hartmann's question as to what must be added to possibility in order to yield reality seems to be answered in this way (Hartmann 1915, p. 13).

According to the above, the possible is the sensuous ideal, i.e. the concrete-ideal and what is founded in it—an essential simplification of the concept of possibility. For a contrasting view, see Gallinger's *Das Problem der objektiven Möglichkeit* (1912) and Meinong's remarks on Gallinger in *Über Möglichkeit und Warscheinlichkeit* (1915, p. 152f.).

Driesch's concept of possibility (Driesch 1912, p. 73f) does not seem to me to have been completely worked out: a triangle whose angles add up to 360 degrees is not possible in our sense of possibility.

(and in these other ideas). This not only allows me to identify the original concretum with progressively more certainty (which is often very important). It also leads me to new ideas, up to the highest and most abstract: all theories of categories have their roots here.[36]

The entire real world, the world of all individuals, is *always* given to us in combinations of such simple ideal concreta or ultimates (combinations that are "intuitable" in comparatively few individual givennesses) and in combinations of the ideas founded in those concreta, independently of however the world may otherwise fluctuate, and whatever empirical laws the world may embody.

What we have, in any event, is a wealth of combinational possibilities and with those a virtually infinite task for phenomenology. Empiricism, by contrast, has to determine which of the intrinsically possible "complexes of qualities" determines an individual being or event (and the species of genera of beings and events) in a given instance, regardless of whether such a combination is actually given or not.

We note that we occasionally call ideas "timeless". Obviously this should only be taken to mean "non-temporally grasped ," because of course we can at least apply temporal determinations to all of our ideas. But the idea is always *something represented, an ideal object:* it is opposed to the presentation, the presenting act, which has the function of referring to the object and determining it referentially. This referential determination can be abstractively detached: as a mere determination it is then obviously *timeless* in an *authentic* sense, as it much it can still mean something temporal. One sees this most clearly in temporal determination [210] itself: the determination 7AM is not 7AM itself.[37] Genuinely timeless determinations (concepts in the narrowest sense) are as such naturally 'non-intuitive' and absolutely do not need to be accompanied by the represented object; in other words, their 'fulfillment' can, in certain circumstances, be completely lacking; more often this fulfillment is merely suggested; it is present in an incomplete way (in the form of so-called 'illustrative pictures'). The idea of a non-intuitive determination for which it is *essential* to have no ideal object is nonsensical.

---

[36] Elsenhans confuses the concretum with the individual when he says that is incomprehensible that there could be a concretum that could not be encountered in experience (Elsenhans 1915, p. 237; incl. in this volume p. 349).

[37] Bolzano's "representation in itself" [*Vorstellung an sich*] (as well as the Twardowskian concept of "representational content" [*Vorstellungsinhalt*] that is oriented around it oscillates between our idea and the authentically *timeless* determination mentioned above.

For the purposes of phenomenological insight, the individual and thus the *fixed* temporal location are matters of complete indifference, and it goes without saying that this holds just as much for those individuals to which I arbitrarily or non-arbitrarily ascribe a temporal location *other than the one that they actually have*; in other words, for fictions. Not because the fictional has a privileged position within phenomenology, but because for phenomenology the particular temporal (and in general, empirical) arrangement of the individuals in the world is a matter of indifference; for this reason I can orient myself phenomenologically just as easily to a fictitious world.[38]

It is, however, a very good litmus test. All of the truths that still persist in such a world are phenomenological truths; one sees here the difference from everything empirical quite clearly. Even if the furniture in my room began to dance in measured intervals, and a green sun moved in spirals at extreme velocity against a yellow sky forming an infinite plane, mathematical laws—even geometrical laws—would remain just as valid as they are now; and the yellow of the sky, as the instantiation of the idea 'yellow' would have the same position on the color spectrum as the one that it has now and that it always will have.

[211] Then again, the *meaning* of the law of gravity and of all physical and empirical laws in general would also survive in this fictional world. I could also bring this meaning to givenness as attached to its objects. What it *means* that gravitational acceleration is 9.8 meters per second is something that I can still easily make *intuitively* clear to myself, and once I have established for myself that the distance fallen is the square of the elapsed time, I can even *prove* this, at least under a presupposition. Namely, if I grasp the law merely as a law of meaning [*Sinngesetz*], a law that, like all mathematical and phenomenological laws, is valid merely for pure possibilities, and of course holds absolutely with respect to those possibilities. The possibilities lie in the ideas, and the ideas, as ultimate *meaning conferring foundations*, remain the same in all worlds that are given to me, be those worlds real or fictitious. The world of pure ideas thus furnishes the only conceivable orientation for each analysis that does not presuppose the correctness—be it factual or methodological—of the results of empirical research from the outset.

---

[38] According to our analysis, therefore, Vaihinger has things exactly reversed (Vaihinger 1911, p. 399 f.): "general concepts" are not fictions; rather, in order to speak sensibly about fictions, "general concepts"—meaning ideas, the roots of everything general—must already be presupposed. The uniqueness and the independence of ideas can be illustrated particularly clearly on the basis of fictions.

How could the world of naïve-practical realism, to which Elsenhans attributes a similar function, provide the same thing (cf. Johannes Volkelt 1915, p. 177)?[39] Admittedly, certain empirical laws—such as the laws that make up the "world of physics"—are put out of action in this world. This may unconsciously have been decisive for him, but otherwise the world of naïve-practical realism consists of a highly unclear mixture of phenomenological and naïve-empirical insights: that the water runs up the mountain appears just as or even more absurd to the naïve man than any pure law of ideas [*Ideengesetz*].

VI Apodictic Evidence and the Criterion

When we consider the foregoing in the correct light, the apodictic evidence of phenomenological claims goes without saying. Naturally this does not mean that for a [212] phenomenologist no error is possible. Even the mathematician occasionally makes errors, but only an extreme, grossly exaggerated psychologism could derive concerns regarding the particular form of mathematical certainty from this fact. Still less does this "secure a fully unassailable position for any opinion of any 'essence researcher' whatever" (Elsenhans 1915, p. 243; incl. in this volume p. 355). But the proposition that Elsenhans takes as the premise of this absurd consequence remains nevertheless true: if an eidetic connection [*Wesenszusammenhang*] has been *correctly* seen, then it can undergo no alteration through observation or induction (Scheler 1973, p. 49). Self-evidently! Could physical laws undergo any alteration on the basis of juridical laws? Naturally they could not, since they concern completely heterogeneous regions. But since it turns out that certain individuals "participate" in certain ideas and the lawful connections between ideas, the reverse is true: we laugh, or at least should laugh, at the empiricist who seeks to contest "essential propositions" such as '2 > 1' or 'to every concrete (real or apparent) movement belongs a velocity and a thing that is moved' on the basis of experiments. What holds with respect to ideas must also hold with respect to their empirical individuation. *A proposition that is false, however, does not even hold with respect to ideas and can obviously not be empirically confirmed.* If one understands this in terms of empirical control, it cannot be denied.

---

[39] If one reflects, from the standpoint of this text, on the question that Volkelt takes up with respect to the objects of the exact sciences, one will observe a very significant simplification of the problem.

In doubtful cases, furthermore, one can always use the simple criterion of the fictional world. Even in the fictional world orange takes its place in the color spectrum between red and yellow. For a *verité de fait*, on the other hand, meaning a proposition that can only be proven on the basis of real individuals, this is absolutely not the case. That mixing red and green together results in white can be seen just as little on the basis of fictional colors as real colors. This simply does not lie in the meaning of red and green. These colors do not come into consideration as ideas, but as things that are merely *determined* by ideas, things that lie, as it were, "behind the ideas," as real facts. The proposition is not equivalent to a proposition about the octahedron; it is a proposition about the crystal [213] that lies in the octahedron. Or does Elsenhans seriously want to contest the Lebnizian-Humean distinction between two broad classes of truths? Therefore, phenomenology does not guarantee an absolute freedom from error, but rather freedom from all sources of error that originate with the *empirical* method in particular.[40] We avail ourselves once again here of our somewhat oversimplified way of speaking: the phenomenologist, who makes "connections of essences" apparent, shows that a given, precisely delineated "property" [*Beschaffenheit*] or "quality" [*Qualität*]—insofar as it is and remains just that quality—includes the existence of another "quality". He reads off, so to speak, merely those characteristics [*Eigenschaften*] that lie in the quality. Only the unavoidable, but always in principle corrigible error of reading, the error which stems from his intellectual capacity, is properly *his* error.

The empiricist, on the other hand, characterizes *individuals* (and individual processes) through such "qualities." But the *individuals*—as we have already grasped in principle—are in and for themselves *independent* of the given "qualities". The individual that is given as red or square (intuitively) does not necessarily need to be red or square, however certainly it is given to me as red and square; and I have no way of resolving this without presupposing the validity of empirically discovered laws, thus without shifting the problem to a level of epistemic dignity [*erkenntnismässigen Dignität*] different from the one at which the original knowledge was derived. From this simple fact, that there is no *absolutely* certain means of determining whether an individual actually has the qualities that are given to me and that I attribute to it follows all of the possibilities for error that are *specifically* characteristic of empiricism. Naturally, therefore, it is the goal of each methodological empiricism to avoid at all cost the errors that

---

[40] I acknowledge that the passage from Geiger (1913, p. 571) that Elsenhans cites (1915, p. 246; incl. in this volume p. 356) is misleading: Geiger appears to hold *induction* solely responsible as the source of error in the empirical method. In principle, however, induction has precisely the opposite task, that of attenuating the source of empirical error.

flow out of this general possibility for error. We all know to what great extent empiricism has reached this goal through the systematic application of the *inductive method*, [214] but we must not forget that it can never *absolutely* reach this goal. Experience is and remains merely an "infinite process," a method of approximation. It is always possible that the domain of experience is analogous to the "blue" mountain in the distance, that is, that *qualities are actually distributed differently* than they appear to be from my perspective.

If on the other hand I am occupied with *qualities as such*, as the phenomenologist is, then it is in the essence of my subject matter that this source of error is excluded. Thus, I see something "as" a mountain and "as" blue, and it is necessarily accompanied with all of the qualities of "mountainness" and "blueness". It has a valley and a degree of brightness as a matter of "essential law". The ideal state of affairs is in each case completely given; we merely highlight certain aspects of it.[41]

According to Elsenhans, evident assertions concerning the color orange would make use of earlier experiences (Elsenhans 1915, p. 246; incl. in this volume p. 356–357). Naturally, no one would challenge that in our assertions, we make use of earlier, psychologically continuous experiences. But what is alone in question here is what the truth[42] of the state of affairs at issue is grounded upon. And to *this* we answer that it is grounded solely in ideal "qualities" themselves, not in psychological processes, just as the truth of a mathematical fact is grounded in certain mathematical ideas (and ultimately in phenomenologically grasped ideas), and not in the use of logarithmic tables, which merely serve to place this fact comfortably at my disposal. Or is it seriously maintained that there could somewhere be an instance of orange that, without ceasing to be orange, would not have the quality of lying between yellow and red? [215] Surely not. But a red that does not result in grey when mixed with green, but rather brown—that could very well be discovered, however improbable it may be.

But how do I *transmit my phenomenological insights to others?* Elsenhans (1915, p. 262; incl. in this volume p. 369) is quite correct: objective criteria are necessary for this purpose; elements that can be 're-lived' by any thinking subject. And phenomenology does not simply have such moments *at its disposal*.

---

[41] I believe that this conception of things also eliminates some of the difficulties that Volkelt (1915, p. 159 ff) locates in the phenomenological method. I confess, incidentally, that I have occupied myself with Volkelt's thought particularly intensively: I have him to thank for the revision of my position with regard to phenomenology, and indirectly therefore for inspiring the ideas presented here.

[42] Elsenhans apparently succumbs here to the confusion to which Volkelt (1915, p. 133) is also subject.

Quite the contrary: it has set itself the task of creating such criteria in areas in which they were not previously available. Its constant emphasis on the need to refer back to intuition, to the things themselves—to the ideal concreta—is also important in this context. Naturally the areas to which it seeks to apply its criteria are, as such, very difficult. And no one will be surprised to learn that phenomenology often fails. In principle, however, phenomenology approaches the "highest" ideas—like justice, truth, etc.—in the same way that we saw in our simple color example, namely, with an eye toward verification: it proceeds from certain available concrete-real details—thus, in our example, from "this" color tablet—and brackets the individualizing moments. Objects cannot be analyzed as they are found in *the* world, in which they interact with one another and can "develop" new properties that do not lie essentially in the given objects themselves. Then, the pure ideal concreta are there, and it is on these that I carry out certain "abstractions," or "acts of foundation" [*Fundierungen*], the sense and justification of which I can again make clear by means of intuitive examples, always proceeding only gradually, so that readers everywhere will be capable of immediately experiencing what is to be understood and (more importantly) of orienting their terminology accordingly. Ultimately, therefore—and with all due qualifications—I should be able to "exhibit" truth and justice just as easily as I can present (the ideal content of) red and yellow. What I mean to say is that either this is the method for dealing [216] with philosophical and philosophical-psychological problems, or there is none.

But—some have objected—if phenomenology occupies itself with determinations of meaning [*Sinnfestellungen*], then does it not simply proceed according to formal logic? Indeed, is phenomenology itself not logic? This is a particularly serious misunderstanding, because phenomenology does not attempt to demonstrate the absurdity that results from certain pre-given definitions and judgments, completely indifferent to whether these are true in themselves, or on what their truth is grounded. Rather, just as empiricism strives to capture the "originary" foundations of all individualizations, phenomenology seeks the ultimate "originary" foundations on which all definitions rest and must rest, insofar as their mere sense, their intuitive-ideal content is in question. For the phenomenologist, meaning is something *positive*; it is not a mere absence of absurdity.

That phenomenology is not logic, however, emerges already from our example. Does logic have anything to do with color? Or with justice? Or with mountains? I do not think it does. The reverse is rather the case: at the level of its ultimate foundations, logic is entirely rooted in phenomenology.[43]

---

[43] Richard Hönigswald has rightly stressed (1913, p. 228) that the meaningful as such is still far

VII Phenomenology and Empirical-Descriptive Psychology

All of the foregoing shows that phenomenology does not contest the legitimacy of empiricism. The domain of phenomenology is totally and completely different. But doesn't phenomenology attempt to challenge *one* of the empirical sciences, namely, empirical psychology? Doesn't it try to claim for itself questions that one previously assigned to empirical-descriptive psychology? Indeed, it does do so, but only because one has so far grouped all sorts of things under the heading of empirical psychology that probably have nothing [217] essential to do with psychology, and which certainly have nothing essential to do with empiricism. One also confused here the grasp of the individual fact with that of the ideal content "under" which it is grasped: one called both of these things perception, in particular, "inner" or self-perception, or even self-*observation*. Later time periods will need to have explicit recourse to the *historical* standpoint—and will have to refer, in particular, to the predominance of misguided theories of abstraction—in order to understand how one could have seriously believed that what the word "intention" [*Absicht*] signifies (the word as such of course being completely indifferent) could be observed, whereas it is certainly just as little observable as the number π, or virtue.

Therefore, it is clear that observation *underscores*, so to speak, the *temporal-individual* moment that already lies in perception (and memory). To give the word 'observation' a meaning in which the relation to what is individual-factual is *not* included conflicts from the outset with all reasonably practicable linguistic usage. I observe—perceptually or in memory—how a thus or thus determined [*beschaffenes*] individual thing, across a certain stretch of time, either remains constant as far as the "qualities" [*Beschaffenheiten*] that are given to me, or is transformed, taking on further, different qualities. To observe means to perceive an individual with an eye toward grasping the *transformations* that it undergoes within a given time, taking constancy as the limiting case of change. Thus can I also observe myself, my conscious-psychic changes. This can only means, however, that I observe how my ego [*Ich*]—or, if one prefers, my stream of consciousness—is qualified in ever new and different ways. For instance, just a few seconds ago, I could remember the title of a newspaper article that interested me

---

from being true. We go further than this: for us, the ideally meaningful, per se, has nothing do with judgments and thought.

yesterday; now, however, I cannot, as much as I try... This is a genuine self-observation, cast in the form of empirical description.

And what have I thus observed? Surely, that my consciousness is now differently determined than it was shortly before. The particular "quale," the "unity of qualities" in which [218] my consciousness is given to me, has given way to a different unity of qualities. Here as well, then, we have a combination of purely "qualitatively" determined aspects, on the one hand, and individualizing factors on the other hand. This surely has to be the case, if indeed we are correct that everything is given in the form of separable, intrinsically temporally indifferent "qualities," that is, in ideal concreta, autonomous ideas. In the case of the memory, in fact, memory as such (namely, memory of "this kind") is already given to me, according to its idea, and thus as the ultimate foundation for the classification of actually occurring memories. Furthermore, it is *completely* given to me, just as in particular cases of duality, duality as such is *completely* given, and just as in particular instances of a shade of red, the shade of red as such is given to me. And I can, indeed I *must* isolate this idea, I must lift it out of the flux of time. I must do this whenever I want to fix the results of my observations. In so doing, I am still obviously empirically oriented; I am directed, as it were, through the idea toward the individual process—I describe what takes place in me during that time, so as, perhaps, to compare it with earlier similar processes and in this way to be able to grasp empirical laws. As we have already stressed, however, similarity, just like equality, leads back to *identity*, to the identity of common ideal determination. Thus, we are again back with the idea. It is here precisely from the very start. And if this is so, then one should not seek to grasp the idea in a mere "vague intention," but rather in the full clarity of its "concrete" intuition, on the ground of genuine phenomenological analysis.

One indeed recognizes this here and there, but tries to dismiss it as the mere analysis of meanings or concepts, as a self-evident triviality. Phenomenology—particularly psychological phenomenology—appears as "the attempt to give reliable conceptual foundations to modern descriptive psychology." Apart from the fact, however, that in phenomenology it is never a matter of mere "concepts," but of *concrete* "things themselves" that one can rightly oppose to concepts (in the standard sense of the word), this characterization actually does nothing more than lower the value of a fundamentally important matter through the use of terminology. [219] In point of fact, of course, with phenomenology it is a question of the creation of such a reliable "conceptual" foundation for many fields, including, among others, psychology. But what would we say to someone who—merely because he happened to lack the organ for mathematics—proposed to capture the essence of mathematics by describing it as an overly-subtle and highly unpleasant discipline, which nevertheless has the role of providing modern natural science with reliable conceptual foundations? Indeed, phenomenology has this role with respect to psychology no less than mathematics does with respect to natural science.

A The "Picture Theory" as Example

Or does one seriously believe that everything is "actually" by and large in wonderful order? To be sure, physics can also be carried out *up to a certain point* without mathematics, but one should not carry it out in this way *as a matter of principle and in general*. Modern *empirical* psychology—which must as far as possible be experimental and folk psychology—certainly has many bright sides, but these are only found in a few, fundamentally quite narrowly delimited areas. I could give many examples of this.[44] I will take the one that lies nearest to hand, which even belongs to our topic in a second sense, because it originates from the essay against which our efforts are directed here. Elsenhans, the author of a psychological compendium that is, in its own way, excellent, and that is absolutely *on* and even *above* the level of traditional psychology, rejects in all seriousness the theory of "intentionality of presentation" [*Intentionalität der Vorstellung*] and gives preference instead to the "picture theory" [*Bildertheorie*] (Elsenhans 1915, p. 270 f.; incl. in this volume p. 375).

At first, the *perceived* thing is simply there. With this, our author finds no problem, except the one that he characterizes as *epistemological*. Only when we form a presentation, in the narrowest sense of the word, do we succeed in "intending" [*meinen*] a thing, namely, the *perceived*. [220] But this means only that we have a *mental picture*. We refer this picture to the thing simply on the basis of its *similarity* with what was previously perceived.

But is this talk of pictures really to be taken in such a literal sense? A picture is at best only a picture, a mere likeness.

The thing is somewhat jagged and is made out of metal. The picture is similar to it, thus must also be jagged and made out of metal. At the same time, as Elsenhans explicitly says, it is in me; "in me," however—for the *naïve* (and Elsenhans refers to the naïve quite explicitly)—in my consciousness, in the sense of my conscious, inner life. But is there jagged metal in my consciousness?

Or is the picture not jagged and not made of metal? Therefore, in what does the similarity consist? Only in the fact that it represents the object, just like every

---

[44] In this regard, and in relation to the whole section, see the work that is mentioned on page 165 above [this volume 386–387].

picture represents its object. Some portion of the thing's qualities must also remain the same here; the white-grey color no less than the particular form. But form and color are also not to be found within my inner life.

Suppose, however, that we did in fact have such a picture. It would be something that could not accomplish what it was supposed to accomplish. Because as a picture it must somehow be similar to, be alike, or agree with, the original.

However, we already know that all agreement or equality refers back to identity, namely, to the identity of *ideal representational content*. This must also be valid for the agreement of picture and object. "Something is a picture of something," in fact, means nothing other than that it has entirely or essentially the same representational content. Both are presented by means of the same *ideal unity*. And since one will probably not recognize ideas that are given otherwise than representationally, one must say: *the picturing function leads back to representation, not the other way around.*[45] It is in fact impossible to understand [221] what the talk of pictures in general is supposed to mean without reference back to representation. "This is the picture of a cat" means only that I represent a cat on the basis of it. In other words, the picture theory of representation involves a veritable *circulus vitiosus*. It is absolutely nothing more than a parable, a coarsely naturalistic parable that owes its dissemination to this coarse naturalism alone, but whose dissemination proves very little in its favor; just as little, for example, as is proved by the coarse naturalism of the image of pressure exerted on someone's psyche, or other arguments in this style.

That I am unable to endorse Elsenhans' argument against the theory of intentionality, made from the standpoint of an empirical epistemology, has hopefully become so clear on the basis of our previous considerations that it would be superfluous to emphasize it yet again. Ultimately, it came down to the foundation of the questions that are particularly meaningful for *psychology*.

Külpe once sought to briefly characterize phenomenology in the following way: "Facts, and not merely words, mean something, and phenomenology is oriented around this meaning" (Külpe 1914, p. 143). Note further that what is meant here by facts is not authentic or individual facts, but rather what is *ideally given*, which is in fact the crux of the matter. All phenomenology—as we have expressed it—is directed toward the *ideal* components of what is presently given, toward the meaning content, the *sense* of the phenomenon. This is phenomenology in the original meaning of the word.

---

[45] It is noteworthy that such a resolute opponent of the picture theory as Heinrich Rickert could miss this important objection. It is not the case, as Rickert says (1915, p. 129 f.) that the "content" of the representation "corresponds" to the perception. Rather, they are ideally one.

In the same place, Külpe stresses the necessity of a more precise description of the phenomenological method and, in this spirit, directs a series of question to the supporters of phenomenology.

Apart from the actual goals of the present work, I hope to have made a contribution here toward answering at least *a few* of these questions.

References

Bauch, Bruno (1911): "Zum Problem der allgemeinen Erfahrung." In: *Studien zur Philosophie der exakten Wissenschaften*. Heidelberg: Winter, pp. 76–107.
Bauch, Bruno (1915): "Schlussbemerkung zu meiner Diskussion mit A. Messer." In: *Kant-Studien* 20, pp. 302–304.
Cassirer, Ernst (1911): *Das Erkenntnisproblem in der Philosophie und Wissenschaft der neuern Zeit* Vol. 2. Berlin: Bruno Cassirer.
Cassirer, Ernst (2004): *Substance and Function & Einstein's Theory of Relativity*. William Curtis Swabey and Marie Collins Swabey (Trans.). New York: Dover.
Driesch, Hans (1912): *Ordnungslehre: ein System des nichtmetaphysischen Teiles der Philosophie. Mit besonderer Berücksichtigung der Lehre vom Werden*. Jena: Diederichs.
Elsenhans, Theodor (1912): *Lehrbuch der Psychologie*. Tübingen: Mohr.
Elsenhans, Theodor (1915): "Phänomenologie, Psychologie, Erkenntnistheorie." *Kant-Studien* 20, pp. 224-275.
Frege, Gottlob (2013): *Basic Laws of Arithmetic*. Philip A. Ebert and Marcus Rossberg (Trans.). Oxford: Oxford University Press.
Frischeisen-Köhler, Max (1912): *Wissenschaft und Wirklichkeit*. Leipzig/Berlin: Teubner.
Gallinger, August (1912): *Das Problem der objektiven Möglichkeit*. Leipzig: Barth.
Gallinger, August (1914): *Zur Grundlegung einer Lehre von der Erinnerung*. Halle an der Saale: Niemeyer.
Geiger, Moritz (1913): "Beiträge zur Phänomenologie des ästhetischen Genusses." In: *Jahrbuch für Philosophie und phänomenologische Forschung* 1, pp. 567-684.
Geyser, Joseph (1909): "Logistik und Relationslogik." In: *Philosophisches Jahrbuch* 22, pp. 123–143.
Guttmann, Julius (1911): *Kants Begriff der objektiven Erkenntnis*. Breslau: Marcus.
Hartmann, Nicolai (1915). "Logische und ontologische Wirklichkeit." In: *Kant-Studien* 20, pp. 1–28.
Hönigswald, Richard (1913). "Prinzipien der Denkpsychologie." In: *Kant-Studien* 18, pp. 205-245.
Husserl, Edmund (2001a): *Logical Investigations* I. J. N. Findlay (Trans.). London/New York: Routledge.
Husserl, Edmund (2001b): *Logical Investigations* II. J. N. Findlay (Trans.). London/New York: Routledge.
Kant, Immanuel (1998): *Critique of Pure Reason*. Paul Guyer and Allen Wood (Trans.). Cambridge: Cambridge University Press.
Külpe, Oswald (1914): *Die Philosophie der Gegenwart in Deutschland*. Leipzig: Teubner.

Lask, Emil (1911): *Die Logik der Philosophie und die Kategorienlehre; eine Studie über den Herrschaftsbereich der logischen Form.* Tübingen: Mohr.

Linke, Paul Ferdinand (1901): "Hume's Lehre vom Wissen." In: *Philosophische Studien* 17, pp. 624-673.

Linke, Paul Ferdinand (1912): *Die phänomenale Sphäre und das reale Bewusstsein.* Halle an der Saale: Niemeyer.

Linke, Paul Ferdinand (1916): "Phänomenologie und Experiment in der Frage der Bewegungsauffassung." In: *Jahrbuch für Philosophie und phänomenologische Forschung* 2, pp. 1–20.

Locke, John (1996): *An Essay Concerning Human Understanding.* Kenneth Winkler (ed.). Indianapolis/Cambridge: Hackett.

Meinong, Alexius (1915): *Über Möglichkeit und Wahrscheinlichkeit.* Leipzig: Barth.

Messer, August (1912a): *Geschichte der Philosophie vom Beginn der Neuzeit bis zum Ende des 18. Jahrhunderts.* Leipzig: Quelle und Meyer.

Messer, August (1912b): "Husserls Phänomenologie in ihrem Verhältnis zur Psychologie." In: *Archiv für die gesamte Psychologie* 22, pp. 117-129.

Messer, August (1914): *Psychologie.* Stuttgart/Berlin: Anstalt.

Messer, August (1915): "Zur Verständigung zwischen Idealismus und Realismus." In: *Kant-Studien* 20, pp. 299-302.

Metzger, Arnold (1915): *Untersuchung zur Frage der Differenz der Phänomenologie und des Kantianismus.* Dissertation: Jena.

Münch, Fritz (1913): "Erlebnis und Geltung." In: *Kant-Studien* Ergänzungsheft 30.

Oesterreich, Konstantin (1910): *Die Phänomenologie des Ich in ihren Grundproblemen.* Leipzig: Barth.

Rickert, Heinrich (1915a): *Der Gegenstand der Erkenntnis: Einführung in die Transzendentalphilosophie.* Tübingen: Mohr Siebeck.

Rickert (1915b): *Zur Lehre von der Definition.* Tübingen: Mohr Siebeck.

Scheler, Max (1973): *Formalism in Ethics and Non-Formal Ethics of Value.* Manfred Frings, Robert Funk (Trans.). Evanston: Northwestern University Press.

Schmied-Kowarzik, Walther (1912): *Umriß einer neuen analytischen Psychologie und ihr Verhältnis zur empirischen Psychologie.* Leipzig: Barth.

Schuppe, Wilhelm (1878): *Erkenntnistheoretische Logik.* Bonn: Weber.

Sigwart, Christoph (1889). *Logik* II. Freiburg: Mohr.

Stern, William (1911): *Die differentielle Psychologie in ihren methodischen Grundlagen.* Leipzig: Barth.

Vaihinger, Hans (1911): *Die Philosophie des Als Ob.* Berlin: Reuther und Reichard.

Volkelt, Johannes (1915): "Der Weg zur Erkenntnistheorie." In: *Zeitschrift für Philosophie und philosophische Kritik* 157, pp. 129–546.

Ziehen, Theodor (1913): *Erkenntnistheorie auf psychophysiologischer und physikalischer Grundlage.* Jena: Fischer.

Translated by Andrea Staiti
Theodor Elsenhans.[1]
Phenomenology and the Empirical

Phänomenologie und Empirie
Kant-Studien 22, pp. 243–261 (1918)
[243] The position of phenomenology in contemporary philosophy is significant enough to secure for it a scientific interest that goes beyond the exposition of isolated substantive disagreements. Concerning Linke's attack on a previous essay of mine devoted to this topic (Elsenhans 1915; incl. in this volume p. 339–381), I must refer readers to the difference in fundamental assumptions that comes to light therein and recommend that the reader compare the arguments made on both sides. What's more, I have no knowledge of the extent to which the founder of phenomenology would subscribe to Linke's analysis. Nevertheless, for the sake of clarifying the whole issue, it seems appropriate to briefly take up the decisive points regarding Linke's argument and the position of phenomenology within science in general.

I The Concept of Experience and Givenness

The first decisive point for Linke is the claim that there exists a "vision of essence" that allegedly grasps ("pure") givennesses on the basis of a non-empirical method, and this despite the fact that I characterize the connection of 'non-empirical' and 'given' as phenomenology's weakest point. Somewhat daringly [244] Linke sees in this vision of essence phenomenology's strongest point.

It is correct that much depends here on the *concept of experience*. I am pleased to acknowledge the priority that the phenomenologist gives to the "highly noteworthy rule, never to depart from natural language without necessity." (Linke 1916; incl. in this volume p. 385–431) Nevertheless, we will have to take our bearings from the meaning that is at issue here, that is, the meaning that phenomenology attributes to the multivalent word 'experience' by way of delineating its basic standpoint and that is determined by the contrast of 'empirical' and '*a priori*', of empirical and 'pure' givenness. In the contemporary idiom, these concepts are absolutely determined by the meanings bestowed upon them by Kant; but Kant's concept of experience lumps together two dif-

---

[1] [For biographical information on Elsenhans, see p. 13–15 of this volume.]

ferent meanings of the word. Kant oscillates between these meanings already in the famous first sentences of the second edition of the *Critique of Pure Reason:* experience as the processing of "the raw material of sensory impression into cognition of objects" and experience as basically[2] coincident with the sensation through which our cognitive faculty is set to work to begin with. The first of these is the genuinely Kantian concept of experience, the one that stands at the center of his critical analyses. Kant employs this first concept of experience when he determines the categories as the principles of a possible experience, or when he transitions from the judgment of perception to the judgment of experience, which is the only universal and necessary form of judgment and which is intended in all of those passages in which Kant discusses experiential cognition or 'empirical' science. When we deal at present with the relationship between phenomenology and empirical psychology, the latter can only be understood (presupposing a connection with existing terminology) as the intellectual processing of the 'raw sensory material' that is 'given' to inner perception.[3]
[245] In this way, the concept of *givenness* finds its appropriate place. What is given is what we find before us, what is present without our active cooperation, what is there before our processing activity is directed toward it. The concepts of receptivity and spontaneity, therefore, pertain respectively to 'sensibility', through which an object is 'given' to us, and to 'intellect', through which an object is 'thought'.

It is certainly true, however, that Kant calls the given an 'empirical given', or what is 'given in experience'. It is also correct that in various passages Kant contrasts this 'empirical given' with another given. Indeed, the 'empirical given' is contrasted partly with 'being given *a priori*' and partly with 'being given as thing-in-itself' [*Ding an sich*] or 'in and of itself' [*an sich selbst*].[4] There is no doubt that the given in the authentic sense for Kant is the 'empirical given,' and hence that the addition of 'empirical' (which in this context can mean nothing but the fact that the given is conditioned by the sensation, i.e. by experience in the second sense of this concept) specifies the mode in which the given is found. If Linke now believes that he can infer from Kant's use of the phrase 'empirical given' that Kant accepts a kind of non-empirical given in the phenomeno-

---

[2] Although here we can disregard completely the difficult question concerning the relationship between outer and inner experience and between outer and inner sense.
[3] I believe that I have shown in my essay (Elsenhans 1915, p. 240f.; incl. in this volume p. 351f.) that we cannot make an exception of 'description'.
[4] The first term of the contrast is particularly evident in the abovementioned passage of the *Critique of Pure Reason*, also quoted by Linke. The second term of the contrast is present particularly in the antinomy of pure reason (Kant 1998, B 401f.).

logical sense, this seems to me completely incorrect. Kant does not have in mind the being-given of a "transcendental object" (Kant 1998, B 404) inaccessible to all cognition. Not even the Kantian 'being-given' of the *a priori* can be understood in the sense of the 'pure givens' of phenomenology, the essence of which is supposed to be cognized in the phenomenological attitude. Kant failed to deal fundamentally with the problem of how we become aware of and cognize the *a priori*. Fries and his followers were the ones who first placed this important issue at the core of epistemological inquiry. However, when Kant brushes against this issue, when he hints at the way in which [246] the *a priori* is given, he uses phrases that—contrary to his fundamental rejection of any involvement of the empirical in the analysis—can only be interpreted in empirical-psychological terms.[5] It is therefore impossible to avoid the following conclusion: the *a priori* has to be the object of an empirical science. Not to the extent that it provides the *foundation* for a universal and necessary cognition, admittedly, but certainly to the extent that it is *given*, in the above sense.

From what we have argued so far it also follows that the attempt to summon Locke as witness for a non-empirical given shifts the focus of the problematic at stake and places it in an odd light. (Linke 1916, p. 172 f.; incl. in this volume p. 391 f.) The following argument is certainly correct: in his attempt to prove that there are no innate ideas from the fact that there is no *consensus omnium*, Locke speaks about something that originates neither in sensation nor in reflection, i.e., something whose origin is by no means in 'experience'. However, all of Locke's analyses of this matter reveal quite unmistakably that he is not considering the possibility of 'pure givens', but rather the possibility of something innate that could be found, for instance, in babies, primitive people, educated and uneducated people. Locke determines the non-existence of this innate element[6] in the same experiential manner that he determines the existence of something that appears in the real world. Thus, the problem of knowledge for Locke becomes the problem of the origin of our ideas [*Vorstellungen*] and he sets out to solve this problem on the basis of an empirical-psychological method. The view that he opposes in his fight against innate 'ideas' is *not apriorism*, but rather *nativism*. The problem at issue here is not the form of our cognition of ideas, but the origin of ideas. The nativist can be an outspoken empiricist with respect to his form of cognition (in the same sense in which the phenomenologist refuses to let "empirical science" stretch to include his

---

5 On this matter see my essay on Fries and Kant (Elsenhans 1906, p. 107 f.).
6 Including mathematical principles (Locke 1996, p. 25).

"pure givens")[7] the moment that he considers the innate (as Locke would have it [247]) as something that is found experientially in the nature of human beings. On this account, innate ideas would naturally become objects of inquiry for the experiential sciences.

As far as *ordinary language* is concerned, finally, it does not seem to me to argue for an extension of the concept of given to the non-empirical. The phrase '*Erfahrungen machen*'[8], from which Linke takes his bearings, means less the 'grasp and the awareness' of something 'given *hic et nunc*' than the conscious accumulation of effects and counter-effects experienced by the speaker and agent in his interplay with the environment, as well as the application of the conscious or unconscious inferences drawn from this accumulation to certain causal nexuses manifesting themselves in that environment. The 'experienced' person is not the person who has had a lot of experiences, but the person who, on the basis of the impressions he has had, surveys the nexus of things in order to choose what is right in the given moment. Every lived experience [*Erlebnis*], and hence every 'given' belongs in 'experience' [*Erfahrung*] in this sense. It belongs to the essence of experience that what is given in the present moment [248] is related to what was given beforehand and that the content of experience is determined by the mutual relationship of such givens. With respect to *this* aspect of its form, 'common experience' is nothing but a preliminary stage of experiential science. However, phenomenology wants to distinguish itself precisely from experiential science, in that, by putting out of play the whole world actually found in experience, it sets out to grasp 'essential states-of-affairs' [*Wesensver-*

---

7 For this reason the appeal to Cassirer's analyses on Locke (Cassirer 1907, 258 f.) is also displacement of the problem. In the fourth book of the *Essay* considered here Locke deals explicitly with "Knowledge and Truth." Incidentally, the extent to which Locke remains an empiricist also in this section seems to me evident precisely in the passages quoted by Cassirer. The fact that we cannot attain any "certain cognition of universal truths regarding natural bodies" and that "our reason can only bring us very little beyond the particular state-of-affairs" does not depend on limits of experience as such determined by some epistemology, but rather on the inability of our senses to penetrate the inside of bodies further than they have so far and, in so doing, attain precise and distinct ideas of their 'primary qualities' beyond our uncertain attempts. "But while we lack senses acute enough to discover the minute particles of bodies and to give us ideas of their fine structure, we must be content to be ignorant of their properties and ways of operation, being assured only of what we can learn from a few experiments." (Locke 1996, p. 246 f.). Hence, Locke is not concerned with fundamental limits of experiential science, but rather with technical limits, as it were, limits that can be partly overcome, for instance, through a perfection of the microscope and that perhaps have already been overcome by creatures in other parts of the universe (Locke 1996, p. 246). It seems to me that here Cassirer could not entirely avoid the temptation of projecting back his own perspective on an earlier, more naïve system.

8 [Translator's note: Literally: to make experiences.]

halte] with immediate insight. Thus, it is apparent that in grounding this standpoint by appealing to a non-empirical given, phenomenology finds no support, at least not from ordinary language.

However, Linke's proposed reference to ordinary language is obviously not decisive. Every researcher has the right, when he coins new concepts, to occasionally create new terms or to change or extend the existing terms according to the new concepts. On the other hand, it is then all the more legitimate to ask a deeper question, namely, whether with the renewal of terminology the envisioned *goal* has been actually attained. When phenomenology, as a "descriptive science of pure experiences," emphasizes that it deals with 'givens', namely, non-empirical givens, then, if we abstain from all terminological disputes, the fundamental *intellectual motif* is that the results of phenomenology should have the same reliability and immediate investigability as we find with the sensory perception of a given, or at least roughly the same. Thereby, phenomenology claims to secure for the whole science of philosophy a point of departure that lies beyond all logical controversy about the issues. 'Pure essences' are indeed out there, we just need to see them. For Husserl, this immediate seeing as "originally giving consciousness" is the "ultimate source of legitimacy of all cognition".[9] But precisely this goal of a philosophical cognition surpassing all others in immediacy and reliability fails to be attained for the following reason: the possibility of starting with the 'evidence' of a given that is *per se* illuminating for everyone *is annulled by the pretension of an 'attitude' that is by no means illuminating for everyone, but that is necessary in order to see this 'given' in the first place.* [249] Whoever is unable to see a given of sensory experience lacks, at least in the moment of his attempt, a normal sensory apparatus. Would it be possible to affirm the same thing of somebody who affirms that all of his attempts to see 'pure essences' on the basis of the prescribed attitude have been in vain? Or of somebody who considers it impossible, in the apprehension of the 'essence' of a 'given', to exclude every relation to apprehensions and earlier cognitions of the same given? In this context, however, we are confronted with another fundamental standpoint of phenomenology: the 'de-individualization' of the singular given.

---

9 For a more thorough discussion of this point, see my essay (Elsenhans 1915, p. 250 f.; incl. in this volume p. 359)

II The Given and 'De-Individualization'

One of my objections to phenomenology was that whoever intends to grasp the essence of some given cannot possibly refrain from consideration and application of what he has otherwise experienced with respect to this given, and of what the experiential sciences have revealed and can continue to reveal about the same object. In that case, however, "essential seeing" [*Wesenserschauung*] cannot be separated from the kind of observation that connects perception with conceptual processes; nor can it be separated from concept-formation in general. This means that essential seeing loses its mysterious character as an immediate seeing of 'ideas'. This objection absolutely cannot be answered with a critique of "abstraction theory"[10], which has been long criticized from all sides. My objection, in fact, is independent of abstraction theory. [250] The point is not how the formation of general concepts is to be explained psychologically, but rather, whether phenomenology is somehow justified in speaking of an apprehension of the *essence* of a 'given' in which every relation to other givens of the same kind and every relation of several such givens to one another (as well as every simultaneous appropriation of the conceptual processing of these relations) is put out of play.

---

[10] Linke (1916, p. 179 f.; incl. in this volume p. 396) very inaptly calls this theory "vagueness theory", although clearly this phrase, which entails a shift from the objective to the subjective, already betrays a negative valuation of the theory. I resist the enticing temptation to entitle a critique of phenomenology 'theory of hallucinations' (see Linke 1916, p. 195, 210, 212 and others; incl. in this volume p. 409, 420 – 423); I must state, however, that Linke made things too easy for himself by taking into consideration the exposition of certain psychological foundations of concept-formation from my manual of psychology (an exposition that has completely different purposes), and believes to have rejected my critique of phenomenology, which actually does not depend on this matter in the slightest. I am very well aware of the fact that abstraction theory, even in its most recent versions and as it is defended from otherwise very different standpoints, for instance by Benno Erdmann, Hans Cornelius and Theodor Ziehen, is opposed quite critically by other scholars. However, I continue to believe that abstraction theory is still the theory that does most justice to the psychological side of concept formation (and the psychological side is the only side at issue in my manual of psychology). Unfortunately, Linke has also completely misunderstood my exposition. This is clear, among other things, by the fact that he attributes to me the view that generality would consist in indeterminacy. He believes to grasp the sense of my exposition with an ironical phrase borrowed from Cassirer about the 'felicitous gift of forgetfulness' as the foundation for the theory of general objects, in order to then repeat Berkeley's arguments. Here it is not possible, but also not necessary, to delve into the other issues touched upon in connection with this point and discussed at length in other sections of my manual (such as, among others, act and object). This is because the present discussion is independent of them.

Phenomenology addresses this concern in that, by 'bracketing' the whole individual and unique spatiotemporal world and thus putting out of play all points of departure for empirical research, it creates a special realm of the non-individual, i.e., non-empirical. (Linke 1916, p. 195 f., 185, 201, 205 f.; incl. in this volume p. 409 f., 401, 413–414, 416–417) Linke distinguishes two stages of this bracketing: first, the putting out of play of spatial reality, which does not mean putting the spatial determinations of the corresponding object out of play, but just its 'reality in the external world'; and second, the putting out play of individual determinacy, which is given with one singular temporal position. With respect to the former, I do not see why the revocation of the reality of the external world should also imply a revocation of 'individuation'. The hallucinated sun adduced as an example can be individual and localized in the 'individually singular spatial world' just as much as the real sun; like the real sun, moreover, it can offer a point of departure for empirical research. The hallucinated sun is a point of departure for empirical research already at the moment in which the hallucinating person, for instance, compares the characteristics of the hallucinated sun with the characteristics of the real sun in order to confirm the non-reality of the former. [251] As for the second point (and remaining with the same example), the fixation of the hallucinated sun in a definite temporal position and the individual determinacy of the same are determined by the fact that the perceptual act has its stable position as an experience in the temporal series of one's own experiences. One is tempted to ask: when Spinoza, at some particular time, contemplates the world *sub specie aeternitatis*, is the world itself temporally determined by the temporal determinacy of his act of contemplation? Couldn't any kind of authentic mysticism be invoked as a counter-example? And is 'essential seeing' itself possible as an apprehension of timeless givens if the temporal determinacy of an act of experiencing carries over to its content, since of course the phenomenologist's act of seeing is no less an act of experiencing at a determinate time? The phenomenologist evidently wants to "let go of every relation to a coinciding experience, along with every relation to a temporal location". (Linke 1916, p. 200; incl. in this volume p. 413) But the perceiver already does the exact same thing. He abstracts completely from the time-point of the perceptual experience and only attends to the individually determined content of perception. The same applies to the example of a memorized series of syllables, for which the time of memorization is irrelevant: with the revocation of the 'time-index', the individualization is by no means revoked. The series of syllables can be present in consciousness with the same accentuation and pronunciation of its original memorization without any relation to the time-location in which it was memorized. The time location is not at all essential for its 'individuality'[11].

Finally, we should add the important fact (which Linke clearly overlooks in several passages) that not only the temporal determination, but also the spatial determinations have an individualizing function and they maintain this function also within a fictional world or vis-à-vis a hallucinated object. If the hallucinated sunset remains the same that "I perceived yesterday," just under disconnection of the time-location [252] of my experience, then the sun that I continue to represent as a "red, round something that is sinking below the horizon", as a "unified complex of imagined qualities" (Linke 1916, p. 196; incl. in this volume p. 409) can remain individual, already by virtue of its inherence in the spatial world, no matter how we think of it. We should hasten to add that if the sun does not remain individual, then we are no longer merely "seeing" it, but we are rather on our way to building a concept of it.

III Comparison and the General

In any case, in order to build a concept, comparison is necessary. By contrast, the phenomenologist rejects this argument, which would provide a straight path toward the formation of abstract concepts in the common sense of this word, to the extent that he leads likeness back to identity. (Linke 1916, p. 184 f.; incl. in this volume p. 400 f.) If I talk about the shade of red of this sheet of blotting paper as having such and such characteristics, and say that the sheet of blotting paper has this shade of red in common with other sheets, this is allegedly only possible because I presuppose the identity of the one color-property, which in this case is meant to be a non-individual entity. Commonality and identity in this case would mean nothing but what they mean in other cases in which their meaning is evident to anyone, for instance, two houses that have a wall in common, two properties that have an owner in common, or two countries that have a king or a government in common. The last examples show that Linke does not have logical identity in mind (according to which what is represented at different times and under different circumstances ought

---

[11] Therefore, Linke's 'joyful surprise' at my distinction between a reproduction with and without relation to time and his belief that he sees in me a phenomenologist (or at least a budding phenomenologist) because of this distinction are a bit premature. (Linke 1916, p. 201; incl. in this volume p. 414) I am a phenomenologist only in the sense that I recognize the enduring significance of phenomenology as a psychology built upon its own distinctive conceptual basis and proceeding according to an autonomous method.

to have the same content) but rather real identity. (Sigwart 1873, p. 105f.) Real identity consists in relating two presentations [*Vorstellungen*] to the same thing or the same process. In the case under scrutiny, the king of one country is 'identical' with the king of the other country. However, what would happen if one could assume that they are actually two distinct persons who are perfectly alike in all their characteristics? In this case, would the kings of the two countries no longer be identical but only alike? Or, to give a slightly more daring example: two iron spheres with a diameter of 10 cm that coincide completely in terms of their properties, or two atoms of the same kind that are completely alike, without therefore [253] being identical. We see that Kant's critique of Leibniz's *principium identitatis indiscernibilium* is well-taken: "Difference of locations, without any further conditions, makes the plurality and distinction of objects, as appearances, not only possible but also necessary."[12] As soon as we consider this *principium individuationis*—much neglected by Linke—which holds both for events happening to objects and for the objects themselves, it necessarily results that the concept of alikeness has to be made independent from the concept of identity and that the departure from the individual and the transition to the general can only be carried out via comparison and concept-formation. One can actually agree with many of Linke's analyses on the relationship of the ideal to the individual if we consistently replace 'idea' with 'concept'. If we do so, there is a lot in Linke's analyses that is immediately geared toward the Kantian interplay of intuitions and concepts. He correctly underscores the timelessness of concepts as such and the need to determine individual reality through concepts ('ideas') and to derive from conceptual relations more and more new conceptual relations "up to the highest and most abstract." (Linke 1916, p. 209; incl. in this volume p. 420) However, in this way the 'ideas' would be derived from experience and this is what phenomenology rejects. For phenomenology, the ideal (and therefore, mediately, also the general) is rather present from the very outset and the 'Copernican turn' of phenomenology consists precisely in making us aware of the fact that 'the whole real world' is 'given to us in timeless ideas'. I admit that here I am unable to follow, unless I assume the perspective of one of the lofty (yet justified in light of their grandiose worldview) systems of the past, such as Plato's or Spinoza's. However, phenomenology wants to provide the foundations for the science of our present and it intends to set also experiential science on a secure foundation. In order for us to be able to attribute

---

[12] In the section of the *Critique of Pure Reason* "On the Amphiboly of the Concepts of Reflection" (Kant *CPR*, B 283–284). Obviously, Leibniz's view is tightly connected to his concept of the individual (Leibniz 1765, Chapter XXVII). See Ernst Cassirer, *Leibniz System in seinen wissnschaftlichen Grundlagen* (1902, p. 384f.)

determinations to the factual individual itself, phenomenology argues, [254] the factual individual must already 'possess' such determinations, i.e., it must already possess a 'sense', something 'ideal'. The test of the timeless validity of ideas should consist in the fact that they remain the same as 'ultimate meaning-giving foundations' in every world, even in a fictional world. Even if "a green sun moved in spirals at extreme velocity against a yellow sky forming an infinite plane" (Linke 1916, p. 210; incl. in this volume, p. 421), the sky's yellow "as the instantiation of the idea 'yellow' would have the same position on the color spectrum as the one that it has now and that it always will have.". Similarly, "the meaning of the law of gravity and of all empirical laws in general would also survive in this fictional world". But can we really doubt that such a fictional world would be basically nothing but an arbitrarily varied replica of the real world? And that therefore the permanence of truths in this fictional world does not add one iota to their validity? Can it be possibly overlooked that we can only speak of the position of yellow on the color spectrum because we already have a color spectrum from empirical observation[13]? Or that we can only speak about the 'sense' of the law of gravity and about 'pure possibilities' of laws in general because the observation of the empirical world already gave us a real law of gravity and other laws, i.e., because the experiential sciences have already done their job? To be sure, non-empirical concepts have already made their contribution in the work of experiential science; but these are *a priori* concepts that make 'experience' and the derivation of singular empirical laws 'possible in the first place', not 'ideas', that can be 'seen' as pure givens in the singular concrete thing.[14]

IV More on the Analogy with Mathematics

However, phenomenologists refer us to a whole domain of inquiry that we have hitherto left out of consideration. In this domain, such 'pure givens' should be

---

[13] For a more extensive treatment of this point, in particular, on the relation between experience and predication see my essay (Elsenhans 1915, p. 246f.; incl. in this volume p. 356f.).
[14] In any case, I remain convinced that I can only conceive of a concrete given as something individual. Linke finds here, as in several other passages, a conflation. (Linke 1916, p. 209; incl. in this volume p. 420) However, in so doing he makes a mistake common to many scholars who work extensively with abstract reasoning. He believes he can presuppose that everyone acknowledges his own conceptual distinctions and, accordingly, that he can quickly drive his point home with the charge of conflation, which, however, is only justified on the basis of said presupposition.

indisputably at hand. I am talking about the domain of mathematics. Let us leave aside here the charge of an illegitimate extension of the concept of givenness discussed above and focus exclusively on the issue at stake. On this matter, we first have to point out that the projection of analyses pertaining to mathematical 'givens' onto non-mathematical entities is fraught with the same weaknesses that are generally (and rightfully) attributed to inferences based on analogy. Obviously, it all depends on whether the presupposed similarity between the two domains under consideration is sufficient to justify the projection. By contrast, we have pointed out the thoroughgoing difference of the two domains. The recognition of this difference is one of the main ferments of development and at the same time one of the most valuable achievements of Kantian philosophy.[15] In fact, it seems to me that Kant's analyses highlight the distinction in the sharpest way possible, perhaps most clearly when he distinguishes between the "employment of reason in accordance with concepts" ("in so employing it we cannot do nothing more than bring appearances under concepts, according to their actual content. These concepts cannot be made determinate in this manner, save only empirically, that is, *a posteriori*, although always in accordance with these concepts as rules of an empirical synthesis") and the "employment of reason through the construction of concepts; and since the concepts here relate to an *a priori* intuition, they are for this very reason themselves *a priori* and can be given in a quite determinate fashion in pure intuition, without the help of any empirical data" (Kant 1998, B 583). To be sure, mathematical determinations are also found in the appearances themselves, however, to the extent that they are found, they are given empirically. By contrast, insofar as they are not empirically given, they are created through 'construction' to begin with. The non-empirical 'pure essences' of phenomenology cannot be produced in the same way independently from experience. Rather, pure essences are bound to the empirical given and to that extent they are perfectly equal [256] to the concepts derived from the given in the experiential sciences.[16] Finally, it is also worrisome that here one should resort to a transference based on analogy where the *terminus a quo* is a domain immediately accessible to ordinary thinking and seeing and the *terminus ad quem* is a domain that discloses itself only on the basis

---

15 See my essay (Elsenhans 1915, p. 230f., 236f.; incl. in this volume p. 343 p. 421f., 348f.) In this respect, one could argue that Husserl's phenomenology reverts back to some of the fundamental thoughts of the grandiose pre-Kantian rationalistic systems. One could see in Husserlian phenomenology a connection of the Cartesian ideal of a universal mathematics to Plato's theory of ideas.

16 For everything else I must refer to the analyses quoted above from my essay (Elsenhans 1915, p. 230f.; incl. in this volume p. 343)

of a special 'attitude', 'bracketing', or 'disconnection'. The argumentative force that phenomenology seeks in the frequently used analogy with mathematics is thus weakened for the following reason: for a person that has to be first convinced—and precisely to the extent that he or she is not convinced yet—at stake here are two different intellectual functions. Therefore, the following question is all the more important: what, ultimately, is the basis for the truth of phenomenological cognitions considered in their own right?

V Phenomenology and the Criterion of Truth

I believe that I have shown in my essay why the question concerning the criterion of truth in phenomenology does not find any satisfactory answer. (Elsenhans 1915, p. 262 f., p. 243 f.; incl. in this volume p. 369 f., 354 f.) I must limit myself to enhancing these analyses by highlighting the main points and by considering Linke's reply. Where it seems necessary, I will have given them a stronger foundation. The phenomenologist grasps in immediate knowledge 'pure givens' and obtains thereby independently from all experience the true cognition of their essence. As Linke recognizes, the phenomenologist must also be able to err, just as the mathematician occasionally errs. (Linke 1916, p. 212 f.; incl. in this volume p. 422) However, an essential nexus that has been seen correctly should not possibly undergo any changes via observation and induction. Let us not consider here the argument by analogy to mathematics that we already criticized, although it would be easy to show that in mathematical knowledge a logical check constantly accompanies, corrects and enhances the cognitive activity. Here we are dealing with givens of the experiential world that, as for instance colors, are at least *also* objects of empirical research. Once it has been seen, the essential nexus should not possibly undergo any change via observation and induction, as little as physical laws can possibly undergo a change via juridical laws. [257] However, at stake here are not two 'heterogeneous domains', but rather the same objects, for which, beside the mode of research otherwise directed toward them where perception and thinking are intertwined (this is, namely, the essence of observation and induction), the phenomenologist claims a special method for immediate essential cognition. Linke's correct question should then be rather the following: is it possible that physical (or juridical) laws undergo a change based on the application of logical laws? Of course they can! (Linke 1916, p. 212; incl. in this volume p. 422) As much as, we add, every apprehension of a 'given' oriented toward cognition can be corrected or enhanced by other or similar apprehensions of the same, or of a similar given and by their logical elaboration. When the phenomenologist reads the properties that inhere in a quality and makes 'reading mistakes' in the process, how can he recognize that he is mistaken and how can he correct the mistakes if not by relating and comparing them to other essential intuitions and by drawing his conclusions from such comparison? However, if this is the case, then the truth of the singular states-of-affairs is no longer grounded in 'seeing' alone, but rather in the cooperation of thinking, which, precisely as it does in empirical research, draws its conclusions from a plurality of 'givens'. It does not help that the truth of the state-of-affairs at issue is not grounded in the psychological process of applying earlier, supposedly unquestionable experiences, but in the "ideal" qualities themselves. (Linke 1916, p. 214; incl. in this volume, p. 424) In fact, the 'verification', the truth-evaluation [*Bewahrheitung*] (which, we obviously agree, does consist in exhibiting the corresponding psychological processes, but rather in the empirical and logical grounding) cannot be separated from the truth-content. As we saw, both verification and truth-content depend on the possibility of distinguishing the correct essential cognition from the incorrect one. However, insofar as this distinction entails comparison and logical processing of what has been compared, [258] seeing and thinking are connected already in the cognition of the essence of singular givens, precisely in the same way in which they are constantly connected in empirical cognition.[17] [259] The impossibility to separat-

---

[17] Linke did not actually consider my more specifically epistemological analyses. His statement that he cannot accept my "reasons against the theory of intentionality" (Linke 1916, p. 221; incl. in this volume p. 429) gives me once again the opportunity to emphasize that all the difficulties he occasionally touches upon only exist on the basis of an insufficient distinction between the naïve and the scientific perspective. For instance, as far as the 'theory of images' is concerned, for the naïve spectator the thing is 'outside' and the image is 'in me', i.e., obviously as an image, which reassures the natural consciousness. For the theorist of knowledge the 'image' is the presentation brought about by the 'affecting element' and it is neither outside, nor 'in me' in the naively spatial sense of this expression. This presentation's relation to the object is mediated by the 'affecting element' at the moment of perception and by 'recognition' in the case of reproduction (Elsenhans 1915, p. 263f.; incl. in this volume p. 370; Linke 1916, p. 219, 190f.; incl. in this volume p. 427–428, 405). Richard Herbertz has recently shown in his *Prolegomena zu einer realistischen Logik* (1916, p. 125f.) that Husserl's concept of profile [*Abschattung*] does not manage to overcome the difficulties pertaining to this issue. Linke responds to my proof that these difficulties only derive from a conflation of the naïve and the epistemological standpoint (Elsenhans 1915, p. 271; incl. in this volume p. 376) with the statement that "the world of naïve-practical realism consists of a highly unclear mixture of phenomenological and naïve-empirical insights". (Linke 1916, p. 211; incl. in this volume p. 422) Unfortunately, I have to abide by my view and I do not consider the argument provided on p. 269f. and p. 271f. refuted (incl. in this volume p. 374f., 376f.). The theory of intentionality in phenomenology begins by speaking about the object as if it were (in accordance with the naïve position) something independent from our activity of representing, to which it can additionally happen to be 'intended' or

ing the scientific application of other experiences from 'seeing' as such in the cognition of essences becomes even more evident if we consider the logical and linguistic form, in which cognition generally finds its expression. For instance, the essential cognition that "in the color spectrum correctly ordered according to similarity, orange has its position between red and yellow"[18] is not yet present as a cognition at the moment in which somebody has experienced the sensory perception of orange beside other colors (which, for instance, an animal could have experienced as well). Rather, the cognition is only present at the moment in which what has been experienced is formed into a truth that can be expressed logically in a judgment and linguistically in a sentence. However, how could this truth speak about a position in the 'color spectrum' without a concurrent consideration of the previous observations or of scientific cognition of the color spectrum? It is correct that an experiential science of this kind can never attain the goal of freedom from error in the absolute sense. All science of givens, which, according to our view, is always empirical in nature, remains an 'infinite process', a 'method of approximation'. A new testimony of this fact is, for instance, the most recent development of natural science, which has shaken a whole set of hitherto apparently absolutely solid principles. However, it seems

---

'aimed at' by us. However, the phenomenologist considers at the same time this 'intending' of an object (including the object) in a scientific sense as a conscious experience. Thereby, he takes into view our participation in the being-present of the object, and in so doing he gives up his right to disregard 'transcendental idealism', which turns the object into a problem. By contrast, I consider it a great advantage to be clear from the beginning that we can by no means give up 'naïve realism' as point of departure and instrument of orientation. As the confrontation between Bruno Bauch (1915a, p. 97f., see in particular p. 100; see in particular 1915b, p. 302f.)) and August Messer (1915a, p. 65f.; 1915b, p. 299f., in particular p. 300) has shown, I believe that on this point I am in agreement with scholars coming from otherwise very different presuppositions. The 'practical realism' that I defend is aware of the fact that naïve realism has to be the point of departure and instrument of orientation, but also that it can be no more than that. This position entails as little a conflation of perspectives as the method of the astronomer, who constantly has to start and orient himself with the picture of the apparent motion of celestial bodies offered by the senses, although his science has long convinced him of the incorrectness of this picture.

18 I have a hard time understanding why Linke (1916, p. 212f. and 214; incl. in this volume p. 422f., 424f.) considers this statement an essential cognition *a priori*, but the other statement, namely, that red and green mixed together produce white, a "*vérité de fait*". The difference between these two statements actually points in a completely different direction. On the one hand we have comparison on the basis of immediate intuition and on the other the observation of a result stemming from a technical procedure that cannot at all be 'seen' in the colors themselves. As far as their rank within the classes of truths is concerned, however, both statements as statements regarding relations among colors are clearly at the same level of *vérité de fait*.

to me that if we presuppose the characteristics of phenomenology's method, then it would be much worse-off in this regard. In fact, it would lack [260] a criterion of truth that transcends the individual statement of an eidetic researcher in such-and-such attitude, and thereby the possibility to impose a statement drawn arbitrarily from this source, in contrast to one's own view considered to be correct.[19]

VI Conclusion

I have made it sufficiently clear that I have a much higher opinion of phenomenology than these analyses would suggest. I admire the sharpness with which its founder pushes forward in the consistent pursuit of his scientific goals. However, I believe that I have to judge the relationship between phenomenology and the empirical differently from how Husserl and his school do.[20] It seems to me that phenomenology in its present form fares exactly like all the other scientific attempts to master the experiential given through cognitive contents that should be obtained independently of experience. In its factual execution it turns out that it cannot do without drawing from experience. It is natural that this aspect is not as prominent in the founder's analyses (geared to found the whole theory to begin with) as it is in the various attempts to apply phenomenology presently available. I believe I have shown that in these variously valuable attempts we should see nothing but a conceptual analysis and an elaboration of some areas of empirical-descriptive psychology carefully developed independently from natural-scientific methods. I am also convinced that, as Husserl himself puts it, a [261] "systematic science of consciousness that investigates the psychical immanently" is a desideratum for the present and that much is missing in the autonomous elaboration of the conceptual foundations and the unitary structure of psychology.[21] It seems to me that we can expect from phenomenology the

---

19 Every invitation to "verify" (Linke 1916, p. 215; incl. in this volume p. 425) entails the requirement of a comparison. Again, this leads straight to an essential cognition that connects seeing and thinking, and, accordingly, beyond mere essential seeing.
20 In so doing, my goal was obviously not to reduce the value of phenomenology "through the use of terminology" (Linke 1916, p. 218f.; incl. in this volume p. 427). Rather, I attempted to situate it objectively according to its value in the philosophical work of our present. It is possible that the disciple of such a 'new science' (who is bound to initially overestimate it almost according to a law of history) does not find the resulting evaluation sufficient. However, it changes nothing about the necessity and the right of an objective appraisal.
21 My "Lehrbuch der Psychologie" (1912; incl. in this volume p. 17–34) is an attempt (beyond the goal of a mere 'compendium') to provide the foundations for the execution of this plan

most valuable contributions in order to fulfill this task. However, these will not come from a 'seeing of pure givens' divorced from all experience but rather in a constant synergy with experiential science and with the connection of intuition and thinking which alone leads, in the wake of Kant's classical testimony, to a universal and necessary cognition.

References

Bauch, Bruno (1915a): "Idealismus und Realismus." In: *Kant-Studien* 20, pp. 97–116.
Bauch, Bruno (1915b): "Schlussbemerkung zu meiner Diskussion mit A. Messer." In: *Kant-Studien* 20, pp. 302–304.
Cassirer, Ernst (1902): *Leibniz System in seinen wissenschaftlichen Grundlagen*. Marburg: Elwert
Cassirer, Ernst (1907): *Das Erkenntnisproblem in der Philosophie und Wissenschaft der neueren Zeit* II. Berlin: Bruno Cassirer.
Elsenhans, Theodor (1906): *Fries und Kant: Ein Beitrag zur Geschichte und zur systematischen Grundlegung der Erkenntnistheorie*. Band I. Gießen: Töpelmann.
Elsenhans, Theodor (1912): *Lehrbuch der Psychologie*. Tübingen: Mohr.
Elsenhans, Theodor (1915): "Phänomenologie, Psychologie, Erkenntnistheorie." In: *Kant-Studien* 20, pp. 224–275.
Herbertz, Richard (1916): *Prolegomena zu einer realistischen Logik*. Halle an der Saale: Niemeyer.
Kant, Immanuel (1998): *Critique of Pure Reason*. Paul Guyer and Allen Wood (Trans.). Cambridge: Cambridge University Press.
Leibniz, Gottfried Wilhelm (1765): *Nouveaux Essais* II. Amsterdam: Raspe.
Linke, Paul Ferdinand (1916): "Das Recht der Phänomenologie. Eine Auseinandersetzung mit Th. Elsenhans." In: *Kant-Studien* 21, pp. 163–221.
Locke, John (1996): *An Essay Concerning Human Understanding*. Kenneth Winkler (ed.). Indianapolis/Cambridge: Hackett.
Messer, August (1915a): "Über Grundfragen der Philosophie der Gegenwart." In: *Kant-Studien* 20, pp. 65–96.
Messer, August (1915b): "Zur Verständigung zwischen Idealismus und Realismus." In: *Kant-Studien* 20, pp. 299–302.
Sigwart, Christoph (1873): *Logik* I. Tübingen: Laup.

---

through a comprehensive treatment of the whole domain of research beside the systematic pursuit of single branches of psychology.

Translated by Evan Clarke
Edmund Husserl and Edith Stein.[1] Critique of Theodor Elsenhans and August Messer (1917) (Edith Stein's Draft)

Zur Kritik an Theodor Elsenhans und August Messer (1917: Edith Steins Ausarbeitung)
Husserliana XXV: Aufsätze und Vorträge (1911-1921)
Thomas Nenon and Hans Rainer Sepp (Eds.)
Dordrecht: Martinus Nijhoff, pp. 226-248 (1987)

[226] The method of phenomenology, its position as regards the theory of knowledge, and its position as regards psychology, have all been the object of lively discussion in recent years: thus, for instance, in a pair of essays by August Messer (1912, 1914; incl. in this volume p. 215–226, 239–253), and in an article by Theodor Elsenhans (1915). Many of the areas of controversy that arise therein will have been clarified by the foregoing. Above all, we have shown that the division between phenomenology and psychology—which is Messer's main object of concern—is a necessary division. By way of an appendix, though, it may be good to enter into several of the additional objections that have been raised.[2]

I The Method of Concept Formation and the Descriptive Sciences

One issue of considerable concern is evidently that of concept acquisition, specifically, the acquisition of those concepts with which phenomenology, as a descriptive science, operates: "*Description is thus always already classification.*," [227] remarks Elsenhans (1915, p. 240; incl. in this volume p. 352). "Thus one has no right to speak of a 'merely descriptive psychology' in the sense of a psychology that could somehow reproduce what is merely factual and that would

---

[1] [For biographical information on Stein, see p. 299–300 of this volume.]
[2] Paul Linke's paper "The Legitimacy of Phenomenology," ostensibly a development of our position, will not come into consideration here, since his "phenomenology" fails to grasp the core content of that science that is called for, methodologically grounded, and carried out by means of exemplary analyses in the *Ideas* (Linke 1917; incl. in this volume, p. 385–431).

not already contain scientific assumptions. Every denomination that picks out a psychical process from the overall psychical nexus and thereby isolates it *is* already such an assumption. At its prescientific level (which certainly at some point must have predated the scientific level) the denomination itself stems from the inheritance of an individual body of language, which, in turn, has to be considered a sediment of multiple experiences. Subsequently, this preliminary delimitation of the concept gives way to a process of exact scientific concept determination and classification, in which modifications that originate with the investigation of the relevant objects are introduced. Science thereby accomplishes one of its most important cultural tasks, namely, forming the knowledge of reality that is laid down in language such that it is free from error and dependable. This process is thus always an *intertwining of experiences, observations, comparisons, and conceptual work*. From the standpoint of these considerations, does it not appear impossible that phenomenology could perform its 'descriptions' of 'essence' completely independently of all conclusions derived from experience? Should we still claim that 'everything that is purely immanent to the experience and, once reduced, is peculiar to it,' is separated by an abyss from all of nature and physics, and no less from psychology? Every attempt at a description seems to me to demonstrate the opposite" (Elsenhans 1915, p. 241; incl. in this volume p. 352–353).

This whole analysis, which is brought forward as an objection to the method of phenomenology, is obviously based on the notion that the relevant concepts—like "concept," "description," "classification," and "experience"—are not adequately clarified. They are just "precipitates" drawn from various "experiences," not from any ultimate source of conceptual meaning. On the contrary, phenomenology follows the principle of not admitting precipitates; instead, all of the concepts that it [228] employs must be clarified anew, in reference precisely to the "original source of concept formation." We will now try to clarify what that means. All original concept formation is the *formation of an expression for something seen*. I must first "have" something before I can grasp it conceptually; it must stand before me in a given intuition. Whether the given intuition is a perception, phantasy, or something else, is irrelevant from the standpoint of concept formation. It is only necessary that "something" is brought to givenness for me to which I can give expression, an intuitional meaning that now becomes a word-meaning when I express it verbally. Whether that "something" exists or not (thus, whether it is "experienced" or not) is completely irrelevant. "Giant," "dwarf," and "fairy" are valid concepts, created on the basis of given intuitions, but do not come from any experience. But we must go still further: it does not matter that it is "this thing here" against which I measure my concept; the correlate of this singular perception or phantasy, the "what" that I intuit and express, is not an absolutely unique individual, but a universal—a universal that is present not just in the example before me right now, but which is, or which can become, present in many other examples, from which just as much could be drawn. Precisely because it expresses a universal, the concept is also universal. But we call that universal an *essence*; and the intuition, to which we owe our insight into the essence, and which "inheres" in each individual intuition, each grasp of an individual, is *eidetic intuition*. That is the source from which *all* concepts, *including* empirical concepts, ultimately originate. The empirical scientist does not need to be clear about this. His leading interest is the formation of determinate statements concerning *existing* objects. The exemplary intuitions, on the basis of which he forms his concepts, are therefore exclusively experiences; thus, he can justifiably claim that he derives his concepts from experience. And experience performs yet another role vis-à-vis concept formation in the empirical sciences. No concept reflects the complete *what* of the intuited object; it expresses this only "by means of" several "prominent features." Like the complete *what*, each individual feature can be "posited in an idea"; in other words, it can be considered as a universal, [229] one that can *ideally* be brought forward by infinitely many examples. In the empirical sciences, however, it is important that in the formation of concepts, we appeal to those features that are common to as many *really existing* examples as possible; because only such concepts are suitable for the formation of empirical "classes," species, and types. Now, there are indeed additional "questions that can only be answered through outer or inner perception, observation, analysis, comparison, etc." (Messer 1914, p. 55; incl. in this volume p. 242). But this takes nothing away from the general essence of concept formation, which we have laid out here.

Naturally, everything we have said here refers just to "valid" concepts and to their ultimate origin. Once concepts are formed, they become fixed acquisitions (or fixed inheritances). One can operate with these acquisitions without inquiring whence they have originated. One can also therefore form new concepts through the combination of concepts. But this process is of doubtful value if carried out in the purely conceptual sphere. If, for example, I have heard of an "equilateral triangle" and a "rectilinear triangle," and I now form the concept of an "equilateral-rectilinear triangle," mathematics will not be very much enlarged. Whether concepts acquired in this way are "valid," or "lawful," can only be decided with reference to giving intuition. So as to avoid playing a game with empty words, phenomenology takes care from the very outset to consider whether the concepts that are customary in a given domain correspond to genuine intuitions. From an external perspective it may therefore look as if phenomenology proceeds by "clarifying meanings (concepts) and of distinguishing those meanings from related concepts by means of reflection on the sense of the words that are associated with them (and partly through the analysis of individual examples)" (Messer 1914, p. 54; incl. in this volume p. 241)." Had one fully grasped the essence of this method, however, then one would not be able to say: "Since the meaning of many colloquial terms and even many scientific terms is not sharply defined or is subject to fluctuation, the resolution of the ensuing disputes is frequently a matter of simply proposing a determinate application [230] for a given word. Where such recommendations ought to be presented as useful linguistic conventions, however, they are occasionally put forward as 'eidetic intuitions'" (Messer 1914, p. 55; incl. in this volume p. 242). One will recognize, on the contrary, that what is at issue here is the discovery of valid and valuable concepts, which can be separated from less valuable concepts (which are either less, or not at all susceptible to fulfillment). One will recognize, moreover, that with this indispensable work, phenomenology creates precise conceptual material for itself and for the other sciences, without which rigorous science would not be possible.

Phenomenology, therefore, should not perform the work of concept clarification just for itself; it should undertake this work for the other sciences as well, and of course *principally for psychology*. As to why psychology should be reliant on the conceptual material provided by phenomenology, this can now be shown through a more detailed account of the procedure of the descriptive sciences, an account that will bring to light the distinctive character of concept formation in the sphere of lived experience (to which we have so far given no consideration).

Things are intuitively given; they are perceived. But they are not given according to what they are, that is, according to their complete *whatness* [*Wasgehalt*]; they are only given according to certain determinations. They are what they are as substrata of real qualities. But real qualities are causal; they are the typical modes of behavior of an identical thing under causal circumstances. Each transformation is causally determined. The absence of transformation is just a limit case of transformation; at the same time, it represents a causally determined persistence in the same condition. The description of things leads therefore to infinite dimensions of causality, dimensions of causality that are, at first, indeterminately open. On the other hand, a finite, closed description is sufficient for characterizing a thing in terms of its type or empirical class—insofar, namely, as self-contained, narrowly delimited sets of attributes are characteristic of these classes, and insofar as the infinity of further attributes, although completely unknown as regards their specific determinations in advance of experience, are posited experientially alongside the established predicates.

In the natural domain, classification results in a mastery of intuitive being: the attributes that are characteristic of, that are sufficient to characterize, or that are distinctive of each class [231] (it is possible that more than one set of attributes would suffice in a given case) can be grouped according to experience, thus from the standpoint of a unified basis for classification. Through knowledge of these characteristic attributes, a pre-given example of each class is determined. Thus, on the ground of the classificatory work undertaken in botany, plants are "determined," meaning that certain attributes are predicated of plants, which make possible their subordination under a class and establish for them a place in a system of classification.

In contrast to this, what are called *immanent* concepts express an absolute given, one that does not gesture towards an infinite series of intuitions. As regards the singular datum of the experiential sphere, there exists no open horizon of infinite possible determinations that would bring to light ever new features of the same object of intuition.

On the other hand, this does not mean that each intuitively given, immanent *what* is determinable through concepts; nor does it mean that the concept represents a more pure and more complete expression of the *what*. Because if the content of the immanent *what* is a continuous flowing, or if the immanent *what* falls along a continuum, such that the content or the individual moments of the content change in a fluid manner, it will not be possible to fix a particular, properly differentiated concept for each phase of the flux. That which flows in this way cannot be fixed by even the lowest-level species concept.

In the material sphere, moreover, there exist "fluid" characteristics. An intuitively given thing, for example, is not directly or exactly describable according to its color, because color is something fluid; and this indeterminacy is transferred to the perception of the thing, because it is characteristic of the perception that it is a perception *of this* red thing, and because the determination of the perceived as such requires a precise determination of the color.

Two obstacles, therefore, stand in the way of an adequate conceptual expression of what is intuitively given:

1. The transcendence of the thing-object includes an infinity of attributes. These are never given completely in a real intuition; nor are they completely given in a finite, self-contained set. [232] The possibility of still unknown attributes always remains open. This infinity of attributes precludes the possibility of an adequate expression of the essence of a thing in terms of intuitive (or "sensuous") concepts.
2. The thing contains fluctuating attributes, continually variable, and probably self-varying.

This suggests another way in which exact description is impossible. The first difficulty applied *only* to transcendent objects; this difficulty applies to immanent objects as well.

Naturally arising typical intuitions, and the corresponding concepts, which are employed in the descriptive sciences, are also *vague*. We have already seen the role that experience plays in such concept formation. Actually encountered examples of men or of particular races are fixed as what is typical or common. The vague concept, to which the vague type-apprehension corresponds, is shaped more "exactly" as one tries to determine which attributes are characteristic of this type, or (as they say) "essential" for that type, and which other attributes "normally" appear alongside these essential attributes in experience. With the help of these attributes the type is systematically established, and where the conceptual demarcation is not sufficient, we draw once again on intuition: "schematic pictures" are introduced, from which what is "characteristic" can easily be extracted. Thus, one distinguishes, for example, between the umbellate and the botryoidal. In the domain of color, one fixes the color designations along a range, or one designates the differences between colors according to instances of color known through experience such as "violet" and "emerald green"; in other domains, we might appeal to events like "vitreous fracture," and so forth.

A parallel form of description, which always falls back on the described thing—appealing either to the thing itself, a picture of the thing, or some presentifying intuition—exists in the *domain of psychology:* in this domain, one describes *types of people*, types of personal qualities, and types of abilities. Such descriptions of "character types" have often been given, indeed since the time of Aristotle and Theophrastus; one proceeds by situating a person (or a certain [233] personality-type more generally) within some concrete set of circumstances, and characterizing his habitual behavior in terms of those circumstances. Just as botany describes how plants behave under causal circumstances of light, warmth, electricity, and so forth, we describe real people in terms of their real, intuitively accessible qualities, and the various forms of behavior that they exhibit. At base, nothing is changed if one employs experiment—even statistical methods—and thus comes to emphasize the empirical laws underlying the behavior of different types of people (for instance, the type "normal person"), or the empirical laws governing their changing physical states. Of course, the development of the individuals described also belongs within the domain of description, so one cannot make here the customary distinction between genetic and descriptive psychology. Next to the descriptive sciences, which investigate the relatively permanent concretions of a particular type (such as a particular species of animal), enters evolutionary theory, which deals with the emergence of one species from another, or with the formation of new species. Each animal species is itself a class of essence, which is not only represented through an enduring type, but through a continuity of type, through a "development" from an initial type to a final type, with reference to normal circumstances, and so forth. Accordingly, the domain of the physical includes not just fully formed types, but also types of development through multiple stages. This development can be described in intuitive terms, whether we are concerned with the development undergone by particular individuals, or with the development that takes place between successive generations in a given species.

This analysis of concrete mental forms, however, is not the sole task of a descriptive psychology; a survey of modern psychology suggests that this is even a relatively unimportant branch. If one is interested in personal qualities, abilities, dispositions, and so forth, then one is lead back to immanent lived experiences; thus, it is the study of the sphere of lived experiences that contemporary psychology takes for the most part as its goal. Here, the conditions of description are essentially different than in the domains examined up to this point. Even the title "psychic phenomenon" is at first a vague classificatory concept, lacking the sharp boundaries [234] that result from a properly scientific workmanship. In everyday reflection, we form concepts like "joy," "sorrow," "perception," "idea," etc. But to content oneself with these general concepts, as psychology has essentially always done, is to deserve the reproach of having treated scientifically posed problems in an inexact, unscientific, and merely verbal fashion. What should one do, then, in order to form scientifically rigorous concepts? Can one take natural science as a model, as Brentano wanted to do, and proceed by way of classification? Are we to follow the natural sciences in forming fluid type-concepts that can only be fixed through concrete examples, through illustrations, or through attachment to some well recognized empirical given. Of course, the psychic, taken here in the broadest sense, also requires fluid type-concepts. To be sure, all of the descriptive concepts of the natural sciences belong within psychology in a certain sense: namely, when we take concrete objects and their types not as types of existing objects, but as types of intentional objectivities, which represent the characteristics of object-intuitions and sense-contents, and which simultaneously prescribe rules to those intuitions and sense-contents as regards possible processes and connections. What is genuinely psychic however—and one must be clear about this—cannot be treated in the same way as other objects. A perception, a feeling of joy, a simple sensation, flows away; and once it has decayed, it has *irretrievably* disappeared. I cannot hold them fast and inspect them, so as to give some determinacy to the fluid descriptive concepts corresponding to them; I cannot hold them up to each other, so as to isolate common attributes and, with their help, to form classificational concepts. If I remain in the domain of purely immanent experience, I have nothing but a flux of unrepeatable and incomparable individualities, which mock any kind of conceptual grasp. *A pure empirical science of the psychic is absolutely impossible.*

As we have already said, however, each individual intuition is simultaneously the intuition of a type, which we can grasp even when its individuation in a singular lived experience has passed, and which we can also therefore recover in a new individuation. These concrete essences of lived experiences can be formulated as type concepts; for reasons already stated, however, [235] these type concepts cannot be employed as a means of empirical classification: I can indeed observe that I have at this moment an experience of a certain type X, one that I had already become acquainted with on previous occasions; but I cannot make comprehensible to anyone else precisely which type I am experiencing, because I cannot show him any example. A *science* of consciousness is only possible on the basis of a certain particularity of the sphere of lived experience: namely, that we are occupied here not just with vague types, but with essences that can be tightly circumscribed. The low-level concretions, that is, the individual empirical essences, are naturally transient; but the universal species—such as thing-perception in general, thing-intuition in general, and even universal perception and universal intuition—are precisely determinable: it is unthinkable that through some continual transformation the perception of a thing would change into the perception of a sensory datum, a feeling of rage, or a predicative judgment—in the way, for example, that the perception of a red thing continually transforms along with the continuous variation of the red itself, or in the same way that in the perception of a thing, our changing eye movements evoke continually changing "representations." Naturally, this quality of the lowest concretions is expressed by the concept of a fluid transition, but one cannot capture the difference between these concretions in precise, descriptive concepts. One can see them, but one cannot differentiate them according to sharply differentiated concepts.

On the other hand, these sharply differentiated generic essences can be grasped scientifically, by "analyzing" them, and by picking out their essential moments. With the analysis of factical givenness, however, we are still not quite done. The fundamental characteristic of intentionality includes ideas of reason and unreason within itself, and thus teleological guidelines for multiplicities of continuous differentiations, all of which coalesce into the unity of a perceptual consciousness towards the progressive givenness of one and the same object. And it is not just these connections of sensory data and appearances that come into question, but also moments such as that of position-taking, which has its own ideally possible variations (certain perception, probable perception, doubtful perception, and so forth) and its own motivations in the nexus of consciousness. These motivations can be investigated and described as a priori necessities and possibilities.

[236] Even though they can play a role in empirical description, it would be foolish to consider the properly essential concepts of number and magnitude as facts pertaining to reality, thus to take them as empirical concepts. Being the kinds of essences that they are, they prescribe an a priori method, a means of entering into systematic possibilities. The same thing is true of consciousness as consciousness of something. Only through the unprejudiced and purely intuitive immersion in intentional consciousness, and only through an immersion in the free domain of possibilities and their ideal lawlike regularities is science, and exact, fruitful concept-formation possible. The eidetic cognition corresponding to this determines an enormous domain of lawlike regularities, governing the forms, modifications, and the genesis of consciousness, while leaving room for merely factual regularities and empirical "accidents." Exactly the same relationship obtains between geometry and nature. In the descriptive natural sciences, we deal with concretions, which, as far as quantity is concerned, are fluid. It is a domain of approximate and vague types. In the sphere of consciousness, on the other hand, we have a domain of intentionality that is strictly and absolutely governed by norms and laws. Similarly, the spatial world has its space and its objective time, its laws of motion and its strict physical order: just as nature is an ordered system, a definite manifold of the specifically mathematical variety, consciousness too is an ordered system; not a mathematically ordered system of dead beings, clearly determinable in terms of mathematical laws, but a system that stands under rational laws and the laws that are conditions of possibility for those rational laws. Rational lawfulness is a merely an element of a more general (and in itself necessary) structural and genetic lawfulness. All in all, these laws do not produce and reproduce a mathematical order; nor is the "causality" that is proper to consciousness a mathematical causality, one that can be characterized in terms of mathematically formalizable laws; rather, it is a motivational causality, having a completely different character. Herein lie immense secrets, the clarification of which does not lead back to a fantastic or verbalistic metaphysics, [237] or to a metaphysics that is speculative in a bad sense, but to a rigorous science.

The forms and the general structure of the concretions of consciousness are analyzable; they can be investigated eidetically according to their possible variations. The modifications which give rise to new types of forms, precisely delineated structures, and ways in which those structures can be fleshed-out stand under essential laws. These ideal operations do not represent possible transformations of empirical beings; rather, they are "operations" that lead from perception to a corresponding perceptual pictorial consciousness, or to possible, precisely corresponding phantasies, and so forth. All possible transformation or real variation stands, therefore, under motivational laws, which are exhibited in eidetic analysis.

One must be clear, therefore, that it is the eidetic science of consciousness that first makes possible psychology as a factual science. To be sure, every psychologist will occasionally express universal propositions that he derives neither from experience, habit, nor induction, and which happen to have the character of a priori propositions. But a science, properly speaking, demands a scientific consciousness of the nature and scope of the principles that are determinative of its method. The physicist would not come very far if he drew his propositions concerning spatial magnitude from actual experience, or from random glimpses of correlations that he grasps in general terms and that he takes for merely contingent empirical universalities; he must actually know that everything material stands, as far as its spatial properties are concerned, under geometrical laws; and he must study geometry, so as to acquire from this science the fundamental standards of his method. Indeed, the basic elements of his method are determined by the fact that spatiality stands under pure mathematical laws, laws which are unconditionally valid for and applicable to all possible, and hence all actual, spatial beings. Something similar is called for in the case of psychology. The psychologist ends up with a skewed methodology when he employs his concepts only as empirical concepts, since those concepts actually embody ideal laws which are valid for every possible consciousness. It is also fundamentally wrong to think of "descriptive psychology" as an incoherent empiricism: what falls under this title, rather, is on the one side an [238] a priori science that considers consciousness in terms of its pure forms and its ideal possibilities; and on the other side, an empiricism, which establishes through descriptive means precisely which forms of consciousness characterize normal people and which forms characterize abnormal people. If we continue to practice psychology as an empirical science, then all of our descriptive concepts will be empirical concepts, meaning that they will be derived from actual experience and bound up with the idea of real existence. Accordingly, Messer is incorrect in claiming that "when the descriptive psychologist wanted to characterize some class of experiences (be it perception, or memory, or volition, etc.) in general terms, he regarded the individual experience from which he took his departure merely as an arbitrary example, as something that would render the sought-after essence intuitive. The existence of the individual experience in the real nexus of nature was of no concern, because the descriptive psychologist was interested not in existence, but essence" (Messer 1914, p. 64; incl. in this volume p. 249–250). By "example," the natural scientist does not mean a particular instance of an essence; he means a representative of an empirical species. And that is also what Messer has in mind, even though he speaks here of "essence." This emerges quite clearly in the following passage from his first treatise, to which he indeed appeals in the passage just quoted: "The singular, real experience in his own consciousness or in the test subject's consciousness only interests the psychologist as an example, as a singular instance, as something from which a general conclusion can be drawn. The psychologist is not interested in these experiences as real events happening with real people, and so does not look to situate them in a *determinate place* within the greater nexus of natural processes" (Messer 1912, p. 123; incl. in this volume p. 220; Husserl's emphasis). A *determinate* place: in general, this is not very important. But it must occupy *some* place in a natural context. It is not necessary that it be *this particular* reality; but it must be *a* reality of some kind. Because "Obviously, the psychologist wants to grasp regularities in the psychical occurrences of real people. He does not want to invent or poetize about anything, he wants to cognize reality." Messer adds here a rhetorical question: "But are things essentially different for 'phenomenologists'?" Indeed! Because for us, the ideally possible is just as important as the actual. "Occasionally," therefore, we can "learn something from novelists" (Messer 1912, p. 123; incl. in this volume p. 220–221); [239] the empirical psychologist can never do so. The fantastic, magical transformations of plants and animals that we find in fairy tales can be quite concrete, having their inner consistency and possibility with the fantasy world. But of course, no natural scientist would appeal to these magical transformations. On the other hand, a natural scientist may recognize that the fantastic machines described by some poet conform to his knowledge of nature and physics, and are thus feasible in the actual world. The scientist may even be inspired to try to implement the poet's ideas, possibly even at the level of exact detail. This possibility is based just on an understanding of nature, and of the concordance between the lawful constitution of the poet's fictional world and the lawful constitution of the actual world. Similarly, the psychologist could make use of novels, plays, and so forth, if he became convinced on the basis of *scientific* experience that the poet has described humanity as it actually is. The concrete description of "possible" characters has no value for the empirical scientist if it has not already been established that "something like" those characters actually exists. Knowledge of what really occurs is the guiding point of view for the empirical psychologist. What he needs, as the basis for his descriptions, is therefore only a small snippet from the domain that phenomenology investigates. He simply needs to fix those forms of consciousness that are actually given; he does not need to fix all possible forms of consciousness. It would be possible, moreover, to separate out these experientially determined, "empirical" parts, from "pure" phenomenology. Descriptive psychology as an exact science can be constructed on this basis.

Of course, one often has something different in mind with the notion of "exact" science. One places descriptive psychology in opposition to a "theoretically explanatory" psychology. Theoretically explanatory, or "nomological" science, strives toward explanatory theory. It aims to distinguish sharply between different domains of investigation, which it arranges in terms of the objects and object classes given within each; it seeks out exact concepts and their associated exact laws, in terms of which the being and the being-thus of the objects, as well as the forms of transformation and constancy associated those objects, can be precisely explained, or clearly determined. The idea of a definite manifold belongs to the idea of a theoretical science. [240] Everything typical must be analyzable in terms of elementary types; these (and subsequently all complex types) can be understood as "approximations" of exact ideas, and determined precisely to any degree of specificity through exact laws.

These ideas can now be extended to the case of a theoretical-nomological psychology. If one has understood the idea of a *mathesis universalis*, and hence the idea of a mathematical multiplicity, one can say: what is sought at this point is the idea of a "mathematical" psychology. Every science that is explanatory, in the strict sense of a science that is clearly and theoretically determined, is "mathematical." Its explanations proceed deductively from principles that necessarily have mathematical form; and the whole deductive system of theorization must be mathematical, and allow itself to be arranged according to its pure mathematical form as a mathematical theory of manifolds.

The only attempt at carrying out a psychology according to this idea has been made by Herbart (though he was not clear in regard to the logical form of the idea, or indeed the idea itself). One could perhaps say a second such attempt was made by Münsterberg, though he did not carry this to completion. As for modern, "physiological," "experimental," or "exact" psychology, this stands absolutely at the level of descriptive psychology, despite all of its psychical-technical methods (which decide nothing). It does not give anything like the theoretical explanations that characterize a genuinely exact science. Indeed, there is not yet any indication of the way in which the idea of an exact science could be realized in the domain of the psychic. And that is probably no accident. Indeed, it should be apparent that any mathematization of the psychic is excluded in principle, that psychology can demand only that particular kind of exactitude that it can achieve on the basis of phenomenological concept formation.

II Eidetic Intuition, Experience and Thought

In discussing concept formation, we must keep the idea of "eidetic intuition" in the foreground. Precisely this idea, however, [241] has been the cause of many headaches, and demands to be clarified in its own right.

An eidetic intuition is said to be "neither a concept nor an empirical intuition" (Elsenhans 1915, p. 229; incl. in this volume p. 343). Essences, meanwhile, are said to [be] "'brought to givenness' through eidetic intuition [...] Thereby it is also shown with full evidence that the phenomenological intuition of essences is not a positive intuition, one that engenders the essence of the object in the act of observing it. Rather, it is a process that, in its degree of passivity, amounts to mere sensuous intuition. *The 'pure essences' are there; it is only a matter of us 'seeing' them.* What we contribute to this is only the 'attitude'" (Elsenhans 1915, p. 233–4; incl. in this volume, p. 347). Before we can reply to this in full, it will first be necessary to examine the concepts that are employed here as a way of characterizing eidetic intuition. *On the one hand*, Elsenhans suggests, we can think of eidetic intuition as a *passive* acquisition: in that case, it is equivalent to sensuous perception (*experience*). *Alternately*, we could think of eidetic intuition as a spontaneous process: in that case, it would represent a kind of productive *thought*, one that *generates* its own objects. In the newest treatise, accordingly, Elsenhans distinguishes between experience in the sense of sensation and authentic experience, meaning experience that is already accompanied by intellectual activity (in the Kantian sense).[3] For us, on the other hand, sensation is completely excluded from consideration, because mere impressions do not in any sense give *objects*; what matters here, however, is precisely the concept of givenness. When Elsenhans continues by saying that "What is given is what we find before us, what is present without our active cooperation, what is there before our processing activity is directed toward it." (Elsenhans 1918, p. 245; incl. in this volume, p. 434)[4], this could conceivably apply to the givenness of impressions in *inner* perception; in external perception, however, we

---

[3] "Kant's concept of experience lumps together two different meanings of the word... Experience as the processing of 'the raw material of sensory impression into cognition of objects' and experience as basically coincident with the sensation through which our cognitive faculty is set to work to begin with... When we deal at present with the relationship between phenomenology and empirical psychology, the latter can only be understood (presupposing a connection with existing terminology) as the intellectual processing of the 'raw sensory material' that is 'given' to inner perception". (Elsenhans 1918, p. 244f.; incl. in this volume, p. 434)

[4] [Translator's note: Stein does not provide a citation for this quote.]

do not find "impressional material"; nor can we say that objects are given along with impressional material.

Experience, for us, means a consciousness in which individual [242] existence comes to givenness (see Husserl 1987, p. 161). This includes "phenomenological experience," in which individual immanent data are given to the reflective grasp. We distinguish this from experience taken narrowly as the grasp of individual *transcendent* objects; it is this experience that is alone at issue here. An example of such empirical consciousness is sensuous perception. Elsenhans does not deny that objects are given in sensuous perception, that we discover therein the proximate things of nature. On the other hand, he maintains, along with Kant, that such experiences are bound up with functions of the understanding. Givenness and spontaneity must not be understood as mutually exclusive. With this, however, the whole argument against eidetic intuition is already invalid. Since this is not just a matter of dialectical wordplay, but the clarification of real things [*Sachen*], we will continue our discussion still further. In experience, things are *given* to us. They are simply there. If we reflect, however, on our empirical consciousness, we encounter the manifold of "appearances" "in" which these unified objects are brought to givenness (in which they are "constituted"), and correlatively, manifold "actions" of the subject united synthetically in the simple intuitive act. Starting, for example, from the movements of perceptual things, and the new appearances that arise from those movements, we progress to the acts of "apprehension" that transform these appearances into "representations" of unified objects, and finally to the unity of consciousness that runs through all of these moments (the expression "activity" is not actually suited to the life of the I, in the sense that the latter simply runs "by itself"; it is not set into motion arbitrarily). What part of this empirical consciousness belongs strictly to thought? The expression "thought" is commonly applied to all kinds of experiences, having more or less to do with one another: thus, it is applied to non-intuitive presentations (I do not "imagine" the landscape that I saw the other day, I "merely think" of it); to memories (I did not "think" that I had a task to carry out); and finally, to actual theoretical thought. If we guard against such conceptual confusions and mark off the expression "exactly," such that it denotes a generically unified class of experiences (and only those experiences), the meaning of *thought* [243] can be understood in terms of *specific logical acts:* relation, comparison, positing as subject, positing as predicate, subordination, unification and differentiation, inference, and proof. The meaning of thought also encompasses what we above called "expression" (in agreement with the *Logical Investigations*): the fusion of a "meaning" with an objective sense; or simply, the "creation of concepts." Understood in this sense, it is clear that we can discover nothing about a given thought in experience. On the contrary, the objects with which the thought is properly engaged become available on the basis of a different kind of givenness. However, if by "thought" Elsenhans means the "acts of apprehension" [*Auffassungen*] and the synthetic consciousness of unity at work in the experience of transcendent objects, then one ought to say that none of the characteristics Elsenhans attributes to thought can be applied to such phenomena: thoughts, for Elsenhans, are not spontaneous acts; they do not "generate" their objects through a freely acting creativity. On the other hand, these qualities do characterize thought in our sense: thought for us is a free act; it does "generate" new objects (through concept formation, for example). It should be noted, however, that the objects that result from these free acts are not "subjective products" of thought (to the extent, at least, that they are rationally evident and are grounded in intuitive givenness); rather, they are "objective" constructions, objects that can be "given" anew in simple intuitive acts, just like sensuous things. Examples of such constructions include "relation," "similarity," "state of affairs," "inference," and "proof." All of these have "that *measure of reality that makes them able to be discovered*" (Elsenhans 1915, p. 234; incl. in this volume, p. 347).[5] The word "reality" is of course out of place here, because reality signifies being insofar as it is related to a spatio-temporal-causal nature, and because nothing is more distant to our purposes than an account of categorial objects as really existing, natural things. Having said that, we can invoke the "being" of categorial objects (independently of whatever subject is occupied with them) with just as much right as we invoke the being of nature, since the giving consciousness corresponding to the former is just as rich as the giving consciousness corresponding to the latter. We therefore have two kinds of existing objects and correlatively, two kinds of originally giving [244] consciousness: nature, constituted in sensuous perception, and categorial (or logical) objects constituted in theoretical thought.

Of course, these two object domains do not exhaust the realm of beings. There remain any number of objects that are neither natural things nor objects of thought (I am thinking, for example, of values, goods, etc.) and hence many forms of giving consciousness that are neither sensuous perception nor thought.

---

5 Elsenhans makes this remark about essence. His claim here is that to speak of the "givenness" of essences amounts to a kind of "Platonic realism."

Let's remain here for a moment with those particular kinds of objects identified in *Ideas* as "*essences*," and with the consciousness in which such essences come to givenness.[6]

The example of mathematics, to which Husserl appeals in the *Ideas* as an example of an eidetic science that is already available, is not decisive, according to Elsenhans: in mathematics—the analogy with which is supposed, among other things, to clarify the possibility of [an apprehension of givens that is independent of any particular experience]—one cannot talk of 'pure givenesses' in the same sense as one does in phenomenology, as Husserl himself admits. There it is a matter of objects, which, as 'irreal possibilities', are produced at will in the manner of 'pure analytic necessity.' Here, it is a matter of objects which are given in the first instance in experience, and which, in the context of phenomenology, are to be grasped 'in the complete fullness of their concreteness', albeit not empirically" (Elsenhans 1915, p. 236 f.).

Our previous analyses have shown that the term "freely generated" is not opposed to the term "discovered," or "given." A closer analysis of the geometrical and phenomenological methods will make this still clearer. At the same time, this will allow the analogy between the two sciences to emerge, which will in turn allow us to employ examples from one science in the context of the other.

The geometer can take as a point of departure some perceived spatial form. But the empirical thesis of perception is not in this way put into action; it contributes nothing to the geometer's reasoning; a phantasized [245] geometrical structure accomplishes exactly the same purpose. In just the same way, the phenomenologist can take as a point of departure some factically present perception, and he can draw his conclusions on the basis of that perception; for him as well, however, the thesis of experience plays no role. A purely phantasized perception can likewise serve just as well as a point of departure. In contrast to this, the natural scientist must grasp existence: he must perceive; he must experience. But it is not just the *thesis* of experience that the eidetic scientist allows to drop away; rather, he begins by "operating freely" with the individual intuitions that are his point of departure. The geometer does not content himself with describing the shapes of fields, trees, and houses, and with forming general propositions about those objects; rather, he runs through all "possible" spatial forms in free, creative phantasy. On the basis of the modifications to which factically encountered shapes can be subjected, the general "idea" of space and spa-

---

[6] A closer analysis than the one that has been possible here would show that eidetic intuition also plays a role with respect to thought (as indeed our treatment of concept formation has already shown).

tial form emerges, and all individual spatial forms come to be seen as *ideal* (or *essential*) *possibilities*. As for the notion of "*possible*" modifications: this means that even the geometer is not completely free in the "generation" of spatial forms, as is sometimes thought. His freedom in this regard reaches just as far as his intuition—because "possibility" is equivalent with "compatibility with an intuition." The structures that are possible are just those that can be intuited in free phantasy. Those spatial forms that are not, in principle, compatible with any intuition whatsoever are impossible (such as the equilateral-rectilinear triangle that we invoked above).

The phenomenologist proceeds in an analogous fashion with an individual perceptual experience: he modifies it as far as possible, he runs through all possible perception in free phantasy, and from these free operations springs the "essence" of "perception in general," which can now be conceptually grasped and expressed in the form of general eidetic laws. On both sides, therefore, we have existing objects (in this case, essences pertaining to lived experience; in the case of geometry, essences pertaining to spatiality) which arise from the free acts of phantasy undertaken by an originally constituting consciousness, but which can also be "discovered" through a simple kind of "inspection"—just like natural objects, which are constituted in a completely different kind of sensuous perception.[7]

[246] The difference between geometry and the science of consciousness (a difference which is strongly emphasized in the *Ideas* and in the preceding works) consists in the fact that consciousness, unlike space, does not have the form of a definite manifold; thus, while geometrical theorems can be derived from axioms "in the manner of pure analytic necessity," this is not possible in the case of phenomenology. But geometry cannot proceed by means of an analytic method alone; otherwise, it would be formal *mathesis* and not a science of space. As such, geometry needs spatial intuition (at least by way of grounding its axioms), and this has the already described form of eidetic intuition.

Therefore, there is a giving consciousness of universal essences that is independent of all experience, and from all positing of individual existence. Since a "fact" is understood in *Ideas* as an individual event (a *matter of fact*, in Humean terms), it must be stressed that phenomenology is not a science of facts. If, in apparent opposition to this, Scheler and Geiger have occasionally seemed to say that phenomenology takes facts as its point of departure, they are actually using the word 'fact' in a different sense: namely, for what is immediately discov-

---

[7] We have taken into account here just universal essences (or "exact" essences, as we said above), because it is principally these essences with which the *Ideas* is concerned.

ered, or intuited, rather than what is only mediately known, deduced, or even simply constructed. If one calls phenomenology a science of fact in this sense, one does not thereby brand phenomenology an empirical science.

III The "Infallibility" of Eidetic Intuition

The independence of phenomenology from all experience, an independence which precludes the possibility of a *correction* of eidetic cognition through psychological experience, has always caused a particular kind of offense. One has seen in this a claim to infallibility, a claim to the impossibility of error. This, however, has never been claimed; nor is this in any way implied by our stress on the particular laws and the particular characteristics of eidetic knowledge. There is no scientific knowledge that is absolutely immune from error. At least in the case of mathematics and logic, however, a history of innumerable errors has not inspired anyone to call into question the idea of complete evidence; [247] which they can claim only because they are eidetic spheres. A mathematician has proven a theorem; he has fully inspected it, and has become convinced by its "incontrovertible certainty." On a later occasion, he returns to this theorem, so as to use it for a new proof. He does not bring it again to intuitive givenness; rather, he contents himself with the mere words, with the formula that remains in his memory. This being so, it is very easy for a mistake to occur which would render the new proof entirely worthless. When the phenomenologist fails to remain within the sphere of given intuitions, when he exploits the conceptual formulation of some analysis without referring back to intuition, the same kind of problem can befall him. And errors can also seep in from different directions: thus, for example, when an investigation is not carried far enough, or when something is accepted as necessary which turns out, upon further investigation, to be subject to modification. The "admission that errors are possible here" does not—contrary to Messer—conflict in any way with the "the confident statement that 'substantial results are immediately given' [within the eidetic attitude]" (Messer 1914, p. 54; incl. in this volume p. 241). But it is not only the eidetic sciences that lay claim to "substantial results"; the factual sciences do so as well, though the further progress of such sciences can always lead to a reevaluation of the results already obtained. What is once again of the first importance in regard to eidetic cognition is the fact that, insofar as it is fully intuitive, it is *intrinsically* indefeasible, which means that it can only be enriched by new intuitions, not invalidated. Every experience, on the other hand—be it the clearest and most distinct perception—is characterized essentially by components that we may describe as "determinately indeterminate" and calls out for the fulfillment of these indeterminate components through new perceptions. These *can* provide merely a more exact determination of the laws already grasped, and hence a confirmation of what is initially posited; on the other hand, they can bring about a consciousness of contradiction and a crossing out of those initial posits.

Supposing that the eidetic scientist runs into an error, therefore, for one of the reasons stated above, how do things stand as regards the possibility of correction? [248] "If empirical science has somehow corrected what is intuited phenomenologically, should he ignore this correction?" (Elsenhans 1915, p. 239 f.; incl. in this volume p. 351). In light of the foregoing, the answer cannot be in doubt: experience can make the eidetic scientist aware that there is an error in his findings; experience can thereby prompt him to check findings against a new intuition, and in that way to justify them; but experience itself cannot serve as a justification, because I can only attain eidetic insights on the basis of eidetic intuition. Suppose that I have concluded that the essence of thing-perception implies the *seeing* of things; and suppose now that I am presented with a person blind since birth, for whom the sense of touch is sufficient for the constitution of spatial things; in that case, I recognize that I have not pursued the free formation of possible modifications of perception far enough. But it is not the *faktum* of the blind person's perception that shows me this; it is the eidetic possibility of such perception, which I grasp in going over from experience to the eidetic attitude.

Elsenhans finds it "strange that the possibility of a knowledge that is free from all errors of experience, and which, once at hand, should lead to absolutely necessary and general acceptance of compelling results, was not realized earlier, and has until now borne no fruit whatsoever[.] Although it is elsewhere employed quite abusively, this argument probably has some evidential force in this context, where it is a matter of adding a new method to the cognitive activities of thought that have been practiced and understood in their particularity for centuries, cognitive activities that are directed toward the essences of things" (Elsenhans 1915, p. 235 f.; incl. In this volume p. 348).

Our remarks here should have shown that this method is not as mysterious, unheard of and absolutely new as Elsenhans suggests. Mathematics has practiced this method systematically for over two thousand years. It has played a role in the concept-formation undertaken in *all* sciences whatsoever, without anyone having been aware that it was performing this role. Now, however, it has been made clear, freed of all confusions and methodically constructed. If through this process new sciences become possible, then we should be glad of this fact, and we should not reproach the founders of these sciences for the fact that no one had arrived at the sciences in question before now.

References

Elsenhans, Theodor (1915): "Phänomenologie, Psychologie, Erkenntnistheorie." In: *Kant-Studien* 20, p. 224-275.

Elsenhans, Theodor (1918): "Phänomenologie und Empirie." In: *Kant-Studien* 22, pp. 243–261.

Husserl, Edmund (1987): "Phänomenologie und Erkenntnistheorie." In: *Husserliana XXV: Aufsätze und Vorträge (1911-1921)*. Dordrecht: Martinus Nijhoff, pp. 161-206.

Linke, Paul Ferdinand (1917): "Das Recht der Phänomenologie." *Kant-Studien* 21, pp. 163–221.

Messer, August (1912): "Husserls Phänomenologie in ihrem Verhältnis zur Psychologie." In: *Archiv für die gesamte Psychologie* 22, pp. 117-129.

Messer, August (1914): "Husserls Phänomenologie in ihrem Verhältnis zur Psychologie (zweiter Aufsatz)." In: *Archiv für die gesamte Psychologie* 32, pp. 52–67.

Contributors

Will Britt: Postdoctoral Fellow, Department of Philosophy, Loyola Marymount University.

Evan Clarke: Academic Administrator, Northeastern University – Toronto.

Adam Knowles: Assistant Professor of Philosophy, Drexel University.

Rodney K.B. Parker: Postdoctoral Fellow, Department of Philosophy/Center for the History of Women Philosophers and Scientists, University of Paderborn.

Erin Stackle: Assistant Professor of Philosophy, Loyola Marymount University.

Andrea Staiti: Rita Levi Montalcini Professor of Philosophy, University of Parma.

Michaela Sobrak-Seaton: Doctoral Student, Boston College.

R. Brian Tracz: Doctoral Student, University of California, San Diego.

Jacob Martin Rump: Postdoctoral Fellow, Boston University.

Jerome Veith: Instructor of Philosophy, Seattle University.

Index

Act   2, 59, 85–87, 92–94, 96f., 128, 138, 141, 233f., 242, 244, 276f., 279, 282, 284–287, 318, 323f., 327–330, 332, 335, 347, 355, 362, 371, 373f., 409f.
– mental ~   42, 46, 336
– ~ of cognition   295
– ~ of experience   311
– ~ of perception   85, 97, 121
– ~ of reflection   37, 329f.
– volitional ~   106, 296
Alexander, Samuel   65, 121, 250, 339, 353, 383
Aliotta, Antonio   54, 65, 67, 69
Anschütz, Georg   140, 215, 218, 222f., 243
Appearance   46, 52, 62, 67, 71, 73, 80–102, 104–111, 118, 122, 124, 127, 133, 217, 221f., 235, 240, 269, 274, 277, 279, 281, 306f., 310f., 326, 328, 344, 346, 354, 385, 387, 410, 441, 443, 456, 462
Apperception   45, 47, 54, 92, 137, 349
Aristotle   132, 325f., 340, 454
Arndt, Karl   229
Ash, Mitchell G.   230
Attention   3, 7, 42, 44, 49, 57f., 63, 66f., 74, 80, 93, 95, 107f., 123, 127, 129, 148, 231, 234, 239, 247, 250, 289, 299, 306, 310, 335, 351, 365, 396, 400, 411
Attitude   3, 100, 109, 216, 221, 223, 241, 243–245, 247, 256, 258, 284, 305, 313, 319f., 326, 344, 347, 349f., 362, 369, 390, 406, 408, 410, 413f., 444, 447, 461, 466f.
– natural ~   214, 243f., 246, 249, 270, 326, 333, 344, 351, 371, 408, 413
– phenomenological ~   312, 333, 344, 348, 362, 369, 376, 435
Avenarius, Richard   371, 377

Bauch, Bruno   395, 406, 415, 446
Becher, Erich   142
Belief
– natural ~   244
Beneke, Friedrich Eduard   87
Bentley, Isaac Madison   83

Benussi, Vittorio   47f.
Bergson, Henri   88, 131, 139, 146, 334
Berkeley, George   88, 90, 399f., 438
Bernstein, A.   65
Binet, Alfred   99
Bleuler, Eugen   56f., 73
Bogdanoff, T.   65
Bolzano, Bernhard   103, 420
Borden, Sarah   299
Brentano, Franz   79, 84, 88, 92, 96, 100, 103, 108, 122, 141, 145, 373, 384, 455
Bühler, Karl   218

Calkins, Mary Whiton   83, 86
Carnap, Rudolf   151
Cassirer, Ernst   152, 317, 392, 399, 436, 438, 441
Christiansen, Broder   148
Cohen, Hermann   125, 133, 225, 317, 324
Cohn, Jonas   115, 117, 129, 252, 261–263, 341
Concept   4, 83, 90, 127, 221f., 224f., 240f., 275–277, 286, 289f., 302f., 322, 324f., 341–343, 347, 349, 352–354, 365–368, 390, 407, 418–420, 438, 440f., 443, 449–457, 460f., 463f., 467
– ~ formation   99, 303, 407, 438, 450, 452, 454, 460f., 463f.
– psychological ~   53, 129, 141, 221, 225, 243, 251
– universal ~   130, 354
Consciousness   1–6, 36, 40–42, 44–46, 48, 50–52, 54–57, 64, 67f., 70f., 82–87, 89, 91f., 94–96, 100–106, 109f., 121, 132–134, 137, 139, 141–143, 146–148, 216–220, 222, 229, 233–236, 240, 244–249, 263, 267, 274, 278–282, 285–287, 295, 306–308, 310f., 314, 318, 320, 328–330, 334f., 337, 341, 343, 346f., 350, 359, 361, 366–368, 370–374, 376, 386, 391f., 396f., 399, 401, 406, 410, 426–428,

437, 439, 445, 447, 456–458, 462–465, 467
– pure ~   140, 219, 263, 283, 306, 317, 320, 329 f., 332–334, 348, 371
Couturat, Louis   289

Dahlstrom, Daniel O.   1
Descartes, Rene   37, 81, 90, 279, 321–323, 328, 361, 371
Dessoir, Max   118, 129
Detto, Carl   52
Deutsch, Max   4
Dilthey, Wilhelm   85, 115, 118, 125 f., 139, 339, 352
Drews, Arthur   146
Driesch, Hans   132, 413, 419

Ebbinghaus, Hermann   100, 106, 109
Ehrenberg, Hans   134
Ehrlich, Walter   230
Elsenhans, Theodor   4 f., 13 f., 17, 270–272, 276 f., 284, 299 f., 339 f., 346, 349, 352, 355, 361, 365, 368, 372, 378, 383, 385, 387 f., 390, 394, 396 f., 399 f., 404 f., 414 f., 418, 420, 422–424, 428 f., 433–435, 437, 442–445, 449, 461–464, 467
Embree, Lester   1
Emotional functions   82 f., 88, 104, 109
Emotional shading   71 f.
Emotional thinking   229, 234, 238
Empiricism   322, 420
Epistemology   13, 79, 115, 119, 139, 141, 148, 151, 233, 235, 271, 276, 344, 370, 377, 379, 405, 429, 436
Epoché   3, 214
Essence   4, 302, 319, 351
– eidetic phenomenology   320, 386
– knowledge of ~   238, 271, 278, 321, 323, 341, 343, 351, 360
Evidence   1, 41, 60, 88, 94 f., 97, 108 f., 133, 151 f., 220, 224, 234, 236 f., 240, 244, 250, 262, 277–279, 317, 321–324, 347, 355, 361 f., 367, 392, 406, 437, 461, 466
– apodictic ~   362, 364, 422
– feeling of ~   363, 369
Experience   2, 4 f., 35 f., 40–45, 47, 49, 53, 65, 80, 83 f., 96, 106, 109, 118, 120, 125 f., 128, 132 f., 137–139, 141, 144, 152, 214, 216 f., 219 f., 225, 230, 233, 236 f., 243, 245–249, 251, 256–258, 264, 272–274, 276–279, 287 f., 292, 294, 301, 303–307, 312, 318, 320–324, 331, 333 f., 344–353, 355, 357–359, 361 f., 364–367, 370–377, 387 f., 390–394, 397, 407, 409, 413, 415, 420, 424, 434–437, 439–444, 446 f., 450, 452–456, 458, 462, 464–467

Farber, Marvin   13
Fichte, Johann Gottlob   343
Fink, Eugen   7
Fischer, Kuno   153, 377
Fisette, Denis   13
Forel, Auguste   52, 131
Franken, August   131
Frege, Gottlob   418
Friedmann, Hugo   143
Fries, Jakob Friedrich   13, 355 f., 435

Gallinger, August   414, 419
Geiger, Moritz   242, 248, 250, 256, 339 f., 356–358, 383 f., 423, 465
Geometry   237, 262, 345
Geyser, Joseph   406
Gibson, William Ralph Boyce   7, 48
Groethuysen, Bernhard   139
Groos, Karl   138
Guttmann, Julius   418

Hall, G. Stanley   130
Hanna, Robert   3
Hartmann, Nicolai   143, 146, 419
Heffernan, George   3
Hegel, Georg Friedrich Wilhelm   121, 133, 136, 282
Heidegger, Martin   1 f., 7, 317
Heilbronner, Karl   58, 60–63
Hellpach, Willy   130, 143
Herbart, Johann   45, 67, 146, 217, 460
Herbertz, Richard   146, 445
Hering, Johannes   302, 411
Hofmann, Heinrich   250
Hönigswald, Richard   369, 425
Hopkins, Burt   1

Hopp, Walter 3
Hume, David 83, 86, 224, 241, 248, 256, 361

Idea 81, 146, 241, 256f., 303, 322, 332f., 393, 402–404, 411, 413–415, 418–420, 427, 441, 451, 458, 466
– ~ in the Kantian sense 318, 334
Idealism 133
– transcendental ~ 3, 415, 446
Ideation 257, 279, 284, 287, 344f., 347
Imagination (see Phantasy) 122, 347, 352, 407
Ingarden, Roman 13, 299
Intentionality 246, 329, 335, 373, 428f., 445, 456f.
Intuition 2–4, 8, 58, 115, 119, 127, 131, 135, 139, 151f., 213, 219, 221f., 224, 234, 236f., 240–243, 245, 248, 261–263, 269, 273f., 276–279, 283, 287f., 290, 294f., 304, 312, 322f., 342–346, 348f., 351, 354, 356, 358–362, 364–369, 375f., 392, 394f., 399, 411, 414, 418, 425, 427, 443, 446, 448, 450f., 453f., 456, 461f., 464–467
Isserlin, Max 63

Jacobs, Hanne 1
James, William 48, 50, 79, 93, 99, 110f., 139
Joachim, Harold H. 133
Judd, Charles Hubbard 46, 132
Jung, Carl 68, 71f.

Kafka, Gustav 148
Kant, Immanuel 38, 81, 89f., 104, 119, 134, 144, 213, 273, 275f., 278f., 282f., 291, 321–323, 325, 327, 333f., 343–345, 349, 361, 366, 369, 375, 377f., 389, 394f., 405, 409, 415, 433–435, 441, 443, 448, 462
Katz, David 250
Kiesow, Federico 49, 64
Klein, Julius 64, 69f.
Klemm, Otto 118
Kronfeld, Arthur 143

Külpe, Oswald 8, 35, 64, 99, 108, 127, 213, 236, 252, 267, 271, 276, 280, 286, 291, 341, 378, 429f.
Kusch, Martin 230

Lange, Carl 55, 110
Lask, Emil 271f., 276, 281f., 290f., 395, 415
Leibniz, Gottfried Wilhelm 81, 84, 86, 96, 279, 325, 441
Linke, Paul Ferdinand 13, 383–385, 387, 396, 402, 405, 407, 433–440, 442, 444–447, 449
Lipps, Theodor 40–46, 50, 59, 85, 134, 138, 146, 339, 359, 383f., 386
Lobsien, Marx 65
Locke, John 84, 361, 391–393, 396, 417, 435f.
Logic 13, 51, 103, 106, 134f., 141, 151, 215, 229, 233f., 245, 257, 271f., 284, 288–295, 313f., 321, 324f., 339, 348, 385f., 398, 403, 407, 425, 466
– pure (formal) ~ 223, 244, 259, 267, 272, 288–295, 303, 313f., 425
Logicism 141
Lotze, Herrmann 79, 84, 86, 97, 118, 127, 291, 400f., 415
Luft, Sebastian 317

Maier, Heinrich 4f., 138, 229–232, 236, 238, 370
Majolino, Claudio 1
Marty, Anton 93, 103, 111
Meaning 305, 308
Meinong, Alexius 7, 93, 101–103, 106, 123, 386, 402, 419
Meisl, Alfred 67
Memory 39
Mercier, Désiré 132
Messer, August 5, 14, 116, 138, 213–220, 223, 239, 241–243, 247, 250f., 255, 257f., 261f., 268–270, 280, 284, 293, 295, 299, 341, 359, 386, 405f., 418, 446, 449, 451f., 458, 466
Metaphysics 50, 67, 87, 131f., 139, 215, 233, 235, 239, 347, 359, 414, 457
Metzger, Arnold 383, 395
Meumann, Ernst 35, 111

Mill, John Stuart 352
Miller, Dickinson S. 83
Modification
– attentional ~ 282, 285
– intentional ~ 335
Moran, Dermot 1
Mormann, Thomas 151
Müller, Georg Elias 46, 56, 61, 64, 96, 107, 109, 138, 218, 222, 229
Münch, Fritz 415
Münsterberg, Hugo 96, 126 f., 129, 137, 142, 145, 460
Myers, Charles S. 131

Natorp, Paul 7, 13, 133, 225, 229, 317 – 320, 335, 343, 375
Natural sciences 115, 123 f., 126, 128, 236, 244, 283, 350, 455, 457
Nenon, Tom 1, 255, 449
Noema 335
– noematic core 286
– noesis and ~ 285, 310, 335

Object 344
Oesterreich, Traugott Konstantin 138, 146 f., 411
Ontology 301
– formal ~ 244, 288, 314
– material ~ 248, 273, 275, 301, 305

Perception 46, 222, 250
Perseveration 60
Pfänder, Alexander 250, 255, 339 f., 353, 383
Phantasy 103, 256, 258 f., 264, 302 f., 344, 346, 349, 450, 464 f.
Phenomenological method 224 f., 241, 250, 262, 272, 308, 340, 358, 390, 395, 424, 430, 464
Phenomenology 1 – 7, 35, 37, 41, 43, 51, 79 f., 115, 123 f., 134, 137, 139, 142, 147, 152, 213 – 216, 219 – 223, 225, 229 f., 234, 236 f., 239 f., 243 – 245, 247 – 251, 255, 257, 263, 267, 269 – 271, 280 f., 283 – 288, 290, 292 – 296, 299, 301, 306, 309, 312 – 314, 317 – 321, 326, 329, 331, 333 f., 336, 339 – 346, 348 – 353, 355 – 361, 365, 369 – 372, 374, 376 f., 379, 383, 385 – 388, 390, 394 – 396, 403 – 406, 408, 410, 415, 417 – 421, 423 – 427, 429 f., 433, 435 – 438, 440 f., 443 – 445, 447, 449 – 452, 459, 464 – 466
Pichler, Hans 276
Pilzecker, Alfons 56, 61, 64
Plato 98, 133, 318, 322 f., 325, 352, 441, 443
Pradelle, Dominique 1
Pribilla, Max, S.J. 213
Psychology 2, 5 f., 13, 35 f., 39 f., 42, 44 f., 49, 51, 53, 67, 75, 79 – 84, 86, 91, 99 f., 106, 108, 110 f., 115, 117 – 119, 121 – 123, 126 f., 129 – 132, 134, 138 f., 141 – 143, 147 f., 151, 213 – 217, 219 – 223, 225, 230 – 238, 242 – 244, 247 – 251, 256 f., 262 f., 268, 270, 279, 284 f., 292 f., 299, 301, 306, 317, 320, 332, 335 f., 339 – 341, 348, 350, 352 f., 359 f., 370, 372, 378, 385 – 388, 393, 396, 403, 426 – 428, 438, 440, 447 – 449, 455, 458, 460
– ~ and phenomenology 5, 214, 248, 257, 268
– descriptive ~ 5, 51, 79, 146, 214, 232, 234, 236, 239, 268, 270, 340 f., 349, 352, 359, 370, 377, 426 f., 447, 449, 454 f., 458, 460
– empirical ~ 215, 217, 230, 247 – 249, 252, 257, 264, 270, 333, 341, 350, 379, 386, 388, 403, 426, 428, 434
– experimental ~ 35, 37, 44, 98, 100, 115, 213, 215, 218, 223, 230, 237, 252
– psychologism 141, 216 f., 234, 236, 240, 269, 285, 292, 294, 324, 359, 387, 422
– rational ~ 257
– reconstructive ~ 336

Ranschburg, Pál 63, 66 f., 109
Reason 3, 7, 86, 88, 97, 102, 106, 120, 130, 134, 142, 219, 221, 223, 229, 248, 270, 274, 312, 323, 330, 356, 363, 378, 393, 396, 421, 434, 436 f., 443, 456
– practical ~ 378
– theoretical ~ 378

Reduction   3, 5, 284, 286, 288, 305–307, 310, 312, 319, 329, 341, 405, 409
– phenomenological ~   3, 6, 214, 245–247, 280, 284, 286 f., 305, 308, 317, 319, 351, 408
Reflection   37, 47, 81, 217, 233, 241, 244 f., 277 f., 282, 284, 287, 305, 307, 313, 328–330, 342, 348, 355, 362, 364–366, 371, 378 f., 391 f., 435, 451, 455
Region   4, 268, 271–273, 287 f., 290, 293–295, 301, 312, 344 f., 359, 396, 409, 417
Rehmke, Johannes   119 f., 122
Reich, S.   75
Reinach, Adolf   241, 256, 299, 339 f., 358, 383
Representation   36, 40, 42, 45, 49 f., 52, 58–62, 64, 68, 74, 85, 92 f., 98–100, 104, 111, 237 f., 282, 350, 373, 375 f., 396, 398, 420, 429
Rickert, Heinrich   125 f., 142, 276, 378 f., 395, 417, 429
Riehl, Alois   99, 377
Riklin, Franz   69, 71

Schapp, Wilhelm   222, 224 f., 250
Scheler, Max   241 f., 248, 339 f., 354–356, 383, 422, 465
Schelling, Friedrich   152, 279, 343
Schmied-Kowarzik, Walther   388–390
Scholem, Gershom   383
Schumann, Friedrich   98, 102, 229
Schuppe, Wilhelm   151, 403
Science   1, 36, 42, 51, 79, 81, 111, 117 f., 121, 123–127, 129, 132, 134, 139, 215–217, 219 f., 223, 231–233, 235–237, 239, 242–245, 247 f., 251, 255–258, 262, 264, 270–273, 275, 279 f., 283 f., 286 f., 293, 295, 299, 303–305, 310, 312, 314, 317, 321, 325, 327, 330 f., 341–345, 347 f., 350–355, 357, 359–361, 363, 366, 370, 372, 376–379, 385, 387, 389 f., 393 f., 405, 409, 415, 418, 422, 426, 428, 433–438, 441, 443, 446 f., 449, 451 f., 454 f., 457 f., 460, 464–467
– human ~   123, 125, 139, 215, 222, 231, 244, 332, 389

Selz, Otto   275
Semon, Richard   52
Sensation   40, 42, 46, 54, 57, 59, 64, 85, 92, 95, 100, 107, 136, 144, 146, 222, 237, 240, 322, 349, 391 f., 409 f., 434 f., 455, 461
Sigwart, Christoph   84, 142, 229, 397, 441
Simmel, Georg   139
Spencer, Herbert   96
Spinoza, Benedict   90, 105, 439, 441
Staiti, Andrea   1, 80, 213, 215, 239, 261, 267, 269, 339, 433
Steffens, Laura   109
Stein, Edith   4–6, 13 f., 268, 299, 301, 449, 461
Steinmann, Heinrich Gustav   4, 6, 267, 269, 276, 299, 301–309, 311–314
Stern, Wilhelm   130, 140, 403
Stransky, Erwin   63, 74
Stratton, George M.   129
Study, Eduard   274
Stumpf, Carl   7, 35, 79 f., 82, 92 f., 96, 101, 103 f., 107, 111, 122 f., 126, 142, 145, 222, 339

Taylor, Clifton   51, 99
Twardowski, Kasimir   386

Vaihinger, Hans   421
Volkelt, Johannes   85, 96, 422, 424

Watt, Henry J.   35–37, 39, 45, 63
Wertheimer, Max   51, 64, 69 f., 72, 237
Wessely, Rudolf   65
Weyer, Edward M.   132
Wolff, Christian   81, 276
Wundt, Wilhelm   35, 38, 47, 55, 86, 115, 119, 126 f., 130, 141 f., 217 f., 229, 271, 367, 383 f.

Ziche, Paul   151
Ziegler, Theobald   131
Ziehen, Theodor   4, 151–153, 402, 438

www.ingramcontent.com/pod-product-compliance
Lightning Source LLC
Chambersburg PA
CBHW031409230426
43668CB00007B/250